**AP** Associated Press
# Stylebook

**Associated Press**

# Stylebook
## and Briefing on Media Law

Editor
**Norm Goldstein**
apstylebook@ap.org

BASIC
BOOKS
A Member of the Perseus Books Group
New York

Published by Basic Books, A Member of the Perseus Books Group,
in cooperation with The Associated Press

Books published by Basic Books are available at special discounts for
bulk purchases in the United States by corporations, institutions,
and other organizations. For more information, please contact the
Special Markets Department at the Perseus Books Group, 2300
Chestnut Street, Suite 200, Philadelphia, PA 19103, or call
(800) 255-1514, or e-mail special.markets@perseusbooks.com.

A CIP catalog record for this book is available from
the Library of Congress.

ISBN-13: 978-0-465-00489-8
ISBN-10: 0-465-00489-X

Design and content management by Satchmo Publishing, Inc.

First Edition, August 1977
42nd Edition, 2007


10  9  8  7  6  5  4  3  2  1

# CONTENTS

# FOREWORD

The first Associated Press Stylebook came out in 1953. It was a booklet of 60 pages, "distilled from a thousand suggestions and ideas, a stack of newspapers and a big dictionary."

The slim, stapled booklet was called the "most definitive and inclusive work ever undertaken by a group of newspapers." Yet it proved to be just the start of a work that is constantly in progress.

In 1977, the AP published a major revision of the original Stylebook, the forerunner of today's editions. Far more than just a collection of rules, the book became part dictionary, part encyclopedia, part textbook — an eclectic source of information for writers and editors of any publication.

Today, the 21st-century Associated Press has become the essential global news network. And the AP Stylebook has become the essential tool for anyone who cares about good writing.

The Stylebook is now available in a variety of electronic formats. It continues to add entries that reflect the language of our fast-changing world. Truly, it is a tool now for wired editors as well as wire editors.

But just as the AP remains dedicated to its fundamental journalistic principles, the AP Stylebook remains committed to its original concept: to provide a uniform presentation of the printed word, to make a story written anywhere understandable everywhere.

And it is still distilled from a thousand suggestions and ideas, and several big desk and online dictionaries.

Our thanks and appreciation go to those who have helped enrich this book by their questions and suggestions on style. Many entries reflect contributions by the AP staff, the AP's members and subscribers, journalism teachers and students, and specialists in a host of fields. There have also been countless contributions from everyday readers of the news, who share with us a distinct pride in the clarity and precision of language.

**TOM CURLEY**
**President and**
**Chief Executive Officer**

# WHAT'S NEW
## In this edition of the AP Stylebook

---------------------------

New entries include: African Union; airstrike; Asperger's syndrome; BlackBerry; Boogie; carry-on; Chennai; datelines (Baghdad); farmers market; female; GPS; headlines; hip-hop; homebuyer, homeowner; intefedah; Islamic holy days; Katmandu; mentally retarded; merger (Business); Mumbai; Swift boat.

Changes and updates include: Baha'i; daylight saving time; editor-in-chief; European Union; Fatah; Mexico; planets; plurals (Broadcast); RSVP; telephone numbers; U.S. time zones map; track and field (Sports); volleyball (Sports); headlines (Filing the Wire); Hold for Release slugs (Filing the Wire).

Deletions: husband, widower; Internet Search Tips; Laundromat; pupil, student; Serbia-Montenegro; U.S. Court of Military Appeals; Woman's Christian Temperance Union.

# BIBLIOGRAPHY

# BIBLIOGRAPHY

Following are reference books used in the preparation of The Associated Press Stylebook. They are the accepted reference sources for material not covered by the Stylebook.

**First reference for spelling, style, usage and foreign geographic names:**
*Webster's New World College Dictionary*, Fourth Edition, Wiley, Hoboken, N.J.

**Second reference for spelling, style and usage:**
*Webster's Third New International Dictionary*, Merriam-Webster, Springfield, Mass.

**Second reference for foreign geographic names:**
*National Geographic Atlas of the World*, National Geographic Society, Washington, D.C. www.nationalgeographic.com/index.html

**For aircraft names:**
*Jane's All the World's Aircraft*; Jane's Yearbooks, London, and Franklin Watts Inc., New York.

**For military ships:**
*Jane's Fighting Ships*; Jane's Yearbooks, London, and Franklin Watts Inc., New York.

**For nonmilitary ships:**
*Lloyd's Register of Shipping*; Lloyd's Register of Shipping Trust Corp. Ltd., London.

**For railroads:**
*Official Railway Guide — Freight Service, and Official Railway Guide — Passenger Service, Travel Edition*; Official Railway Guide, New York.

**For federal government questions:**
*Official Congressional Directory*; U.S. Government Printing Office, Washington, D.C.

**For foreign government questions:**
*Political Handbook of the World*; CQ Press, Washington, D.C.

**For the formal name of a business:**
*Standard & Poor's Register of Corporations, Directors and Executives*; Standard & Poor's Corp., New York.

**For religion questions:**
*Handbook of Denominations in the United States*; Abingdon Press, Nashville, Tenn., and New York.
*World Christian Encyclopedia*; Second Edition; Oxford University Press, New York, N.Y.
*Yearbook of American and Canadian Churches*; Abingdon Press, Nashville, Tenn., and New York, for the National Council of Churches of Christ in the U.S.A., New York.

Other references consulted in the preparation of the AP Stylebook:
Bernstein, Theodore M. *The Careful Writer: A Modern Guide to English Usage.* Atheneum, 1965.
Bernstein, Theodore M. *More Language That Needs Watching.* Channel Press, 1962.
Bernstein, Theodore M. *Watch Your Language.* Atheneum, 1958.
Cappon, Rene J. *The Word.* The Associated Press, 1982; second edition, 1991.
Follett, Wilson (edited and completed by Jacques Barzun). *Modern American Usage.* Hill & Wang, 1966.
Fowler, H.W. *A Dictionary of Modern English Usage.* Oxford University Press, 1965.
*The Chicago Manual of Style,* 15th Edition. University of Chicago Press, 2003.
Morris, William and Morris, Mary. *Harper Dictionary of Contemporary Usage.* Harper & Row, 1975; second edition, 1985.
Newton, Harry, *Newton's Telecom Dictionary,* 15th Edition. Miller Freeman, Inc., 1999.
Shaw, Harry. *Dictionary of Problem Words & Expressions.* McGraw-Hill Book Co., 1975.
Skillin, Marjorie E. and Gay, Robert M. *Words into Type.* Prentice-Hall Inc., 1974.
Strunk, William Jr. and White, E.B. *The Elements of Style,* second edition. The Macmillan Co., 1972.
Also consulted were the stylebooks of the Boston Globe, Indianapolis News, Kansas City Star, Los Angeles Times, Miami Herald, Milwaukee Journal Sentinel, Newsday, New York Times, Wall Street Journal, Wilmington (Del.) News-Journal, and the U.S. Government Printing Office.

# STYLEBOOK

# STYLEBOOK KEY

This updated and revised version of The Associated Press Stylebook has been organized like a dictionary. Need the acronym for a government agency? Look under the agency's name. Should you capitalize a word? Check the word itself or the **capitalization** entry. What's the format for baseball boxes? See **baseball**.

Following is a key to the entries:

**airport** Capitalize as part of a proper name: *La Guardia Airport, Newark International Airport.*

The first name of an individual and the word *international* may be deleted from a formal airport name while the remainder is capitalized: *John F. Kennedy International Airport, Kennedy International Airport,* or *Kennedy Airport.* Use whichever is appropriate in the context.

Do not make up names, however. There is no *Boston Airport,* for example. The *Boston airport* (lowercase *airport*) would be acceptable if for some reason the proper name, *Logan International Airport,* were not used.

Entry words, in alphabetical order, are in **boldface**. They represent the accepted word forms unless otherwise indicated.

Text explains usage.

Examples of correct and incorrect usage are in italics.

**airtight**

**air traffic controller** (no hyphen.)

Many entries simply give the correct spelling, hyphenation and/or capitalization.

**airways** The system of routes that the federal government has established for airplane traffic.

See the **airline, airlines** entry for its use in carriers' names.

Abbrev. indicates the correct abbreviation of a word.

**Alabama** Abbrev.: *Ala.* See **state names**.

Related topics are in **boldface**.

Other abbreviations used in the Stylebook:

| | |
|---|---|
| **n.:** noun form | **adj.:** adjectives |
| **v.:** verb form | **adv.:** adverbs |

**a-** The rules of **prefixes** apply, but in general no hyphen. Some examples:

achromatic          atonal

**AAA** Formerly the American Automobile Association. On second reference, *the automobile association* or *the association* is acceptable.

Headquarters is in Heathrow, Fla.

**a, an** Use the article *a* before consonant sounds: *a historic event*, *a one-year term* (sounds as if it begins with a *w*), *a united stand* (sounds like *you*).

Use the article *an* before vowel sounds: *an energy crisis*, *an honorable man* (the *h* is silent), *an NBA record* (sounds like it begins with the letter *e*), *an 1890s celebration*.

**A&P** Acceptable in all references for *Great Atlantic & Pacific Tea Co. Inc.* Headquarters is in Montvale, N.J.

**AARP** Use only the initials for the organization formerly known as the American Association of Retired Persons.

**abbreviations and acronyms** The notation *abbrev.* is used in this book to identify the abbreviated form that may be used for a word in some contexts.

A few universally recognized abbreviations are required in some circumstances. Some others are acceptable depending on the context. But in general, avoid alphabet soup. Do not use abbreviations or acronyms that the reader would not quickly recognize.

Guidance on how to use a particular abbreviation or acronym is provided in entries alphabetized according to the sequence of letters in the word or phrase.

An *acronym* is a word formed from the first letter or letters of a series of words: *laser* (light amplification by stimulated emission of radiation). An *abbreviation* is not an *acronym*.

Some general principles:

BEFORE A NAME: Abbreviate titles when used before a full name: *Dr., Gov., Lt. Gov., Mr., Mrs., Rep., the Rev., Sen.* and certain military designations listed in the **military titles** entry.

For guidelines on how to use titles, see **courtesy titles; legislative titles; military titles; religious titles**; and the entries for the most commonly used titles.

AFTER A NAME: Abbreviate *junior* or *senior* after an individual's name. Abbreviate *company, corporation, incorporated* and *limited* when used after the name of a corporate entity. See entries under these words and **company names**.

In some cases, an academic degree may be abbreviated after an individual's name. See **academic degrees**.

WITH DATES OR NUMERALS: Use the abbreviations *A.D., B.C., a.m., p.m., No.,* and abbreviate certain months when used with the day of the month.

Right: *In 450 B.C.; at 9:30 a.m.; in room No. 6; on Sept. 16.*

Wrong: *Early this a.m. he asked for the No. of your room.* The abbreviations are correct only with figures.

Right: *Early this morning he asked for the number of your room.*

See **months** and individual entries for these other terms:

IN NUMBERED ADDRESSES: Abbreviate *avenue, boulevard* and *street* in numbered addresses: *He lives on Pennsylvania Avenue. He lives at 1600 Pennsylvania Ave.*

See **addresses**.

STATES: The names of certain states and the *United States* are abbreviated with periods in some circumstances.

See **state names**; **datelines**; and individual entries.

ACCEPTABLE BUT NOT RE-QUIRED: Some organizations and government agencies are widely recognized by their initials: *CIA, FBI, GOP.*

If the entry for such an organization notes that an abbreviation is acceptable in all references or on second reference, that does not mean that its use should be automatic. Let the context determine, for example, whether to use *Federal Bureau of Investigation* or *FBI.*

See **second reference**.

AVOID AWKWARD CON-STRUCTIONS: Do not follow an organization's full name with an abbreviation or acronym in pa-

rentheses or set off by dashes. If an abbreviation or acronym would not be clear on second reference without this arrangement, do not use it.

Names not commonly before the public should not be reduced to acronyms solely to save a few words.

SPECIAL CASES: Many abbreviations are desirable in tabulations and certain types of technical writing. See individual entries.

CAPS, PERIODS: Use capital letters and periods according to the listings in this book. For words not in this book, use the first-listed abbreviation in Webster's New World College Dictionary. Generally, omit periods in acronyms unless the result would spell an unrelated word. But use periods in two-letter abbreviations: *U.S., U.N., U.K., B.A., B.C.* (*AP,* a trademark, is an exception. Also, no periods in *GI* and *EU.*)

Use all caps, but no periods, in longer abbreviations and acronyms when the individual letters are pronounced: *ABC, CIA, FBI.*

Use only an initial cap and then lowercase for acronyms of more than six letters, unless listed otherwise in this Stylebook or Webster's New World College Dictionary.

**ABC** Acceptable in all references for *American Broadcasting Cos.* (the plural is part of the corporate name).

Divisions are *ABC News, ABC Radio* and *ABC-TV.*

**ABCs**

**able-bodied**

**ABM, ABMs** Acceptable in all references for *anti-ballistic missile(s),* but the term should be defined in the story. (The hyphen is an exception to Webster's.)

Avoid the redundant phrase *ABM missiles.*

**A-bomb** Use *atomic bomb* unless a direct quotation is involved.

See **Hiroshima**.

**Aborigine** Capitalize when referring to Australian indigenous people.

**abortion** Use *anti-abortion* instead of *pro-life* and *abortion rights* instead of *pro-abortion* or *pro-choice.* Avoid *abortionist,* which connotes a person who performs clandestine abortions.

**aboveboard**

**absent-minded**

**absent without leave** *AWOL* is acceptable on second reference.

**academic degrees** If mention of degrees is necessary to establish someone's credentials, the preferred form is to avoid an abbreviation and use instead a phrase such as: *John Jones, who has a doctorate in psychology.*

Use an apostrophe in *bachelor's degree, a master's,* etc., but there is no possessive in *Bachelor of Arts* or *Master of Science.*

Also: an *associate degree* (no possessive).

Use such abbreviations as *B.A., M.A., LL.D.* and *Ph.D.* only when the need to identify many individuals by degree on first reference would make the preferred form cumbersome. Use these abbreviations only after a full name — never after just a last name.

When used after a name, an academic abbreviation is set off by commas: *John Snow, Ph.D., spoke.*

Do not precede a name with a courtesy title for an academic degree and follow it with the abbreviation for the degree in the same reference:

Wrong: *Dr. Pam Jones, Ph.D.*

Right: *Dr. Pam Jones, a chemist.*

See **doctor**.

**academic departments** Use lowercase except for words that are proper nouns or adjectives: *the department of history, the history department, the department of English, the English department,* or when *department* is part of the official and formal name: *University of Connecticut Department of Medicine.*

**academic titles** Capitalize and spell out formal titles such as *chancellor, chairman,* etc., when they precede a name. Lowercase elsewhere.

Lowercase modifiers such as *department* in *department Chairman Jerome Wiesner.*

See **doctor** and **titles**.

**academy** See **military academies**.

**Academy Awards** Presented annually by the Academy of Motion Picture Arts and Sciences. Also known as the *Oscars.* (Both *Academy Awards* and *Oscars* are trademarks.)

Lowercase *the academy* and *the awards* whenever they stand alone.

**accent marks** Do not use any diacritical marks on general wires because they cause garble in many newspaper computers.

**accept, except** *Accept* means to receive. *Except* means to exclude.

**accommodate**

**accused** A person is *accused of*, not *with*, a crime.

To avoid any suggestion that an individual is being judged before a trial, do not use a phrase such as *accused slayer John Jones;* use *John Jones, accused of the slaying.*

For guidelines on related words, see **allege**; **arrest**; and **indict**.

**Ace** A trademark for a brand of elastic bandage.

**acknowledgment**

**acre** Equal to 43,560 square feet or 4,840 square yards. The metric equivalent is 0.4 (two-fifths) of a hectare or 4,047 square meters.

One square mile is 640 acres.

To convert to hectares, multiply by 0.4 (5 acres x 0.4 equals 2 hectares).

See **hectare**.

**acronyms** See the **abbreviations and acronyms** entry.

**act** Capitalize when part of the name for pending or implemented legislation: *the Taft-Hartley Act.*

**acting** Always lowercase, but capitalize any formal title that may follow before a name: *acting Mayor Peter Barry.*

See **titles**.

**act numbers** Use Arabic figures and capitalize *act: Act 1; Act 2, Scene 2.* But: *the first act, the second act.*

**actor** (man) **actress** (woman)

**Actors' Equity Association** Headquarters is in New York.

**A.D.** Acceptable in all references for *anno Domini:* in the year of the Lord.

Because the full phrase would read *in the year of the Lord 96,* the abbreviation *A.D.* goes before the figure for the year: *A.D. 96.*

Do not write: *The fourth century A.D. The fourth century* is sufficient. If *A.D.* is not specified with a year, the year is presumed to be A.D.

See **B.C.**

**addresses** Use the abbreviations *Ave., Blvd.* and *St.* only with a numbered address: *1600 Pennsylvania Ave.* Spell them out and capitalize when part of a formal street name without a number: *Pennsylvania Avenue.* Lowercase and spell out when used alone or with more than one street name: *Massachusetts and Pennsylvania avenues.*

All similar words (*alley, drive, road, terrace,* etc.) always are spelled out. Capitalize them when part of a formal name without a number; lowercase when used alone or with two or more names.

Always use figures for an address number: *9 Morningside Circle.*

Spell out and capitalize *First* through *Ninth* when used as street names; use figures with two letters for *10th* and above: *7 Fifth Ave., 100 21st St.*

Abbreviate compass points used to indicate directional ends of a street or quadrants of a city in a numbered address: *222 E. 42nd St., 562 W. 43rd St., 600 K St. N.W.* Do not abbreviate if the number is omitted: *East 42nd*

*Street, West 43rd Street, K Street Northwest.*
See **highway designations**.
Use periods in the abbreviation *P.O.* for P.O. Box numbers.

**adjectives** The abbreviation *adj.* is used in this book to identify the spelling of the adjectival forms of words that frequently are misspelled.
The **comma** entry provides guidance on punctuating a series of adjectives.
The **hyphen** entry provides guidance on handling compound modifiers used before a noun.

**ad-lib** (n., v., adj.)

**administration** Lowercase: *the administration, the president's administration, the governor's administration, the Reagan administration.*
See the **government, junta, regime** entry for distinctions that apply in using these terms and *administration.*

**administrative law judge** This is the federal title for the position formerly known as *hearing examiner.* Capitalize it when used as a formal title before a name.
To avoid the long title, seek a construction that sets the title off by commas: *The administrative law judge, John Williams, disagreed.*

**administrator** Never abbreviate. Capitalize when used as a formal title before a name.
See **titles**.

**admiral** See **military titles**.

**admissible**

**admit, admitted** These words may in some contexts give the erroneous connotation of wrongdoing.
A person who acknowledges that he is a recovering alcoholic, for example, is not *admitting* it. *Said* is usually sufficient.

**ad nauseam**

**Adobe Acrobat** Software for creating, displaying and printing PDF files.

**adopt, approve, enact, pass** Amendments, ordinances, resolutions and rules are *adopted* or *approved.*
Bills are *passed.*
Laws are *enacted.*

**Adrenalin** A trademark for the synthetic or chemically extracted forms of epinephrine, a substance produced by the adrenal glands.
The nonproprietary terms are *epinephrine hydrochloride* or *adrenaline.*

**Adventist** See **Seventh-day Adventist Church**.

**adverbs** The abbreviation *adv.* is used in this book to identify the spelling of adverbial forms of words frequently misspelled.
See the **hyphen** entry in the **Punctuation** chapter for guidelines on when an adverb should be followed by a hyphen in constructing a compound modifier.

**adverse, averse** *Adverse* means unfavorable: *He predicted adverse weather.*
*Averse* means reluctant, opposed: *She is averse to change.*

**adviser** Not *advisor.*

**advisory**

**Aer Lingus** The headquarters of this airline is in Dublin, Ireland.

**Aeroflot** The headquarters of this airline is in Moscow.

**Aeromexico** Headquarters is in Mexico City.

**aesthetic**

**affect, effect** *Affect*, as a verb, means to influence: *The game will affect the standings.*

*Affect*, as a noun, is best avoided. It occasionally is used in psychology to describe an emotion, but there is no need for it in everyday language.

*Effect*, as a verb, means to cause: *He will effect many changes in the company.*

*Effect*, as a noun, means result: *The effect was overwhelming. He miscalculated the effect of his actions. It was a law of little effect.*

**Afghan** (adj.) *Afghani* is the *Afghan* unit of currency.

**AFL-CIO** Acceptable in all references for the *American Federation of Labor and Congress of Industrial Organizations.*

**A-frame**

**African** Of or pertaining to Africa, or any of its peoples or languages. Do not use the word as a synonym for *black* or *Negro*.

In some countries of Africa, *colored* is used to describe those of mixed white and black ancestry. In other societies *colored* is considered a derogatory word.

Because of the ambiguity, avoid the term in favor of a phrase such as *mixed racial ancestry*. If the word cannot be avoided, place it in quotation marks and provide its meaning. See **colored**.

**African-American** The preferred term is *black*. Use *African-American* only in quotations or the names of organizations or if individuals describe themselves so.

See **black**.

**African Union** The African Union, established in 2002 to succeed the Organization of African Unity, has the following members:

Algeria, Angola, Benin, Botswana, Burkina Faso, Burundi, Cameroon, Cape Verde, Central African Republic, Chad, Comoros, Democratic Republic of Congo, Djibouti, Egypt, Equatorial Guinea, Eritrea, Ethiopia, Gabon, Gambia, Ghana, Guinea Bissau, Guinea, Ivory Coast, Kenya, Lesotho, Liberia, Libya, Madagascar, Malawi, Mali, Mauritania, Mauritius, Mozambique, Namibia, Niger, Nigeria, Republic of Congo, Rwanda, Sao Tome and Principe, Senegal, Seychelles, Sierra Leone, Somalia, South Africa, Sudan, Swaziland, Tanzania, Togo, Tunisia, Uganda, Western Sahara, Zambia, Zimbabwe.

**after-** No hyphen after this prefix when it is used to form a noun:

aftereffect      afterthought

Follow *after* with a hyphen when it is used to form compound modifiers:

after-dinner drink    after-theater snack

**afterward** Not *afterwards*.

**Agency for International Development** *AID* is acceptable on second reference.

**agenda** A list. It takes singular verbs and pronouns: *The agenda has run its course.* The plural is *agendas.*

**agent** Lowercase unless it is a formal title used before a name. In the FBI, the formal title is *special agent.* Use *Special Agent William Smith* if appropriate in a special context. Otherwise, make it *agent William Smith* or *FBI agent William Smith.* See **titles**.

**ages** Always use figures for people and animals (but not for inanimates): *The girl is 15 years old; the law is eight years old.* When the context does not require *years* or *years old*, the figure is presumed to be *years.*
Use hyphens for ages expressed as adjectives before a noun or as substitutes for a noun.
Examples: *A 5-year-old boy*, but *the boy is 5 years old. The boy, 7, has a sister, 10. The woman, 26, has a daughter 2 months old. The race is for 3-year-olds. The woman is in her 30s* (no apostrophe).
See also **boy; girl; infant;** and **youth**.
See **comma** in **punctuation guidelines**.

**ages of history** See the **historical periods and events** entry.

**agnostic, atheist** An *agnostic* is a person who believes it is impossible to know whether there is a God.
An *atheist* is a person who believes there is no God.

**aid, aide** *Aid* is assistance.

An *aide* is a person who serves as an assistant.

**aide-de-camp, aides-de-camp** A military officer who serves as assistant and confidential secretary to a superior.

**AIDS** Acceptable in all references for *acquired immune deficiency syndrome*, sometimes called *acquired immunodeficiency syndrome.*
*AIDS* is a disease that weakens the immune system, gradually destroying the body's ability to fight infections and certain cancers. It is caused by *human immunodeficiency virus*, or *HIV.* (*HIV virus* is redundant.)
*HIV* is spread most often through sexual contact; contaminated needles or syringes shared by drug abusers; infected blood or blood products; and from infected women to their babies at birth or through breast feeding.
Several types of tests are available for *HIV.* One is a blood test that looks for antibodies the body has made to defend against *HIV.* Other tests look for parts of the virus itself in blood. Those who test positive are often described as being *HIV-positive.*
People infected with the virus do not have *AIDS* until they develop serious symptoms. Many remain infected but apparently healthy for years.

**ain't** A dialectical or nonstandard contraction. Use it only in quoted matter or special contexts.

**air bag** Two words.

**air base** Two words. Follow the practice of the U.S. Air Force, which uses *air force base* as part of the proper name for its bases in the United States and *air base* for its installations abroad.

On second reference: *the Air Force base, the air base,* or *the base.*

Do not abbreviate, even in datelines:

*LACKLAND AIR FORCE BASE, Texas (AP) —*

**Air Canada** Headquarters is in Montreal.

**air-condition, air-conditioned** (v. and adj.) The nouns are: *air conditioner, air conditioning.*

**aircraft names** Use a hyphen when changing from letters to figures; no hyphen when adding a letter after figures.

Some examples for aircraft often in the news: *B-1, BAC-111, C-5A, DC-10, FH-227, F-15 Eagle, F-16 Falcon, L-1011, MiG-21, Tu-144, 727-100C, 747, 747B, VC-10. Airbus A300* or *A300* (no hyphen) is an exception.

This hyphenation principle is the one used most frequently by manufacturers and users. Apply it in all cases for consistency. For other elements of a name, use the form adopted by the manufacturer or user. If in doubt, consult Jane's All the World's Aircraft.

NO QUOTES: Do not use quotation marks for aircraft with names: *Air Force One, the Spirit of St. Louis.*

PLURALS: *DC-10s, 747s.* But: *747B's.* (As noted in plurals, the apostrophe is used in forming the plural of a single letter.)

SEQUENCE: Use Arabic figures to establish the sequence of aircraft, spacecraft and missiles: *Apollo 10.* Do not use hyphens.

**aircraft terms** Use *engine,*

not *motor,* for the units that propel aircraft: a *twin-engine* plane (not *twin engined*).

Use *jet plane* or *jetliner* to describe only those aircraft driven solely by jet engines. Use *turboprop* to describe an aircraft on which the jet engine is geared to a propeller. Turboprops sometimes are called *propjets.*

See the **engine, motor** entry.

**airfare** One word.

**air force** Capitalize when referring to U.S. forces: *the U.S. Air Force, the Air Force, Air Force regulations.* Do not use the abbreviation *USAF.*

Congress established the Army Air Forces (note the *s*) in 1941. Prior to that, the air arm was known as the U.S. Army Air Corps. The U.S. Air Force (no *s*) was created as a separate service in 1947.

Use lowercase for the forces of other nations: *the Israeli air force.*

This approach has been adopted for consistency, because many foreign nations do not use *air force* as the proper name.

See the **military academies** and **military titles** entries.

**air force base** See **air base**.

**Air Force One** The Air Force applies this name to any of its aircraft the president of the United States may be using.

In ordinary usage, however, *Air Force One* is the name of the Air Force plane normally reserved for the president's use.

**Air France** Headquarters is in Paris.

**Air-India** The hyphen is part of the formal name.

Headquarters is in Mumbai, India.

**Air Jamaica** Headquarters is in Kingston, Jamaica.

**airline, airlines** Capitalize *airlines*, *air lines* and *airways* when used as part of a proper airline name.

Major airlines are listed in this book separately by name.

Companies that use *airlines* include Alitalia, American, Continental, Hawaiian, Iberia, Japan, Northwest, Southwest, and United.

Companies that use *airways* include British, JetBlue, Qantas and US.

Companies that use none of these include Aer Lingus, Aeromexico, Air Canada, Air France, Air-India, Air Jamaica, and KLM.

On second reference, use just the proper name (*Delta*), an abbreviation if applicable, or *the airline*. Use *airlines* when referring to more than one line.

Do not use *air line*, *air lines* or *airways* in generic references to an airline.

**airmail**

**airman** See **military titles**.

**Air National Guard**

**airport** Capitalize as part of a proper name: *La Guardia Airport*, *O'Hare International Airport*.

The first name of an individual and the word *international* may be deleted from a formal airport name while the remainder is capitalized: *John F. Kennedy International Airport*, *Kennedy International Airport*, or *Kennedy Airport*. Use whichever is appropriate in the context.

Do not make up names, however. There is no *Boston Airport*, for example. The *Boston airport* (lowercase *airport*) would be acceptable if for some reason the proper name, *Logan International Airport*, were not used.

**airstrike**

**airtight**

**air traffic controller** (no hyphen)

**airways** The system of routes that the federal government has established for airplane traffic.

See the **airline, airlines** entry for its use in carriers' names.

**aka** (no spacing is an exception to Webster's)

**Alabama** Abbrev.: *Ala.* See **state names**.

**a la carte**

**a la king, a la mode**

**Alaska** Do not abbreviate. Largest land area of the 50 states. See **state names**.

**Alaska Standard Time** The time zone used in all of Alaska, except the western Aleutian Islands and St. Lawrence Island, which are on *Hawaii-Aleutian Standard Time*.

There is also an *Alaska Daylight Time*.

See **time zones**.

**Alberta** A province of western Canada. Do not abbreviate. See **datelines**.

**albino, albinos**

**Alcoa Inc.** *Alcoa* is acceptable in all references to the formerly named Aluminum Company of America.
*Alcoa* also is a city in Tennessee.

**alcoholic** Use *recovering*, not *reformed*, in referring to those afflicted with the disease of alcoholism.

**alderman** Do not abbreviate. See **legislative titles**.

**alert** See **weather terms**.

**align**

**Alitalia Airlines** Headquarters is in Rome.

**Al-Jazeera**

**all-** Use a hyphen:
all-around (not all-round)    all-out
all-clear                     all-star
See **all right** and the **all time, all-time** entries.

**Allahu akbar** The Arabic phrase for "God is great."

**allege** The word must be used with great care.
Some guidelines:
—Avoid any suggestion that the writer is making an allegation.
—Specify the source of an allegation. In a criminal case, it should be an arrest record, an indictment or the statement of a public official connected with the case.
—Use *alleged bribe* or similar phrase when necessary to make it clear that an unproved action is not being treated as fact. Be sure that the source of the charge is specified elsewhere in the story.

—Avoid redundant uses of *alleged*. It is proper to say: *The district attorney alleged that she took a bribe.* Or: *The district attorney accused her of taking a bribe.* But not: *The district attorney accused her of allegedly taking a bribe.*
—Do not use *alleged* to describe an event that is known to have occurred, when the dispute is over who participated in it. Do not say: *He attended the alleged meeting* when what you mean is: *He allegedly attended the meeting.*
—Do not use *alleged* as a routine qualifier. Instead, use a word such as *apparent, ostensible* or *reputed*.
For guidelines on related words, see **accused**; **arrest**; and **indict**.

**Allegheny Mountains** Or simply: *the Alleghenies*.

**alley** Do not abbreviate. See **addresses**.

**allies, allied** Capitalize *allies* or *allied* only when referring to the combination of the United States and its Allies during World War I or World War II: *The Allies defeated Germany. He was in the Allied invasion of France.*

**allot, allotted, allotting**

**all right** (adv.) Never *alright*. Hyphenate only if used colloquially as a compound modifier: *He is an all-right guy.*

**all time, all-time** An *all-time high*, but *the greatest runner of all time*.
Avoid the redundant phrase *all-time record*.

**allude, refer** To *allude* to something is to speak of it without specifically mentioning it. To *refer* is to mention it directly.

**allusion, illusion** *Allusion* means an indirect reference: *The allusion was to his opponent's war record.*
*Illusion* means an unreal or false impression: *The scenic director created the illusion of choppy seas.*

**alma mater**

**almost never** Do not use the phrase. Instead use *seldom* or *hardly ever.*

**al-Qaida** International terrorist organization headed by Osama bin Laden.

**also-ran** (n.)

**altar, alter** An *altar* is a tablelike platform used in a religious service.
To *alter* is to change.

**alumnus, alumni, alumna, alumnae** Use *alumnus* (*alumni* in the plural) when referring to a man who has attended a school.
Use *alumna* (*alumnae* in the plural) for similar references to a woman.
Use *alumni* when referring to a group of men and women.

**Alzheimer's disease** This is a progressive, irreversible neurological disorder. Most victims are older than 65, but Alzheimer's can strike in the 40s or 50s.
Symptoms include gradual memory loss, impairment of judgment, disorientation, personality change, difficulty in learning and loss of language skills.
No cure is known.

**AM** Acceptable in all references to the *amplitude modulation* system of radio transmission.

**Amalgamated Transit Union** Use this full name on first reference.
Headquarters is in Washington.

**ambassador** Use for both men and women. Capitalize as a formal title before a name.
See **titles**.

**Amber Alert** A procedure for rapidly publicizing the disappearance of a child.

**amendments to the Constitution** Use *First Amendment, 10th Amendment,* etc.
Colloquial references to the Fifth Amendment's protection against self-incrimination are best avoided, but where appropriate: *He took the Fifth seven times.*

**American** An acceptable description for a citizen of the United States.

**American Airlines** Headquarters is in Fort Worth, Texas.

**American Baptist Association** See **Baptist churches**.

**American Baptist Churches in the U.S.A.** See **Baptist churches**.

**American Bar Association** *ABA* is acceptable on second reference. Also: *the bar association, the association.*
Headquarters is in Chicago.

**American Broadcasting Cos.** See **ABC**.

**American Civil Liberties Union** *ACLU* is acceptable on second reference.

Headquarters is in New York.

**American Federation of Government Employees** Use this full name on first reference to prevent confusion with other unions that represent government workers.

Headquarters is in Washington.

**American Federation of Labor and Congress of Industrial Organizations** *AFL-CIO* is acceptable in all references.

Headquarters is in Washington.

**American Federation of Musicians** Use this full name on first reference.

The shortened form *Musicians' union* is acceptable on second reference.

Headquarters is in New York.

**American Federation of State, County and Municipal Employees** Use this full name on first reference to prevent confusion with other unions that represent government workers.

Headquarters is in Washington.

**American Federation of Teachers** Use this full name on first reference to prevent confusion with other unions that represent teachers.

Headquarters is in Washington.

**American Federation of Television and Radio Artists** *AFTRA* is acceptable on second reference.

Headquarters is in New York.

**American Hospital Association** *AHA* is acceptable on second reference. Also: *the hospital association, the association.*

Headquarters is in Chicago.

**Americanisms** Words and phrases that have become part of the English language as spoken in the United States are listed with a star in Webster's New World College Dictionary.

Most Americanisms are acceptable in news stories, but let the context be the guide.

See **word selection**.

**American Legion** Capitalize also *the Legion* in second reference. Members are *Legionnaires*, just as members of the Lions Club are *Lions*.

*Legion* and *Legionnaires* are capitalized because they are not being used in their common noun sense. A *legion* (lowercase) is a large group of soldiers or, by derivation, a large number of items: *His friends are legion.* A *legionnaire* (lowercase) is a member of such a legion.

See the **fraternal organizations and service clubs** entry.

**American Medical Association** *AMA* is acceptable on second reference. Also: *the medical association, the association.*

Headquarters is in Chicago.

**American Newspaper Publishers Association** See **Newspaper Association of America**.

**American Petroleum Institute** *API* is acceptable on second reference.

Headquarters is in Washington.

## American Postal Workers Union
This union represents clerks and similar employees who work inside post offices.

Use the full name on first reference to prevent confusion with the National Association of Letter Carriers. The shortened form *Postal Workers union* is acceptable on second reference.

Headquarters is in Washington.

## American Press Institute
*API* is acceptable on second reference.

Headquarters is in Reston, Va.

## American Society for the Prevention of Cruelty to Animals
This organization is limited to the five boroughs of New York City and neighboring Suffolk County in providing animal adoption services, although it has offices elsewhere that offer legal advice and other services to other animal welfare organizations. *ASPCA* is acceptable on second reference.

See **Society for the Prevention of Cruelty to Animals**.

## American Society of Composers, Authors and Publishers
*ASCAP* is acceptable on second reference.

Headquarters is in New York.

## American Stock Exchange
In second reference: *the American Exchange, the Amex,* or *the exchange*.

## American Telephone & Telegraph Co.
See **AT&T Corp.**

## America West
Headquarters is in Tempe, Ariz.

**Amex** See **American Stock Exchange**.

**amid** Not *amidst.*

**amidships**

**ammunition** See **weapons**.

**amnesty** See the entry that reads **pardon, parole, probation**.

**amok** Not *amuck.*

**among, between** The maxim that *between* introduces two items and *among* introduces more than two covers most questions about how to use these words: *The funds were divided among Ford, Carter and McCarthy.*

However, *between* is the correct word when expressing the relationships of three or more items considered one pair at a time: *Negotiations on a debate format are under way between the network and the Ford, Carter and McCarthy committees.*

As with all prepositions, any pronouns that follow these words must be in the objective case: *among us, between him and her, between you and me.*

**ampersand (&)** Use the ampersand when it is part of a company's formal name or composition title: *House & Garden, Procter & Gamble, Wheeling & Lake Erie Railway.*

The ampersand should not otherwise be used in place of *and.*

**amplitude modulation** *AM* is acceptable in all references.

**a.m., p.m.** Lowercase, with periods. Avoid the redundant *10 a.m. this morning.*

**Amtrak** This acronym, drawn from the words *American travel by track*, may be used in all references to the *National Railroad Passenger Corp.* Do not use *AMTRAK*.

The corporation was established by Congress in 1970 to take over intercity passenger operations from railroads that wanted to drop passenger service. Amtrak contracts with railroads for the use of their tracks and of certain other operating equipment and crews.

Amtrak is subsidized in part by federal funds appropriated yearly by Congress and administered through the Department of Transportation.

*Amtrak* should not be confused with *Conrail* (see separate entry). However, the legislation that established Conrail provided for Amtrak to gradually take over ownership of certain trackage in the Boston-Washington corridor and from Philadelphia to Harrisburg, Pa.

Amtrak headquarters is in Washington.

**AMVETS** Acceptable in all references for *American Veterans*, the organization formerly known as *American Veterans of World War II, Korea, and Vietnam.*

Headquarters is in Washington.

**anchorman, anchorwoman** (not *anchor* or *co-anchor*)

**anemia, anemic**

**Anglican Communion** This is the name for the worldwide association of the 22 separate national Anglican churches.

Each national church is independent. A special position of honor is accorded to the archbishop of Canterbury, as the pre-eminent officer in the original Anglican body, the Church of England.

The test of membership in the Anglican Communion traditionally has been whether a church has been in communion with the See of Canterbury. No legislative or juridical ties exist, however.

BELIEFS: Anglicans believe in the Trinity, the humanity and divinity of Christ, the virginity of Mary, salvation through Christ, and everlasting heaven and hell.

A principal difference between Roman Catholics and Anglicans is still the dispute that led to the formation of the Church of England — refusal to acknowledge that the pope, as bishop of Rome, has ruling authority over other bishops. See **catholic, catholicism**.

ANGLICAN CHURCHES: Members of the Anglican Communion, in addition to the Church of England, include the Scottish Episcopal Church, the Anglican Church of Canada, and, in the United States, the Protestant Episcopal Church.

See **Episcopal Church**.

**Anglo-** Always capitalized. No hyphen when the word that follows is in lowercase:

Anglomania     Anglophobe
Anglophile

Use a hyphen when the word that follows is capitalized:

Anglo-American     Anglo-Indian
Anglo-Catholic     Anglo-Saxon

**angry** *At* someone or *with* someone.

**animals** Do not apply a personal pronoun to an animal unless its sex has been established or the animal has a name:

*The dog was scared; it barked. Rover was scared; he barked. The cat, which was scared, ran to its basket. Susie the cat, who was scared, ran to her basket. The bull tosses his horns.*

Capitalize the name of a specific animal, and use Roman numerals to show sequence: *Bowser, Whirlaway II.*

For breed names, follow the spelling and capitalization in Webster's New World College Dictionary. For breeds not listed in the dictionary, capitalize words derived from proper nouns; use lowercase elsewhere: *basset hound, Boston terrier.*

**anniversary** Avoid *first anniversary*, the redundant *one-year anniversary* and terms such as *six-month anniversary* (or other time spans less than a year). Similarly, avoid *first annual.*

**anno Domini** See **A.D.**

**annual** An event cannot be described as *annual* until it has been held in at least two successive years.

Do not use the term *first annual.* Instead, note that sponsors plan to hold an event annually.

**annual meeting** Lowercase in all uses.

**anoint**

**anonymous sources** Use anonymous attribution only when essential and even then provide the most specific possible identification of the source. Simply quoting "a source," unmodified, is almost always prohibited.

Do not attribute information to sources — anonymous or otherwise — when it is obvious, common sense or well-known.

The basic guidelines for use of anonymous sources:

The material must be information and not opinion and it must provide information of significant value to the news report.

The information must not be available except under the conditions of anonymity imposed by the source. In some cases, it may be appropriate to say why the source requested anonymity.

The source must be in a position to have accurate information and, to the best of the reporter's ability to determine, must be understood to be reliable.

Be sure to seek more than one source for the story.

**another** *Another* is not a synonym for *additional*; it refers to an element that somehow duplicates a previously stated quantity.

Right: *Ten people took the test; another 10 refused.*

Wrong: *Ten people took the test; another 20 refused.*

Right: *Ten people took the test; 20 others refused.*

## Antarctic, Antarctica, Antarctic Ocean

**ante-** The rules in **prefixes** apply, but in general, no hyphen. Some examples:

antebellum     antedate

**anthems** See **composition titles**. Lowercase the term *national anthem.*

**anti-** Hyphenate all except the following words, which have specific meanings of their own:

antibiotic          antiparticle*
antibody           antipasto
anticlimax         antiperspirant
antidepressant     antiphon

| | |
|---|---|
| antidote | antiphony |
| antifreeze | antiseptic |
| antigen | antiserum |
| antihistamine | antithesis |
| antiknock | antitoxin |
| antimatter | antitrust |
| antimony | antitussive |

*And similar terms in physics such as *antiproton*.

This approach has been adopted in the interests of readability and easily remembered consistency.

Note these exceptions to Webster's New World:

| | |
|---|---|
| anti-abortion | anti-labor |
| anti-aircraft | anti-social |
| anti-bias | anti-war |
| anti-inflation | |

See **Antichrist, anti-Christ**.

**Antichrist, anti-Christ**
*Antichrist* is the proper name for the individual the Bible says will challenge Christ.

The adjective *anti-Christ* would be applied to someone or something opposed to Christ.

**anticipate, expect** *Anticipate* means to expect and prepare for something; *expect* does not include the notion of preparation:
*They expect a record crowd.*
*They have anticipated it by adding more seats to the auditorium.*

**Antiochian Orthodox Christian Archdiocese of North America** Formed in 1975 by the merger of the Antiochian Orthodox Christian Archdiocese of New York and All North America and the Archdiocese of Toledo, Ohio, and Dependencies in North America. It is under the jurisdiction of the patriarch of Antioch.

See **Eastern Orthodox churches**.

**anybody, any body, anyone, any one** One word for an indefinite reference: *Anyone can do that.*

Two words when the emphasis is on singling out one element of a group: *Any one of them may speak up.*

**AP** Use in logotypes. Acceptable on second reference for *The Associated Press*.

Do not capitalize *the* when it precedes *AP*.

See **Associated Press**.

**apostolic delegate, papal nuncio** An *apostolic delegate* is a Roman Catholic diplomat chosen by the pope to be his envoy to the church in a nation that does not have formal diplomatic relations with the Vatican.

A *papal nuncio* is the pope's envoy to a nation with which the Vatican has diplomatic relations.

**apostrophe (')** See entry in **Punctuation** section.

**Appalachia** In the broadest sense, the word applies to the entire region along the Appalachian Mountains, which extend from Maine into northern Alabama.

In a sense that often suggests economic depression and poverty, the reference is to sections of eastern Tennessee, eastern Kentucky, southeastern Ohio and the western portion of West Virginia.

The Appalachian Regional Commission, established by federal law in 1965, has a mandate to foster development in 397 counties in 13 states — all of West Virginia and parts of Alabama, Georgia, Kentucky, Maryland, Mississippi, New York, North Carolina, Ohio, Pennsylvania, South Carolina, Tennessee and Virginia.

When the word *Appalachia* is used, specify the extent of the area in question.

## Appalachian Mountains
Or simply: *the Appalachians.*

## appeals court See U.S. Court of Appeals.

**apposition** A decision on whether to put commas around a word, phrase or clause used in apposition depends on whether it is essential to the meaning of the sentence (no commas) or not essential (use commas).

See the **essential phrases, nonessential phrases** entry for examples.

**approve** See the entry that reads **adopt, approve, enact, pass.**

## April See months.

## April Fools' Day

**Aqua-Lung** A trademark for an underwater breathing apparatus.
See **scuba.**

**Arabic names** In general, use an English spelling that approximates the way a name sounds in Arabic.

If an individual has a preferred spelling in English, use that. If usage has established a particular spelling, use that.

Problems in transliteration of Arabic names often are traceable to pronunciations that vary from region to region. The *g*, for example, is pronounced like the *g* of *go* in North Africa, but like the *j* of *joy* in the Arab Peninsula. Thus it is *Gamal* in Egypt and *Jamal* in nations on the peninsula. Follow local practice in deciding which letter to use.

Arabs commonly are known by two names (*Fuad Butros*), or by three (*Ahmed Zaki Yamani*). Follow the individual's preference on first reference. On second reference, use only the final name in the sequence.

The articles *al-* or *el-* may be used or dropped depending on the person's preference or established usage. *Osama el-Baz, el-Baz* or *Moammar Gadhafi, Gadhafi.*

The Arabic word for son (*ibn* or *bin* depending on personal preference and the nation) is sometimes part of a name (*Rashid bin Humaid*). On second reference, use only the final word in the name: *Humaid.*

The word *abu*, meaning *father of*, occasionally is used as a last name (*Abdul Mohsen Abu Maizer*). Capitalize and repeat it on second reference: *Abu Maizer.*

The titles *king, emir, sheik* and *imam* are used, but *prince* usually replaces *emir.* Some Arabs are known only by the title and a given name on first reference (*King Hussein*). Others are known by a complete name (*Sheik Sabah Salem Sabah*). Follow the common usage on first reference. On second reference, drop the title, using only the given name if it stood alone (*Hussein*) or the final name in the sequence if more than one was used on first reference (*Sabah*). Make an exception to this procedure for second reference if an individual commonly is known by some other one of the names used on first reference.

The *al*, when found in front of many newspaper names, means *the.* It should be capitalized, as in *The New York Times, El Pais, Die Welt.*

**Arabic numerals** The numerical figures *0, 1, 2, 3, 4, 5, 6, 7, 8, 9.*

In general, use Arabic forms unless denoting the sequence of wars or establishing a personal sequence for people or animals. See **Roman numerals**.

Separate entries list more details and examples. For a full list, see the **numerals** entry.

**arbitrate, mediate** Both terms are used in reports about labor negotiations, but they should not be interchanged.

One who *arbitrates* hears evidence from all people concerned, then hands down a decision.

One who *mediates* listens to arguments of both parties and tries by the exercise of reason or persuasion to bring them to an agreement.

**arch-** No hyphen after this prefix unless it precedes a capitalized word:

| | |
|---|---|
| archbishop | arch-Republican |
| archenemy | archrival |

**archaeology**

**archbishop** See **Episcopal Church; Roman Catholic Church**; and **religious titles**.

**archbishop of Canterbury** In general, lowercase *archbishop* unless it is used before the name of the individual who holds the office.

Capitalize *Archbishop of Canterbury* standing alone only when it is used in a story that also refers to members of Britain's nobility. See the **nobility** entry for the relevant guidelines.

**archdiocese** Capitalize as part of a proper name: *the Archdiocese of Chicago, the Chicago*

*Archdiocese.* Lowercase when it stands alone.

See the entry for the particular denomination in question.

**arctic** (lowercase for adjective meaning frigid; capitalize for region around the North Pole), **Arctic Circle, arctic fox, Arctic Ocean**

**are** A unit of surface measure in the metric system, equal to 100 square meters.

An *are* is equal to approximately 1,076.4 square feet or 119.6 square yards.

See **hectare** and **metric system**.

**area codes** See **telephone numbers**.

**Arizona** Abbrev.: *Ariz.* See **state names**.

**Arkansas** Abbrev.: *Ark.* See **state names**.

**Armenian Church of America** The term encompasses two independent dioceses that cooperate in some activities: the Eastern Diocese of the Armenian Church of America, for areas outside California, and the Western Diocese of the Armenian Church of America, which serves California.

See **Eastern Orthodox Churches**.

**Armistice Day** It is now *Veterans Day.*

**army** Capitalize when referring to U.S. forces: *the U.S. Army, the Army, Army regulations.* Do not use the abbreviation *USA.*

Use lowercase for the forces of other nations: *the French army.*

This approach has been adopted for consistency, because many foreign nations do not use *army* as the proper name.
See **military academies** and **military titles**.

**arrest** To avoid any suggestion that someone is being judged before a trial, do not use a phrase such as *arrested for killing*. Instead, use *arrested on a charge of killing*.
For guidelines on related words, see **accused**; **allege**; and **indict**.

**arrive** It requires the preposition *at*. Do not omit, as airline dispatchers often do in: *He will arrive La Guardia.*

**artifact**

**artificial intelligence** Ideally, computers that think like humans. Currently, computers cannot apply experience, logic, and prediction to problem-solving. They act only on instructions, either from the program or from the user.

**artillery** See **weapons**.

**artworks** See **composition titles**.

**as** See **like, as**.

**ASCII** An acronym for *American Standard Code for Information Interchange*. A numeric code used to represent the letters of the Roman alphabet, numbers and punctuation marks. Use of the acronym on first reference is acceptable if it is identified as a code.

**ashcan, ashtray**

**Ash Wednesday** The first day of Lent, 46 days before Easter.
See **Easter** and **Lent**.

**Asian, Asiatic** Use *Asian* or *Asians* when referring to people.
Some Asians regard *Asiatic* as offensive when applied to people.

**Asian flu**

**Asian subcontinent** In popular usage the term applies to Bangladesh, Bhutan, India, Nepal, Pakistan, Sikkim and the island nation of Sri Lanka (formerly Ceylon) at the southeastern tip of India.
For definitions of the terms that apply to other parts of Asia, see **Far East**; **Middle East**; and **Southeast Asia**.

**as if** The preferred form, but *as though* is acceptable.

**assassination** Use the term only if it involves the murder of a politically important or prominent individual by surprise attack.

**assassination, date of** A prominent person is shot one day and dies the next. Which day was he assassinated? The day he was attacked.

**assassin, killer, murderer** An *assassin* is a politically motivated killer.
A *killer* is anyone who kills with a motive of any kind.
A *murderer* is one who is convicted of murder in a court of law.
See **execute** and the **homicide, murder, manslaughter** entry.

**assault, battery** Popularly, *assault* almost always implies physical contact and sudden, intense violence.

Legally, however, *assault* means simply to threaten violence, as in pointing a pistol at an individual without firing it. *Assault and battery* is the legal term when the victim was touched by the assaulter or something the assaulter put in motion.

**assembly** Capitalize when part of the proper name for the lower house of a legislature: *the California Assembly.* Retain capitalization if the state name is dropped but the reference is specific:

*SACRAMENTO, Calif. (AP)* — *The state Assembly ...*

If a legislature is known as a general assembly: *the Missouri General Assembly, the General Assembly, the assembly. Legislature* also may be used as the proper name, however. See **legislature**.

Lowercase all plural uses: *the California and New York assemblies.*

**assemblyman, assemblywoman** Do not abbreviate. See **legislative titles**.

**assistant** Do not abbreviate. Capitalize only when part of a formal title before a name: *Assistant Secretary of State George Ball.* Whenever practical, however, an appositional construction should be used: *George Ball, assistant secretary of state.* See **titles**.

**associate** Never abbreviate. Apply the same capitalization norms listed under **assistant**.

**Associated Press, The** The newsgathering cooperative dating from 1846.

Use *The Associated Press* on first reference (the capitalized article is part of the formal name).

On second reference, *AP* or *the AP* (no capital on *the*) may be used.

The address is 450 West 33rd Street, New York, NY 10001. The telephone number is (212) 621-1500.

The World Wide Web address is www.ap.org.

The following are service names used most frequently by the AP.

DataFeature
DataSpeed
DataStream
GraphicsNet
Newsfeatures
NewsPhoto
NewsPower
Network News
PhotoColor
PhotoExpress
PhotoStream
SportsStats
See the **AP** entry.

**Association** Do not abbreviate. Capitalize as part of a proper name: *American Medical Association.*

**asterisk** Do not use the symbol in standard AP wire transmissions. It rarely translates and in many cases cannot be seen by AP computers or received by newspaper computers.

**astronaut** It is not a formal title. Do not capitalize when used before a name: *astronaut John Glenn.*

**AT&T Inc.** The full name of the business formerly known as American Telephone & Telegraph

Co. AT&T was acquired in 2005 by its former subsidiary, SBC Communications Inc., which renamed itself AT&T and is headquartered in San Antonio.

**Atchison, Topeka & Santa Fe Railway** Now a part of Burlington Northern Santa Fe Railway.

**atheist** See the **agnostic, atheist** entry.

**athlete's foot, athlete's heart**

**Atlanta** The city in Georgia stands alone in datelines.

**Atlantic Ocean**

**Atlantic Richfield Co.** *Arco* is acceptable on second reference.
Headquarters is in Los Angeles.

**Atlantic Standard Time, Atlantic Daylight Time** Used in the Maritime Provinces of Canada and in Puerto Rico.
See **time zones**.

**at large** Usually two words for an individual representing more than a single district: *congressman at large, councilman at large.*
But it is *ambassador-at-large* for an ambassador assigned to no particular country.

**ATM** Acceptable in first reference for *automated teller machine.* It should be spelled out somewhere in the story.
Do not use the redundant *ATM machine.*

**Atomic Age** It began Dec. 2, 1942, at the University of Chicago with the creation of the first self-sustaining nuclear chain reaction.

**Atomic Energy Commission** It no longer exists. See **Nuclear Regulatory Commission**.

**attache** It is not a formal title. Always lowercase.

**attorney general, attorneys general** Never abbreviate. Capitalize only when used as a title before a name: *Attorney General Alberto Gonzales.*
See **titles**.

**attorney, lawyer** In common usage the words are interchangeable.
Technically, however, an *attorney* is someone (usually, but not necessarily, a lawyer) empowered to act for another. Such an individual occasionally is called an *attorney in fact.*
A *lawyer* is a person admitted to practice in a court system. Such an individual occasionally is called an *attorney at law.*
Do not abbreviate. Do not capitalize unless it is an officeholder's title: *defense attorney Perry Mason, attorney Perry Mason, District Attorney Hamilton Burger.*
See **lawyer**.

**augur** A transitive verb. Do not follow it with the preposition for: *The tea leaves augur a time of success.*

**August** See **months**.

**author** A noun used for both men and women. Do not use it as a verb.

**automaker, automakers**

**automatic** See **pistol** and **weapons** entries.

**automobiles** Capitalize brand names: *Buick, Ford, Mustang, Accord, Toyota, Taurus, Saturn.* Lowercase generic terms: *Sunfire convertible, Windstar minivan.*

**Auto Train** Rail service that carries passengers and their cars. Owned and operated by Amtrak.

**autoworker, autoworkers** One word when used generically.

But *Auto Worker* when referring specifically to the membership and the activities of the United Automobile, Aerospace and Agricultural Implement Workers of America.

**autumn** See **seasons**.

**avenue** Abbreviate only with a numbered address. See **addresses**.

**average, mean, median, norm** *Average* refers to the result obtained by dividing a sum by the number of quantities added together: *The average of 7, 9, 17 is 33 divided by 3, or 11.*

*Mean*, in its sense used in arithmetic and statistics, is an *average* and is determined by adding the series of numbers and dividing the sum by the number of cases: *The mean temperature of five days with temperatures of 67, 62, 68, 69, 64 is 66.*

*Median* is the middle number of points in a series arranged in order of size: *The median grade in the group of 50, 55, 85, 88, 92 is 85. The average is 74.*

*Norm* implies a standard of average performance for a given group: *The child was below the norm for his age in reading comprehension.*

**average of** The phrase takes a plural verb in a construction such as: *An average of 100 new jobs are created daily.*

**averse** See **adverse, averse**.

**Avianca** The headquarters of this airline is in Bogota, Colombia.

**aviator** Use for both men and women.

**awards and decorations** Capitalize them: *Bronze Star, Medal of Honor,* etc.

See **Nobel Prize** and **Pulitzer Prizes**.

**awe-struck**

**awhile, a while** *He plans to stay awhile.*

*He plans to stay for a while.*

**AWOL** Acceptable on second reference for *absent without leave.*

**ax** Not *axe.*

The verb forms: *ax, axed, axing.*

**Axis** The alliance of Germany, Italy and Japan during World War II.

# B

**Baby Bells** A collective description of the regional telephone companies formed out of the breakup of the Bell System of AT&T. Avoid except in quotes.

**baby boomer** Lowercase, no hyphen.

**baby-sit, baby-sitting, baby-sat, baby sitter**

**baccalaureate**

**Bachelor of Arts, Bachelor of Science** A *bachelor's degree* or *bachelor's* is acceptable in any reference. See **academic degrees** for guidelines on when the abbreviations *B.A.* or *B.S.* are acceptable.

**backfire** In wildfires, this term is for a fire set along the inner edge of a fireline to consume the fuel in the fire's path or change its direction.

**back up** (v.) **backup** (n. and adj.)

**backward** Not backwards.

**backyard** One word in all uses.

**bad, badly** *Bad* should not be used as an adverb. It does not lose its status as an adjective, however, in a sentence such as *I feel bad.* Such a statement is the idiomatic equivalent of *I am in bad health.* An alternative, *I feel badly*, could be interpreted as meaning that your sense of touch was bad.
See the **good, well** entry.

**Baha'i** A monotheistic religion founded in the 1860s by Baha'u'llah, a Persian nobleman considered a prophet by the Baha'is. Baha'u'llah taught that all religions represent progressive stages in the revelation of God's will, leading to the unity of all people and faiths. The Baha'is have no clergy; they are governed by local, national and international elected councils. The international governing body, the Universal House of Justice, is based in Haifa, Israel. Its U.S. offices are in Evanston, Ill.

**Bahamas** In datelines, give the name of the city or town followed by *Bahamas:*
NASSAU, Bahamas (AP) —
In stories, use *Bahamas, the Bahamas or the Bahama Islands* as the construction of a sentence dictates.
Identify a specific island in the text if relevant.

**bail** *Bail* is money or property that will be forfeited to the court if an accused individual fails to appear for trial. It may be posted as follows:

—The accused may deposit with the court the full amount or its equivalent in collateral such as a deed to property.

—A friend or relative may make such a deposit with the court.

—The accused may pay a professional bail bondsman a percentage of the total figure. The bondsman, in turn, guarantees the court that it will receive from him the full amount in the event the individual fails to appear for trial.

It is correct in all cases to say that an accused *posted bail* or *posted a bail bond* (the money held by the court is a form of bond). When a distinction is desired, say that the individual *posted his own bail*, that *bail was posted by a friend or relative*, or that *bail was obtained through a bondsman*.

**Bakelite** A trademark for a type of plastic resin.

**baker's dozen** It means 13.

**Bakery, Confectionery, Tobacco Workers and Grain Millers International Union** The shortened form *Bakery Workers union* is acceptable in all references.

Headquarters is in Washington.

**balance of payments, balance of trade** The *balance of payments* is the difference between the amount of money that leaves a nation and the amount that enters it during a period of time.

The *balance of payments* is determined by computing the amount of money a nation and

its citizens send abroad for all purposes — including goods and services purchased, travel, loans, foreign aid, etc. — and subtracting from it the amount that foreign nations send into the nation for similar purposes.

The *balance of trade* is the difference between the monetary value of the goods a nation imports and the goods it exports.

An example illustrating the difference between the two:

The United States and its citizens might send $10 billion abroad — $5 billion for goods, $3 billion for loans and foreign aid, $1 billion for services and $1 billion for tourism and other purposes.

Other nations might send $9 billion into the United States — $6 billion for U.S. goods, $2 billion for services and $1 billion for tourism and other purposes.

The United States would have a *balance-of-payments* deficit of $1 billion but a *balance-of-trade* surplus of $1 billion.

**ball carrier**

**ballclub, ballpark, ballplayer, ballroom**

**ball point pen**

**baloney** Foolish or exaggerated talk.

The sausage or luncheon meat is *bologna*.

**Baltimore** The city in Maryland stands alone in datelines.

**B'nai B'rith** See the **fraternal organizations and service clubs** entry.

**Band-Aid** A trademark for a type of adhesive bandage.

## Bank of America Corp.

Formed from the 1998 merger of BankAmerica and NationsBank and the 2004 merger with Fleet-Boston Financial. Headquarters is in Charlotte, N.C.

**bankruptcy** See entry in **Business Guidelines**.

**baptism** See **sacraments**.

**baptist, Baptist** A person who baptizes is a *baptist* (lowercase).

A *Baptist* (uppercase) is a person who is a member of the Protestant denomination described in the next entry.

## Baptist churches

It is incorrect to apply the term *church* to any Baptist unit except the local church.

The largest of the more than 20 Baptist bodies in the United States is the Southern Baptist Convention. It has more than 12 million members, most of them in the South, although it has churches in 50 states.

The largest Northern body is American Baptist Churches in the U.S.A., with about 1.5 million members.

Blacks predominate in three other large Baptist bodies, the National Baptist Convention of America, the National Baptist Convention U.S.A. Inc., and the Progressive National Baptist Convention Inc.

The roster of Baptist bodies in the United States also includes the Baptist General Conference, the Conservative Baptist Association of America, the General Association of Regular Baptist Churches, the General Association of General Baptists, and the North American Baptist General Conference.

The Baptist World Alliance, a voluntary association of Baptist bodies throughout the world, organizes the Baptist World Congress meetings generally held every five years. Headquarters is in Washington.

CLERGY: All members of the Baptist clergy may be referred to as *ministers*. *Pastor* applies if a minister leads a congregation.

On first reference, use *the Rev.* before the name of a man or woman. On second reference, use only the last name.

See **religious titles**.

See **religious movements** for definitions of some descriptive terms that often apply to Baptists but are not limited to them.

**barbecue** Not *barbeque* or *Bar-B-Q*.

## barbiturate

## barmaid

**bar mitzvah** The Jewish religious ritual and family celebration that marks a boy's 13th birthday. Judaism regards the age of 13 as the benchmark of religious maturity. *Bar mitzvah* translates as "one who is responsible for the Commandments."

Some congregations have instituted the *bas mitzvah* or *bat mitzvah*, a similar ceremony for girls.

**baron, baroness** See **nobility**.

**barrel** A standard barrel in U.S. measure contains 31.5 gallons.

A standard barrel in British and Canadian measure contains 36 imperial gallons.

In international dealings with crude oil, a standard barrel contains 42 U.S. gallons or 35 imperial gallons.

See the **oil** entry for guidelines on computing the volume and weight of petroleum products.

### barrel, barreled, barreling

### barrel-chested, barrelhouse Also: *double-barreled shotgun*.

### barrister See **lawyer**.

### barroom

**BASIC** A computer programming language. Acronym for *Beginners' All-Purpose Symbolic Instruction Code*. Use of acronym on first reference is acceptable if it is identified as a programming language.

**battalion** Capitalize when used with a figure to form a name: *the 3rd Battalion, the 10th Battalion*.

**battlefield** Also: *battlefront, battleground, battleship*. But *battle station*.

### Bavarian cream

**bay** Capitalize as an integral part of a proper name: *Hudson Bay, San Francisco Bay*.

Capitalize also *San Francisco Bay Area* or *the Bay Area* as the popular name for the nine-county region that has San Francisco as its focal point.

**bazaar** A fair. *Bizarre* means unusual.

**B.C.** Acceptable in all references to a calendar year in the period *before Christ*.

Because the full phrase would be *in the year 43 before Christ*, the abbreviation *B.C.* is placed after the figure for the year: *43 B.C.*

See **A.D.**

**because, since** Use *because* to denote a specific cause-effect relationship: *He went because he was told*.

*Since* is acceptable in a causal sense when the first event in a sequence led logically to the second but was not its direct cause: *They went to the game, since they had been given the tickets*.

### before Christ See **B.C.**

**Beijing** The city in China (formerly Peking) stands alone in datelines.

**Bell Labs** The research and development division of Lucent Technologies. It was previously called AT&T Bell Laboratories after the breakup of the Bell system in 1984 and was spun off from AT&T in 1996 as part of the formation of Lucent Technologies.

### bellwether

### benefit, benefited, benefiting

**Benelux** Belgium, the Netherlands and Luxembourg.

If *Benelux* is used, explain that it is an inclusive word for these three nations.

### Ben-Gurion International Airport Located at Lod, Israel, about 10 miles south of Tel Aviv.

See **airport**.

**Berlin** Stands alone in datelines.

**Berlin Wall** On second reference, *the wall.*

**Bermuda collar, Bermuda grass, Bermuda shorts**

**beside, besides** *Beside* means at the side of. *Besides* means in addition to.

**besiege**

**best-seller** Hyphenate in all uses.

**betting odds** Use figures and a hyphen: *The odds were 5-4, he won despite 3-2 odds against him.*

The word *to* seldom is necessary, but when it appears it should be hyphenated in all constructions: *3-to-2 odds, odds of 3-to-2, the odds were 3-to-2.*

**bettor** A person who bets.

**between** See the **among, between** entry.

**bi-** The rules in **prefixes** apply, but in general, no hyphen. Some examples:

| | |
|---|---|
| bifocal | bimonthly |
| bilateral | bipartisan |
| bilingual | |

**biannual, biennial** *Biannual* means twice a year and is a synonym for the word semiannual.
*Biennial* means every two years.

**Bible** Capitalize, without quotation marks, when referring to the Scriptures in the Old Testament or the New Testament. Capitalize also related terms such as the *Gospels, Gospel of St. Mark, the Scriptures, the Holy Scriptures.*
Lowercase *biblical* in all uses.

Lowercase *bible* as a nonreligious term: *My dictionary is my bible.*

Do not abbreviate individual books of the Bible.

Old Testament is a Christian designation; Hebrew Bible or Jewish Bible is the appropriate term for stories dealing with Judaism alone.

The standard names and order of Old Testament books as they appear in Protestant Bibles are: Genesis, Exodus, Leviticus, Numbers, Deuteronomy, Joshua, Judges, Ruth, 1 Samuel, 2 Samuel, 1 Kings, 2 Kings, 1 Chronicles, 2 Chronicles, Ezra, Nehemiah, Esther, Job, Psalms, Proverbs, Ecclesiastes, Song of Solomon, Isaiah, Jeremiah, Lamentations, Ezekiel, Daniel, Hosea, Joel, Amos, Obadiah, Jonah, Micah, Nahum, Habakkuk, Zephaniah, Haggai, Zechariah, Malachi.

Jewish Bibles contain the same 39 books, in different order. Roman Catholic Bibles follow a different order, usually use some different names, and include the seven Deuterocanonical books (called the Apocrypha by Protestants): Tobit, Judith, 1 Maccabees, 2 Maccabees, Wisdom, Sirach, Baruch.

The books of the New Testament, in order: Matthew, Mark, Luke, John, Acts, Romans, 1 Corinthians, 2 Corinthians, Galatians, Ephesians, Philippians, Colossians, 1 Thessalonians, 2 Thessalonians, 1 Timothy, 2 Timothy, Titus, Philemon, Hebrews, James, 1 Peter, 2 Peter, 1 John, 2 John, 3 John, Jude, Revelation.

Citation listing the number of chapter and verse(s) use this form: *Matthew 3:16, Luke 21:1-13, 1 Peter 2:1.*

**Bible Belt** Those sections

of the United States, especially in the South and Middle West, where fundamentalist religious beliefs prevail. Use with care, because in certain contexts it can give offense.

See **religious movements**.

**bicycle**

**Big Board** Acceptable on second reference for *the New York Stock Exchange*.

**big brother** One's older brother is a *big brother*. *Big Brother* (capitalized) means under the watchful eye of big government, from George Orwell's "1984."

Capitalize also in reference to members of Big Brothers Big Sisters of America Inc. The organization has headquarters in Philadelphia.

**Big Three automakers** A phrase generally referring to General Motors, Ford and Chrysler (a unit of DaimlerChrysler).

**bigwig**

**billion** A thousand million. For forms, see the **millions, billions** entry.

**Bill of Rights** The first 10 amendments to the Constitution.

**bimonthly** Means every other month. *Semimonthly* means twice a month.

**bioterrorism**

**birthday** Capitalize as part of the name for a holiday: *Washington's Birthday*. Lowercase in other uses.

**bishop** See **religious titles** and the entry for the denomination in question.

**bit** Acceptable in all references as an acronym for *binary digit*. Actual data take the form of electrical impulses. These can be thought of as either on or off or 1 and 0. The pulses are bits.

**biweekly** Means every other week. *Semiweekly* means twice a week.

**bizarre** Unusual. A fair is a *bazaar*.

**black** Preferred usage for those of the Negroid or black race. (Use *Negro* only in names of organizations or in quotations.) Do not use *colored* as a synonym. See the **colored** entry.

**BlackBerry**

**Black Muslims** See **Muslim(s)**.

**blackout, brownout** A *blackout* is a total power failure over a large area or the concealing of lights that might be visible to enemy raiders.

The term *rolling blackout* is used by electric companies to describe a situation in which electric power to some sections temporarily is cut off on a rotating basis to assure that voltage will meet minimum standards in other sections.

A *brownout* is a small, temporary voltage reduction, usually from 2 percent to 8 percent, implemented to conserve electric power.

**blast off** (v.) **blastoff** (n. and adj.)

**Blessed Sacrament, Blessed Virgin**

**blind** See **disabled, handicapped, impaired**.

**blizzard** See **weather terms**.

**bloc, block** A *bloc* is a coalition of people, groups or nations with the same purpose or goal.

*Block* has more than a dozen definitions, but a political alliance is not one of them.

**blond, blonde** Use *blond* as a noun for males and as an adjective for all applications: She has *blond* hair.

Use *blonde* as a noun for females.

**bloodbath** One word, an exception to Webster's.

**bloodhound**

**Bloody Mary** A drink made of vodka and tomato juice. The name is derived from the nickname for Mary I of England.

**blue blood** (n.) **blue-blooded** (adj.)

**blue chip stock** Stock in a company known for its long-established record of making money and paying dividends.

**board** Capitalize only when an integral part of a proper name. See **capitalization**.

**board of aldermen** See **city council**.

**board of directors, board of trustees** Always lowercase. See the **organizations and institutions** entry.

**board of supervisors** See **city council**.

**boats, ships** A *boat* is a watercraft of any size but generally is used to indicate a small craft. A *ship* is a large, seagoing vessel.

The word *boat* is used, however, in some words that apply to large craft: *ferryboat, PT boat*.

Use *it*, not the pronoun *she*, in references to boats and ships.

Use Arabic or Roman numerals in the names of boats and ships: *the Queen Elizabeth 2* or *QE2; Titan I, Titan II.*

The reference for military ships is Jane's Fighting Ships; for nonmilitary ships, Lloyd's Register of Shipping.

**Bobcat** Trademark for a brand of skid-steer loaders, excavators and backhoes.

**Boeing Co.** Formerly Boeing Aircraft Co.

Headquarters is in Chicago.

**bologna** The sausage. *Baloney* is foolish or exaggerated talk.

**bona fide**

**bonbon**

**boo-boo**

**Boogie** A trademark for a type of surfing bodyboard. Use the generic term.

**Books on Tape** A trademark for a brand of audiotapes. Use a generic term such as audiotape or audiocassette.

**book titles** See **composition titles**.

**borscht**

**Bosnia-Herzegovina** The country has been divided into a Bosnian Serb republic and a Muslim-Croat federation since 1995. Both have wide autonomy but share a common presidency, parliament and government. In datelines: *SARAJEVO, Bosnia-Herzegovina.* The people are *Bosnians.*

**Bosporus, the** Not the Bosporus Strait.

**Boston** The city in Massachusetts stands alone in datelines.

**Boston brown bread, Boston cream pie, Boston terrier**

**boulevard** Abbreviated only with a numbered address. See **addresses**.

**bowlegged**

**box office** (n.) **box-office** (adj.)

**boy** Applicable until 18th birthday is reached. Use *man* or *young man* afterward.

**boycott, embargo** A *boycott* is an organized refusal to buy a particular product or service, or to deal with a particular merchant or group of merchants.

An *embargo* is a legal restriction against trade. It usually prohibits goods from entering or leaving a country.

**boyfriend, girlfriend**

**Boy Scouts** The full name of the national organization is *Boy Scouts of America.* Headquarters is in Irving, Texas.

*Cub Scouting* is for boys 8 through 10. Members are *Cub Scouts* or *Cubs.*

*Boy Scouting* is for boys 11 through 17. Members are *Boy Scouts* or *Scouts.*

*Exploring* is a separate program open to boys and girls from high school age through 20. Members are *Explorers*, not *Explorer Scouts.* Members of units that stress nautical programs are *Sea Explorers.*

*Venturing*, originally part of the *Exploring* division, is for young adults, 14 through 20.

See **Girl Scouts**.

**BP Amoco PLC** Formerly British Petroleum. *BP* is acceptable on second reference.

Headquarters is in London.

**bra** Acceptable in all references for *brassiere.*

**brackets** See entry in **Punctuation** chapter.

**Brahman, Brahmin** *Brahman* applies to the priestly Hindu caste and a breed of cattle.

*Brahmin* applies to aristocracy in general: *Boston Brahmin.*

**brand names** When they are used, capitalize them.

Brand names normally should be used only if they are essential to a story.

Sometimes, however, the use of a brand name may not be essential but is acceptable because it lends an air of reality to a story: *He fished a Camel from his shirt pocket* may be preferable to the less specific cigarette.

When a company sponsors an event such as a tennis tournament, use the company's name for the event in first reference and the generic term in subsequent references.

Also use a separate paragraph to provide the name of a sponsor when the brand name is not part of the formal title.

Brand name is a nonlegal term for *service mark* or *trademark.* See entries under those words.

**brand-new** (adj.)

**break in** (v.) **break-in** (n. and adj.)

**break up** (v.) **breakup** (n. and adj.)

**bride, bridegroom, bridesmaid** *Bride* is appropriate in wedding stories, but use *wife* or *spouse* in other circumstances.

**brigadier** See **military titles**.

**Bright's disease** After Dr. Richard Bright, the London physician who first diagnosed this form of kidney disease.

**Brill's disease** After Nathan E. Brill, a U.S. physician. A form of epidemic typhus fever in which the disease recurs years after the original infection.

**Britain** Acceptable in all references for *Great Britain*, which consists of England, Scotland and Wales.
See **United Kingdom**.

**British Airways** Headquarters is in Hounslow, England.

**British, Briton(s)** The people of Great Britain: the English, the Scottish, the Welsh. *Brits* is slang.

**British Broadcasting Corp.** *BBC* is acceptable in all references within contexts such as a television column. Otherwise, do not use *BBC* until second reference.

**British Columbia** The Canadian province bounded on the west by the Pacific Ocean. Do not abbreviate.

See **datelines**.

**British Commonwealth** See **Commonwealth, the**.

**British Petroleum** See **BP Amoco PLC**.

**British thermal unit** The amount of heat required to increase the temperature of a pound of water 1 degree Fahrenheit. *Btu* (the same for singular and plural) is acceptable on second reference.

**British ton** See **ton**.

**British Virgin Islands** Use with a community name in datelines on stories from these islands. Do not abbreviate.
Specify an individual island in the text if relevant.
See **datelines**.

**broadcast** The past tense also is *broadcast*, not *broadcasted*.

**Broadway, off-Broadway, off-off-Broadway** When applied to stage productions, these terms refer to distinctions made by union contracts, not to location of a theater.
Actors' Equity Association and unions representing craft workers have one set of pay scales for *Broadway* productions (generally those in New York City theaters of 300 or more seats) and a lower scale for smaller theaters, classified as *off-Broadway* houses.
The term *off-off-Broadway* refers to workshop productions that may use Equity members for a limited time at substandard pay. Other unions maintain a hands-off policy, agreeing with the Equity attitude that actors should have an opportunity to whet their talents in offbeat roles without

losing their Equity memberships.

**broccoli**

**Bronze Age** The age characterized by the development of bronze tools and weapons, from 3500 to 1000 B.C. Regarded as coming between the Stone Age and the Iron Age.

**brother** See **Roman Catholic Church**.

**Brotherhood of Locomotive Engineers and Trainmen** *BLET* is acceptable on second reference.
Headquarters is in Cleveland.

**brothers** Abbreviate as *Bros.* in formal company names: *Warner Bros.*
For possessives: *Warner Bros.' profits.*

**brownout** See the **blackout, brownout** entry.

**brunet, brunette** Use *brunet* as a noun for males, and as the adjective for both sexes.
Use *brunette* as a noun for females.

**brussels sprouts**

**Btu** The same in singular and plural. See **British thermal unit**.

**Bubble Wrap** A registered trademark. Unless the trademark name is important to the story, use *cushioning* or *packaging material.*

**Budapest** The capital of Hungary. In datelines, follow it with *Hungary.*

**Buddha, Buddhism** A major religion founded in India

about 500 B.C. by Buddha. Buddha, which means enlightened one, was the name given to Siddhartha Gautama by his followers.
Buddhism has about 325 million followers, mostly in India, Tibet, China, Japan, Korea and Southeast Asia. About 2 million practice Buddhism in North America.
Buddhists believe that correct thinking and self-denial will enable the soul to reach nirvana, a state of release into ultimate enlightenment and peace. Until nirvana is reached, believers cannot be freed from the cycle of death and rebirth.
There are four major groups within Buddhism.
—Hinayana or Theravada: Followers stress monastic discipline and attainment of nirvana by the individual through meditation. It is dominant among Buddhists in Cambodia, Laos, Myanmar, Thailand and Sri Lanka.
—Mahayana: Followers lay stress on idealism. The ideal life is that of virtue and wisdom. The sect is found mostly in Japan, Korea and eastern China.
—Mantrayana: Major centers for this group are in the Himalayas, Mongolia and Japan. It is similar to Mahayana but also has a structure of spiritual leaders and disciples, believes in various evil spirits and deities, uses magic, and has secret rituals.
—Zen: Followers seek enlightenment through introspection and intuition. The doctrines are again similar to Mahayana and like Mantrayana there is a loose structure of leaders and disciples. This group is found mostly in Japan.

**Bufferin** A trademark for

buffered aspirin.

**bug, tap** A concealed listening device designed to pick up sounds in a room, an automobile, or such is a *bug*.

A *tap* is a device attached to a telephone circuit to pick up conversations on the line.

**building** Never abbreviate. Capitalize the proper names of buildings, including the word *building* if it is an integral part of the proper name: *the Empire State Building*.

**build up** (v.) **buildup** (n. and adj.)

**bull's-eye**

**bullet** See **weapons**.

**bullfight, bullfighter, bullfighting**

**bullpen** One word, for the place where baseball pitchers warm up, and for a pen that holds cattle.

**bureau** Capitalize when part of the formal name for an organization or agency: *the Bureau of Labor Statistics*.

Lowercase when used alone or to designate a corporate subdivision: *the Washington bureau of The Associated Press*.

**Bureau of Alcohol, Tobacco, Firearms and Explosives** *ATF* is acceptable in subsequent references to this agency of the Department of Justice. (Note the *Explosives* part of the name.)

**burglary, larceny, robbery, theft** Legal definitions of *burglary* vary, but in general a *burglary* involves entering a building (not necessarily by breaking in) and remaining unlawfully with the intention of committing a crime.

*Larceny* is the legal term for the wrongful taking of property. Its nonlegal equivalents are *stealing* or *theft*.

*Robbery* in the legal sense involves the use of violence or threat in committing larceny. In a wider sense it means to plunder or rifle, and may thus be used even if a person was not present: *His house was robbed while he was away*.

*Theft* describes a larceny that did not involve threat, violence or plundering.

USAGE NOTE: You *rob* a person, bank, house, etc., but you *steal* the money or the jewels.

**burqa** The all-covering dress worn by some Muslim women.

**bus, buses** Transportation vehicles. The verb forms: *bus, bused, busing*.
See **buss, busses**.

**bushel** A unit of dry measure equal to 4 pecks or 32 dry quarts. The metric equivalent is approximately 35.2 liters.

To convert to liters, multiply by 35.2 (5 bushels x 35.2 equals 176 liters).
See **liter**.

**business editor** Capitalize when used as a formal title before a name. See **titles**.

**business names** See **company names**.

**buss, busses** Kisses. The verb forms: *buss, bussed, bussing*.
See **bus, buses**.

**by-** The rules in **prefixes** apply, but in general, no hyphen. Some examples:

| | |
|---|---|
| byline | byproduct |
| bypass | bystreet |

*By-election* is an exception. See the next entry.

**by-election** A special election held between regularly scheduled elections. The term most often is associated with special elections to the British House of Commons.

**bylaw**

**bylines** Use only if the reporter was in the datelined community to gather the information reported.

Nicknames should not be used unless they specifically are requested by the writer.

**byte** A computer "word" made up of bits. The most common size *byte* contains eight bits, or binary digits. *Bytes* are a measure of information storage.

**cabinet** Capitalize references to a specific body of advisers heading executive departments for a president, king, governor, etc.: *The president-elect said he has not made his Cabinet selections.*

The capital letter distinguishes the word from the common noun meaning cupboard, which is lowercase.

See **department** for a listing of all the U.S. Cabinet departments.

**cactus, cactuses**

**cadet** See **military academies**.

**Caesarean section**

**caliber** The form: *.38-caliber pistol.*
See **weapons**.

**California** Abbrev.: *Calif.* See **state names**.

**call letters** Use all caps. Use hyphens to separate the type of station from the base call letters: *WBZ-AM, WBZ-FM, WBZ-TV.*

Citizens band operators, since 1983, are not required to be licensed by the Federal Communications Commission. Identification of such stations, either by the call sign previously assigned or made up by the operator, com-

prised of the letter *K*, the operator's initials and the operator's ZIP code, is optional.

Shortwave stations, which operate with greater power than citizens band stations and on different frequencies, typically mix letters and figures: *K2LRX.*

See **channel**; **citizens band**; **radio station**; and **television station**.

**call up** (v.) **call-up** (n. and adj.)

**Cambodia** Use this rather than *Kampuchea* in datelines since the country continues to be known more widely by this name. In the body of stories *Kampuchea* may be used as long as it is identified as another name for *Cambodia.*

**Cameroon** Not *Camerouns* or *Cameroun*. See **geographic names**.

**campaign manager** Do not treat as a formal title. Always lowercase.
See **titles**.

**Camp Fire Boys and Girls** The full name of the national organization formerly known as Camp Fire, Inc. Founded in 1910 as Camp Fire Girls, the name was changed to Camp Fire, Inc., in 1979, and again in 1993 to reflect the inclusion of boys. Headquarters is in Kansas City, Mo.

Both girls and boys are included in all levels of the organization. Boys and girls in kindergarten through second grades are *Starflights*. Children in third through fifth grades are *Adventure* club members. Children in sixth through eighth grades are *Discovery* members. Youths in ninth through 12th grades are *Horizon* members.

**Canada** Montreal, Ottawa, Quebec City and Toronto stand alone in datelines. For all other datelines, use the city name and the name of the province or territory spelled out.

The 10 provinces of Canada are Alberta, British Columbia, Manitoba, New Brunswick, Newfoundland and Labrador (but usually known as just Newfoundland), Nova Scotia, Ontario, Prince Edward Island, Quebec and Saskatchewan.

The three territories are the Yukon, the Northwest Territories, and Nunavut (created April 1, 1999).

The provinces have substantial autonomy from the federal government.

The territories are administered by the federal government, although residents of the territories do elect their own legislators and representatives to Parliament.

See **datelines**.

**Canada goose** Not *Canadian goose*.

**Canadian Broadcasting Corp.** *CBC* is acceptable in all references within contexts such as a television column. Otherwise, do not use *CBC* until second reference.

**canal** Capitalize as an integral part of a proper name: *the Suez Canal.*

**Canal Zone** Do not abbreviate. No longer used except when referring to the Panama Canal area during the time it was controlled by the United States, exclusively or jointly with Panama, 1904-1999.

**can't hardly** A double negative is implied. Better is: *can hardly.*

**cancel, canceled, canceling, cancellation**

**cannon, canon** A *cannon* is a weapon. See the **weapons** entry.

A *canon* is a law or rule, particularly of a church.

**cannot**

**cant** The distinctive stock words and phrases used by a particular sect or class.

See **dialect**.

**cantor** See **Jewish congregations**.

**Canuck** This reference to a Canadian is sometimes considered a derogatory term. It should be avoided except when in quoted matter or in terms used in Canada, such as references to the hockey team, the *Vancouver Canucks.*

**canvas, canvass** *Canvas* is heavy cloth.

*Canvass* is a noun and a verb denoting a survey.

**cape** Capitalize as part of a proper name: *Cape Cod, Cape Hatteras.* Lowercase when standing alone.

Although local practice may call for capitalizing *the Cape* when the rest of the name is clearly understood, always use the full name on first reference.

**Cape Canaveral, Fla.** Formerly Cape Kennedy. See **John F. Kennedy Space Center**.

**capital** The city where a seat of government is located. Do not capitalize.

When used in a financial sense, *capital* describes money, equipment or property used in a business by a person or corporation.

**capitalization** In general, avoid unnecessary capitals. Use a capital letter only if you can justify it by one of the principles listed here.

Many words and phrases, including special cases, are listed separately in this book. Entries that are capitalized without further comment should be capitalized in all uses.

If there is no relevant listing in this book for a particular word or phrase, consult Webster's New World College Dictionary. Use lowercase if the dictionary lists it as an acceptable form for the sense in which the word is being used.

As used in this book, *capitalize* means to use uppercase for the first letter of a word. If additional capital letters are needed, they are called for by an example or a phrase such as use *all caps.*

Some basic principles:
PROPER NOUNS: Capitalize nouns that constitute the unique identification for a specific person, place, or thing: *John, Mary, America, Boston, England.*

Some words, such as the examples just given, are always proper nouns. Some common nouns receive proper noun status when they are used as the name of a particular entity: *General Electric, Gulf Oil.*

PROPER NAMES: Capitalize common nouns such as *party, river, street* and *west* when they are an integral part of the full name for a person, place or thing: *Democratic Party, Mississippi River, Fleet Street, West Virginia.*

Lowercase these common nouns when they stand alone in subsequent references: *the party, the river, the street.*

Lowercase the common noun elements of names in all plural uses: *the Democratic and Republican parties, Main and State streets, lakes Erie and Ontario.*

Among entries that provide additional guidelines are:

| | |
|---|---|
| animals | historical periods |
| brand names | and events |
| building | holidays and |
| committee | holy days |
| congress | legislature |
| datelines | months |
| days of the week | monuments |
| directions and | nationalities |
| regions | and races |
| family names | nicknames |
| food | organizations and |
| foreign | institutions |
| governmental | planets |
| bodies | plants |
| foreign | police |
| legislative | department |
| bodies | religious |
| geographic | references |
| names | seasons |
| governmental | trademarks |
| bodies | unions |
| heavenly bodies | |

POPULAR NAMES: Some places and events lack officially designated proper names but have popular names that are the effective equivalent: *the Combat Zone* (a section of downtown Boston), *the Main Line* (a group of Philadelphia suburbs), *the South Side* (of Chicago), *the Badlands* (of South Dakota), *the Street* (the financial community in the Wall Street area of New York).

The principle applies also to shortened versions of the proper names of one-of-a-kind events: *the Series* (for the World Series), *the Derby* (for the Kentucky Derby). This practice should not, however, be interpreted as a license to ignore the general practice of lowercasing the common noun elements of a name when they stand alone.

DERIVATIVES: Capitalize words that are derived from a proper noun and still depend on it for their meaning: *American, Christian, Christianity, English, French, Marxism, Shakespearean.*

Lowercase words that are derived from a proper noun but no longer depend on it for their meaning: *french fries, herculean, manhattan cocktail, malapropism, pasteurize, quixotic, venetian blind.*

SENTENCES: Capitalize the first word in a statement that stands as a sentence. See **sentences** and **parentheses**.

In poetry, capital letters are used for the first words of some phrases that would not be capitalized in prose. See **poetry**.

COMPOSITIONS: Capitalize the principal words in the names of books, movies, plays, poems, operas, songs, radio and television programs, works of art, etc. See **composition titles**; **magazine names**; and **newspaper names**.

TITLES: Capitalize formal titles when used immediately before a name. Lowercase formal titles when used alone or in constructions that set them off from a name by commas.

Use lowercase at all times for terms that are job descriptions rather than formal titles.

See **academic titles**; **courtesy titles**; **legislative titles**; **military titles**; **nobility titles**; **religious titles**; and **titles**.

ABBREVIATIONS: Capital letters apply in some cases. See the **abbreviations and acronyms** entry.

**Capitol** Capitalize *U.S. Capitol* and *the Capitol* when referring to the building in Washington: *The meeting was held on Capitol Hill in the west wing of the Capitol.*

Follow the same practice when referring to state capitols: *The Virginia Capitol is in Richmond. Thomas Jefferson designed the Capitol of Virginia.*

**captain** See **military titles** for military and police usage.

Lowercase and spell out in such uses as *team captain Carl Yastrzemski.*

**carat, caret, karat** The weight of precious stones, especially diamonds, is expressed in *carats.* A carat is equal to 200 milligrams or about 3 grains.

A *caret* is a writer's and a proofreader's mark.

The proportion of pure gold used with an alloy is expressed in *karats.*

**carbine** See **weapons**.

**cardinal** See **Roman Catholic Church**.

**cardinal numbers** See **numerals**.

**CARE** Acceptable in all references for *Cooperative for Assistance and Relief Everywhere. CARE USA* is headquartered in Atlanta; *CARE International* is headquartered in Brussels, Belgium.

**carefree**

**caretaker**

**Caribbean** See **Western Hemisphere**.

**carmaker, carmakers**

**car pool**

**carry-on**

**carry-over** (n. and adj.)

**cash on delivery** *c.o.d.* is preferred in all references.

**caster, castor** *Caster* is a roller.
*Castor* is the spelling for the oil and the bean from which it is derived.

**catalog, cataloged, cataloger, cataloging, catalogist**

**Caterpillar** A trademark for a brand of crawler tractor.
Use lowercase for the worm-like larva of various insects.

**catholic, catholicism** Use *Roman Catholic Church, Roman Catholic* or *Roman Catholicism* in the first references to those who believe that the pope, as bishop of Rome, has the ultimate authority in administering an earthly organization founded by Jesus Christ.
Most subsequent references may be condensed to *Catholic Church, Catholic* or *Catholicism. Roman Catholic* should continue to be used, however, if the context requires a distinction between Roman Catholics and members of other denominations who often describe themselves as Catholic. They include some high church

Episcopalians (who often call themselves *Anglo-Catholics*), members of Eastern Orthodox churches, and members of some national Catholic churches that have broken with Rome. Among churches in this last category are the Polish National Catholic Church and the Lithuanian National Catholic Church.
Lowercase *catholic* where used in its generic sense of general or universal, meanings derived from a similar word in Greek.
Those who use *Catholic* in a religious sense are indicating their belief that they are members of a universal church that Jesus Christ left on Earth.

**cats** See **animals**.

**CAT scan** See **CT scan**.

**cattle** See **animals**.

**Caucasian**

**cave in** (v.) **cave-in** (n. and adj.)

**CB** See **citizens band radio**.

**CBS** Acceptable in all references for *CBS Inc.*, the former Columbia Broadcasting System.
Divisions include *CBS News, CBS Radio* and *CBS-TV.*

**CD** See **compact disc** entry.

**CD-ROM** Acronym for *compact disc* acting as *read-only memory.*
*CD-ROM disc* is redundant.

**cease-fire, cease-fires** (n. and adj.) The verb form is *cease fire.*

**celebrant, celebrator** Reserve *celebrant* for someone who conducts a religious rite: *He was*

*the celebrant of the Mass.*
Use *celebrator* for someone having a good time: *The celebrators kept the party going until 3 a.m.*

**cellophane** Formerly a trademark, now a generic term.

**cell phone** Two words; an exception to Webster's.

**Celsius** Use this term rather than *centigrade* for the temperature scale that is part of the metric system.

The Celsius scale is named for Anders Celsius, a Swedish astronomer who designed it. In it, zero represents the freezing point of water, and 100 degrees is the boiling point at sea level.

To convert to Fahrenheit, multiply a Celsius temperature by 9, divide by 5 and add 32 (25 x 9 equals 225, divided by 5 equals 45, plus 32 equals 77 degrees Fahrenheit).

When giving a Celsius temperature, use these forms: *40 degrees Celsius* or *40 C* (note the space and no period after the capital *C*) if degrees and Celsius are clear from the context.

See **Fahrenheit** and **metric system** entries.

**cement** *Cement* is the powder mixed with water and sand or gravel to make *concrete.* The proper term is *concrete* (not *cement*) *pavement, blocks, driveways,* etc.

**censer, censor, censure**
A *censer* is a container in which incense is burned.

To *censor* is to prohibit or restrict the use of something.

To *censure* is to condemn.

**census** Capitalize only in specific references to the *U.S. Census Bureau.* Lowercase in other uses: *the census data was released Tuesday.*

**Centers for Disease Control and Prevention** The centers, located in Atlanta, are the U.S. Public Health Service's national agencies for control of infectious and other preventable diseases. It works with state health departments to provide specialized services that they are unable to maintain on an everyday basis.

The normal form for first reference is the national *Centers for Disease Control and Prevention.* *CDC* is acceptable on second reference and takes a singular verb.

On the Net:
www.cdc.gov

**centi-** A prefix denoting one-hundredth of a unit. Move a decimal point two places to the left in converting to the basic unit: *155.6 centimeters equals 1.556 meters.*

**centigrade** See **Celsius**.

**centimeter** One-hundredth of a meter.

There are 10 millimeters in a centimeter.

A centimeter is approximately the width of a large paper clip.

To convert to inches, multiply by 0.4 (5 centimeters x 0.4 equals 2 inches).

See **meter**; **metric system**; and **inch**.

**Central America** See **Western Hemisphere**.

**Central Asia** The region includes Kyrgyzstan, Kazakhstan,

Turkmenistan, Tajikistan, and Uzbekistan.

**Central Conference of American Rabbis** See **Jewish Congregations**.

**Central Intelligence Agency** *CIA* is acceptable in all references.

The formal title for the individual who heads the agency is *director of central intelligence*. On first reference: *Director George Tenet of the CIA, Director of Central Intelligence George Tenet*, or *CIA Director George Tenet*.

**Central Standard Time (CST), Central Daylight Time (CDT)** See **time zones**.

**cents** Spell out the word cents and lowercase, using numerals for amounts less than a dollar: *5 cents, 12 cents*. Use the $ sign and decimal system for larger amounts: *$1.01, $2.50*.

Numerals alone, with or without a decimal point as appropriate, may be used in tabular matter.

**century** Lowercase, spelling out numbers less than 10: *the first century, the 20th century*.

For proper names, follow the organization's practice: *20th Century Fox, Twentieth Century Fund, Twentieth Century Limited*.

**Ceylon** It is now *Sri Lanka*, which should be used in datelines and other references to the nation.

The people may be referred to as *Ceylonese* (n. or adj.) or *Sri Lankans*. The language is *Sinhalese*.

**cha-cha**

**Chagas' disease** After Charles Chagas, a Brazilian physician who identified the chronic wasting disease caused by the parasite that is carried by insects.

**chain saw** (two words)

**chairman, chairwoman** Capitalize as a formal title before a name: *company Chairman Henry Ford, committee Chairwoman Margaret Chase Smith*.

Do not capitalize as a casual, temporary position: *meeting chairman Robert Jones*.

Do not use *chairperson* unless it is an organization's formal title for an office.

See **titles**.

**chamber of deputies** See **foreign legislative bodies**.

**chancellor** The translation to English for the first minister in the governments of Germany and Austria. Capitalize when used before a name.

See the **premier, prime minister** entry and **titles**.

**changeable**

**changeover**

**change up** (v.) **change-up** (n. and adj.)

**channel** Capitalize when used with a figure; lowercase elsewhere: *She turned to Channel 3. No channel will broadcast the game*.

Also: *the English Channel*, but the channel on second reference.

**chapters** Capitalize *chapter* when used with a numeral in reference to a section of a book or legal code. Always use Arabic fig-

ures: *Chapter 1, Chapter 20.*
Lowercase when standing
alone.

## character, reputation

*Character* refers to moral qualities.
*Reputation* refers to the way a
person is regarded by others.

## charismatic groups See religious movements.

## Charleston, Charlestown, Charles Town

*Charleston* is
the name of the capital of West
Virginia and a port city in South
Carolina.
*Charlestown* is a section of
Boston.
*Charles Town* is the name of a
small city in West Virginia.

## chauffeur

## chauvinism, chauvinist

The words mean unreasoning
devotion to one's race, sex, country, etc., with contempt for other
races, sexes, countries, etc.
The terms come from Nicolas
Chauvin, a soldier of Napoleon I,
who was famous for his devotion
to the lost cause.

## check up (v.) checkup (n.)

## Chemical Mace

A trade-
mark, usually shortened to *Mace*,
for a brand of tear gas that is
packaged in an aerosol canister
and temporarily stuns its victims.

## Chennai

Indian city formerly
known as Madras.

## chess

In stories, the names
and pieces are spelled out, lowercase: *king, queen, bishop, pawn,
knight, rook, kingside, queenside,
white, black.*
Use the algebraic notation in

providing tabular summaries.
In algebraic notation, the
"ranks" are the horizontal rows
of squares. The ranks take numbers, 1 to 8, beginning on white's
side of the board.
The "files" are the vertical rows
of squares. They take letters, a
through h, beginning on white's
left.
Thus, each square is identified
by its file letter and rank number.
In the starting position,
white's queen knight stands on
*b1*, the queen on *d1*, the king on
*e1*; black's queen knight stands
on *b8*, the queen on *d8*, the king
on *e8*, and so on.
Other features of the system
follow:
—DESIGNATION OF PIECES:
The major pieces are shown by
a capital letter: *K* for king, *Q* for
queen, *R* for rook, *B* for bishop
and *N* for knight. No symbol is
used for the pawn.
—MOVES BY PIECES: Shown
by the letter of the piece (except
for the pawn) and the destination
square. For instance, *Bb5* means
the bishop moves to square b5.
—MOVES BY PAWNS: Pawn
moves are designated only by the
name of the destination square.
Thus, *e4* means the pawn on the
e file moves to e4.
—CASTLING: It is written as
*0-0* for the kingside and *0-0-0*
for the queenside. *Kingside* is
the side of the board (right half
from white's point of view, left
half from black's), on which each
player's king starts. The other
half is *queenside.*
—CAPTURES BY PIECES: A
capture is recorded using an x
after the letter for the capturing piece. For instance, if white's
bishop captures the black pawn
at the f6 square, it is written
*Bxf6.*

—CAPTURES BY PAWNS: When a pawn captures a piece, the players name the file the pawn was on and the square where it made the capture. If white's pawn on a g file captured black's pawn on f6 square, the move would be *gxf6*. If black's pawn on an f file captured white's, it would be *fxg5*.

—CHECK: Use plus sign.

—AMBIGUITY: If more than one piece of the same type can move to a square, the rank number or file letter of the origination square is added. Thus, if a rook on d1 were to move to d4, but another rook also could move there, instead of Rd4 the move would be given as *R1d4*. If there are black knights on c6 and e6, and the one on e6 moves to d4, the move is given as *Ned4*.

The form, taken from a 1993 championship match:

| | Short (White) | Karpov (Black) |
|---|---|---|
| 1. | e4 | c5 |
| 2. | Nf3 | d6 |
| 3. | d4 | cxd4 |
| 4. | Nxd4 | Nf6 |
| 5. | Nc3 | a6 |
| 6. | Bc4 | e6 |
| 7. | Bb3 | Nbd7 |
| 8. | f4 | Nc5 |
| 9. | f5 | Be7 |
| 10. | Qf3 | 0-0 |
| 11. | Be3 | e5 |
| 12. | Nde2 | b5 |
| 13. | Bd5 | Rb8 |
| 14. | b4 | Ncd7 |
| 15. | 0-0 | Nxd5 |
| 16. | Nxd5 | Bb7 |
| 17. | Nec3 | Nf6 |
| 18. | Rad1 | Bxd5 |
| 19. | Nxd5 | Nxd5 |
| 20. | Rxd5 | Rc8 |
| 21. | Qg4 | f6 |
| 22. | Rf3 | Rxc2 |
| 23. | Rh3 | Rf7 |
| 24. | Qh5 | h6 |
| 25. | Qg6 | Kf8 |
| 26. | Bxh6 | gxh6 |
| 27. | Rxh6 | Qb6+ |
| 28. | Rc5 | Bd8 |
| 29. | Rh8+ | Ke7 |
| 30. | Rh7 | Rxh7 |
| 31. | Qxh7+ | Kf8 |

Draw agreed.

**Chevron Corp.** Created by the merger of Chevron (formerly Standard Oil Co. of California) and Texaco in 2001. Headquarters is in San Ramon, Calif. (Name changed from Chevron-Texaco in 2005.)

**Chevy** Not *Chevie* or *Chevvy*. This nickname for the *Chevrolet* should be used only in automobile features or in quoted matter.

**Chicago** The city in Illinois stands alone in datelines.

**chief** Capitalize as a formal title before a name: *She spoke to police Chief Michael Codd. He spoke to Chief Michael Codd of the New York police.*

Lowercase when it is not a formal title: *union chief Walter Reuther.*

See **titles**.

**chief justice** Capitalize only as a formal title before a name: *Chief Justice William Rehnquist.* The officeholder is the chief justice of the United States, not of the Supreme Court.

See **judge**.

**child care** Two words, no hyphen, in all cases. (An exception to Webster's.)

**children** In general, call children 15 or younger by their first name on second reference. Use the last name, however, if the seriousness of the story calls for it, as in a murder case, for example.

For ages 16 and 17, use judgment, but generally go with the surname unless it's a light story. Use the surname for those 18 and older.

Avoid *kids* as a universal synonym, unless the tone of the story dictates less formal usage.

**Chile** The nation.

**chili, chilies** The peppers.

**chilly** Moderately cold.

**China** When used alone, it refers to the mainland nation. Use it in datelines and other routine references.

Use *People's Republic of China, Communist China, mainland China* or *Red China* only in direct quotations or when needed to distinguish the mainland and its government from Taiwan.

For datelines on stories from the island of Taiwan, use the name of a community and *Taiwan*. In the body of a story, use *Nationalist China* or *Taiwan* for references to the government based on the island. Use the formal name of the government, the *Republic of China*, when required for legal precision.

**Chinaman** A patronizing term. Confine it to quoted matter.

**Chinese names** For most Chinese place names and personal names, use the official Chinese spelling system known as Pinyin: *Senior leader Deng Xiaoping, Beijing*, or *Zhejiang province*.

Note that the Chinese usually give the family name first (*Deng*) followed by the given name (*Xiaoping*). Second reference should be the family name only: *Deng*.

The Pinyin spelling system eliminates the hyphen or apostrophe previously used in many given names. Use the new spelling for *Mao Zedong* and *Zhou Enlai*, but keep the traditional American spelling for such historical figures as *Sun Yat-sen* and *Chiang Kai-shek*.

If the new Pinyin spelling of a proper noun is so radically different from the traditional American spelling that a reader might be confused, provide the Pinyin spelling followed by the traditional spelling in parentheses. For example, the city of *Fuzhou* (*Foochow*). Or use a descriptive sentence: *Fuzhou is the capital of Fujian province, on China's eastern coast.*

Use the traditional American spellings for these place names: *China, Inner Mongolia, Shanghai, Tibet.*

Follow local spellings in stories dealing with Hong Kong and Taiwan.

Some Chinese have Westernized their names, putting their given names or the initials for them first: *P.Y. Chen, Jack Wang.* In general, follow an individual's preferred spelling.

Normally Chinese women do not take their husbands' surnames. Use the courtesy titles *Mrs., Miss,* or *Ms.* only when specifically requested.

**chip** An integrated computer circuit.

**chip-maker, chip-making** Hyphenate as adjectives (but two words as nouns).

**Christian Church (Disciples of Christ)** The parentheses and the words they surround are part of the formal name.

The body owes its origins to an early 19th-century frontier movement to unify Christians.

The Disciples, led by Alexander Campbell in western Pennsylvania, and the Christians, led by Barton W. Stone in Kentucky, merged in 1832.

The local church is the basic organizational unit.

National policies are developed by the General Assembly, made up of representatives chosen by local churches and regional organizations.

The church lists 831,000 members.

All members of the clergy may be referred to as *ministers. Pastor* applies if a minister leads a congregation.

On first reference, use *the Rev.* before the name of a man or woman. On second reference, use only the last name.

See **religious titles**.

## Christian Science Church

See **Church of Christ, Scientist**.

## Christmas, Christmas Day

Dec. 25. The federal legal holiday is observed on Friday if Dec. 25 falls on a Saturday, on Monday if it falls on a Sunday.

Never abbreviate *Christmas* to *Xmas* or any other form.

**church** Capitalize as part of the formal name of a building, a congregation or a denomination; lowercase in other uses: *St. Mary's Church, the Roman Catholic Church, the Catholic and Episcopal churches, a Roman Catholic church, a church.*

Lowercase in phrases where the church is used in an institutional sense: *She believes in the separation of church and state. The pope said the church opposes abortion.*

See **religious titles** and the entry for the denomination in question.

## Churches of Christ

Approximately 18,000 independent congregations with a total U.S. membership of more than 2 million cooperate under this name. They sponsor numerous educational activities, primarily radio and television programs.

Each local church is autonomous and operates under a governing board of elders. The minister is an evangelist, addressed by members as *Brother.* The ministers do not use clergy titles. Do not precede their names by a title.

The churches do not regard themselves as a denomination. Rather, they stress a nondenominational effort to preach what they consider basic Bible teachings. The churches also teach that baptism is an essential part of the salvation process.

See **religious movements**.

## churchgoer

## Church of Christ, Scientist

This denomination was founded in 1879 by Mary Baker Eddy. Her teachings are contained in "Science and Health with Key to the Scriptures," which, along with the Bible, she ordained as the impersonal pastor of the church.

The Mother Church in Boston is the international headquarters. Its government provides for a board of directors, which transacts the business of the Mother Church.

A branch church, governed by its own democratically chosen board, is named First Church of Christ, Scientist, or Second Church, etc., according to the order of its establishment in a community.

The terms *Christian Science Church* or *Churches of Christ, Scientist,* are acceptable in all references to the denomination.

The word *Christian* is used because its teachings are based on the word and works of Jesus Christ. The word *Science* is used to reflect the concept that the laws of God are replicable and can be proved in healing sickness and sin.

The church is composed entirely of lay members and does not have clergy in the usual sense. Both men and women may serve as *readers, practitioners,* or *lecturers.*

The preferred form for these titles is to use a construction that sets them off from a name with commas. Capitalize them only when used as a formal title immediately before a name. Do not continue use of the title in subsequent references.

The terms *reverend* and *minister* are not applicable. Do not use *the Rev.* in any references.

See **religious titles**.

## Church of England See Anglican Communion.

## Church of Jesus Christ of Latter-day Saints, The

Note the capitalization and punctuation of *Latter-day. Mormon church, LDS church* or *the Latter-day Saints* can be used, but the official name is preferred in first reference in a story dealing primarily with church activities.

Members are referred to as *Latter-day Saints* or *Mormons,* the latter based on the church's sacred Book of Mormon.

The church is based on revelations that Joseph Smith said were brought to him in the 1820s by heavenly messengers.

The headquarters in Salt Lake City, Utah, lists membership at 5.2 million for the United States and 11 million worldwide.

Church hierarchy is composed of men known as general authorities. Among them, the policy-making body is the First Presidency, made up of a president and two or more counselors. It has final authority in all spiritual and worldly matters.

CLERGY: All worthy young men over the age of 12 are members of the priesthood. They can be ordained elders after age 18, usually after graduating from high school and before serving as missionaries. They may later become high priests, or bishops.

The only formal titles are *president* (for the head of the First Presidency), *bishop* (for members of the Presiding Bishopric and for local bishops) and *elder* (for other general authorities and church missionaries). Capitalize these formal titles before a name on first reference; use only the last name on second reference.

The terms *minister* or *the Rev.* are not used.

See **religious titles**.

SPLINTER GROUPS: The term *Mormon* is not properly applied to the other Latter Day Saints churches that resulted from the split after Smith's death.

The largest is the Community of Christ, headquartered in Independence, Mo., with 137,000 U.S. members. From 1860 to 2001, it was called the Reorganized Church of Jesus Christ of Latter Day Saints (note the lack of a hyphen and the capitalized Day).

**CIA** Acceptable in all references for *Central Intelligence Agency.*

**cigarette**

**Cincinnati** The city in Ohio stands alone in datelines.

**CIO** See **AFL-CIO**.

**Citibank** The former First National City Bank. The parent holding company is Citicorp of New York.

**cities and towns** Capitalize them in all uses. See **datelines** for guidelines on when they should be followed by a state or a country name.

Capitalize official titles, including separate political entities such as *East St. Louis, Ill.*, or *West Palm Beach, Fla.*

The preferred form for the section of a city is lowercase: *the west end, northern Los Angeles.* But capitalize widely recognized names for the sections of a city: *South Side* (Chicago), *Lower East Side* (New York).

Spell out the names of cities unless in direct quotes: *A trip to Los Angeles*, but: *"We're going to L.A."*

See **city**.

**citizen, resident, subject, national, native** A *citizen* is a person who has acquired the full civil rights of a nation either by birth or naturalization. Cities and states in the United States do not confer citizenship. To avoid confusion, use *resident*, not *citizen*, in referring to inhabitants of states and cities.

*Citizen* is also acceptable for those in the United Kingdom, or other monarchies where the term *subject* is often used.

*National* is applied to a person

residing away from the nation of which he or she is a citizen, or to a person under the protection of a specified nation.

*Native* is the term denoting that an individual was born in a given location.

**citizens band** Without an apostrophe after the *s*, based on widespread practice.

*CB* is acceptable on second reference.

The term describes a group of radio frequencies set aside by the Federal Communications Commission for local use at low power by individuals or businesses.

The Federal Communications Commission no longer requires a license to operate a CB station. Identification of such stations, either by the call sign previously assigned or made up by the operator, comprised of the letter *K*, the operator's initials and the operator's ZIP code, is optional.

**city** Capitalize *city* if part of a proper name, an integral part of an official name, or a regularly used nickname: *Kansas City, New York City, Windy City, City of Light, Fun City.*

Lowercase elsewhere: *a Texas city; the city government; the city Board of Education;* and all *city of* phrases: *the city of Boston.*

Capitalize when part of a formal title before a name: *City Manager Francis McGrath.* Lowercase when not part of the formal title: *city Health Commissioner Frank Smith.*

See **city council** and **governmental bodies**.

**city commission** See the next entry.

**city council** Capitalize when part of a proper name: *the Boston*

*City Council.*
Retain capitalization if the reference is to a specific council but the context does not require the city name:
*BOSTON (AP) — The City Council ...*
Lowercase in other uses: *the council, the Boston and New York city councils, a city council.*
Use the proper name if the body is not known as a city council: *the Miami City Commission, the City Commission, the commission; the Louisville Board of Aldermen, the Board of Aldermen, the board.*
Use *city council* in a generic sense for plural references: *the Boston, Louisville and Miami city councils.*

**city editor** Capitalize as a formal title before a name. See **titles**.

**city hall** Capitalize with the name of a city, or without the name of a city if the reference is specific: *Boston City Hall, City Hall.*
Lowercase plural uses: *the Boston and New York city halls.*
Lowercase generic uses, including: *You can't fight city hall.*

**citywide**

**civil cases, criminal cases**
A *civil case* is one in which an individual, business or agency of government seeks damages or relief from another individual, business or agency of government. Civil actions generally involve a charge that a contract has been breached or that someone has been wronged or injured.
A *criminal case* is one that the state or the federal government brings against an individual

charged with committing a crime.

**Civil War**

**claptrap**

**clean up** (v.) **cleanup** (n. and adj.)

**clear-cut** (adj.)

**clerical titles** See **religious titles**.

**Cleveland** The city in Ohio stands alone in datelines.

**clientele**

**cloak-and-dagger**

**Clorox** A trademark for a brand of bleach.

**closed shop** A *closed shop* is an agreement between a union and an employer that requires workers to be members of a union before they may be employed.
A *union shop* requires workers to join a union within a specified period after they are employed.
An *agency shop* requires that the workers who do not want to join the union pay the union a fee instead of union dues.
A *guild shop*, a term often used when the union is The Newspaper Guild, is the same as a *union shop.*
See the **right-to-work** entry for an explanation of how some states prohibit contracts that require workers to join unions.

**close-up** (n. and adj.)

**cloture** Not *closure*, for the parliamentary procedure for closing debate.
Whenever practical, use a phrase such as closing debate or

ending debate instead of the technical term.

**CNN** Acceptable in all references for the *Cable News Network.*

**co-** Retain the hyphen when forming nouns, adjectives and verbs that indicate occupation or status:

| | |
|---|---|
| co-author | co-pilot |
| co-chairman | co-respondent |
| | (in a divorce suit) |
| co-defendant | co-signer |
| co-host | co-sponsor |
| co-owner | co-star |
| co-partner | co-worker |

(Several are exceptions to Webster's New World in the interests of consistency.)

Use no hyphen in other combinations:

| | |
|---|---|
| coed | cooperate |
| coeducation | cooperative |
| coequal | coordinate |
| coexist | coordination |
| coexistence | |

*Cooperate, coordinate* and related words are exceptions to the rule that a hyphen is used if a prefix ends in a vowel and the word that follows begins with the same vowel.

**Co.** See **company**.

**coast** Lowercase when referring to the physical shoreline: *Atlantic coast, Pacific coast, east coast.*

Capitalize when referring to regions of the United States lying along such shorelines: *the Atlantic Coast states, a Gulf Coast city, the West Coast, the East Coast.*

Do not capitalize when referring to smaller regions: *the Virginia coast.*

Capitalize *the Coast* when standing alone only if the reference is to the West Coast.

**coastal waters** See **weather terms**.

**Coast Guard** Capitalize when referring to this branch of the U.S. armed forces, a part of the Department of Homeland Security: *the U.S. Coast Guard, the Coast Guard, Coast Guard policy.* Do not use the abbreviation *USCG,* except in quotes.

Use lowercase for similar forces of other nations.

This approach has been adopted for consistency, because many foreign nations do not use *coast guard* as the proper name.

See **military academies**.

**Coast Guardsman** Note spelling. Capitalize as a proper noun when referring to an individual in a U.S. Coast Guard unit: *He is a Coast Guardsman.*

Lowercase *guardsman* when it stands alone.

See **military titles**.

**coastline**

**coattails**

**Coca-Cola, Coke** Trademarks for a brand of cola drink.

**cocaine** The slang term *coke* should appear only in quoted matter.

*Crack* is a refined cocaine in crystalline rock form.

**c.o.d.** Acceptable in all references for *cash on delivery* or *collect on delivery.* (The use of lowercase is an exception to the first listing in Webster's New World.)

**Cold War** Capitalize when referring specifically to the post-World War II rivalry between the United States and the former

Soviet Union. Use only in the historic sense.

**collective nouns** Nouns that denote a unit take singular verbs and pronouns: *class, committee, crowd, family, group, herd, jury, orchestra, team.*

Some usage examples: *The committee is meeting to set its agenda. The jury reached its verdict. A herd of cattle was sold.*

Team names and band names, however, take plural verbs.

PLURAL IN FORM: Some words that are plural in form become collective nouns and take singular verbs when the group or quantity is regarded as a unit.

Right: *A thousand bushels is a good yield.* (A unit.)

Right: *A thousand bushels were created.* (Individual items.)

Right: *The data is sound.* (A unit.)

Right: *The data have been carefully collected.* (Individual items.)

**collectors' item**

**college** Capitalize when part of a proper name: *Dartmouth College.*

See the **organizations and institutions** entry.

**College of Cardinals** See **Roman Catholic Church**.

**collide, collision** Two objects must be in motion before they can *collide.* An automobile cannot *collide* with a utility pole, for example.

**colloquialisms** The word describes the informal use of a language. It is not local or regional in nature, as dialect is.

Webster's New World College Dictionary identifies many words as colloquial with the label *Informal.*

Many colloquial words and phrases characteristic of informal writing and conversation are acceptable in some contexts but out of place in others. Examples include *bum* and *phone.*

Other colloquial words normally should be avoided because they are substandard. Webster's New World College Dictionary notes, for example, that *ain't* is informal, a "dialectal or nonstandard usage," although "widely used informally by educated speakers." Many still consider it illiterate and it should not be used in news stories unless needed to illustrate nonstandard speech in writing.

See the **dialect** and **word selection** entries.

**colon** See the entry in the **Punctuation** chapter.

**colonel** See **military titles**.

**colonial** Capitalize *Colonial* as a proper adjective in all references to the *Colonies.* (See the next entry.)

**colonies** Capitalize only for the British dependencies that declared their independence in 1776, now known as the United States.

**Colorado** Abbrev.: *Colo.* See **state names**.

**colorblind**

**colored** In some societies, including the United States, the word is considered derogatory and should not be used.

In some countries of Africa,

it is used to denote individuals of mixed racial ancestry. Whenever the word is used, place it in quotation marks and provide an explanation of its meaning.

### Columbia Broadcasting System It no longer exists. See CBS.

### Columbus Day Oct. 12. The federal legal holiday is the second Monday in October.

### combat, combated, combating

### comedian Use for both men and women.

### comma See entry in Punctuation chapter.

### commander See military titles.

### commander in chief Capitalize only if used as a formal title before a name.
See titles.

### commissioner Do not abbreviate. Capitalize when used as a formal title.
See titles.

### commitment

### committee Do not abbreviate. Capitalize when part of a formal name: *the House Appropriations Committee.*

Do not capitalize committee in shortened versions of long committee names: *the Special Senate Select Committee to Investigate Improper Labor-Management Practices*, for example, became *the rackets committee.*
See subcommittee.

### commodity When used in

a financial sense, the word describes the products of mining and agriculture before they have undergone extensive processing.

### commonwealth A group of people united by their common interests.
See state.

### Commonwealth of Independent States Founded Dec. 8, 1991, the organization is made up of 12 of the former republics of the USSR, or Soviet Union. Russia is the largest and richest. Three other former republics — Latvia, Lithuania and Estonia — became independent nations earlier in 1991. (The Soviet Union was formally dissolved in December 1991. Its last leader, Mikhail Gorbachev, resigned on Dec. 25, 1991.)

The republics (with adjective form in parentheses):

Armenia (Armenian); Azerbaijan (Azerbaijani); Belarus (Belarusian); Georgia (Georgian); Kazakhstan (Kazakh); Kyrgyzstan (Kyrgyz); Moldova (Moldovan); Russia (Russian); Tajikistan (Tajik); Turkmenistan (Turkmen); Ukraine (no *the*) (Ukrainian); Uzbekistan (Uzbek).

DATELINES: MOSCOW stands alone. Follow all other datelines with the name of the state. *AL-MATY, Kazakhstan.*

### Commonwealth, the Formerly the British Commonwealth. The members of this free association of sovereign states recognize the British sovereign as head of the Commonwealth. Some also recognize the sovereign as head of their state; others do not.

The members are: Antigua and Barbuda, Australia, Bahamas, Bangladesh, Barbados, Belize,

Botswana, Brunei, Cameroon, Canada, Cyprus, Dominica, Fiji, Gambia, Ghana, Grenada, Guyana, India, Jamaica, Kenya, Kiribati, Lesotho, Malawi, Malaysia, Maldives, Malta, Mauritius, Mozambique, Namibia, Nauru, New Zealand, Nigeria, Pakistan (suspended after the 1999 military coup; suspension lifted 2004), Papua New Guinea, St. Kitts and Nevis, St. Lucia, St. Vincent and the Grenadines, Samoa, Seychelles, Sierra Leone, Singapore, Solomon Islands, South Africa, Sri Lanka, Swaziland, Tanzania, Tonga, Trinidad and Tobago, Tuvalu, Uganda, United Kingdom, Vanuatu and Zambia. (Zimbabwe withdrew in 2003.)

### Communicable Disease Center
The former name of the *Centers for Disease Control and Prevention.* See entry under that name.

### Communications Satellite Corp.
See **Comsat Corp**.

### Communications Workers of America
The shortened form *Communications Workers union* is acceptable in all references.

Headquarters is in Washington.

### communism, communist
See the **political parties and philosophies** entry.

### commutation
A legal term for a change of sentence or punishment to one that is less severe.

See the **pardon, parole, probations** entry.

### compact disc
*CD* is acceptable in all references.

### company, companies

Use *Co.* or *Cos.* when a business uses either word at the end of its proper name: *Ford Motor Co., American Broadcasting Cos.*

If *company* or *companies* appears alone in second reference, spell the word out.

The forms for possessives: *Ford Motor Co.'s profits, American Broadcasting Cos.' profits.*

THEATRICAL: Spell out *company* in names of theatrical organizations: *the Martha Graham Dance Company.*

### company (military)
Capitalize only when part of a name: *Company B.* Do not abbreviate.

### company names
Consult the company or Standard & Poor's Register of Corporations if in doubt about a formal name. Do not, however, use a comma before Inc. or Ltd.

Generally, follow the spelling and capitalization preferred by the company: *eBay.* But capitalize the first letter if it begins a sentence.

Do not use all capital letter names unless the letters are individually pronounced: *BMW.* Others should be uppercase and lowercase.

Do not use symbols such as exclamation points, plus signs or asterisks that form contrived spellings that might distract or confuse a reader. Use an ampersand only if it is part of the company's formal name, but not otherwise in place of "and."

Use "the" lowercase unless it is part of the company's formal name.

See the **organizations and institutions** entry.

### compared to, compared with
Use *compared to* when the intent is to assert, without the

need for elaboration, that two or more items are similar: *She compared her work for women's rights to Susan B. Anthony's campaign for women's suffrage.*

Use *compared with* when juxtaposing two or more items to illustrate similarities and/or differences: *His time was 2:11:10, compared with 2:14 for his closest competitor.*

### compatible

### complacent, complaisant

*Complacent* means self-satisfied. *Complaisant* means eager to please.

### complementary, complimentary

*The husband and wife have complementary careers.*

*They received complimentary tickets to the show.*

### complement, compliment

*Complement* is a noun and a verb denoting completeness or the process of supplementing something: *The ship has a complement of 200 sailors and 20 officers. The tie complements his suit.*

*Compliment* is a noun or a verb that denotes praise or the expression of courtesy: *The captain complimented the sailors. She was flattered by the compliments on her outfit.*

### compose, comprise, constitute

*Compose* means to create or put together. It commonly is used in both the active and passive voices: *She composed a song. The United States is composed of 50 states. The zoo is composed of many animals.*

*Comprise* means to contain, to include all or embrace. It is best used only in the active voice,

followed by a direct object: *The United States comprises 50 states. The jury comprises five men and seven women. The zoo comprises many animals.*

*Constitute,* in the sense of form or make up, may be the best word if neither *compose* nor *comprise* seems to fit: *Fifty states constitute the United States. Five men and seven women constitute the jury. A collection of animals can constitute a zoo.*

Use *include* when what follows is only part of the total: *The price includes breakfast. The zoo includes lions and tigers.*

### composition titles

Apply the guidelines listed here to book titles, computer game titles, movie titles, opera titles, play titles, poem titles, album and song titles, radio and television program titles, and the titles of lectures, speeches and works of art.

The guidelines, followed by a block of examples:

—Capitalize the principal words, including prepositions and conjunctions of four or more letters.

—Capitalize an article — *the, a, an* — or words of fewer than four letters if it is the first or last word in a title.

—Put quotation marks around the names of all such works except the Bible and books that are primarily catalogs of reference material. In addition to catalogs, this category includes almanacs, directories, dictionaries, encyclopedias, gazetteers, handbooks and similar publications. Do not use quotation marks around such software titles as WordPerfect or Windows.

—Translate a foreign title into English unless a work is known to the American public by its foreign name.

EXAMPLES: *"The Star-Spangled Banner," "The Rise and Fall of the Third Reich," "Gone With the Wind," "Of Mice and Men," "For Whom the Bell Tolls," "Time After Time,"* the NBC-TV *"Today"* program, the *"CBS Evening News," "The Mary Tyler Moore Show."* See television program names for further guidelines and examples.

Reference works: *Jane's All the World's Aircraft; Encyclopaedia Britannica; Webster's New World Dictionary of the American Language, Second Edition.*

Foreign works: *Rousseau's "War,"* not *Rousseau's "La Guerre."* But: *Leonardo da Vinci's "Mona Lisa," Mozart's "The Marriage of Figaro"* and *"The Magic Flute."* But: *"Die Walkuere"* and *"Gotterdammerung" from* Wagner's *"The Ring of the Nibelungen."*

**compound adjectives** See the **hyphen** entry in the **Punctuation** chapter.

**comptroller, controller** *Comptroller* generally is the accurate word for government financial officers.

The U.S. comptroller of the currency is an appointed official in the Treasury Department who is responsible for the chartering, supervising and liquidation of banks organized under the federal government's National Bank Act.

*Controller* generally is the proper word for financial officers of businesses and for other positions such as *air traffic controller.*

Capitalize *comptroller* and *controller* when used as the formal titles for financial officers. Use lowercase for *aircraft controller* and similar occupational applica-

tions of the word.
See **titles**.

**Comsat Corp.** Formerly known as Communications Satellite Corp. Headquarters is in Bethesda, Md.

**conclave** A private or secret meeting. In the Roman Catholic Church it describes the private meeting of cardinals to elect a pope.

**concrete** See **cement**.

**Confederate States of America** The formal name of the states that seceded during the Civil War. The shortened form *the Confederacy* is acceptable in all references.

**confess, confessed** In some contexts the words may be erroneous.
See **admit**.

**confirmation** See **sacraments**.

**Congo** In datelines:
*KINSHASA, Democratic Republic of Congo (AP) —*
*BRAZZAVILLE, Republic of Congo (AP) —*
Use *Congo* or *the Congo*, as the construction of a sentence dictates, in second references.

**Congress** Capitalize *U.S. Congress* and *Congress* when referring to the U.S. Senate and House of Representatives. Although *Congress* sometimes is used as a substitute for the House, it properly is reserved for reference to both the Senate and House.

Capitalize *Congress* also if referring to a foreign body that uses the term, or its equivalent in

a foreign language, as part of its formal name: *the Argentine Congress, the Congress.*
See **foreign legislative bodies**.
Lowercase when used as a synonym for *convention* or in second reference to an organization that uses the word as part of its formal name: *the Congress of Racial Equality, the congress.*

**congressional** Lowercase unless part of a proper name: *congressional salaries, the Congressional Quarterly, the Congressional Record.*

## Congressional Directory
Use this as the reference source for questions about the federal government that are not covered by this stylebook.

## congressional districts
Use figures and capitalize district when joined with a figure: *the 1st Congressional District, the 1st District.*
Lowercase *district* whenever it stands alone.

## Congressional Record A
daily publication of the proceedings of Congress including a complete stenographic report of all remarks and debates.

## congressman, congresswoman Use only in
reference to members of the U.S. House of Representatives.
See **legislative titles**.

## Congress of Racial Equality *CORE* is acceptable on second
reference.
Headquarters is in New York.

## Connecticut Abbrev.: *Conn.*
See **state names**.

**connote, denote** *Connote* means to suggest or imply something beyond the explicit meaning: *To some people, the word marriage connotes too much restriction.*
*Denote* means to be explicit about the meaning: *The word demolish denotes destruction.*

## Conrail This acronym is acceptable in all references to *Consolidated Rail Corp.* (The corporation originally used *ConRail,* but later changed to *Conrail.*)
A private, for-profit corporation, *Conrail* was set up by Congress as a monopoly in 1976 to reorganize and consolidate six bankrupt Northeast freight railroads — the Penn Central, the Erie Lackawanna, Reading, Central of New Jersey, Lehigh Valley, and Lehigh & Hudson River.
Philadelphia-based *Conrail* was sold to the public in 1987.
In 1999, CSX and Norfolk Southern completed their acquisition of *Conrail,* splitting the assets and sharing *Conrail* tracks and facilities in Detroit, Philadelphia and most of New Jersey. Norfolk Southern acquired 58 percent of *Conrail* and CSX 42 percent. Norfolk Southern, based in Norfolk, Va., operates a 21,600-mile rail system in 22 states, the District of Columbia, and Ontario, Canada. CSX, based in Richmond, Va., formed a 22,300-mile system serving 23 states, the District of Columbia, and Montreal and Ontario, Canada.
Do not confuse *Conrail* and *Amtrak* (see separate entry).

## consensus

## conservative See the political parties and philosophies
entry.

**Conservative Judaism** See **Jewish congregations**.

**constable** Capitalize when used as a formal title before a name.
See **titles**.

**constitute** See the **compose, comprise, constitute** entry.

**constitution** Capitalize references to the U.S. Constitution, with or without the *U.S.* modifier: *The president said he supports the Constitution.*

When referring to constitutions of other nations or of states, capitalize only with the name of a nation or a state: *the French Constitution, the Massachusetts Constitution, the nation's constitution, the state constitution, the constitution.*

Lowercase in other uses: *the organization's constitution.*

Lowercase *constitutional* in all uses.

**consulate** A *consulate* is the residence of a consul in a foreign city. It handles the commercial affairs and personal needs of citizens of the appointing country.

Capitalize with the name of a nation; lowercase without it: *the French Consulate, the U.S. Consulate, the consulate.*

See **embassy** for the distinction between a consulate and an embassy.

**consul, consul general, consuls general** Capitalize when used as a formal title before a noun.
See **titles**.

**consumer price index** A measurement of changes in the retail prices of a constant market-basket of goods and services. It is computed by comparing the cost of the marketbasket at a fixed time with its cost at subsequent or prior intervals.

Capitalize when referring to the U.S. index, issued monthly by the Bureau of Labor Statistics, an agency of the Labor Department.

The *U.S. Consumer Price Index* should not be referred to as a *cost-of-living index,* because it does not include the impact of income taxes and Social Security taxes on the cost of living, nor does it reflect changes in buying patterns that result from inflation. It is, however, the basis for computing cost-of-living raises in many union contracts.

The preferred form for second reference is *the index.* Confine *CPI* to quoted material.

**Consumer Product Safety Commission**

**contagious**

**contemptible**

**continent** The seven continents, in order of their land size: Asia, Africa, North America, South America, Europe, Antarctica and Australia.

Capitalize *the Continent* and *Continental* only when used as synonyms for Europe or European. Lowercase in other uses such as: *the continent of Europe, the European continent, the African and Asian continents.*

**Continental Airlines** Use this spelling of *Airlines,* which Continental has adopted for its public identity. Only its incorporation papers still read *Air Lines.* Headquarters is in Houston.

**Continental Divide** The ridge along the Rocky Mountains that separates rivers flowing east from those that flow west.

**continental shelf, continental slope** Lowercase. The *shelf* is the part of a continent that is submerged in relatively shallow sea at gradually increasing depths, generally up to about 600 feet below sea level.

The *continental slope* begins at the point where the descent to the ocean bottom becomes very steep.

**continual, continuous**

*Continual* means a steady repetition, over and over again: *The merger has been the source of continual litigation.*

*Continuous* means uninterrupted, steady, unbroken: *All she saw ahead of her was a continuous stretch of desert.*

**Contra, Contras** Uppercase when used to describe former Nicaraguan rebel groups.

**contractions** Contractions reflect informal speech and writing. Webster's New World College Dictionary includes many entries for contractions: *aren't* for *are not*, for example.

Avoid excessive use of contractions. Contractions listed in the dictionary are acceptable, however, in informal contexts where they reflect the way a phrase commonly appears in speech or writing.

See **colloquialisms**; **quotations in the news**; and **word selection**.

**contrasted to, contrasted with** Use *contrasted to* when the intent is to assert, without the need for elaboration, that two items have opposite characteristics: *He contrasted the appearance of the house today to its ramshackle look last year.*

Use *contrasted with* when juxtaposing two or more items to illustrate similarities and/or differences: *He contrasted the Republican platform with the Democratic platform.*

**control, controlled, controlling**

**controller** See the **comptroller, controller** entry.

**controversial** An overused word; avoid it. A *controversial issue* is redundant. See **noncontroversial**.

**convention** Capitalize as part of the name for a specific national or state political convention: *the Democratic National Convention, the Republican State Convention.*

Lowercase in other uses: *the national convention, the state convention, the convention, the annual convention of the American Medical Association.*

**convict** (v.) Follow with preposition *of*, not *for*: *He was convicted of murder.*

**convince, persuade** You may be *convinced that* something or *of* something. You must be *persuaded to do* something.

Right: *The robbers persuaded him to open the vault.*

Wrong: *The robbers convinced him to open the vault.*

Right: *The robbers convinced him that it was the right thing to do.*

Wrong: *The robbers persuaded*

*him that it was the right thing to do.*

## cookie, cookies

## cooperate, cooperative
But *co-op* as a short term of *cooperative*, to distinguish it from *coop*, a cage for animals.

## Cooperative for Assistance and Relief Everywhere See CARE.

## coordinate, coordination

**cop** Be careful in the use of this colloquial term for *police officer*. It may be used in lighter stories and in casual, informal descriptions, but often is a derogatory term out of place in serious police stories.

**copter** Acceptable shortening of *helicopter*. But use it only as a noun or adjective. It is not a verb.

**copy editor** Seldom a formal title. See **titles**.

**copyright** (n., v. and adj.) *A copyright story.*
Use *copyrighted* only as the past tense of the verb: *He copyrighted the article.*
See **Copyright Infringement** in **Briefing on Media Law** section.

**co-respondent** In a divorce suit.

**Corn Belt** The region in the north central Midwest where much corn and corn-fed livestock are raised. It extends from western Ohio to eastern Nebraska and northeastern Kansas.

**Corp.** See **corporation**.

**corporal** See **military titles**.

**corporate names** See **company names**.

**corporation** An entity that is treated as a person in the eyes of the law. It is able to own property, incur debts, sue and be sued.
Abbreviate *corporation* as *Corp.* when a company or government agency uses the word at the end of its name: *Gulf Oil Corp., the Federal Deposit Insurance Corp.*
Spell out *corporation* when it occurs elsewhere in a name: *the Corporation for Public Broadcasting.*
Spell out and lowercase *corporation* whenever it stands alone.
The form for possessives: *Gulf Oil Corp.'s profits.*

**corps** Capitalize when used with a word or a figure to form a proper name: *the Marine Corps, the Signal Corps, the 9th Corps.*
Capitalize when standing alone only if it is a shortened reference to *U.S. Marine Corps.*
The possessive form is *corps'* for both singular and plural: *one corps' location, two corps' assignments.*

## corral, corralled, corralling

## correctional facility, correctional institution See the **prison, jail** entry.

**Corsica** Use instead of *France* in datelines on stories from communities on this island.

**Cortes** The Spanish parliament. See **foreign legislative bodies**.

**cosmonaut** The applicable occupational term for astronauts of the former Soviet Union. Always use lowercase.

See **titles**.

**cost of living** The amount of money needed to pay taxes and to buy the goods and services deemed necessary to make up a given standard of living, taking into account changes that may occur in tastes and buying patterns.

The term often is treated incorrectly as a synonym for the *U.S. Consumer Price Index*, which does not take taxes into account and measures only price changes, keeping the quantities constant over time.

Hyphenate when used as a compound modifier: *The cost of living went up, but he did not receive a cost-of-living raise.*

See the **consumer price index** and **inflation** entries.

**Cotton Belt** The region in the South and Southwestern sections of the United States where much cotton is grown.

**council, councilor, councilman, councilwoman** A deliberative body and those who are members of it.

See the **counsel** entry and **legislative titles**.

**Council of Economic Advisers** A group of advisers who help the U.S. president prepare his annual economic report to Congress and recommend economic measures to him throughout the year.

**counsel, counseled, counseling, counselor, counselor at law** To *counsel* is to advise. A *counselor* is one who advises.

A *counselor at law* (no hyphens for consistency with *attorney at law*) is a lawyer. See **lawyer**.

**count, countess** See **nobility**.

**counter-** The rules in **prefixes** apply, but in general, no hyphen. Some examples:

| | |
|---|---|
| counteract | counterproposal |
| countercharge | counterspy |
| counterfoil | |

**countryside**

**county** Capitalize when an integral part of a proper name: *Dade County, Nassau County, Suffolk County.*

Capitalize the full names of county governmental units: *the Dade County Commission, the Orange County Department of Social Services, the Suffolk County Legislature.*

Retain capitalization for the name of a county body if the proper noun is not needed in the context; lowercase the word *county* if it is used to distinguish an agency from state or federal counterparts: *the Board of Supervisors, the county Board of Supervisors; the Department of Social Services, the county Department of Social Services.* Lowercase *the board, the department,* etc. whenever they stand alone.

Capitalize *county* if it is an integral part of a specific body's name even without the proper noun: *the County Commission, the County Legislature.* Lowercase *the commission, the legislature,* etc. when not preceded by the word *county.*

Capitalize as part of a formal title before a name: *County Manager John Smith.* Lowercase when it is not part of the formal title: *county Health Commissioner Frank Jones.*

Avoid *county of* phrases where possible, but when necessary, always lowercase: *the county of Westchester.*

Lowercase plural combinations: *Westchester and Rockland counties.*

Apply the same rules to similar terms such as *parish.*

See **governmental bodies**.

**county court** In some states, it is not a court but the administrative body of a county. In most cases, the *court* is presided over by a *county judge*, who is not a judge in the traditional sense but the chief administrative officer of the county.

The terms should be explained if they are not clear in the context.

Capitalize all references to a specific *county court*, and capitalize *county judge* when used as a formal title before a name. Do not use *judge* alone before a name except in direct quotations.

Examples:

*SEVIERVILLE, Tenn. (AP) — A reluctant County Court approved a school budget today that calls for a 10 percent tax increase for property owners.*

*The county had been given an ultimatum by the state: Approve the budget or shut down the schools.*

*The chief administrative officer, County Judge Ray Reagan, said ...*

**coup d'etat** The word *coup* usually is sufficient.

**couple** When used in the sense of two people, the word takes plural verbs and pronouns: *The couple were married Saturday and left Sunday on their honeymoon. They will return in two weeks.*

In the sense of a single unit, use a singular verb: *Each couple was asked to give $10.*

**couple of** The *of* is necessary. Never use *a couple tomatoes* or a similar phrase.

The phrase takes a plural verb in constructions such as: *A couple of tomatoes were stolen.*

**course numbers** Use Arabic numerals and capitalize the subject when used with a numeral: *History 6, Philosophy 209.*

**court decisions** Use figures and a hyphen: *The Supreme Court ruled 5-4, a 5-4 decision.* The word *to* is not needed, but use hyphens if it appears in quoted matter: *"The court ruled 5-to-4, the 5-to-4 decision."*

**court districts** See **court names**.

**courtesy titles** Refer to both men and women by first and last name: *Susan Smith* or *Robert Smith.* Use the courtesy titles *Mr., Miss, Ms.* or *Mrs.* only in direct quotations or in other special situations:

—When it is necessary to distinguish between two people who use the same last name, as in married couples or brothers and sisters, use the first and last name.

—When a woman specifically requests it; for example, where a woman prefers to be known as *Mrs. Susan Smith* or *Ms. Susan Smith.*

In cases where a person's gender is not clear from the first name or from the story's context, indicate the gender by using *he* or *she* in subsequent reference.

**courthouse** Capitalize with the name of a jurisdiction: *the Cook County Courthouse, the U.S. Courthouse.* Lowercase in other uses: *the county courthouse, the courthouse, the federal courthouse.*

*Court House* (two words) is used in the proper names of some communities: *Appomattox Court House, Va.*

**court-martial, court-martialed, courts-martial**

**court names** Capitalize the full proper names of courts at all levels.

Retain capitalization if *U.S.* or a state name is dropped: *the U.S. Supreme Court, the Supreme Court, the state Superior Court, the Superior Court, Superior Court.*

For courts identified by a numeral: *2nd District Court, 8th U.S. Circuit Court of Appeals.*

For additional details on federal courts, see **judicial branch** and separate listings under **U.S.** and the court name.

See **judge** for guidelines on titles before the names of judges.

**Court of St. James's** Note the *'s.* The formal name for the royal court of the British sovereign. Derived from St. James's Palace, the former scene of royal receptions.

**courtroom**

**cover up** (v.) **cover-up** (n. and adj.) *He tried to cover up the scandal. He was prosecuted for the cover-up.*

**crack up** (v.) **crackup** (n. and adj.)

**crawfish** Not *crayfish.* An exception to Webster's New World based on the dominant spelling in Louisiana, where it is a popular delicacy.

**criminal cases** See the **civil cases, criminal cases** entry.

**Crisco** A trademark for a brand of vegetable shortening.

**crisis, crises**

**crisscross**

**criterion, criteria**

**cross-examine, cross-examination**

**cross-eye** (n.) **cross-eyed** (adj.)

**crossfire** (one word)

**crossover** (n. and adj.)

**cross section** (n.) **cross-section** (v.)

**CRT** Abbreviation for *cathode ray tube.* Do not use. In stories referring to the TV component, *picture tube* is preferred.

**CT scan** *Computerized tomography,* a method of making multiple X-ray images of the body or parts of the body and using a computer to construct, from those images, cross-sectional views. (Formerly known as *CAT scan.*)

**Cub Scouts** See **Boy Scouts**.

**cuckoo clock**

**cup** Equal to 8 fluid ounces. The approximate metric equivalents are 240 milliliters or 0.24 of a liter.

To convert to liters, multiply by 0.24 (14 cups x 0.24 = 3.36 liters, or 3,360 milliliters). See **liter**.

**cupful, cupfuls** Not *cupsful*.

**curate** See **religious titles**.

**cure-all**

**Curia** See **Roman Catholic Church**.

**currency depreciation, currency devaluation** A nation's money *depreciates* when its value falls in relation to the currency of other nations or in relation to its own prior value.

A nation's money is *devalued* when its value is reduced in relation to the currency of other nations, either deliberately by the government or through market forces.

When a nation devalues its currency, the goods it imports tend to become more expensive. Its exports tend to become less expensive in other nations and thus more competitive. See **devaluations**.

**curtain raiser**

**Customs** Capitalize in U.S. Immigration and Customs Enforcement and in U.S. Customs and Border Protection, both agencies of the Department of Homeland Security.

Lowercase elsewhere: *a customs official, a customs ruling, she went through customs.*

**cut back** (v.) **cutback** (n. and adj.) *He cut back spending. The cutback will require frugality.*

**cut off** (v.) **cutoff** (n. and adj.) *He cut off his son's allow-*

ance. *The cutoff date for applications is Monday.*

**cyber-, cyberspace** *Cyberspace* is a term popularized by William Gibson in the novel "Neuromancer" to refer to the digital world of computer networks. It has spawned numerous words with *cyber-* prefixes, but try to avoid most of these cutesy coinages. When the combining form is used, follow the general rule for prefixes and do not use a hyphen before a word starting with a consonant: *cybercafe*.

**cyclone** See **weather terms**.

**Cyclone** A trademark for a brand of chain-link fence.

**cynic, skeptic** A *skeptic* is a doubter.

A *cynic* is a disbeliever.

**czar** Not *tsar*. It was a formal title only for the ruler of Russia and some other Slavic nations. Lowercase in all other uses.

**Dacron** A trademark for a brand of polyester fiber.

**dad** Uppercase only when the noun substitutes for a name as a term of address: *Hi, Dad!*

**DaimlerChrysler AG** Merger of Chrysler Corp. and Daimler-Benz AG.
Dual headquarters in Auburn Hills, Mich., and Stuttgart, Germany.

**dalai lama** The traditional high priest of Lamaism, a form of Buddhism practiced in Tibet and Mongolia. *Dalai lama* is a title rather than a name, but it is all that is used when referring to the man. Capitalize *Dalai Lama* in references to the holder of the title, in keeping with the principles outlined in the **nobility** entry.

**Dallas** The city in Texas stands alone in datelines.

**Dalles, The** A city in Oregon.

**dam** Capitalize when part of a proper name: *Hoover Dam.*

**damage, damages** *Damage* is destruction: *Authorities said damage from the storm would total more than $1 billion.*
*Damages* are awarded by a court as compensation for injury,

loss, etc.: *The woman received $25,000 in damages.*

**dame** See **nobility**.

**damn it** Use instead of *dammit*, but like other profanity it should be avoided unless there is a compelling reason.
See the **obscenities, profanities, vulgarities** entry.

**dangling modifiers** Avoid modifiers that do not refer clearly and logically to some word in the sentence.
Dangling: *Taking our seats, the game started.* (*Taking* does not refer to the subject, *game*, nor to any other word in the sentence.)
Correct: *Taking our seats, we watched the opening of the game.* (*Taking* refers to *we*, the subject of the sentence.)

**Danish pastry**

**Dardanelles, the** Not *the Dardanelles Strait.*

**Dark Ages** The period beginning with the fall of Rome in 476 and ending about the 10th century. The term is derived from the idea that this period in Europe was characterized by intellectual stagnation, widespread ignorance and poverty.

**dark horse**

**dash** See entry in the **Punctuation** chapter.

**data** A plural noun, it normally takes plural verbs and pronouns.

See the **collective nouns** entry, however, for an example of when *data* may take singular verbs and pronouns.

**databank**

**database** One word, in keeping with widespread usage. The collection of all data used and produced by a computer program.

**data processing** (n. and adj.) Do not hyphenate the adjective.

**date line** Two words for the imaginary line that separates one day from another.

See the **international date line** entry.

**datelines** Datelines on stories should contain a city name, entirely in capital letters, followed in most cases by the name of the state, county or territory where the city is located.

DOMESTIC DATELINES: A list of domestic cities that stand alone in datelines follows. The norms that influenced the selection were the population of the city, the population of its metropolitan region, the frequency of the city's appearance in the news, the uniqueness of its name, and experience that has shown the name to be almost synonymous with the state or nation where it is located.

No state with the following:

| | |
|---|---|
| ATLANTA | MILWAUKEE |
| BALTIMORE | MINNEAPOLIS |
| BOSTON | NEW ORLEANS |
| CHICAGO | NEW YORK |
| CINCINNATI | OKLAHOMA CITY |
| CLEVELAND | PHILADELPHIA |
| DALLAS | PHOENIX |
| DENVER | PITTSBURGH |
| DETROIT | ST. LOUIS |
| HONOLULU | SALT LAKE CITY |
| HOUSTON | SAN ANTONIO |
| INDIANAPOLIS | SAN DIEGO |
| LAS VEGAS | SAN FRANCISCO |
| LOS ANGELES | SEATTLE |
| MIAMI | WASHINGTON |

Stories from all other U.S. cities should have both the city and state name in the dateline, including *KANSAS CITY, Mo.*, and *KANSAS CITY, Kan.*

Spell out *Alaska, Hawaii, Idaho, Iowa, Maine, Ohio, Texas* and *Utah.* Abbreviate others as listed in this book under the full name of each state.

Use *Hawaii* on all cities outside Honolulu. Specify the island in the text if needed.

Follow the same practice for communities on islands within the boundaries of other states: *EDGARTOWN, Mass.*, for example, not *EDGARTOWN, Martha's Vineyard.*

REGIONAL CIRCUITS: On state wires, additional cities in a state or region may stand alone if requested by the newspapers served.

When this is done, provide a list to all offices in the region, to all newspapers affected and to New York headquarters.

U.S. POSSESSIONS: Apply the guidelines listed below in the ISLAND NATIONS AND TERRITORIES section and the OVERSEAS TERRITORIES section.

FOREIGN CITIES: These foreign locations stand alone in datelines:

| | |
|---|---|
| BAGHDAD | MEXICO CITY |
| BEIJING | MONACO |

BERLIN MONTREAL
DJIBOUTI MOSCOW
GENEVA NEW DELHI
GIBRALTAR OTTAWA
GUATEMALA CITY PARIS
HAVANA QUEBEC CITY
HONG KONG ROME
JERUSALEM SAN MARINO
KUWAIT CITY SINGAPORE
LONDON TOKYO
LUXEMBOURG TORONTO
MACAU VATICAN CITY

In addition, use *UNITED NA-TIONS* alone, without a *N.Y.* designation, in stories from *U.N.* headquarters.

BALKANS: With the independence of Montenegro from Serbia-Montenegro formalized in 2006, use a Montenegro-only dateline, such as *PODGORICA, Montenegro*. Stories originating in Serbia carry a Serbia-only dateline: *BELGRADE, Serbia*. Stories originating in Kosovo carry Serbia in the dateline.

CANADIAN DATELINES: Datelines on stories from Canadian cities other than Montreal, Ottawa, Quebec City and Toronto should contain the name of the city in capital letters followed by the name of the province. Do not abbreviate any province or territory name.

COMMONWEALTH OF INDEPENDENT STATES: For cities in the former Soviet Union, datelines include city and republic name: *ALMATY, Kazakhstan*.

OTHER FOREIGN NATIONS: Stories from other foreign cities that do not stand alone in datelines should contain the name of the country or territory (see the next section) spelled out.

SPELLING AND CHOICE OF NAMES: In most cases, the name of the nation in a dateline is the conventionally accepted short form of its official name: *Argentina*, for example, rather than *Republic of Argentina*. (If in doubt, look for an entry in this book. If none is found, follow Webster's New World College Dictionary.)

Note these special cases:
—Instead of *United Kingdom*, use *England, Northern Ireland, Scotland* or *Wales*.
—For divided nations, use the commonly accepted names based on geographic distinctions: *North Korea, South Korea*.
—Use an article only with *El Salvador*. For all others, use just a country name — *Gambia, Netherlands, Philippines*, etc.

See **geographic names** for guidelines on spelling the names of foreign cities and nations not listed here or in separate entries.

ISLAND NATIONS AND TERRITORIES: When reporting from nations and territories that are made up primarily of islands but commonly are linked under one name, use the city name and the general name in the dateline. Identify an individual island, if needed, in the text:
Examples:
British Virgin Islands
Netherlands Antilles
Indonesia        Philippines

OVERSEAS TERRITORIES: Some overseas territories, colonies and other areas that are not independent nations commonly have accepted separate identities based on their geographic character or special status under treaties. In these cases, use the commonly accepted territory name after a city name in a dateline.
Examples:
Bermuda          Martinique
Corsica          Puerto Rico
Faeroe Islands   Sardinia
Greenland        Sicily
Guadeloupe       Sikkim
Guam             Tibet

WITHIN STORIES: In citing other cities within the body of a story:

—No further information is necessary if a city is in the same state as the datelined city. Make an exception only if confusion would result.

—Follow the city name with further identification in most cases where it is not in the same state or nation as the dateline city. The additional identification may be omitted, however, if no confusion would result — there is no need, for example, to refer to *Boston, Mass.*, in a story datelined *NEW YORK.*

—Provide a state or nation identification for the city if the story is undated. However, cities that stand alone in datelines may be used alone in undated stories if no confusion would result.

**dateline selection** A dateline should tell the reader that the AP obtained the basic information for the story in the datelined city.

Do not, for example, use a Washington dateline on a story written primarily from information that a newspaper reported under a Washington dateline. Use the home city of the newspaper instead.

This rule does not preclude the use of a story with a dateline different from the home city of a newspaper if it is from the general area served by the newspaper.

Use a foreign dateline only if the basic information in a story was obtained by a full- or part-time correspondent physically present in the datelined community.

If a radio broadcast monitored in another city was the source of information, use the dateline of the city where the monitoring took place and mention the fact in the story.

When a story has been assembled from sources in widely separated areas, use no dateline.

When a datelined story contains supplementary information obtained in another city, make that point clear in the context. Do not put parentheses around such material, however, unless the correspondent in the datelined community was cut off from incoming communications. Note the following examples:

—Material from another area was available in the datelined city:

*LONDON (AP) — Prime Minister Wilson submitted his resignation today.*

*In Washington, a State Department spokesman said the change in government leadership would have no effect on negotiations involving the Common Market.*

—Material from another area was not available to the correspondent in the dateline city because communications from the outside world were cut off:

*PHNOM PENH, Cambodia (AP) — Khmer Rouge troops pushed into Phnom Penh today, barely hours after the United States ran down the Stars and Stripes and abandoned Cambodia to the Communists.*

*(In Washington, the State Department said Americans evacuated in a mass airlift had arrived safely aboard aircraft carriers and at bases in Thailand.)*

**dates** Always use Arabic figures, without *st, nd, rd* or *th.* See **months** for examples and **punctuation** guidelines.

**daughter-in-law, daugh-**

ters-in-law

**Daughters of the American Revolution** DAR is acceptable on second reference.
Headquarters is in Washington.

**day care** Two words, no hyphen, in all uses. (An exception to Webster's use as an adjective.)

**daylight saving time** Not savings. No hyphen.
When linking the term with the name of a time zone, use only the word daylight: Eastern Daylight Time, Pacific Daylight Time, etc.
Lowercase daylight saving time in all uses and daylight time whenever it stands alone.
A federal law specifies that, starting in 2007, daylight time applies from 2 a.m. on the second Sunday of March until 2 a.m. on the first Sunday of November in areas that do not specifically exempt themselves.
See **time zones**.

**daylong**

**days of the week** Capitalize them. Do not abbreviate, except when needed in a tabular format: Sun, Mon, Tue, Wed, Thu, Fri, Sat (three letters, without periods, to facilitate tabular composition).
See **time element**.

**daytime**

**day to day, day-to-day** Hyphenate when used as a compound modifier: They have extended the contract on a day-to-day basis.

**D.C.** See **District of Colum-**

bia.

**D-Day** June 6, 1944, the day the Allies invaded Europe in World War II.

**DDT** Preferred in all references for the insecticide dichloro-diphenyltrichloroethane.

**de** See **foreign names** entry.

**deacon** See the entry for the individual's denomination.

**dead center**

**dead end** (n.) **dead-end** (adj.) She reached a dead end. He has a dead-end job.

**Dead Sea Scrolls**

**deaf** See **disabled, handicapped, impaired**.

**deaf-mute** Avoid the term. The preferred form is to say that an individual cannot hear or speak. A mute person may be deaf or may be able to hear.
Do not use deaf and dumb.

**dean** Capitalize when used as a formal title before a name: Dean John Jones, Deans John Jones and Susan Smith.
Lowercase in other uses: John Jones, dean of the college; the dean.

**dean's list** Lowercase in all uses: He is on the dean's list. She is a dean's list student.

**deathbed** (n. and adj.)

**decades** Use Arabic figures to indicate decades of history. Use an apostrophe to indicate numerals that are left out; show plural by adding the letter s: the

*1890s, the '90s, the Gay '90s, the 1920s, the mid-1930s.* See the **historical periods and events** entry.

**December** See **months**.

**deci-** A prefix denoting one-tenth of a unit. Move the decimal point one place to the left in converting to the basic unit: 15.5 decigrams = 1.55 grams.

**decimal units** Use a period and numerals to indicate decimal amounts. Decimalization should not exceed two places in textual material unless there are special circumstances.

For amounts less than 1, use the numeral zero before the decimal point: *0.03.* See **fractions**.

**Declaration of Independence** Lowercase *the declaration* whenever it stands alone.

**decorations** See the **awards and decorations** entry.

**Deepfreeze** A trademark for a brand of home freezer.

If something is being postponed indefinitely, use two words: *The project is in the deep freeze.*

**deep-sea** (adj.)

**Deep South** Capitalize both words when referring to the region that consists of Alabama, Georgia, Louisiana, Mississippi and South Carolina.

**deep water** (n.) **deep-water** (adj.) *The creature swam in deep water. The ship needs a deep-water port.*

**defendant**

**defense** Do not use it as a verb.

**defense attorney** Always lowercase, never abbreviate. See **attorney** and **titles**.

**defense spending** *Military spending* usually is the more precise term.

**definitely** Overused as a vague intensifier. Avoid it.

**degree-day** See **weather terms**.

**degrees** See **academic degrees**.

**deity** Lowercase. See **gods** and **religious references**.

**dek-** (before a vowel), **deka-** (before a consonant) A prefix denoting 10 units of a measure. Move the decimal point one place to the right to convert to the basic unit: 15.6 dekameters = 156 meters.

**Delaware** Abbrev.: *Del.* Only Rhode Island is smaller in area. See **state names**.

**delegate** The formal title for members of the lower houses of some legislatures. Do not abbreviate. Capitalize only before their names. See **legislative titles**.

Always lowercase in other uses: *convention delegate Richard Henry Lee.*

**Delta Air Lines** Headquarters is in Atlanta.

**demagogue, demagoguery** Not *demagog.*

**democrat, democratic, Democratic Party** See the **political parties and philosophies** entry.

**Democratic Governors' Association** Note the apostrophe.

**Democratic National Committee** On the second reference: *the national committee, the committee.*
Similarly: *Democratic State Committee, Democratic County Committee, Democratic City Committee, the state committee, the city committee, the committee.*

**demolish, destroy** Both mean to do away with something completely. Something cannot be partially *demolished* or *destroyed.* It is redundant to say *totally demolished* or *totally destroyed.*

**denote** See the **connote, denote** entry.

**Denver** The city in Colorado stands alone in datelines.

**depart** Follow it with a preposition: *He will depart from La Guardia. She will depart at 11:30 a.m.*
Do not drop the preposition as some airline dispatchers do.

**Department of Agriculture; Department of Commerce; Department of Defense; Department of Education; Department of Energy** (*DOE* acceptable on second reference); **Department of Health and Human Services** (formerly the Department of Health, Education and Welfare); **Department of Homeland Security; Department of Housing and Urban Development** (*HUD* acceptable on second reference); **Department of the Interior; Department of Justice; Department of Labor; Department of State; Department of Transportation** (*DOT* acceptable on second reference); **Department of the Treasury, Department of Veterans Affairs** (*VA* on second reference).

If, as is common practice, the title is flopped, drop the *of* and retain the capitalization: *the State Department, the Treasury Department.*
Avoid acronyms when possible. A phrase such as *the department* is preferable on second reference because it is more readable and avoids alphabet soup.
Lowercase *department* in plural uses, but capitalize the proper name element: *the departments of Labor and Justice.*
A shorthand reference to the proper name element also is capitalized: *Kissinger said, "State and Justice must resolve their differences."* But: *Henry Kissinger, the secretary of state.*
Lowercase *the department* whenever it stands alone.
Do not abbreviate *department* in any usage.
See **academic departments**.

**dependent** (n. and adj.) Not *dependant.*

**depreciation** The reduction in the value of capital goods due to wear and tear or obsolescence.
*Estimated depreciation* may be deducted from income each year as one of the costs of doing business.

**depression** Capitalize *Depression* and *the Great Depression* when referring to the worldwide economic hard times generally regarded as having begun with the stock market collapse of Oct. 28-29, 1929.
Lowercase in other uses: *the depression of the 1970s.*

**depths** See **dimensions**.

**deputy** Capitalize as a formal title before a name. See **titles**.

**derogatory terms** Do not use derogatory terms such as *krauts* (for Germans) or *niggers* (for blacks) except in direct quotes, and then only when their use is an integral, essential part of the story.

See the **obscenities, profanities, vulgarities** entry and **word selection**.

**-designate** Hyphenate: *chairman-designate*. Capitalize only the first word if used as a formal title before a name. See **titles**.

**destroy** See the **demolish, destroy** entry.

**detective** Do not abbreviate. Capitalize before a name only if it is a formal rank: *police Detective Frank Serpico, private detective Richard Diamond*. See **titles**.

**detente**

**detention center** See the **prison, jail** entry.

**Detroit** The city in Michigan stands alone in datelines.

**devaluations** Devaluations occur when the value of a country's currency goes down in its relation to another currency. This may happen by government decree, or through market forces. Devaluations are expressed in percentages, but the normal method of figuring a percentage change won't work. Use the following rules:

Say currency A is quoted in a set of units to currency B. When currency A is devalued, 1) take the new exchange rate and subtract the old exchange rate, 2) divide the answer by the new exchange rate and 3) multiply the answer by 100 to get the percentage devaluation.

Example:

9.5 (new rate) minus 6.3 (old rate) = 3.2

3.2 divided by 9.5 = 0.3368

0.3368 times 100 = 33.68421 (or 34 percent).

The ruble has been devalued against the dollar by 34 percent.

**devil** But capitalize *Satan*.

**DEW line** See **North Warning System**.

**Dexedrine** A trademark for a brand of appetite suppressant. It also may be called *dextroamphetamine sulfate*.

**dialect** The form of language peculiar to a region or a group, usually in matters of pronunciation or syntax. Dialect should be avoided, even in quoted matter, unless it is clearly pertinent to a story.

There are some words and phrases in everyone's vocabulary that are typical of a particular region or group. Quoting dialect, unless used carefully, implies substandard or illiterate usage.

When there is a compelling reason to use dialect, words or phrases are spelled phonetically, and apostrophes show missing letters and sounds: *"Din't ya yoosta live at Toidy-Toid Street and Sekun' Amya? Across from da moom pitchers?"*

See **colloquialisms**; **quotes in the news**; and **word selection**.

**dialogue** (n.)

**diarrhea**

**Dictaphone** A trademark for a brand of dictation recorder.

**dictionaries** For spelling, style and usage questions not covered in this stylebook, consult Webster's New World College Dictionary, Fourth Edition, published by Wiley.

Use the first spelling listed in Webster's New World unless a specific exception is listed in this book.

If Webster's New World provides different spellings in separate entries (*tee shirt* and *T-shirt*, for example), use the spelling that is followed by a full definition (*T-shirt*).

If Webster's New World provides definitions under two different spellings for the same sense of a word, either use is acceptable. For example, *although* or *though*.

If there is no listing in either this book or Webster's New World, the backup dictionary is Webster's Third New International Dictionary, published by Merriam-Webster Inc.

Webster's New World is also the first reference for geographic names not covered in this stylebook. See **geographic names**.

**die-hard** (n. and adj.)

**Diet** The Japanese parliament. See **foreign legislative bodies**.

**dietitian** Not *dietician*.

**different** Takes the preposition *from*, not *than*.

**differ from, differ with** To *differ from* means to be unlike.

To *differ with* means to disagree.

**dilemma** It means more than a problem. It implies a choice between two unattractive alternatives.

**dimensions** Use figures and spell out *inches, feet, yards*, etc., to indicate depth, height, length and width. Hyphenate adjectival forms before nouns.

EXAMPLES: *He is 5 feet 6 inches tall, the 5-foot-6-inch man, the 5-foot man, the basketball team signed a 7-footer.*

*The car is 17 feet long, 6 feet wide and 5 feet high. The rug is 9 feet by 12 feet, the 9-by-12 rug.*

*The storm left 5 inches of snow.*

Use an apostrophe to indicate feet and quote marks to indicate inches (5'6") only in very technical contexts.

**Diners Club** No apostrophe, in keeping with the practice the company has adopted for its public identity. Only its incorporation papers still read *Diners' Club*.

Headquarters is in New York.

**diocese** Capitalize as part of a proper name: *the Diocese of Rochester, the Rochester Diocese, the diocese*.

See **Episcopal Church** and **Roman Catholic Church**.

**directions and regions** In general, lowercase *north, south, northeast, northern*, etc., when they indicate compass direction; capitalize these words when they designate regions.

Some examples:

COMPASS DIRECTIONS: *He drove west. The cold front is moving east.*

REGIONS: *A storm system that developed in the Midwest is spreading eastward. It will bring* showers to the East Coast by morning and to the entire Northeast by late in the day. High temperatures will prevail throughout the Western states.

The North was victorious. The South will rise again. Settlers from the East went to the West in search of new lives. The customs of the East are different from those of the West. The Northeast depends on the Midwest for its food supply.

She has a Southern accent. He is a Northerner. Asian nations are opening doors to Western businessmen. The candidate developed a Southern strategy. She is a Northern liberal.

The storm developed in the South Pacific. European leaders met to talk about supplies of oil from Southeast Asia.

WITH NAMES OF NATIONS: Lowercase unless they are part of a proper name or are used to designate a politically divided nation: northern France, eastern Canada, the western United States.

But: Northern Ireland, South Korea.

WITH STATES AND CITIES: The preferred form is to lowercase compass points only when they describe a section of a state or city: western Texas (not West Texas), southern Atlanta.

But capitalize compass points:

—When part of a proper name: North Dakota, West Virginia.

—When used in denoting widely known sections: Southern California, the South Side of Chicago, the Lower East Side of New York. If in doubt, use lowercase.

IN FORMING PROPER NAMES: When combining with another common noun to form the name for a region or location: the North Woods, the South Pole, the Far East, the Middle East, the West Coast (the entire region, not the coastline itself — see coast), the Eastern Shore (see separate entry), the Western Hemisphere.

**dis-** The rules in **prefixes** apply, but in general, no hyphen. Some examples:

| | |
|---|---|
| dismember | disservice |
| dissemble | dissuade |

## disabled, handicapped, impaired

In general, do not describe an individual as disabled or handicapped unless it is clearly pertinent to a story. If such a description must be used, make it clear what the handicap is and how much the person's physical or mental performance is affected.

Avoid such euphemisms as mentally challenged and descriptions that connote pity, such as afflicted with or suffers from multiple sclerosis. Rather, has multiple sclerosis.

Some terms include:

cripple Often considered offensive when used to describe a person who is lame or disabled.

disabled A general term used for a physical or cognitive condition that substantially limits one or more of the major daily life activities.

handicap It should be avoided in describing a disability.

blind Describes a person with complete loss of sight. For others, use terms such as visually impaired or person with low vision.

deaf Describes a person with total hearing loss. For others, use partial hearing loss or partially deaf. Avoid using deaf-mute. Do not use deaf and dumb.

mute Describes a person who physically cannot speak. Others with speaking difficulties are speech impaired.

wheelchair-user People use wheelchairs for independent mobility. Do not use confined to a *wheelchair,* or *wheelchair-bound.* If a wheelchair is needed, say why.

**disc, disk** Use the *disc* spelling for phonograph records and related terms (*disc jockey*), optical and laser-based devices (*laserdisc, videodisc*) and for *disc brake.* Use *disk* for computer-related references: (*floppy disk, hard disk*) and medical references such as *slipped disk.*

**disc jockey** *DJ* is acceptable on second reference in a column or other special context. Use announcer in other contexts.

**discreet, discrete** *Discreet* means prudent, circumspect: *"I'm afraid I was not very discreet,"* she wrote.
*Discrete* means detached, separate: *There are four discrete sounds from a quadraphonic system.*

**diseases** Do not capitalize *arthritis, emphysema, leukemia, migraine, pneumonia,* etc.
When a disease is known by the name of a person identified with it, capitalize only the individual's name: *Alzheimer's disease, Parkinson's disease,* etc.

**disinterested, uninterested** *Disinterested* means impartial, which is usually the better word to convey the thought.
*Uninterested* means that someone lacks interest.

**disk** See **disc, disk**.

**diskette** A generic term that means *floppy disk.* Not synonymous with *disk.*

**dispel, dispelled, dispelling**

**disposable personal income** The income that a person retains after deductions for income taxes, Social Security taxes, property taxes and for other payments such as fines and penalties to various levels of government.

**Disposall** A trademark for a type of mechanical garbage disposer.

**dissociate** Not *disassociate.*

**distances** Use figures for 10 and above, spell out one through nine: *He walked four miles.*

**district** Always spell it out. Use a figure and capitalize *district* when forming a proper name: *the 2nd District.*

**district attorney** Do not abbreviate. Capitalize when used as a formal title before a name: *District Attorney Hamilton Burger.*
Use *DA* (no periods) only in quoted matter.
See **titles**.

**district court** See **court names** and **U.S. District Court**.

**District of Columbia** Abbreviate as *D.C.* Spell out when used alone. Do not use *D.C.* in conjunction with the federal district of Washington unless it could be confused with other Washingtons.
*The district,* rather than *D.C.,* should be used in subsequent references.

**ditto marks** They can be made with quotation marks, but their use in newspapers, even in tabular material, is confusing. Don't use them.

**dive, dived, diving** Not

*dove* for the past tense.

**divided nations** See **datelines** and entries under the names of these nations.

**dividend** See entry in **Business Guidelines**.

**division** See the **organizations and institutions** entry; **military units**; and **political divisions**.

**divorcee** The fact that a woman has been divorced should be mentioned only if a similar story about a man would mention his marital status.

When the woman's marital status is relevant, it seldom belongs in the lead. Avoid stories that begin: *A 35-year-old divorcee* ...

The preferred form is to say in the body of the story that a woman is divorced.

**Dixie cup** A trademark for a paper drinking cup.

**DNS** Acronym for the *domain name system*, an international network of *Internet* domain servers, names and addresses.

**doctor** Use *Dr.* in first reference as a formal title before the name of an individual who holds a doctor of dental surgery, doctor of medicine, doctor of optometry, doctor of osteopathy, or doctor of podiatric medicine degree: *Dr. Jonas Salk.*

The form *Dr.*, or *Drs.*, in a plural construction, applies to all first-reference uses before a name, including direct quotations.

If appropriate in the context, *Dr.* also may be used on first reference before the names of individuals who hold other types of doctoral degrees. However, because the public frequently identifies *Dr.* only with physicians, care should be taken to assure that the individual's specialty is stated in first or second reference. The only exception would be a story in which the context left no doubt that the person was a dentist, psychologist, chemist, historian, etc.

In some instances it also is necessary to specify that an individual identified as *Dr.* is a physician. One frequent case is a story reporting on joint research by physicians, biologists, etc.

Do not use *Dr.* before the names of individuals who hold only honorary doctorates.

Do not continue the use of *Dr.* in subsequent references.

See **academic degrees**; **courtesy titles**; and **religious titles**.

**Doctors Without Borders** The group's preference is the French name, Medecins Sans Frontieres.

**dogs** See **animals**.

**dollars** Always lowercase. Use figures and the $ sign in all except casual references or amounts without a figure: *The book cost $4. Dad, please give me a dollar. Dollars are flowing overseas.*

For specified amounts, the word takes a singular verb: *He said $500,000 is what they want.*

For amounts of more than $1 million, use the $ and numerals up to two decimal places. Do not link the numerals and the word by a hyphen: *It is worth $4.35 million. It is worth exactly $4,351,242. He proposed a $300 billion budget.*

The form for amounts less

than $1 million: *$4, $25, $500, $1,000, $650,000.* See **cents**.

**domain names** The address used to locate a particular Web site or reach an e-mail system. In e-mail addresses, it is the portion to the right of the @ sign. It includes a suffix defining the type of entity, such as .com (for commerce, the most common suffix); .net (primarily for the network service providers); .org (organizations); .edu (reserved for educational institutions); .gov (reserved for U.S. government); .mil (for military); .int (reserved for organizations established by international treaty); .arpa (reserved for Internet infrastructure functions). There are also country-code suffixes (such as .fr for France, .us for the United States).

Seven more domain suffixes were approved in 2000: *.info, .biz, .name, .pro, .museum, .aero, .coop.*

**domino, dominoes**

**door to door, door-to-door** Hyphenate when used as a compound modifier: *He is a door-to-door salesman.*

But: *He went from door to door.*

**DOS** An acronym for *disk operating system.* Spell out.

**dot-com** As an informal adjective describing companies that do business mainly on the Internet.

**double-click**

**double-faced**

**doughnut** Not *donut.*

**Dow Jones & Co.** The com-

pany publishes The Wall Street Journal and Barron's National Business and Financial Weekly. It also operates the Dow Jones News Service.

For stock market watchers, it provides the Dow Jones industrial average, the Dow Jones transportation average, the Dow Jones utility average, and the Dow Jones composite average.

Headquarters is in New York.

**-down** Follow Webster's New World. Some examples, all nouns and/or adjectives:

| | |
|---|---|
| breakdown | rundown |
| countdown | sit-down |

All are two words when used as verbs.

**down-** The rules in **prefixes** apply, but in general, no hyphen. Some examples:

| | |
|---|---|
| downgrade | downtown |

**Down East** Use only in reference to Maine.

**downstate** Lowercase unless part of a proper name: *downstate Illinois.* But: *the Downstate Medical Center.*

**Down syndrome** Not *Down's,* for the genetic, chromosomal disorder first reported in 1866 by Dr. J. Langdon Down.

**Down Under** Australia, New Zealand and environs.

**Dr.** See **doctor**.

**draft beer** Not *draught beer.*

**drama** See **composition titles**.

**Dramamine** A trademark for a brand of motion sickness remedy.

**Drambuie** A trademark for a brand of Scottish liqueur.

**dressing room**

**drive** See **addresses**.

**drive-in** (n.)

**driver's license(s)**

**drop out** (v.) **dropout** (n.)

**drought**

**drowned, was drowned**
If a person suffocates in water or other fluid, the proper statement is that the individual *drowned*. To say that someone *was drowned* implies that another person caused the death by holding the victim's head under the water.

**Dr Pepper** A trademark (no period after Dr) for a brand of soft drink.
Headquarters is in Dallas.

**Drug Enforcement Administration** *DEA* on second reference.

**drugs** Because the word *drugs* has come to be used as a synonym for narcotics in recent years, *medicine* is frequently the better word to specify that an individual is taking medication.

**drunk, drunken** *Drunk* is the spelling of the adjective used after a form of the verb *to be*: *He was drunk.*
*Drunken* is the spelling of the adjective used before nouns: *a drunken driver, drunken driving.*

**drunkenness**

**DSL** Acronym for *digital subscriber line*, for high-speed access to the Internet over a telephone network.

**duel** A contest between two people. Three people cannot duel.

**duffel** Not *duffle.*

**duke, duchess** See **nobility**.

**Dumpster** Trademark for a large metal trash bin.
Use trash bin or trash container instead.

**Dunkirk** Use this spelling rather than *Dunkerque*, in keeping with widespread practice.

**du Pont, E.I.** Note the spelling of the name of the U.S. industrialist born in France. Use *du Pont* on second reference.
The company named after him is *E.I. du Pont de Nemours & Co.* of Wilmington, Del. Capitalize the shortened form *DuPont* (no space, capital P) in keeping with company practice. The shortened form is acceptable in all references.
See **foreign names**.

**dust storm** See **weather terms**.

**Dutch oven, Dutch treat, Dutch uncle**

**DVD** Acronym for *digital video disc* (or *digital versatile disc*), similar to CD-ROMs, but able to hold more music, video or data.
The acronym is acceptable in all references in most stories, but spell out somewhere in a story in which the context may not be familiar to readers.

**dyed-in-the-wool** (adj.)

**dyeing, dying** *Dyeing* refers to changing colors.
*Dying* refers to death.

**each** Takes a singular verb.

**each other, one another**
Two people look at *each other*.
More than two look at *one another*.
Either phrase may be used when the number is indefinite: *We help each other. We help one another.*

**earl, countess** See **nobility**.

**earmark**

**earth** Generally lowercase; capitalize when used as the proper name of the planet. *She is down-to-earth. How does the pattern apply to Mars, Jupiter, Earth, the sun and the moon? The astronauts returned to Earth. He hopes to move heaven and earth.*
See **planets**.

**earthquakes** Hundreds of earthquakes occur each year. Most are so small they cannot be felt.
The best source for information on major earthquakes is the National Earthquake Information Service operated by the U.S. Geological Survey in Golden, Colo.
On the Net:
www.usgs.gov
Earthquake magnitudes are measures of earthquake size calculated from ground motion recorded on seismographs. The Richter scale, named for Dr.

Charles F. Richter, is no longer widely used.
Magnitudes are usually reported simply as *magnitude 6.7*, for example, without specifying the scale being used. The various scales differ only slightly from one another.
In the first hours after a quake, earthquake size should be reported as a *preliminary magnitude of 6.7*, for example. Early estimates are often revised, and it can be several days before seismologists calculate a final figure.
Magnitudes are measured on several different scales. The most commonly used measure is the *moment magnitude*, related to the area of the fault on which an earthquake occurs, and the amount the ground slips.
The magnitude scale being used should be specified only when necessary. An example would be when two centers are reporting different magnitudes because they are using different scales.
With each scale, every increase of one number, say from 5.5 to 6.5, means that the quake's magnitude is 10 times as great. Theoretically, there is no upper limit to the scales.
A quake of magnitude 2.5 to 3 is the smallest generally felt by people.
—Magnitude 4: The quake can cause moderate damage.
—Magnitude 5: The quake can

cause considerable damage.
—Magnitude 6: The quake can cause severe damage.
—Magnitude 7: A major earthquake, capable of widespread, heavy damage.
—Magnitude 8: An earthquake capable of tremendous damage.

NOTABLE QUAKES: Earthquakes noted for both their magnitude and the amount of damage they caused include:
—Shensi province of China, January 1556: Killed 830,000 people, the largest number of fatalities on record from an earthquake.
—Hopeh province of northern China, July 28, 1976: Magnitude 7.5. A government document later said 655,237 people were killed and 779,000 injured. The fatality total was second only to the toll in the Shensi quake of 1556.
—Tokyo and Yokohama, Japan, September 1923: Magnitude later computed as 7.9. The quake and subsequent fires destroyed most of both cities, killing an estimated 200,000 people. Until the China quake of 1976, this was the highest fatality toll in the 20th century.
—Indian Ocean quake Dec. 26, 2004, off Indonesia's island of Sumatra with a magnitude 9, killed more than 162,000 people in 11 countries in the ensuing tsunami.
—South Asia quake, Oct. 8, 2005, with a magnitude of 7.6, killed an estimated 87,000 people in Pakistan and the part of Kashmir controlled by India.
—San Francisco, April 1906: Moment magnitude later computed as 7.8. The quake and subsequent fire were blamed for an estimated 700 deaths, although some estimates put the loss above 3,000 and possibly as high as 6,000.
—Chile, May 1960: Magnitude 9.5, considered the largest recorded quake. Killed 5,700 people.
—Alaska, March 1964: Magnitude 9.2. Killed 125 people, most from the seismic sea wave that followed.
—Guatemala, February 1976: Magnitude 7.5. Authorities reported more than 23,000 deaths.
—Mexico, Sept. 19, 1985: A quake registered at 8.1 left 9,500 people dead.
—Kobe, Japan, Jan. 17, 1995: A magnitude 6.9 quake killed about 5,500 people in collapsed buildings and fires.

OTHER TERMS: The word *temblor* (not *tremblor*) is a synonym for earthquake.
The word *epicenter* refers to the point on Earth's surface above the underground center, or focus, of an earthquake.

**east, eastern** See the **directions and regions** entry.

**Easter** In the computation used by the Latin Rite of the Roman Catholic Church and by Protestant churches, it falls on the first Sunday after the first full moon that occurs on or after March 21. If the full moon falls on a Sunday, Easter is the next Sunday.
Easter may fall, therefore, between March 22 and April 25 inclusive.

**Easter egg** A hidden "surprise" in a program or on a Web site, such as an extra level of a computer game or a message.

**Eastern Europe** No longer a separate political unit, but can be used in specific references to the region. Use only in historic sense. (Also *Western Europe.*)

**Eastern Hemisphere** The half of the Earth made up primarily of Africa, Asia, Australia and Europe.

**Eastern Orthodox churches** The term applies to a group of churches that have roots in the earliest days of Christianity and do not recognize papal authority over their activities.

Churches in this tradition were part of the undivided Christendom that existed until the Great Schism of 1054. At that time, many of the churches in the western half of the old Roman Empire accorded the bishop of Rome supremacy over other bishops. The result was a split between eastern and western churches.

The autonomous churches that constitute Eastern Orthodoxy are organized along mostly national lines. They recognize the patriarch of Constantinople (modern-day Istanbul) as their leader. He convenes councils, but his authority is otherwise that of a "first among equals."

Eastern orthodox churches today count about 200 million members. They include the Greek Orthodox Church and the Russian Orthodox Church.

In the United States, organizational lines are based on the national backgrounds of various ethnic groups. The largest is the Greek Orthodox Archdiocese of America, with about 2 million members. Next is the Orthodox Church in America, with about 1 million members, including people of Bulgarian, Romanian, Russian and Syrian descent.

The churches have their own disciplines on matters such as married clergy — a married man may be ordained, but a priest may not marry after ordination.

Some of these churches call the archbishop who leads them a *metropolitan;* others use the term *patriarch.* He normally heads the principal archdiocese within a nation. Working with him are other archbishops, bishops, priests and deacons.

Archbishops and bishops frequently follow a monastic tradition in which they are known only by a first name. When no last name is used, repeat the title before the sole name in subsequent references.

Some forms: *Metropolitan Theodosius, archbishop of Washington and metropolitan of America and Canada.* On second reference: *Metropolitan Theodosius. Archbishop* may be replaced by *the Most Rev.* on first reference. *Bishop* may be replaced by *the Rt. Rev.* on first reference.

Use *the Rev.* before the name of a priest on first reference. See **religious titles**.

**Eastern Rite churches** The term applies to a group of Catholic churches that are organized along ethnic lines traceable to the churches established during the earliest days of Christianity.

These churches accept the authority of the pope, but they have considerable autonomy in ritual and questions of discipline such as married clergy — a married man may be ordained, but marriage is not permitted after ordination.

Worldwide membership totals more than 10 million.

Among the churches of the Eastern Rite are the Antiochean-Maronite, Armenian Catholic, Byzantine-Byelorussian, Byzantine-Russian, Byzantine-Ruthe-

nian, Byzantine-Ukrainian and Chaldean Catholic.
See **Roman Catholic Church**.

**Eastern Shore** A region on the east side of Chesapeake Bay, including parts of Maryland and Virginia.
*Eastern Shore* is not a synonym for *East Coast*.

**Eastern Standard Time (EST), Eastern Daylight Time (EDT)** See **time zones**.

**easygoing**

**ecology** The study of the relationship between organisms and their surroundings. It is not synonymous with *environment*.
Right: *The laboratory is studying the ecology of man and the desert.*
Wrong: *Even so simple an undertaking as maintaining a lawn affects ecology.* (Use *environment* instead.)

**Ecstasy** Capitalize (no quote marks) this and other synthetic drug names.

**Ecuadorean**

**editor** Capitalize *editor* before a name only when it is an official corporate or organizational title. Do not capitalize as a job description.
See **titles**.

**editorial, news** In references to a newspaper, reserve *news* for the news department, its employees and news articles. Reserve *editorial* for the department that prepares the editorial page, its employees and articles that appear on the editorial page.

**editor-in-chief** Use hyphens and capitalize when used as a formal title before a name: *Editor-in-Chief Horace Greeley.* (The hyphens, reflecting industry usage, are an exception to Webster's New World College Dictionary.)
See **titles**.

**eerie** Not *eery*.

**effect** See the **affect, effect** entry.

**e.g.** Meaning *for example*, it is always followed by a comma.

**Eglin Air Force Base, Fla.** Not *Elgin*.

**Eid al-Adha** Meaning "Feast of Sacrifice," this most important Islamic holiday marks the willingness of the Prophet Ibrahim (Abraham to Christians and Jews) to sacrifice his son. During the holiday, which in most places lasts four days, Muslims slaughter sheep or cattle, distribute part of the meat to the poor and eat the rest. The holiday begins on the 10th day of the Islamic lunar month of Dhul-Hijja, during the annual hajj pilgrimage to Mecca.

**Eid al-Fitr** A three-day holiday marking the end of Ramadan, Islam's holy month of fasting.

**either** Use it to mean one or the other, not both.
Right: *She said to use either door.*
Wrong: *There were lions on either side of the door.*
Right: *There were lions on each side of the door. There were lions on both sides of the door.*

**either...or, neither...nor** The nouns that follow these words do not constitute a compound subject; they are alternate subjects and require a verb that agrees with the nearer subject: *Neither they nor he is going. Neither he nor they are going.*

**El Al** Israel Airlines. An *El Al* airliner is acceptable in any reference. Headquarters in Tel Aviv.

**elder** For its use in religious contexts, see the entry for an individual's denomination.

**elderly** Use this word carefully and sparingly. Do not refer to a person as *elderly* unless it is clearly relevant to the story.

It is appropriate in generic phrases that do not refer to specific individuals: *concern for the elderly, a home for the elderly,* etc.

If the intent is to show that an individual's faculties have deteriorated, cite a graphic example and give attribution for it.

Apply the same principle to terms such as *senior citizen.*

**-elect** Always hyphenate and lowercase: *President-elect Reagan.*

**Election Day** The first Tuesday after the first Monday in November.

**election returns** Use figures, with commas every three digits starting at the right and counting left. Use the word *to* (not a hyphen) in separating different totals listed together: *Jimmy Carter defeated Gerald Ford 40,827,292 to 39,146,157 in 1976* (this is the actual final figure).

Use the word *votes* if there is any possibility that the figures could be confused with a ratio: *Nixon defeated McGovern 16 votes to 3 votes in Dixville Notch.*

Do not attempt to create adjectival forms such as *the*

*40,827,292-39,146,157 vote.* See **vote tabulations**.

**Electoral College** But *electoral vote(s).*

**electrocardiogram** *EKG* is acceptable on second reference.

**eleventh** Spell out only in the phrase *the eleventh hour,* meaning at the last moment; otherwise use the numeral.

**ellipsis** See entry in **Punctuation** chapter.

**El Salvador** The use of the article in the name of the nation helps to distinguish it from its capital, *San Salvador.*

Use *Salvadoran(s)* in references to citizens of the nation.

**e-mail** Short form of *electronic mail.* Many *e-mail* or Internet addresses use symbols such as the *at* symbol (@), or the *tilde* (~) that cannot be transmitted correctly in some member computing systems. When needed, spell them out and provide an explanatory editor's note.

(Also *e-book, e-commerce, e-business.*)

**embargo** See the **boycott, embargo** entry.

**embargo times** See **release times**.

**embarrass, embarrassing, embarrassed, embarrassment**

**embassy** An *embassy* is the official office of an ambassador in a foreign country and the office that handles the political relations of one nation with another.

A *consulate*, the office of a consul in a foreign city, handles the commercial affairs and personal needs of citizens of the appointing country.

Capitalize with the name of a nation; lowercase without it: *the French Embassy, the U.S. Embassy, the embassy.*

**emcee, emceed, emceeing** A colloquial verb and noun best avoided. A phrase such as: *He was the master of ceremonies* is preferred.

**emeritus** This word often is added to formal titles to denote that individuals who have retired retain their rank or title.

When used, place *emeritus* after the formal title, in keeping with the general practice of academic institutions: *Professor Emeritus Samuel Eliot Morison, Dean Emeritus Courtney C. Brown, Publisher Emeritus Barnard L. Colby.*

Or: *Samuel Eliot Morison, professor emeritus of history; Courtney C. Brown, dean emeritus of the faculty of business; Barnard L. Colby, publisher emeritus.*

**emigrate, immigrate** One who leaves a country *emigrates* from it.

One who comes into a country *immigrates.*

The same principle holds for *emigrant* and *immigrant.*

**Emmy, Emmys** The annual awards by the Academy of Television Arts & Sciences (for prime-time programming; based in Los Angeles) and the National Academy of Television Arts and Sciences (for daytime, news and sports; based in New York).

**emoticon** A typographical cartoon or symbol generally used to indicate mood or appearance,

as :-) and often looked at sideways. Also known as *smileys.*

**Empirin** A trademark for a brand of aspirin compound.

**employee** Not *employe.*

**empty-handed**

**enact** See the **adopt, approve, enact, pass** entry.

**encyclopedia** But follow the spelling of formal names: *Encyclopaedia Britannica.*

**enforce** But *reinforce.*

**engine, motor** An *engine* develops its own power, usually through internal combustion or the pressure of air, steam or water passing over vanes attached to a wheel: *an airplane engine, an automobile engine, a jet engine, a missile engine, a steam engine, a turbine engine.*

A *motor* receives power from an outside source: *an electric motor, a hydraulic motor.*

**England** London stands alone in datelines. Use *England* after the names of other English communities in datelines.

See **datelines** and **United Kingdom**.

**English muffin, English setter**

**enquire, enquiry** The preferred words are *inquire, inquiry.*

**enroll, enrolled, enrolling**

**en route** Always two words.

**ensign** See **military titles**.

**ensure, insure** Use *ensure* to mean guarantee: *Steps were taken to ensure accuracy.*
Use *insure* for references to insurance: *The policy insures his life.*

**entitled** Use it to mean a right to do or have something. Do not use it to mean titled.
Right: *She was entitled to the promotion.*
Right: *The book was titled "Gone With the Wind."*

**enumerations** See examples in the **dash** and **periods** entries in the **Punctuation** chapter.

**envelop** Other verb forms: *enveloping, enveloped.* But: *envelope* (n.)

**environment** See **ecology**.

**Environmental Protection Agency** *EPA* is acceptable on second reference.

**envoy** Not a formal title. Lowercase.
See **titles**.

**epicenter** The point on the Earth's surface above the underground center, or focus, of an earthquake.
See **earthquakes**.

**epidemiology**

**Episcopal Church** Acceptable in all references for the *Protestant Episcopal Church in the United States of America*, the U.S. national church that is a member of the Anglican Communion.
The church is governed nationally by two bodies — the permanent Executive Council and the General Convention, which meets every three years.
After the council, the principal organizational units are, in descending order of size, provinces, dioceses or missionary districts, local parishes and local missions.
The National Council is composed of bishops, priests, laymen and laywomen. One bishop is designated the leader and holds the formal title of presiding bishop.
The General Convention has final authority in matters of policy and doctrine. All acts must pass both of its houses — the House of Bishops and the House of Deputies. The latter is composed of an equal number of clergy and lay delegates from each diocese.
A province is composed of several dioceses. Each has a provincial synod made up of a house of bishops and a house of deputies. The synod's primary duty is to coordinate the work of the church in its area.
Within a diocese, a bishop is the principal official. He is helped by the Diocesan Convention, which consists of all the clergy in the diocese and lay representatives from each parish.
The parish or local church is governed by a vestry, composed of the pastor and lay members elected by the congregation.
The clergy consists of bishops, priests, deacons and brothers. A priest who heads a parish is described as a *rector* rather than a pastor.
For first reference to bishops, use *Bishop* before the individual's name: *Bishop John M. Allin.* An acceptable alternative in referring to U.S. bishops is *the Rt. Rev.* The designation *the Most Rev.* is used before the names of the archbishops of Canterbury and York.

For first references, use *the Rev.* before the name of a priest, *Deacon* before the name of a deacon.
See **Anglican Communion** and **religious titles**.

### Episcopal, Episcopalian

*Episcopal* is the adjective form; use *Episcopalian* only as a noun referring to a member of the Episcopal Church: *She is an Episcopalian.* But: *She is an Episcopal priest.*

Capitalize *Episcopal* when referring to the Episcopal Church. Use lowercase when the reference is simply to a body governed by bishops.

**epoch** See the **historical periods and events** entry.

**equal** An adjective without comparative forms.

When people speak of a *more equal* distribution of wealth, what is meant is *more equitable.*

### Equal Employment Opportunity Commission *EEOC*

is acceptable on second reference.

### equal, equaled, equaling

**equally as** Do not use the words together; one is sufficient.

Omit the *equally* shown here in parentheses: *She was (equally) as wise as Marilyn.*

Omit the *as* shown here in parentheses: *She and Marilyn were equally (as) liberal.*

### Equal Rights Amendment

*ERA* is acceptable on second reference.

Ratification required approval by three-fourths (38) of the 50 states by June 30, 1982. Ratification failed when only 35 states

had approved the amendment by the deadline. The original deadline was March 22, 1979, but was extended by Congress.

The text:

Section 1. Equality of rights under the law shall not be denied or abridged by the United States or by any state on account of sex.

Section 2. The Congress shall have the power to enforce, by appropriate legislation, the provisions of this article.

Section 3. This amendment shall take effect two years after the date of ratification.

**equal time** *Equal time* applies to the Federal Communications Commission regulation that requires a radio or television station to provide a candidate for political office with air time equal to any time that an opponent receives beyond the coverage of news events.

**equator** Always lowercase.

**equitable** See **equal**.

**ERA** Acceptable in all references to baseball's *earned run average.*

Acceptable on second reference for *Equal Rights Amendment.*

**eras** See the **historical periods and events** entry.

**escalator** Formerly a trademark, now a generic term.

**escalator clause** A clause in a contract providing for increases or decreases in wages, prices, etc., based on fluctuations in the cost of living, production, expenses, etc.

**Eskimo, Eskimos** Some, especially in northern Canada,

use the term *Inuit* for these native peoples of northern North America. Follow the preference of those involved in the story.

**espresso** The coffee is *espresso*, not *expresso*.

**essential clauses, nonessential clauses** These terms are used in this book instead of *restrictive clause* and *nonrestrictive clause* to convey the distinction between the two in a more easily remembered manner.

Both types of clauses provide additional information about a word or phrase in the sentence.

The difference between them is that the *essential clause* cannot be eliminated without changing the meaning of the sentence — it so *restricts* the meaning of the word or phrase that its absence would lead to a substantially different interpretation of what the author meant.

The *nonessential clause*, however, can be eliminated without altering the basic meaning of the sentence — it does not *restrict* the meaning so significantly that its absence would radically alter the author's thought.

PUNCTUATION: An essential clause must not be set off from the rest of a sentence by commas. A nonessential clause must be set off by commas.

The presence or absence of commas provides the reader with critical information about the writer's intended meaning. Note the following examples:

—*Reporters who do not read the Stylebook should not criticize their editors.* (The writer is saying that only one class of reporters, those who do not read the Stylebook, should not criticize their editors. If the *who ... Stylebook* phrase were deleted, the meaning of the sentence would be changed substantially.)

—*Reporters, who do not read the Stylebook, should not criticize their editors.* (The writer is saying that all reporters should not criticize their editors. If the *who ... Stylebook* phrase were deleted, this meaning would not be changed.)

USE OF WHO, WHOM, THAT, WHICH. See separate entries on **that (conjunction); that, which (pronouns); who, whom**.

*That* is the preferred pronoun to introduce essential clauses that refer to an inanimate object or an animal without a name. *Which* is the only acceptable pronoun to introduce a nonessential clause that refers to an inanimate object or an animal without a name.

The pronoun *which* occasionally may be substituted for *that* in the introduction of an essential clause that refers to an inanimate object or an animal without a name. In general, this use of *which* should appear only when *that* is used as a conjunction to introduce another clause in the same sentence: *He said Monday that the part of the army which suffered severe casualties needs reinforcement.*

See **that (conjunction)** for guidelines on the use of *that* as a conjunction.

**essential phrases, nonessential phrases** These terms are used in this book instead of *restrictive phrase* and *nonrestrictive phrase* to convey the distinction between the two in a more easily remembered manner.

The underlying concept is the one that also applies to clauses:

An *essential phrase* is a word

or group of words critical to the reader's understanding of what the author had in mind.

A *nonessential phrase* provides more information about something. Although the information may be helpful to the reader's comprehension, the reader would not be misled if the information were not there.

PUNCTUATION: Do not set an essential phrase off from the rest of a sentence by commas:

*We saw the award-winning movie "One Flew Over the Cuckoo's Nest."* (No comma, because many movies have won awards, and without the name of the movie the reader would not know which movie was meant.)

*They ate dinner with their daughter Julie.* (Because they have more than one daughter, the inclusion of Julie's name is critical if the reader is to know which daughter is meant.)

Set off nonessential phrases by commas:

*We saw the 1975 winner in the Academy Award competition for best picture, "One Flew Over the Cuckoo's Nest."* (Only one movie won the award. The name is informative, but even without the name no other movie could be meant.)

They ate dinner with their daughter Julie and her husband, David. *(Julie has only one husband. If the phrase read and her husband David, it would suggest that she had more than one husband.)*

*The company chairman, Henry Ford II, spoke.* (In the context, only one person could be meant.)

*Indian corn, or maize, was harvested.* (*Maize* provides the reader with the name of the corn, but its absence would not change the meaning of the sentence.)

DESCRIPTIVE WORDS: Do not confuse punctuation rules for nonessential clauses with the correct punctuation when a nonessential word is used as a descriptive adjective. The distinguishing clue often is the lack of an article or pronoun:

Right: *Julie and husband Jeff went shopping. Julie and her husband, Jeff, went shopping.*

Right: *Company Chairman Henry Ford II made the announcement. The company chairman, Henry Ford II, made the announcement.*

**Eurasian** Of European and Asian descent.

**euro** The common currency of some of the European Union members.

Austria, Belgium, Finland, France, Germany, Ireland, Italy, Luxembourg, Netherlands, Portugal and Spain adopted the euro as of Jan. 1, 1999; Greece officially joined them Jan. 1, 2001.

The Vatican also adopted the euro as its official currency.

Euro bank notes and coins went into circulation Jan. 1, 2002.

**European Community** See **European Union**.

**European Union** *EU* (no periods, the more common practice). *The European Union,* based in Brussels, Belgium, was created by the Treaty on European Union signed in February 1992 and took effect Nov. 1, 1993. It is an outgrowth of the 1958 European Economic Community, which itself was formed out of the 1952 European Coal and Steel Community. The six founding members of the *European Union* are France,

Germany, Italy, Netherlands, Belgium, and Luxembourg. Other members are Denmark, Greece, Ireland, Portugal, Spain and the United Kingdom, with Austria, Sweden and Finland joining as of Jan. 1, 1995. Cyprus, Czech Republic, Estonia, Hungary, Latvia, Lithuania, Malta, Poland, Slovenia, and Slovakia joined May 1, 2004, and Bulgaria and Romania on Jan. 1, 2007.

**evangelical** See **religious movements**.

**Evangelical Friends Alliance** See **Quakers**.

**evangelism** See **religious movements**.

**evangelist** Capitalize only in reference to the men credited with writing the Gospels: *The four Evangelists were Matthew, Mark, Luke and John.*

In lowercase, it means a preacher who makes a profession of seeking conversions.

**eve** Capitalize when used after the name of a holiday: *New Year's Eve, Christmas Eve.* But: *the eve of Christmas.*

**even-steven** Not *even-ste-phen.*

**every day** (adv.) **everyday** (adj.) *She goes to work every day. He wears everyday shoes.*

**every one, everyone** Two words when it means each individual item: *Every one of the clues was worthless.*

One word when used as a pronoun meaning all persons: *Everyone wants his life to be happy.* (Note that *everyone* takes singular verbs and pronouns.)

**ex-** Use no hyphen for words that use *ex-* in the sense of *out of:* excommunicate    expropriate

Hyphenate when using *ex-* in the sense of *former:* ex-convict          ex-president

Do not capitalize *ex-* when attached to a formal title before a name: *ex-President Nixon.* The prefix modifies the entire term: *ex-New York Gov. Mario Cuomo;* not *New York ex-Gov.* Usually *former* is better.

**exaggerate**

**Excedrin** A trademark for a brand of aspirin compound.

**except** See the **accept, except** entry.

**exclamation point** See entry in **Punctuation** chapter.

**execute** To *execute* a person is to kill him in compliance with a military order or judicial decision. See the **assassin, killer, murderer** entry and the **homicide, murder, manslaughter** entry.

**executive branch** Always lowercase.

**executive director** Capitalize before a name only if it is a formal corporate or organizational title. See **titles**.

**Executive Mansion** Capitalize only in references to the White House.

**executor** Use for both men and women.

Not a formal title. Always lowercase. See **titles**.

**exorcise, exorcism** Not *exorcize.*

**expel, expelled, expelling**

**Explorers** See **Boy Scouts**.

**Export-Import Bank of the United States** *Export-Import Bank* is acceptable in all references; *Ex-Im Bank* is acceptable on second reference.

Headquarters is in Washington.

**extol, extolled, extolling**

**extra-** Do not use a hyphen when *extra* means *outside of* unless the prefix is followed by a word beginning with *a* or a capitalized word:

extralegal    extraterrestrial
extramarital    extraterritorial

But:

extra-alimentary    extra-Britannic

Follow *extra-* with a hyphen when it is part of a compound modifier describing a condition beyond the usual size, extent or degree:

extra-base hit    extra-large book
extra-dry drink    extra-mild taste

**extrasensory perception** *ESP* is acceptable on second reference.

**extreme unction** See **sacraments**.

**Exxon Mobil Corp.** Energy corporation formed from the 1999 merger of Exxon and Mobil, both formerly part of Standard Oil. *ExxonMobil* is acceptable as a subsequent reference to the official corporate name.

Headquarters is in Irving, Texas, with exploration, production and chemical operations based in Houston.

**eye, eyed, eyeing**

**eyestrain**

**eye to eye, eye-to-eye** Hyphenate when used as a compound modifier: *an eye-to-eye confrontation.*

**eyewitness**

# F

**face to face** When a story says two people meet for discussions, talks or debate, it is unnecessary to say they met *face to face.*

**fact-finding** (adj.)

**Faeroe Islands** Use in datelines after a community name in stories from this group of Danish islands in the northern Atlantic Ocean between Iceland and the Shetland Islands.

**Fahrenheit** The temperature scale commonly used in the United States.

The scale is named for Gabriel Daniel Fahrenheit, a German physicist who designed it. In it, the freezing point of water is 32 degrees and the boiling point is 212 degrees.

To convert to Celsius, subtract 32 from Fahrenheit figure, multiply by 5 and divide by 9 (77 - 32 = 45, times 5 = 225, divided by 9 = 25 degrees Celsius.)

In cases that require mention of the scale, use these forms: *86 degrees Fahrenheit* or *86 F* (note the space and no period after the *F*) if degrees and Fahrenheit are clear from the context.

See **Celsius** and **Kelvin**.

For guidelines on when Celsius temperatures should be used, see **metric system** entry.

TEMPERATURE CONVERSIONS

Following is a temperature conversion table. Celsius temperatures have been rounded to the nearest whole number.

| F | C | F | C | F | C |
|---|---|---|---|---|---|
| -26 | -32 | 19 | -7 | 64 | 18 |
| -24 | -31 | 21 | -6 | 66 | 19 |
| -22 | -30 | 23 | -5 | 68 | 20 |
| -20 | -29 | 25 | -4 | 70 | 21 |
| -18 | -28 | 27 | -3 | 72 | 22 |
| -17 | -27 | 28 | -2 | 73 | 23 |
| -15 | -26 | 30 | -1 | 75 | 24 |
| -13 | -25 | 32 | 0 | 77 | 25 |
| -11 | -24 | 34 | 1 | 79 | 26 |
| -9 | -23 | 36 | 2 | 81 | 27 |
| -8 | -22 | 37 | 3 | 82 | 28 |
| -6 | -21 | 39 | 4 | 84 | 29 |
| -4 | -20 | 41 | 5 | 86 | 30 |
| -2 | -19 | 43 | 6 | 88 | 31 |
| 0 | -18 | 45 | 7 | 90 | 32 |
| 1 | -17 | 46 | 8 | 91 | 33 |
| 3 | -16 | 48 | 9 | 93 | 34 |
| 5 | -15 | 50 | 10 | 95 | 35 |
| 7 | -14 | 52 | 11 | 97 | 36 |
| 9 | -13 | 54 | 12 | 99 | 37 |
| 10 | -12 | 55 | 13 | 100 | 38 |
| 12 | -11 | 57 | 14 | 102 | 39 |
| 14 | -10 | 59 | 15 | 104 | 40 |
| 16 | -9 | 61 | 16 | 106 | 41 |
| 18 | -8 | 63 | 17 | 108 | 42 |

**fall** See **seasons**.

**fallout** (n.)

**false titles** Often derived from occupational titles or other labels.

Always lowercase. See **titles**.

**family names** Capitalize

words denoting family relationships only when they precede the name of a person or when they stand unmodified as a substitute for a person's name: *I wrote to Grandfather Smith. I wrote Mother a letter. I wrote my mother a letter.*

**Fannie Mae** See entry in **Business Guidelines**.

**Fannie May** A trademark for a brand of candy.

**FAQ** Acronym for *frequently asked questions*, a format often used to summarize information on the *Internet*. Spell it out in copy.

**Far East** The easternmost portions of the continent of Asia: China, Japan, North and South Korea, Taiwan, Hong Kong and the eastern portions of Russia.
Confine *Far East* to this restricted sense. Use the *Far East and Southeast Asia* when referring to a wider portion of eastern Asia.
See the **Asian subcontinent** and **Southeast Asia** entries.

**far-flung** (adj.)

**farmers market** No apostrophe.

**farmworker**

**far-off** (adj.)

**far-ranging** (adj.)

**farsighted** When used in a medical sense, it means that a person can see objects at a distance but has difficulty seeing materials at close range.

**farther, further** Farther refers to physical distance: *He*

*walked farther into the woods.*
*Further* refers to an extension of time or degree: *She will look further into the mystery.*

**Far West** For the U.S. region, generally west of the Rocky Mountains.

**fascism, fascist** See the **political parties and philosophies** entry.

**Fatah** A secular Palestinian party and former guerrilla movement founded by Yasser Arafat. Do not use with the prefix *al-*.

**father** Use *the Rev.* in first reference before the names of Episcopal, Orthodox and Roman Catholic priests. Use *Father* before a name only in direct quotations.
See **religious titles**.

**Father's Day** The third Sunday in June.

**father-in-law, fathers-in-law**

**Father Time**

**fax** (n.) or (v.) Acceptable as short version of facsimile or facsimile machine in all uses.

**faze, phase** *Faze* means to embarrass or disturb: *The snub did not faze her.*
*Phase* denotes an aspect or stage: *They will phase in a new system.*

**FBI** Acceptable in all references for *Federal Bureau of Investigation.*

**feather bedding, featherbedding** *Feather bedding* is a mattress stuffed with feathers.

*Featherbedding* is the practice of requiring an employer to hire more workers than needed to handle a job.

**features** They are not exempt from normal style rules. See **special contexts** for guidelines on some limited exceptions.

**February** See **months**.

**federal** Use a capital letter for the architectural style and for corporate or governmental bodies that use the word as part of their formal names: *the Federal Trade Commission.* (See separate entries for governmental agencies.)

Lowercase when used as an adjective to distinguish something from state, county, city, town or private entities: *federal assistance, federal court, the federal government, a federal judge.*

Also: *federal District Court* (but *U.S. District Court* is preferred) and *federal Judge Ann Aldrich* (but *U.S. District Judge Ann Aldrich* is preferred).

**Federal Aviation Administration** *FAA* is acceptable on second reference.

**Federal Bureau of Investigation** *FBI* is acceptable in all references. To avoid alphabet soup, however, use *the bureau* in some references.

**Federal Communications Commission** *FCC* is acceptable on second reference.

**federal court** Always lowercase.

The preferred form for first reference is to use the proper name of the court. See entries under **U.S.** and the court name.

Do not create nonexistent entities such as *Manhattan Federal Court.* Instead, use *a federal court in Manhattan.*

See **judicial branch**.

**Federal Crop Insurance Corp.** Do not abbreviate.

**Federal Deposit Insurance Corp.** *FDIC* is acceptable on second reference.

**Federal Emergency Management Agency** *FEMA* is acceptable on second reference.

**Federal Energy Regulatory Commission** This agency replaced the Federal Power Commission in 1977. It regulates interstate natural gas and electricity transactions.

*FERC* is acceptable on second reference, but *the agency* or *the commission* is preferred.

**Federal Farm Credit Board** Do not abbreviate.

**Federal Highway Administration** Reserve the *FHA* abbreviation for the *Federal Housing Administration.*

**Federal Home Loan Bank Board** Do not abbreviate.

**Federal Home Loan Mortgage Corp.** See **Freddie Mac** entry in **Business** section.

**Federal Housing Administration** *FHA* is acceptable on second reference.

**federal legal holidays** See the **holidays and holy days** entry.

**Federal Mediation and Conciliation Service** Do not

abbreviate. Use *the service* on
second reference.

**Federal National Mort-
gage Association** See **Fannie
Mae** entry in **Business** section.

**Federal Register** This publication, issued every workday,
is the legal medium for recording
and communicating the rules and
regulations established by the
executive branch of the federal
government.

Individuals or corporations
cannot be held legally responsible
for compliance with a regulation
unless it has been published in
the Register.

In addition, executive agencies are required to publish in
advance some types of proposed
regulations.

**Federal Reserve System,
Federal Reserve Board** On
second reference, use the *Federal
Reserve, the Reserve, the Fed, the
system* or *the board.*

Also: *the Federal Reserve Bank
of New York* (*Boston*, etc.), *the
bank.*

**Federal Trade
Commission** *FTC* is acceptable
on second reference.

**FedEx** Use this official brand
name for the Federal Express
delivery service company. The formal name of the parent company
is FedEx Corp.

**felony, misdemeanor** A
*felony* is a serious crime. A *misdemeanor* is a minor offense against
the law.

A fuller definition of what constitutes a felony or misdemeanor
depends on the governmental jurisdiction involved.

At the federal level, a *misde-*

*meanor* is a crime that carries a
potential penalty of no more than
a year in jail. A *felony* is a crime
that carries a potential penalty of
more than a year in prison. Often,
however, a statute gives a judge
options such as imposing a fine
or probation in addition to or instead of a jail or prison sentence.

A *felon* is a person who has
been convicted of a *felony,* regardless of whether the individual
actually spends time in confinement or is given probation or a
fine instead.

*Convicted felon* is redundant.
See the **prison, jail** entry.

**female** This is the preferred
adjective, not *woman.*

**Ferris wheel**

**ferryboat**

**fertility rate** As calculated
by the federal government, it
is the number of live births per
1,000 females age 15 through 44
years.

**fewer, less** In general, use
*fewer* for individual items, *less* for
bulk or quantity.

Wrong: *The trend is toward
more machines and less people.*
(People in this sense refers to individuals.)

Wrong: *She was fewer than
60 years old.* (Years in this sense
refers to a period of time, not individual years.)

Right: *Fewer than 10 appli-
cants called.* (Individuals.)

Right: *I had less than $50 in
my pocket.* (An amount.) But: *I
had fewer than 50 $1 bills in my
pocket.* (Individual items.)

**fiance** (man) **fiancee**
(woman)

**Fiberglas** Note the single *s*. A trademark for fiberglass or glass fiber.

**field house**

**figuratively, literally** *Figuratively* means in an analogous sense, but not in the exact sense. *He bled them white.* Literally means in an exact sense; do not use it figuratively. Wrong: *He literally bled them white.* (Unless the blood was drained from their bodies.)

**figure** The symbol for a number: *the figure 5.* See **numerals**.

**filibuster** To *filibuster* is to make long speeches to obstruct the passage of legislation. A legislator who used such methods also is a *filibuster*, not a *filibusterer*.

**Filipinos** The people of the Philippines.

**film ratings** See **movie ratings**.

**financial editor** Capitalize only as a formal title before a name. See **titles**.

**Finland** A Nordic state, not part of Scandinavia.

**firearms** See **weapons**.

**fire department** See the **governmental bodies** entry for the basic rules on capitalization. See **titles** and **military titles** for guidelines on titles.

**firefighter, fireman** The preferred term to describe a person who fights fire is *firefighter*.

One meaning of *fireman* is a person who tends fires in a furnace. *Fireman* is also an acceptable synonym for *firefighter*.

**firewall** Software that monitors incoming and outgoing Internet traffic to your computer and checks for suspicious patterns.

**firm** A business partnership is correctly referred to as a *firm*. *He joined a law firm.* Do not use *firm* in references to an incorporated business entity. Use *the company* or *the corporation* instead.

**first degree, first-degree** Hyphenate when used as a compound modifier: *It was murder in the first degree. He was convicted of first-degree murder.*

**first family** Always lowercase.

**first lady** Not a formal title. Do not capitalize, even when used before the name of a chief of state's wife. See **titles**.

**first quarter, first-quarter** Hyphenate when used as a compound modifier: *He scored in the first quarter. The team took the lead on his first-quarter goal.*

**fiscal, monetary** *Fiscal* applies to budgetary matters. *Monetary* applies to money supply.

**fiscal year** See entry in **Business Guidelines**.

**fitful** It means restless, not a condition of being fit.

**fjord**

**flack, flak** *Flack* is slang for

press agent.

*Flak* is a type of anti-aircraft fire, hence figuratively a barrage of criticism.

**flagpole, flagship**

**flail, flay** To *flail* is to swing the arms widely.

To *flay* is, literally, to strip off the skin by whipping. Figuratively, *to flay* means to tongue-lash a person.

**flair, flare** *Flair* is conspicuous talent.

*Flare* is a verb meaning to blaze with sudden, bright light or to burst out in anger. It is also a noun meaning a flame.

**flak** See the **flack, flak** entry.

**flare up** (v.) **flare-up** (n.) See the **flair, flare** entry.

**flash flood** See **weather terms**.

**flaunt, flout** To *flaunt* is to make an ostentatious or defiant display: *She flaunted her intelligence.*

To *flout* is to show contempt for: *He flouts the law.*

**flautist** The preferred word is *flutist*.

**fleet** Use figures and capitalize *fleet* when forming a proper name: *the 6th Fleet.*

Lowercase *fleet* whenever it stands alone.

**flier, flyer** *Flier* is the preferred term for an aviator or a handbill. *Flyer* is the proper name of some trains and buses: *The Western Flyer.*

**flimflam, flimflammed**

**flip-flop**

**floods, flood stage** See **weather terms**.

**floodwaters**

**floor leader** Treat it as a job description, lowercased, rather than a formal title: *Republican floor leader John Smith.*

Do not use when a formal title such as *majority leader, minority leader* or *whip* would be the accurate description.

See the **legislative titles** and **titles** entries.

**floppy disk** Use *diskette.*

**Florida** Abbrev.: *Fla.* See **state names**.

**Florida Keys** A chain of small islands extending southwest from the southern tip of mainland Florida.

Cities, or the islands themselves, are followed by *Fla.* in datelines:

*KEY WEST, Fla. (AP) —*

**flounder, founder** A *flounder* is a fish; to *flounder* is to move clumsily or jerkily, to flop about: *The fish floundered on land.*

To *founder* is to bog down, become disabled or sink: *The ship floundered in the heavy seas for hours, then foundered.*

**flout** See the **flaunt, flout** entry.

**flowers** See **plants**.

**fluid ounce** Equal to 1.8 cubic inches, two tablespoons or six teaspoons. The metric equivalent is approximately 30 milliliters.

To convert to milliliters, multiply by 30 (3 ounces x 30 equals 90 milliliters).
See **liter**.

**fluorescent**

**flush** To become red in the face. See **livid**.

**flutist** The preferred term, rather than *flautist.*

**flyer** See the **flier, flyer** entry.

**FM** Acceptable in all references for the *frequency modulation* system of radio transmission.

**f.o.b.** Acceptable on first reference for *free on board.* The concept should be explained, however, in contexts not addressed to business-oriented audiences: The seller agrees to put an item on a truck, ship, etc., at no charge, but the transportation costs must be paid by the buyer.

**-fold** No hyphen:
twofold            fourfold

**folk singer, folk song**

**following** The word usually is a noun, verb or adjective: *He has a large following. He is following his conscience. The following statement was made.*

Although Webster's New World records its use as a preposition, the preferred word is *after: He spoke after dinner.* Not: *He spoke following dinner.*

**follow-up** (n. and adj.) Use two words (no hyphen) in verb form.

**food** Most food names are lowercase: *apples, cheese, peanut butter.*

Capitalize brand names and trademarks: *Roquefort cheese, Tabasco sauce.*

Most proper nouns or adjectives are capitalized when they occur in a food name: *Boston brown bread, Russian dressing, Swiss cheese, Waldorf salad.*

Lowercase is used, however, when the food does not depend on the proper noun or adjective for its meaning: *french fries, graham crackers, manhattan cocktail.*

If a question arises, check the separate entries in this book. If there is no entry, follow Webster's New World. Use lowercase if the dictionary lists it as an acceptable form for the sense in which the word is used.

The same principles apply to foreign names for foods: *mousse de saumon* (salmon mousse), *pomme de terre* (literally, "apple of the earth" — for potato), *salade Russe* (Russian salad).

**Food and Agriculture Organization** Not *Agricultural. FAO* is acceptable on second reference to this U.N. agency.

**Food and Drug Administration** *FDA* is acceptable on second reference.

**foot** The basic unit of length in the measuring system that has been used in the United States. Its origin was a calculation that this was the length of the average human foot.

The metric equivalent is exactly 30.48 centimeters, which may be rounded to 30 centimeters for most comparisons.

For most conversions to centimeters, it is adequate to multiply 30 (5 feet x 30 equals 150 centimeters). For more exact figures, multiply by 30.48 (5 feet x 30.48 equals 152.4 centimeters).

To convert to meters, multiply

by .3 (5 feet x .3 equals 1.5 meters).
See **centimeter**; **meter;** and **dimensions.**

**foot-and-mouth disease**
Not *hoof-and-mouth disease.*

**forbear, forebear** *To forbear* is to avoid or shun.
A *forebear* is an ancestor.

**forbid, forbade, forbidding**

**forcible rape** A redundancy that usually should be avoided. It may be used, however, in stories dealing with both rape and statutory rape, which does not necessarily involve the use of force.

**Ford Motor Co.** Use *Ford,* not *FMC,* on second reference.
Headquarters is in Dearborn, Mich.

**fore-** The rules in **prefixes** apply, but in general, no hyphen. Some examples:

| | |
|---|---|
| forebrain | foregoing |
| forefather | foretooth |

There are three nautical exceptions, based on long-standing practice:

| | |
|---|---|
| fore-topgallant | fore-topsail |
| fore-topmast | |

**forecast** Use *forecast* also for the past tense, not *forecasted.*
See **weather terms.**

**forego, forgo** *To forego* means to go before, as in *foregone conclusion.*
*To forgo* means to abstain from.

**foreign governmental bodies** Capitalize the names of the specific foreign governmental agencies and departments, either with the name of the nation or without it if clear in the context: *French Foreign Ministry, the Foreign Ministry.*
Lowercase *the ministry* or a similar term when standing alone.

**foreign legislative bodies** In general, capitalize the proper name of a specific legislative body abroad: *the Knesset, the Diet.*
The most frequent names in use are *Congress, National Assembly* and *Parliament.*
GENERIC USES: Lowercase *parliament* or a similar term only when used generically to describe a body for which the foreign name is being given: *the Diet, Japan's parliament.*
PLURALS: Lowercase *parliament* and similar terms in plural constructions: *the parliaments of England and France, the English and French parliaments.*
INDIVIDUAL HOUSES: The principle applies also to individual houses of the nation's legislature, just as *Senate* and *House* are capitalized in the United States:
*ROME (AP) — New leaders have taken control in the Chamber of Deputies.*
Lowercase *assembly* when used as a shortened reference to national assembly.
In many countries, *national assembly* is the name of a unicameral legislative body. In some, such as France, it is the name for the lower house of a legislative body known by some other name such as *parliament.*

**foreign money** Generally, amounts of foreign money mentioned in news stories should be converted to dollars. If it is necessary to mention the foreign amount, provide the dollar equivalent in parentheses.

The basic monetary units of nations are listed in Webster's New World College Dictionary under "Monetary Units." Use, as appropriate, the official exchange rates, which change from day to day on the world's markets.

**foreign names** For foreign place names, use the primary spelling in Webster's New World College Dictionary. If it has no entry, follow the National Geographic Atlas of the World.

For personal names, follow the individual's preference for an English spelling if it can be determined. Otherwise:

—Use the nearest phonetic equivalent in English if one exists: *Alexander Solzhenitsyn*, for example, rather than *Aleksandr*, the spelling that would result from a transliteration of the Russian letters into the English alphabet.

If a name has no close phonetic equivalent in English, express it with an English spelling that approximates the sound in the original language: *Anwar Sadat.*

In general, lowercase particles such as *de, der, la, le,* and *van, von* when part of a given name: *Charles de Gaulle, Baron Manfred von Richthofen.* But follow individual preferences, as in *bin Laden,* or Dutch names such as *Van Gogh* or *Van der Graaf.* Capitalize the particles when the last names start a sentence: *De Gaulle spoke to von Richthofen.*

For additional guidelines, see **Arabic names; Chinese names; Portuguese names; Russian names; Spanish names**.

**foreign words** Some foreign words and abbreviations have been accepted universally into the English language: *bon voyage; versus, vs.; et cetera, etc.* They may be used without explanation if they are clear in the context.

Many foreign words and their abbreviations are not understood universally, although they may be used in special applications such as medical or legal terminology. If such a word or phrase is needed in a story, place it in quotation marks and provide an explanation: *"ad astra per aspera," a Latin phrase meaning "to the stars through difficulty."*

**foreman, forewoman** Seldom a formal title.

**formal titles** See **titles**.

**former** Always lowercase. But retain capitalization for a formal title used immediately before a name: *former President Nixon.*

**Formica** A trademark for a brand of laminated plastic.

**Formosa** See **Taiwan**.

**Formosa Strait** Not *the straits of Taiwan.*

**formula, formulas** Use figures in writing formulas, as illustrated in the entries on metric units.

**forsake, forsook, forsaken**

**fort** Do not abbreviate, for cities or for military installations.

In datelines for cities:
*FORT LAUDERDALE, Fla. (AP)*
—

In datelines for military instal-

lations:
*FORT BRAGG, N.C. (AP)* —

**fortnight** The expression
*two weeks* is preferred.

**fortuneteller,
fortunetelling**

**forty, forty-niner** *'49er* is
acceptable.

**forward** Not *forwards*.

**foul, fowl** *Foul* means offensive, out of line.
A *fowl* is a bird, especially the larger domestic birds used as food: chickens, ducks, turkeys.

**founder** See the **flounder, founder** entry.

**Founding Fathers** Capitalize when referring to the creators of the U.S. Constitution.

**four-flush** (stud poker)

**Four-H Club** *4-H Club* is preferred. Members are *4-H'ers*.

**four-star general**

**Fourth Estate** Capitalize when used as a collective name for journalism and journalists.
The description is attributed to Edmund Burke, who is reported to have called the reporters' gallery in Parliament a "Fourth Estate."
The three estates of early English society were the Lords Spiritual (the clergy), the Lords Temporal (the nobility) and the Commons (the bourgeoisie).

**Fourth of July, July Fourth** Also *Independence Day*. The federal legal holiday is observed on Friday if July 4 falls on a Saturday, on Monday if it falls on a Sunday.

**4x4** *Four-wheel drive* is preferred, unless *4x4* is part of the car model's proper name.

**fractions** Spell out amounts less than 1 in stories, using hyphens between the words: *two-thirds, four-fifths, seven-sixteenths,* etc.
Use figures for precise amounts larger than 1, converting to decimals whenever practical.
When using fractional characters, remember that most newspaper type fonts can set only 1/8, 1/4, 3/8, 1/2, 5/8, 3/4 and 7/8 as one unit; for mixed numbers, use *1 1/2, 2 5/8,* etc. with a full space between the whole number and the fraction. Other fractions require a hyphen and individual figures, with a space between the whole number and the fraction: *1 3-16, 2 1-3, 5 9-10.*
In tabular material, use figures exclusively, converting to decimals if the amounts involve extensive use of fractions that cannot be expressed as a single character.
See **percent**.

**fragment, fragmentary**
*Fragment* describes a piece or pieces broken from the whole: *She sang a fragment of the song.*
*Fragmentary* describes disconnected and incomplete parts: *Early returns were fragmentary.*

**frame up** (v.) **frame-up** (n.)

**frankfurters** They were first called hot dogs in 1906 when a cartoonist, T.A. "Tad" Dorgan, showed a dachshund inside an elongated bun.

**fraternal organizations and service clubs** Capitalize the proper names: *American Legion, Lions Club, Independent Order of Odd Fellows, Rotary Club.*
Capitalize also words describing membership: *He is a Legionnaire, a Lion, an Odd Fellow, an Optimist and a Rotarian.* See **American Legion** for the rationale on *Legionnaire.*
Capitalize the formal titles of officeholders when used before a name.
See **titles**.

**free-for-all** (n. and adj.)

**freelance** (v. and adj.) The noun: *freelancer.* (No hyphen is a change in AP style.)

**free on board** See **f.o.b.**

**freewheeling**

**Free World** An imprecise description. Use only in quoted matter.

**freeze-dry, freeze-dried, freeze-drying**

**freezing drizzle, freezing rain** See **weather terms**.

**French Canadian, French Canadians** Without a hyphen. An exception to the normal practice in describing a dual ethnic heritage.

**French Foreign Legion** Retain capitalization if shortened to the Foreign Legion.
Lowercase *the legion* and *legionnaires.* Unlike the situation with the American Legion, the French Foreign Legion is a group of active soldiers.

**french fries** See **capitaliza-**

tion and **food**.

**frequency modulation** *FM* is acceptable in all references.

**Friday** See **days of the week**.

**Friends General Conference, Friends United Meeting** See **Quakers**.

**Frigidaire** A trademark for a brand of refrigerator.

**Frisbee** A trademark for a plastic disc thrown as a toy. Use *Frisbee disc* for the trademarked version and *flying disc* for other generic versions.

**front line** (n.) **front-line** (adj.)

**front page** (n.) **front-page** (adj.)

**front-runner**

**frost** See **weather terms**.

**fruits** See **food**.

**FTP** *File transfer protocol,* a common procedure for transferring files on the *Internet.* The acronym is acceptable in second reference.

**fulfill, fulfilled, fulfilling**

**full-** Hyphenate when used to form compound modifiers:
full-dress          full-page
full-fledged        full-scale
full-length

See the listings that follow and Webster's New World College Dictionary for the spelling of other combinations.

**full house** (poker)

**full time, full-time** Hyphenate when used as a compound modifier: *He works full time. She has a full-time job.*

**fulsome** It means disgustingly excessive. Do not use it to mean lavish or profuse.

**fundamentalist** See **religious movements**.

**fundraising, fundraiser** One word in all cases.

**funnel cloud** See **weather terms**.

**furlough**

**further** See the **farther, further** entry.

**fuselage**

**fusillade**

# G

**G** The general audience rating. See **movie ratings**.

**gage, gauge** A *gage* is a security or a pledge.

A *gauge* is a measuring device. *Gauge* is also a term used to designate the size of shotguns. See **weapons**.

**gaiety**

**gale** See **weather terms**.

**gallon** Equal to 128 fluid ounces. The metric equivalent is approximately 3.8 liters.

To convert to liters, multiply by 3.8 (3 gallons x 3.8 = 11.4 liters).

See **imperial gallon**; **liter**; and **metric system**.

**Gallup Poll** Prepared by the Gallup Organization, Princeton, N.J.

**Game Boy** The video game system from Nintendo. Also, Game Boy Advance.

**game plan**

**gamut, gantlet, gauntlet** A *gamut* is a scale of notes or any complete range or extent.

A *gantlet* is a flogging ordeal, literally or figuratively.

A *gauntlet* is a glove. *To throw down the gauntlet* means to issue a challenge. To *take up the gauntlet* means to accept a challenge.

**gamy, gamier, gamiest**

**garnish, garnishee** *Garnish* means to adorn or decorate.

As a verb, *garnishee* (*garnisheed, garnisheeing*) means to attach a debtor's property or wages to satisfy a debt. As a noun, it identifies the individual whose property was attached.

**gauge** See the **gage, gauge** entry.

**gay** Used to describe men and women attracted to the same sex, though *lesbian* is the more common term for women. Preferred over *homosexual* except in clinical contexts or references to sexual activity.

Include sexual orientation only when it is pertinent to a story, and avoid references to "sexual preference" or to a gay or alternative "lifestyle."

**G-8** Use a hyphen in the abbreviated form for the *Group of Eight*, made up of representatives of the major industrial nations, the United States, France, Russia, Great Britain, Germany, Japan, Italy, and Canada. (The *G-7* or *Group of Seven* — all the aforementioned except Russia — deals with economic issues.)

**general assembly** See **legislature** for its treatment as the name of a state's legislative body.

Capitalize when it is the formal name for the ruling or consultative body of an organization: *the General Assembly of the World Council of Churches.*

**General Assembly (U.N.)** *General Assembly* may be used on the first reference in a story under a United Nations dateline.

Use *U.N. General Assembly* in other first references, *the General Assembly* or *the assembly* in subsequent references.

**general court** Part of the official proper name for the legislatures in Massachusetts and New Hampshire. Capitalize specific references with or without the state name: *the Massachusetts General Court, the General Court.*

In keeping with the accepted practice, however, *Legislature* may be used instead and treated as a proper name. See **legislature**.

Lowercase *legislature* in a generic use such as: *The General Court is the legislature in Massachusetts.*

**General Electric Co.** *GE* is acceptable on second reference.

Headquarters is in Fairfield, Conn.

**general, general of the air force, general of the army** See **military titles**.

**general manager** Capitalize only as a formal title before a name.

See **titles**.

**General Motors Corp.** *GM* is acceptable on second reference. Headquarters is in Detroit.

**General Services Administration** *GSA* is acceptable on second reference.

**Geneva Conventions** Note the final *s*.

**genie** Not *jinni.*

**gentile** Generally, any person not a Jew; often, specifically a Christian. But to Mormons it is anyone not a Mormon.

**gentleman** Do not use as a synonym for *man.* See **lady**.

**genus, species** In scientific or biological names, capitalize the first, or generic, Latin name for the class of plant or animal and lowercase the species that follows: *Homo sapiens, Tyrannosaurus rex.*

In second references, use the abbreviated form: *P. borealis, T. rex.*

**geographic names** The basic guidelines:

DOMESTIC: Do not use the postal abbreviations for state names. For acceptable abbreviations, see entries in this book under each state's name. See **state names** for rules on when the abbreviations may be used.

Abbreviate *Saint* as *St.* (But abbreviate *Sault Sainte Marie* as *Sault Ste. Marie.*)

FOREIGN: The first source for the spelling of all foreign place names is Webster's New World College Dictionary as follows:

—Use the first-listed spelling if an entry gives more than one.

—If the dictionary provides different spellings in separate entries, use the spelling that is followed by a full description of the location.

If the dictionary does not have

an entry, use the first-listed spelling in the National Geographic Atlas of the World.

On the Net: www.nationalgeographic.com NEW NAMES: Follow the styles adopted by the United Nations and the U.S. Board on Geographic Names on new cities, new independent nations and nations that change their names.

DATELINES: See the **datelines** entry.

CAPITALIZATION: Capitalize common nouns when they form an integral part of a proper name, but lowercase them when they stand alone: *Pennsylvania Avenue, the avenue; the Philippine Islands, the islands; the Mississippi River, the river.*

Lowercase common nouns that are not a part of a specific name: *the Pacific islands, the Swiss mountains, Zhejiang province.*

For additional guidelines, see **addresses**; **capitalization**; the **directions and regions** entry; and **island**.

**Georgia** Abbrev.: *Ga.* See **state names**.

**German measles** Also known as *rubella.*

**Germany** *East Germany* and *West Germany* were reunited as of Oct. 3, 1990. *Berlin* stands alone in datelines.

**getaway** (n.)

**get-together** (n.)

**ghetto, ghettos** Do not use indiscriminately as a synonym for the sections of cities inhabited by minorities or the poor. *Ghetto* has a connotation that government

decree has forced people to live in a certain area.

In most cases, *section, district, slum area* or *quarter* is the more accurate word. Sometimes a place name alone has connotations that make it best: *Harlem, Watts.*

**gibe, jibe** To *gibe* means to taunt or sneer: *They gibed him about his mistakes.*

*Jibe* means to shift direction or, colloquially, to agree: *They jibed their ship across the wind. Their stories didn't jibe.*

**Gibraltar, Strait of** Not *Straits.* The entrance to the Mediterranean from the Atlantic Ocean. The British colony on the peninsula that juts into the strait stands alone in datelines as *GIBRALTAR.*

**GIF** Acronym for *graphics interchange format,* a compression format for images. The acronym is acceptable in copy, but it should be explained somewhere in the story. Use lowercase in a file name.

**giga-** A prefix denoting 1 billion units of a measure. Move a decimal point nine places to the right, adding zeros if necessary, to convert to the basic unit: 5.5 gigatons = 5,500,000,000 tons.

**gigabyte** A unit of storage capacity in a computer system, loosely equal to 1 billion bytes. Abbrev.: *GB.*

**GI, GIs** Believed to have originated as an abbreviation for *government issue* supplies, it describes military personnel in general, but normally is used for the Army. (No periods is an exception to the general rule for two-letter abbreviations.)

Soldier is preferred unless the story contains the term in quoted matter or involves a subject such as the GI Bill of Rights.

**girl** Applicable until 18th birthday is reached. Use woman or young woman afterward.

**girlfriend, boyfriend**

**Girl Scouts** The full name of the national organization is Girl Scouts of the United States of America. Headquarters is in New York.

Girls 6 through 8 are Brownie Girl Scouts or Brownies. Girls 9 through 11 are Junior Girl Scouts or Juniors. Girls 12 through 14 are Cadette Girl Scouts or Cadettes. Girls 15 through 17 are Senior Girl Scouts or Seniors.

See **Boy Scouts**.

**glamour** One of the few our endings still used in American writing. But the adjective is glamorous.

**Global Positioning System** See **GPS**.

**globe-trotter, globe-trotting** But the proper name of the basketball team is the Harlem Globetrotters.

**GMT** For Greenwich Mean Time. See **time zones**.

**gobbledygook**

**go-between** (n.)

**godchild, goddaughter** Also: godfather, godliness, godmother, godsend, godson, godspeed. Always lowercase.

**gods and goddesses** Capitalize God in references to the deity of all monotheistic religions. Capitalize all noun references to the deity: God the Father, Holy Ghost, Holy Spirit, etc. Lowercase personal pronouns: he, him, thee, thou.

Lowercase gods and goddesses in references to the deities of polytheistic religions.

Lowercase god, gods and goddesses in references to false gods: He made money his god.

See **religious references**.

**go-go**

**goodbye** Not goodby.

**Good Conduct Medal**

**Good Friday** The Friday before Easter.

**good, well** Good is an adjective that means something is as it should be or is better than average.

When used as an adjective, well means suitable, proper, healthy. When used as an adverb, well means in a satisfactory manner or skillfully.

Good should not be used as an adverb. It does not lose its status as an adjective in a sentence such as I feel good. Such a statement is the idiomatic equivalent of I am in good health. An alternative, I feel well, could be interpreted as meaning that your sense of touch was good.

See the **bad, badly** entry and **well**.

**good will** (n.) **goodwill** (adj.)

**Google** A trademark for a Web search engine.

**GOP** See **Grand Old Party**.

## Gospel(s), gospel Capitalize when referring to any or all of the first four books of the New Testament: *the Gospel of St. John, the Gospels.*
Lowercase in other references: *She is a famous gospel singer.*

## gourmand, gourmet A *gourmand* is a person who likes good food and tends to eat to excess; a glutton.
A *gourmet* is a person who likes fine food and is an excellent judge of food and drink.

## government Always lowercase, never abbreviate: *the federal government, the state government, the U.S. government.*

## Government Accountability Office The *Government Accountability Office* is a nonpartisan congressional agency that audits federal programs. (Formerly the General Accounting Office.)
*GAO* is acceptable on second reference.

## governmental bodies Follow these guidelines:
FULL NAME: Capitalize the full proper names of governmental agencies, departments, and offices: *The U.S. Department of State, the Georgia Department of Human Resources, the Boston City Council, the Chicago Fire Department.*
WITHOUT JURISDICTION: Retain capitalization in referring to a specific body if the dateline or context makes the name of the nation, state, county, city, etc. unnecessary: *The Department of State* (in a story from Washington), *the Department of Human Resources* or *the state Department of Human Resources* (in a story from Georgia), *the City Council* (in a story from Boston), *the Fire De-*

*partment* or *the city Fire Department* (in a story from Chicago).
Lowercase further condensations of the name: *the department, the council,* etc.
For additional guidance see **assembly**; **city council**; **committee**; **congress**; **legislature**; **house of representatives**; **senate**; **Supreme Court of the United States**; and **supreme courts of the states**.
FLIP-FLOPPED NAMES: Retain capital names for the name of a governmental body if its formal name is flopped to delete the word *of: the State Department, the Human Resources Department.*
GENERIC EQUIVALENTS: If a generic term has become the equivalent of a proper name in popular use, treat it as a proper name: *Walpole State Prison,* for example, even though the proper name is the *Massachusetts Correctional Institute-Walpole.*
For additional examples, see **legislature**; **police department**; and the **prison, jail** entry.
PLURALS, NONSPECIFIC REFERENCES: All words that are capitalized when part of a proper name should be lowercased when they are used in the plural or do not refer to a specific, existing body. Some examples:
All states except Nebraska have a state senate. The town does not have a fire department. The bill requires city councils to provide matching funds. The president will address the lower houses of the New York and New Jersey legislatures.
FOREIGN BODIES: The same principles apply. See **foreign governmental bodies** and **foreign legislative bodies**.

## government, junta, regime A *government* is an established system of political adminis-

tration: *the U.S. government.*

A *junta* is a group or council that often rules after a coup: *A military junta controls the nation.* A *junta* becomes a government after it establishes a system of political administration.

The word *regime* is a synonym for *political system: a democratic regime, an authoritarian regime.* Do not use *regime* to mean government or junta. For example, use *the Franco government* in referring to the government of Spain under Francisco Franco, not *Franco regime.* But: *The Franco government was an authoritarian regime.*

An *administration* consists of officials who make up the executive branch of a government: *the Reagan administration.*

**governor** Capitalize and abbreviate as *Gov.* or *Govs.* when used as a formal title before one or more names.

See the next entry and **titles**.

**governor general, governors general** The formal title for the British sovereign's representatives in Canada and elsewhere.

Do not abbreviate in any use.

**GPS** Acceptable in all references to *Global Positioning System.* If a descriptive word is used following, use it in lowercase: *The GPS satellite.*

**grade, grader** Hyphenate in combining forms: *a fourth-grade pupil, a 12th-grade student, first-grader, 10th-grader.*

**graduate** (v.) *Graduate* is correctly used in the active voice: *She graduated from the university.*

It is correct, but unnecessary, to use the passive voice: *He was*

graduated from the university. Do not, however, drop *from: John Adams graduated from Harvard.* Not: *John Adams graduated Harvard.*

**graham, graham crackers** The crackers are made from a finely ground whole-wheat flour named for Sylvester Graham, a U.S. dietary reformer.

**grain** The smallest unit in the system of weights that has been used in the United States. It originally was defined as the weight of 1 grain of wheat.

It takes 437.5 grains to make an ounce. There are 7,000 grains to a pound.

See **ounce (weight)** and **pound**.

**gram** The basic unit of weight in the metric system. It is the weight of 1 cubic centimeter of water at 4 degrees Celsius.

A gram is roughly equivalent to the weight of a paper clip, or approximately one-twenty-eighth of an ounce.

To convert to ounces, multiply by .035 (86 grams x .035 equals 3 ounces).

See **metric system**.

**grammar**

**granddad, granddaughter** Also: *grandfather, grandmother, grandson.*

**grand jury** Always lowercase: *a Los Angeles County grand jury, the grand jury.*

This style has been adopted because, unlike the case with city council and similar governmental units, a jurisdiction frequently has more than one grand jury session.

**Grand Old Party** *GOP* is acceptable as a synonym for *Republican Party* without first spelling out *Grand Old Party.*

**grant-in-aid, grants-in-aid**

**gray** Not grey. But: *greyhound.*

**great-** Hyphenate *great-grandfather, great-great-grandmother,* etc.
Use *great grandfather* only if the intended meaning is that the grandfather was a great man.

**Great Atlantic & Pacific Tea Co. Inc.** *A&P* is acceptable in all references.
Headquarters is in Montvale, N.J.

**Great Britain** It consists of England, Scotland and Wales, but not Northern Ireland.
*Britain* is acceptable in all references.
See **United Kingdom.**

**Great Depression** See **Depression.**

**greater** Capitalize when used to define a community and its surrounding region: *Greater Boston.*

**Great Lakes** The five, from the largest to the smallest: Lake Superior, Lake Huron, Lake Michigan, Lake Erie, Lake Ontario.

**Great Plains** Capitalize *Great Plains* or *the Plains* when referring to the U.S. prairie lands that extend from North Dakota to Texas and from the Rocky Mountains east toward the Mississippi River valley. Use *northern* *Plains, southwestern Plains,* etc., when referring to a portion of the region.

**Greek Orthodox Archdiocese of America** See **Eastern Orthodox churches.**

**Greek Orthodox Church** See **Eastern Orthodox churches.**

**Green Berets** See **special forces.**

**Green Revolution** The substantial increase in agricultural yields that resulted from the development of new varieties of grains.

**Greenwich Mean Time (GMT)** See **time zones** and **meridians.**

**gringo** See the **nationalities and races** entry.

**grisly, grizzly** *Grisly* is horrifying, repugnant.
*Grizzly* means grayish or is a short form for *grizzly bear.*

**grits** Ground hominy. The word normally takes plural verbs and pronouns: *Grits are to country ham what Yorkshire pudding is to roast beef.*

**gross domestic product** The sum of all goods and services produced within U.S. borders, it is calculated quarterly by the Commerce Department.
Lowercase in all uses, but *GDP* is acceptable in later references.

**Groundhog Day** Feb. 2.

**groundskeeper**

**groundswell**

**ground zero**

**group** Takes singular verbs and pronouns: *The group is reviewing its position.*

**grown-up** (n. and adj.)

**G-string**

**Guadalupe** (Mexico)

**Guadeloupe** (West Indies)

**Guam** Use in datelines after the name of a community. See **datelines**.

**guarantee** Preferred to *guaranty*, except in proper names.

**guard** Usually a job description, not a formal title. See **titles**.

**guardsman** See **National Guard** and **Coast Guardsman**.

**Guatemala City** Stands alone in datelines.

**gubernatorial**

**guerrilla** Unorthodox soldiers and their tactics.

**guest** Do not use as a verb except in quoted matter. (An exception to a use recorded by Webster's New World.)

**Guild, The** See **Newspaper Guild, The**.

**Guinness World Records** The book is published by Guinness World Records Ltd.

**Gulf Coast** Capitalize when referring to the region of the United States lying along the Gulf of Mexico.
See **coast**.

**Gulf Stream** But the racetrack is *Gulfstream Park.*

**gunbattle, gunboat, gunfight, gunfire, gunpoint, gunpowder**

**gung-ho** A colloquialism to be used sparingly.

**guns** See **weapons**.

**guru**

**Gypsy, Gypsies** Capitalize references to the nomadic Caucasoid people found throughout the world. Also known as *Roma.*
Lowercase when used generically to mean one who is constantly on the move.

**gypsy moth**

**habeas corpus** A writ ordering a person in custody to be brought before a court. It places the burden of proof on those detaining the person to justify the detention.

When *habeas corpus* is used in a story, define it.

**hacker** In common usage, the term has evolved to mean one who uses computer skills to unlawfully penetrate proprietary computer systems.

**Hades** But lowercase *hell.*

**Hague, The** In datelines:
*THE HAGUE, Netherlands (AP)*
—
In text: *The Hague.*

**half** It is not necessary to use the preposition *of: half the time* is correct, but *half of the time* is not wrong.

**half-** Follow Webster's New World College Dictionary. Hyphenate if not listed there.

Some frequently used words without a hyphen:

| | |
|---|---|
| halfback | halftone |
| halfhearted | halftrack |

Also: *halftime*, in keeping with widespread practice in sports copy.

Some frequently used combinations that are two words without a hyphen:

| | |
|---|---|
| half brother | half size |
| half dollar | half sole (n.) |
| half note | half tide |

Some frequently used combinations that include a hyphen:

| | |
|---|---|
| half-baked | half-life |
| half-blood | half-moon |
| half-cocked | half-sole (v.) |
| half-hour | half-truth |

**half-mast, half-staff**
On ships and at naval stations ashore, flags are flown at *half-mast.*

Elsewhere ashore, flags are flown at *half-staff.*

**hallelujah**

**Halley's comet** After Edmund Halley, an English astronomer who predicted the comet's appearance once every 75 years. It was last seen in 1985-86.

**Halloween**

**halo, halos**

**hand-held**

**handicapped** See **disabled, handicapped, impaired**.

**handmade**

**hand-picked**

**hands off, hands-off**
Hyphenate when used as a compound modifier: *He kept his*

*hands off the matter. He follows a hands-off policy.*

**hand to hand, hand-to-hand, hand to mouth, hand-to-mouth** Hyphenate when used as compound modifiers: *The cup was passed from hand to hand. They live a hand-to-mouth existence.*

**hangar, hanger** A *hangar* is a building.
A *hanger* is used for clothes.

**hang, hanged, hung** One *hangs* a picture, a criminal or oneself.
For past tense or the passive, use *hanged* when referring to executions or suicides, *hung* for other actions.

**hangover**

**hanky-panky**

**Hanukkah** The Jewish Festival of Lights, an eight-day commemoration of rededication of the Temple by the Maccabees after their victory over the Syrians.
Usually occurs in December but sometimes falls in late November.

**harass, harassment**

**harelip** Avoid. *Cleft lip* is preferred.

**Harper's Magazine** Not to be confused with Harper's Bazaar.

**Harris Poll** Prepared by Harris Interactive of New York.

**Havana** The city in Cuba stands alone in datelines.

**Hawaii** Do not abbreviate the state name. *Hawaiians* are members of an ethnic group indigenous to the Hawaiian Islands and are also called *Native Hawaiians.* Use *Hawaii resident* or *islander* for anyone living in the state.
The state comprises 132 islands about 2,400 miles southwest of San Francisco. Collectively, they are the *Hawaiian Islands.*
The largest island in land area is Hawaii. Honolulu and Pearl Harbor are on Oahu, where more than 80 percent of the state's residents live.
*Honolulu* stands alone in datelines. Use *Hawaii* after all other cities in datelines, specifying the island in the text, if needed.
See **datelines** and **state names**.

**Hawaiian Airlines** Headquarters is in Honolulu.

**Hawaii Standard Time** The time zone used in Hawaii. There is no daylight-saving time in Hawaii.

**H-bomb** Use *hydrogen bomb* unless a direct quotation is involved.

**headlines** Only the first word and proper nouns are capitalized.
Follow story style in spelling, but use numerals for all numbers and single quotes for quotation marks.
**Online:** For online subscribers so desiring, AP systems convert headlines to a version with all words capitalized.

**headlong**

**head-on** (adj., adv.)

**headquarters** May take a singular or a plural verb. Do not use *headquarter* as a verb.

**health care** Two words, no hyphen, in all uses. (An exception to Webster's first listing.)

**hearing examiner** See **administrative law judge**.

**hearsay**

**heaven**

**heavenly bodies** Capitalize the proper names of planets, stars, constellations, etc.: *Mars, Arcturus, the Big Dipper, Aries.* See **earth**.

For comets, capitalize only the proper noun element of the name: *Halley's comet.*

Lowercase sun and moon, but capitalize them if their Greek or Latin names are used: *Helios, Luna.*

Capitalize nouns and adjectives derived from the proper names of planets: *Martian, Venusian,* but lowercase adjectives derived from other heavenly bodies: *solar, lunar.*

**hect-** (before a vowel), **hecto-** (before a consonant) A prefix denoting 100 units of a measure. Move a decimal point two places to the right, adding zeros if necessary, to convert to the basic unit: 5.5 hectometers = 550 meters.

**hectare** A unit of surface measure in the metric system equal to 100 ares or 10,000 square meters.

A hectare is equal to 2.47 acres, 107,639.1 square feet or 11,959.9 square yards.

To convert to acres, multi-ply by 2.47 (5 hectares x 2.47 = 12.35 acres).

See **are** and **metric system**.

**he, him, his, thee, thou** Personal pronouns referring to the deity are lowercase. See **deity**.

**heights** See **dimensions**.

**heliport**

**hell** But capitalize *Hades.*

**helter-skelter**

**hemisphere** Capitalize *Northern Hemisphere, Western Hemisphere,* etc. Lowercase *hemisphere* in other uses: *the Eastern and Western hemispheres, the hemisphere.*

**hemorrhage**

**hemorrhoid**

**her** Do not use this pronoun in reference to nations or ships, except in quoted matter. Use *it* instead.

**here** The word is frequently redundant, particularly in the lead of a datelined story. Use only if there is some specific need to stress that the event being reported took place in the community.

If the location must be stressed in the body of the story, repeat the name of the datelined community, both for the reader's convenience and to avoid problems if the story is topped with a different dateline.

**Her Majesty** Capitalize when it appears in quotations or is appropriate before a name as the long form of a formal title.

For other purposes, use the

woman's name or *the queen.*
See **nobility.**

**heroin** The narcotic, originally a trademark.

**hertz** This term, the same in singular or plural, has been adopted as the international unit of frequency equal to one cycle per second.

In contexts where it would not be understood by most readers, it should be followed by a parenthetical explanation: *15,400 hertz (cycles per second).*

Do not abbreviate.

**hideaway**

**hi-fi**

**high-tech**

**highway designations**
Use these forms, as appropriate in the context, for highways identified by number: *U.S. Highway 1, U.S. Route 1, U.S. 1, state Route 34, Route 34, Interstate Highway 495, Interstate 495.* On second reference only for *Interstate: I-495.*

When a letter is appended to a number, capitalize it but do not use a hyphen: *Route 1A.*

See **addresses.**

**highway patrol** Capitalize if used in the formal name of a police agency: *the Kansas Highway Patrol, the Highway Patrol.* Lowercase *highway patrolman* in all uses.

See **state police.**

**hike** People take *hikes* through the woods, but they *increase* prices.

**hillbilly** Usually a derogatory term for an Appalachian back-

woods or mountain person. Avoid unless in direct quotes or special context. *Mountaineer* is a suggested alternative.

**Hindu, Hinduism** The dominant religion of India. It has about 811 million followers worldwide, making it the world's third largest religion after Christianity and Islam. There are more than 1 million followers in the United States.

The basic teaching is that the soul never dies, but is reborn each time the body dies. The soul may be reborn in either human or animal form. The following rule is that of karma and states that no matter how small the action or thought of an individual, it will affect how the soul will be reborn in the next generation. The cycle of death and rebirth continues until a soul reaches spiritual perfection. At that point the soul is united in total enlightenment and peace with the supreme being and the cycle is ended.

There are a number of gods and goddesses, all of whom are different focuses of the one supreme being. The primary gods are Brahma, Vishnu, called the preserver, and Siva, the destroyer. Vishnu has had important human incarnations as Krishna and Rama. The primary goddess is Devi, who is also known as Durga, Kali, Sarasvati, Lakshimi and other names. She represents in her forms either motherhood and good fortune or destruction. There are thousands of other deities and saints which also may receive prayers and offerings.

Hindus also believe that animals have souls and many are worshiped as gods. There are thousands of sects and organization runs from virtually none to very strict depending on the group. There is no formal clergy.

**hip-hop**

**Hiroshima** On Aug. 6, 1945, this Japanese city and military base were the targets of the first atomic bomb dropped as a weapon. The explosion had the force of 20,000 tons (20 kilotons) of TNT. It destroyed more than four square miles and killed or injured 140,000 people, according to an official count taken between August and December 1945. Hiroshima city officials say the toll may be 220,000 if including those who died after December 1945 of non-acute injuries or radiation.

**his, her** Do not presume maleness in constructing a sentence, but use the pronoun *his* when an indefinite antecedent may be male or female: *A reporter attempts to protect his sources.* (Not *his or her* sources, but note the use of the word *reporter* rather than *newsman.*)

Frequently, however, the best choice is a slight revision of the sentence: *Reporters attempt to protect their sources.*

**His Majesty** Capitalize when it appears in quotations or is appropriate before a name as the long form of a formal title.

For other purposes, use the man's name or *king.*

See **nobility**.

**Hispanic** The preferred term for those whose ethnic origin is in a Spanish-speaking country. *Latino* is acceptable for *Hispanics* who prefer that term. (The feminine form is *Latina.*) Use a more specific identification when possible, such as *Cuban, Puerto Rican* or *Mexican-American* or the name of an indigenous group in a Latin

American country. Avoid *Chicano* as a synonym for *Mexican-American.* Refer to people of Brazilian and Portuguese origin as such, not as *Hispanic.*

**Hispaniola** The island shared by the Dominican Republic and Haiti.
See **Western Hemisphere**.

**historical periods and events** Capitalize the names of widely recognized epochs in anthropology, archaeology, geology and history: *the Bronze Age, the Dark Ages, the Middle Ages, the Pliocene Epoch.*

Capitalize also widely recognized popular names for the periods and events: *the Atomic Age, the Boston Tea Party, the Civil War, the Exodus* (of the Israelites from Egypt), *the Great Depression, Prohibition.*

Lowercase *century: the 18th century.*

Capitalize only the proper nouns or adjectives in general descriptions of a period: *ancient Greece, classical Rome, the Victorian era, the fall of Rome.*

For additional guidance, see separate entries in this book for many epochs, events and historical periods. If this book has no entry, follow the capitalization in Webster's New World College Dictionary, using lowercase if the dictionary lists it as an acceptable form for the sense in which the word is used.

**historic, historical** A *historic* event is an important occurrence, one that stands out in history.

Any occurrence in the past is a *historical* event.

**history** Avoid the redundant *past history.*

**hit and run** (v.) **hit-and-run** (n. and adj.) *The coach told him to hit and run. He scored on a hit-and-run. She was struck by a hit-and-run driver.*

**hitchhike, hitchhiker**

**HIV** See **AIDS** entry.

**hocus-pocus**

**hodgepodge**

**Hodgkin's disease** After Dr. Thomas Hodgkin, the English physician who first described the disease of the lymph nodes.

*Non-Hodgkin's* lymphoma is the more common type and spreads rapidly, especially among older people and those with HIV infections.

**ho-hum**

**hold up** (v.) **holdup** (n. and adj.)

**holidays and holy days** Capitalize them: *New Year's Eve, New Year's Day, Groundhog Day, Easter, Hanukkah,* etc.

The legal holidays in federal law are New Year's, Martin Luther King Jr. Day, Washington's Birthday, Memorial Day, Independence Day, Labor Day, Columbus Day, Veterans Day, Thanksgiving and Christmas. See individual entries for the official dates and when they are observed if they fall on a weekend.

The designation of a day as a federal legal holiday means that federal employees receive the day off or are paid overtime if they must work. Other requirements that may apply to holidays generally are left to the states. Many follow the federal lead in desig-

nating a holiday, but they are not required to do so.

**Holy Communion** See **sacraments**.

**Holy Father** The preferred form is to use *the pope* or *the pontiff,* or to give the individual's name.

Use *Holy Father* in direct quotations or special contexts where a particular literary effect is desired.

**holy orders** See **sacraments**.

**Holy See** The headquarters of the Roman Catholic Church in Vatican City.

**Holy Spirit** Now preferred over *Holy Ghost* in most usage.

**Holy Week** The week before Easter.

**homebuyer, homeowner**

**homemade**

**home page** (two words) The "front" page of a particular Web site.

**home schooling, home-schooled, home-schooler**

**hometown** Use a comma to set off an individual's hometown when it is placed in apposition to a name, whether *of* is used or not: *Tim Johnson, of Vermillion, S.D.; Mary Richards, Minneapolis.*

**homicide, murder, manslaughter** *Homicide* is a legal term for slaying or killing.

*Murder* is malicious, premeditated homicide. Some states define certain homicides as murder if the killing occurs in the course of armed robbery, rape, etc. *Manslaughter* is homicide without malice or premeditation.

A person should not be described as a *murderer* until convicted of the charge.

Unless authorities say premeditation was obvious, do not say that a victim *was murdered* until someone has been convicted in court. Instead, say that a victim *was killed* or *slain.*

See **execute** and the **assassin, killer, murderer** entry.

**Hong Kong** Stands alone in datelines.

**Honolulu** The city in Hawaii stands alone in datelines. It is on the island of Oahu.
See **Hawaii**.

**honorary degrees** All references to honorary degrees should specify that the degree was honorary.

Do not use *Dr.* before the name of an individual whose only doctorate is honorary.

**honorary titles** See **nobility**.

**hoof-and-mouth disease** Use *foot-and-mouth disease.*

**hooky** Not *hookey.*

**hopefully** It means in a hopeful manner. Do not use it to mean it is hoped, let us or we hope.

Right: *It is hoped that we will complete our work in June.*

Right: *We hope that we will complete our work in June.*

Wrong as a way to express the thought in the previous two sentences: *Hopefully, we will com-*
*plete our work in June.*

**horsepower**

**horse races** Capitalize their formal names: *Kentucky Derby, Preakness, Belmont Stakes,* etc.

**horses' names** Capitalize. See **animals**.

**hotel** Capitalize as part of the proper name for a specific hotel: *the Waldorf-Astoria Hotel.*

Lowercase when standing alone or used in an indefinite reference to one hotel in a chain: *The city has a Sheraton hotel.*

**hot line** A direct telephone line for use in an emergency or crisis, especially between government leaders. (Two words, lowercase.)

**Hotshot** Capitalize when referring to the elite firefighting crews or their members.

**hot spot** Two words, for descriptions of the area where computers can connect wirelessly, or for global trouble spots, or areas of intense heat in general.

**household, housing unit** In the sense used by the Census Bureau, a *household* is made up of all occupants of a *housing unit.* A *household* may contain more than one family or may be used by one person.

A *housing unit*, as defined by the bureau, is a group of rooms or single room occupied by people who do not live and eat with any other person in the structure. It must have either direct access from the outside or through a common hall, or have a kitchen or cooking equipment for the exclusive use of the occupants.

**House of Commons, House of Lords** The two houses of the British Parliament. On second reference: *Commons* or *the Commons, Lords* or *the Lords.*

**house of delegates** See the next entry.

**House of Representatives** Capitalize when referring to a specific governmental body: *the U.S. House of Representatives, the Massachusetts House of Representatives.*

Capitalize shortened references that delete the words *of Representatives: the U.S. House, the Massachusetts House.*

Retain capitalization if *U.S.* or the name of a state is dropped but the reference is to a specific body.

*BOSTON (AP) — The House has adjourned for the year.*

Lowercase plural uses: *the Massachusetts and Rhode Island houses.*

Apply the same principle to similar legislative bodies such as *the Virginia House of Delegates.*

See the **organizations and institutions** entry for guidelines on how to handle the term when it is used by a nongovernmental body.

**Houston** The city in Texas stands alone in datelines.

**howitzer** See **weapons**.

**HTML** For *hypertext markup language.* (Lowercase in Web addresses.)

**HTTP** For *hypertext transfer protocol.* (Lowercase in Web addresses.)

**human, human being** *Human* is preferred, but either is acceptable.

**Humane Society of the United States** An animal protection agency headquartered in Washington. It operates 10 regional offices across the country, but has no formal affiliation with the many local organizations that use the name *Humane Society.*

**hurly-burly**

**hurricane** Capitalize hurricane when it is part of the name that weather forecasters assign to a storm: *Hurricane Hazel.*

But use *it* and *its* — not *she, her* or *hers* or *he, him* or *his* — in pronoun references.

And do not use the presence of a woman's name as an excuse to attribute sexist images of women's behavior to a storm. Avoid, for example, such sentences as: *The fickle Hazel teased the Louisiana coast.*

See **weather terms**.

**hush-hush**

**Hyannis Port, Mass.**

**hydro-** The rules in **prefixes** apply, but in general, no hyphen. Some examples:

hydroelectric       hydrophobia

**hyper-** The rules in **prefixes** apply, but in general, no hyphen. Some examples:

hyperactive       hypercritical

**hyperlink** A link from one part of an Internet page to another page, as a restaurant home page with a link to its menu.

**hypertext** A system of linking electronic documents.

**hyphen** See entry in **Punctuation** chapter.

# I

## Iberia Airlines of Spain
An *Iberia airliner* is acceptable in any reference.
Headquarters is in Madrid.

**IBM** Acceptable as first reference for *International Business Machines*.
Headquarters is in Armonk, N.Y.

**ICBM, ICBMs** Acceptable on first reference for *intercontinental ballistic missile(s)*, but the term should be defined in the body of a story.
Avoid the redundant *ICBM missiles*.

**ice age** Lowercase, because it denotes not a single period but any of a series of cold periods marked by glaciation alternating with periods of relative warmth.
Capitalize the proper nouns in the names of individual ice ages, such as the *Wisconsin ice age*.
The most recent series of ice ages happened during the *Pleistocene* epoch, which began about 1.6 million years ago. During that time, glaciers sometimes covered much of North America and northwestern Europe.
The present epoch, the *Holocene* or *Recent*, began about 10,000 years ago, when the continental glaciers had retreated to Antarctica and Greenland.

**Icelandair** Headquarters is in Reykjavik, Iceland.

**ice storm** See **weather terms**.

**Idaho** Do not abbreviate. See **state names**.

**i.e.** Abbreviation for the Latin *id est* or *that is* and is always followed by a comma.

**illegal** Use *illegal* only to mean a violation of the law. Be especially careful in labor-management disputes, where one side often calls an action by the other side illegal. Usually it is a charge that a contract or rule, not a law, has been violated.

**illegal immigrant** Used to describe those who have entered the country illegally, it is the preferred term, rather than *illegal alien* or *undocumented worker*.
Do not use the shortened term *illegals*.

**Illinois** Abbrev.: *Ill.* See **state names**.

**illusion** See the **allusion, illusion** entry.

**imam** Lowercase when describing the leader of a prayer in a Muslim mosque. Capitalize before a name when used as the

formal title for a Muslim leader or ruler.
See **religious titles**.

**immigrate** See the **emigrate, immigrate** entry.

**impassable, impassible, impassive** *Impassable* means that passage is impossible: *The bridge was impassable.*
*Impassible* and *impassive* describe lack of sensitivity to pain or suffering. Webster's New World notes, however, that *impassible* suggests an inability to be affected, while *impassive* implies only that no reaction was noticeable: *She was impassive throughout the ordeal.*

**impeachment** The constitutional process accusing an elected official of a crime in an attempt to remove the official from office. Do not use as a synonym for convicted or removed from office.

**impel, impelled, impelling**

**imperial gallon** The standard British gallon, equal to 277.42 cubic inches or about 1.2 U.S. gallons.
The metric equivalent is approximately 4.5 liters.
See **liter**.

**imperial quart** One-fourth of an imperial gallon.

**implausible**

**imply, infer** Writers or speakers *imply* in the words they use.
A listener or reader *infers* something from the words.

**impostor** Not *imposter*.

**impromptu** It means without preparation or advance thought.

**in, into** *In* indicates location: *He was in the room.*
*Into* indicates motion: *She walked into the room.*

**-in** Precede with a hyphen:

| | |
|---|---|
| break-in | walk-in |
| cave-in | write-in |

**in-** No hyphen when it means *not*:

| | |
|---|---|
| inaccurate | insufferable |

Often solid in other cases:

| | |
|---|---|
| inbound | infighting |
| indoor | inpatient (n., adj.) |
| infield | |

A few combinations take a hyphen, however:

| | |
|---|---|
| in-depth | in-house |
| in-group | in-law |

Follow Webster's New World when in doubt.

**"in"** When employed to indicate that something is in vogue, use quotation marks only if followed by a noun: *It was the "in" thing to do. Raccoon coats are in again.*

**inasmuch as**

**Inauguration Day** Capitalize only when referring to the total collection of events that include inauguration of a U.S. president; lowercase in other uses: *Inauguration Day is Jan. 20. The inauguration day for the change has not been set.*

**inbox**

**Inc.** See **incorporated**.

**inch** Equal to one-twelfth of a foot.
The metric equivalent is exactly 2.54 centimeters.
To convert to centimeters,

multiply by 2.54 (6 inches x 2.54 equals 15.24 centimeters).
See **centimeter**; **foot**; and **dimensions**.

**inches per second** A rating used for the speed of tape recorders.

The abbreviation *ips* (no periods) is acceptable on first reference in specialized contexts such as a records column; otherwise do not use *ips* until second reference.

**include** Use *include* to introduce a series when the items that follow are only part of the total: *The price includes breakfast. The zoo includes lions and tigers.*

Use *comprise* when the full list of individual elements is given: *The zoo comprises 100 types of animals, including lions and tigers.*

See the **compose, comprise, constitute** entry.

**incorporated** See entry in **Business Guidelines**.

**incorporator** Do not capitalize when used before a name.
See **titles**.

**incredible, incredulous** *Incredible* means unbelievable.
*Incredulous* means skeptical.

**incur, incurred, incurring**

**Independence Day** *July Fourth* or *Fourth of July* also are acceptable.

The federal legal holiday is observed on Friday if July 4 falls on a Saturday, on Monday if it falls on a Sunday.

**index, indexes**

**Index of Leading Economic Indicators** A composite of 10 economic measurements that was developed to help forecast likely shifts in the U.S. economy as a whole.

It is compiled by the Conference Board, a private business-sponsored research group.

**Indiana** Abbrev.: *Ind.* See **state names**.

**Indianapolis** The city in Indiana stands alone in datelines.

**Indian Ocean** See **oceans**.

**Indians** *American Indian* is the preferred term for those in the United States. Where possible, be precise and use the name of the tribe: *He is a Navajo commissioner. Native American* is acceptable in quotations and names of organizations.

In news stories about American Indians, such words as *wampum, warpath, powwow, tepee, brave, squaw*, etc., can be disparaging and offensive. Be careful and certain of their usage.

**indict** Use *indict* only in connection with the legal process of bringing charges against an individual or corporation.

To avoid any suggestion that someone is being judged before a trial, do not use phrases such as *indicted for killing* or *indicted for bribery.* Instead, use *indicted on a charge of killing* or *indicted on a bribery charge.*

For guidelines on related words, see the entries under **accuse**; **allege**; and **arrest**.

**indiscreet, indiscrete** *Indiscreet* means lacking prudence. Its noun form is *indiscretion.*

*Indiscrete* means not separated into distinct parts. Its noun form is *indiscreteness.*

**indiscriminate, indiscriminately**

**indispensable**

**indo-** Usually hyphenated and capitalized:

Indo-Aryan     Indo-Hittite
Indo-German   Indo-Iranian

But: *Indochina.*

**Indochina** Formerly French Indochina, now divided into Cambodia, Laos and Vietnam.

**Indochinese peninsula** Located here are the nations of Cambodia, Laos, Myanmar, Thailand and Vietnam.

**Indonesia** Use after the name of a community in datelines on stories from this nation.

Specify an individual island, if needed, in the text.

**indoor** (adj.) **indoors** (adv.) *He plays indoor tennis. He went indoors.*

**infant** Applicable to children through 12 months old.

**infantile paralysis** The preferred term is *polio.*

**inflation** A sustained increase in prices. The result is a decrease in the purchasing power of money.

There are two basic types of inflation:

—*Cost-push inflation* occurs when rising costs are the chief reason for the increased prices.

—*Demand-pull inflation* occurs when the amount of money available exceeds the amount of goods and services available for sale.

**infra-** The rules in **prefixes** apply, but in general, no hyphen.

Some examples:

infrared        infrastructure

**initials** Use periods and no space when an individual uses initials instead of a first name: *H.L. Mencken.*

This format has been adopted to assure that in typesetting the initials are set on the same line.

Do not give a name with a single initial (*J. Jones*) unless it is the individual's preference or a first name cannot be learned.

See **middle initials**.

**injuries** They are *suffered*, not *sustained* or *received*.

**in-law**

**Inner Light** See **Quakers**.

**innocent, not guilty** In court cases, plea situations and trials, *not guilty* is preferable to *innocent*, because it is more precise legally. (However, special care must be taken to prevent omission of the word *not*.) When possible, say a defendant was *acquitted* of criminal charges.

**innocuous**

**innuendo**

**inoculate**

**input** Do not use as a verb in describing the introduction of data into a computer.

**inquire, inquiry** Not *enquire, enquiry*.

**insignia** Same form for singular and plural.

**insofar as**

**in spite of** *Despite* means

the same thing and is shorter.

**intefadeh** An Arabic term for the Palestinian uprising against Israel.

**intelligence quotient** *IQ* is acceptable in all references.

**inter-** The rules in **prefixes** apply, but in general, no hyphen. Some examples:

inter-American interstate
interracial

**intercontinental ballistic missile** See **ICBM, ICBMs**.

**Internal Revenue Service** *IRS* is acceptable on second reference.

Capitalize also *Internal Revenue*, but lowercase *the revenue service*.

**International Association of Machinists and Aerospace Workers** The shortened form *Machinists* union is acceptable in all references.

Headquarters is in Washington.

**International Bank for Reconstruction and Development** *World Bank* is acceptable in all references.

Headquarters is in Washington.

**International Brotherhood of Electrical Workers** Use the full name on first reference to avoid confusion with the United Electrical, Radio and Machine Workers of America.

*IBEW* is acceptable on second reference.

Headquarters is in Washington.

**International Court of Justice** The principal judicial organ of the United Nations, established at The Hague in 1945.

The court is not open to individuals. It has jurisdiction over all matters specifically provided for either in the U.N. charter or in treaties and conventions in force. It also has jurisdiction over cases referred to it by U.N. members and by nonmembers such as Switzerland that subscribe to the court statute.

The court serves as the successor to the Permanent Court of International Justice of the League of Nations, which also was known as the World Court.

On second reference use *international court* or *world court* in lowercase. Do not abbreviate.

**International Criminal Police Organization** *Interpol* is acceptable in all references.

Headquarters is in Lyon, France.

**international date line** The imaginary line drawn north and south through the Pacific Ocean, largely along the 180th meridian.

By international agreement, when it is 12:01 a.m. Sunday just west of the line, it is 12:01 a.m. Saturday just east of it.

See **time zones**.

**International Labor Organization** *ILO* is acceptable on second reference.

Headquarters is in Geneva.

**International Longshore and Warehouse Union** *ILWU* is acceptable on second reference.

Headquarters is in San Francisco.

## International Longshoremen's Association ILA is acceptable on second reference.

Headquarters is in New York.

## International Monetary Fund IMF is acceptable on second reference.

Headquarters is in Washington.

## International Telecommunications Satellite Organization ITSO is acceptable on first reference, but the body of the story should identify it as the shortened form of the full name.

(The original name was International Telecommunications Satellite Consortium.)

Headquarters is in Washington.

**Internet** A decentralized, worldwide network of computers that can communicate with each other. In later references, *the Net* is acceptable.

Be acutely aware of the potential dangers of using information from *Internet* and e-mail sources. Be sure of the authenticity and correctness before using the information. All such electronic information -- from computer disk data to e-mail to material posted on the *Internet* -- falls into the "tangible form" category that is subject to copyright protection as well as libel guidelines.

Use care, too, in copying online jargon and abbreviated forms, unless they are generally understood.

*Internet* addresses include e-mail addresses and Web site designations. Follow the spelling and capitalization of the Web site owner. If an *Internet* address falls at the end of a sentence, use a period. (If an address breaks between lines, split it directly after a slash or a dot that is part of the address, without an inserted hyphen.) Use the *http://* protocol at the start of a Web address, as well as other starts, such as *ftp://*.

When a story mentions a specific Web site or Web service, include the Internet address, the URL, within the text. This is essential information for the reader.

Add *Internet* addresses (URLs) to the end of a story when they provide additional information, but aren't specifically referred to in a story.

An example:

*PASADENA, Calif. (AP) -- NASA abandoned any real hope Tuesday for the missing-in-action Mars Polar Lander and promised to investigate every aspect of the failed mission and delay future expeditions to the Red Planet if necessary.*

*The last, best chance to make radio contact with the spacecraft yielded only silence early Tuesday. A somber Richard Cook, the spacecraft's operations manager at NASA's Jet Propulsion Laboratory, said the flight team had "played its last ace." ...*

---

*On the Net: NASA Mars site: http://marslander.jpl.nasa.gov*

*UCLA site on experiments aboard the mission: http://mars. ucla.edu*

Avoid URLs that are particularly lengthy and complicated, unless essential to guide the reader to a particular document.

Some symbols in Internet addresses, such as the "at" sign, the equal sign, the underscore, and the tilde, result in garbles in some newspaper computers. Spell them out instead and provide an explanatory note. (See **Nontransmitting Symbols** in the **Filing Practices** section.)

See separate listings for some commonly used Internet, computer and telecommunications terms.

**Interpol** Acceptable in all references for *International Criminal Police Organization.*

**infra-** The rules in **prefixes** apply, but in general, no hyphen. Some examples:
infrared     infrastructure

**intranet** A private network inside a company or organization, only for internal use. Lowercase.

**IOU, IOUs**

**Iowa** Do not abbreviate. See **state names.**

**IP address** *Internet Protocol* address, a numeric address given to a computer connected to the Internet.

**ips** See **inches per second.**

**IQ** Acceptable in all references for **intelligence quotient.**

**Iran** The nation formerly called Persia. It is not an Arab country.
The people are *Iranians,* not *Persians* or *Irani.*
The official language is *Persian,* also known as *Farsi.*

**Iraq** The Arab nation coinciding roughly with ancient Mesopotamia.
Its people are *Iraqis.* The dialect of Arabic is *Iraqi.*

**Ireland** Acceptable in most references to the independent nation known formally as the Irish Republic.
Use *Irish Republic* when a dis-

tinction must be made between this nation and *Northern Ireland,* a part of the United Kingdom.

**Irish coffee** Brewed coffee containing Irish whiskey, topped with cream or whipped cream.

**Irish Republican Army** An outlawed paramilitary group committed to overthrowing Northern Ireland and its links with Britain. Its formal name is Provisional IRA. It was founded in 1969 with the aim of abolishing Northern Ireland as a predominantly British Protestant state. Its members claim direct lineage to the old IRA, which wrested the predominantly Catholic rest of Ireland from British control following a 1919-21 rebellion.
*IRA* is acceptable, but *Irish Republican Army* should be spelled out somewhere in the story.
*Sinn Fein* (pronounced "shin fane") is a legal political party that is linked with the *IRA,* but not technically a wing of it.

**Iron Curtain**

**irregardless** A double negative. *Regardless* is correct.

**Islam** Followers are called Muslims. Their holy book is the Quran, which according to Islamic belief was revealed by Allah (God) to the Prophet Muhammad in the seventh century in Mecca and Medina. The place of worship is a mosque. The weekly holy day, the equivalent of the Christian sabbath, is Friday.
It is the religion of more than 1 billion people in the world, making it the world's second largest faith, after Christianity. Although Arabic is the language of the Quran and Muslim prayers,

not all Arabs are Muslims and not all Muslims are Arabs. Most of the world's Muslims live in a wide belt that stretches halfway around the world: across West Africa and North Africa, through the Arab countries of the Middle East and on to Turkey, Iran, Afghanistan, Pakistan and other Asian countries, parts of the former Soviet Union and western China, to Indonesia and the southern Philippines.

There are two major divisions in Islam:

—*Sunni* The biggest single sect in Islam, comprising about 85 percent of all Muslims. Nations with Sunni majorities include Egypt, Saudi Arabia and most other Arab nations, as well as non-Arab Turkey and Afghanistan. Most Palestinian Muslims and most West African Muslims are Sunnis.

The Saudis sometimes are referred to as Wahhabi Muslims. This is a subgroup within the Sunni branch of Islam.

—*Shiite* The second-largest sect, after the Sunni. Iran is the only nation with an overwhelming Shiite majority. Iraq, Lebanon and Bahrain have large Shiite communities, in proportion to their overall populations.

(The schism between Sunni and Shiite stems from the very early days of Islam and arguments over Muhammad's successors as caliph, the spiritual and temporal leader of Muslims. The Shiites wanted the caliphate to descend through Ali, Muhammad's son-in-law. Ali eventually became the fourth caliph, but he was murdered; Ali's son al-Hussein was massacred with his fighters at Karbala, in what is now Iraq. Shiites considered the later caliphs to be usurpers. The Sunnis no longer have a caliph.)

Titles for the clergy vary from sect to sect and from country to country, but these are the most common:

*Grand Mufti* — The highest authority in Quranic law and interpretation, a title used mostly by Sunnis.

*Sheik* — Used by most clergymen in the same manner that *the Rev.* is used as a Christian clerical title, especially common among Sunnis. (Not all sheiks are clergymen. *Sheik* can also be a secular title of respect or nobility.)

*Ayatollah* — Used by Shiites, especially in Iran, to denote senior clergymen, such as *Ayatollah Ruhollah Khomeini.*

*Hojatoleslam* — A rank below ayatollah.

*Mullah* — Lower level clergy.

*Imam* — Used by some sects as a title for the prayer leader at a mosque. Among the Shiites, it usually has a more exalted connotation.

The adjective is *Islamic.*

See **Muslims** and **Nation of Islam**.

**Islamic holy days** See separate entries for **Eid al-Adha**, **Eid al-Fitr** and **Ramadan**.

**island** Capitalize *island* or *islands* as part of a proper name: *Prince Edward Island, the Hawaiian Islands.*

Lowercase *island* and *islands* when they stand alone or when the reference is to the islands in a given area: *the Pacific islands.*

Lowercase all *island of* constructions: *the island of Nantucket.*

U.S. DATELINES: For communities on islands within the boundaries of the United States, use the community name and the

state name:
*EDGARTOWN, Mass. (AP)* —
*Honolulu* stands alone, however.
DATELINES ABROAD: If an island has an identity of its own (*Bermuda, Prince Edward Island, Puerto Rico, Sardinia, Taiwan,* etc.) use the community name and the island name:
*HAMILTON, Bermuda (AP)* —
*Havana, Hong Kong, Macau* and *Singapore* stand alone, however.
If the island is part of a chain, use the community name and the name of the chain:
*MANILA, Philippines (AP)* —
Identify the name of the island in the text if relevant: *Manila is on the island of Luzon.*
For additional guidelines, see **datelines**.

**it** Use this pronoun, rather than *she*, in references to nations and ships.

**IT** Acronym for *information technology*; spell it out.

**italic** Type face cannot be sent through AP computers. (It is used in this book only to indicate style examples and in using a word as a word.)
See **words as words**.

**it's, its** *It's* is a contraction for *it is* or *it has*: *It's up to you. It's been a long time.*
*Its* is the possessive form of the neuter pronoun: *The company lost its assets.*

**IUD** Acceptable on second reference for *intrauterine device.*

**Ivy League** Brown University, Columbia University, Cornell University, Dartmouth College, Harvard University, Princeton University, the University of Pennsylvania and Yale University.

**Jacuzzi** Trademark for a brand of whirlpool products. Generic terms are whirlpool bath or whirlpool spa.

**jail** Not interchangeable with *prison.* See the **prison, jail** entry.

**Jamaica rum** Not *Jamaican rum.*

**Jane's All the World's Aircraft, Jane's Fighting Ships** The reference sources for questions about aircraft and military ships not covered in this book.

The reference for nonmilitary ships is Lloyd's Register of Shipping.

**January** See **months.**

**Japan Airlines** *JAL* is acceptable on second reference. Headquarters is in Tokyo.

**Japan Current** A warm current flowing from the Philippine Sea east of Taiwan and northeast past Japan.

**jargon** The special vocabulary and idioms of a particular class or occupational group.

In general, avoid jargon. When it is appropriate in a special context, include an explanation of any words likely to be unfamiliar to most readers.

See **dialect** and **word selection**.

**Java** A trademark of Sun Microsystems Inc. for a computer programming language that can be run across the Internet.

**JavaScript** A scripting language, developed by Netscape, designed to run inside Web pages.

**Jaws of Life** Trademark name for the tool used to pry open parts of a vehicle to free those trapped inside.

**Jaycees** Members of the U.S. Junior Chamber of Commerce, affiliated with the worldwide body, Junior Chamber International.

See the **fraternal organizations and service clubs** and **Junior Chamber of Commerce** entries.

**J.C. Penney Co.** Headquarters is in Plano, Texas.

**jeep, Jeep** Lowercase the military vehicle.

Capitalize if referring to the rugged, four-wheel-drive civilian vehicle so trademarked.

**Jehovah's Witnesses** The denomination was founded in Pittsburgh in 1872 by Charles Taze Russell, a former Congregationalist layman.

Witnesses do most of their work through three legal corporations: the Watch Tower Bible and Tract Society of Pennsylvania, the Watchtower Bible and Tract Society of New York Inc., and, in England, the International Bible Students Association. A governing body consisting largely of the principal officers of the corporations oversees the denomination.

Worldwide membership is listed at more than 6 million and U.S. membership at 988,000.

Jehovah's Witnesses believe that they adhere to the oldest religion on Earth, the worship of Almighty God revealed in the Bible as Jehovah.

They regard civil authority as necessary and obey it "as long as its laws do not contradict God's law." Witnesses refuse to bear arms, salute the flag or participate in secular government.

They refuse blood transfusions as being against the Bible, citing the section of Leviticus that reads: "Whatsoever man ... eats any manner of blood, I will cut him off from among his people."

There are no formal titles, but there are three levels of ministry: *publishers* (baptized members who do evangelistic work), *regular pioneers*, who devote greater time to activities, and *special pioneers* (full-time workers).

**Jell-O** A trademark for a brand of gelatin dessert.

**Jerusalem** Stands alone in datelines.

**Jesus** The central figure of Christianity, he also may be called *Jesus Christ* or *Christ.*

Personal pronouns referring to him are lowercase.

**JetBlue Airways** Based in New York.

**jet, jetliner, jet plane** See **aircraft terms**.

**Jet Ski** A registered trademark of Kawasaki for a type of personal watercraft.

**Jew** Use for men and women. Do not use *Jewess.*

**Jewish congregations** A Jewish congregation is autonomous. No synods, assemblies or hierarchies control the activities of an individual synagogue.

In the United States, there are three major expressions of Judaism:

1. Orthodox Judaism. Most of its congregations are represented nationally by the Union of Orthodox Jewish Congregations of America. Most of its rabbis are members of the Rabbinical Council of America.

2. Reform Judaism. Its national representatives are the Union for Reform Judaism and the Central Conference of American Rabbis.

3. Conservative Judaism. Its national representatives are the United Synagogue of Conservative Judaism and the Rabbinical Assembly.

Conservative and Reform are the largest branches of Judaism, well exceeding the Orthodox and the very small Reconstructionist branches.

Jews generally believe that a divine kingdom will be established on Earth, opening a messianic era that will be marked by peace and bliss. They also believe that they have a mandate from God to work toward this kingdom.

The only formal titles in use are *rabbi*, for the spiritual leader of a congregation, and *cantor*, for the individual who leads the congregation in song. Capitalize these titles before an individual's full name on first reference. On second reference, use only the last name.

See **religious titles** and **Zionism**.

**Jewish holy days** See separate listings for **Hanukkah**, **Passover**, **Purim**, **Rosh Hashana**, **Shavuot**, **Sukkot** and **Yom Kippur**.

The High Holy Days are Rosh Hashana and Yom Kippur. All Jewish holy days and the Jewish Sabbath start at sunset before the day marked on most calendars.

**jibe** See the **gibe, jibe** entry.

**jihad** Arabic noun used to refer to the Islamic concept of the struggle to do good. In particular situations, that can include *holy war*, the meaning extremist Muslims commonly use.

**job descriptions** Always lowercase. See **titles**.

**John F. Kennedy Space Center** Located in Cape Canaveral, Fla., it is the National Aeronautics and Space Administration's principal launch site for manned spacecraft.

*Kennedy Space Center* is acceptable in all references.

For datelines on launch stories:

CAPE CANAVERAL, Fla. (AP) —

See **Lyndon B. Johnson Space Center**.

**Johns Hopkins University** No apostrophes.

**Joint Chiefs of Staff** Also: *the Joint Chiefs*. But lowercase *the chiefs* or *the chiefs of staff*.

**JPEG, JPG** Acronyms for *Joint Photographic Experts Group*, one of two common types of image compression mechanisms used on the World Wide Web (along with *GIF*).

**Jr.** See the **junior, senior** entry.

**judge** Capitalize before a name when it is the formal title for an individual who presides in a court of law. Do not continue to use the title in second reference.

Do not use *court* as part of the title unless confusion would result without it:

—No *court* in the title: *U.S. District Judge James Robertson, District Judge James Robertson, federal Judge James Robertson, Judge James Robertson, U.S. Circuit Judge Homer Thornberry, appellate Judge John Blair.*

—*Court* needed in the title: *Juvenile Court Judge John Jones, Criminal Court Judge John Jones, Superior Court Judge Robert Harrison, state Supreme Court Judge William Cushing.*

When the formal title *chief judge* is relevant, put the court name after the judge's name: *Chief Judge John Sirica of the U.S. District Court in Washington, D.C.; Chief Judge Clement F. Haynsworth Jr. of the 4th U.S. Circuit Court of Appeals.*

Do not pile up long court names before the name of a judge. Make it *Judge John Smith of Allegheny County Common Pleas Court.* Not: *Allegheny County Common Pleas Court Judge John Smith.*

Lowercase *judge* as an occupational designation in phrases such as *beauty contest judge Bert Parks.*

See **administrative law judge**; **court names**; **judicial branch**; **justice**; and **magistrate**.

**judge advocate** The plural:

*judge advocates.* Also: *judge advocate general, judge advocates general.*
Capitalize as a formal title before a name.
See **titles**.

**judgment** Not *judgement.*

**judicial branch** Always lowercase.
The federal court system that exists today as the outgrowth of Article 3 of the Constitution is composed of the Supreme Court of the United States, the U.S. Court of Appeals, U.S. District Courts, and the U.S. Customs Court. There are also four district judges for U.S. territories.
U.S. bankruptcy and magistrate judges are fixed-term judges serving in U.S. District Courts. Magistrate judges are generalist judges who preside in cases referred from U.S. district judges. Bankruptcy judges are specialized judges whose authority is restricted to bankruptcy issues.
The U.S. Tax Court and the U.S. Court of Military Appeals are not part of the judicial branch as such.
For more detail on all federal courts, see separate entries under the names listed here.

**Judicial Conference of the United States** This policy-making body for the courts of the judicial branch meets twice a year. Its 27 members are the chief justice of the United States, the chief judges of the 12 regional circuit courts of appeals, the chief judge of the Federal Circuit Court of Appeals, a district judge from each of the regional circuits, and the chief judge of the Court of International Trade.
Day-to-day functions are handled by the Administrative Office of U.S. Courts.

**jukebox**

**July** See **months**.

**jumbo jet** Any very large jet plane, including the Airbus A380, Boeing 747, the DC-10, the L-1011 and the C-5A.

**June** See **months**.

**Junior Chamber of Commerce** A volunteer organization of young men and women involved in civic service and leadership training.
Members are called *Jaycees.*
U.S. headquarters is in Tulsa, Okla.; international headquarters in Coral Gables, Fla.
See **Jaycees**.

**junior, senior** Abbreviate as *Jr.* and *Sr.* only with full names of persons or animals. Do not precede by a comma: *Joseph P. Kennedy Jr.*
The notation *II* or *2nd* may be used if it is the individual's preference. Note, however, that *II* and *2nd* are not necessarily the equivalent of *junior* — they often are used by a grandson or nephew.
If necessary to distinguish between father and son in second reference, use the *elder Smith* or the *younger Smith.*
See **names**.

**junta** See the **government, junta, regime** entry.

**jury** The word takes singular verbs and pronouns: *The jury has been sequestered until it reaches a verdict.*
Do not use awkward phrases such as *seven-man, five-woman jury.* Make it: *a jury of seven men*

*and five women.*

Do not capitalize: *a U.S. District Court jury, a federal jury, a Massachusetts Superior Court jury, a Los Angeles County grand jury.*

See **grand jury**.

**justice** Capitalize before a name when it is the formal title. It is the formal title for members of the U.S. Supreme Court and for jurists on some state courts. In such cases, do not use *judge* in first or subsequent references.

See **judge**; **Supreme Court of the United States**; and **titles**.

**justice of the peace** Capitalize as a formal title before a name. Do not abbreviate.

See **titles**.

**juvenile delinquent** Juveniles may be declared delinquents in many states for anti-social behavior or for breaking the law. In some states, laws prohibit publishing or broadcasting the names of juvenile delinquents.

Follow the local practice unless there is a compelling reason to the contrary. Consult with the National Desk if you believe such an exception is warranted.

**K** Use *K* in references to modem transmission speeds, in keeping with standard usage: *a 56K modem* (no space after numeral).

The abbreviation should not be used to mean 1,000 or $1,000.

**Kansas** Abbrev.: *Kan.* See **state names**.

**Kansas City** Use *KANSAS CITY, Kan.*, or *KANSAS CITY, Mo.*, in datelines to avoid confusion between the two.

**karat** See the **carat, caret, karat** entry.

**Katmandu** Preferred spelling for the capital of Nepal.

**Kelvin scale** A scale of temperature based on, but different from, the Celsius scale. It is used primarily in science to record very high and very low temperatures. The Kelvin scale starts at zero and indicates the total absence of heat (absolute zero).

Zero on the Kelvin scale is equal to minus 273.16 degrees Celsius and minus 459.67 degrees Fahrenheit.

The freezing point of water is 273.16 kelvins. The boiling point of water is 373.16 kelvins. (Note temperatures on the Kelvin scale are called *kelvins*, not *degrees*. The symbol, a capital K, stands alone with no degree symbol.)

To convert from Celsius to Kelvin, add 273.16 to the Celsius temperature.

See **Celsius** and **Fahrenheit**.

**Kennedy Space Center** See **John F. Kennedy Space Center**.

**Kentucky** Abbrev.: *Ky.* Legally a commonwealth, not a state. See **state** and **state names**.

**kerosene** Formerly a trademark, now a generic term.

**ketchup** Not *catchup* or *catsup*.

**keynote address** Also: *keynote speech*.

**Keystone Kops**

**KGB** Acceptable on first reference, but the story should contain a phrase identifying it as the former Russian secret police and intelligence agency.

The initials stand for the Russian words meaning *Committee for State Security*.

**kibbutz** An Israeli collective settlement.

The plural is *kibbutzim*.

**kidnap, kidnapped, kidnapping, kidnapper**

**killer** See the **assassin, killer, murderer** entry.

**kilo-** A prefix denoting 1,000 units of a measure. Move a decimal point three places to the right, adding zeros if necessary, to convert to the basic unit: 10.5 kilograms equals 10,500 grams.

**kilobyte** A unit of measurement for digital data storage. In the metric system, a *kilobyte* is 1,000 bytes; in computer binary terms, it is 1,024 bytes. Thus, 64KB means 64 times 1,024 bytes, or 65,536 bytes (not 64,000). Abbrev.: *KB*. (Similarly, *MB* for megabytes, *GB* for gigabytes.) Note no space when used with numerals: *a 400KB file.*
   Use *Kb* in abbreviations for kilobits and *Kbps* for kilobits per second.

**kilocycles** The new term is *kilohertz.*

**kilogram** The metric term for 1,000 grams.
   A kilogram is equal to approximately 2.2 pounds or 35 ounces.
   To convert to pounds, multiply by 2.2 (9 kilograms x 2.2 equals 19.8 pounds).
   See **gram**; **metric system**; and **pound**.

**kilohertz** Equals 1,000 hertz (1,000 cycles per second), replacing *kilocycles* as the correct term in applications such as broadcast frequencies. Abbrev.: *kHz.*

**kilometer** The metric term for 1,000 meters. (Abbrev.: *km.*)
   A kilometer is equal to approximately 3,281 feet, or five-eighths (0.62) of a mile.
   To convert to miles, multiply by 0.62 (5 kilometers x 0.62 equals 3.1 miles).

See **meter**; **metric system**; and **miles**.

**kiloton, kilotonnage** A unit used to measure the power of nuclear explosions. One kiloton has the explosive force of 1,000 tons of TNT.
   The atomic bomb dropped Aug. 6, 1945, on Hiroshima, Japan, in the first use of the bomb as a weapon had an explosive force of 20 kilotons.
   A *megaton* has the force of a million tons of TNT. A *gigaton* has the force of a billion tons of TNT.

**kilowatt-hour** The amount of electrical energy consumed when 1,000 watts are used for one hour.
   The abbreviation *kwh* is acceptable on second reference.

**kindergarten**

**king** Capitalize only when used before the name of royalty: *King George VI.* Continue in subsequent references that use the king's given name: *King George,* not *George.*
   Lowercase *king* when it stands alone.
   Capitalize in plural uses before names: *Kings George and Edward.*
   Lowercase in phrases such as *chess king Bobby Fischer.*
   See **nobility** and **titles**.

**Kitty Litter** A brand of absorbent material used in cat litter boxes. Use a generic term such as *cat box filler.*

**Klan in America** See **Ku Klux Klan**.

**Kleenex** A trademark for a brand of facial tissue.

**KLM Royal Dutch Airlines**
A *KLM airliner* is acceptable in
any reference.
Headquarters is in Amsterdam, Netherlands.

**Kmart** No hyphen, no space,
lowercase *m.*
See **Sears Holdings Corp.**

**Knesset** The Israeli parliament. See **foreign legislative
bodies.**

**knickknack**

**knight** See **nobility.**

**Knights of Columbus** *K. of
C.* or *the Knights* may be used on
second reference.
See the **fraternal organizations and service clubs** entry.

**K-9**

**knot** A knot is 1 nautical mile
(6,076.10 feet) per hour. It is redundant to say *knots per hour.*
To convert knots into approximate statute miles per hour, multiply knots by 1.15.
Always use figures: *Winds
were at 7 to 9 knots; a 10-knot
wind.*
See **nautical mile.**

**know-how**

**Kodak** A trademark for cameras and other photographic
products made by Eastman
Kodak Co. of Rochester, N.Y.

**Koran** See **Quran.**

**Korean names** North Korean names are generally three
separate words, each starting
with a capital letter: *Kim Il Sung.*
South Korean names are three
words with the second two names

hyphenated and a lowercase letter after the hyphen: *Kim Young-
sam.*
In all cases, the family name
comes first.
For South Korean place
names, use the revised Roman-
ized spellings introduced by the
government in 2000: *Incheon* (formerly Inchon), *Busan* (formerly
Pusan).

**Korean War** But lowercase
*Korean conflict.*

**kosher** Always lowercase.

**kowtow**

**Kriss Kringle** Not *Kris.*

**kudos** It means credit or
praise for an achievement.
The word is singular and takes
singular verbs.

**Ku Klux Klan** There are a
number of separate organizations
known as the *Klan in America.*
Some of them do not use the
full name *Ku Klux Klan,* but each
may be called that, and the *KKK*
initials may be used for any of
them on second reference.
The two largest Klan organizations are the National Knights of
the Ku Klux Klan, based at Stone
Mountain, Ga., and the United
Klans of America, based at Tusca-
loosa, Ala.
An Imperial Board, composed
of leaders from the various
groups, meets occasionally to coordinate activities.

**Kuomintang** The Chinese
Nationalist political party. Do not
follow with the word *party. Tang*
means party.

**Kuril Islands** Use in datelines after a community name in

stories from these islands. Name an individual island, if needed, in the text.

Explain in the text that a small portion of the archipelago is claimed by Japan but most are part of Russia.

**Kuwait City** This capital city of Kuwait stands alone in datelines.

**Kwanzaa** A seven-day celebration, based on African festivals, from Dec. 26 through Jan. 1. The name comes from the Swahili for "first fruits."

**la** See **foreign names** entry.

**Labor Day** The first Monday in September.

**Laborers' International Union of North America** The shortened form *Laborers' union* is acceptable in all references.
Headquarters is in Washington.

**Labrador** The mainland portion of the Canadian province of Newfoundland and Labrador.
Use *Newfoundland* in datelines after the name of a community. Specify in the text that it is in Labrador.

**Ladies' Home Journal**

**lady** Do not use as a synonym for *woman*. *Lady* may be used when it is a courtesy title or when a specific reference to fine manners is appropriate without patronizing overtones.
See **nobility**.

**lager** (beer)

**lake** Capitalize as part of a proper name: *Lake Erie, Canandaigua Lake, the Finger Lakes.*
Lowercase in plural uses: *lakes Erie and Ontario; Canandaigua and Seneca lakes.*

**lamebrain**

**lame duck** (n.) **lame-duck** (adj.)

**LAN** Acronym for *local area network*, which links computers within a geographically limited area.

**Land Rover** No hyphen. A trademark for a brand of all-terrain vehicle.

**languages** Capitalize the proper names of languages and dialects: *Aramaic, Cajun, English, Gullah, Persian, Serbo-Croatian, Yiddish.*

**lanolin** Formerly a trademark, now a generic term.

**larceny** See the **burglary, larceny, robbery, theft** entry.

**last** Avoid the use of last as a synonym for latest if it might imply finality. *The last time it rained, I forgot my umbrella,* is acceptable. But: *The last announcement was made at noon* may leave the reader wondering whether the announcement was the final announcement, or whether others are to follow.
The word *last* is not necessary to convey the notion of most recent when the name of a month or day is used:
Preferred: *It happened Wednesday. It happened in April.* Correct,

but redundant: *It happened last Wednesday.*

But: *It happened last week. It happened last month.*

**Lastex** A trademark for a type of elastic yarn.

## Last Supper

**Las Vegas** The city in Nevada stands alone in datelines. Do not confuse with Las Vegas, N.M.

**late** Do not use it to describe someone's actions while alive.

Wrong: *Only the late senator opposed this bill.* (The senator was not dead at that time.)

**latex** A resin-based substance used in making elastic materials and paints.

**Latin America** See **Western Hemisphere**.

**Latin Rite** See **Roman Catholic Church**.

## latitude and longitude

*Latitude*, the distance north or south of the equator, is designated by parallels. *Longitude*, the distance east or west of Greenwich, England, is designated by meridians.

Use these forms to express degrees of latitude and longitude: *New York City lies at 40 degrees 45 minutes north latitude and 74 degrees 0 minutes west longitude*; *New York City lies south of the 41st parallel north and along the 74th meridian west.*

**Latter Day Saints, Latter-day Saints** See **Church of Jesus Christ of Latter-day Saints**.

**laws** Capitalize legislative acts but not bills: *the Taft-Hartley Act, the Kennedy bill.*

**lawsuit** *Civil lawsuit* is redundant.

**lawyer** A generic term for all members of the bar.

An *attorney* is someone legally appointed or empowered to act for another, usually, but not always, a lawyer. An *attorney at law* is a lawyer.

A *barrister* is an English lawyer who is specially trained and appears exclusively as a trial lawyer in higher courts. He is retained by a solicitor, not directly by the client. There is no equivalent term in the United States.

*Counselor*, when used in a legal sense, means a person who conducts a case in court, usually, but not always, a lawyer. A *counselor at law* is a lawyer. *Counsel* frequently is used collectively for a group of counselors.

A *solicitor* in England is a lawyer who performs legal services for the public. A solicitor appears in lower courts but does not have the right to appear in higher courts, which are reserved to barristers.

A *solicitor* in the United States is a lawyer employed by a governmental body. *Solicitor* is generally a job description, but in some agencies it is a formal title.

*Solicitor general* is the formal title for a chief law officer (where there is no attorney general) or for the chief assistant to the law officer (when there is an attorney general). Capitalize when used before a name.

Do not use *lawyer* as a formal title.

See the **attorney, lawyer** entry and **titles**.

**lay, lie** The action word is

*lay.* It takes a direct object. *Laid* is the form for its past tense and its past participle. Its present participle is *laying.*

*Lie* indicates a state of reclining along a horizontal plane. It does not take a direct object. Its past tense is *lay.* Its past participle is *lain.* Its present participle is *lying.*

When *lie* means to make an untrue statement, the verb forms are *lie, lied, lying.*

Some examples:

PRESENT OR FUTURE TENSES:

Right: *I will lay the book on the table. The prosecutor tried to lay the blame on him.*

Wrong: *He lays on the beach all day. I will lay down.*

Right: *He lies on the beach all day. I will lie down.*

IN THE PAST TENSE:

Right: *I laid the book on the table. The prosecutor has laid the blame on him.*

Right: *He lay on the beach all day. He has lain on the beach all day. I lay down. I have lain down.*

WITH THE PRESENT PARTICIPLE:

Right: *I am laying the book on the table. The prosecutor is laying the blame on him.*

Right: *He is lying on the beach. I am lying down.*

## Leaning Tower of Pisa

**leatherneck** Lowercase this nickname for a member of the U.S. Marine Corps. It is derived from the leather lining that was formerly part of the collar on the Marine uniform.

**lectern, podium, pulpit, rostrum** A speaker stands *behind a lectern, on a podium or rostrum, or in the pulpit.*

**lecturer** A formal title in the Christian Science Church. An occupational description in other uses.

**lectures** Capitalize and use quotation marks for their formal titles, as described in **composition titles**.

**left hand** (n.) **left-handed** (adj.) **left-hander** (n.)

**leftist, ultra-leftist** In general, avoid these terms in favor of a more precise description of an individual's political philosophy.

As popularly used today, particularly abroad, *leftist* often applies to someone who is merely liberal or believes in a form of democratic socialism.

*Ultra-leftist* suggests an individual who subscribes to a communist view or one holding that liberal or socialist change cannot come within the present form of government.

See **radical** and the **rightist, ultra-rightist** entry.

**left wing** (n.) But: *left-wing* (adj.), *left-winger* (n.).

**legal holiday** See the **holidays and holy days** entry.

**legerdemain**

**legion, legionnaire** See **American Legion** and **French Foreign legion**.

**Legionnaires' disease** The disease takes its name from an outbreak at the Pennsylvania American Legion convention held at the Bellevue-Stratford Hotel in Philadelphia in July 1976. Thirty-four people died — 29 Legionnaires or family members and five other people who had been near the hotel. The disease was diagnosed for the first time after 221 people contracted the illness in Philadelphia.

The bacterium believed to be responsible is found in soil and grows in water, such as air-conditioning ducts, storage tanks and rivers.

## legislative titles

FIRST REFERENCE FORM: Use *Rep., Reps., Sen.* and *Sens.* as formal titles before one or more names. Spell out and lowercase *representative* and *senator* in other uses.

Spell out other legislative titles in all uses. Capitalize formal titles such as *assemblyman, assemblywoman, city councilor, delegate,* etc., when they are used before a name. Lowercase in other uses.

Add *U.S.* or state before a title only if necessary to avoid confusion: *U.S. Sen. Nancy Kassebaum spoke with state Sen. Hugh Carter.*

FIRST REFERENCE PRACTICE: The use of a title such as *Rep.* or *Sen.* in first reference is normal in most stories. It is not mandatory, however, provided an individual's title is given later in the story.

Deletion of the title on first reference is frequently appropriate, for example, when an individual has become well known: *Barry Goldwater endorsed President Ford today. The Arizona senator said he believes the president deserves another term.*

SECOND REFERENCE: Do not use legislative titles before a name on second reference unless they are part of a direct quotation.

CONGRESSMAN, CONGRESSWOMAN: *Rep.* and *U.S. Rep.* are the preferred first-reference forms when a formal title is used before the name of a U.S. House member. The words *congressman* or *congresswoman,* in lowercase, may be used in subsequent references that do not use an individual's name, just as senator is used in references to members of the Senate.

*Congressman* and *congresswoman* should appear as capitalized formal titles before a name only in direct quotation.

ORGANIZATIONAL TITLES: Capitalize titles for formal, organizational offices within a legislative body when they are used before a name: *Speaker Thomas P. O'Neill, Majority Leader Robert C. Byrd, Minority Leader John J. Rhodes, Democratic Whip James C. Wright, Chairman John J. Sparkman of the Senate Foreign Relations Committee, President Pro Tem John C. Stennis.*

See **party affiliation** and **titles**.

**legislature** Capitalize when preceded by the name of a state: *the Kansas Legislature.*

Retain capitalization when the state name is dropped but the reference is specifically to that state's legislature:

*TOPEKA, Kan. (AP) — Both houses of the Legislature adjourned today.*

Capitalize *legislature* in subsequent specific references and in such constructions as: *the 100th Legislature, the state Legislature.*

Although the word *legislature* is not part of the formal, proper name for the lawmaking bodies in many states, it commonly is used that way and should be treated as such in any story that does not use the formal name.

If a given context or local practice calls for the use of a formal name such as *Missouri General Assembly*, retain the capital letters if the name of the state can be dropped, but lowercase the word *assembly* if it stands alone. Lowercase *legislature* if a story uses it in a subsequent reference to a body identified as a general assembly.

Lowercase *legislature* when used generically: *No legislature has approved the amendment.*

Use *legislature* in lowercase for all plural references: *The Arkansas and Colorado legislatures are considering the amendment.*

In 49 states the separate bodies are a senate and a *house* or *assembly*. The *Nebraska Legislature* is a unicameral body.

See **assembly**; **general assembly**; **governmental bodies**; **house of representatives**; and **senate**.

**Lent** The period from Ash Wednesday through Holy Saturday, the day before Easter. The 40-day Lenten period for penance, suggested by Christ's 40 days in the desert, does not include the six Sundays between Ash Wednesday and Easter.

See **Easter** for the method of computing when Easter occurs.

**lesbian** See **gay**.

**-less** No hyphen before this suffix:

| | |
|---|---|
| childless | waterless |
| tailless | |

**less** See the **fewer, less** entry.

**let up** (v.) **letup** (n. and adj.)

**Levi's** A trademark for a brand of jeans.

**liaison**

**liberal, liberalism** See the **political parties and philosophies** entry.

**lie** See the **lay, lie** entry.

**lie in state** Only people who are entitled to a state funeral may formally lie in state. In the United States, this occurs in the rotunda in the Capitol.

Those entitled to a state funeral are a president, a former president, a president-elect or any other person designated by the president.

Members of Congress may lie in state, and a number have done so. The decision is either house's to make, although the formal process normally begins with a request from the president.

Those entitled to an official funeral, but not to lie in state, are the vice president, the chief justice, Cabinet members and other government officials when designated by the president.

**lieutenant** See **military titles**.

**lieutenant governor** Capitalize and abbreviate as *Lt. Gov.* or *Lt. Govs.* when used as a formal title before one or more names in regular text. Capitalize and spell out when used as a formal title before one or more names in direct quotations.

Lowercase and spell out in all other uses.

See **titles**.

**Life Saver, Life Savers** Trademarks for a brand of roll candy.

**life-size**

**lifestyle**

**lifetime**

**lift off** (v.) **liftoff** (n. and adj.)

**light, lighted, lighting** *Lit* is acceptable as the past tense form.

**lightning** The electrical discharge.

**light-year** The distance that light travels in one year at the rate of 186,282 miles per second. It works out to about 5.88 trillion miles (5,878,612,800,000 miles).

**likable** Not *likeable*.

**-like** Do not precede this suffix by a hyphen unless the letter l would be tripled or the main element is a proper noun:

| | |
|---|---|
| bill-like | Norwalk-like |
| businesslike | shell-like |

**like-** Follow with a hyphen when used as a prefix meaning similar to:

| | |
|---|---|
| like-minded | like-natured |

No hyphen in words that have meanings of their own:

| | |
|---|---|
| likelihood | likewise |
| likeness | |

**like, as** Use *like* as a preposition to compare nouns and pronouns. It requires an object: *Jim blocks like a pro.*

The conjunction *as* is the correct word to introduce clauses: *Jim blocks the linebacker as he should.*

**limousine**

**linage, lineage** *Linage* is the number of lines.

*Lineage* is ancestry or descent.

**Lincoln's Birthday** Capitalize *birthday* in references to the holiday.

Lincoln was born Feb. 12. His birthday is not a federal legal holiday.

**line numbers** Use figures and lowercase the word line in naming individual lines of a text: *line 1, line 9.* But: *the first line, the 10th line.*

**Line of Control**

**linoleum** Formerly a trademark, now a generic term.

**Linotype** A trademark for a brand of typesetting machine that casts an entire line of type in one bar or slug.

**lion's share** The term comes from an Aesop fable in which the lion took all the spoils of a joint hunt.

Use it to mean the whole of something, or the best and biggest portion.

Do not use it to mean majority.

**liquefy**

**liter** The basic unit of volume in the metric system. It is defined as the volume occupied by 1 kilogram of distilled water at 4 degrees Celsius. It works out to a total of 1,000 cubic centimeters (1 cubic decimeter).

It takes 1,000 milliliters to make a liter.

A liter is equal to approximately 34 fluid ounces or 1.06 liquid quarts. A liter equals .91 of a dry quart. The metric system makes no distinction between dry volume and liquid volume.

To convert to liquid quarts,

multiply by 1.06 (4 liters x 1.06 equals 4.24 liquid quarts).
To convert to dry quarts, multiply by .91 (4 liters x .91 equals 3.64 dry quarts).
To convert to liquid gallons, multiply by .26 (8 liters x .26 equals 2.08 gallons).
See **gallon**; **kilogram**; **metric system**; **quart (dry)**; and **quart (liquid)**.

**literally** See the **figuratively, literally** entry.

**literature** See **composition titles**.

**Little League, Little League Baseball** The official name of the worldwide youth baseball and softball organization and its affiliated local leagues.

**livable** Not *liveable.*

**livid** It is not a synonym for *fiery, bright, crimson, red* or *flaming.* If a person turns *livid* with rage, his face becomes ashen or pale. It can mean *blue, bluish gray, gray, dull white, dull purple* or *grayish black.*

**Lloyds Bank International Ltd.** A prominent bank with headquarters in London.

**Lloyd's of London** A self-regulating market of insurance. Founded in Britain in 1680, it relies on individual investors worldwide, known as Names, along with several hundred companies, to provide the money for underwriting insurance.

**Lloyd's Register of Shipping** The reference source for questions about nonmilitary ships not covered in this book.
It is published by Lloyd's Register of Shipping Trust Corp. Ltd. in London.

**local** Avoid the irrelevant use of the word.
Irrelevant: *The injured were taken to a local hospital.*
Better: *The injured were taken to a hospital.*

**local of a union** Always use a figure and capitalize *local* when giving the name of a union subdivision: *Local 222 of The Newspaper Guild.*
Lowercase *local* standing alone in plural uses: *The local will vote Tuesday. He spoke to locals 2, 4 and 10.*

**Lockheed Martin Corp.** (No hyphen.) Headquarters is in Bethesda, Md.

**lodges** See the **fraternal organizations and service clubs** entry.

**login, logon, logoff** (n.) But use as two words in verb form: *I log in to my computer.*

**London** The city in England stands alone in datelines.

**long distance, long-distance** Always a hyphen in reference to telephone calls: *We keep in touch by long-distance. He called long-distance. She took the long-distance call.*
In other uses, hyphenate only when used as a compound modifier: *She traveled a long distance. She made a long-distance trip.*

**longitude** See the **latitude and longitude** entry.

**longshoreman** Capitalize *longshoreman* only if the intended meaning is that the individual is a member of the International Longshore and Warehouse Union or the International Longshoremen's Association.

**long term, long-term** Hyphenate when used as a compound modifier: *We will win in the long term. He has a long-term assignment.*

**long time, longtime** *They have known each other a long time. They are longtime partners.*

**long ton** Also known as a *British ton.* Equal to 2,240 pounds. See **ton**.

**Lord's Supper** See **sacraments**.

**Los Angeles** The city in California stands alone in datelines. Confine *L.A.* to quoted matter.

**LOT Polish Airlines** Headquarters is in Warsaw, Poland.

**Louisiana** Abbrev.: *La.* See **state names**.

**Low Countries** Belgium, Luxembourg and Netherlands.

**lowercase** One word (n., v., adj.) when referring to the absence of capital letters. Originally from printers' practice.

**LSD** Acceptable in all references for *lysergic acid diethylamide.*

**Lt. Gov.** See **lieutenant governor**.

**Lucite** A trademark for an acrylic plastic.

**Lufthansa German Airlines** A *Lufthansa airliner* is ac-

ceptable in any reference. Headquarters is in Cologne, Germany.

**Lutheran churches** The basic unit of government in Lutheran practice is the congregation. It normally is administered by a council, headed either by the senior pastor or a lay person elected from the membership of the council. The council customarily consists of a congregation's clergy and elected lay people.

The three major Lutheran bodies in the United States merged on Jan. 1, 1988, into a new organization, the Evangelical Lutheran Church in America, with about 5.3 million members in more than 11,000 congregations.

The Lutheran Church in America was the largest and most geographically spread of the three and was formed in 1962 from a merger of four bodies with Danish, Finnish, German and Swedish backgrounds. It merged with the American Lutheran Church, a mostly Midwestern group formed in 1960 through a merger of four bodies with Danish, German and Norwegian backgrounds, and the relatively small west-central Association of Evangelical Lutheran Churches.

The Lutheran Church—Missouri Synod, founded in 1847, has 2.6 million members and is a separate and distinct body.

Lutheran teachings go back to Martin Luther, a 16th-century Roman Catholic priest whose objections to elements of Roman Catholic practice began the movement known as the Protestant Reformation.

Members of the clergy are known as *ministers. Pastor* applies if a minister leads a congregation.

On first reference, use *the Rev.* before the name of a man or woman. On second reference, use only the last name.

See **religious titles**.

**Luxembourg** Stands alone in datelines.

**-ly** Do not use a hyphen between adverbs ending in *-ly* and adjectives they modify: *an easily remembered rule, a badly damaged island, a fully informed woman.*

See the compound modifiers section of the **hyphen** entry.

**Lycra** Unless referring to the trademark fiber or fabric, use a generic term such as spandex or elastic or stretch fabric.

**Lyndon B. Johnson Space Center** Formerly the Manned Spacecraft Center. Located in Houston, it is the National Aeronautics and Space Administration's principal control and training center for manned spaceflight.

*Johnson Space Center* is acceptable in all references.

In datelines:

*HOUSTON (AP) —*

See **John F. Kennedy Space Center**.

# M

**Macau** Stands alone in datelines. (Spelling is an exception to Webster's New World.)

**Mace** A trademark, shortened from *Chemical Mace*, for a brand of tear gas that is packaged in an aerosol canister and temporarily stuns its victims.

**machine gun** (n.) But: *machine-gun* (v. and adj.), *machine-gunner*.
See **weapons**.

**Mach number** Named for Ernst Mach, an Austrian physicist, the figure represents the ratio of the speed of an object to the speed of sound in the surrounding medium, such as air, through which the object is moving.
A rule of thumb for speed of sound is approximately 750 miles per hour at sea level and approximately 660 miles per hour at 30,000 feet above sea level.
A body traveling at *Mach 1* would be traveling at the speed of sound. *Mach 2* would equal twice the speed of sound.

**Mafia** Lowercase as a synonym for organized crime. (A cap *M* can be used when referring to the secret society of criminals.)

**magazine names** Capitalize the initial letters of the name but do not place it in quotes. Lowercase *magazine* unless it is part of the publication's formal title: *Harper's Magazine, Newsweek magazine, Time magazine.*
Check the masthead if in doubt.

**magistrate** Capitalize when used as a formal title before a name. Use *magistrate judge* when referring to the fixed-term judge who presides in U.S. District Court and handles cases referred by U.S. district judges. See **titles**.

**Magna Carta** Not Magna Charta. The charter the English barons forced King John of England to grant at Runnymede in June 1215. It guaranteed certain civil and political liberties.

**Mailgram** A trademark for a telegram sent to a post office near the recipient's address and delivered to the address by a letter carrier.

**mailman** *Letter carrier* or *postal worker* is preferable because many women hold this job.

**Maine** Do not abbreviate. See **state names**.

**mainland China** See **China**.

**major** See **military titles**.

**majority leader** Capitalize when used as a formal title before a name: *Majority Leader Bill Frist.* Lowercase elsewhere.
See **legislative titles** and **titles**.

**majority, plurality** *Majority* means more than half of an amount.
*Plurality* means more than the next highest number.
COMPUTING MAJORITY: To describe how large a majority is, take the figure that is more than half and subtract everything else from it: If 100,000 votes were cast in an election and one candidate received 60,000 while opponents received 40,000, the winner would have a *majority* of 20,000 votes.
COMPUTING PLURALITY: To describe how large a plurality is, take the highest number and subtract from it the next highest number: If, in the election example above, the second-place finisher had 25,000 votes, the winner's *plurality* would be 35,000 votes.
Suppose, however, that no candidate in this example had a majority. If the first-place finisher had 40,000 votes and the second-place finisher had 30,000, for example, the leader's *plurality* would be 10,000 votes.
USAGE: When *majority* and *plurality* are used alone, they take singular verbs and pronouns: *The majority has made its decision.*
If a plural word follows an *of* construction, the decision on whether to use a singular or plural verb depends on the sense of the sentence: *A majority of two votes is not adequate to control the committee. The majority of the houses on the block were destroyed.*

**make up** (v.) **makeup** (n., adj.)

**malarkey** Not *malarky.*

**Maldives** Use this official name with a community name in a dateline. The body of the story should note that the nation frequently is called the *Maldive Islands.*

**Mallorca** Use instead of Spain in datelines on stories from communities on this island.

**manageable**

**manager** Capitalize when used as a formal title before a name: *General Manager Dick O'Connell.*
Do not capitalize in job descriptions such as *equipment manager John Smith.*
See **titles**.

**managing editor** Capitalize when used as a formal title before a name.
See **titles**.

**Manitoba** A province of central Canada. Do not abbreviate.
See **datelines**.

**man, mankind** Either may be used when both men and women are involved and no other term is convenient. In these cases, do not use duplicate phrases such as *a man or a woman* or *mankind and womankind.*
Frequently the best choice is a substitute such as *humanity, a person* or *an individual.*
See **women**.

**manslaughter** See the **homicide, murder, manslaughter** entry.

**mantel, mantle** A *mantel* is a shelf. A *mantle* is a cloak.

**Maoism (Maoist)** The communist philosophy and policies of Mao Zedong. See the **political parties and philosophies** entry.

**March** See **months**.

**Mardi Gras** Literally *fat Tuesday*, the term describes a day of merrymaking on the Tuesday before Ash Wednesday.

In New Orleans and many Roman Catholic countries, the Tuesday celebration is preceded by a week or more of parades and parties.

**marijuana** Not *marihuana*.

**Marines** Capitalize when referring to U.S. forces: *the U.S. Marines, the Marines, the Marine Corps, Marine regulations*. Do not use the abbreviation *USMC*.

Capitalize *Marine* when referring to an individual in a Marine Corps unit: *He is a Marine*.

Do not describe *Marines* as soldiers, which is generally associated with the Army. Use *troops* if a generic term is needed.

**Maritime Provinces** The Canadian provinces of Nova Scotia, New Brunswick and Prince Edward Island.

**marketbasket, marketplace**

**marquess, marchioness, marquis, marquise** See **nobility**.

**Marshall Islands** Named for John Marshall, a British explorer. In datelines, give the name of a city and *Marshall Islands*. List the name of an individual island in the text.

**marshal, marshaled, marshaling, Marshall** *Marshal* is the spelling for both the verb and the noun: *Marilyn will marshal her forces. Erwin Rommel was a field marshal.*

*Marshall* is used in proper names: *George C. Marshall, John Marshall, the Marshall Islands*.

**Martin Luther King Jr. Day** Federal holiday honoring Martin Luther King Jr., who was born Jan. 15, 1929, is on the third Monday in January. It was first celebrated in 1986.

**Marxism (Marxist)** The system of thought developed by Karl Marx and Friedrich Engels. See the **political parties and philosophies** entry.

**Maryland** Abbrev.: *Md.* See **state names**.

**Mason-Dixon Line** The boundary line between Pennsylvania and Maryland, generally regarded as separating the North from the South. (Named for 18th-century surveyors Charles Mason and Jeremiah Dixon, the line later was extended to West Virginia.)

**Mass** It is *celebrated*, not *said*. Always capitalize when referring to the ceremony, but lowercase any preceding adjectives: *high Mass, low Mass, requiem Mass*.

In Eastern Orthodox churches the correct term is *Divine Liturgy*. See **Roman Catholic Church**.

**Massachusetts** Abbrev.: *Mass.* Legally a commonwealth, not a state.
See **state** and **state names**.

**Master of Arts, Master of Science** A *master's degree* or a *master's* is acceptable in any reference.
See **academic degrees**.

**matrimony** See **sacraments**.

**maturity** In a financial sense, the date on which a bond, debenture or note must be repaid.
See **loan terminology** in Business Guidelines.

**May** See **months**.

**May Day, mayday** *May Day* is May 1, often observed as a festive or political holiday.
*Mayday* is the international distress signal, from the French *m'aider*, meaning "help me."

**mayors' conference** See **U.S. Conference of Mayors**.

**MC** For *master of ceremonies*, but only in quoted matter. See **emcee**.

**M.D.** A word such as *physician* or *surgeon* is preferred. (The periods in the abbreviation are an exception to Webster's.)
See **doctor** and **academic titles**.

**meager**

**mean** See the **average, mean, median, norm** entry.

**mecca** Lowercase in the metaphorical sense; capitalize the city in Saudi Arabia.

**Medal of Freedom** It is now the *Presidential Medal of Freedom.* See entry under that name.

**Medal of Honor** The nation's highest military honor, awarded by Congress for risk of life in combat beyond the call of duty. Use *Medal of Honor recipient* or a synonym, but not *winner*.
There is no *Congressional Medal of Honor*.

**medevac** Acceptable abbreviation for *medical evacuation*, especially in referring to aircraft used to transport wounded military personnel.

**Medfly** Mediterranean fruit fly. The capital *M* is an exception to Webster's.

**media** In the sense of mass communication, such as magazines, newspapers, the news services, radio and television, the word is plural: *The news media are resisting attempts to limit their freedom.*

**median** See the **average, mean, median, norm** entry.

**mediate** See the **arbitrate, mediate** entry.

**Medicaid** A federal-state program that helps pay for health care for the needy, aged, blind and disabled, and for low-income families with children.
A state determines eligibility and which health services are covered. The federal government reimburses a percentage of the state's expenditures.

**Medicare** The federal health care insurance program for

people aged 65 and over, and for the disabled. Eligibility is based mainly on eligibility for Social Security.

Medicare helps pay charges for hospitalization, for stays in skilled nursing facilities, for physician's charges and for some associated health costs. There are limitations on the length of stay and type of care.

In Canada, *Medicare* refers to the nation's national health insurance program.

**medicine** See the **drugs, medicine** entry.

**medieval**

**mega-** A prefix denoting 1 million units of a measure. Move the decimal point six places to the right, adding zeros if necessary, to convert to the basic unit: 5.5 megatons = 5,500,000 tons.

**megabyte** A unit of storage capacity in computer systems, loosely 1 million bytes. Abbrev.: *MB*.

**megahertz** A measure of radio frequency or the speed of a computer processor, equal to a million hertz, or cycles per second. Abbrev.: *MHz*.

**melee**

**Melkite Church** See **Eastern Rite churches**.

**memento, mementos**

**memo, memos**

**memorandum, memorandums**

**Memorial Day** Formerly May 30. The federal legal holiday is the last Monday in May.

**menage a trois**

**menswear** Not *men's wear.*

**mentally retarded** The preferred term for those with significantly subaverage intellectual functioning. Do not use *retard* as a noun.

**Mercedes-Benz** Note hyphen in this division of DaimlerChrysler.

**merchant marine** Lowercase in referring to the ships of a nation used in commerce. Capitalize only in references to the organization the Merchant Marine or the U.S. Merchant Marine Academy. Members are *merchant mariners* or *merchant crewmen*, but not marines.

**meridians** Use numerals and lowercase to identify the imaginary locater lines that ring the globe from north to south through the poles. They are measured in units of 0 to 180 degrees east and west of the *prime meridian*, which runs through Greenwich, England.

Examples: *33rd meridian* (if location east or west of Greenwich is obvious), *1st meridian west, 100th meridian.*

See the **latitude and longitude** entry.

**merry-go-round**

**messiah** Capitalize in religious uses. Lowercase when used generically to mean a liberator.

**meter** The basic unit of length in the metric system.

It is equal to approximately 39.37 inches, which may be rounded off to 39.5 inches in most comparisons.

It takes 100 centimeters to make a meter.

It takes 1,000 meters to make a kilometer.

To convert to inches, multiply by 39.37 (5 meters x 39.37 = 196.85 inches).

To convert to yards, multiply by 1.1 (5 meters x 1.1 = 5.5 yards).

See **inch**; **metric system**; and **yards**.

**Methodist churches** The term *Methodist* originated as a nickname applied to a group of 18th-century Oxford University students known for their methodical application to Scripture study and prayer.

The principal Methodist body in the United States is the United Methodist Church, which also has some member conferences outside the United States. It was formed in 1968 by the merger of the Methodist Church and the Evangelical United Brethren Church. It has about 10 million members.

The government of the United Methodist Church follows a stratified pattern from the General Conference through several intermediate conferences down to the local congregation.

The General Conference, which meets every four years, has final authority in all matters. Its members, half lay and half clergy, are elected by the annual conferences.

A Methodist bishop presides over a "church area," which may embrace one or more annual conferences. Bishops have extensive administrative powers, including the authority to place, transfer and remove local church pastors, usually in consultation with district superintendents.

Districts in each conference are responsible for promotion of mission work, support of colleges, hospitals and publications, and examination of candidates for the ministry.

Members of a congregation form a charge conference. It elects officers to a board that assists the pastor.

Methodism in the United States also includes three major black denominations: the African Methodist Episcopal Church, the African Methodist Episcopal Zion Church and the Christian Methodist Episcopal Church.

Methodists believe in the Trinity and the humanity and divinity of Christ. There are two sacraments, baptism and the Lord's Supper.

Ordained individuals are known as *bishops* and *ministers*. *Pastor* applies if a minister leads a congregation.

For first references to bishops use the word: *Bishop W. Kenneth Goodson of Richmond, Va.*

For first reference to ministers, use *the Rev.* before the name of a man or woman. On second reference, use only the last name.

See **religious titles**.

**metric system** For U.S. members, use metric terms only in situations where they are universally accepted forms of measurement (*16 mm film*) or where the metric distance is an important number in itself: *He vowed to walk 100 kilometers (62 miles) in a week.*

Normally, the equivalent

should be in parentheses after the metric figure. A general statement, however, such as *A kilometer equals about five-eighths of a mile*, would be acceptable to avoid repeated use of parenthetical equivalents in a story that uses *kilometers* many times.

To avoid the need for long strings of figures, prefixes are added to the metric units to denote fractional elements or large multiples. The prefixes are: *pico-* (one-trillionth), *nano-* (one-billionth), *micro-* (one-millionth), *milli-* (one-thousandth), *centi-* (one-hundredth), *deci-* (one-tenth), *deka-* (10 units), *hecto-* (100 units), *kilo-* (1,000 units), *mega-* (1 million units), *giga-* (1 billion units), *tera-* (1 trillion units). Entries for each prefix show how to convert a unit preceded by the prefix to the basic unit.

In addition, separate entries for **gram**, **meter**, **liter**, **Celsius** and other frequently used metric units define them and give examples of how to convert them to equivalents in the terminology that has been used in the United

# METRIC CONVERSION CHART

### INTO METRIC

| multiply | by this number | to get |
|---|---|---|

### OUT OF METRIC

| multiply | by this number | to get |
|---|---|---|

#### LENGTH

| multiply | by this number | to get | multiply | by this number | to get |
|---|---|---|---|---|---|
| inches | 2.54 | centimeters | millimeters | 0.04 | inches |
| foot | 30 | centimeters | centimeters | 0.39 | inches |
| yards | 0.91 | meters | meters | 3.28 | feet |
| miles | 1.61 | kilometers | kilometers | 0.62 | miles |

#### AREA

| multiply | by this number | to get | multiply | by this number | to get |
|---|---|---|---|---|---|
| sq. inches | 6.45 | sq. centimeters | sq. centimeters | 0.16 | sq. inches |
| sq. feet | 0.09 | sq. meters | sq. meters | 0.2 | sq. yards |
| sq. yards | 0.84 | sq. meters | sq. kilometers | 0.39 | sq. miles |
| sq. miles | 2.59 | sq. kilometers | hectares | 2.47 | acres |
| acres | 0.39 | hectares | | | |

#### MASS (weight)

| multiply | by this number | to get | multiply | by this number | to get |
|---|---|---|---|---|---|
| ounces | 28 | grams | grams | 0.035 | ounces |
| pounds | 0.45 | kilograms | kilograms | 2.2 | pounds |
| short ton | 0.91 | metric ton | metric ton | 1.1 | short tons |

#### VOLUME

| multiply | by this number | to get | multiply | by this number | to get |
|---|---|---|---|---|---|
| teaspoons | 5 | milliliters | milliliters | 0.03 | fluid ounces |
| tablespoons | 15 | milliliters | liters | 2.1 | pints |
| fluid ounces | 30 | milliliters | liters | 1.06 | quarts |
| cups | 0.24 | liters | liters | 0.26 | gallons |
| pints | 0.47 | liters | cubic meters | 35 | cubic feet |
| quarts | 0.95 | liters | cubic meters | 1.3 | cubic yards |
| gallons | 3.79 | liters | | | |
| cubic feet | 0.03 | cubic meters | | | |
| cubic yards | 0.76 | cubic meters | | | |

#### TEMPERATURE

| | | |
|---|---|---|
| Fahrenheit to Celsius | Subtract 32, then divide by 1.8 | Celsius to Fahrenheit | Multiply by 1.8, then add 32 |

States.

Similarly, entries for **pound**, **inch**, **quart**, **Fahrenheit**, etc., contain examples of how to convert these terms to metric forms.

On the Net: http://www.megaconverter.com/mega2.

ABBREVIATIONS: The abbreviation *mm* for millimeter is acceptable in references to film widths (*8 mm film*) and weapons (*a 105 mm cannon*). (Note space between numeral and abbreviation.)

The principal abbreviations, for reference in the event they are used by a source, are: *g* (gram), *kg* (kilogram), *t* (metric ton), *m* (meter), *cm* (centimeter), *km* (kilometer), *mm* (millimeter), *L* (liter, capital *L* to avoid confusion with the figure *1*) and *mL* (milliliter).

**metric ton** Equal to approximately 2,204.62 pounds. See **ton**.

**Metro-Goldwyn-Mayer Inc.** *MGM* is acceptable in all references.

Headquarters is in Santa Monica, Calif.

**Mexico** There are 31 states and Mexico City, the capital and an independent federal district run by a city government. The states are Aguascalientes, Baja California, Baja California Sur, Campeche, Coahuila, Colima, Chiapas, Chihuahua, Durango, Guanajuato, Guerrero, Hidalgo, Jalisco, Mexico, Michoacan, Morelos, Nayarit, Nuevo Leon, Oaxaca, Puebla, Queretaro, Quintana Roo, San Luis Potosi, Sinaloa, Sonora, Tabasco, Tamaulipas, Tlaxcala, Veracruz, Yucatan and Zacatecas.

Mexican states elect their own governor and legislators. Congress is made up of two houses: the lower House of Deputies, with 500 members, and the Senate, with 128 members.

In datelines, use only the city and country.

**Mexico City** The city in Mexico stands alone in datelines.

**Miami** The city in Florida stands alone in datelines.

**Michigan** Abbrev.: *Mich.* See **state names**.

**micro-** A prefix denoting one-millionth of a unit.

Move the decimal point six places to the left in converting to the basic unit: 2,999,888.5 microseconds = 2.9998885 seconds.

**mid-** No hyphen unless a capitalized word follows:

mid-America     midsemester
mid-Atlantic     midterm

But use a hyphen when *mid-* precedes a figure: *mid-30s*.

**Middle Ages** A.D. 476 to approximately A.D. 1450.

**Middle Atlantic States** As defined by the U.S. Census Bureau, they are New Jersey, New York and Pennsylvania.

Less formal references often consider Delaware part of the group.

See **Northeast region**.

**middle class, middle-class** *He is a member of the middle class. She has middle-class values.*

**Middle East** The term applies to southwest Asia west of Pakistan and Afghanistan (Iran, Iraq, Israel, Kuwait, Jordan, Lebanon, Oman, Bahrain,

Qatar, Saudi Arabia, Syria, Turkey, United Arab Emirates and Yemen), and northeastern Africa (Egypt and Sudan).

Popular usage once distinguished between the *Near East* (the westerly nations in the listing) and the *Middle East* (the easterly nations), but the two terms now overlap, with current practice favoring *Middle East* for both areas.

Use *Middle East* unless *Near East* is used by a source in a story.

*Mideast* is also acceptable, but *Middle East* is preferred.

**middle initials** In general, use them. They are an integral part of a person's name.

Particular care should be taken to include middle initials in stories where they help identify a specific individual. Examples include casualty lists and stories naming the accused in a crime.

A middle initial may be dropped if a person does not use one or is publicly known without it: *Mickey Mantle* (not *Mickey C.*), *the Rev. Billy Graham* (not *Billy F.*).

See **names**.

**middleman**

**middle names** Use them only with people who are publicly known that way (*James Earl Jones*), or to prevent confusion with people of the same name.

See **middle initials**; **names**.

**Middle West** Definitions vary, but the term generally applies to the 12 states that the U.S. Census Bureau includes in the *Midwest* region. See **Midwest region** entry.

The shortened form *Midwest* is

acceptable in all references.

The forms for adjectives are *Middle Western, Midwestern*.

See the **directions and regions** entry.

**midnight** Do not put a *12* in front of it. It is part of the day that is ending, not the one that is beginning.

**midshipman** See **military academies**.

**Midwest region** As defined by the U.S. Census Bureau, the region (previously designated the North Central region) is broken into two divisions.

The East North Central states are Indiana, Illinois, Michigan, Ohio and Wisconsin.

The West North Central states are Iowa, Kansas, Minnesota, Missouri, Nebraska, North Dakota and South Dakota.

See **Northeast region**; **South**; and **West** for the bureau's other regional breakdowns.

**MiG** The *i* in this designation for a type of Russian fighter is lowercase because it is the Russian word for *and*. The initials are from the last names of the designers, Arten Mikoyan and Mikhail Gurevich.

The forms: *MiG-19, MiG-21s*. See **aircraft names**.

**mile** Also called a statute mile, it equals 5,280 feet.

The metric equivalent is approximately 1.6 kilometers.

To convert to kilometers, multiply by 1.6 (5 miles x 1.6 equals 8 kilometers).

See **foot**; **kilometer**; **knot**; and **nautical mile**.

Use figures for amounts under 10 in dimensions, formulas and speeds: *The farm measures 5 miles by 4 miles. The car slowed to 7 mph. The new model gets 4 miles more per gallon.*

Spell out below 10 in distances: *He drove four miles.*

**miles per gallon** The abbreviation *mpg* is acceptable on second reference.

**miles per hour** The abbreviation *mph* (no periods) is acceptable in all references.

**military academies** Capitalize *U.S. Air Force Academy, U.S. Coast Guard Academy, U.S. Merchant Marine Academy, U.S. Military Academy, U.S. Naval Academy.* Retain capitalization if the *U.S.* is dropped: *the Air Force Academy,* etc.

Lowercase *academy* whenever it stands alone.

*Cadet* is the proper title on first reference for men and women enrolled at the Army, Air Force, Coast Guard and Merchant Marine academies. *Midshipman* is the proper title for men and women enrolled at the Naval Academy.

Use the appropriate title on first reference. On second reference, use only the last name.

**military titles** Capitalize a military rank when used as a formal title before an individual's name.

See the lists that follow to determine whether the title should be spelled out or abbreviated in regular text.

On first reference, use the appropriate title before the full name of a member of the military.

In subsequent references, do not continue using the title before a name. Use only the last name.

Spell out and lowercase a title when it is substituted for a name: *Gen. John J. Pershing arrived today. An aide said the general would review the troops.*

In some cases, it may be necessary to explain the significance of a title: *Army Sgt. Maj. John Jones described the attack. Jones, who holds the Army's highest rank for enlistees, said it was unprovoked.*

In addition to the ranks listed on the next page, each service has ratings such as *machinist, radarman, torpedoman,* etc., that are job descriptions. Do not use any of these designations as a title on first reference. If one is used before a name in a subsequent reference, do not capitalize or abbreviate it.

ABBREVIATIONS: The abbreviations, with the highest ranks listed first:

### MILITARY TITLES

| Rank | Usage before a name |
|---|---|

### ARMY

#### Commissioned Officers

| | |
|---|---|
| general | Gen. |
| lieutenant general | Lt. Gen. |
| major general | Maj. Gen. |
| brigadier general | Brig. Gen. |
| colonel | Col. |
| lieutenant colonel | Lt. Col. |
| major | Maj. |
| captain | Capt. |
| first lieutenant | 1st Lt. |
| second lieutenant | 2nd Lt. |

#### Warrant Officers

| | |
|---|---|
| chief warrant officer | Chief Warrant Officer |
| warrant officer | Warrant Officer |

#### Enlisted Personnel

| | |
|---|---|
| sergeant major of the Army | Sgt. Maj. of the Army |
| command sergeant major | Command Sgt. Maj. |
| sergeant major | Sgt. Maj. |
| first sergeant | 1st Sgt. |
| master sergeant | Master Sgt. |

| | |
|---|---|
| sergeant first class | Sgt. 1st Class |
| staff sergeant | Staff Sgt. |
| sergeant | Sgt. |
| corporal | Cpl. |
| specialist | Spc. |
| private first class | Pfc. |
| private | Pvt. |

## NAVY, COAST GUARD

### Commissioned Officers

| | |
|---|---|
| admiral | Adm. |
| vice admiral | Vice Adm. |
| rear admiral upper half | Rear Adm. |
| rear admiral lower half | Rear Adm. |
| captain | Capt. |
| commander | Cmdr. |
| lieutenant commander | Lt. Cmdr. |
| lieutenant | Lt. |
| lieutenant junior grade | Lt. j.g. |
| ensign | Ensign |

### Warrant Officers

| | |
|---|---|
| chief warrant officer | Chief Warrant Officer |

### Enlisted Personnel

| | |
|---|---|
| master chief petty officer of the Navy | Master Chief Petty Officer of the Navy |
| master chief petty officer | Master Chief Petty Officer |
| senior chief petty officer | Senior Chief Petty Officer |
| chief petty officer | Chief Petty Officer |
| petty officer first class | Petty Officer 1st Class |
| petty officer second class | Petty Officer 2nd Class |
| petty officer third class | Petty Officer 3rd Class |
| seaman | Seaman |
| seaman apprentice | Seaman Apprentice |
| seaman recruit | Seaman Recruit |

## MARINE CORPS

Ranks and abbreviations for commissioned officers are the same as those in the Army. Warrant officer ratings follow the same system used in the Navy. There are no specialist ratings.

### Others

| | |
|---|---|
| sergeant major of the Marine Corps | Sgt. Maj. of the Marine Corps |

| | |
|---|---|
| sergeant major | Sgt. Maj. |
| master gunnery sergeant | Master Gunnery Sgt. |
| first sergeant | 1st Sgt. |
| master sergeant | Master Sgt. |
| gunnery sergeant | Gunnery Sgt. |
| staff sergeant | Staff Sgt. |
| sergeant | Sgt. |
| corporal | Cpl. |
| lance corporal | Lance Cpl. |
| private first class | Pfc. |
| private | Pvt. |

## AIR FORCE

Ranks and abbreviations for commissioned officers are the same as those in the Army.

### Enlisted Designations

| | |
|---|---|
| chief master sergeant of the Air Force | Chief Master Sgt. of the Air Force |
| chief master sergeant | Chief Master Sgt. |
| senior master sergeant | Senior Master Sgt. |
| master sergeant | Master Sgt. |
| technical sergeant | Tech. Sgt. |
| staff sergeant | Staff Sgt. |
| senior airman | Senior Airman |
| airman first class | Airman 1st Class |
| airman | Airman |
| airman basic | Airman |

PLURALS: Add *s* to the principal element in the title: *Majs. John Jones and Robert Smith; Maj. Gens. John Jones and Robert Smith; Spcs. John Jones and Robert Smith.*

RETIRED OFFICERS: A military rank may be used in first reference before the name of an officer who has retired if it is relevant to a story. Do not, however, use the military abbreviation *Ret.*

Instead, use *retired* just as *former* would be used before the title of a civilian: *They invited retired Army Gen. John Smith.*

FIREFIGHTERS, POLICE OFFICERS: Use the abbreviations listed here when a military-style title is used before the name of a firefighter or police officer outside a direct quotation. Add *police* or *fire* before the title if needed for clarity: *police Sgt. William Smith,*

*fire Capt. David Jones.*
Spell out titles such as *detective* that are not used in the armed forces.

**military units** Use Arabic figures and capitalize the key words when linked with the figures: *1st Infantry Division* (or *the 1st Division*), *5th Battalion, 395th Field Artillery, 7th Fleet.*
But: *the division, the battalion, the artillery, the fleet.*

**millennium**

**milli-** A prefix denoting one-thousandth of a unit. Move the decimal three places to the left in converting to the basic unit: 1,567.5 millimeters equals 1.5675 meters.

**milligram** One-thousandth of a gram.
Equal to approximately one-twenty-eight-thousandth of an ounce.
To convert to ounces, multiply by 0.000035 (140 milligrams x 0.000035 equals 0.0049 ounces).
See **metric system**.

**milliliter** One-thousandth of a liter.
Equal to approximately one-fifth of a teaspoon.
Thirty milliliters equals 1 fluid ounce.
To convert to teaspoons, multiply by 0.2 (5 milliliters x 0.2 equals 1 teaspoon).
See **liter** and **metric system**.

**millimeter** One-thousandth of a meter.
It takes 10 millimeters to make a centimeter.
A millimeter is roughly equal to the thickness of a paper clip.

To convert to inches, multiply by .04 (5 millimeters x .04 is 0.2 of an inch).
May be abbreviated as *mm* when used with a numeral in first or subsequent references to film or weapons: *35 mm film, 105 mm artillery piece.* (Note space after numeral.)
See **meter**; **metric system**; and **inch**.

**millions, billions** Use figures with *million* or *billion* in all except casual uses: *I'd like to make a billion dollars.* But: *The nation has 1 million citizens. I need $7 billion.*
Do not go beyond two decimal places. *7.51 million people, $256 billion, 7,542,500 people, $2,565,750,000.* Decimals are preferred where practical: *1.5 million.* Not: *1 1/2 million.*
Do not mix *millions* and *billions* in the same figure: *2.6 billion.* Not: *2 billion 600 million.*
Do not drop the word *million* or *billion* in the first figure of a range: *He is worth from $2 million to $4 million.* Not: *$2 to $4 million,* unless you really mean $2.
Note that a hyphen is not used to join the figures and the word *million* or *billion,* even in this type of phrase: *The president submitted a $300 billion budget.*

**milquetoast** Not *milk toast* when referring to a shrinking, apologetic person. Derived from Caspar Milquetoast, a character in a comic strip by Harold T. Webster.

**Milwaukee** The city in Wisconsin stands alone in datelines.

**mimeograph** Formerly a trademark, now a generic term.

**mini-** The rules in **prefixes**

apply, but in general, no hyphen.
Some examples:

miniseries     miniskirt
minivan

**minister** It is not a formal
title in most religions, with exceptions such as the Nation of Islam,
and is not capitalized. Where it is
a formal title, it should be capitalized before the name: *Minister
John Jones.*
    See **religious titles** and the
entry for an individual's denomination.

**ministry** See **foreign governmental bodies**.

**Minneapolis** The city in
Minnesota stands alone in datelines.

**Minnesota** Abbrev.: *Minn.*
See **state names**.

**Minnesota Mining and
Manufacturing** See **3M** entry.

**minority leader** Treat the
same as *majority leader*. See that
entry and **legislative titles**.

**minuscule** Not *miniscule.*

**minus sign** Use a hyphen,
not a dash, but use the word
*minus* if there is any danger of
confusion.
    Use a word, not a minus sign,
to indicate temperatures below
zero: *minus 10* or *5 below zero.*

**mips** Acronym for *million instructions per second.* Spell out
on first reference.

**MIRV, MIRVs** Acceptable
on first reference for *multiple in-
dependently targetable re-entry
vehicle(s).*

Explain in the text that a *MIRV*
is an intercontinental ballistic
missile with several warheads,
each of which can be directed to a
different target.

**misdemeanor** See the **felony, misdemeanor** entry.

**mishap** A minor misfortune.
People are not killed in *mishaps.*

**Miss** See **courtesy titles**.

**missile names** Use Arabic
figures and capitalize the proper
name but not the word *missile*:
*Pershing 2 missile.*
    See **ABM**; **ICBM**; **MIRV**; and
**SAM**.

**Mississippi** Abbrev.: *Miss.*
See **state names**.

**Missouri** Abbrev.: *Mo.* See
**state names**.

**mix up** (v.) **mix-up** (n. and
adj.)

**Mobil Corp.** See **Exxon
Mobil**.

**mock-up** (n.)

**model numbers** See **serial
numbers**.

**modem** Acceptable in all references for the acronym formed
from *modulator* and *demodulator.*

**mom** Uppercase only when
the noun substitutes for a name
as a term of address: *Hi, Mom!*

**Monaco** After the Vatican,
the world's smallest state.
    The *Monaco* section stands
alone in datelines. The other
two sections, *La Condamine* and

*Monte Carlo*, are followed by *Monaco*:

MONTE CARLO, Monaco (AP) —

**Monday** See **days of the week**.

**Monday morning quarterback** One who second-guesses.

**M-1, M-14** See **weapons**.

**monetary** See the **fiscal, monetary** entry.

**monetary units** See **cents**; **dollars**; and **pounds**.

**moneymaker**

**monsignor** See **Roman Catholic Church**.

**Montana** Abbrev.: *Mont.* See **state names**.

**Montessori method** After Maria Montessori, a system of training young children. It emphasizes training of the senses and guidance to encourage self-education.

**monthlong**

**months** Capitalize the names of months in all uses. When a month is used with a specific date, abbreviate only *Jan., Feb., Aug., Sept., Oct., Nov.* and *Dec.* Spell out when using alone, or with a year alone.

When a phrase lists only a month and a year, do not separate the year with commas. When a phrase refers to a month, day and year, set off the year with commas.

EXAMPLES: *January 1972 was a cold month. Jan. 2 was the coldest day of the month. His*

birthday *is May 8. Feb. 14, 1987, was the target date. She testified that it was Friday, Dec. 3, when the accident occurred.*

In tabular material, use these three-letter forms without a period: *Jan, Feb, Mar, Apr, May, Jun, Jul, Aug, Sep, Oct, Nov, Dec.*

See **dates** and **years**.

**Montreal** The city in Canada stands alone in datelines.

**monuments** Capitalize the popular names of monuments and similar public attractions: *Lincoln Memorial, Statue of Liberty, Washington Monument, Leaning Tower of Pisa*, etc.

**moon** Lowercase. See **heavenly bodies**.

**mo-ped** Hyphen is an exception to Webster's.

**mop up** (v.) **mop-up** (n. and adj.)

**Moral Majority** Not *the* Moral Majority.

**more than** See **over**.

**Mormon church** Acceptable in references to *The Church of Jesus Christ of Latter-day Saints*, but the official name is preferred in first reference in a story dealing primarily with church activities.

See the entry under the formal name.

**Moscow** The city in Russia stands alone in datelines.

**Moslem(s)** The preferred term to describe adherents of Islam is *Muslim(s)*.

**mosquito, mosquitoes**

**Mother's Day** The second
Sunday in May.

**mother-in-law, mothers-in-law**

**Mother Nature**

**motor** See the **engine, motor** entry.

**mount** Spell out in all uses, including the names of communities and of mountains: *Mount Clemens, Mich.*; *Mount Everest.*

**mountains** Capitalize as part of a proper name: *Appalachian Mountains, Ozark Mountains, Rocky Mountains.*
Or simply: *the Appalachians, the Ozarks, the Rockies.*

**Mountain Standard Time (MST), Mountain Daylight Time (MDT)** See **time zones**.

**Mountain States** As defined by the U.S. Census Bureau, the eight are Arizona, Colorado, Idaho, Montana, Nevada, New Mexico, Utah and Wyoming.

**movie ratings** The ratings used by the Motion Picture Association of America are:
*G — General audiences.* All ages admitted.
*PG — Parental guidance suggested.* Some material may not be suitable for children.
*PG-13 — Special parental guidance* strongly suggested for children under 13. Some material may be inappropriate for young children.
*R — Restricted.* Under 17 requires accompanying parent or adult guardian.
*NC-17 —* No one under 17 admitted.

When the ratings are used in news stories or reviews, use these forms as appropriate: *the movie has an R rating, an R-rated movie, the movie is R-rated.*

**movie titles** See **composition titles**.

**mph** Acceptable in all references for *miles per hour* or *miles an hour.*

**MP3** A popular audio compression format on the Internet.

**Mr., Mrs.** See **courtesy titles**.

**Ms.** This is the spelling and punctuation for all uses of the courtesy title, including direct quotations.
There is no plural. If several women who prefer *Ms.* must be listed in a series, repeat *Ms.* before each name.
See **courtesy titles** for guidelines on when to use *Ms.*

**Muhammad** The prophet and founder of the Islamic religion, *Prophet Muhammad.* Use other spellings only if preferred by a specific person for his own name or in a title or the name of an organization.

**mujahedeen** Lowercase when using the Arabic for *holy warriors*; uppercase if it is part of the name of a group.

**mullah** An Islamic leader or teacher, often a general title of respect for a learned man.

**multi-** The rules in prefixes apply, but in general, no hyphen. Some examples:

| | |
|---|---|
| multicolored | multimillion |
| multilateral | multimillionaire |

**Mumbai** India's largest city, formerly known as Bombay.

**murder** See the **homicide, murder, manslaughter** entry.

**murderer** See the **assassin, killer, murderer** entry.

**Murphy's law** The law is: *If something can go wrong, it will.*

**music** Capitalize, but do not use quotation marks, on descriptive titles for orchestral works: *Bach's Suite No. 1 for Orchestra; Beethoven's Serenade for Flute, Violin and Viola.* If the instrumentation is not part of the title but is added for explanatory purposes, the names of the instruments are lowercased: *Mozart's Sinfonia Concertante in E flat major* (the common title) *for violin and viola.* If in doubt, lowercase the names of the instruments.

Use quotation marks for nonmusical terms in a title: *Beethoven's "Eroica" Symphony.* If the work has a special full title, all of it is quoted: *"Symphonie Fantastique," "Rhapsody in Blue."*

In subsequent references, lowercase *symphony, concerto*, etc.

**musket** See **weapons**.

**Muslims** The preferred term to describe adherents of Islam.

A *Black Muslim* is a member of a predominantly black Islamic sect in the United States. However, the term is considered derogatory by members of the sect, who call themselves *Muslims*.

**Muzak** A trademark for a type of recorded background music.

**Myanmar** Use this name for the country and the language. Use *Myanmar people* or *Myanmar* for the inhabitants. (Formerly Burma.)

# N

**n.** See **nouns**.

**naive**

**names** In general, use last names only on second reference.

When it is necessary to distinguish between two people who use the same last name, as in married couples or brothers and sisters, use the first and last name. (See **courtesy titles**.)

In stories involving youngsters, generally refer to them by first name on second reference if they are 15 or younger and by their surname at 18 and older.

However, use news judgment and refer to children under 15 by their last name if the story is a serious one involving, for example, a major crime. With 16- or 17-year-olds, use the surname unless it's a light-hearted story.

**nano-** A prefix denoting one-billionth of a unit. Move the decimal point nine places to the left in converting to the basic unit: 2,999,888,777.5 nanoseconds equals 2.9998887775 seconds.

**naphtha**

**narrow-minded**

**national** See the **citizen, resident, subject, national, native** entry.

**National Aeronautics and Space Administration** *NASA* is acceptable in all references.

**national anthem** Lowercase. But: *"The Star-Spangled Banner."*

**National Association for the Advancement of Colored People** *NAACP* is acceptable on first reference to avoid a cumbersome lead, but provide the full name in the body of the story.

Headquarters is in Baltimore.

**National Association of Letter Carriers** The shortened form *Letter Carriers union* is acceptable in all references.

Headquarters is in Washington.

**National Baptist Convention of America** See **Baptist churches**.

**National Baptist Convention U.S.A. Inc.** See **Baptist churches**.

**National Broadcasting Co.** See **NBC**.

**national chairman** Capitalize when used before the name of the individual who heads a political party: *Democratic National Chairman Kenneth M. Curtis.*

## National Council of the Churches of Christ in the U.S.A.
This interdenominational, cooperative body includes most major Protestant and Eastern Orthodox denominations in the United States.

The shortened form *National Council of Churches* is acceptable in all references.

Headquarters is in New York. See **World Council of Churches**.

## National Education Association
*NEA* is acceptable on second reference.

Headquarters is in Washington.

## National FFA Organization
Formerly the Future Farmers of America. *FFA* is acceptable on second reference.

Headquarters is in Alexandria, Va.

## National Governors Association
Represents the governors of the 50 states and five territories.

Its office is in Washington.

## National Guard
Capitalize when referring to U.S. or state-level forces, or foreign forces when that is the formal name: *the National Guard, the Guard, the Iowa National Guard, Iowa's National Guard, National Guard troops, the Iraqi National Guard.*

When referring to an individual in a National Guard unit, use National Guardsman: *He is a National Guardsman.*

Lowercase *guardsman* when it stands alone.

See **military titles**.

## National Hurricane Center
See **weather terms**.

## National Institutes of Health
This agency within the Department of Health and Human Services is the principal biomedical research arm of the federal government.

Its agencies are: National Cancer Institute; National Center for Research Resources; National Eye Institute; National Human Genome Research Institute; National Heart, Lung and Blood Institute; National Institute on Aging; National Institute on Alcohol Abuse and Alcoholism; National Institute of Allergy and Infectious Diseases; National Institute of Arthritis and Musculoskeletal and Skin Diseases; National Institute of Child Health and Human Development; National Institute on Drug Abuse; National Institute on Deafness and Other Communication Disorders; National Institute of Diabetes and Digestive and Kidney Diseases; National Institute of Dental and Craniofacial Research; National Institute of Environmental Health Sciences; National Institute of General Medical Sciences; National Institute of Mental Health; National Institute of Neurological Disorders and Stroke; National Institute of Nursing Research; National Library of Medicine; Office of Alternative Medicine; Office of Medical Applications of Research; Office of Research on Women's Health; National Institutes of Health Clinical Center; Center for Scientific Review; Center for Information Technology.

All the agencies are in Bethesda, Md., except the National Institute of Environmental Health Sciences, which is in Research Triangle Park, N.C.

## nationalist
Lowercase when referring to a partisan of a coun-

try. Capitalize only when referring to alignment with a political party for which this is the proper name.

See the **political parties and philosophies** entry.

## Nationalist China See China.

## nationalities and races

Capitalize the proper names of nationalities, peoples, races, tribes, etc.: *Arab, Arabic, African, American, Caucasian, Cherokee, Chinese* (both singular and plural), *Eskimo* (plural *Eskimos*), *French Canadian, Gypsy (Gypsies), Japanese* (singular and plural), *Jew, Jewish, Latin, Negro (Negroes), Nordic, Sioux, Swede,* etc.

Lowercase *black* (noun or adjective), *white, red, mulatto,* etc. See **colored**.

See **race** for guidelines on when racial identification is pertinent in a story.

Use derogatory terms only in direct quotes when essential to the story and flag the contents in an editor's note.

## National Labor Relations Board *NLRB* is acceptable on second reference.

## National League of Cities

Its members are the governments of cities with 30,000 or more residents, and some state and municipal leagues.

It is separate from the U.S. Conference of Mayors, whose membership is limited to mayors of cities with 30,000 or more residents. The organizations often engage in joint projects, however. The office is in Washington.

## National Newspaper Association A newspaper asso-

ciation representing community newspapers, their owners, publishers and editors. *NNA* is acceptable on second reference.

Headquarters is at the Missouri School of Journalism, Columbia, Mo.

See www.nna.org

## National Organization for Women Not *of. NOW* is acceptable on second reference.

Headquarters is in Washington.

## National Rifle Association *NRA* is acceptable on second reference.

Headquarters is in Washington.

## National Weather Service No longer the U.S. Weather Bureau. *The weather service* (lowercase) may be used in any reference.

See **weather terms**.

## Nation of Islam The nationalist religious movement traces its origins in 1930 to W.D. Fard, also known as Wali Fard, who called for racial separation. Elijah Muhammad took over the leadership in 1934, holding the post until his death in 1975. A son, Warith (Wallace) Dean Muhammad, succeeded to the leadership and pointed the movement toward integration and traditional Islam. Louis Farrakhan led a militant faction into a separatist movement in 1976.

The Nation of Islam does not release membership figures, but published estimates have ranged from 10,000 to more than 20,000.

Use the title *minister* on first reference to clergymen: *Minister Louis Farrakhan.*

## nationwide

**native** See the **citizen, resident, subject, national, native** entry.

**NATO** Acceptable in all references for the *North Atlantic Treaty Organization*, but use it sparingly. A phrase such as *the alliance* is less burdensome to the reader.

**Naugahyde** A trademark for a brand of simulated leather.

**nautical mile** It equals 1 minute of arc of a great circle of the Earth or 6,076.11549 feet, or 1,852 meters. To convert to approximate statute miles (5,280 feet), multiply the number of nautical miles by 1.15.
See **knot**.

**naval, navel** Use *naval* in copy pertaining to a navy.
A *navel* is a bellybutton.
A *navel orange* is a seedless orange, so named because it has a small depression, like a navel.

**naval station** Capitalize only as part of a proper name: *Norfolk Naval Station.*

**navy** Capitalize when referring to U.S. forces: *the U.S. Navy, the Navy, Navy policy.* Do not use the abbreviation *USN.*
Lowercase when referring to the naval forces of other nations: *the British navy.*
This approach has been adopted for consistency, because many foreign nations do not use *navy* as the proper name.
See **military academies** and **military titles**.

**Nazi, Nazism** Derived from the German for the National Socialist German Workers' Party, the fascist political party founded in 1919 and abolished in 1945. Under Adolf Hitler, it seized control of Germany in 1933.
See the **political parties and philosophies** entry.

**NBC** Acceptable in all references to the *National Broadcasting Co.*
Divisions are *NBC News, NBC Radio* and *NBC-TV.*

**NC-17** The movie rating that denotes individuals under 17 are not admitted. (Previously, an *X rating.*)

**NCR Corp.** Formerly National Cash Register Co.
Headquarters is in Dayton, Ohio.

**Near East** There is no longer a substantial distinction between this term and *Middle East.*
See the **Middle East** entry.

**nearsighted** When used in a medical sense, it means an individual can see well at close range but has difficulty seeing objects at a distance.

**Nebraska** Abbrev.: *Neb.* See **state names**.

## negligee

**neither...nor** See the **either...or, neither...nor** entry.

**Netherlands** In datelines, give the name of the community followed by *Netherlands*:
*AMSTERDAM, Netherlands (AP)*
—
In stories: *the Netherlands* or *Netherlands* as the construction of a sentence dictates.

**Netherlands Antilles** In datelines, give the name of the community followed by *Nether-*

*lands Antilles.* Do not abbreviate.

Identify an individual island, if needed, in the text.

### net income, net profit
See **profit terminology** in the Business Guidelines and Style section.

### neutron weapon
A small warhead designed to be mounted on a Lance missile or fired from an 8-inch gun. It produces twice the deadly radiation of older, tactical nuclear warheads but less than one-tenth as much explosive power, heat and fallout. This means the warhead can kill people while causing little damage to buildings and other structures.

It is not a *bomb.* It is a *weapon* or a *warhead.*

If *neutron bomb* is used in a direct quote, explain in a subsequent paragraph that the warhead would be fired on a missile or from artillery and not dropped, like a bomb, from a plane.

The weapon officially is known as an *enhanced radiation weapon.*

### Nevada
Abbrev.: *Nev.* See **state names**.

### New Brunswick
One of the three Maritime Provinces of Canada. Do not abbreviate.
See **datelines**.

### New England
Connecticut, Maine, Massachusetts, New Hampshire, Rhode Island and Vermont.

### Newfoundland
This Canadian province, officially renamed Newfoundland and Labrador in 2001, comprises the island of Newfoundland and the mainland section of Labrador. Do not ab-breviate.

In datelines, use Newfoundland after the names of all cities and towns. Specify in the text whether the community is on the island or in Labrador.
See **datelines**.

### New Hampshire
Abbrev.: *N.H.* See **state names**.

### New Jersey
Abbrev.: *N.J.* See **state names**.

### New Mexico
Abbrev.: *N.M.* See **state names**.

### New Orleans
The city in Louisiana stands alone in date-lines.

### New South
The era that began in the South in the 1960s with a thriving economy and the election of state officials who advocated the abolition of racial segregation.

*Old South* applies to the South before the Civil War.

### Newspaper Association of America
Formerly the American Newspaper Publishers Association. *NAA* is acceptable in second reference. Also *the newspaper association, the association.*

Headquarters is in Vienna, Va.

### Newspaper Guild, The
Formerly the American Newspaper Guild, it is a union for newspaper and news service employees, generally those in the news and business departments.

On second reference: *the Guild.*

Headquarters is in Washington.

### newspaper names
Capitalize *the* in a newspaper's name if that is the way the publication

prefers to be known. Do not place name in quotes.

Lowercase *the* before newspaper names if a story mentions several papers, some of which use *the* as part of the name and some of which do not.

Where location is needed but is not part of the official name, use parentheses: *The Huntsville (Ala.) Times.*

Consult the International Year Book published by Editor & Publisher to determine whether a two-name combination is hyphenated.

### newsstand

### New Testament See **Bible**.

### New World The Western Hemisphere.

### New Year's, New Year's Day, New Year's Eve But:
*What will the new year bring?*

The federal legal holiday is observed on Friday if Jan. 1 falls on a Saturday, on Monday if it falls on a Sunday.

### New York Abbrev.: *N.Y.* Use *New York state* when a distinction must be made between state and city. See **state names**.

### New York City Use *NEW YORK* in datelines, not the name of an individual community or borough such as *Flushing* or *Queens*.

Identify the borough in the body of the story if pertinent.

### New York Stock Exchange See entry in **Business Guidelines**.

### nicknames A nickname should be used in place of a person's given name in news stories only when it is the way the individual prefers to be known: *Jimmy Carter.*

When a nickname is inserted into the identification of an individual, use quotation marks: *Sen. Henry M. "Scoop" Jackson.* Also: *Jackson is known as "Scoop."*

In sports stories and sports columns, commonly used nicknames may be substituted for a first name without the use of quotation marks: *Woody Hayes, Bear Bryant, Catfish Hunter, Bubba Smith,* etc. But in sports stories where the given name is used, and in all news stories: *Paul "Bear" Bryant.*

Capitalize without quotation marks such terms as *Sunshine State, the Old Dominion, Motown, the Magic City, Old Hickory, Old Glory, Galloping Ghost.*

See **names**.

### nightclub

### nighttime

### 9/11 *Sept. 11* is the preferred term to use in describing the terrorist attacks in the United States Sept. 11, 2001.

### nitpicking

### nitty-gritty

### No. Use as the abbreviation for *number* in conjunction with a figure to indicate position or rank: *No. 1 man, No. 3 choice.*

Do not use in street addresses, with this exception: *No. 10 Downing St.,* the residence of Britain's prime minister.

Do not use in the names of schools: *Public School 19.*

### Nobel Prize, Nobel Prizes
The five established under terms of the will of Alfred Nobel are:

Nobel Peace Prize, Nobel Prize in chemistry, Nobel Prize in literature, Nobel Prize in physics, Nobel Prize in physiology or medicine. (Note the capitalization styles.)

The Nobel Memorial Prize in Economic Sciences (officially it is the cumbersome Bank of Sweden Prize in Economic Sciences in Memory of Alfred Nobel) is not a Nobel Prize in the same sense. The Central Bank of Sweden established it in 1968 as a memorial to Alfred Nobel. References to this prize should include the word *Memorial* to help make this distinction. Explain the status of the prize in the story when appropriate.

Nobel Prize award ceremonies are held on Dec. 10, the anniversary of Alfred Nobel's death in 1896. The award ceremony for peace is in Oslo and the other ceremonies are in Stockholm.

Capitalize prize in references that do not mention the category: *He is a Nobel Prize winner. She is a Nobel Prize-winning scientist.*

Lowercase *prize* when not linked with the word Nobel: *The peace prize was awarded Monday.*

**nobility** References to members of the nobility in nations that have a system of rank present special problems because nobles frequently are known by their titles rather than their given or family names. Their titles, in effect, become their names.

The guidelines here relate to Britain's nobility. Adapt them as appropriate to members of nobility in other nations.

Orders of rank among British nobility begin with the royal family. The term *royalty* is reserved for the families of living and deceased sovereigns.

Next, in descending order, are dukes, marquesses (also called marquises), earls, viscounts and barons. Many hold inherited titles; others have been raised to the nobility by the sovereign for their lifetimes. Occasionally the sovereign raises an individual to the nobility and makes the title inheritable by the person's heirs, but the practice is increasingly rare.

Sovereigns also confer honorary titles, which do not make an individual a member of the nobility. The principal designations, in descending order, are baronet and knight.

In general, the guidelines in **courtesy titles** and **titles** apply. However, honorary titles and titles of nobility are capitalized when they serve as an alternate name.

Some guidelines and examples:

ROYALTY: Capitalize *king, queen, prince* and *princess* when they are used directly before one or more names; lowercase when they stand alone:

*Queen Elizabeth II, Queen Elizabeth II of the United Kingdom of Great Britain and Northern Ireland, the queen. Kings George and Edward. Queen Mother Elizabeth, the queen mother.*

Also capitalize a longer form of the sovereign's title when its use is appropriate in a story or it is being quoted: *Her Majesty Queen Elizabeth.*

Use *Prince* or *Princess* before the names of a sovereign's children: *Princess Anne, the princess.*

The male heir to the throne normally is designated *Prince of Wales,* and the title becomes, in common usage, an alternate name. Capitalize when used: *The queen invested her eldest son as Prince of Wales. Prince Charles is now the Prince of Wales. The prince is a bachelor. Charles, Prince of Wales, was married today. His wife is known as the Princess of Wales.*

DUKE: The full title — *Duke of Wellington*, for example — is an alternate name, capitalized in all uses. Lowercase duke when it stands alone.

The designation *Arthur, Duke of Wellington*, is appropriate in some cases, but never *Duke Arthur* or *Lord Arthur*.

The wife of a *duke* is a *duchess: the Duchess of Wellington, the duchess*, but never *Duchess Diana* or *Lady Diana.*

A duke normally also has a lesser title. It is commonly used for his eldest son if he has one. Use the courtesy titles *Lord* or *Lady* before the first names of a duke's children.

Some examples:

*Lady Jane Wellesley, only daughter of the eighth Duke of Wellington, has been linked romantically with Prince Charles, heir to the British throne. The eldest of Lady Jane's four brothers is Arthur Charles, the Marquess Douro. The Wellingtons, whose family name is Wellesley, are not of royal blood. However, they rank among the nation's most famous aristocrats thanks to the first duke, the victor at Waterloo.*

MARQUESS, MARQUIS, EARL, VISCOUNT, BARON: The full titles serve as alternate names and should be capitalized. Frequently, however, the holder of such a title is identified as a lord: *The Marquess of Bath*, for example, more commonly is known as *Lord Bath.*

Use *Lady* before the name of a woman married to a man who holds one of these titles. The wife of a marquess is a marchioness, the wife of a marquis is a marquise, the wife of an earl is a countess (earl is the British equivalent of count), the wife of a viscount is a viscountess, the wife of a baron is a baroness.

Use *Lord* or *Lady* before the first names of the children of a marquess.

Use *Lady* before the first name of an earl's daughter.

*The Honorable* often appears before the names of sons of earls, viscounts and barons who do not have titles. Their names should stand alone in news stories, however.

*The Honorable* also appears frequently before the names of unmarried daughters of viscounts and barons. In news stories, however, use a full name on first reference, a last name preceded by *Miss* on second.

Some examples:

*Queen Elizabeth gave her sister's husband, Antony Armstrong-Jones, the title Earl of Snowdon. Their son, David, is the Viscount Linley. They also have a daughter, Lady Sarah Armstrong-Jones. Lord Snowdon, a photographer, was known as Antony Armstrong-Jones before he received his title.*

BARONET, KNIGHT: Use *Sir* before a name if appropriate in the context; otherwise follow routine practice for names: *Sir Harold Wilson* on first reference, *Sir Harold* (not *Sir Wilson*) on second. Or: *Prime Minister Harold Wilson* on first reference, *Wilson* on second.

Do not use both an honorary title and a title of authority such as *prime minister* before a name.

Use *Lady* before the name of the wife of a baronet or knight.

For a woman who has received an honor in her own right, use

*Dame* before her name if it is the way she is known or it is appropriate in the context: *Dame Margot Fonteyn* on first reference, *Dame Margot* on second.

## nobody

## noisome, noisy *Noisome* means offensive, noxious.
*Noisy* means clamorous.

## nolo contendere The literal meaning is, "I do not wish to contend." Terms such as *no contest* or *no-contest plea* are acceptable in all references.

When a defendant in a criminal case enters this plea, it means that he is not admitting guilt but is stating that he will offer no defense. The person is then subject to being judged guilty and punished as if he had pleaded guilty or had been convicted. The principal difference is that the defendant retains the option of denying the same charge in another legal proceeding.

## no man's land

## non- The rules of **prefixes** apply, but in general no hyphen when forming a compound that does not have special meaning and can be understood if *not* is used before the base word. Use a hyphen, however, before proper nouns or in awkward combinations, such as *non-nuclear*.

## nonaligned nations A political rather than economic or geographic term used primarily during the Cold War. Although nonaligned nations do not belong to Western or Eastern military alliances or blocs, they profess not to be neutral, like Switzerland, but activist alternatives.

Do not confuse *nonaligned* with *Third World*, although some Third World nations may belong to the nonaligned group.
See the **Third World** entry.

## noncontroversial All issues are controversial. A *noncontroversial issue* is impossible. A *controversial issue* is redundant.

## none It usually means no single one. When used in this sense, it always takes singular verbs and pronouns: *None of the seats was in its right place.*
Use a plural verb only if the sense is no two or no amount: *None of the consultants agree on the same approach. None of the taxes have been paid.*

## nonrestrictive clauses See **essential clauses, nonessential clauses**.

## noon Do not put a *12* in front of it.
See **midnight** and **times**.

## no one

## norm See the **average, mean, median, norm** entry.

## North America See **Western Hemisphere**.

## North Atlantic Treaty Organization *NATO* is acceptable in all references, but use it sparingly. A phrase such as *the alliance* is less burdensome to the reader.

## North Carolina Abbrev.: *N.C.* See **state names**.

## North Dakota Abbrev.: *N.D.* See **state names**.

## Northeast region As de-

fined by the U.S. Census Bureau, the nine-state region is broken into two divisions — the *New England* states and the *Middle Atlantic* states.

Connecticut, Maine, Massachusetts, New Hampshire, Rhode Island and Vermont are the *New England* states.

New Jersey, New York and Pennsylvania are classified as the *Middle Atlantic* states.

See **Midwest region**; **South**; and **West** for the bureau's other regional breakdowns.

**Northern Ireland** Use *Northern Ireland* after the names of all communities in datelines.

See **datelines** and **United Kingdom**.

**north, northern, northeast, northwest** See the **directions and regions** entry.

**Northrop Grumman Corp.** Headquarters is in Los Angeles.

**North Slope** The portion of Alaska north of Brooks Range, a string of mountains extending across the northern part of the state.

**North Warning System** A system of long-range radar stations along the 70th parallel in North America. Previous system, known as the Distant Early Warning (DEW) line, was deactivated in 1985.

**Northwest Airlines** Headquarters is in Eagan, Minn.

**Northwest Territories** A territorial section of Canada. Do not abbreviate. Use in datelines after the names of all cities and towns in the territory.

See **Canada**.

**nouns** The abbreviation *n.* is used in this book to identify the spelling of the noun forms of words frequently misspelled.

**Nova Scotia** One of the three Maritime Provinces of Canada. Do not abbreviate.

See **datelines**.

**November** See **months**.

**Novocain** A trademark for a drug used as a local anesthetic. It also may be called *procaine*.

**nowadays** Not *nowdays*.

**Nuclear Regulatory Commission** This commission has taken over the regulatory functions previously performed by the Atomic Energy Commission.

*NRC* is acceptable on second reference, but *the agency* or *the commission* is preferred.

**nuclear terminology** In reporting on nuclear energy, include the definitions of appropriate terms, especially those related to radiation.

**core** The part of a nuclear reactor that contains its fissionable fuel. In a reactor core, atoms of fuel, such as uranium, are split. This releases energy in the form of heat which, in turn, is used to boil water for steam. The steam powers a turbine, and the turbine drives a generator to produce electricity.

**fission** The splitting of the nucleus of an atom, releasing energy.

**meltdown** The worst possible

nuclear accident in which the reactor core overheats to such a degree that the fuel melts. If the fuel penetrates its protective housing, radioactive materials will be released into the environment.

**rad** The standard unit of measurement for absorbed radiation. A *millirad* is a thousandth of a rad. There is considerable debate among scientists whether there is any safe level of absorption.

**radiation** Invisible particles or waves given off by radioactive material, such as uranium. Radiation can damage or kill body cells, resulting in latent cancers, genetic damage or death.

**rem** The standard unit of measurement of absorbed radiation in living tissue, adjusted for different kinds of radiation so that 1 rem of any radiation will produce the same biological effect. A millirem is a thousandth of a rem.

A diagnostic chest X-ray involves between 20 millirems and 30 millirems of radiation. Each American, on average, receives 100 millirems to 200 millirems of radiation a year from natural "background" sources, such as cosmic rays, and man-made sources, such as diagnostic X-rays. There is considerable debate among scientists over the safety of repeated low doses of radiation.

**roentgen** The standard measure of X-ray exposure.

**uranium** A metallic, radioactive element used as fuel in nuclear reactors.

**numerals** A numeral is a figure, letter, word or group of words expressing a number.

Roman numerals use the letters *I, V, X, L, C, D* and *M*. Use Roman numerals for wars and to show personal sequence for animals and people: *World War II, Native Dancer II, King George VI, Pope John XXIII*. See **Roman numerals**.

Arabic numerals use the figures *1, 2, 3, 4, 5, 6, 7, 8, 9* and *0*. Use Arabic forms unless Roman numerals are specifically required. See **Arabic numerals**.

The figures *1, 2, 10, 101*, etc. and the corresponding words — *one, two, ten, one hundred one*, etc. — are called cardinal numbers. The term ordinal number applies to *1st, 2nd, 10th, 101st, first, second, tenth, one hundred first*, etc.

Follow these guidelines in using numerals:

SENTENCE START: Spell out a numeral at the beginning of a sentence. If necessary, recast the sentence. There is one exception — a numeral that identifies a calendar year.

Wrong: *993 freshmen entered the college last year.*

Right: *Last year 993 freshmen entered the college.*

Right: *1976 was a very good year.*

CASUAL USES: Spell out casual expressions:

*A thousand times no! Thanks a million. He walked a quarter of a mile.*

PROPER NAMES: Use words or numerals according to an organization's practice: *3M, Twentieth Century Fund, Big Ten.*

FRACTIONS: See the **fractions** entry.

DECIMALS: See the **decimal units** entry.

FIGURES OR WORDS?
For ordinals:
—Spell out *first* through *ninth*

when they indicate sequence in time or location: *first base, the First Amendment, he was first in line.* Starting with *10th* use figures.

—Use *1st, 2nd, 3rd, 4th,* etc. when the sequence has been assigned in forming names. The principal examples are geographic, military and political designations such as *1st Ward, 7th Fleet* and *1st Sgt.* See examples in the separate entries listed below.

For cardinal numbers, consult the following separate entries:

| | |
|---|---|
| **act numbers** | **latitude and longitude** |
| **addresses** | **mile** |
| **ages** | **millions, billions** |
| **aircraft names** | **monetary units** |
| **amendments to the Constitution** | **No.** |
| **betting odds** | **page numbers** |
| **century** | **parallels** |
| **channel** | **percent** |
| **chapters** | **political divisions** |
| **congressional districts** | **proportions** |
| **course numbers** | **ratios** |
| **court decisions** | **recipes** |
| **court names** | **room numbers** |
| **dates** | **route numbers** |
| **decades** | **scene numbers** |
| **decimal units** | **serial numbers** |
| **dimensions** | **sizes** |
| **district** | **spacecraft designations** |
| **earthquakes** | **speeds** |
| **election returns** | **telephone** |
| **fleet** | **temperatures** |
| **formula** | **times** |
| **fractions** | **weights** |
| **handicaps (sports)** | **years** |
| **highway designations** | |

SOME PUNCTUATION AND USAGE EXAMPLES:
—*Act 1, Scene 2*
—*a 5-year-old girl*
—*DC-10* but *747B*
—*a 5-4 court decision*
—*2nd District Court*
—*the 1980s, the '80s*
—*the House voted 230-205.*
(Fewer than 1,000 votes.)
—*Jimmy Carter defeated*

*Gerald Ford 40,827,292 to 39,146,157.* (More than 1,000 votes.)
—*Carter defeated Ford 10 votes to 2 votes in Little Junction.* (To avoid confusion with ratio.)
—*5 cents, $1.05, $650,000, $2.45 million*
—*No. 3 choice,* but *Public School 3*
—*0.6 percent, 1 percent, 6.5 percent*
—*a pay increase of 12 percent to 15 percent.* Or: *a pay increase of between 12 percent and 15 percent*
Also: *from $12 million to $14 million*
—*a ratio of 2-to-1, a 2-1 ratio*
—*a 4-3 score*
—*(350) 262-4600*
—*minus 10, zero, 60 degrees*
OTHER USES: For uses not covered by these listings: Spell out whole numbers below 10, use figures for 10 and above. Typical examples: *They had three sons and two daughters. They had a fleet of 10 station wagons and two buses.*

IN A SERIES: Apply the appropriate guidelines: *They had 10 dogs, six cats and 97 hamsters. They had four four-room houses, 10 three-room houses and 12 10-room houses.*

**nuns** See **sister**.

**Nuremberg** Use this spelling for the city in Germany, instead of Nuernberg, in keeping with widespread practice.

**nylon** Not a trademark.

# O

**oasis, oases**

**obscenities, profanities, vulgarities** Do not use them in stories unless they are part of direct quotations and there is a compelling reason for them.

Try to find a way to give the reader a sense of what was said without using the specific word or phrase. If a profanity, obscenity or vulgarity must be used, flag the story at the top:
**Eds: Note contents of 4th graf.**

Confine the offending language, in quotation marks, to a separate paragraph that can be deleted easily by editors who do not want to use it.

In reporting profanity that normally would use the words *damn* or *god*, lowercase *god* and use the following forms: *damn, damn it, goddamn it.* (Do not change *damn it* to *darn it.*)

If a full quote that contains an obscenity, profanity or vulgarity cannot be dropped but there is no compelling reason for the offensive language, replace the letters of the offensive word with hyphens, using only an initial letter.

When the subject matter of a story may be considered offensive, but the story does not contain quoted profanity, obscenities or vulgarities, flag the story at the top:

**Eds: Note contents.**
For guidelines on racial or ethnic slurs, see the **nationalities and races** entry.

**Occidental Petroleum Corp.** Headquarters is in Los Angeles.

**Occident, Occidental** Capitalize when referring to Europe, the Western Hemisphere or an inhabitant of these regions.

**Occupational Safety and Health Administration** *OSHA* is acceptable on second reference.

**occupational titles** They are always lowercase. See **titles**.

**occur, occurred, occurring** Also: *occurrence.*

**ocean** The five, from the largest to the smallest: Pacific Ocean, Atlantic Ocean, Indian Ocean, Antarctic Ocean, Arctic Ocean.

Lowercase *ocean* standing alone or in plural uses: *the ocean, the Atlantic and Pacific oceans.*

**oceangoing**

**October** See **months**.

**odd-** Follow with a hyphen:
odd-looking     odd-numbered
See **betting odds**.

## oddsmaker

### off-Broadway, off-off-Broadway See the **Broadway, off-Broadway, off-off-Broadway** entry.

**office** Capitalize *office* when it is part of an agency's formal name: *Office of Management and Budget.*
Lowercase all other uses, including phrases such as: *the office of the attorney general, the U.S. attorney's office.*
See **Oval Office**.

### officeholder

**offline** (No hyphen is an exception to Webster's.)

**off of** The *of* is unnecessary: *He fell off the bed.* Not: *He fell off of the bed.*

**off-, -off** Follow Webster's New World College Dictionary. Hyphenate if not listed there.
Some commonly used combi-nations with a hyphen:

| | |
|---|---|
| off-color | off-white |
| off-peak | send-off |

Some combinations without a hyphen:

| | |
|---|---|
| cutoff | offside |
| liftoff | offstage |
| offhand | playoff |
| offset | standoff |
| offshore | takeoff |

**Ohio** Do not abbreviate. See **state names**.

**oil** In shipping, oil and oil products normally are measured by the ton. For news stories, convert these tonnage figures to gallons.
There are 42 gallons to each barrel of oil. The number of barrels per ton varies, depending on the type of oil product.
To convert tonnage to gallons:
—Determine the type of oil.
—Consult the table below to find out how many barrels per ton for that type of oil.
—Multiply the number of tons by the number of barrels per ton.

## OIL EQUIVALENCY TABLE

| Type of Product | Barrels Per Short Ton (2,000 lbs.) | Barrels Per Metric Ton (2,204.6 lbs.) | Barrels Per Long Ton (2,240 lbs.) |
|---|---|---|---|
| crude oil, foreign | 6.349 | 6.998 | 7.111 |
| crude oil, domestic | 6.770 | 7.463 | 7.582 |
| gasoline and naphtha | 7.721 | 8.511 | 8.648 |
| kerosene | 7.053 | 7.775 | 7.900 |
| distillate fuel oil | 6.580 | 7.253 | 7.369 |
| residual fuel oil | 6.041 | 6.660 | 6.766 |
| lubricating oil | 6.349 | 6.998 | 7.111 |
| lubricating grease | 6.665 | 7.346 | 7.464 |
| wax | 7.134 | 7.864 | 7.990 |
| asphalt | 5.540 | 6.106 | 6.205 |
| coke | 4.990 | 5.500 | 5.589 |
| road oil | 5.900 | 6.503 | 6.608 |
| jelly and petrolatum | 6.665 | 7.346 | 7.464 |
| liquefied pet. gas | 10.526 | 11.603 | 11.789 |
| Gilsonite | 5.515 | 6.080 | 6.177 |

The result is the number of barrels in the shipment.

—Multiply the number of barrels by 42. The result is the number of gallons.

EXAMPLE: A tanker spills 20,000 metric tons of foreign crude petroleum. The table shows 6.998 barrels of foreign crude petroleum per metric ton. Multiply 6.998 x 20,000 equals 139,960 barrels. Multiply 139,960 x 42 is 5,878,320 gallons.

TABLE: The table on the previous page is based on figures supplied by the American Petroleum Institute.

**OK, OK'd, OK'ing, OKs** Do not use *okay*.

**Oklahoma** Abbrev.: *Okla.* See **state names**.

**Oklahoma City** Stands alone in datelines.

**Old City of Jerusalem** The walled part of the city.

**Old South** The South before the Civil War. See **New South**.

**Old Testament** See **Bible**.

**old-time, old-timer, old times**

**Old West** The American West as it was being settled in the 19th century.

**Old World** The Eastern Hemisphere: Asia, Europe, Africa. The term also may be an allusion to European culture and customs.

**Olympic Airways** Headquarters is in Athens, Greece.

**Olympics** Capitalize all references to the international athletic contests: *the Olympics, the Winter Olympics, the Olympic Games, an Olympic-size pool,* but lowercase *the games* when used alone.

An Olympic-size pool is 50 meters long by 25 meters wide.

**on** Do not use *on* before a date or day of the week when its absence would not lead to confusion, except at the beginning of a sentence: *The meeting will be held Monday. He will be inaugurated Jan. 20. On Sept. 3, the committee will meet to discuss the issue.*

Use *on* to avoid an awkward juxtaposition of a date and a proper name: *John met Mary on Monday. He told Reagan on Thursday that the bill was doomed.*

Use *on* also to avoid any suggestion that a date is the object of a transitive verb: *The House killed on Tuesday a bid to raise taxes. The Senate postponed on Wednesday its consideration of a bill to reduce import duties.*

**one-** Hyphenate when used in writing fractions:

one-half       one-third

Use phrases such as *a half* or *a third* if precision is not intended.

See **fractions**.

**one another** See the **each other, one another** entry.

**one person, one vote** The adjective form: *one-person, one-vote. He supports the principle of one person, one vote. The one-man, one-vote rule.*

Supreme Court rulings all use the phrase *one person, one vote,* not *one man, one vote.*

**one-sided**

**one time, one-time** *He did it one time. She is a one-time friend.*

**online** One word in all cases for the computer connection term.

**Ontario** This Canadian province is the nation's first in total population and second to Quebec in area. Do not abbreviate.
See **datelines**.

**operas** See **composition titles**.

**opinion polls** See the **polls and surveys** entry.

**opossum** The only North American marsupial. No apostrophe is needed to indicate missing letters in a phrase such as *playing possum.*

**oral, verbal, written** Use *oral* to refer to spoken words: *He gave an oral promise.*

Use *written* to refer to words committed to paper: *We had a written agreement.*

Use *verbal* to compare words with some other form of communication: *His tears revealed the sentiments that his poor verbal skills could not express.*

**ordinal numbers** See **numerals**.

**Oregon** Abbrev.: *Ore.* See **state names**.

**Oreo** A trademark for a brand of chocolate sandwich cookie held together by a white filling.

The use of the word by blacks indicates belief that another black is "black outside but white inside."

**Organization of American States** *OAS* is acceptable on second reference. Headquarters is in Washington.

**Organization of Petroleum Exporting Countries** Use the full name for most first references. *OPEC* may be used on first reference in business-oriented copy, but the body of the story should identify it as the shortened form of the name.

The 11 OPEC members: Algeria, Indonesia, Iran, Iraq, Kuwait, Libya, Nigeria, Qatar, Saudi Arabia, United Arab Emirates, Venezuela.

Headquarters is in Vienna, Austria.

**organizations and institutions** Capitalize the full names of organizations and institutions: *the American Medical Association; First Presbyterian Church; General Motors Corp.; Harvard University, Harvard University Medical School; the Procrastinators Club; the Society of Professional Journalists.*

Retain capitalization if *Co., Corp.* or a similar word is deleted from the full proper name: *General Motors.* See **company**; **corporation**; and **incorporated**.

SUBSIDIARIES: Capitalize the names of major subdivisions: *the Pontiac Motor Division of General Motors.*

INTERNAL ELEMENTS: Use lowercase for internal elements of an organization when they have names that are widely used generic terms: *the board of directors of General Motors, the board of trustees of Columbia University, the history department of Harvard University, the sports department of the Daily Citizen-Leader.*

Capitalize internal elements

of an organization when they have names that are not widely used generic terms: *the General Assembly of the World Council of Churches, the House of Delegates of the American Medical Association, the House of Bishops and House of Deputies of the Episcopal Church.*

FLIP-FLOPPED NAMES: Retain capital letters when commonly accepted practice flops a name to delete the word of: *College of the Holy Cross, Holy Cross College; Harvard School of Dental Medicine, Harvard Dental School.*

Do not, however, flop formal names that are known to the public with the word of: *Massachusetts Institute of Technology,* for example, not *Massachusetts Technology Institute.*

ABBREVIATIONS AND ACRONYMS: Some organizations and institutions are widely recognized by their abbreviations: *Alcoa, GOP, NAACP, NATO.* For guidelines on when such abbreviations may be used, see the individual listings and the entries under **abbreviations and acronyms** and **second reference**.

**Orient, Oriental** Capitalize when referring to the Far East nations of Asia and nearby islands. *Asian* is the preferred term for an inhabitant of these regions.

Also: *Oriental rug, Oriental cuisine.*

**Orlon** A trademark for a form of acrylic fiber similar to nylon.

**orthodox** Capitalize when referring to membership in or the activities of an Eastern Orthodox church. See **Eastern Orthodox Churches**.

Capitalize also in phrases such as *Orthodox Judaism* or *Or-*

*thodox Jew.* See **Jewish congregations**.

Do not describe a member of an Eastern Orthodox church as a *Protestant.* Use a phrase such as *Orthodox Christian* instead.

Lowercase *orthodox* in nonreligious uses: *an orthodox procedure.*

**Orthodox Church in America** See **Eastern Orthodox churches**.

**Osama bin Laden** Use *bin Laden* on second reference, an exception to the general rule on Arabic names. It is the family preference for the last name. .

**Oscar, Oscars** See **Academy Awards**.

**Ottawa** The capital of Canada stands alone in datelines.

**Ouija** A trademark for a board used in seances.

**ounce (dry)** Units of dry volume are not customarily carried to this level.

See **pint (dry)**.

**ounce (liquid)** See **fluid ounce**.

**ounce (weight)** It is defined as 437.5 grains.

The metric equivalent is approximately 28 grams.

To convert to grams, multiply by 28 (5 ounces x 28 = 140 grams).

See **grain** and **gram**.

**-out** Follow Webster's New World. Hyphenate nouns and adjectives not listed there.

Some frequently used words (all nouns):

| | |
|---|---|
| cop-out | hide-out |

fade-out          pullout
fallout           walkout
flameout          washout

Two words for verbs:

fade out          walk out
hide out          wash out
pull out

**out-** Follow Webster's New World. Hyphenate if not listed there.

Some frequently used words:

outargue          outpost
outbox            output
outdated          outscore
outfield          outstrip
outfox            outtalk
outpatient (n., adj.)

**Outer Banks** The sandy islands along the North Carolina coast.

**out of bounds** But as a modifier: *out-of-bounds. The ball went out of bounds. He took an out-of-bounds pass.*

**out of court, out-of-court** *They settled out of court. He accepted an out-of-court settlement.*

**Oval Office** The White House office of the president.

**-over** Follow Webster's New World Dictionary. Hyphenate if not listed there.

Some frequently used words (all are nouns, some also are used as adjectives):

carry-over        stopover
holdover          walkover
takeover

Use two words when any of these occurs as a verb.

See **suffixes**.

**over** It generally refers to spatial relationships: *The plane flew over the city.*

*More than* is preferred with numerals: *Their salaries went up more than $20 a week.*

**over-** Follow Webster's New World. A hyphen seldom is used. Some frequently used words:

overbuy           overrate
overexert         override

See the **overall** entry.

**overall** A single word in adjectival and adverbial use: *Overall, the Democrats succeeded. Overall policy.*

The word for the garment is *overalls.*

**owner** Not a formal title. Always lowercase: *Atlanta Braves owner Ted Turner.*

**Oyez** Not *oyes.* The cry of court and public officials to command silence.

**Ozark Mountains** Or simply: *the Ozarks.*

# P

**Pablum** A trademark for a soft, bland food for infants.

In lowercase, *pablum* means any over-simplified or bland writing or idea.

**pacemaker** Formerly a trademark, now a generic term for a device that electronically helps a person's heart maintain a steady beat.

**Pacific Ocean** See **ocean**.

**Pacific Standard Time (PST), Pacific Daylight Time (PDT)** See **time zones**.

**page numbers** Use figures and capitalize *page* when used with a figure. When a letter is appended to the figure, capitalize it but do not use a hyphen: *Page 1, Page 10, Page 20A.*

One exception: *It's a Page One story.*

**paintings** See **composition titles**.

**palate, palette, pallet** *Palate* is the roof of the mouth.

A *palette* is an artist's paint board.

A *pallet* is a bed.

**Palestine Liberation Organization** Not *Palestinian. PLO* is acceptable in all references.

**pan-** Prefix meaning "all" takes no hyphen when combined with a common noun:

panchromatic    pantheism

Most combinations with *pan-* are proper nouns, however, and both *pan-* and the proper name it is combined with are capitalized:

Pan-African    Pan-Asiatic
Pan-American

**Panama City** Use *PANAMA CITY, Fla.,* or *PANAMA CITY, Panama,* in datelines to avoid confusion between the two.

**pantsuit** Not *pants suit.*

**pantyhose**

**papal nuncio** Do not confuse with an *apostolic delegate.* See the **apostolic delegate, papal nuncio** entry.

**Pap test** (or **smear**) After George Papanicolaou, the U.S. anatomist who developed this test for cervical and uterine cancer.

**parallel, paralleled, paralleling**

**parallels** Use figures and lowercase to identify the imaginary locater lines that ring the globe from east to west. They are measured in units of 0 to 90 degrees north or south of the equator.

Examples: *4th parallel north,*

*89th parallel south*, or, if location north or south of the equator is obvious: *19th parallel.*
See the **latitude and longitude** entry.

**pardon, parole, probation** The terms often are confused, but each has a specific meaning. Do not use them interchangeably.

A *pardon* forgives and releases a person from further punishment. It is granted by a chief of state or a governor. By itself, it does not expunge a record of conviction, if one exists, and it does not by itself restore civil rights.

A *general pardon*, usually for political offenses, is called *amnesty.*

*Parole* is the release of a prisoner before the sentence has expired, on condition of good behavior. It is granted by a parole board, part of the executive branch of government, and can be revoked only by the board.

*Probation* is the suspension of sentence for a person convicted, but not yet imprisoned, on condition of good behavior. It is imposed and revoked only by a judge.

**parentheses** See the entry in the **Punctuation** chapter.

**parent-teacher association** *PTA* is acceptable in all references. Capitalize when part of a proper name: *the Franklin School Parent-Teacher Association* or *the Parent-Teacher Association of the Franklin School.*

**pari-mutuel**

**Paris** The city in France stands alone in datelines.

**parish** Capitalize as part of the formal name for a church congregation or a governmental jurisdiction: *St. John's Parish, Jefferson Parish.*

Lowercase standing alone or in plural combinations: *the parish, St. John's and St. Mary's parishes, Jefferson and Plaquemines parishes.*

See **county** for additional guidelines on governmental jurisdictions.

**parishioner** Note spelling for this member of a parish, an administrative district of various churches, particularly Roman Catholic and Anglican churches. Do not use for Judaism or non-hierarchal Protestant denominations.

**Parkinson's disease** After James Parkinson, the English physician who described this degenerative disease of later life.

**Parkinson's law** After C. Northcote Parkinson, the British economist who came to the satirical conclusion that work expands to fill the time allotted to it.

**parliament** See **foreign legislative bodies**.

**parliamentary** Lowercase unless part of a proper name.

**parole** See the **pardon, parole, probation** entry.

**partial quotes** See **quotation marks** in the **Punctuation** chapter.

**particles** See **foreign names** entry.

**part time, part-time** Hyphenate when used as a compound modifier: *She works part time. She has a part-time job.*

**party** See the **political parties and philosophies** entry.

**party affiliation** Let relevance be the guide in determining whether to include a political figure's party affiliation in a story.

Party affiliation is pointless in some stories, such as an account of a governor accepting a button from a poster child.

It will occur naturally in many political stories.

For stories between these extremes, include party affiliation if readers need it for understanding or are likely to be curious about what it is.

GENERAL FORMS: When party designation is given, use any of these approaches as logical in constructing a story:

—*Democratic Sen. Hubert Humphrey of Minnesota said ...*

—*Sen. Hubert Humphrey, D-Minn., said ...*

—*Sen. Hubert Humphrey also spoke. The Minnesota Democrat said ...*

—*Rep. Morris Udall of Arizona is seeking the Democratic presidential nomination.* Not: *Rep. Morris Udall, D-Ariz., is seeking the Democratic ...*

In stories about party meetings, such as a report on the Republican National Convention, no specific reference to party affiliation is necessary unless an individual is not a member of the party in question.

SHORT-FORM PUNCTUATION: Set short forms such as *D-Minn.* off from a name by commas, as illustrated above.

Use the abbreviations listed in the entries for each state. (No

abbreviations for *Alaska, Hawaii, Idaho, Iowa, Maine, Ohio, Texas* and *Utah.*)

Use *R-* for Republicans, *D-* for Democrats, and three-letter combinations for other affiliations: *Sen. James Buckley, R-Con-N.Y., spoke with Sen. Harry Byrd, D-Ind-Va.*

FORM FOR U.S. HOUSE MEMBERS: The normal practice for U.S. House members is to identify them by party and state. In contexts where state affiliation is clear and home city is relevant, such as a state election roundup, identify representatives by party and city: *U.S. Reps. Thomas P. O'Neill Jr., D-Cambridge, and Margaret Heckler, R-Wellesley.* If this option is used, be consistent throughout the story.

FORM FOR STATE LEGISLATORS: Short-form listings showing party and home city are appropriate in state wire stories. For trunk wire stories, the normal practice is to say that the individual is a *Republican* or *Democrat.* Use a short-form listing only if the legislator's home city is relevant.

See **legislative titles**.

**pass** See the **adopt, approve, enact, pass** entry.

**passenger lists** When providing a list of victims in a disaster, arrange names alphabetically according to last name, include street addresses if available, and use a paragraph for each name:

*Jones, Joseph, 260 Town St., Sample, N.Y.*

*Williams, Susan, 780 Main St., Example, N.J.*

**passenger mile** One passenger carried one mile, or its equivalent, such as two passengers carried one-half mile.

### passer-by, passers-by

**Passover** The weeklong Jewish commemoration of the deliverance of the ancient Hebrews from slavery in Egypt. Occurs in March or April.
Capitalize *Seder* in references to the *Passover* feast commemorating the exodus.

### pasteurize

**pastor** See **religious titles** and the entry for the individual's denomination.

**patriarch** Lowercase when describing someone of great age and dignity.
Capitalize as a formal title before a name in some religious uses. See **Eastern Orthodox churches**; **religious titles**; and **Roman Catholic Church**.

### patrolman, patrolwoman
Capitalize before a name only if the word is a formal title. In some cities, the formal title is *police officer*.
See **titles**.

### patrol, patrolled, patrolling

### payload

**PDA** *Personal digital assistant.*

**PDF** *Portable Document Format*, a file format for Adobe Acrobat.

### peacekeeping

### peacemaker, peacemaking

### peace offering

### peacetime

**peacock** It applies only to the male. The female is a *peahen.* Both are *peafowl.*

**peasant** Avoid the term, which is often derogatory, in referring to farm laborers (except in quotes or an organization name).

**peck** A unit of dry measure equal to 8 dry quarts or one-fourth of a bushel.
The metric equivalent is approximately 8.8 liters.
To convert to liters, multiply by 8.8 (5 pecks x 8.8 = 44 liters). See **liter**.

**pedal, peddle** When riding a bicycle or similar vehicle, you *pedal* it.
When selling something, you may *peddle* it.

### peddler

### pell-mell

**penance** See **sacraments**.

**peninsula** Capitalize as part of a proper name: *the Florida Peninsula, the Upper Peninsula of Michigan.*

**penitentiary** See the **prison, jail** entry.

**Pennsylvania** Abbrev.: *Pa.* Legally a commonwealth, not a state.
See **state** and **state names**.

**Pennsylvania Dutch** The individuals are of German descent. The word *Dutch* is a corruption of *Deutsch*, the German word for "German."

**penny-wise** See **-wise**.
Also: *pound-foolish*.

**Pentecost** The seventh Sunday after Easter.

**Pentecostalism** See **religious movements**.

**people's** Use this possessive form when the word occurs in the formal name of a nation: *the People's Republic of China*.
Use this form also in such phrases as *the people's desire for freedom*.

**people, persons** Use *person* when speaking of an individual: *One person waited for the bus*.
The word *people* is preferred to persons in all plural uses. For example: *Thousands of people attended the fair. What will people say? There were 17 people in the room*.
*Persons* should be used only when it is in a direct quote or part of a title as in *Bureau of Missing Persons*.
*People* also is a collective noun that takes a plural verb when used to refer to a single race or nation: *The American people are united*. In this sense, the plural is *peoples*: *The peoples of Africa speak many languages*.

**PepsiCo Inc.** Note the in-capped *C*. Formerly the Pepsi-Cola Co.
Headquarters is in Purchase, N.Y.

**Pepsi, Pepsi-Cola** Trademarks for a brand of cola soft drink.

**percent** One word. It takes a singular verb when standing alone or when a singular word follows an *of* construction: *The teacher said 60 percent was a failing grade. He said 50 percent of the membership was there*.
It takes a plural verb when a plural word follows an *of* construction: *He said 50 percent of the members were there*.
*Use figures: 1 percent, 2.5 percent* (use decimals, not fractions), *10 percent*.
For amounts less than 1 percent, precede the decimal with a zero: *The cost of living rose 0.6 percent*.

**periods** See the entry in the **Punctuation** chapter.

**perk** A shortened form of *perquisite*, often used by legislators to describe fringe benefits. In the state of New York, legislators also use the word *lulu* to describe the benefits they receive in lieu of pay.
When either word is used, define it.

**permissible**

**Persian Gulf** Use this long-established name for the body of water off the southern coast of Iran.
Some Arab nations call it the *Arabian Gulf*. Use *Arabian Gulf* only in direct quotations and explain in the text that the body of water is more commonly known as the *Persian Gulf*.

**personifications** Capitalize them: *Grim Reaper, John Barleycorn, Mother Nature, Old Man Winter, Sol*, etc.

**-persons** Do not use coined words such as *chairperson* or *spokesperson* in regular text.
Instead, use *chairman* or

*spokesman* if referring to a man or the office in general. Use *chairwoman* or *spokeswoman* if referring to a woman. Or, if applicable, use a neutral word such as *leader* or *representative.*

Use *chairperson* or similar coinage only in direct quotations or when it is the formal description for an office.

**persons** See the **people, persons** entry.

**persuade** See the **convince, persuade** entry.

**Peter Principle** It is: Employees are promoted until they reach their level of incompetence.

From the book by Laurence J. Peter.

**petty officer** See **military titles**.

**PG, PG-13** The *parental guidance* ratings. See **movie ratings**.

**phase** See the **faze, phase** entry.

**Ph.D., Ph.D.s** The preferred form is to say a person *holds a doctorate* and name the individual's area of specialty.

See **academic degrees** and **doctor**.

**phenomenon, phenomena**

**Philadelphia** The city in Pennsylvania stands alone in datelines.

**Philippines** In datelines, give the name of a city or town followed by *Philippines*:

MANILA, Philippines (AP) —

Specify the name of an individual island, if needed, in the text.

In stories: *the Philippines* or *the Philippine Islands* as the construction of a sentence dictates.

The people are *Filipinos*. The language is *Filipino*, an offshoot of Tagalog.

**Phoenix** The city in Arizona stands alone in datelines.

**Photoshop** Trademark for a brand of photo editing software.

**Photostat** A trademark for a type of photocopy.

**physician assistant** No apostrophe in this medical profession title.

**piano, pianos**

**pica** A unit of measure in printing, equal to a fraction less than one-sixth of an inch.

A pica contains 12 points.

**picket, pickets, picketed, picket line** *Picket* is both the verb and the noun. Do not use *picketer.*

**picnic, picnicked, picnicking, picnicker**

**pico-** A prefix denoting one-trillionth of a unit. Move the decimal point 12 places to the left in converting to the basic unit: 2,999,888,777,666.5 picoseconds equals 2.9998887776665 seconds.

**pigeon**

**pigeonhole** (n. and v.)

**Pikes Peak** No apostrophe. After Zebulon Montgomery Pike, a U.S. general and explorer. The 14,115-foot peak is in the Rockies of central Colorado.

**pile up** (v.) **pileup** (n., adj.)

**pill** Do not capitalize in references to oral contraceptives. Use *birth control pill* on first reference if necessary for clarity.

**pilot** Not a formal title. Do not capitalize before a name. See **titles**.

**pingpong** A synonym for *table tennis*.
The trademark name is *Ping-Pong*.

**pint (dry)** Equal to 33.6 cubic inches, or one-half of a dry quart.
The metric equivalent is approximately 0.55 of a liter.
To convert to liters, multiply by 0.55 (5 dry pints x 0.55 is 2.75 liters).
See **liter** and **quart (dry)**.

**pint (liquid)** Equal to 16 fluid ounces, or two cups.
The approximate metric equivalents are 470 milliliters or 0.47 of a liter.
To convert to liters, multiply by 0.47 (4 pints x 0.47 is 1.88 liters).
See **liter**.

**Pinyin** The official Chinese spelling system.
See **Chinese names**.

**pipeline**

**Pittsburgh** The city in Pennsylvania stands alone in datelines.
The spelling is *Pittsburg* (no *h*) for communities in California, Illinois, Kansas, New Hampshire, Oklahoma and Texas.

**plains** See **Great Plains**.

**planets** Capitalize the proper names of planets: *Jupiter, Mars, Mercury, Neptune, Saturn, Uranus, Venus*. (*Pluto* was redefined as a dwarf planet by the International Astronomical Union in 2006.)
Capitalize *Earth* when used as the proper name of our planet: *The astronauts returned to Earth*.
Capitalize nouns and adjectives derived from the proper names of planets and other heavenly bodies: *Martian, Venusian*. But lowercase adjectives derived from other heavenly bodies: *solar, lunar*.
See **earth** and **heavenly bodies**.

**planning** Avoid the redundant *future planning*.

**plants** In general, lowercase the names of plants, but capitalize proper nouns or adjectives that occur in a name.
Some examples: *tree, fir, white fir, Douglas fir; Scotch pine; clover, white clover, white Dutch clover*.
If a botanical name is used, capitalize the first word; lowercase others: *pine tree* (*Pinus*), *red cedar* (*Juniperus virginiana*), *blue azalea* (*Callicarpa americana*), *Kentucky coffee tree* (*Gymnocladus dioica*).

**play titles** See **composition titles**.

**plead, pleaded, pleading** Do not use the colloquial past tense form, *pled*.

**Plexiglas** Note the single *s*. A trademark for plastic glass.

**plow** Not *plough*.

**plurality** See the **majority,**

Comp - 8    1nt - 4
G7th 11    SL - 5

Writing 17    format 19

Ethics 20

Conc 23
Doc 2C    Cro2 - ref - 24
25

Ex
#1 RADIO news
Copy

EX 2 - What not to
wear

Ex 3 - Press release
short

Ex 4 Press release
long

Ex 5 - PR web
Ex 5 Press R. PR Press release 200

**plurality** entry.

**plurals** Follow these guidelines in forming and using plural words:

MOST WORDS: Add *s*: *boys, girls, ships, villages.*

WORDS ENDING IN CH, S, SH, SS, X and Z: Add *es*: *churches, lenses, parishes, glasses, boxes, buzzes.* (*Monarchs* is an exception.)

WORDS ENDING IN IS: Change *is* to *es*: *oases, parentheses, theses.*

WORDS ENDING IN Y: If *y* is preceded by a consonant or *qu*, change *y* to *i* and add *es*: *armies, cities, navies, soliloquies.* (See PROPER NAMES below for an exception.)

Otherwise add *s*: *donkeys, monkeys.*

WORDS ENDING IN O: If *o* is preceded by a consonant, most plurals require *es*: *buffaloes, dominoes, echoes, heroes, potatoes.* But there are exceptions: *pianos.* See individual entries in this book for many of these exceptions.

WORDS ENDINGS IN F: In general, change *f* to *v* and add *es*: *leaves, selves.* (*Roof, roofs* is an exception.)

LATIN ENDINGS: Latin-root words ending in *us* change *us* to *i*: *alumnus, alumni.* (Words that have taken on English endings by common usage are exceptions: *prospectuses, syllabuses.*)

Most ending in *a* change to *ae*: *alumna, alumnae* (*formula, formulas* is an exception).

Most ending in *um* add *s*: *memorandums, referendums, stadiums.* Among those that still use the Latin ending: *addenda, curricula, media.*

Use the plural that Webster's New World lists as most common for a particular sense of word.

FORM CHANGE: *man, men; child, children; foot, feet; mouse, mice;* etc.

Caution: When *s* is used with any of these words it indicates possession and must be preceded by an apostrophe: *men's, children's,* etc.

WORDS THE SAME IN SINGULAR AND PLURAL: *corps, chassis, deer, moose, sheep,* etc.

The sense in a particular sentence is conveyed by the use of a singular or plural verb.

WORDS PLURAL IN FORM, SINGULAR IN MEANING: Some take singular verbs: *measles, mumps, news.*

Others take plural verbs: *grits, scissors.*

COMPOUND WORDS: Those written solid add *s* at the end: *cupfuls, handfuls, tablespoonfuls.*

For those that involve separate words or words linked by a hyphen, make the most significant word plural:

—Significant word first: *adjutants general, aides-de-camp, attorneys general, courts-martial, daughters-in-law, passers-by, postmasters general, presidents-elect, secretaries-general, sergeants major.*

—Significant word in the middle: *assistant attorneys general, deputy chiefs of staff.*

—Significant word last: *assistant attorneys, assistant corporation counsels, deputy sheriffs, lieutenant colonels, major generals.*

WORDS AS WORDS: Do not use *'s*: *His speech had too many "ifs," "ands" and "buts."* (Exception to Webster's New World.)

PROPER NAMES: Most ending in *es* or *s* or *z* add *es*: *Charleses, Joneses, Gonzalezes.*

Most ending in *y* add *s* even if preceded by a consonant: *the*

*Duffys, the Kennedys, the two Kansas Cities.* Exceptions include *Alleghenies* and *Rockies.*

For others, add *s: the Carters, the McCoys, the Mondales.*

FIGURES: Add *s: The custom began in the 1920s. The airline has two 727s. Temperatures will be in the low 20s. There were five size 7s.*

(No apostrophes, an exception to Webster's New World guideline under "apostrophe.")

SINGLE LETTERS: Use *'s: Mind your p's and q's. He learned the three R's and brought home a report card with four A's and two B's. The Oakland A's won the pennant.*

MULTIPLE LETTERS: Add *s: She knows her ABCs. I gave him five IOUs. Four VIPs were there.*

PROBLEMS, DOUBTS: Separate entries in this book give plurals for troublesome words and guidance on whether certain words should be used with singular or plural verbs and pronouns. See also **collective nouns** and **possessives**.

For questions not covered by this book, use the plural that Webster's New World lists as most common for a particular sense of a word.

Note also the guidelines that the dictionary provides under its "plural" entry.

**p.m., a.m.** Lowercase, with periods. Avoid the redundant *10 p.m. tonight.*

**pocket veto** Occurs only when Congress has adjourned. If Congress is in session, a bill that remains on the president's desk for 10 days becomes law without his signature. If Congress adjourns, however, a bill that fails to get his signature within 10 days is vetoed.

Many states have similar procedures, but the precise requirements vary.

**podium** See the **lectern, podium, pulpit, rostrum** entry.

**poetic license** It is valid for poetry, not news or feature stories.

See **colloquialisms** and **special contexts**.

**poetry** See **composition titles** for guidelines on the names of poems.

Capitalize the first word in a line of poetry unless the author deliberately has used lowercase for a special effect. Do not, however, capitalize the first word on indented lines that must be created simply because the writer's line is too long for the available printing width.

**poinsettia** Note the *ia.*

**point** Do not abbreviate. Capitalize as part of a proper name: *Point Pleasant.*

**point-blank**

**point (printing)** As a unit of measure in printing, a *point* equals a fraction less than a seventy-second of an inch. A pica contains 12 *points.*

See **pica**.

**Polaroid** A trademark for Polaroid Land instant-picture cameras and for transparent material containing embedded crystals capable of polarizing light.

**police department** In communities where this is the formal name, capitalize *police department* with or without the name of the community: *the Los Angeles Police Department, the Police Department.*

If a police agency has some other formal name such as *Division of Police,* use that name if it is the way the department is known to the public. If the story uses *police department* as a generic term for such an agency, put *police department* in lowercase.

If a police agency with an unusual formal name is known to the public as a *police department,* treat *police department* as the name, capitalizing it with or without the name of the community. Use the formal name only if there is a special reason in the story.

If the proper name cannot be determined for some reason, such as the need to write about a police agency from a distance, treat *police department* as the proper name, capitalizing it with or without the name of the community.

Lowercase *police department* in plural uses: *the Los Angeles and San Francisco police departments.*

Lowercase *the department* whenever it stands alone.

**police titles** See **military titles** and **titles**.

**policymaker, policymaking**

**polio** The preferred term for *poliomyelitis* and *infantile paralysis.*

**Politburo** Acceptable in all references for the *Political Bureau of the Communist Party.*

**political divisions** Use Arabic figures and capitalize the accompanying word when used with the figures: *1st Ward, 10th Ward,* *3rd Precinct, 22nd Precinct, the ward, the precinct.*

**political parties and philosophies** Capitalize both the name of the party and the word *party* if it is customarily used as part of the organization's proper name: *the Democratic Party, the Republican Party.*

Capitalize *Communist, Conservative, Democrat, Liberal, Republican, Socialist,* etc., when they refer to a specific party or its members. Lowercase these words when they refer to political philosophy (see examples below).

Lowercase the name of a philosophy in noun and adjective forms unless it is the derivative of a proper name: *communism, communist; fascism, fascist.* But: *Marxism, Marxist; Nazism, Nazi.*

EXAMPLES: *John Adams was a Federalist, but a man who subscribed to his philosophy today would be described as a federalist. The liberal Republican senator and his Conservative Party colleague said they believe that democracy and communism are incompatible. The Communist said he is basically a socialist who has reservations about Marxism.*

See **convention** and **party affiliation**.

**politicking**

**politics** Usually it takes a plural verb: *My politics are my own business.*

As a study or science, it takes a singular verb: *Politics is a demanding profession.*

**polls and surveys** Stories based on public opinion polls must include the basic information for an intelligent evaluation of the results. Such stories must be carefully worded to avoid exaggerating the meaning of the poll results.

Information that should be in every story based on a poll includes the answers to these questions:

1. Who did the poll and who paid for it? (The place to start is the polling firm, media outlet or other organization that conducted the poll. Be wary of polls paid for by candidates or interest groups. The release of poll results is often a campaign tactic or publicity ploy.

Any reporting of such polls must highlight the poll's sponsor, so that readers can be aware of the potential for bias from such sponsorship.)

2. How many people were interviewed? How were they selected? (Only a poll based on a scientific, random sample of a population — in which every member of the population has a known probability of inclusion — can be used as a reliable and accurate measure of that population's opinions. Polls based on submissions to Web sites or calls to 900-numbers may be good entertainment but have no validity. They should be avoided because the opinions come from people who select themselves to participate. If such unscientific pseudopolls are reported for entertainment value, they must never be portrayed as accurately reflecting public opinion and their failings must be highlighted.)

3. Who was interviewed? (A valid poll reflects only the opinions of the population that was sampled. A poll of business executives can only represent the views of business executives, not of all adults. Surveys conducted via the Internet — even if at-

tempted in a random manner, not based on self-selection — face special sampling difficulties that limit how the results may be generalized, even to the population of Internet users. Many political polls are based on interviews only with registered voters, since registration is usually required for voting. Close to the election, polls may be based only on "likely voters." If "likely voters" are used as the base, ask the pollster how that group was identified.)

4. How was the poll conducted — by telephone or some other way? (Avoid polls in which computers conduct telephone interviews using a recorded voice. Among the problems of these surveys are that they do not randomly select respondents within a household, as reliable polls do, and they cannot exclude children from polls in which adults or registered voters are the population of interest.)

5. When was the poll taken? (Opinion can change quickly, especially in response to events.)

6. What are the sampling error margins for the poll and for subgroups mentioned in the story? (The polling organization should provide sampling error margins, which are expressed as "plus or minus X percentage points," not "percent." The margin varies inversely with sample size: the fewer people interviewed, the larger the sampling error. Although some pollsters state sampling error or even poll results to a tenth of a percentage point, that implies a greater degree of precision than is possible from a sampling; sampling error margins should be rounded to the nearest half point and poll results to the nearest full point. If the opinions of a subgroup — women, for ex-

ample — are important to the story, the sampling error for that subgroup should be included. Subgroup error margins are always larger than the margin for the entire poll.)

7. What questions were asked and in what order? (Small differences in question wording can cause big differences in results. The exact question texts need not be in every poll story unless it is crucial or controversial.)

When writing and editing poll stories, here are areas for close attention:

—Do not exaggerate poll results. In particular, with pre-election polls, these are the rules for deciding when to write that the poll finds one candidate is leading another:

If the difference between the candidates is more than twice the sampling error margin, then the poll says one candidate is leading.

If the difference is less than the sampling error margin, the poll says that the race is close, that the candidates are "about even." (Do not use the term "statistical dead heat," which is inaccurate if there is any difference between the candidates; if the poll finds the candidates are tied, say they're tied.)

If the difference is at least equal to the sampling error but no more than twice the sampling error, then one candidate can be said to be "apparently leading" or "slightly ahead" in the race.

—Comparisons with other polls are often newsworthy. Earlier poll results can show changes in public opinion. Be careful comparing polls from different polling organizations. Different poll techniques can cause differing results.

—Sampling error is not the only source of error in a poll, but it is one that can be quantified. Question wording and order, interviewer skill and refusal to participate by respondents randomly selected for a sample are among potential sources of error in surveys.

—No matter how good the poll, no matter how wide the margin, the poll does not say one candidate will win an election. Polls can be wrong and the voters can change their minds before they cast their ballots.

## pom-pom, pompom

*Pom-pom* is sometimes used to describe a rapid firing automatic weapon. Define the word if it must be used.

A *pompom* (also sometimes spelled *pompon*) is a large ball of crepe paper or fluffed cloth, often waved by cheerleaders or atop a hat. It is also a flower that appears on some varieties of chrysanthemums.

**pontiff** Not a formal title. Always lowercase.

## pooh-pooh

**pope** Capitalize when used as a formal title before a name; lowercase in all other uses: *Pope Paul spoke to the crowd. At the close of his address, the pope gave his blessing.*

See **Roman Catholic Church** and **titles**.

**Popsicle** A trademark for a brand of flavored ice on a stick.

**popular names** See **capitalization**.

**pore, pour** The verb *pore* means to gaze intently or steadily:

*She pored over her books.*

The verb *pour* means to flow in a continuous stream: *It poured rain. He poured the coffee.*

## port, starboard

Nautical for left and right (when facing the bow, or forward). Port is left. Starboard is right. Change to *left* or *right* unless in direct quotes.

## Portuguese names

The family names of both the father and mother usually are considered part of a person's full name. In everyday use, customs sometimes vary with individuals and countries.

The normal sequence is given name, mother's family name, father's family name: *Maria Santos Ferreira.*

On second reference, use only the father's family name (*Ferreira*), unless the individual prefers or is widely known by a multiple last name (*Ferreira Castro*).

Some Portuguese use an *e* (for *and*) between the two names: *Joao Canto e Castro.* This would not be split on second reference, but would be *Canto e Castro.*

When a surname is preceded by *da, do, dos,* or *das*, include it in the second reference. *Jorge da Costa,* for example, would be *da Costa* on second reference.

A married woman adds her husband's surname to the end of hers. If *Maria Santos Ferreira* married *Joao Costa da Silva*, her full name would be *Maria Ferreira da Silva.*

Occasionally, a woman may choose not to take her husband's surname for personal reasons or because the mother's family has an aristocratic or famous surname. Use both surnames if the individual's choice is not known.

## possessives

Follow these guidelines:

PLURAL NOUNS NOT ENDING IN S: Add *'s*: *the alumni's contributions, women's rights.*

PLURAL NOUNS ENDING IN S: Add only an apostrophe: *the churches' needs, the girls' toys, the horses' food, the ships' wake, states' rights, the VIPs' entrance.*

NOUNS PLURAL IN FORM, SINGULAR IN MEANING: Add only an apostrophe: *mathematics' rules, measles' effects.* (But see INANIMATE OBJECTS below.)

Apply the same principle when a plural word occurs in the formal name of a singular entity: *General Motors' profits, the United States' wealth.*

NOUNS THE SAME IN SINGULAR AND PLURAL: Treat them the same as plurals, even if the meaning is singular: *one corps' location, the two deer's tracks, the lone moose's antlers.*

SINGULAR NOUNS NOT ENDING IN S: Add *'s*: *the church's needs, the girl's toys, the horse's food, the ship's route, the VIP's seat.*

Some style guides say that singular nouns ending in *s* sounds such as *ce, x,* and *z* may take either the apostrophe alone or *'s*. See SPECIAL EXPRESSIONS, but otherwise, for consistency and ease in remembering a rule, always use *'s* if the word does not end in the letter *s*: *Butz's policies, the fox's den, the justice's verdict, Marx's theories, the prince's life, Xerox's profits.*

SINGULAR COMMON NOUNS ENDING IN S: Add *'s* unless the next word begins with *s*: *the hostess's invitation, the hostess' seat; the witness's answer, the witness' story.*

SINGULAR PROPER NAMES ENDING IN S: Use only an apostrophe: *Achilles' heel, Agnes' book, Ceres' rites, Descartes' theories, Dickens' novels, Euripides' dramas, Hercules' labors, Jesus' life, Jules' seat, Kansas' schools, Moses' law, Socrates' life, Tennessee Williams' plays, Xerxes' armies.*

SPECIAL EXPRESSIONS: The following exceptions to the general rule for words not ending in *s* apply to words that end in an *s* sound and are followed by a word that begins with *s: for appearance' sake, for conscience' sake, for goodness' sake.* Use 's otherwise: *the appearance's cost, my conscience's voice.*

PRONOUNS: Personal interrogative and relative pronouns have separate forms for the possessive. None involve an apostrophe: *mine, ours, your, yours, his, hers, its, theirs, whose.*

Caution: If you are using an apostrophe with a pronoun, always double-check to be sure that the meaning calls for a contraction: *you're, it's, there's, who's.*

Follow the rules listed above in forming the possessives of other pronouns: *another's idea, others' plans, someone's guess.*

COMPOUND WORDS: Applying the rules above, add an apostrophe or 's to the word closest to the object possessed: *the major general's decision, the major generals' decisions, the attorney general's request, the attorneys general's request.* See the **plurals** entry for guidelines on forming the plurals of these words.

Also: *anyone else's attitude, John Adams Jr.'s father, Benjamin Franklin of Pennsylvania's motion.* Whenever practical, however, recast the phrase to avoid ambiguity: *the motion by Benjamin Franklin of Pennsylvania.*

JOINT POSSESSION, INDIVIDUAL POSSESSION: Use a possessive form after only the last word if ownership is joint: *Fred and Sylvia's apartment, Fred and Sylvia's stocks.*

Use a possessive form after both words if the objects are individually owned: *Fred's and Sylvia's books.*

DESCRIPTIVE PHRASES: Do not add an apostrophe to a word ending in *s* when it is used primarily in a descriptive sense: *citizens band radio, a Cincinnati Reds infielder, a teachers college, a Teamsters request, a writers guide.*

Memory Aid: The apostrophe usually is not used if *for* or *by* rather than *of* would be appropriate in the longer form: *a radio band for citizens, a college for teachers, a guide for writers, a request by the Teamsters.*

An 's is required, however, when a term involves a plural word that does not end in *s: a children's hospital, a people's republic, the Young Men's Christian Association.*

DESCRIPTIVE NAMES: Some governmental, corporate and institutional organizations with a descriptive word in their names use an apostrophe; some do not. Follow the user's practice: *Actors' Equity, Diners Club, the Ladies' Home Journal, the National Governors Association.* See separate entries for these and similar names frequently in the news.

QUASI POSSESSIVES: Follow the rules above in composing the possessive form of words that occur in such phrases as *a day's pay, two weeks' vacation, three days' work, your money's worth.*

Frequently, however, a hyphenated form is clearer: *a two-week vacation, a three-day job.*

DOUBLE POSSESSIVE: Two conditions must apply for a double possessive — a phrase such as *a friend of John's* — to occur: 1. The word after *of* must refer to an animate object, and 2. The word before *of* must involve only a portion of the animate object's possessions.

Otherwise, do not use the possessive form of the word after *of*: *The friends of John Adams mourned his death.* (All the friends were involved.) *He is a friend of the college.* (Not *college's*, because college is inanimate.)

Memory Aid: This construction occurs most often, and quite naturally, with the possessive forms of personal pronouns: *He is a friend of mine.*

INANIMATE OBJECTS: There is no blanket rule against creating a possessive form for an inanimate object, particularly if the object is treated in a personified sense. See some of the earlier examples, and note these: *death's call, the wind's murmur.*

In general, however, avoid excessive personalization of inanimate objects, and give preference to an *of* construction when it fits the makeup of the sentence. For example, the earlier references to *mathematics' rules* and *measles' effects* would better be phrased: *the rules of mathematics, the effects of measles.*

**post-** Follow Webster's New World. Hyphenate if not listed there.

Some words without a hyphen:

| | |
|---|---|
| postdate | postnuptial |
| postdoctoral | postoperative |
| postelection | postscript |
| postgraduate | postwar |

Some words that use a hyphen:

| | |
|---|---|
| post-bellum | post-mortem |

**post office** It may be used but it is no longer capitalized because the agency is now the *U.S. Postal Service.*

Use lowercase in referring to an individual office: *I went to the post office.*

**potato, potatoes**

**pothole**

**pound (monetary)** The English pound sign is not used. Convert the figures to dollars in most cases. Use a figure and spell out *pounds* if the actual figure is relevant.

**pound (weight)** Equal to 16 ounces. The metric equivalent is approximately 454 grams, or .45 kilograms.

To convert to kilograms, multiply the number of pounds by .45 (20 pounds x .45 equals 9 kilograms).

See **gram** and **kilogram**.

**pour** See the **pore, pour** entry.

**poverty level** An income level judged inadequate to provide a family or individual with the essentials of life. The figure for the United States is adjusted regularly to reflect changes in the Consumer Price Index.

**practitioner** See **Church of Christ, Scientist**.

**pre-** The rules in **prefixes** apply. The following examples of exceptions to first-listed spellings in Webster's New World are based on the general rule that a hyphen is used if a prefix ends in a vowel and the word that follows begins with the same vowel:

| | |
|---|---|
| pre-election | pre-establish |

pre-eminent    pre-exist
pre-empt

Otherwise, follow Webster's New World, hyphenating if not listed there. Some examples:

prearrange     prehistoric
precondition   preignition
precook        prejudge
predate        premarital
predecease     prenatal
predispose     pretax
preflight      pretest
preheat        prewar

Some hyphenated coinage, not listed in the dictionary:

pre-convention    pre-dawn

**preacher** A job description, not a formal religious title. Do not capitalize.

See **titles** and **religious titles**.

**precincts** See **political divisions**.

**predominant, predominantly** Use these primary spellings listed in Webster's New World for the adjectival and adverbial forms. Do not use the alternates it records, *predominate* and *predominately*.

The verb form, however, is *predominate*.

**prefixes** See separate listings for commonly used prefixes.

Generally do not hyphenate when using a prefix with a word starting with a consonant.

Three rules are constant, although they yield some exceptions to first-listed spellings in Webster's New World College Dictionary:

—Except for *cooperate* and *coordinate*, use a hyphen if the prefix ends in a vowel and the word that follows begins with the same vowel.

—Use a hyphen if the word that follows is capitalized.

—Use a hyphen to join dou-

bled prefixes: *sub-subparagraph*.

**premiere** A first performance.

**premier, prime minister** These two titles often are used interchangeably in translating to English the title of an individual who is the first minister in a national government that has a council of ministers.

*Prime minister* is the correct title throughout the Commonwealth, formerly the British Commonwealth. See **Commonwealth** for a list of members.

*Prime minister* is the best or traditional translation from most other languages. For consistency, use it throughout the rest of the world with these exceptions:

—Use *chancellor* in Austria and Germany.

—Follow the practice of a nation if there is a specific preference that varies from this general practice.

*Premier* is also the correct title for the individuals who lead the provincial governments in Canada and Australia.

See **titles**.

**Presbyterian churches** Presbyterian denominations typically have four levels of authority — individual congregations, presbyteries, synods and a general assembly.

Congregations are led by a pastor, who provides guidance in spiritual matters, and by a session, composed of ruling elders chosen by the congregation to represent the members in matters of government and discipline.

A presbytery is composed of all the ministers and an equal number of ruling elders, including at least one from each congregation, in a given district. Although the next two levels are technically higher, the presbytery has the authority to rule on many types of material and spiritual questions.

Presbyteries unite to form a synod, whose members are elected by the presbyteries. A synod generally meets once a year to decide matters such as the creation of new presbyteries and to pass judgment on appeals and complaints that do not affect the doctrine or constitution of the church.

A general assembly, composed of delegations of pastors and ruling elders from each presbytery, meets yearly to decide issues of doctrine and discipline within a Presbyterian body. It also may create new synods, divide old ones and correspond with general assemblies of other Presbyterian bodies.

The northern and southern branches of Presbyterianism merged in 1983 to become the Presbyterian Church (U.S.A.). Its membership totals 3.5 million. Formerly, Presbyterianism in the United States was concentrated in two bodies. The principal body in the North was the United Presbyterian Church in the United States of America. The Presbyterian Church in the United States was the principal Southern body.

There are also several distinctly conservative Presbyterian denominations, the largest of them the Presbyterian Church in America. Be careful to specify the denomination being written about.

Presbyterians believe in the Trinity and the humanity and divinity of Christ. Baptism, which may be administered to children, and the Lord's Supper are the only sacraments.

All Presbyterian clergymen may be described as *ministers*. *Pastor* applies if a minister leads a congregation.

On first reference, use *the Rev.* before the name of a man or woman. On second reference, use only the last name.

See **religious titles**.

**presently** Use it to mean *in a little while* or *shortly*, but not to mean *now*.

**presidency** Always lowercase.

**president** Capitalize *president* only as a formal title before one or more names: *President Reagan, Presidents Ford and Carter.*

Lowercase in all other uses: *The president said today. He is running for president. Lincoln was president during the Civil War.*

See **titles**.

FIRST NAMES: In most cases, the first name of a current or former U.S. president is not necessary on first reference. Use first names when necessary to avoid confusion: *President Andrew Johnson, President Lyndon Johnson.* First names also may be used for literary effect, or in feature or personality contexts.

For presidents of other nations and of organizations and institutions, capitalize president as a formal title before a full name: *President Askar Akayev of Kyrgyzstan* (not: *President Akayev* on first reference), *President John Smith of Acme Corp.*

On second reference, use only the last name.

**presidential** Lowercase unless part of a proper name.

**Presidential Medal of Freedom** This is the nation's highest civilian honor. It is given by the president, on the recommendation of the Distinguished Civilian Service Board, for "exceptionally meritorious contribution to the security of the United States or other significant public or private endeavors."

Until 1963 it was known as the Medal of Freedom.

**Presidents Day** Not adopted by the federal government as the official name of the Washington's Birthday holiday. However, some federal agencies, states and local governments use the term.

**presiding officer** Always lowercase.

**press conference** *News conference* is preferred.

**press secretary** Seldom a formal title. For consistency, always use lowercase, even when used before an individual's name.

(The formal title for the person who serves a U.S. president in this capacity is *assistant to the president for press relations*.)

See **titles**.

**pretense, pretext** A *pretext* is something that is put forward to conceal a truth: *He was discharged for tardiness, but the reason given was only a pretext for general incompetence.*

A *pretense* is a false show, a more overt act intended to conceal personal feelings: *My profuse compliments were all pretense.*

**preventive** Not *preventative*.

**priest** A vocational description, not a formal title. Do not capitalize.

See **religious titles** and the entries for the **Roman Catholic Church** and **Episcopal Church**.

**prima-facie** (adj.)

**primary** Do not capitalize: *the New Hampshire primary, the Democratic primary, the primary.*

**primary day** Use lowercase for any of the days set aside for balloting in a primary.

**prime meridian** See **meridians**.

**prime minister** See the **premier, prime minister** entry.

**prime rate** See entry in **Business Guidelines**.

**Prince Edward Island** One of the three Maritime Provinces of Canada. Do not abbreviate.

See **datelines**.

**prince, princess** Capitalize when used as a royal title before a name; lowercase when used alone: *Prince Charles, the prince.*

See **nobility**.

**principal, principle** *Principal* is a noun and adjective meaning someone or something first in rank, authority, importance or degree: *She is the school principal. He was the principal player in the trade. Money is the principal problem.*

*Principle* is a noun that means a fundamental truth, law, doctrine or motivating force: *They fought for the principle of self-determination.*

**prior to** *Before* is less stilted for most uses. *Prior to* is appropriate, however, when a notion of requirement is involved: *The fee must be paid prior to the examina-*

*tion.*

### prisoner(s) of war *POW(s)*
is acceptable on second reference.

Hyphenate when used as a compound modifier: *a prisoner-of-war trial.*

### prison, jail Do not use the
two words interchangeably.

DEFINITIONS: *Prison* is a generic term that may be applied to the maximum security institutions often known as *penitentiaries* and to the medium security facilities often called *correctional institutions* or *reformatories.* All such facilities confine people serving sentences for felonies.

A *jail* is a facility normally used to confine people serving sentences for misdemeanors, people awaiting trial or sentencing on either felony or misdemeanor charges, and people confined for civil matters such as failure to pay alimony and other types of contempt of court.

See the **felony, misdemeanor** entry.

The guidelines for capitalization:

PRISONS: Many states have given elaborate formal names to their prisons. They should be capitalized when used, but commonly accepted substitutes should also be capitalized as if they were proper names. For example, use either *Massachusetts Correctional Institution-Walpole* or *Walpole State Prison* for the maximum security institution in Massachusetts.

Do not, however, construct a substitute when the formal name is commonly accepted: It is the *Colorado State Penitentiary,* for example, not *Colorado State Prison.*

On second reference, any of the following may be used, all in lowercase: *the state prison, the prison, the state penitentiary, the penitentiary.*

Use lowercase for all plural constructions: *the Colorado and Kansas state penitentiaries.*

JAILS: Capitalize *jail* when linked with the name of the jurisdiction: *Los Angeles County Jail.* Lowercase *county jail, city jail* and *jail* when they stand alone.

FEDERAL INSTITUTIONS: Maximum security institutions are known as *penitentiaries: the U.S. Penitentiary at Lewisburg* or *Lewisburg Penitentiary* on first reference; *the federal penitentiary* or *the penitentiary* on second reference.

Medium security institutions include the word *federal* as part of their formal names: *the Federal Correctional Institution at Danbury, Conn.* On second reference: *the correctional institution, the federal prison, the prison.*

Most federal facilities used to house people awaiting trial or serving sentences of a year or less have the proper name *Federal Detention Center.* The term *Metropolitan Correctional Center* is being adopted for some new installations. On second reference: *the detention center, the correctional center.*

### private See **military titles**.

### privilege, privileged

### pro- Use a hyphen when coining words that denote support for something. Some examples:

| | |
|---|---|
| pro-labor | pro-business |
| pro-peace | pro-war |

No hyphen when *pro* is used in other senses: *produce, profile, pronoun,* etc.

### probation See the **pardon,**

**parole, probation** entry.

**Procter & Gamble Co.** *P&G* is acceptable on second reference. Headquarters is in Cincinnati.

**profanity** See the **obscenities, profanities, vulgarities** entry.

**professor** Never abbreviate. Lowercase before a name. Do not continue in second reference unless part of a quotation.

See **academic titles** and **titles**.

**profit-sharing** (n. and adj.) The hyphen for the noun is an exception to Webster's New World.

**Prohibition** Capitalize when referring to the period that began when the 18th Amendment to the Constitution prohibited the manufacture, sale or transportation of alcoholic liquors.

The amendment was declared ratified Jan. 29, 1919, and took effect Jan. 16, 1920. It was repealed by the 21st Amendment, which took effect Dec. 5, 1933, the day it was declared ratified.

**pronouncers** When necessary to use a *pronouncer*, put it in parentheses immediately following the word or name. The syllable to be stressed should be in caps with an apostrophe: *Ayatollah Khomeini (koh-MAY'-nee).*

Here are the basic sounds represented by AP phonetic symbols:

| Vowels | Consonants |
|---|---|
| a — apple, bat | g — got, beg |
| ah — father, hot | j — gem, job |
| ar — far, harm | k — cap, keep |
| aw — law, long | ch — chair |
| ay — ace, fate | s — see |
| e — bed | sh — shut |
| ehr — merry | y — yes |
| ee — see, tea | z — zoom |
| i — pin, middle | zh — mirage |

| | |
|---|---|
| oh — go, oval | kh — guttural "k" |
| oo — food, two | |
| or — for, torn | |
| ow — cow | |
| oy — boy | |
| u — foot, put | |
| uh — puff | |
| ur — burden, curl | |
| y, eye — ice, time | |

**propeller**

**proper nouns** See **capitalization**.

**prophecy** (n.) **prophesy** (v.)

**proportions** Always use figures: *2 parts powder to 6 parts water.*

**proposition** Do not abbreviate. Capitalize when used with a figure in describing a ballot question: *He is uncommitted on Proposition 15.*

**prosecutor** Capitalize before a name when it is the formal title. In most cases, however, the formal title is a term such as *attorney general, state's attorney* or *U.S. attorney.* If so, use the formal title on first reference.

Lowercase *prosecutor* if used before a name on a subsequent reference, generally to help the reader distinguish between prosecutor and defense attorney without having to look back to the start of the story.

See **titles**.

**prostate gland** Not *prostrate.*

**Protestant Episcopal Church** See **Episcopal Church**.

**Protestant, Protestantism** Capitalize these words when they refer either to denominations formed as a result of the break from the Roman Catholic Church in the 16th century or to the members of these denominations.

Church groups covered by the term include Anglican, Baptist, Congregational, Methodist, Lutheran, Presbyterian and Quaker denominations. See separate entries for each.

*Protestant* is not generally applied to Christian Scientists, Jehovah's Witnesses or Mormons.

Do not use *Protestant* to describe a member of an Eastern Orthodox church. Use a phrase such as *Orthodox Christian* instead.

See **religious movements**.

**protester** Not *protestor*.

**prove, proved, proving**
Use *proven* only as an adjective: *a proven remedy.*

**provinces** Names of provinces are set off from community names by commas, just as the names of U.S. states are set off from city names: *They went to Halifax, Nova Scotia, on their vacation.*

Do not capitalize province: *They visited the province of Nova Scotia. The earthquake struck Shensi province.*

See **datelines**.

**proviso, provisos**

**provost marshal** The plural: *provost marshals.*

**PTA** See **parent-teacher association**.

**PT boat** It stands for *patrol torpedo boat.*

**Public Broadcasting Service** It is not a network, but an association of public television stations organized to buy and distribute programs selected by a vote of the members.

*PBS* is acceptable on first reference only within contexts such as a television column. Otherwise, do not use *PBS* until second reference.

**public schools** Use figures and capitalize *public school* when used with a figure: *Public School 3, Public School 10.*

If a school has a commemorative name: *Benjamin Franklin School.*

**publisher** Capitalize when used as a formal title before an individual's name: *Publisher Isaiah Thomas of the Massachusetts Spy.*

See **titles**.

**Puerto Rico** Do not abbreviate. See **datelines**.

**Pulitzer Prizes** These yearly awards for outstanding work in journalism and the arts were endowed by the late Joseph Pulitzer, publisher of the old New York World, and first given in 1917. They are awarded by the trustees of Columbia University on recommendation of an advisory board.

Capitalize *Pulitzer Prize*, but lowercase the categories: *Pulitzer Prize for public service, Pulitzer Prize for fiction*, etc.

Also: *She is a Pulitzer Prize winner. He is a Pulitzer Prize-winning author.*

**pull back** (v.) **pullback** (n.)

**pull out** (v.) **pullout** (n.)

**pulpit** See the **lectern, podium, pulpit, rostrum** entry.

**punctuation** Think of it as

a courtesy to your readers, designed to help them understand a story.

Inevitably, a mandate of this scope involves gray areas. For this reason, the punctuation entries in this book refer to guidelines rather than rules. Guidelines should not be treated casually, however.

See **Punctuation** chapter for separate entries under: **apostrophe**; **brackets**; **colon**; **comma**; **dash**; **ellipsis**; **exclamation point**; **hyphen**; **parentheses**; **periods**; **question mark**; **quotation marks**; and **semicolon**.

**Purim** The Jewish Feast of Lots, commemorating Esther's deliverance of the Jews in Persia from a massacre plotted by Haman. Occurs in February or March.

**push-button** (n., adj.)

**push up** (v.) **push-up** (n., adj.)

**put out** (v.) **putout** (n.)

**pygmy** Capitalize only when referring specifically to any of several races of unusually small African or Asian peoples.

**Pyrex** A trademark for a brand of oven glassware.

**Q-and-A format** See **question mark** in **Punctuation** chapter.

**Qantas Airways** Headquarters is in Sydney, Australia.

**QE2** Acceptable on second reference for the ocean liner Queen Elizabeth 2.

(But use a Roman numeral for the monarch: *Queen Elizabeth II*.)

**Q-tips** A trademark for a brand of cotton swabs.

**Quakers** This informal name may be used in all references to members of the *Religious Society of Friends*, but always include the full name in a story dealing primarily with Quaker activities.

The denomination originated with George Fox, an Englishman who objected to Anglican emphasis on ceremony. In the 1640s, he said he heard a voice that opened the way for him to develop a personal relationship with Christ, described as the Inner Light, a term based on the Gospel description of Christ as the "true light."

Brought to court for opposing the established church, Fox tangled with a judge who derided him as a "quaker" in reference to his agitation over religious matters.

The basic unit of Quaker organization is the weekly meeting, which corresponds to the congregation in other churches.

Various yearly meetings form larger associations that assemble at intervals of a year or more. The largest is the Friends United Meeting. Its 15 yearly meeting members represent about half the Friends in the world.

Others include the Evangelical Friends Alliance and the Friends General Conference. Members of the conference include some yearly meetings that also are affiliated with the Friends United Meeting.

Overall, Friends count about 120,000 members in the United States and Canada and a total of 200,000 worldwide.

Fox taught that the Inner Light emancipates a person from adherence to any creed, ecclesiastical authority or ritual forms.

There is no recognized ranking of clergy over lay people. However, there are meeting officers, called *elders* or *ministers*. Many Quaker ministers, particularly in the Midwest and West, use *the Rev.* before their names and describe themselves as *pastors*.

Capitalize *elder, minister* or *pastor* when used as a formal title before a name. Use *the Rev.* before a name on first reference

if it is a minister's practice. On second reference, use only the last name.
See **religious titles**.

**quakes** See **earthquakes**.

**quart (dry)** Equal in volume to 67.2 cubic inches. The metric equivalent is approximately 1.1 liters.
To convert to liters, multiply by 1.1 (5 dry quarts x 1.1 is 5.5 liters).
See **liter**.

**quart (liquid)** Equal in volume to 57.75 cubic inches. Also equal to 32 fluid ounces.
The approximate metric equivalents are 950 milliliters or .95 of a liter.
To convert to liters, multiply by .95 (4 quarts x .95 is 3.8 liters).
See **liter**.

**quasar** Acceptable in all references for a *quasi-stellar astronomical object*, often a radio source.

**Quebec** Use *Quebec City* without the name of the province in datelines.
Do not abbreviate any reference to the province of *Quebec*, Canada's largest in area and second largest in population.
The people are *Quebecois*.
See **datelines**.

**queen** Capitalize only when used before the name of royalty: *Queen Elizabeth II*. Continue in second references that use the queen's given name: *Queen Elizabeth*.
Lowercase *queen* when it stands alone.
Capitalize in plural uses:

*Queens Elizabeth and Victoria*.
See **nobility** and **titles**.

**queen mother** A widowed queen who is mother of the reigning monarch. See **nobility**.

**question mark** See entry in **Punctuation** chapter.

**questionnaire**

**quick-witted**

**quotation marks** See entry in **Punctuation** chapter.

**quotations in the news**
Never alter quotations even to correct minor grammatical errors or word usage. Casual minor tongue slips may be removed by using ellipses but even that should be done with extreme caution. If there is a question about a quote, either don't use it or ask the speaker to clarify.
If a person is unavailable for comment, detail attempts to reach that person. (*Smith was out of the country on business; Jones did not return phone messages left at the office.*)
Do not use substandard spellings such as *gonna* or *wanna* in attempts to convey regional dialects or informal pronunciations, except to help a desired touch in a feature.
Follow basic writing style and use abbreviations where appropriate, as in *No. 1* or *St.*
FULL vs. PARTIAL QUOTES:
In general, avoid fragmentary quotes. If a speaker's words are clear and concise, favor the full quote. If cumbersome language can be paraphrased fairly, use an indirect construction, reserving quotation marks for sensitive or controversial passages that must

be identified specifically as coming from the speaker.

CONTEXT: Remember that you can misquote someone by giving a startling remark without its modifying passage or qualifiers. The manner of delivery sometimes is part of the context. Reporting a smile or a deprecatory gesture may be as important as conveying the words themselves.

OFFENSIVE LANGUAGE: See the **obscenities, profanities, vulgarities** entry.

PUNCTUATION: See the **quotation marks** entry in the **Punctuation** chapter.

**Quran** The preferred spelling for the Muslim holy book. Use the spelling *Koran* only if preferred by a specific organization or in a specific title or name.

# R

**R** The *restricted* rating. See **movie ratings**.

**rabbi** See **Jewish congregations**.

**Rabbinical Assembly** See **Jewish congregations**.

**Rabbinical Council of America** See **Jewish congregations**.

**raccoon**

**race** Identification by race is pertinent:

—In biographical and announcement stories, particularly when they involve a feat or appointment that has not routinely been associated with members of a particular race.

—When it provides the reader with a substantial insight into conflicting emotions known or likely to be involved in a demonstration or similar event.

In some stories that involve a conflict, it is equally important to specify that an issue cuts across racial lines. If, for example, a demonstration by supporters of busing to achieve racial balance in schools includes a substantial number of whites, that fact should be noted.

Do not use racially derogatory terms unless they are part of a quotation that is essential to the story.

See the **obscenities, profanities, vulgarities** entry and the **nationalities and races** entry.

**racket** Not *racquet*, for the light bat used in tennis and badminton.

**rack, wrack** The noun *rack* applies to various types of framework; the verb *rack* means to arrange on a rack, to torture, trouble or torment: *He was placed on the rack. She racked her brain.*

The noun *wrack* means ruin or destruction, and generally is confined to the phrase *wrack and ruin.*

The verb *wrack* has substantially the same meaning as the verb *rack*, the latter being preferred.

**radar** A lowercase acronym for *radio detection and ranging.*

**radical** In general, avoid this description in favor of a more precise definition of an individual's political views.

When used, it suggests that an individual believes change must be made by tearing up the roots or foundation of the present order.

Although *radical* often is applied to individuals who hold strong socialist or communist views, it also is applied at times to individuals who believe an existing form of government must be replaced by a more authoritarian or militaristic one.

See the **leftist, ultra-leftist** and **rightist, ultra-rightist** entries.

**radio** Capitalize and use before a name to indicate an official voice of the government: *Voice of America.*

Lowercase and place after the name when indicating only that the information was obtained from broadcasts in a city. *Havana radio*, for example, is the form used in referring to reports that are broadcast on various stations in the Cuban capital.

**radio station** Use lowercase: *radio station WHEC.*
See **call letters**.

**railroads** Capitalize when part of a name: *the Illinois Central Gulf Railroad.*

Railroad companies vary the spellings of their names, using *Railroad, Rail Road, Railway*, etc.

Use *the railroad* for all lines in second references.

Use *railroads* in lowercase for all plurals: *the Penn Central and Santa Fe railroads.*

See **Amtrak** and **Conrail**.

**rainstorm** See **weather terms**.

**raised, reared** Only humans may be *reared.*

All living things, including humans, may be *raised.*

**RAM** Acronym for *random access memory*, the "working memory" of a computer into which programs can be introduced and then executed.

**Ramadan** The Muslim holy month, a period of daily fasting from sunrise to sunset, ending with the Islamic holiday of Eid al-Fitr.

**ranges** The form: *$12 million to $14 million.* Not: *$12 to $14 million.*

**rank and file** (n.) The adjective form: *rank-and-file.*

**rarely** It means seldom. *Rarely ever* is redundant, but *rarely if ever* often is the appropriate phrase.

**ratios** Use figures and hyphens: *the ratio was 2-to-1, a ratio of 2-to-1, a 2-1 ratio.* As illustrated, the word *to* should be omitted when the numbers precede the word *ratio.*

Always use the word *ratio* or a phrase such as *a 2-1 majority* to avoid confusion with actual figures.

**ravage, ravish** *To ravage* is to wreak great destruction or devastation: *Union troops ravaged Atlanta.*

*To ravish* is to abduct, rape or carry away with emotion: *Soldiers ravished the women.*

Although both words connote an element of violence, they are not interchangeable. Buildings and towns cannot be *ravished.*

**rayon** Not a trademark.

**re-** The rules in **prefixes** apply. The following examples of exceptions to first-listed spellings in Webster's New World are based on the general rule that a hyphen is used if a prefix ends in a vowel and the word that follows begins with the same vowel:

re-elect       re-enlist

re-election     re-enter
re-emerge     re-entry
re-employ     re-equip
re-enact     re-establish
re-engage     re-examine

For many other words, the sense is the governing factor:

recover (regain)     re-cover (cover again)
reform (improve)     re-form (form again)
resign (quit)     re-sign (sign again)

Otherwise, follow Webster's New World. Use a hyphen for words not listed there unless the hyphen would distort the sense.

**reader** See **Church of Christ, Scientist**.

**Realtor** The term *real estate agent* is preferred. Use *Realtor* only if there is a reason to indicate that the individual is a member of the National Association of Realtors.

See **service marks**.

**reared** See **raised, reared** entry.

**rebut, refute** *Rebut* means to argue to the contrary: *He rebutted his opponent's statement.*

*Refute* connotes success in argument and almost always implies an editorial judgment. Instead, use *deny, dispute, rebut* or *respond to.*

**recipes** Always use figures. See **fractions**.

Do not use abbreviations. Spell out *teaspoon, tablespoon,* etc.

See the **food** entry for guidelines on when to capitalize the names of foods.

**recision** The preferred spelling is *rescission.*

**reconnaissance**

**Reconstruction** The pro-

cess of reorganizing the Southern states after the Civil War.

**record** Avoid the redundant *new record.*

**rector** See **religious titles**.

**recur, recurred, recurring** Not *reoccur.*

**Red** Capitalize when used as a political, geographic or military term: *the Red army.*

**Red China** See **China**.

**red-haired, redhead, redheaded** All are acceptable for a person with red hair.

*Redhead* also is used colloquially to describe a type of North American diving duck.

**red-handed** (adj. and adv.)

**red-hot**

**redneck** From the characteristic sunburned neck acquired in the fields by farm laborers. It refers to poor, white rural residents of the South and often is a derogatory term.

**re-elect, re-election**

**refer** See the **allude, refer** entry.

**referable**

**reference works** Capitalize their proper names.

Do not use quotation marks around the names of books that are primarily catalogs of reference material. In addition to catalogs, this category includes almanacs, directories, dictionaries, encyclopedias, gazetteers, handbooks and similar publications.

EXAMPLES: *Congressional Directory, Webster's New World College Dictionary, the AP Stylebook.* But: *"The Careful Writer" and "Modern American Usage."*

See the bibliography for the principal reference works used in preparing this book.

### referendum, referendums

**reformatory** See the **prison, jail** entry.

### Reform Judaism See Jewish congregations.

**refute** See the **rebut, refute** entry.

**regime** See the **government, junta, regime** entry.

**regions** See the **directions and regions** entry.

**reign, rein** The leather strap for controlling a horse is a *rein*, hence figuratively: *seize the reins, give free rein to, put a checkrein on.*

*Reign* is the period a ruler is on the throne: *The king began his reign.*

**release times** Follow these guidelines:

TIME SET BY SOURCE FOR PUBLICATION OR BROADCAST OF A STORY: If a source provides material on condition that it not be published or broadcast until a specific time (sometimes known as a release embargo), the story should contain a statement to that effect.

TIME SET BY SOURCE FOR WIRE MOVEMENT: If a source provides material on condition that it not be transmitted in any form to members or subscribers until a specific time (sometimes known as a wire embargo or wire movement embargo), the material should be held until that time. Consult New York if any problems arise.

"MORNING" OR "EVENING" NEWSPAPER RELEASE SPECIFIED BY SOURCE: If a source does not specify a particular hour but says material is for release in morning papers or afternoon papers, consider the release time for print and broadcast to be 6:30 p.m. the day before publication or 6:30 a.m. Eastern time the day of publication, respectively.

AP ADVANCES: AP stories sent in advance for use on a specific date are considered released for publication and broadcast at 6:30 p.m. Eastern time the night before that date.

**religious affiliations** Capitalize the names and the related terms applied to members of the orders: *He is a member of the Society of Jesus. He is a Jesuit.*

### religious movements

The terms that follow have been grouped under a single entry because they are interrelated and frequently cross denominational lines.

**evangelical** Historically, *evangelical* was used as an adjective describing dedication to conveying the message of Christ. Today it also is used as a noun, referring to a category of doctrinally conservative Christians. They emphasize the need for a definite, adult commitment or conversion to faith in Christ and the duty of all believers to persuade others to accept Christ.

*Evangelicals* make up some conservative denominations and

are numerous in broader denominations. Evangelicals stress both doctrinal absolutes and vigorous efforts to win others to belief.

The National Association of Evangelicals is an interdenominational, cooperative body of relatively small, conservative Protestant denominations. It says it has 60 member denominations with 45,000 churches and represents millions of evangelicals.

**evangelism** The word refers to activity directed outside the church fold to influence others to commit themselves to faith in Christ, to his work of serving others and to infuse his principles into society's conduct.

Styles of evangelism vary from direct preaching appeals at large public meetings to practical deeds of carrying the name of Christ, indirectly conveying the same call to allegiance to him.

The word *evangelism* is derived from the Greek *evangelion*, which means the gospel or good news of Christ's saving action in behalf of humanity.

**fundamentalist** The word gained usage in an early 20th century fundamentalist-modernist controversy within Protestantism. In recent years, however, *fundamentalist* has to a large extent taken on pejorative connotations except when applied to groups that stress strict, literal interpretations of Scripture and separation from other Christians.

In general, do not use *fundamentalist* unless a group applies the word to itself.

**liberal** In general, avoid this word as a descriptive classification in religion. It has objectionable implications to many believers.

Acceptable alternate descriptions include *activist, more flexible* and *broadview.*

*Moderate* is appropriate when used by the contending parties, as is the case in the conflict between the moderate or more flexible wing of the Lutheran Church-Missouri Synod and conservatives, who argue for literal interpretations of biblical passages others consider symbolic.

Do not use the term *Bible-believing* to distinguish one faction from another, because all Christians believe the Bible. The differences are over interpretations.

**neo-Pentecostal, charismatic** These terms apply to a movement that has developed within mainline Protestant and Roman Catholic denominations since the mid-20th century. It is distinguished by its emotional expressiveness, spontaneity in worship, speaking or praying in "unknown tongues" and healing. Participants often characterize themselves as "spirit-filled" Christians.

Unlike the earlier Pentecostal movement, which led to separate denominations, this movement has swelled within major churches.

**Pentecostalism** A movement that arose in the early 20th century and separated from historic Protestant denominations. It is distinguished by the belief in tangible manifestations of the Holy Spirit, often in demonstrative, emotional ways such as speaking in "unknown tongues" and healing.

Pentecostal denominations include the Assemblies of God, the Pentecostal Holiness Church, the United Pentecostal Church Inc. and the International Church of the Foursquare Gospel founded by Aimee Semple McPherson.

**religious references** The basic guidelines:

DEITIES: Capitalize the proper names of monotheistic deities: *God, Allah, the Father, the Son, Jesus Christ, the Son of God, the Redeemer, the Holy Spirit,* etc.

Lowercase pronouns referring to the deity: *he, him, his, thee, thou, who, whose, thy,* etc.

Lowercase *gods* in referring to the deities of polytheistic religions.

Capitalize the proper names of pagan and mythological gods and goddesses: *Neptune, Thor, Venus,* etc.

Lowercase such words as *god-awful, goddamn, godlike, godliness, godsend.*

LIFE OF CHRIST: Capitalize the names of major events in the life of Jesus Christ in references that do not use his name: *The doctrines of the Last Supper, the Crucifixion, the Resurrection and the Ascension are central to Christian belief.*

But use lowercase when the words are used with his name: *The ascension of Jesus into heaven took place 40 days after his resurrection from the dead.*

Apply the principle also to events in the life of his mother: *He cited the doctrines of the Immaculate Conception and the Assumption.* But: *She referred to the assumption of Mary into heaven.*

RITES: Capitalize proper names for rites that commemorate the Last Supper or signify a belief in Christ's presence: *the Lord's Supper, Holy Communion, Holy Eucharist.*

Lowercase the names of other sacraments. See the **sacraments** entry.

Capitalize *Benediction* and the

*Mass.* But: *a high Mass, a low Mass, a requiem Mass.*

HOLY DAYS: Capitalize the names of holy days. See the **holidays and holy days** entry and separate entries for major Christian and Jewish feasts.

OTHER WORDS: Lowercase *heaven, hell, devil, angel, cherub, an apostle, a priest,* etc.

Capitalize *Hades* and *Satan.*

For additional details, see **Bible**, entries for frequently used religious terms, the entries for major denominations, **religious movements** and **religious titles**.

**Religious Society of Friends** See **Quakers**.

**religious titles** The first reference to a clergyman or clergywoman normally should include a capitalized title before the individual's name.

In many cases, *the Rev.* is the designation that applies before a name on first reference. Use *the Rev. Dr.* only if the individual has an earned doctoral degree (doctor of divinity degrees frequently are honorary) and reference to the degree is relevant.

On second reference to members of the clergy, use only a last name: *the Rev. Billy Graham* on first reference, *Graham* on second. If known only by a religious name, repeat the title: *Pope Paul VI* or *Pope Paul* on first reference, *Pope Paul, the pope* (not Paul) or *the pontiff* on second; *Metropolitan Ireney* on first reference, *Metropolitan Ireney* or *the metropolitan* on second.

Detailed guidance on specific titles and descriptive words such as *priest* and *minister* is provided in the entries for major denominations. In general, however:

CARDINALS, ARCHBISHOPS,

BISHOPS: The preferred form for first reference is to use *Cardinal, Archbishop* or *Bishop* before the individual's name: *Cardinal Timothy Manning, archbishop of Los Angeles.* On second reference: *Manning* or *the cardinal.*

Substitute *the Most Rev.* if applicable and appropriate in the context: *He spoke to the Most Rev. Anthony Bevilacqua, archbishop of Philadelphia.* On second reference: *Bevilacqua* or *the archbishop.*

Entries for individual denominations tell when *the Most Rev., the Very Rev.,* etc., are applicable.

MINISTERS AND PRIESTS: Use *the Rev.* before a name on first reference.

Substitute *Monsignor* before the name of a Roman Catholic priest who has received this honor.

Do not routinely use *curate, father, pastor* and similar words before an individual's name. If they appear before a name in a quotation, capitalize them.

RABBIS: Use *Rabbi* before a name on first reference. On second reference, use only the last name.

NUNS: Always use *Sister,* or *Mother* if applicable, before a name: *Sister Agnes Rita* in all references if the nun uses only a religious name; *Sister Clare Regina Torpy* on first reference if she uses a surname, *Sister Torpy* on second reference.

OFFICEHOLDERS: The preferred first-reference form for those who hold church office but are not ordained clergy in the usual sense is to use a construction that sets the title apart from the name by commas. Capitalize the formal title of an office, however, if it is used directly before an individual's name.

**reluctant, reticent** *Reluctant* means unwilling to act: *He is reluctant to enter the primary.*

*Reticent* means unwilling to speak: *The candidate's husband is reticent.*

**Reorganized Church of Jesus Christ of Latter Day Saints** Not properly described as a *Mormon church.* See the explanation under **Church of Jesus Christ of Latter-day Saints**.

**representative, Rep.** See **legislative titles** and **party affiliation**.

**republic** Capitalize *republic* when used as part of a nation's full, formal name: *the Republic of Argentina.*

See **datelines**.

**Republican Governors Association** No apostrophe.

**Republican National Committee** On second reference: *the national committee, the committee.*

Similarly: *Republican State Committee, Republican County Committee, Republican City Committee, the state committee, the county committee, the city committee, the committee.*

**republican, Republican Party** *GOP* may be used on second reference.

See the **political parties and philosophies** entry.

**reputation** See the **character, reputation** entry.

**rescission** Not *recision.*

**Reserve** Capitalize when referring to U.S. armed forces, as in

*Army Reserve.* Lowercase in reference to members of these backup forces: *reserves,* or *reservists.*

**Reserve Officers' Training Corps** The *s'* is military practice. *ROTC* is acceptable in all references.

When the service is specified, use *Army ROTC, Navy ROTC* or *Air Force ROTC,* not *AROTC, NROTC* or *AFROTC.*

**resident** See the **citizen, resident, subject, national, native** entry.

**resistible**

**restaurateur** No *n.* Not *restauranteur.*

**restrictive clauses** See the **essential clauses, nonessential clauses** entry.

**restrictive phrases** See the **essential phrases, nonessential phrases** entry.

**Retail Clerks International Union** See **United Food and Commercial Workers International Union.**

**retarded** See **mentally retarded.**

**Reuters** The British news agency, part of the public company Reuters Group PLC, is named for Baron Paul Julius von Reuter, the founder.

Based in London, the official name is *Reuters Ltd.,* but it is referred to as *Reuters.*

**Rev.** When this description is used before an individual's name, precede it with the word *"the"* because, unlike the case with *Mr.* and *Mrs.,* the abbreviation *Rev.*

does not stand for a noun.

If an individual also has a secular title such as *Rep.,* use whichever is appropriate to the context.

See **religious titles.**

**revolution** Capitalize when part of a name for a specific historical event: *the American Revolution, the Bolshevik Revolution, the French Revolution.*

*The Revolution,* capitalized, also may be used as a shorthand reference to the *American Revolution.* Also: *the Revolutionary War.*

Lowercase in other uses: *a revolution, the revolution, the American and French revolutions.*

**revolutions per minute** The abbreviation *rpm* is acceptable on first reference in specialized contexts such as an auto column. Otherwise do not use it until second reference.

**Rh factor** Also: *Rh negative, Rh positive.*

**Rhode Island** Abbrev.: *R.I.* Smallest of the 50 states in total land area: 1,049 square miles.

See **state names.**

**Rhodes scholar** Lowercase *scholar* and *scholarship.*

**Richter scale** See **earthquakes.**

**RICO** An acronym for *Racketeer Influenced and Corrupt Organizations Act.* Acceptable on second reference, but *anti-racketeering* or *anti-corruption law* is preferred.

**riffraff**

**rifle** See **weapons.**

**rifle, riffle** *To rifle* is to plunder or steal.

*To riffle* is to leaf rapidly through a book or pile of papers.

**right hand** (n.) **right-handed** (adj.) **right-hander** (n.)

**rightist, ultra-rightist** In general, avoid these terms in favor of more precise descriptions of an individual's political philosophy.

As popularly used today, particularly abroad, *rightist* often applies to someone who is conservative or opposed to socialism. It also often indicates an individual who supports an authoritarian government that is militantly anti-communist or anti-socialist.

*Ultra-rightist* suggests an individual who subscribes to rigid interpretations of a conservative doctrine or to forms of fascism that stress authoritarian, often militaristic, views.

See **radical** and the **leftist, ultra-leftist** entry.

**right of way, rights of way**

**right-to-work** (adj.) A *right-to-work* law prohibits a company and a union from signing a contract that would require the affected workers to be union members.

See **closed shop** for definitions of various agreements that require union membership.

**right wing** (n.) But: *right-wing* (adj.), *right-winger* (n.).

**Ringling Bros. and Barnum & Bailey** Note the *and*, &..

The circus is owned by Feld Entertainment Inc., headquartered in Vienna, Va.

**Rio Grande** Not *Rio Grande River*. (*Rio* means river.)

**rip off** (v.) **rip-off** (n., adj.)

**river** Capitalize as part of a proper name: *the Mississippi River.*

Lowercase in other uses: *the river, the Mississippi and Missouri rivers.*

**road** Do not abbreviate. See **addresses**.

**Roaring '20s** See **decades**.

**robbery** See the **burglary, larceny, robbery, theft** entry.

**rock 'n' roll** But *Rock and Roll Hall of Fame.*

**Rocky Mountains** Or simply: *the Rockies.*

**roll call** (n.) **roll-call** (adj.)

**Rollerblade** A trademark for a brand of in-line skates.

**Rolls-Royce** Note the hyphen in this trademark for a make of automobile.

**Rolodex** A trademark for a brand of rotary card file.

**roly-poly**

**ROM** Acronym for *read-only memory*, computer memory whose contents cannot be modified.

**Roman Catholic Church** The church teaches that its bishops have been established as the successors of the apostles through generations of ceremonies in which authority was passed down by a laying-on of hands.

Responsibility for teaching the faithful and administering the church rests with the bishops. However, the church holds that the pope has final authority over their actions because he is the bishop of Rome, the office that it teaches was held by the Apostle Peter at his death.

Although the pope is empowered to speak infallibly on faith and morals, he does so only in formal pronouncements that specifically state he is speaking from the chair (*ex cathedra*) of St. Peter. This rarely used prerogative was most recently invoked in 1950, when Pope Pius XII declared that Mary was assumed bodily into heaven.

The Curia serves as a form of governmental cabinet. Its members, appointed by the pope, handle both administrative and judicial functions.

The pope also chooses members of the College of Cardinals, who serve as his principal counselors. When a new pope must be chosen, they meet in a conclave to select a new pope by majority vote. In practice, cardinals are bishops, but there is no requirement that a cardinal be a bishop.

In the United States, the church's principal organizational units are archdioceses and dioceses. They are headed, respectively, by archbishops and bishops, who have final responsibility for many activities within their jurisdictions and report directly to Rome.

The church counts more than 1 billion members worldwide. In the United States it has more than 62 million members, making it the largest single body of Christians in the nation.

Roman Catholics believe in the Trinity — that there is one God who exists as three divine persons, the Father, the Son and the Holy Spirit. They believe that the Son became man as Jesus Christ.

In addition to the Holy Eucharist, there are six other sacraments — baptism, confirmation, penance (often called the sacrament of reconciliation), matrimony, holy orders, and the sacrament of the sick (formerly extreme unction).

The clergy below pope are, in descending order, cardinal, archbishop, bishop, monsignor, priest and deacon. In religious orders, some men who are not priests have the title *brother.*

Capitalize pope when used as a title before a name: *Pope Paul VI, Pope Paul.* Lowercase in all other uses. See the **titles** entry.

The first-reference forms for other titles follow. Use only last names on second reference.

Cardinals: *Cardinal Timothy Manning.* The usage *Timothy Cardinal Manning,* a practice traceable to the nobility's custom of identifications such as *William, Duke of Norfolk,* is still used in formal documents but otherwise is considered archaic.

Archbishops: *Archbishop Joseph L. Bernardin,* or *the Most Rev. Joseph L. Bernardin, archbishop of Cincinnati.*

Bishops: *Bishop Bernard J. Flanagan,* or *the Most Rev. Bernard J. Flanagan, bishop of Worcester.*

Monsignors: *Monsignor Joseph E. Vogt.* Do not use the abbreviation *Msgr.* Do not use *the Rt. Rev.* or *the Very Rev.* — this distinction between types of monsignors no longer is made.

Priests: *the Rev. John J. Paret.* See **religious titles** and **sister.**

**Romania** Not *Rumania.*

**Romanian Orthodox Church** The Romanian Orthodox Church in America is an autonomous archdiocese of the Romanian Orthodox Church. The Romanian Orthodox Episcopate of America is an autonomous archdiocese within the Orthodox Church in America.

See **Eastern Orthodox churches**.

**Roman numerals** They use letters (*I*, *X*, etc.) to express numbers.

Use Roman numerals for wars and to establish personal sequence for people and animals: *World War I, Native Dancer II, King George V.* Also for certain legislative acts (*Title IX*) and pro football Super Bowls.

Use Arabic numerals in all other cases. See **Arabic numerals** and **numerals**.

In Roman numerals, the capital letter *I* equals 1, *V* equals 5, *X* equals 10, *L* equals 50, *C* equals 100, *D* equals 500 and *M* equals 1,000. Do not use *M* to mean million, as some newspapers occasionally do in headlines.

Other numbers are formed from these by adding or subtracting as follows:

—The value of a letter following another of the same or greater value is added: *III* equals 3.

—The value of a letter preceding one of greater value is subtracted: *IV* equals 4.

**Rome** The city in Italy stands alone in datelines.

**room numbers** Use figures and capitalize *room* when used with a figure: *Room 2, Room 211.*

**rooms** Capitalize the names of specially designated rooms: *Blue Room, Lincoln Room, Oval Office, Persian Room.*

**Roquefort cheese, Roquefort dressing** A certification mark for a type of blue cheese cured in Roquefort, France.

It is not a trademark.

**rosary** It is *recited* or *said,* never *read.* Always lowercase.

**Rosh Hashana** The Jewish new year. Occurs in September or October.

**rostrum** See the **lectern, podium, pulpit, rostrum** entry.

**ROTC** See **Reserve Officers' Training Corps**.

**round up** (v.) **roundup** (n.)

**route numbers** Do not abbreviate *route.* Use figures and capitalize route when used with a figure: *U.S. Route 70, state Route 1A.*

See **highway designations**.

**Royal Dutch Shell PLC** A 2005 unification of Royal Dutch Petroleum and Shell Transport & Trading Co., with headquarters in The Hague, Netherlands. The company specializes in petroleum and related products. Holdings include Shell Oil Co., a U.S. corporation, with headquarters in Houston.

**royal titles** See **nobility**.

**RSVP** The abbreviation for the French *repondez s'il vous plait,* it means *please reply.*

**Rt. Rev.** See the entry for an

individual denomination.

**rubber stamp** (n.) **rubber-stamp** (v. and adj.)

**rubella** Also known as *German measles*.

**runner-up, runners-up**

**running mate**

**rush hour** (n.) **rush-hour** (adj.)

**Russia** See **Commonwealth of Independent States** entry.

**Russian names** When a first name in Russian has a close phonetic equivalent in English, use the equivalent in translating the name: *Alexander Solzhenitsyn* rather than *Aleksandr*, the spelling that would result from a transliteration of the Russian letter into the English alphabet.

When a first name has no close phonetic equivalent in English, express it with an English spelling that approximates the sound in Russian: *Nikita*, for example.

For last names, use the English spelling that most closely approximates the pronunciation in Russian.

If an individual has a preference for an English spelling that is different from the one that would result by applying these guidelines, follow the individual's preference.

Women's last names have feminine endings. But use them only if the woman is not married or if she is known under that name (*the ballerina Maya Plissetskaya*). Otherwise, use the masculine form: *Raisa Gorbachev*, not *Gorbacheva*.

Russian names never end in *off*, except for common mistransliterations such as *Rachmaninoff*. Instead, the transliterations should end in *ov*: *Romanov*.

**Russian Orthodox Church** See **Eastern Orthodox churches**.

**Russian Revolution** Also: *the Bolshevik Revolution*.

**Rust Belt**

# S

**Sabbath** Capitalize in religious references; lowercase to mean a period of rest.

**saboteur**

**Sacagawea**

**sacraments** Capitalize the proper names used for a sacramental rite that commemorates the life of Jesus Christ or signifies a belief in his presence: *the Lord's Supper, Holy Communion, Holy Eucharist.*

Lowercase the names of other sacraments: *baptism, confirmation, penance* (now often called the *sacrament of reconciliation*), *matrimony, holy orders,* and *the sacrament of anointing the sick* (formerly *extreme unction*).

See entries for the major religious denominations and **religious references**.

**sacrilegious**

**Saddam** Use *Saddam* in second reference to Iraq's Saddam Hussein.

**Safeway Inc.** Formerly Safeway Stores. Headquarters is in Pleasanton, Calif.

**saint** Abbreviate as *St.* in the names of saints, cities and other places: *St. Jude; St. Paul, Minn.; St. John's, Newfoundland; St. Lawrence Seaway.*

But see the entries for **Saint John** and **Sault Ste. Marie**.

**Saint John** The spelling for the city in New Brunswick.

To distinguish it from *St. John's, Newfoundland.*

**salable**

**SALT** See **Strategic Arms Reduction Treaty (START)**

**Salt Lake City** Stands alone in datelines.

**salvo, salvos**

**SAM, SAMs** Acceptable on second reference for *surface-to-air missile(s).*

**San'a** It's NOT an apostrophe (') in the Yemen capital's name. It's a reverse apostrophe ('), or a single opening quotation mark.

**San Antonio** The city in Texas stands alone in datelines.

**sandbag** (n.) The verbs: *sandbagged, sandbagging.* And: *sandbagger.*

**San Diego** The city in California stands alone in datelines.

**sandstorm** See **weather terms**.

**sandwich**

**San Francisco** The city in California stands alone in date-lines.

**sanitarium, sanitariums**

**San Marino** Use alone in datelines on stories from the Republic of San Marino.

**Santa Claus**

**Sardinia** Use instead of Italy in datelines on stories from communities on this island.

**SARS** Acceptable in all references for *severe acute respiratory syndrome*, but it should be spelled out somewhere in the story.

**Saskatchewan** A province of Canada north of Montana and North Dakota. Do not abbreviate. See **datelines**.

**SAT** Use only the initials in referring to the previously designated Scholastic Aptitude Test or the Scholastic Assessment Test.

**Satan** But lowercase *devil* and *satanic*.

**satellite communications** The following are some generally used technical terms dealing with satellite communications.
—*uplink* The transmission from the ground to the satellite.
—*downlink* The transmission from the satellite to the ground.
— *footprint* The area on the ground in which a transmission from a particular satellite can be received.
—*earth station* Sending or receiving equipment on the ground for a satellite.
—*transponder* The equipment

on a satellite that receives from the ground and sends to the ground. A satellite usually has a number of *transponders.*
—*geosynchronous* A satellite orbit in which the satellite appears to always be in the same place in reference to the Earth. Most communications satellites are in geosynchronous orbits. Also *geostationary.*

**satellites** See **spacecraft designations**.

**Saturday** See **days of the week**.

**Saturday night special** See **weapons**.

**Saudi Arabian Oil Co.**
*Saudi Aramco* is acceptable on second reference. (Formerly the Arabian American Oil Co.)

**Sault Ste. Marie, Mich., Sault Ste. Marie, Ontario**
The abbreviation is *Ste.* instead of *St.* because the full name is *Sault Sainte Marie.*

**savings and loan associations** See entry in **Business Guidelines**.

**savior** Use this spelling for all senses, rather than the alternate form, *saviour.*

**Scandinavian Airlines System** SAS is acceptable on second reference.
Headquarters is in Stockholm, Sweden.

**scene numbers** Capitalize scene when used with a figure: *Scene 2; Act 2, Scene 4.*
But: *the second scene, the third scene.*

**scheme** Do not use as a synonym for *a plan* or *a project.*

**school** Capitalize when part of a proper name: *Public School 3, Madison Elementary School, Doherty Junior High School, Crocker High School.*

**scissors** Takes plural verbs and pronouns: *The scissors are on the table. Leave them there.*

**scotch barley, scotch broth, scotch salmon, scotch sour**

**Scotch tape** A trademark for a brand of transparent tape.

**Scotch whisky** A type of whiskey distilled in Scotland from malted barley. The malt is dried over a peat fire.

Capitalize *Scotch* and use the spelling *whisky* only when the two words are used together.

Lowercase *scotch* standing alone: *Give me some scotch.*

Use the spelling *whiskey* for generic references to the beverage, which may be distilled from any of several grains.

The verb *to scotch* means to stamp out, put an end to.

**Scotland** Use *Scotland* after the names of Scottish communities in datelines.

See **datelines** and **United Kingdom**.

**Scot, Scots, Scottish** A native of Scotland is a *Scot*. The people are the *Scots*, not the *Scotch*.

Somebody or something is *Scottish.*

**screen saver** Two words.

**Scripture, Scriptures** Capitalize when referring to the religious writings in the Bible.

See **Bible**.

**scuba** Lowercased acronym for *self-contained underwater breathing apparatus.*

**Scud missile**

**sculptor** Use for both men and women.

**scurrilous**

**Sea Islands** A chain of islands off the coasts of South Carolina, Georgia and Florida.

Islands within the boundaries of South Carolina include Parris Island, Port Royal Island, and St. Helena Island.

Those within Georgia include Cumberland Island (largest in the chain), St. Simons Island and St. Catherines Island (no apostrophes), and Sea Island.

Amelia Island is within the boundaries of Florida.

Several communities have names taken from the island name — Port Royal is a town on Port Royal Island, Sea Island is a resort on Sea Island, and St. Simons Island is a village on St. Simons Island.

In datelines:
*PORT ROYAL, S.C. (AP) —*
*ST. SIMONS ISLAND, Ga. (AP) —*

**SEAL(s)** A special operations force of the Navy. The acronym is for *sea, air, land.*

(See also **special forces**.)

**seaman** See **military titles**.

**Sears Holdings Corp.** A 2005 merger of Kmart and Sears, Roebuck and Co. Based in Hoffman Estates, Ill.

**seasons** Lowercase *spring, summer, fall, winter* and derivatives such as *springtime* unless part of a formal name: *Dartmouth Winter Carnival, Winter Olympics, Summer Olympics*.

**Seattle** The city in the state of Washington stands alone in datelines.

**second guess** (n.) The verb form: *second-guess*. Also: *second-guesser*.

**second hand** (n.) **secondhand** (adj. and adv.) *Secondhand Rose had a watch with a second hand that she bought secondhand.*

**second-rate** (adj.) All uses: *A second-rate play. The play is second-rate.*

**second reference** When used in this book, the term applies to all subsequent references to an organization or individual within a story.

Acceptable abbreviations and acronyms for organizations frequently in the news are listed under the organization's full name. A few prominent acronyms acceptable on first reference also are listed alphabetically according to the letters of the acronym.

The listing of an acceptable term for second reference does not mean that it always must be used after the first reference. Often a generic word such as *the agency, the commission* or *the company* is more appropriate and less jarring to the reader. At other times, the full name may need to be repeated for clarity.

For additional guidelines that

apply to organizations, see the **abbreviations and acronyms** entry and **capitalization**.

For additional guidelines that apply to individuals, see **courtesy titles** and **titles**.

**secretary** Capitalize before a name only if it is an official corporate or organizational title. Do not abbreviate.

See **titles**.

**secretary-general** With a hyphen. Capitalize as a formal title before a name: *Secretary-General Dag Hammarskjold.*

See **titles**.

**secretary of state** Capitalize as a formal title before a name.

See **titles**.

**secretary-treasurer** With a hyphen. Capitalize as a formal title before a name.

See **titles**.

**Secret Service** A federal agency administered by the Department of Homeland Security.

The *Secret Service Uniformed Division*, which protects the president's residence and offices and the embassies in Washington, formerly was known as the Executive Protective Service.

**section** Capitalize when used with a figure to identify part of a law or bill: *Section 14B of the Taft-Hartley Act.*

**Securities and Exchange Commission** *SEC* is acceptable on second reference.

The related legislation is the *Securities Exchange Act* (no *and*).

**Security Council (U.N.)** *Security Council* may be used on first reference in stories under a United Nations dateline. Use *U.N. Security Council* in other first references.

Retain capitalization of *Security Council* in all references.

Lowercase *council* whenever it stands alone.

**Seeing Eye dog** A trademark for a guide dog trained by Seeing Eye Inc. of Morristown, N.J.

**seesaw**

**self-** Always hyphenate:
self-assured        self-government
self-defense

**sell out** (v.) **sellout** (n.)

**semi-** The rules in **prefixes** apply, but in general, no hyphen. Some examples:
semifinal        semiofficial
semi-invalid        semitropical

**semiannual** Twice a year, a synonym for *biannual.*

Do not confuse it with *biennial*, which means every two years.

**semicolon** See entry in **Punctuation** chapter.

**semitrailer** Or *tractor-trailer* (but not semi-tractor trailer).

**Senate** Capitalize all specific references to governmental legislative bodies, regardless of whether the name of the nation is used: *the U.S. Senate, the Senate, the Virginia Senate, the state Senate, the Senate.*

Lowercase plural uses: *the Virginia and North Carolina senates.*

See **governmental bodies**.

The same principles apply to foreign bodies. See **foreign legislative bodies**.

Lowercase references to nongovernmental bodies: *the student senate at Yale.*

**senatorial** Always lowercase.

**senator, Sen.** See **legislative titles** and **party affiliation**.

**send off** (v.) **send-off** (n.)

**senior** See the **junior, senior** entry.

**senior citizen** Use the term sparingly. See **elderly**.

**sentences** Capitalize the first word of every sentence, including quoted statements and direct questions:
*Patrick Henry said, "I know not what course others may take, but as for me, give me liberty or give me death."*

Capitalize the first word of a quoted statement if it constitutes a sentence, even if it was part of a larger sentence in the original: *Patrick Henry said, "Give me liberty or give me death."*

In direct questions, even without quotation marks: *The story answers the question, Where does true happiness really lie?*

Use a single space between sentences.

See **ellipsis** in the **Punctuation** chapter and poetry.

**Sept. 11** The preferred term for describing the terrorist attacks in the United States Sept. 11, 2001. Use 2001 if needed for clarity. See **9/11** entry.

**September** See **months**.

**sergeant** See **military titles**.

**sergeant-at-arms**

**serial numbers** Use figures and capital letters in solid form (no hyphens or spaces unless the source indicates they are an integral part of the code): *A1234567*.

**server** On the World Wide Web, a computer that is host to a Web site.

### serviceable

**service clubs** See the **fraternal organizations and service clubs** entry.

**service mark** A brand, symbol, word, etc. used by a supplier of services and protected by law to prevent a competitor from using it: *Realtor*, for a member of the National Association of Realtors, for example.

When a service mark is used, capitalize it.

The preferred form, however, is to use a generic term unless the service mark is essential to the story.

See **brand names** and **trademark**.

**sesquicentennial** A 150-year period.

**set up** (v.) **setup** (n. and adj.)

**7-Eleven** Trademark for stores operated and licensed by Southland Corp. Headquarters in Dallas.

**Seven Seas** Arabian Sea, Atlantic Ocean, Bay of Bengal, Mediterranean Sea, Persian Gulf, Red Sea, South China Sea.

**Seven Sisters** The colleges are: Barnard, Bryn Mawr, Mount Holyoke, Radcliffe, Smith, Vassar and Wellesley.

Also an outdated nickname for the world's largest privately operated oil companies. They were: British Petroleum, Exxon, Gulf, Mobil, Royal Dutch Shell, Texaco, and Chevron, formerly Standard Oil Co. of California. Chevron has since taken over Gulf and merged with Texaco. Exxon and Mobil have merged.

**Seventh-day Adventist Church** The denomination is traceable to the preaching of William Miller of New Hampton, N.Y., a Baptist layman who said his study of the Book of Daniel showed that the end of the world would come in the mid-1840s.

When the prediction did not come true, the Millerites split into smaller groups. One, influenced by visions described by Ellen Harmon, later the wife of James White, is the precursor of the Seventh-day Adventist practice today.

The church has four constituent levels: 1. Local churches. 2. Local conferences of churches for a state or part of a state. 3. Union conferences of a number of local conferences. 4. The General Conference.

The General Conference in Session, which meets every five years, and the General Conference Executive Committee are the highest administrative authorities.

The headquarters in Silver Spring, Md., lists membership at 862,000 for the United States and more than 12 million worldwide.

The description *adventist* is based on the belief that a second coming of Christ is near. *Seventh-day* derives from the contention that the Bible requires observing the seventh day of the week as the Sabbath.

Baptism, by immersion, is reserved for those old enough to understand its meaning. Baptism and the Lord's Supper are the only sacraments.

The head of the General Conference holds the formal title of *president*. The formal titles for ministers are *pastor* or *elder*. Capitalize them when used immediately before a name on first reference. On second reference, use only the last name.

The designation *the Rev.* is not used.

See **religious titles**.

**7UP** Trademark for a brand of soft drink. Also *7 UP*, or *Seven-Up*.

**Seven Wonders of the World** The Egyptian pyramids, the hanging gardens of Babylon, the Mausoleum at Halicarnassus, the temple of Artemis at Ephesus, the Colossus of Rhodes, the statue of Zeus by Phidias at Olympia and the Pharos or lighthouse at Alexandria.

**sewage** Use this term, not *sewerage*, for both the waste matter and the drainage system.

**sexism** See the **man, mankind** and **women** entries.

**shah** Capitalize when used as a title before a name: *Shah Mohammad Reza Pahlavi of Iran.*

The Shah of Iran commonly is known only by this title, which is, in effect, an alternate name. Capitalize *Shah of Iran* in references to the holder of the title; lowercase subsequent references as *the shah.*

The practice is based on the guidelines in the **nobility** entry.

**shake up** (v.) **shake-up** (n. and adj.)

**shall, will** Use *shall* to express determination: *We shall overcome. You and he shall stay.*

Either *shall* or *will* may be used in first-person constructions that do not emphasize determination: *We shall hold a meeting. We will hold a meeting.*

For second- and third-person constructions, use *will* unless determination is stressed: *You will like it. She will not be pleased.*

See the **should, would** entry and **subjunctive mood**.

**shape up** (v.) **shape-up** (n. and adj.)

**Shariah** Islamic law.

**Shavuot** The Jewish Feast of Weeks, commemorating the receiving of the Ten Commandments. Occurs in May or June.

**she** Do not use this pronoun in references to ships or nations. Use *it* instead.

**Sheet Metal Workers International Association** The shortened form *Sheet Metal Workers union* is acceptable in all references.

Headquarters is in Washington.

**Sheetrock** A trademark for a brand of gypsum wallboard.

**sheik** Use this spelling unless the individual named personally prefers *sheikh.*

**shell** See **weapons**.

**Shell Oil Co.** This U.S. company, with headquarters in Houston, is part of Royal Dutch Shell

PLC, which owns more than half of the stock in Shell Oil.

**sheriff** Capitalize when used as a formal title before a name. See **titles**.

**ships** See the **boats, ships** entry.

**Shiite** The spelling for this branch of Islam. Plural is *Shiites.* (See **Islam**.)

**shirt sleeve, shirt sleeves** (n.) **shirt-sleeve** (adj.)

**shoeshine, shoestring**

**shopworn**

**shortchange**

**short-lived** (adj.) *A short-lived plan. The plan was short-lived.*

**short ton** Equal to 2,000 pounds. See **ton**.

**shot** See **weapons**.

**shotgun** See **weapons**.

**should, would** Use *should* to express an obligation: *We should help the needy.*

Use *would* to express a customary action: *In the summer we would spend hours by the seashore.*

Use *would* also in constructing a conditional past tense, but be careful:

Wrong: *If Soderholm would not have had an injured foot, Thompson would not have been in the lineup.*

Right: *If Soderholm had not had an injured foot, Thompson would not have been in the lineup.*

See **subjunctive mood**.

**showcase, showroom**

**show off** (v.) **showoff** (n.)

**shrubs** See **plants**.

**shut down** (v.) **shutdown** (n.)

**shut-in**

**shut off** (v.) **shut-off** (n.)

**shut out** (v.) **shutout** (n.)

**(sic)** Do not use (*sic*) unless it is in the matter being quoted. To show that an error, peculiar usage or spelling is in the original, use a note to editors at the top of the story, below the summary line but ahead of a byline.

— — —

**Eds. note: [ Eds: The spelling cabob is in the original copy. ]**
*or*
**Eds. note: [ Eds: The spelling Jorga is correct. ]**

**Sicily** Use instead of Italy in datelines on stories from communities on this island.

**side by side, side-by-side** *They walked side by side. The stories received side-by-side display.*

**Sierra Nevada, the** Not *Sierra Nevada mountains* or *Sierra Nevada mountain range.* (*Sierra* means mountain range.)

**sightseeing, sightseer**

**sign-up** (n. and adj.) Use two words (no hyphen) in verb form.

**Simoniz** A trademark for a brand of auto wax.

**Sinai** Not the *Sinai.* But: *the*

*Sinai Desert, the Sinai Peninsula.*

**Singapore** Stands alone in datelines.

**single-handed, single-handedly**

**sir** See **nobility**.

**sister** Capitalize in all references before the names of nuns.

If no surname is given, the name is the same in all references: *Sister Agnes Rita.*

If a surname is used in first reference, drop the given name on second reference: *Sister Clair Regina Torpy* on first reference, *Sister Torpy* in subsequent references.

Use *Mother* the same way when referring to a woman who heads a group of nuns.

See **religious titles**.

**sister-in-law, sisters-in-law**

**sit down** (v.) **sit-down** (n. and adj.)

**sit in** (v.) **sit-in** (n. and adj.)

**sizable**

**sizes** Use figures: *a size 9 dress, size 40 long, 10 1/2B shoes, a 34 1/2 sleeve.*

**skeptic** See the **cynic, skeptic** entry.

**Skid Road, Skid Row** The term originated as *Skid Road* in the Seattle area, where dirt roads were used to skid logs to the mill. Over the years, *Skid Road* became a synonym for the area where loggers gathered, usually down among the rooming houses and saloons.

In time, the term spread to other cities as a description for sections, such as the Bowery in New York, that are havens for derelicts. In the process, *row* replaced *road* in many references.

Use *Skid Road* for this section in Seattle; either *Skid Road* or *Skid Row* for other areas.

**skillful**

**ski, skis, skier, skied, skiing** Also: *ski jump, ski jumping.*

**slang** In general, avoid slang, the highly informal language that is outside of conventional or standard usage.

See **colloquialisms**; **dialect**; and **word selection**.

**slash** Acceptable in descriptive phrases such as *24/7* or *9/11*, but otherwise confine its use to special situations, as with fractions or denoting the ends of a line in quoted poetry.

**slaying** See the **homicide, murder, manslaughter** entry.

**sledgehammer**

**sleet** See **weather terms**.

**sleight of hand**

**slowdown** (n.) Two words in verb form.

**slumlord**

**slush fund**

**small-arms fire**

**small-business man**

**smash up** (v.) **smashup** (n. and adj.)

**Smithfield Ham** A trademark for a ham dry-cured, smoked and aged in Smithfield, Va.

**Smithsonian Institution** Not *Smithsonian Institute.*

**smoke bomb, smoke screen**

**smokejumper** One word, lowercase, for the firefighter who gets to fires by aircraft and parachute.

**Smokey** Or *Smokey Bear.* Not *Smokey the Bear.*
But: *A smoky room.*

**smolder** Not *smoulder.*

**sneaked** Preferred as past tense of *sneak.* Do not use the colloquial *snuck.*

**snowdrift, snowfall, snowflake, snowman, snowplow, snowshoe, snowstorm, snowsuit**

**so called** (adv.) **so-called** (adj.)

**socialist, socialism** See the **political parties and philosophies** entry.

**Social Security** Capitalize all references to the U.S. system.
The number groups are hyphenated: *123-45-6789*
Lowercase generic uses such as: *Is there a social security program in Sweden?*

**social titles** See **courtesy titles**.

**Society for the Prevention of Cruelty to Animals** *SPCA* is acceptable on second

reference.
The *American Society for the Prevention of Cruelty to Animals* is limited to the five boroughs of New York City.
The autonomous chapters in other cities ordinarily precede the organization by the name of the city: On first reference, *the San Francisco Society for the Prevention of Cruelty to Animals;* on second, *the San Francisco SPCA* or *SPCA* as appropriate in the context.

**Society of Friends** See **Quakers**.

**Society of Professional Journalists** (no longer the Society of Professional Journalists, Sigma Delta Chi). On second reference: *SPJ.*

**soft-spoken**

**software titles** Capitalize but do not use quotation marks around such titles as WordPerfect or Windows, but use quotation marks for computer games: *"Where in the World is Carmen Sandiego?"*

**solicitor** See **lawyer**.

**Solid South** Those Southern states traditionally regarded as supporters of the Democratic Party.

**soliloquy, soliloquies**

**song titles** See **composition titles**.

**son-in-law, sons-in-law**

**SOS** The distress signal.
*S.O.S* (no final period) is a trademark for a brand of soap pad.

**sound barrier** The speed of sound is no longer a true barrier because aircraft have exceeded it. See **Mach number**.

**source code** The basic blueprint of any computer program. Without the *source code* it is not possible to understand how a program works internally.

**South** As defined by the U.S. Census Bureau, the 16-state region is broken into three divisions.

The four *East South Central* states are Alabama, Kentucky, Mississippi and Tennessee.

The eight *South Atlantic* states are Delaware, Florida, Georgia, Maryland, North Carolina, South Carolina, Virginia and West Virginia.

The four *West South Central* states are Arkansas, Louisiana, Oklahoma and Texas.

There is no official U.S. Census Bureau definition of Southeast.

See **Midwest region**; **Northeast region**; and **West** for the bureau's other regional breakdowns.

**South America** See **Western Hemisphere**.

**South Carolina** Abbrev.: *S.C.* See **state names**.

**South Dakota** Abbrev.: *S.D.* See **state names**.

**Southeast Asia** The nations of the Indochinese Peninsula and the islands southeast of it: Cambodia, Indonesia, Laos, Malaysia, Myanmar, Papua New Guinea, the Philippines, Singapore, Thailand and Vietnam.

See **Asian subcontinent** and Far East.

**south, southern, southeast, southwest** See the **directions and regions** entry.

**Southwest Airlines** Headquarters is in Dallas.

**Soviet Union** See **Commonwealth of Independent States**.

**Space Age** It began with the launching of Sputnik 1 on Oct. 4, 1957.

**space agency** See **National Aeronautics and Space Administration**.

**space centers** See **John F. Kennedy Space Center** and **Lyndon B. Johnson Space Center**.

**spacecraft designations** Use Arabic figures and capitalize the name: *Gemini 7, Apollo 11, Pioneer 10*.

**spaceship**

**space shuttle** Lowercase *space shuttle*, but capitalize a proper name.

The space shuttle is a reusable winged aircraft capable of carrying people and cargo into Earth orbit. It is designed to take off vertically with the aid of booster rockets. After an orbital mission, re-entry begins with the firing of engines that send the craft back into Earth's atmosphere. The final leg of the return trip is a powerless glide to a landing strip.

**spacewalk**

**Spanish-American War**

**Spanish names** The family names of both the father and

mother usually are considered part of a person's full name. In everyday use, customs sometimes vary with individuals and countries.

The normal sequence is given name, father's family name, mother's family name: *Jose Lopez Portillo.*

On second reference, use only the father's family name (*Lopez*), unless the individual prefers or is widely known by a multiple last name (*Lopez Portillo*).

Some individuals use a *y* (for *and*) between the two surnames to ensure that both names are used together (including second references): *Jose Lopez y Portillo.*

A married woman frequently uses her father's name, followed by the particle *de* (for *of*) and her husband's name. A woman named *Irma Perez* who married a man named *Anibal Gutierrez* would be known as *Irma Perez de Gutierrez.*

**speaker** Capitalize as a formal title before a name. Generally, it is a formal title only for the speaker of a legislative body: *Speaker Thomas P. O'Neill.*
See **titles**.

**special contexts** When this term is used in this book, it means that the material described may be used in a regular column devoted to a specialized subject or when a particular literary effect is suitable.

Special literary effects generally are suitable only in feature copy, but even there they should be used with care. Most feature material should follow the same style norms that apply to regular news copy.

**special forces** Do not use interchangeably with *special operations forces.* Capitalize when referring specifically to the *U.S. Army Special Forces*, also known as Green Berets. Others, such as Navy SEALs or Army Rangers, should be called *special operations forces.*

**species** Same in singular and plural. Use singular or plural verbs and pronouns depending on the sense: *The species has been unable to maintain itself. Both species are extinct.*
See **genus, species**.

**speeches** Capitalize and use quotation marks for their formal titles, as described in **composition titles**.

**speechmaker, speechmaking**

**speed of sound** See **Mach number**.

**speeds** Use figures. *The car slowed to 7 miles per hour, winds of 5 to 10 miles per hour, winds of 7 to 9 knots, 10-knot wind.*

Avoid extensively hyphenated constructions such as *5-mile-per-hour winds.*

**speed up** (v.) **speedup** (n. and adj.)

**spelling** The basic rule when in doubt is to consult this book followed by, if necessary, a dictionary under conditions described in the **dictionaries** entry.

Memory Aid: Noah Webster developed the following rule of thumb for the frequently vexing question of whether to double a final consonant in forming the present participle and past tense of a verb:

—If the stress in pronunciation is on the first syllable, do not double the consonant: *combat, combating, combated; cancel, canceling, canceled.*

—If the stress in pronunciation is on the second syllable, double the consonant unless confusion would result: *incur, incurred, incurring.* An exception, to avoid confusion with *buss,* is *bus, bused, busing.*

Avoid spelling simplifications such as *thru* or *lite.*

British spellings, when they differ from American, are acceptable only in particular cases such as formal or composition titles: *Jane's Defence Weekly, Labour Party.*

**spill, spilled, spilling** Not *spilt* in the past tense.

**split infinitive** See **verbs**.

**spokesman, spokeswoman** But not *spokesperson.* Use a *representative* if you do not know the sex of the individual.

**sport utility vehicle** No plural *s* in *sport*; no hyphen.

*SUV* is acceptable on second reference.

**spouse** Use when some of the people involved may be men. For example: *physicians and their spouses,* not *physicians and their wives.*

**spring** See **seasons**.

**springtime**

**sputnik** Usually lowercase, but capitalize when followed by a figure as part of a proper name: *Sputnik 1.*

It is Russian for *satellite.*

**squall** See **weather terms**.

**square** Do not abbreviate. Capitalize when part of a proper name: *Washington Square.*

**squinting modifier** A misplaced adverb that can be interpreted as modifying either of two words: *Those who lie often are found out.*

Place the adverb where there can be no confusion, even if a compound verb must be split: *Those who often lie are found out.* Or if that was not the sense: *Those who lie are often found out.*

**Sri Lanka** Formerly Ceylon. Use *Sri Lanka* in datelines and other references to the nation.

The people may be called either *Sri Lankans* or *Ceylonese.*

Before the nation was called Ceylon, it was Serendip, whence comes the word *serendipity.*

**SRO** Acceptable on second reference for *standing room only.*

**SST** Acceptable in all references for a *supersonic transport.*

**stadium, stadiums** Capitalize only when part of a proper name: *Shea Stadium.*

**Stalin, Josef** Not *Joseph.*

**stall** Use care when using *stall* in this sense. When an automobile *stalls,* the engine stops. This may not be true when an airplane *stalls*; it pitches forward or sideways because of a lack of air speed.

**stamp, stomp** Both are acceptable, but *stamp* is preferred.

**stanch, staunch** *Stanch* is a verb: *He stanched the flow of* *blood.*

*Staunch* is an adjective: *She is a staunch supporter of equality.*

### Standard & Poor's Register of Corporations The

source for determining the formal name of a business. See **company names**.

The register is published by Standard & Poor's of New York.

### standard-bearer

### standard time Capitalize

*Eastern Standard Time, Pacific Standard Time,* etc., but lowercase *standard time* when standing alone.

See **time zones**.

### stand in (v.) stand-in (n. and adj.)

### standing room only SRO

is acceptable on second reference.

### stand off (v.) standoff (n. and adj.)

### stand out (v.) standout (n. and adj.)

### starboard Nautical for *right*,

when facing the bow, or forward. See **port, starboard** entry.

### "The Star-Spangled Banner" But lowercase *the*

*national anthem.*

### startup One word (n. and

adj.) to describe a new business venture. (An exception to Webster's preference.)

### state Lowercase in all *state of*

constructions: *the state of Maine, the states of Maine and Vermont.*

Four states — Kentucky, Massachusetts, Pennsylvania and Virginia — are legally common-

wealths rather than states. The distinction is necessary only in formal uses: *The commonwealth of Kentucky filed a suit.* For simple geographic reference: *Tobacco is grown in the state of Kentucky.*

Do not capitalize *state* when used simply as an adjective to specify a level of jurisdiction: *state Rep. William Smith, the state Transportation Department, state funds.*

Apply the same principle to phrases such as *the city of Chicago, the town of Auburn,* etc.

See also **state names**.

### statehouse Capitalize all

references to a specific statehouse, with or without the name of the state: *The Vermont Statehouse is in Montpelier. The governor will visit the Statehouse today.*

Lowercase plural uses: *the Massachusetts and Rhode Island statehouses.*

### state names Follow these

guidelines:

STANDING ALONE: Spell out the names of the 50 U.S. states when they stand alone in textual material. Any state name may be condensed, however, to fit typographical requirements for tabular material.

EIGHT NOT ABBREVIATED: The names of eight states are never abbreviated in datelines or text: *Alaska, Hawaii, Idaho, Iowa, Maine, Ohio, Texas* and *Utah.*

Memory Aid: Spell out the names of the two states that are not part of the contiguous United States and of the continental states that are five letters or fewer.

ABBREVIATIONS REQUIRED: Use the state abbreviations listed at the end of this section:

—In conjunction with the name of a city, town, village or military base in most datelines. See **datelines** for examples and exceptions for large cities.

—In conjunction with the name of a city, county, town, village or military base in text. See examples in Punctuation section below. See **datelines** for guidelines on when a city name may stand alone in the body of a story.

—In short-form listings of party affiliation: *D-Ala., R-Mont.* See **party affiliation** entry for details.

Following are the state abbreviations, which also appear in the entries for each state (ZIP code abbreviations in parentheses):

| | | |
|---|---|---|
| Ala. (AL) | Md. (MD) | N.D. (ND) |
| Ariz. (AZ) | Mass. (MA) | Okla. (OK) |
| Ark. (AR) | Mich. (MI) | Ore. (OR) |
| Calif. (CA) | Minn. (MN) | Pa. (PA) |
| Colo. (CO) | Miss. (MS) | R.I. (RI) |
| Conn. (CT) | Mo. (MO) | S.C. (SC) |
| Del. (DE) | Mont. (MT) | S.D. (SD) |
| Fla. (FL) | Neb. (NE) | Tenn. (TN) |
| Ga. (GA) | Nev. (NV) | Vt. (VT) |
| Ill. (IL) | N.H. (NH) | Va. (VA) |
| Ind. (IN) | N.J. (NJ) | Wash. (WA) |
| Kan. (KS) | N.M. (NM) | W.Va. (WV) |
| Ky. (KY) | N.Y. (NY) | Wis. (WI) |
| La. (LA) | N.C. (NC) | Wyo. (WY) |

(These are the ZIP code abbreviations for the eight states that are not abbreviated in datelines or text: AK (Alaska), HI (Hawaii), ID (Idaho), IA (Iowa), ME (Maine), OH (Ohio), TX (Texas), UT (Utah). Also: District of Columbia (DC).

Use the two-letter Postal Service abbreviations only with full addresses, including ZIP code.

PUNCTUATION: Place one comma between the city and the state name, and another comma after the state name, unless ending a sentence or indicating a dateline: *He was traveling from Nashville, Tenn., to Austin, Texas, en route to his home in Albuquerque, N.M. She said Cook County, Ill., was Mayor Daley's stronghold.*

MISCELLANEOUS: Use *New York state* when necessary to distinguish the state from New York City.

Use *state of Washington* or *Washington state* when necessary to distinguish the state from the District of Columbia. (*Washington State* is the name of a university in the state of Washington.)

**State of the Union** Capitalize all references to the president's annual address.

Lowercase other uses: *"The state of the union is confused,"* the editor said.

**state police** Capitalize with a state name if part of the formal description for a police agency: *the New York State Police, the Virginia State Police.*

In most cases, state police standing alone is a shorthand reference for *state policemen* rather than a reference to the agency. For consistency and to avoid hairline distinctions about whether the reference is to the agency or the officers, lowercase the words *state police* whenever they are not preceded by a state name.

See **highway patrol**.

**states' rights**

**statewide**

**stationary, stationery** To stand still is to be *stationary.* Writing paper is *stationery.*

**station wagon**

**statute mile** It equals 5,280 feet, or approximately 1.6 kilometers.

To convert to approximate nautical miles, multiply the number of statute miles by .869.

See **kilometer**; **knot**; **mile**; and **nautical mile**.

**staunch** See the **stanch, staunch** entry.

**stealth** When used in connection with military aircraft, ships and vehicles it means the equipment is masked from various types of electronic detection. Stealth equipment can range from radar wave absorbing paint to electronic jamming devices. Like the *cruise* missile, always lowercase, no quotation marks.

**stepbrother, stepfather** Also: *stepsister, stepmother.*

**steppingstone**

**stifling**

**St. John's** The city in the Canadian province of Newfoundland and Labrador.

Not to be confused with *Saint John, New Brunswick.*

**St. Louis** The city in Missouri stands alone in datelines.

**stool pigeon**

**stopgap**

**storm** See **weather terms**.

**storyteller**

**straight-laced, strait-laced** Use *straight-laced* for someone strict or severe in behavior or moral views.

Reserve *strait-laced* for the notion of confinement, as in a corset.

**strait** Capitalize as part of a proper name: *Bering Strait, Strait of Gibraltar.*

But: *the Bosporus* and *the Dardanelles.* Neither is followed by *Strait.*

**straitjacket** Not *straightjacket.*

**Strategic Arms Reduction Treaty** *START* is acceptable on first reference to the treaty as long as it is made immediately clear which is being referred to.

Use the *strategic arms treaty* or *the treaties* in some references to avoid alphabet soup.

There are two treaties, START I (1991) and START II (1993).

Do not confuse with the *Strategic Arms Limitation Treaty* of 1979, known as *SALT.*

**Strategic Defense Initiative** This is the official name of the research and development work on defense against a nuclear attack. *SDI* is the acronym and is acceptable on second reference. "Star Wars" has become synonymous with both and was derived from the movie series. If used, it must always be within quotation marks.

**street** Abbreviate only with a numbered address. See **addresses**.

**strikebreaker**

**strong-arm** (v., adj.)

**strong-willed**

**stylebook** One word when referring to the *AP Stylebook* and to *stylebooks* generically.

**Styrofoam** A trademark for a brand of plastic foam. Use the term plastic foam unless referring specifically to the trademark product. (Note: Cups and other serving items are not made of *Styrofoam* brand plastic foam.)

**sub-** The rules in **prefixes** apply, but in general, no hyphen. Some examples:

| | |
|---|---|
| subbasement | submachine gun |
| subcommittee | suborbital |
| subculture | subtotal |
| subdivision | subzero |

**subcommittee** Lowercase when used with the name of a legislative body's full committee: *a Ways and Means subcommittee.*

Capitalize when a subcommittee has a proper name of its own: *the Senate Permanent Subcommittee on Investigations.*

**subject** See the **citizen, resident, subject, national, native** entry.

**subjunctive mood** Use the subjunctive mood of a verb for contrary-to-fact conditions, and expressions of doubts, wishes or regrets:

*If I were a rich man, I wouldn't have to work hard.*

*I doubt that more money would be the answer.*

*I wish it were possible to take back my words.*

Sentences that express a contingency or hypothesis may use either the subjunctive or the indicative mood depending on the context. In general, use the subjunctive if there is little likelihood that a contingency might come true:

*If I were to marry a millionaire, I wouldn't have to worry about money.*

*If the bill passes as expected, it*

*will provide an immediate tax cut.* See the **should, would** entry.

**submachine gun** See **weapons**.

**subpoena, subpoenaed, subpoenaing**

**Sucaryl** A trademark for a brand of noncaloric sweetener.

**successor**

**suffixes** See separate listing for commonly used suffixes.

Follow Webster's New World College Dictionary for words not in this book.

If a word combination is not listed in Webster's New World, use two words for the verb form; hyphenate any noun or adjective forms.

**suit, suite** You may have a *suit* of clothes, a *suit* of cards, or be faced with a *lawsuit.*

There are *suites* of music, rooms and furniture.

**Sukkot** The Jewish Feast of Tabernacles, celebrating the fall harvest and commemorating the desert wandering of the Jews during the Exodus. Occurs in September or October.

**summer** See **seasons**.

**summertime**

**sun** Lowercase. See **heavenly bodies**.

**sunbathe** The verb forms: *sunbathed, sunbathing.* Also: *sunbather.*

**Sun Belt** Generally those states in the South and West, ranging from Florida and Georgia through the Gulf states into California.

**Sunday** See **days of the week**.

**super** Avoid the slang tendency to use it in place of *excellent, wonderful,* etc.

**super-** The rules in **prefixes** apply, but in general, no hyphen. Some frequently used words:

| | |
|---|---|
| superagency | superhighway |
| supercarrier | superpower |
| supercharge | supertanker |

As with all prefixes, however, use a hyphen if the word that follows is capitalized: *super-Republican.*

**Super Bowl**

**superconducting super collider**

**superintendent** Do not abbreviate. Capitalize when used as a formal title before a name.
See **titles**.

**superior court** See **court names**.

**supersede**

**supersonic** See **Mach number**.

**supersonic transport** *SST* is acceptable in all references.

**supra-** The rules in **prefixes** apply, but in general, no hyphen. Some examples:

supragovernmental  supranational

**Supreme Court of the United States** Capitalize *U.S. Supreme Court* and also *the Su-preme Court* when the context makes the *U.S.* designation unnecessary.

The chief justice is properly the *chief justice of the United States,* not *of the Supreme Court: Chief Justice William Rehnquist.*

The proper title for the eight other members of the court is *associate justice.* When used as a formal title before a name, it should be shortened to justice unless there are special circumstances: *Justice Sandra Day O'Connor, Associate Justice Sandra Day O'Connor.*

See **judge**.

**supreme courts of the states** Capitalize with the state name (*the New Jersey Supreme Court*) and without the state name when the context makes it unnecessary: *the state Supreme Court, the Supreme Court.*

If a court with this name is not a state's highest tribunal, the fact should be noted. In New York, for example, the Supreme Court is a trial court. Appeals are directed to the Appellate Division of the Supreme Court. The state's highest court is the Court of Appeals.

**surface-to-air missile(s)** *SAM(s)* may be used on second reference. Avoid the redundant *SAM missiles.*

**suspensive hyphenation** The form: *The 5- and 6-year-olds attend morning classes.*

**SWAT** Acronym for *Special Weapons and Tactics.*

**swastika**

**sweat pants, sweat shirt, sweat suit**

**Swift boat** Use a cap S for this particular type of Navy boat.

**Swiss** Switzerland's national airline is formally Swiss International Air Lines. Headquarters is in Zurich, Switzerland.

### syllabus, syllabuses

**synagogue** Capitalize only when part of a formal name.

### Synagogue Council of America See Jewish congregations.

**sync** Short for synchronization; not *synch*. Also, *syncing*.

**synod** A council of churches or church officials. See the entry for the denomination in question.

# T

**Tabasco** A trademark for a brand of hot pepper sauce.

**tablecloth**

**tablespoon, tablespoonfuls** Equal to three teaspoons or one-half a fluid ounce.

The metric equivalent is approximately 15 milliliters.

See **liter** and **recipes**.

**table tennis** See **pingpong**.

**tabular matter** Exceptions may be made to the normal rules for abbreviations, as necessary to make material fit. But make any abbreviations as clear as possible.

**tailspin**

**tail wind**

**Taiwan** Use *Taiwan*, not *Formosa*, in references to the Nationalist government in Taiwan and to the island itself.

See **China**.

**take-home pay**

**take off** (v.) **takeoff** (n. and adj.)

**take out** (v.) **takeout** (n. and adj.)

**take over** (v.) **takeover** (n. and adj.)

**take up** (v.) **takeup** (n. and adj.)

**Taliban** Extremist Islamic movement that ruled Afghanistan until driven out by U.S.-led coalition after the Sept. 11, 2001, terrorist attacks. Arabic for *religious students*, it takes a plural verb. The singular is *Talib*.

**Talmud** The collection of writings that constitute the Jewish civil and religious law.

**Tammany, Tammany Hall, Tammany Society**

**tanks** Use Arabic figures, separated from letters by a hyphen: *M-60*. Plural: *M-60s*.

**tape recording** The noun. But hyphenate the verb form: *tape-record*.

**taps** Lowercase (without quotation marks) the bugle call for "lights out," also sounded at military funerals.

**Taser** Trademark for an electronic control device or stun gun. (Acronym for Thomas A. Swift's Electric Rifle.)

**Tass** Acceptable on first reference for the Russian government's news agency that is officially *ITAR-Tass*. *ITAR* is an acronym for *Information Telegraph Agency of Russia.* Copy from other parts of the former Soviet Union should carry the logo of the local agency plus *Tass.*

**tattletale**

**teachers college** No apostrophe.

**team** See **collective nouns**.

**teammate**

**teamster** Capitalize *teamster* only if the intended meaning is that the individual is a member of the International Brotherhood of Teamsters, Chauffeurs, Warehousemen and Helpers of America.

**Teamsters union** Acceptable in all references to the *International Brotherhood of Teamsters, Chauffeurs, Warehousemen and Helpers of America.*
See the entry under that name.

**tear gas** Two words. See also **Chemical Mace**.

**teaspoon** Equal to one-sixth of a fluid ounce, or one-third of a tablespoon.
The metric equivalent is approximately 5 milliliters.
See **liter**.

**teaspoonful, teaspoonfuls** Not *teaspoonsful.* See **recipes**.

**Technicolor** A trademark for a process of making color motion pictures.

**teen, teenager** (n.) **teenage** (adj.) No hyphen is a change in AP style. Do not use *teen-aged.*

**Teflon** A trademark for a type of nonstick coating.

**telecast** (n.) **televise** (v.)

**telephone numbers** Use figures. The form: *212-621-1500.* For international numbers use 011 (from the United States), the country code, the city code and the telephone number: *011-44-20-7535-1515.* Use hyphens, not periods.
The form for toll-free numbers: *800-111-1000.*
If extension numbers are needed, use a comma to separate the main number from the extension: *212-621-1500, ext. 2.*

**teleprompter** It has become a generic term, no longer a trademark, for a type of television cuing device.

**Teletype** A trademark for a brand of teleprinters and teletypewriters.

**television program titles** Follow the guidelines in **composition titles**.
Put quotation marks around *show* only if it is part of the formal name. The word *show* may be dropped when it would be cumbersome, such as in a set of listings.
(Italics are used here only to illustrate examples; do not use italics on the wires.)
In text or listing, treat programs named after the star in any of the following ways: *"The Mary Tyler Moore Show," "Mary Tyler Moore"* or *the Mary Tyler Moore show.* But be consistent in a story or set of listings.
Use quotation marks also for the title of an episode: *"Chuckles Bites the Dust," an episode of "The Mary Tyler Moore Show."* Also:

"NBC Nightly News," the "Today" show, "The Tonight Show."

**television station** The call letters alone are frequently adequate, but when this phrase is needed, use lowercase: *television station WTEV.*

**telex, Telex** (n.) A communications system. Use lowercase when not referring to a specific company. Use uppercase only when referring to the company. Never used as a verb.

**telltale**

**temblor** See **earthquakes**.

**temperatures** Use figures for all except *zero.* Use a word, not a minus sign, to indicate temperatures below zero.

Right: *The day's low was minus 10.*

Right: *The day's low was 10 below zero.*

Wrong: *The day's low was -10.*

Right: *The temperature rose to zero by noon.*

Right: *The day's high was expected to be 9 or 10.*

Also: *5-degree temperatures, temperatures fell 5 degrees, temperatures in the 30s* (no apostrophe).

Temperatures get *higher* or *lower,* but they don't get *warmer* or *cooler.*

Wrong: *Temperatures are expected to warm up in the area Friday.*

Right: *Temperatures are expected to rise in the area Friday.*

See **Fahrenheit**; **Celsius;** and **weather terms**.

**Ten Commandments** Do not abbreviate or use figures.

**tenderhearted**

**tenfold**

**Ten Most Wanted Fugitives** The FBI's official list.

**Tennessee** Abbrev.: *Tenn.* See **state names**.

**Tennessee Valley Authority** *TVA* is acceptable on second reference.

Headquarters is in Knoxville, Tenn.

**tera-** A prefix denoting 1 trillion units of a measure. Move the decimal point 12 places to the right, adding zeros if necessary, to convert to the basic unit: 5.5 teratons = 5,500,000,000,000 tons.

**terrace** Do not abbreviate. See **addresses**.

**Texaco** See **ChevronTexaco**.

**Texas** Do not abbreviate. Second in total land area.

See **state names**.

**Texas Hold 'em** The poker game.

**texts, transcripts** Follow normal style guidelines for capitalization, spelling and abbreviations in handling a text or transcript.

Use quotation marks only for words or phrases that were quoted in the text or by the person who spoke.

Identify a change in speakers by starting a paragraph with the new speaker's name and a colon. Use normal second-reference forms if the speaker has been identified earlier; provide a full name and identification if the individual is being mentioned for the first time.

Use *Q:* for *question* and *A:* for *answer* at the start of paragraphs when these notations are adequate to identify a change in speakers.

See **ellipsis** in the **Punctuation** chapter for guidelines on condensing texts and transcripts.

**Thai** A native or the language of Thailand.

*Siam* and *Siamese* are historical only.

Use *siamese* for the cat.

**Thanksgiving, Thanksgiving Day** The fourth Thursday in November.

**that (conjunction)** Use the conjunction *that* to introduce a dependent clause if the sentence sounds or looks awkward without it. There are no hard-and-fast rules, but in general:

—*That* usually may be omitted when a dependent clause immediately follows a form of the verb *to say*: *The president said he had signed the bill.*

—*That* should be used when a time element intervenes between the verb and the dependent clause: *The president said Monday that he had signed the bill.*

—*That* usually is necessary after some verbs. They include: *advocate, assert, contend, declare, estimate, make clear, point out, propose* and *state.*

—*That* is required before subordinate clauses beginning with conjunctions such as *after, although, because, before, in addition to, until* and *while*: *Haldeman said that after he learned of Nixon's intention to resign, he sought pardons for all connected with Watergate.*

When in doubt, include *that.* Omission can hurt. Inclusion never does.

**that, which (pronouns)** Use *that* and *which* in referring to inanimate objects and to animals without a name. Use *that* for essential clauses, important to the meaning of a sentence, and without commas: *I remember the day that we met.* Use *which* for nonessential clauses, where the pronoun is less necessary, and use commas: *The team, which finished last a year ago, is in first place.*

(Tip: If you can drop the clause and not lose the meaning of the sentence, use *which*; otherwise, use *that.* A *which* clause is surrounded by commas; no commas are used with *that* clauses.)

See the **essential clauses, nonessential clauses** entry for guidelines on using *that* and *which* to introduce phrases and clauses.

**theater** Use this spelling unless the proper name is *Theatre*: *Shubert Theatre.*

**theft** See the **burglary, larceny, robbery, theft** entry.

**their, there, they're** *Their* is a possessive pronoun: *They went to their house.*

*There* is an adverb indicating direction: *We went there for dinner.*

*There* also is used with the force of a pronoun for impersonal constructions in which the real subject follows the verb: *There is no food on the table.*

*They're* is a contraction for *they are.*

**theretofore** Use *until then.*

**thermos** Formerly a trademark, now a generic term for any vacuum bottle, although one manufacturer still uses the word as a brand name.

Lowercase *thermos* when it is used to mean any vacuum bottle; use *Thermos* when referring to the specific brand.

**Third World** The economically developing nations of Africa, Asia and Latin America.

Do not confuse with nonaligned, which is a political term. See **nonaligned** nations.

**three-D** *3-D* is preferred.

**3M** Trademark and official name of the company formerly known as Minnesota Mining & Manufacturing. Its products are known under the names *3M* and *Scotch.* Headquarters is in Maplewood, Minn.

**three R's** They are: *reading, 'riting and 'rithmetic.*

**threesome**

**throwaway** (n. and adj.)

**thunderstorm** See **weather terms**.

**Thursday** See **days of the week**.

**tidbit**

**tie in** (v.) **tie-in** (n. and adj.)

**tie, tied, tying**

**tie up** (v.) **tie-up** (n. and adj.)

**tilde** Do not use the symbol

in standard AP wire transmissions. If necessary for Internet addresses, write out the word and put it in parentheses.

**till** Or *until.* But not *'til.*

**time element** Use the days of the week, not *today* or *tonight* in print copy.

Use the month and a figure where appropriate. See **months** for forms and punctuation.

Avoid such redundancies as *last Tuesday* or *next Tuesday.* The past, present or future tense used for the verb usually provides adequate indication of which Tuesday is meant: *He said he finished the job Tuesday. She will return on Tuesday.*

Avoid awkward placements of the time element, particularly those that suggest the day of the week is the object of a transitive verb: *The police jailed Tuesday.* Potential remedies include the use of the word on (see the on entry), rephrasing the sentence, or placing the time element in a different sentence.

**time of day** The exact time of day that an event has happened or will happen is not necessary in most stories. Follow these guidelines to determine when it should be included and in what form:

SPECIFY THE TIME:

—Whenever it gives the reader a better picture of the scene: Did the earthquake occur when people were likely to be home asleep or at work? A clock reading for the time in the datelined community is acceptable although *predawn hours* or *rush hour* often is more graphic.

—Whenever the time is critical to the story: When will the rocket be launched? When will a major political address be broadcast? What is the deadline for meeting a demand?

DECIDING ON CLOCK TIME: When giving a clock reading, use the time in the datelined community.

If the story is undated, use the clock time in force where the event happened or will take place.

The only exception is a nationwide story or tabular listing that involves television or radio programs. Always use Eastern time, followed by *EDT* or *EST*, and specify whether the program will be broadcast simultaneously nationwide or whether times will vary because of separate transmissions for different time zones. If practical, specify those times in a separate paragraph.

ZONE ABBREVIATIONS: Use *EST*, *CDT*, *PST*, etc., after a clock time only if:

—The story involves travel or other activities, such as the closing hour for polling places or the time of a televised speech, likely to affect people or developments in more than one time zone.

—The item involves television or radio programs. (See above.)

—The item is undated.

—The item is an advisory to editors.

CONVERT TO EASTERN TIME? Do not convert clock times from other time zones in the continental United States to Eastern time. If there is high interest in the precise time, add *CDT*, *PST*, etc., to the local reading to help readers determine their equivalent local time.

If the time is critical in a story from outside the continental United States, provide a conversion to Eastern time using this form:

*The kidnappers set a 9 a.m. (3 a.m. EDT) deadline.*

See **time zones** for additional guidance on forms.

**times** Use figures except for *noon* and *midnight*. Use a colon to separate hours from minutes: *11 a.m., 1 p.m., 3:30 p.m.*

Avoid such redundancies as *10 a.m. this morning, 10 p.m. tonight* or *10 p.m. Monday night*. Use *10 a.m.* or *10 p.m. Monday*, etc., as required by the norms in time element.

The construction *4 o'clock* is acceptable, but time listings with *a.m.* or *p.m.* are preferred.

See **midnight**, **noon** and **time zones**.

**time sequences** Spell out: *50 hours, 23 minutes, 14 seconds*. When using the abbreviated form, as in sports statistics or similar agate use, or subsequent references, the form is: 2:30:21.65 (hours, minutes, seconds, tenths, hundredths).

**Time Warner Inc.** Time Warner, which merged with America Online in January 2000, includes Time Warner Cable, CNN, Time magazine, TBS, TNT, Cartoon Network, HBO, Fortune, Sports Illustrated, Entertainment Weekly and Looney Tunes. The online company AOL includes Netscape Communications, MovieFone and CompuServe.

A name change to AOL Time Warner Inc. was rescinded in 2003.

**time zones** Capitalize the full name of the time in force within a particular zone: *Eastern Standard Time, Eastern Daylight Time, Central Standard Time*, etc.

Lowercase all but the region

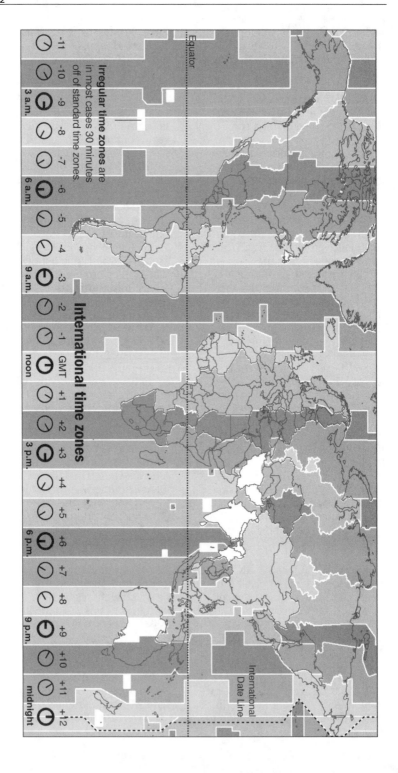

# United States time zones

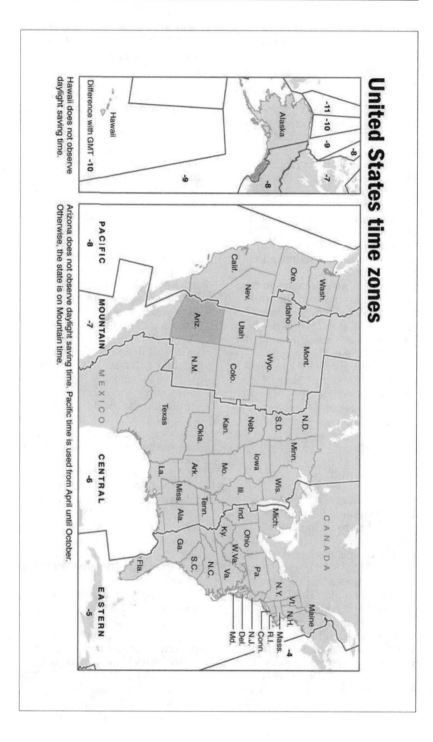

-11 -10 -9 -8

Alaska

-9

-8 -7

Hawaii

Difference with GMT -10

Hawaii does not observe
daylight saving time.

PACIFIC
-8

MOUNTAIN
-7

CENTRAL
-6

EASTERN
-5

Calif.

Ore.

Wash.

Nev.

Idaho

Ariz.

Utah

Mont.

N.M.

Colo.

Wyo.

N.D.

Texas

Okla.

Kan.

Neb.

S.D.

Minn.

La.

Ark.

Mo.

Iowa

Wis.

Miss.

Tenn.

Ill.

Ind.

Mich.

Ala.

Ga.

Ky.

Ohio

W.Va.

Pa.

Fla.

S.C.

N.C.

Va.

N.Y.

Vt. N.H.

Maine

Mass.
R.I.
Conn.
N.J.
Del.
Md.

-4

MEXICO

CANADA

Arizona does not observe daylight saving time. Pacific time is used from April until October.
Otherwise, the state is on Mountain time.

in short forms: *the Eastern time zone, Eastern time, Mountain time*, etc.

See **time of day** for guidelines on when to use clock time in a story.

Spell out *time zone* in references not accompanied by a clock reading: *Chicago is in the Central time zone.*

The abbreviations *EST, CDT*, etc., are acceptable on first reference for zones used within the continental United States, Canada and Mexico only if the abbreviation is linked with a clock reading: *noon EST, 9 a.m. PST.* (Do not set off the abbreviations with commas.)

Spell out all references to time zones not used within the contiguous United States: *When it is noon EDT, it is 1 p.m. Atlantic Standard Time and 8 a.m. Alaska Standard Time.*

One exception to the spelled-out form: *Greenwich Mean Time* may be abbreviated as *GMT* on second reference if used with a clock reading.

**tiptop**

**titleholder**

**titles** In general, confine capitalization to formal titles used directly before an individual's name.

The basic guidelines:

LOWERCASE: Lowercase and spell out titles when they are not used with an individual's name: *The president issued a statement. The pope gave his blessing.*

Lowercase and spell out titles in constructions that set them off from a name by commas: *The vice president, Nelson Rockefeller, declined to run again. Paul VI, the current pope, does not plan to retire.*

COURTESY TITLES: See the **courtesy titles** entry for guidelines on when to use *Miss, Mr., Mrs., Ms.* or no titles.

The forms *Mr., Mrs., Miss* and *Ms.* apply both in regular text and in quotations.

FORMAL TITLES: Capitalize formal titles when they are used immediately before one or more names: *Pope Paul, President Washington, Vice Presidents John Jones and William Smith.*

A formal title generally is one that denotes a scope of authority, professional activity or academic activity: *Sen. Dianne Feinstein, Dr. Marcus Welby, Pvt. Gomer Pyle.*

Other titles serve primarily as occupational descriptions: *astronaut John Glenn, movie star John Wayne, peanut farmer Jimmy Carter.*

A final determination on whether a title is formal or occupational depends on the practice of the governmental or private organization that confers it. If there is doubt about the status of a title and the practice of the organization cannot be determined, use a construction that sets the name or the title off with commas.

ABBREVIATED TITLES: The following formal titles are capitalized and abbreviated as shown when used before a name outside quotations: *Dr., Gov., Lt. Gov., Rep., Sen.* and certain military ranks listed in the **military titles** entry.

All other formal titles are spelled out in all uses.

ROYAL TITLES: Capitalize *king, queen*, etc., when used directly before a name. See individual entries and **nobility**.

TITLES OF NOBILITY: Capitalize a full title when it serves as the alternate name for an individual. See **nobility**.

PAST AND FUTURE TITLES: A formal title that an individual formerly held, is about to hold or holds temporarily is capitalized if used before the person's name. But do not capitalize the qualifying word: *former President Ford, deposed King Constantine, Attorney General-designate Griffin B. Bell, acting Mayor Peter Barry.*

LONG TITLES: Separate a long title from a name by a construction that requires a comma: *Charles Robinson, the undersecretary for economic affairs, spoke.* Or: *The undersecretary for economic affairs, Charles Robinson, spoke.*

UNIQUE TITLES: If a title applies only to one person in an organization, insert the word *the* in a construction that uses commas: *John Jones, the deputy vice president, spoke.*

ADDITIONAL GUIDANCE: Many commonly used titles and occupational descriptions are listed separately in this book, together with guidelines on whether and/or when they are capitalized. In these entries, the phrases *before a name* or *immediately before a name* are used to specify that capitalization applies only when a title is not set off from a name by commas.

See **academic titles; composition titles; legislative titles; military titles**; and **religious titles**.

**TNT** Acceptable in all references for *trinitrotoluene.*

**tobacco, tobaccos**

**Tobago** See the **Trinidad and Tobago** entry.

**today, tonight** Use only in direct quotations and in phrases that do not refer to a specific day: *Customs today are different from those of a century ago.*

Use the day of the week in copy, not *today* or *tonight.*

**Tokyo** Stands alone in datelines.

**tollhouse, tollhouse cookies**

**Tommy gun** Alternative name for Thompson submachine gun, from John T. Thompson, its co-inventor.

See **weapons**.

**tomorrow** Use only in direct quotations and in phrases that do not refer to a specific day: *The world of tomorrow will need additional energy resources.*

Use the day of the week in other cases.

**ton** There are three different types:

A *short ton* is equal to 2,000 pounds.

A *long ton*, also known as a *British ton*, is equal to 2,240 pounds.

A *metric ton* is equal to 1,000 kilograms, or approximately 2,204.62 pounds.

CONVERSION EQUATIONS:

Short to long: Multiply by 0.89 (5 short tons x 0.89 = 4.45 long tons).

Short to metric: Multiply by 0.9 (5 short tons x 0.9 = 4.5 metric tons).

Long to short: Multiply by 1.12 (5 long tons x 1.12 = 5.6 short tons).

Long to metric: Multiply by 1.02 (5 long tons x 1.02 = 5.1 metric tons).

Metric to short: Multiply by

1.1 (5 metric tons x 1.1 = 5.5 short tons).

Metric to long: Multiply by 0.98 (5 metric tons x 0.98 = 4.9 long tons).

See **metric system**.

See **kiloton** for units used to measure the power of nuclear explosions.

See **oil** for formulas to convert the tonnage of oil shipments to gallons.

**tonight** See **today, tonight** entry.

**tornado(es)** See **weather terms**.

**Toronto** The city in Canada stands alone in datelines.

**Tory, Tories** An exception to the normal practice when forming the plural of a proper name ending in *y*.

The words are acceptable on second reference to the Conservative Party in Britain and its members.

**total, totaled, totaling**
The phrase *a total of* often is redundant.

It may be used, however, to avoid a figure at the start of a sentence: *A total of 650 people were killed in holiday traffic accidents.*

**touch-screen**

**touch-tone** A generic term for a push-button telephone dialing service.

**toward** Not *towards*.

**town** Apply the capitalization principles in **city**.

**town council** Apply the

capitalization principles in **city council**.

**Toys "R" Us**

**trade in** (v.) **trade-in** (n. and adj.)

**trademark** A trademark is a brand, symbol, word, etc., used by a manufacturer or dealer and protected by law to prevent a competitor from using it: *Astro-Turf*, for a type of artificial grass, for example.

In general, use a generic equivalent unless the trademark name is essential to the story.

When a trademark is used, capitalize it.

Many trademarks are listed separately in this book, together with generic equivalents.

For questions about trademarks not listed in this book, the International Trademark Association, located in New York, is a helpful source of information.

On the Net:

http://www.inta.org/index. php

See **brand names** and **service marks**.

**trade off** (v.) **trade-off** (n. and adj.)

**traffic, trafficked, trafficking**

**trampoline** Formerly a trademark, now a generic term.

**trans-** The rules in **prefixes** apply, but in general, no hyphen. Some examples:

| | |
|---|---|
| transcontinental | transsexual |
| transmigrate | transship |
| transoceanic | trans-Siberian |

Also: *trans-Atlantic* and *trans-Pacific*. These are exceptions to Webster's New World in keeping with the general rule that a hyphen is needed when a prefix precedes a capitalized word.

**transcripts** See the **texts, transcripts** entry.

**transfer, transferred, transferring**

**transgender** Use the pronoun preferred by the individuals who have acquired the physical characteristics of the opposite sex or present themselves in a way that does not correspond with their sex at birth.

If that preference is not expressed, use the pronoun consistent with the way the individuals live publicly.

**Transjordan** Earlier name for Jordan.

**Transportation Communications International Union** Formerly the Brotherhood of Railway, Airline and Steamship Clerks, Freight Handlers, Express and Station Employees. *TCU* is acceptable on second reference.

Headquarters is in Rockville, Md.

**transsexual** See **transgender**.

**Trans World Airlines** Formed in 1930 from the merger of Western Air Express and Transcontinental Air Transport, *TWA* was acquired by American Airlines in 2001.

**travelogue** Not *travelog*.

**travel, traveled, traveling, traveler**

**treasurer** Capitalize when used as a formal title immediately before a name. See **titles**.

Caution: The secretary of the U.S. Department of the Treasury is not the same person as the U.S. treasurer.

**trees** See **plants**.

**tribes** See the **nationalities and races** entry.

**trigger-happy**

**TriMotor** The proper name of a three-engine airplane once made by Ford Motor Co.

**Trinidad and Tobago** In datelines on stories from this island nation, use a community name followed by either *Trinidad* or *Tobago* — but not both — depending on where the community is located.

**Trojan horse, Trojan War**

**troop, troops, troupe** A *troop*, in its singular form, is a group of people, often military, or animals. *Troops*, in the plural, means several such groups. But when the plural appears with a large number, it is understood to mean individuals: *There were an estimated 150,000 troops in Iraq.* (But not: *Three troops were injured.*)

Use *troupe* only for ensembles of actors, dancers, singers, etc.

**tropical depression** See **weather terms**.

**Truman, Harry S.** With a period after the initial. Truman once said there was no need for the period because the S did not stand for a name. Asked in the early 1960s about his preference, he replied, "It makes no difference to me."

AP style has called for the period since that time.

**trustee** A person to whom another's property or the management of another's property is entrusted.

Do not capitalize if used before a name.

**trusty** A prison inmate granted special privileges as a trustworthy person.

Do not capitalize if used before a name.

**try out** (v.) **tryout** (n.)

**tsar** Use *czar.*

**T-shirt**

**tuberculosis** *TB* is acceptable on second reference.

**Tuesday** See **days of the week**.

**tune up** (v.) **tuneup** (n. and adj.)

**turboprop** See **aircraft terms**.

**turnpike** Capitalize as part of a proper name: *the Pennsylvania Turnpike.* Lowercase *turnpike* when it stands alone.

See **highway designations**.

**TV** Acceptable as an abbreviated form of *television,* as a noun or adjective.

**Twelve Apostles** The disciples of Jesus. An exception to the normal practice of using figures for 10 and above.

**20th Century Fox, Twentieth Century Limited** Follow an organization's practice. See **company names**.

**20-something**

**two-by-four** Spell out the noun, which refers to any length of building lumber 2 inches thick by 4 inches wide.

**typhoons** Capitalize typhoon when it is part of the name that weather forecasters assign to a storm: *Typhoon Tilda.*

But use *it* and *its* — not *she, her* or *hers* — in pronoun references.

And do not use the presence of a woman's name as an excuse to attribute sexist images of women's behavior to a typhoon.

See **weather terms**.

# U

**U** In Burmese names *U* is an honorific prefix. It means something like Mr., and is used for adult males only. It should not be used. For example, *U Nu* is only *Nu* in all references. Women retain their given names after marriage. No courtesy titles apply.

**U-boat** A German submarine. Anything referring to a submarine should be *submarine* unless directly referring to a German vessel of World War I or II vintage.

**UFO, UFOs** Acceptable in all references for *unidentified flying object(s)*.

**UHF** Acceptable in all references for *ultrahigh frequency*.

**Ukrainian Catholic Church** See **Eastern Rite churches**.

**ukulele**

**Ulster** Historically, one of the four Irish provinces, covering nine counties. Six of the counties became Northern Ireland, three became part of the Republic of Ireland. Avoid use as a synonym for *Northern Ireland*. See **United Kingdom**.

**ultra-** The rules in **prefixes** apply, but in general, no hyphen. Some examples:

| | |
|---|---|
| ultramodern | ultrasonic |
| ultranationalism | ultraviolet |

**ultrahigh frequency** *UHF* is acceptable in all references.

**umlaut** This diacritical mark (two dots placed over the vowel to change its sound) should not be used in standard AP transmissions. Instead, use two regular letters when needed.

**U.N.** The periods in *U.N.*, for consistency with U.S., are an exception to Webster's New World College Dictionary.
See **United Nations**.

**un-** The rules in **prefixes** apply, but in general, no hyphen. Some examples:

| | |
|---|---|
| un-American | unnecessary |
| unarmed | unshaven |

**Uncle Sam**

**Uncle Tom** A term of contempt applied to a black person, taken from the main character in Harriet Beecher Stowe's novel "Uncle Tom's Cabin." It describes the practice of kowtowing to whites to curry favor.

Do not apply it to an individual. It carries potentially libelous connotations of having sold one's convictions for money, prestige or political influence.

**under-** The rules in **prefixes** apply, but in general, no hyphen. Some examples:

| | |
|---|---|
| underdog | undersheriff |
| underground | undersold |

**underscore** Do not use the symbol in Internet addresses; write out the word and put it in parentheses.

**undersecretary** One word. See **titles**.

**under way** Two words in virtually all uses: *The project is under way. The naval maneuvers are under way.*

One word only when used as an adjective before a noun in a nautical sense: *an underway flotilla.*

**unemployment rate** In the United States, this estimate of the number of unemployed residents seeking work is compiled monthly by the Bureau of Labor Statistics, an agency of the Labor Department.

Each month the bureau selects a nationwide cross section of the population and conducts interviews to determine the size of the U.S. work force. The work force is defined as the number of people with jobs and the number looking for jobs.

The unemployment rate is expressed as a percentage figure. The essential calculation involves dividing the total work force into the number of people looking for jobs, followed by adjustments to reflect variable factors such as seasonal trends.

**UNESCO** Acceptable on first reference for the *United Nations Educational, Scientific and Cultural Organization*, but a subsequent reference should give the full name.

**UNICEF** Acceptable in all references for the *United Nations Children's Fund*. The words *International* and *Emergency*, origi-nally part of the name, have been dropped.

**unidentified flying object(s)** *UFO* and *UFOs* are acceptable in all references.

**Uniform Code of Military Justice** The laws covering members of the U.S. armed forces.

**uninterested** See the **disinterested, uninterested** entry.

**union** Capitalize when used as a proper name of the Northern states during the Civil War: *The Union defeated the Confederacy.*

**union names** The formal names of unions may be condensed to conventionally accepted short forms that capitalize characteristic words from the full name followed by *union* in lowercase.

Follow union practice in the use of the word *worker* in shortened forms: *United Auto Workers, United Mine Workers.*

When *worker* is used generically, make *autoworkers* and *steelworkers* one word in keeping with widespread practice; use two words for other job descriptions: *bakery workers, mine workers.*

See the local of a union entry and the individual entries for these unions frequently in the news:

**Amalgamated Transit Union**
**American Federation of Government Employees**
**American Federation of Labor and Congress of Industrial Organizations**
**American Federation of Musicians**
**American Federation of State, County and Municipal Employees**
**American Federation of Teachers**
**American Federation of Television and Radio Artists**

American Postal Workers Union

Bakery, Confectionery, Tobacco Workers and Grain Millers International Union

Bricklayers, Masons and Plasterers' International Union of America

Communications Workers of America

International Association of Machinists and Aerospace Workers

International Brotherhood of Electrical Workers

International Brotherhood of Teamsters, Chauffeurs, Warehousemen and Helpers of America

International Longshore and Warehouse Union

International Longshoremen's Association

International Union of Bricklayers and Allied Craftworkers

International Union of Painters and Allied Trade

Laborers' International Union of North America

National Association of Letter Carriers

Newspaper Guild, The

Sheet Metal Workers International Association

Transportation Communications International Union

UNITE-HERE (A merger of the Union of Needletrades, Industrial and Textile Employees with the Hotel Employees and Restaurant Employees.)

United Automobile, Aerospace and Agricultural Implement Workers of America

United Brotherhood of Carpenters and Joiners of America

United Electrical, Radio and Machine Workers of America

United Farm Workers of America

United Food and Commercial Workers International Union

United Mine Workers of America

United Steel, Paper and Forestry, Rubber, Manufacturing, Energy, Allied Industrial and Service Workers International Union

**union shop** See **closed shop**.

**unique** It means one of a kind. Do not describe something as *rather unique* or *most unique.*

**United Airlines** A subsidiary of UAL Corp.

Headquarters is in Chicago.

**United Arab Emirates** Do not abbreviate, even in datelines.

Use *U.A.E.* (with periods) if quoted matter requires the abbreviation.

**United Brotherhood of Carpenters and Joiners of America** The shortened form *Carpenters union* is acceptable in all references.

Headquarters is in Washington.

**United Church of Christ**
The Evangelical and Reformed Church merged with the Congregational Christian Churches in 1957 to form the United Church of Christ. It has some 1.4 million members.

The word *church* is correctly applied only to an individual local church. Each such church is responsible for the doctrine, ministry and ritual of its congregation.

A small body of churches that did not enter the United Church of Christ is known as the National Association of Congregational Churches.

Churches in the association have more than 100,000 members.

Jesus is regarded as man's savior, but no subscription to a set creed is required for membership.

Members of the clergy are known as *ministers*. *Pastor* applies if a minister leads a congregation.

On first reference, use *the Rev.* before the name of a man or woman. On second reference, use only the last name.

See **religious titles**.

### United Electrical, Radio and Machine Workers of America

The shortened form *Electrical Workers union* is acceptable in all references.

Headquarters is in New York.

### United Food and Commercial Workers International Union

Formed by the merger of the Retail Clerks International Union and the Amalgamated Meat Cutters and Butcher Workmen of North America.

The shortened form *Food and Commercial Workers union* is acceptable in all references.

Headquarters is in Washington.

### United Kingdom

It consists of Great Britain and Northern Ireland.

Great Britain (or Britain) consists of England, Scotland and Wales.

Ireland is independent of the United Kingdom.

The abbreviation *U.K.* is acceptable as a noun or adjective.

See **datelines** and **Ireland**.

### United Methodist Church

See **Methodist churches**.

### United Mine Workers of

America

The shortened forms *United Mine Workers* and *United Mine Workers union* are acceptable in all references.

*UMW* and *Mine Workers* are acceptable on second reference.

Use *mine workers* or *miners*, lowercase, in generic references to workers in the industry.

Headquarters is in Washington.

### United Nations

Abbrev: *U.N.* (no space). The periods in *U.N.*, for consistency with U.S., are an exception to the first listing in Webster's New World College Dictionary.

In datelines: *UNITED NATIONS (AP)* —

Use *U.N. General Assembly, U.N. Secretariat* and *U.N. Security Council* in first references not under a United Nations dateline.

*General Assembly, the Secretariat* and *Security Council* are acceptable in all references under a United Nations dateline and on second reference under other datelines.

Lowercase *the assembly* and *the council* when they stand alone.

See **UNESCO** and **UNICEF**.

### United Presbyterian Church in the United States of America

It no longer exists. See **Presbyterian churches** entry.

### United Press International

A privately owned news agency formed in 1958 as a merger of United Press and International News Service.

Use the full name on first reference. *UPI* is acceptable on second reference.

Headquarters is in Washington.

### United Service Organizations

*USO* is acceptable on second reference.

**United States** Use periods in the abbreviation, *U.S.*

---

**For organizations with names beginning with the words United States, see entries alphabetized under U.S.**

**United States Conference of Catholic Bishops** Formerly the National Conference of Catholic Bishops, it is the national organization of Roman Catholic bishops.

**United Synagogue of Conservative Judaism** Not *synagogues*. See **Jewish congregations**.

**-up** Follow Webster's New World College Dictionary. Hyphenate if not listed there.

Some frequently used words (all are nouns, some also are used as adjectives):

| | |
|---|---|
| breakup | makeup |
| call-up | mix-up |
| change-up | mock-up |
| checkup | pileup |
| cleanup | push-up |
| close-up | roundup |
| cover-up | runners-up |
| crackup | setup |
| follow-up | shake-up |
| frame-up | shape-up |
| grown-up | smashup |
| holdup | speedup |
| letup | tie-up |
| lineup | walk-up |
| | windup |

Use two words when any of these occurs as a verb.

See **suffixes**.

**up-** The rules in **prefixes** apply, but in general, no hyphen. Some examples:

| | |
|---|---|
| upend | upstate |
| upgrade | uptown |

**UPI** Acceptable on second references for *United Press International.*

**uppercase** One word (n., v., adj.) when referring to the use of capital letters, in keeping with printers' practice.

**UPS** Acceptable in all references to the *United Parcel Service.*

**upside down** (adv.) **upside-down** (adj.) *The car turned upside down. The book is upside-down.*

**upstate** Always lowercase: *upstate New York.*

**upward** Not *upwards.*

**URL** *Uniform Resource Locator,* an *Internet* address. An example:
*http://politics.ap.org/states/mi.html*
*http:* is the protocol, or method of transfer.
*//* indicates a computer name follows.
*politics* is the server.
*ap.org* is the domain.
*/states* is the folder.
*/mi.html* indicates a file (*.html* is the file type).
When the *URL* does not fit entirely on one line, break it into two or more lines without adding a hyphen or other punctuation mark.
The URL should always be the last line on a story; other underdash material, such as a list of contributors to the story, goes above the *URL.*

**U.S.** The abbreviation is acceptable as a noun or adjective for *United States.*

**USA** No periods in the abbreviated form for United States of America.

**U.S. Air Force** See **air force**;

**military academies**; and **military titles**.

**US Airways** Formerly USAir. Acquired by America West Holdings Corp. in 2005. The combined company retains the *US Airways* name. Headquarters in Tempe, Ariz.

**U.S. Army** See **army**; **military academies**; and **military titles**.

**U.S. Coast Guard** See **coast guard**; **military academies**; and **military titles**.

**U.S. Conference of Mayors** The members are the mayors of cities with 30,000 or more residents. See **National League of Cities**.

Use *the conference* or *the mayors' conference* on second reference.

There is no organization with the name *National Mayors' Conference*.

**U.S. Court of Appeals** The court is divided into 13 circuits as follows:

District of Columbia Circuit.

Federal Circuit.

1st Circuit: Maine, Massachusetts, New Hampshire, Rhode Island, Puerto Rico. Based in Boston.

2nd Circuit: Connecticut, New York, Vermont. Based in New York.

3rd Circuit: Delaware, New Jersey, Pennsylvania, Virgin Islands. Based in Philadelphia.

4th Circuit: Maryland, North Carolina, South Carolina, Virginia, West Virginia. Based in Richmond, Va.

5th Circuit: Louisiana, Mississippi, Texas. Based in New Orleans.

6th Circuit: Kentucky, Michigan, Ohio, Tennessee. Based in Cincinnati.

7th Circuit: Illinois, Indiana, Wisconsin. Based in Chicago.

8th Circuit: Arkansas, Iowa, Minnesota, Missouri, Nebraska, North Dakota, South Dakota. Based in St. Louis.

9th Circuit: Alaska, Arizona, California, Hawaii, Idaho, Montana, Nevada, Oregon, Washington, Guam. Based in San Francisco.

10th Circuit: Colorado, Kansas, New Mexico, Oklahoma, Utah, Wyoming. Based in Denver.

11th Circuit: Alabama, Florida and Georgia. Based in Atlanta.

The courts do not always sit in the cities where they are based. Sessions may be held in other major cities within each region.

REFERENCE FORMS: A phrase such as a *federal appeals court* is acceptable on first reference.

On first reference to the full name, use *U.S. Court of Appeals* or a full name: *8th U.S. Circuit Court of Appeals* or *the U.S. Court of Appeals for the 8th Circuit*.

*U.S. Circuit Court of Appeals* without a circuit number is a misnomer and should not be used.

In shortened and subsequent references: *the Court of Appeals, the 2nd Circuit, the appeals court, the appellate court(s), the circuit court(s), the court.*

Do not create nonexistent entities such as *the San Francisco Court of Appeals*. Make it *the U.S. Court of Appeals in San Francisco*.

JURISTS: The formal title for the jurists on the court is *judge*: *U.S. Circuit Judge Homer Thornberry* is preferred to *U.S. Appeals Judge Homer Thornberry*, but either is acceptable.

See **judge**.

**U.S. Court of Appeals for the Armed Forces** This court, not part of the judicial branch as such, is a civilian body established by Congress to hear appeals from actions of the Defense Department. It is based in Washington. (Formerly the U.S. Court of Military Appeals.)

**U.S. Court of Appeals for the Federal Circuit** Commonly known as the CAFC, it replaced U.S. Court of Claims and U.S. Court of Customs and Patent Appeals. It handles suits against the federal government and appeals involving customs, patents and copyright. It is based in Washington.

**U.S. Court of Military Appeals** This court, not part of the judicial branch as such, is a civilian body established by Congress to hear appeals from actions of the Defense Department. It is based in Washington.

**U.S. Customs and Border Protection** An agency of the Department of Homeland Security, it includes the Border Patrol.

**U.S. Customs Court** This court, based in New York City, handles disputes over customs duties that arise at any U.S. port of entry.

**U.S. District Courts** There are 94. In shortened and subsequent references: *the District Court, the District Courts, the court.*

*Judge* is the formal title for District Court jurists: *U.S. District Judge Frank Johnson.* See **judge**.

**user friendly** Avoid. For example: *The system is easy to use,* not *the system is user friendly.*

**usher** Use for both men and women.

**U.S. Immigration and Customs Enforcement** *ICE* is the acronym for this investigative arm of the Department of Homeland Security. It incorporates the functions of the former Immigration and Naturalization Service, the former Customs service, the Federal Air Marshals and the Federal Protective Service.

**U.S. Marshals Service** No apostrophe.

**U.S. Military Academy** See **military academies**.

**U.S. Navy** See **navy**; **military academies**; and **military titles**.

**U.S. Postal Service** Use *U.S. Postal Service* or *the Postal Service* on first reference. Retain capitalization of *Postal Service* in subsequent references to the agency.

Lowercase *the service* when it stands alone. Lowercase *post office* in generic references to the agency and to an individual office: *I went to the post office.*

**USS** For *United States Ship, Steamer* or *Steamship,* preceding the name of a vessel: *the USS Iowa.*

In datelines:
*ABOARD USS IOWA (AP) —*

**U.S. Supreme Court** See **Supreme Court of the United States**.

**U.S. Tax Court** This court handles appeals in tax cases.

**Utah** Do not abbreviate. See **state names**.

**U-turn** (n. and adj.)

**v.** See **verbs**.

**vacuum**

**Valium** A trademark for a brand of tranquilizer and muscle relaxant. It also may be called *diazepam.*

**valley** Capitalize as part of a full name: *the Mississippi Valley.*
Lowercase in plural uses: *the Missouri and Mississippi valleys.*

**van, von** See **foreign names** entry.

**Vandyke beard, Vandyke collar**

**Varig** Headquarters of Brazil's flagship airline is in Rio de Janeiro.

**Vaseline** A trademark for a brand of petroleum jelly.

**Vatican City** Stands alone in datelines.

**v-chip**

**VCR** Acceptable in all references to *videocassette recorder.*

**VDT** Abbreviation for *video display terminal.* Spell out.

**V-E Day** May 8, 1945, the day the surrender of Germany was announced, officially ending the European phase of World War II.

**vegetables** See **food**.

**V-8** The engine.

**Velcro** Trademark for a nylon material that can be pressed together or pulled apart for easy fastening and unfastening. Use a generic term such as fabric fastener.

**vendor**

**venereal disease** *VD* is acceptable on second reference.

**verbal** See the **oral, verbal, written** entry.

**verbs** The abbreviation v. is used in this book to identify the spelling of the verb forms of words frequently misspelled.
SPLIT FORMS: In general, avoid awkward constructions that split infinitive forms of a verb (*to leave, to help,* etc.) or compound forms (*had left, are found out,* etc.)
Awkward: *She was ordered to immediately leave on an assignment.*
Preferred: *She was ordered to leave immediately on an assignment.*
Awkward: *There stood the wagon that we had early last autumn left by the barn.*
Preferred: *There stood the wagon that we had left by the barn early last autumn.*
Occasionally, however, a split

is not awkward and is necessary to convey the meaning:

*He wanted to really help his mother.*

*Those who lie are often found out.*

*How has your health been?*

*The budget was tentatively approved.*

**Vermont** Abbrev.: *Vt.* See **state names**.

**vernacular** The native language of a country or place. A vernacular term that has achieved widespread recognition may be used without explanation if appropriate in the context.

Terms not widely known should be explained when used. In general, they are appropriate only when illustrating vernacular speech.

See **colloquialisms** and **dialect**.

**verses** See **poetry** for guidelines on how to handle verses of poetry typographically.

**versus** Spell it out in ordinary speech and writing: *The proposal to revamp Medicare versus proposals to reform Medicare and Medicaid at the same time* ... In short expressions, however, the abbreviation *vs.* is permitted: *The issue of guns vs. butter has long been with us.*

For court cases, use *v*: *Marbury v. Madison.*

**vertical takeoff aircraft** See the **V-STOL** and **VTOL** entries.

**very high frequency** *VHF* is acceptable in all references.

**Very Rev.** See **Episcopal Church**; **religious titles**; and

**Roman Catholic Church**.

**Veterans Affairs** Formerly Veterans Administration, it became Cabinet level in March 1989 with the full title Department of Veterans Affairs. *VA* (no periods) is still used on second reference.

**Veterans Day** Formerly Armistice Day, Nov. 11, the anniversary of the armistice that ended World War I in 1918.

The federal legal holiday, observed on the fourth Monday in October during the mid-1970s, reverted to Nov. 11 in 1978.

**Veterans of Foreign Wars** *VFW* is acceptable on second reference.

Headquarters in Kansas City, Mo.

**veto, vetoes** (n.) The verb forms: *vetoed, vetoing.*

**VHF** Acceptable in all references for *very high frequency.*

**vice-** Use two words: *vice admiral, vice chairman, vice chancellor, vice consul, vice president, vice principal, vice regent, vice secretary.*

Several are exceptions to Webster's New World. The two-word rule has been adopted for consistency in handling the similar terms.

**vice president** Capitalize or lowercase following the same rules that apply to *president*. See **president** and **titles**.

Do not drop the first name on first reference.

**vice versa**

**Victrola** A trademark for a brand of record player.

**videocassette recorder** *VCR* is acceptable in all references.

**videodisc**

**video game** Two words in all uses.

**videotape** (n. and v.)

**vienna bread, vienna coffee, vienna sausages** See **food**.

**Viet Cong**

**Vietnam** Not *Viet Nam.*

**Vietnam War**

**vie, vied, vying**

**village** Apply the capitalization principles in **city**.

**VIP, VIPs** Acceptable in all references for *very important person(s).*

**Virginia** Abbrev.: *Va.* Legally a commonwealth, not a state.
See **state** and **state names**.

**Virgin Islands** Use with a community name in datelines on stories from the U.S. Virgin Islands. Do not abbreviate.
Identify an individual island in the text if relevant.
See **datelines** and **British Virgin Islands**.

**virus, worm** A computer *virus* is any malicious, invasive program designed to infect and disrupt computers. A *worm* is a type of virus that spreads on networks such as the Internet, copying itself from one computer to another without human intervention.

**viscount, viscountess** See **nobility**.

**vitamins** Lowercase *vitamin,* use a capital letter and/or a figure for the type: *vitamin A, vitamin B-12.*

**V-J Day** The day of victory for the Allied forces over Japan in World War II.
It is calculated both as Aug. 15, 1945, the day the fighting with Japan ended, and as Sept. 2, 1945, the day Japan officially surrendered.

**V-neck** (n. and adj.)

**voice mail** Two words.

**Voice of America** *VOA* is acceptable on second reference.

**volatile** Something that evaporates rapidly. It may or may not be explosive.

**Volkswagen of America Inc.** The name of the U.S. subsidiary of the German company named *Volkswagen AG.*
U.S. headquarters is in Auburn Hills, Mich.

**volley, volleys**

**Volunteers in Service to America** *VISTA* is acceptable in second reference.

**voodoo** Capitalize when referring specifically to the religion, practiced primarily in Haiti and parts of Africa. Lowercase in other uses, especially when ascribing magical solutions to problems, as in *voodoo economics.*

**vote-getter**

**vote tabulations** Always

use figures for the totals.

Spell out below 10 in other phrases related to voting: *by a five-vote majority, with three abstentions, four votes short of the necessary two-thirds majority.*

For results that involve fewer than 1,000 votes on each side, use these forms: *The House voted 230-205, a 230-205 vote.*

To make totals that involve more than 1,000 votes on a side easier to read, separate the figures with the word *to* to avoid hyphenated adjectival constructions. See **election returns** for examples.

**V-STOL** Acceptable on second reference for an aircraft capable of *vertical* or *short takeoff or landing.*

**VTOL** Acceptable on second reference for an aircraft capable of *vertical takeoff or landing.*

**vulgarities** See the **obscenities, profanities, vulgarities** entry.

# W

**Wac, WAC** *Wac* is no longer used by the military but is an acceptable term in a reference to a woman who served in what used to be the *Women's Army Corps.*

*WAC* is acceptable on second reference to the corps.

**Waf, WAF** *Waf* no longer is used by the military but is acceptable in a reference to a woman who served in the Air Force.

*WAF* is acceptable on second reference to *Women in the Air Force,* an unofficial organizational distinction formerly made by the Air Force but never authorized by Congress.

**waiter** (male) **waitress** (female)

**Wales** Use *Wales* after the names of Welsh communities in datelines.

See **datelines** and **United Kingdom**.

**walk up** (v.) **walk-up** (n. and adj.)

**Wall Street** When the reference is to the entire complex of financial institutions in the area rather than the actual street itself, *the Street* is an acceptable short form.

See **capitalization**.

**Wal-Mart**

**war** Capitalize when used as part of the name for a specific conflict: *the Civil War, the Cold War, the Korean War, the Vietnam War, the War of 1812, World War II, Gulf War.*

**warden** Capitalize as a formal title before a name. See **titles**.

**wards** Use figures. See **political divisions**.

**warhead**

**war horse, warhorse** Two words for a horse used in battle.

One word for a veteran of many battles: *He is a political warhorse.*

**warlike**

**warlord**

**warrant officer** See **military titles**.

**wartime**

**washed-up** (adj.)

**Washington** Abbreviate the state as *Wash.*

Never abbreviate when referring to the U.S. capital.

Use *state of Washington* or

*Washington state* and *Washington, D.C.,* or *District of Columbia* when the context requires distinction between the state and the federal district.

See **state** and **state names**.

### Washington's Birthday

Capitalize *birthday* in references to the holiday.

The date he was born is computed as Feb. 22. The federal legal holiday is the third Monday in February.

Some states and some organizations refer to it as *Presidents Day,* but the formal name has not changed.

### wastebasket

**waterspout** See **weather terms**.

**watt** A unit of power, mostly associated with electricity. Electrical energy is measured in watt-hours (or kilowatt-hours or megawatt-hours). Do not use "megawatts per hour." Abbrev.: *W, kW, MW.*

**Wave, WAVES** *Wave* no longer is used by the military but is acceptable in a reference to a woman who served in the Navy.

*WAVES* is acceptable on second reference to the *Women Accepted for Volunteer Emergency Service,* an organizational distinction made for women during World War II but subsequently discontinued.

### weak-kneed

**weapons** *Gun* is an acceptable term for any firearm. Note the following definitions and forms in dealing with weapons and ammunition:

**anti-aircraft** A cannon that fires explosive shells. It is designed for defense against air attack. The form: *a 105 mm anti-aircraft gun.*

**artillery** A carriage-mounted cannon.

**assault-style weapon** Any semiautomatic pistol, rifle or shotgun originally designed for military or police use with a large ammunition capacity. Also, firearms that feature two or more accessories such as a detachable magazine, folding or telescopic stock, silencer, pistol grip, bayonet mount or a device to suppress the flash emitted while shooting in the dark.

**automatic** An autoloading action that will fire a succession of cartridges while the trigger is depressed or until the ammunition supply is exhausted. The form: *a .22-caliber automatic.*

**buckshot** See **shot** below.

**bullet** The projectile fired by a rifle, pistol or machine gun. Together with metal casing, primer and propellant, it forms a *cartridge.*

**caliber** A measurement of the diameter of the inside of a gun barrel except for most shotguns. Measurement is in either millimeters or decimal fractions of an inch. The word *caliber* is not used when giving the metric measurement. The forms: *a 9 mm pistol, a .22-caliber rifle.*

**cannon** A weapon, usually supported on some type of carriage, that fires explosive projectiles. The form: *a 105 mm cannon.*

**carbine** A short, lightweight rifle, usually having a barrel length of less than 20 inches. The form: *an M-3 carbine.*

**cartridge** See **bullet** above.

**clip** A device used to store multiple rounds of ammunition together as a unit, ready for insertion into the magazine of a repeating firearm.

**Colt** Named for Samuel Colt, it designates a make of weapon or ammunition developed for Colt handguns. The forms: *a Colt .45-caliber revolver, .45 Long Colt ammunition.*

**gauge** This word describes the size of a shotgun. Gauge is expressed in terms of the number per pound of round lead balls with a diameter equal to the size of the barrel. The bigger the number, the smaller the shotgun.

Some common shotgun gauges:

| Gauge | Interior Diameter |
|-------|-------------------|
| 10    | .775 inches       |
| 12    | .729 inches       |
| 16    | .662 inches       |
| 20    | .615 inches       |
| 28    | .550 inches       |
| .410  | .410 inches       |

The .410 actually is a caliber, but commonly is called a gauge.

The forms: *a 12-gauge shotgun, a .410-gauge shotgun.*

**howitzer** A cannon shorter than a gun of the same caliber employed to fire projectiles at relatively high angles at a target, such as opposing forces behind a ridge. The form: *a 105 mm howitzer.*

**M-1, M-16** These and similar combinations of a letter and figure(s) designate rifles used by the military. The forms: *an M-1 rifle, an M-16 rifle.*

**machine gun** An automatic gun that fires as long as the trigger is depressed. The form: *a .50-caliber Browning machine gun.*

**magazine** The ammunition storage and feeding device within or attached to a firearm. It may be fixed to the firearm or detachable.

**Magnum** A trademark for a type of high-powered cartridge with a larger case and a larger powder charge than other cartridges of approximately the same caliber. The form: *a .357-caliber Magnum, a .44-caliber Magnum.*

**mortar** Device used to launch a mortar shell; it is the shell, not the mortar, that is fired.

**musket** A heavy, large-caliber shoulder firearm fired by means of a matchlock, a wheel lock, a flintlock or a percussion lock. Its ammunition is a musket ball.

**pistol** A small firearm or handgun, it can be a single shot, a semiautomatic or a revolver. Its size is measured in calibers. The form: *a .45-caliber pistol.*

**revolver** A handgun. Its cartridges are held in chambers in a cylinder that revolves. The form: *a .45-caliber revolver.*

**rifle** A firearm designed or made to be fired from the shoulder and having a rifled bore. It uses bullets or cartridges for ammunition. Its size is measured in calibers. The form: *a .22-caliber rifle.*

**Saturday night special** The popular name for the type of cheap pistol used for impulsive crimes.

**shell** The word applies to military or naval ammunition and to shotgun ammunition.

**shot** Small lead or steel pellets fired by shotguns. A shotgun shell usually contains 1 to 2 ounces of shot. Do not use *shot* interchangeably with *buckshot*, which refers only to the largest shot sizes.

**shotgun** A firearm typically used to fire small spherical pellets called shot. *Shotguns* usually have a smooth bore barrel, but some contain a rifled barrel, which is used to fire a single projectile. Size is measured in gauges. The form: *a 12-gauge shotgun.*

**submachine gun** A lightweight automatic gun firing handgun ammunition.

## weather-beaten

**weather bureau** See **National Weather Service**.
On the Net:
www.noaa.gov

**weatherman** The preferred term is *weather forecaster.*

**weather terms** The following are based on definitions used by the National Weather Service. All temperatures are Fahrenheit.
**blizzard** Wind speeds of 35 mph or more and considerable falling and/or blowing of snow with visibility near zero.
**coastal waters** The waters within about 20 miles of the coast, including bays, harbors and sounds.
**cyclone** A storm with strong winds rotating about a moving center of low atmospheric pressure.
The word sometimes is used in the United States to mean *tornado* and in the Indian Ocean area to mean *hurricane.*
**degree-day** A unit of measurement describing how much the temperature differs from a standard average for one day. It is usually used to gauge the amount of heating or cooling needed for a building. If the standard average temperature for a day is 65 degrees, then a temperature of 10 below zero for 24 hours yields 75 degree-days.
**dust storm** Visibility of one-half mile or less due to dust, wind speeds of 30 mph or more.
**flash flood** A sudden, violent flood. It typically occurs after a

heavy rain or the melting of a heavy snow.
**flash flood warning** Warns that flash flooding is imminent or in progress. Those in the affected area should take necessary precautions immediately.
**flash flood watch** Alerts the public that flash flooding is possible. Those in the affected area are urged to be ready to take additional precautions if a flash flood warning is issued or if flooding is observed.
**flood** Stories about floods usually tell how high the water is and where it is expected to crest. Such a story should also, for comparison, list flood stage and how high the water is above, or below, flood stage.
Wrong: *The river is expected to crest at 39 feet.*
Right: *The river is expected to crest at 39 feet, 12 feet above flood stage.*
**freeze** Describes conditions when the temperature at or near the surface is expected to be below 32 degrees during the growing season. Adjectives such as *severe* or *hard* are used if a cold spell exceeding two days is expected.
A freeze may or may not be accompanied by the formation of frost. However, use of the term *freeze* usually is restricted for occasions when wind or other conditions prevent frost.
**freezing drizzle, freezing rain** Synonyms for *ice storm.*
**frost** Describes the formation of very small ice crystals, which might develop under conditions similar to dew except for the minimum temperatures involved. Phrases such as *frost in low places* or *scattered light frost* are used when appropriate.
**funnel cloud** A violent, ro-

tating column of air that does not touch the ground, usually a pendant from a cumulonimbus cloud.

**gale** Sustained winds within the range of 39 to 54 mph (34 to 47 knots).

**heavy snow** It generally means:

a. A fall accumulating to 4 inches or more in depth in 12 hours, or

b. A fall accumulating to 6 inches or more in depth in 24 hours.

**high wind** Normally indicates that sustained winds of 39 mph or greater are expected to persist for one hour or longer.

**hurricane categories** Hurricanes are ranked 1 to 5 according to what is known as the Saffir-Simpson scale of strength:

Category 1 — Hurricane has central barometric pressure of 28.94 inches or more and winds of 74 to 95 mph, is accompanied by a 4-5 foot storm surge and causes minimal damage.

Category 2 — Pressure 28.50 to 28.93 inches, winds from 96 to 110 mph, storm surge 6-8 feet, damage moderate.

Category 3 — Pressure 27.91 to 28.49 inches, winds from 111 to 130 mph, storm surge 9-12 feet, damage extensive.

Category 4 — Pressure 27.17 to 27.90 inches, winds from 131 to 155 mph, storm surge 13-18 feet, damage extreme.

Category 5 — Pressure less than 27.17 inches, winds greater than 155 mph, storm surge higher than 18 feet, damage catastrophic.

Only three *Category 5* storms have hit the United States since record-keeping began: the 1935 Labor Day hurricane that hit the Florida Keys and killed 600 people; Hurricane Camille, which devastated the Mississippi coast in 1969, killing 256 and leaving $1.4 billion damage, and Hurricane Andrew, which hit South Florida in 1992, killing 43 and causing $30.5 billion in damage.

**hurricane eye** The relatively calm area in the center of the storm. In this area winds are light and the sky often is covered only partly by clouds.

**hurricane or typhoon** A warm-core tropical cyclone in which the minimum sustained surface wind is 74 mph or more.

Hurricanes are spawned east of the international date line. Typhoons develop west of the line. They are known as cyclones in the Indian Ocean.

When a hurricane or typhoon loses strength (wind speed), usually after landfall, it is reduced to *tropical storm* status.

**hurricane season** The portion of the year that has a relatively high incidence of hurricanes. In the Atlantic, Caribbean and Gulf of Mexico, this is from June through November. In the eastern Pacific, it is May 15 through Nov. 30. In the central Pacific, it is June 1 through Nov. 30.

**hurricane tide** Same as **storm tide**.

**hurricane warning** Warns that one or both of these dangerous effects of a hurricane are expected in specified areas in 24 hours or less:

a. Sustained winds of 74 mph (64 knots) or higher, and/or

b. Dangerously high water or a combination of dangerously high water and exceptionally high waves, even though winds expected may be less than hurricane force.

**hurricane watch** An announcement for specific areas

that a hurricane or incipient hurricane conditions may pose a threat to coastal and inland communities.

**ice storm warning** Reserved for occasions when significant, and possibly damaging, accumulations of ice are expected.

**ice storm, freezing drizzle, freezing rain** Describes the freezing of drizzle or rain on objects as it strikes them. *Freezing drizzle* and *freezing rain* are synonyms for *ice storm.*

**National Hurricane Center** The National Weather Service's National Hurricane Center in Miami has overall responsibility for tracking and providing information about tropical depressions, tropical storms and hurricanes in the Atlantic Ocean, Gulf of Mexico, Caribbean Sea and eastern Pacific Ocean.

The service's Central Pacific Hurricane Center in Honolulu is responsible for hurricane information in the Pacific Ocean area north of the equator from 140 degrees west longitude to 180 degrees.

On the Net: www.nhc.noaa.gov

**nearshore waters** The waters extended to five miles from shore.

**nor'easter** The term used by the National Weather Service for storms that either exit or move north along the East Coast, producing winds blowing from the northeast.

**offshore waters** The waters extending to about 250 miles from shore.

**sandstorm** Visibility of one-half mile or less due to sand blown by winds of 30 mph or more.

**severe blizzard** Wind speeds of 45 mph or more, great density of falling and/or blowing snow with visibility frequently near zero and a temperature of 10 degrees or lower.

**severe thunderstorm** Describes either of the following:

a. Winds — Thunderstorm-related surface winds sustained or gusts 50 knots or greater.

b. Hail — Surface hail three-quarters of an inch in diameter or larger. The word *hail* in a watch implies hail at the surface and aloft unless qualifying phrases such as *hail aloft* are used.

**sleet** (one form of ice pellet) Describes generally solid grains of ice formed by the freezing of raindrops or the refreezing of largely melted snowflakes. Sleet, like small hail, usually bounces when hitting a hard surface.

**sleet (heavy)** Heavy sleet is a fairly rare event in which the ground is covered to a depth of significance to motorists and others.

**snow avalanche bulletin** Snow avalanche bulletins are issued by the U.S. Forest Service for avalanche-prone areas in the western United States.

**squall** A sudden increase of wind speed by at least 16 knots and rising to 25 knots or more and lasting for at least one minute.

**storm tide** Directional wave(s) caused by a severe atmospheric disturbance.

**tidal wave** A term often used incorrectly for *seismic sea wave.* Use *tsunami,* but explain the term. These waves are caused by underwater earthquakes, landslides or volcanoes and are sometimes referred to as *great sea waves.*

**tornado** A violent rotating column of air forming a pendant usually from a cumulonimbus cloud, and touching the ground.

It usually starts as a funnel cloud and is accompanied by a loud roaring noise. On a local scale, it is the most destructive of all atmospheric phenomena.

**tornado warning** Warns the public of an existing tornado or one suspected to be in existence.

**tornado watch** Alerts the public to the possibility of a tornado.

**traveler's advisory** Alerts the public that difficult traveling or hazardous road conditions are expected to be widespread.

**tropical depression** A tropical cyclone in which the maximum sustained surface wind is 38 mph (33 knots) or less.

**tropical storm** A warm-core tropical cyclone in which the maximum sustained surface winds range from 39 to 73 mph (34 to 63 knots) inclusive.

**tsunami** See **tidal wave** in this listing.

**typhoon** See **hurricane or typhoon** in this listing.

**waterspout** A tornado over water.

**wind chill index** Also known as the *wind chill factor*. No hy-

## Heat index table

RELATIVE HUMIDITY

| TEMP. F | 40% | 45% | 50% | 55% | 60% | 65% | 70% | 75% | 80% | 85% | 90% | 95% | 100% |
|---|---|---|---|---|---|---|---|---|---|---|---|---|---|
| 110 | 136 | | | | | | | | | | | | |
| 108 | 130 | 137 | | | | | | | | | | | |
| 106 | 124 | 130 | 137 | | | | | | | | | | |
| 104 | 119 | 124 | 131 | 137 | | | APPARENT TEMPERATURE | | | | | | |
| 102 | 114 | 119 | 124 | 130 | 137 | | | | | | | | |
| 100 | 109 | 114 | 118 | 124 | 129 | 136 | | | | | | | |
| 98 | 105 | 109 | 113 | 117 | 123 | 128 | 134 | | | | | | |
| 96 | 101 | 104 | 108 | 112 | 116 | 121 | 126 | 132 | | | | | |
| 94 | 97 | 100 | 102 | 106 | 110 | 114 | 119 | 124 | 129 | 135 | | | |
| 92 | 94 | 96 | 99 | 101 | 105 | 108 | 112 | 116 | 121 | 126 | 131 | | |
| 90 | 91 | 93 | 95 | 97 | 100 | 103 | 106 | 109 | 113 | 117 | 122 | 127 | 132 |
| 88 | 88 | 89 | 91 | 93 | 95 | 98 | 100 | 103 | 106 | 110 | 113 | 117 | 121 |
| 86 | 85 | 87 | 88 | 89 | 91 | 93 | 95 | 97 | 100 | 102 | 105 | 108 | 112 |
| 84 | 83 | 84 | 85 | 86 | 88 | 89 | 90 | 92 | 94 | 96 | 98 | 100 | 103 |
| 82 | 81 | 82 | 83 | 84 | 84 | 85 | 86 | 88 | 89 | 90 | 91 | 93 | 95 |
| 80 | 80 | 80 | 81 | 81 | 82 | 82 | 83 | 84 | 84 | 85 | 86 | 86 | 87 |

## Wind chill factor table

AIR TEMPERATURE

| WIND MPH | 40 | 35 | 30 | 25 | 20 | 15 | 10 | 5 | 0 | -5 | -10 | -15 | -20 | -25 | -30 | -35 | -40 | -45 |
|---|---|---|---|---|---|---|---|---|---|---|---|---|---|---|---|---|---|---|
| | | | | | | APPARENT TEMPERATURE | | | | | | | | | | | | |
| 5 | 36 | 31 | 25 | 19 | 13 | 7 | 1 | -5 | -11 | -16 | -22 | -28 | -34 | -40 | -46 | -52 | -57 | -63 |
| 10 | 34 | 27 | 21 | 15 | 9 | 3 | -4 | -10 | -16 | -22 | -28 | -35 | -41 | -47 | -53 | -59 | -66 | -72 |
| 15 | 32 | 25 | 19 | 13 | 6 | 0 | -7 | -13 | -19 | -26 | -32 | -39 | -45 | -51 | -58 | -64 | -71 | -77 |
| 20 | 30 | 24 | 17 | 11 | 4 | -2 | -9 | -15 | -22 | -29 | -35 | -42 | -48 | -55 | -61 | -68 | -74 | -81 |
| 25 | 29 | 23 | 16 | 9 | 3 | -4 | -11 | -17 | -24 | -31 | -37 | -44 | -51 | -58 | -64 | -71 | -78 | -84 |
| 30 | 28 | 22 | 15 | 8 | 1 | -5 | -12 | -19 | -26 | -33 | -39 | -46 | -53 | -60 | -67 | -73 | -80 | -87 |
| 35 | 28 | 21 | 14 | 7 | 0 | -7 | -14 | -21 | -27 | -34 | -41 | -48 | -55 | -62 | -69 | -76 | -82 | -89 |
| 40 | 27 | 20 | 13 | 6 | -1 | -8 | -15 | -22 | -29 | -36 | -43 | -50 | -57 | -64 | -71 | -78 | -84 | -91 |
| 45 | 26 | 19 | 12 | 5 | -2 | -9 | -16 | -23 | -30 | -37 | -44 | -51 | -58 | -65 | -72 | -79 | -86 | -93 |
| 50 | 26 | 19 | 12 | 4 | -3 | -10 | -17 | -24 | -31 | -38 | -45 | -52 | -60 | -67 | -74 | -81 | -88 | -95 |
| 55 | 25 | 18 | 11 | 4 | -3 | -11 | -18 | -25 | -32 | -39 | -46 | -54 | -61 | -68 | -75 | -82 | -89 | -97 |
| 60 | 25 | 17 | 10 | 3 | -4 | -11 | -19 | -26 | -33 | -40 | -48 | -55 | -62 | -69 | -76 | -84 | -91 | -98 |

FROSTBITE TIME — 30 min. — 10 min. — 5 min.

phen.

The *wind chill* is a calculation that describes the combined effect of the wind and cold temperatures on exposed skin. The *wind chill index* would be minus 4, for example, if the temperature was 15 degrees and the wind was blowing at 25 mph — in other words, a temperature of 4 below zero with no wind.

The higher the wind at a given temperature, the lower the wind chill reading, although wind speeds above 40 mph have little additional cooling effect.

**wind shear** It is caused when a mass of cooled air rushes downward out of a thunderstorm in what is called a *microburst*, hits the ground and rushes outward in all directions. Wind shear itself is described as a sudden shift in wind direction and speed. A plane flying through a microburst at low altitude, as on final approach or takeoff, would at first experience a strong headwind and increased lift, followed by a strong tail wind and sharply decreased lift.

**winter storm warning** Notifies the public that severe winter weather conditions are almost certain to occur.

**winter storm watch** Alerts the public to the possibility of severe winter weather conditions.

### weather vane

**Web** Short form of *World Wide Web*, it is a service, or set of standards, that enables the publishing of multimedia documents on the Internet. The *Web* is not the same as the Internet, but is a subset; other applications, such as e-mail, exist on the Internet.

It is generally credited as the concept of researcher Tim Bern-ers-Lee who developed the first practical system in 1989.

Also, *Web site* (an exception to Webster's first listing), and *Web page.*

But *webcam, webcast, webmaster.*

———

### Caution:

Do not mistake the Internet for an encyclopedia, and the search engine for a table of contents. The Internet is a sprawling databank that's about one-quarter wheat and three-quarters chaff. Any information you find should be assessed with the same care that you use for everything else. In particular, check these points:

• Who is sponsoring the page? Is the author identifiable? You should avoid anonymous pages just as you avoid anonymous sources.

• Is there contact information in case you want to follow up? One way to check who owns a page is the Whois query at http://www.networksolutions.com/whois/.

• Is the domain type (.edu or .gov, for example) appropriate for the information provided? Web sites set up by professional groups are generally more reliable than personal home pages.

• The source for the information on the page should be clearly stated, whether original or borrowed. Is it a primary or secondary source? Can it be checked somewhere else?

• Based on what you know, how accurate does the information seem? If there's something on the site that you know is incorrect, it's likely there are errors elsewhere.

• Are there any obvious signs of bias? One possible clue: The

type of sites that this site links to.
• Is the page current? If it hasn't been updated lately, the information may be outdated. Right-click on the page and choose "View Info"; that often includes the date when the page was last modified.

### Webster's New World College Dictionary See dictionaries.

### Webster's Third New International Dictionary See dictionaries.

### Wednesday See days of the week.

### weekend

### weeklong One word as an adjective; an exception to Webster's.

### weights Use figures: *The baby weighed 9 pounds, 7 ounces. She had a 9-pound, 7-ounce boy.*

### weird, weirdo

### Welcome Wagon A trademark of Welcome Wagon International Inc.

### well Hyphenate as part of a compound modifier: *She is a well-dressed woman.*
See **hyphen** in the **Punctuation** chapter for guidelines on compound modifiers.

### well-being

### well-to-do

### well-wishers

### West As defined by the U.S. Census Bureau, the 13-state region is broken into two divisions.
The eight *Mountain division*

states are Arizona, Colorado, Idaho, Montana, Nevada, New Mexico, Utah and Wyoming.
The five *Pacific division* states are Alaska, California, Hawaii, Oregon and Washington.
See **Midwest region**; **Northeast region**; and **South** for the bureau's other three regional breakdowns.

### Western Capitalize for the film or book genre, but lowercase the style of music better known as *country*.

### Western Hemisphere The continents of North and South America, and the islands near them.
It frequently is subdivided as follows:

### Caribbean The islands from the tip of Florida to the continent of South America, plus French Guiana, Guyana and Suriname on the northeastern coast of South America.
Major island elements are Cuba, Hispaniola (the island shared by the Dominican Republic and Haiti), Jamaica, Puerto Rico, and the West Indies islands.

### Central America The narrow strip of land between Mexico and Colombia. Located there are Belize, Costa Rica, El Salvador, Guatemala, Honduras, Nicaragua and Panama.

### Latin America The area of the Americas south of the United States where Romance languages (those derived from Latin) are dominant. It applies to most of the region south of the United States except areas with a British heritage: the Bahamas, Barbados, Belize, Grenada, Guyana, Jamaica, Trinidad and Tobago,

and various islands in the West Indies. Suriname, the former Dutch Guiana, is an additional exception.

**North America** Canada, Mexico, the United States and the Danish territory of Greenland. When the term is used in more than its continental sense, it also may include the islands of the Caribbean.

**South America** Argentina, Bolivia, Brazil, Chile, Colombia, Ecuador, Paraguay, Peru, Uruguay, Venezuela, and in a purely continental sense, French Guiana, Guyana and Suriname. Politically and psychologically, however, the latter three regard themselves as part of the Caribbean.

**West Indies** An island chain extending in an eastward arc between the southeastern United States and the northern shore of South America, separating the Caribbean Sea from the Atlantic Ocean and including the Bahamas, the Greater Antilles, and the Lesser Antilles.

Major island elements are the nations of Barbados, Grenada, and Trinidad and Tobago, plus smaller islands dependent in various degrees on:

—Britain: British Virgin Islands, Anguilla, and the West Indies Associated States, including Antigua, Dominica, St. Lucia, St. Vincent and St. Christopher-Nevis.

—France: Guadeloupe (composed of islands known as Basse-Terre and Grande-Terre, plus five other islands) and Martinique.

—Netherlands: Netherlands Antilles, composed of Aruba, Bonaire, Curacao, Saba, St. Eustatius and the southern portion of St. Martin Island (the northern half is held by France and is part of Guadeloupe).

—United States: U.S. Virgin Islands, principally St. Croix, St. John and St. Thomas.

**West Indies** See **Western Hemisphere**.

**West Point** Acceptable on second reference to the *U.S. Military Academy.*
See **military academies**.
In datelines:
*WEST POINT, N.Y. (AP) —*

**West Virginia** Abbrev.: *W.Va.* (no space between *W.* and *Va.*). See **state names**.

**west, western** See the **directions and regions** entry.

**wheat** It is measured in bushels domestically, in metric tons for international trade.
There are 36.7 bushels of wheat in a metric ton.

**wheelchair** See **disabled, handicapped, impaired** entry.

**wheeler-dealer**

**whereabouts** Takes a singular verb:
*His whereabouts is a mystery.*

**wherever**

**which** See the **essential clauses, nonessential clauses** entry; the **that, which** entry; and the **who, whom** entry.

**whip** Capitalize when used as a formal title before a name. See **legislative titles** and **titles**.

**whiskey, whiskeys** Use the spelling *whisky* only in conjunc-

tion with *Scotch*.
See the **Scotch whisky** entry.

### white-collar (adj.)

**White House** Do not personify it with phrases such as *the White House said*. Instead, use a phrase such as *a White House official said*.

**white paper** Two words, lowercase, when used to refer to a special report.

**whitewash** (n. and v. and adj.)

**who's, whose** *Who's* is a contraction for *who is*, not a possessive: *Who's there?*
*Whose* is the possessive: *I do not know whose coat it is.*

### wholehearted

### wholesale price index
A measurement of the changes in the average prices that businesses pay for a selected group of industrial commodities, farm products, processed foods and feed for animals.
Capitalize when referring to the U.S. index, issued monthly by the Bureau of Labor Statistics, an agency of the Labor Department.

### whole-wheat

**who, whom** *Who* is the pronoun used for references to human beings and to animals with a name. It is grammatically the subject (never the object) of a sentence, clause or phrase: *The woman who rented the room left the window open. Who is there?*
*Whom* is used when someone is the object of a verb or preposition: *The woman to whom the room was rented left the window open. Whom do you wish to see?*

See the **essential clauses, nonessential clauses** entry for guidelines on how to punctuate clauses introduced by *who, whom, that* and *which*.

**whom** See **who, whom** entry.

**-wide** No hyphen. Some examples:

| | |
|---|---|
| citywide | nationwide |
| continentwide | statewide |
| countrywide | worldwide |
| industrywide | |

**wide-** Usually hyphenated. Some examples:

| | |
|---|---|
| wide-angle | wide-eyed |
| wide-awake | wide-open |
| wide-brimmed | |

Exception: *widespread*.

**widow, widower** In obituaries: A man is *survived by his wife*, or *leaves his wife*. A woman is *survived by her husband*, or *leaves her husband*.
Guard against the redundant *widow (widower) of the late*.

**widths** See **dimensions**.

**Wi-Fi** For the wireless networking standards.

### wigwag

### wildlife

### Wilkes-Barre, Pa.

**will** See the **shall, will** entry and **subjunctive mood**.

**Wilson's disease** After Samuel A. Wilson, an English neurologist. A disease characterized by abnormal accumulation of copper in the brain, liver and other organs.

**Windbreaker** A trademark for a brand of wind-resistant

sports jacket.

**wind chill index** See **weather terms**.

**window dressing** The noun. But as a verb: *window-dress.*

**wind-swept**

**wind up** (v.) **windup** (n. and adj.)

**wingspan**

**winter** See **seasons**.

**wintertime**

**wiretap, wiretapper** The verb forms: *wiretap, wiretapped, wiretapping.*

**Wisconsin** Abbrev.: *Wis.* See **state names**.

**-wise** No hyphen when it means *in the direction of* or *with regard to.* Some examples:

| | |
|---|---|
| clockwise | otherwise |
| lengthwise | slantwise |

Avoid contrived combinations such as *moneywise, religionwise.*

The word *penny-wise* is spelled with a hyphen because it is a compound adjective in which *wise* means *smart*, not an application of the suffix *-wise.* The same for *street-wise* in the *street-wise youth* (an exception to Webster's).

**women** Women should receive the same treatment as men in all areas of coverage. Physical descriptions, sexist references, demeaning stereotypes and condescending phrases should not be used.

To cite some examples, this means that:

—Copy should not assume maleness when both sexes are involved, as in *Jackson told newsmen* or in *the taxpayer ... he* when it easily can be said *Jackson told reporters* or *taxpayers ... they.*

—Copy should not express surprise that an attractive woman can be professionally accomplished, as in: *Mary Smith doesn't look the part, but she's an authority on ...*

—Copy should not gratuitously mention family relationships when there is no relevance to the subject, as in: *Golda Meir, a doughty grandmother, told the Egyptians today ...*

—Use the same standards for men and women in deciding whether to include specific mention of personal appearance or marital and family situation.

In other words, treatment of the sexes should be evenhanded and free of assumptions and stereotypes. This does not mean that valid and acceptable words such as *mankind* or *humanity* cannot be used. They are proper.

See **courtesy titles**; **divorcee**; the **man, mankind** entry; and **-persons**.

**Women's Army Corps** See the **Wac, WAC** entry.

**word-of-mouth** (n. and adj.)

**word processing** (adj.) Do not hyphenate.

**words as words** The meaning of this phrase, which appears occasionally in this book and similar manuals that deal with words, is best illustrated by an example: In this sentence, *woman* appears solely as a word rather than as the means of representing the concept normally associated with the word.

When italics are available, a word used as a word should be italicized.

Italics are not available to highlight this type of word use on the news wires. When a news story must use a word as a word, place quotation marks around it. See **plurals**.

**word selection** In general, any word with a meaning that universally is understood is acceptable unless it is offensive or below the normal standards for literate writing.

This Stylebook lists many words with cautionary notes about how they should be used. The entries in Webster's New World College Dictionary provide cautionary notes, comparisons and usage guidelines to help a writer choose the correct word for a particular context.

Any word listed in Webster's New World may be used for the definitions given unless this Stylebook restricts its use to only some definitions recorded by the dictionary or specifies that the word be confined to certain contexts.

If the dictionary cautions that a particular usage is objected to by some linguists or is not accepted widely, be wary of the usage unless there is a reason in the context.

The dictionary provides guidance on many idiomatic expressions under the principal word in the expression. The definition and spelling of *under way*, for example, are found in the *way* entry.

If it is necessary to use an archaic word or an archaic sense of a word, explain the meaning.

Additional guidance on the acceptability of a word is provided in this book under:

| | |
|---|---|
| **Americanisms** | **jargon** |
| **colloquialisms** | **special contexts** |
| **dialect** | **vernacular** |
| **foreign words** | |

See also the **obscenities, profanities, vulgarities** entry.

**workday**

**workers' compensation**

**work force**

**working class** (n.)
**working-class** (adj.)

**workout**

**workplace**

**workweek**

**World Bank** Acceptable in all references for *International Bank for Reconstruction and Development.*

**World Council of Churches** This is the main international, interdenominational cooperative body of Anglican, Eastern Orthodox, Protestant and old or national Catholic churches.

The Roman Catholic church is not a member but cooperates with the council in various programs.

Headquarters is in Geneva, Switzerland.

**World Court** This was an alternate name for the *Permanent Court of International Justice* set up by the League of Nations.

See the entry for the **International Court of Justice**, which has replaced it.

**World Health Organization** *WHO* is acceptable on second reference.

Headquarters is in Geneva, Switzerland.

**World Series** Or *the Series* on second reference. A rare exception to the general principles under **capitalization**.

**World War I, World War II**

**worldwide**

**worn-out**

**worship, worshipped, worshipper**

**worthwhile**

**would** See the **should, would** entry.

**wrack** See the **rack, wrack** entry.

**write in** (v.) **write-in** (n. and adj.)

**wrongdoing**

**Wyoming** Abbrev.: *Wyo.* See **state names**.

# XYZ

**Xerox** A trademark for a brand of photocopy machine. Never a verb. Use a generic term, such as photocopy.

**XML** For *extensible markup language*, used to sort, search and format information.

**X-ray** (n., v. and adj.) Use for both the photographic process and the radiation particles themselves.

**Yahoo** A trademark for an online computer service.

**yam** Botanically, yams and sweet potatoes are not related, although several varieties of moist-fleshed sweet potatoes are popularly called *yams* in some parts of the United States.

**yard** Equal to 3 feet.
The metric equivalent is approximately 0.91 meter.
To convert to meters, multiply by 0.91 (5 yards x 0.91 = 4.55 meters).
See **foot**; **meter**; and **distances**.

**year-end** (adj.)

**yearlong**

**years** Use figures, without commas: *1975*. Use commas only with a month and day: *Dec. 18, 1994*, was a special day. Use an *s* without an apostrophe to indicate spans of decades or centuries: *the 1890s, the 1800s.*
Years are the lone exception to the general rule in numerals that a figure is not used to start a sentence: *1976 was a very good year.*
See **A.D.**; **B.C.**; **centuries**; **historical periods and events**; and **months**.

**yellow journalism** The use of cheaply sensational methods to attract or influence readers. The term comes from the "Yellow Kid," a comic strip in the New York World in 1895.

**Yellow Pages** Capitalize in describing the business telephone directory.

**yesterday** Use only in direct quotations and in phrases that do not refer to a specific day: *Yesterday we were young.*
Use the day of the week in other cases.

**yesteryear**

**Yom Kippur** The Jewish Day of Atonement. Occurs in September or October.

**Young Men's Christian Association** *YMCA* is acceptable in all references.

Headquarters is in Chicago.

## Young Women's Christian Association

*YWCA* is acceptable in all references.

Headquarters is in New York.

**youth** Applicable to boys and girls from age 13 until 18th birthday. Use *man* or *woman* for individuals 18 and older.

**yo-yo** Formerly a trademark, now a generic term.

**Yukon** A territorial section of Canada. Do not abbreviate. Use in datelines after the names of communities in the territory.

See **Canada**.

## yule, yuletide

## zero-base budgeting

A process that requires an agency, department or division to justify budget requests as if its programs were starting from scratch, or from a base of zero. In theory this assures a review of all programs at budget time.

## zero, zeros

## zigzag

**Zionism** The effort of the Jews to regain and retain their biblical homeland. It is based on the promise of God in the Book of Genesis that Israel would forever belong to Abraham and his descendants as a nation.

The term is named for Mount Zion, the site of the ancient temple in Jerusalem. The Bible also frequently uses *Zion* in a general sense to denote the place where God is especially present with his people.

**ZIP code** Use all-caps *ZIP* for *Zoning Improvement Plan*, but always lowercase the word *code*.

Run the five digits together without a comma, and do not put a comma between the state name and the ZIP code: *New York, NY 10020.*

# SPORTS GUIDELINES AND STYLE

# SPORTS GUIDELINES AND STYLE

Sports is entertainment. It is big business. It is news that extends beyond games, winners and losers.

It is also statistics — agate.

Writing about sports requires a broad understanding of law and economics and psychology and sociology and mores.

As the appetite grows, so too does the need for writing with style and consistency.

The constant is the need to write with clarity and accuracy.

Good sports writing depends on the same writing and reporting tools as any other story.

A stylebook, a sports section of a stylebook, is an aid in reaching that goal.

**A note on BC filing of sports items:**

The 24-hour BC cycle requires the following procedures to differentiate between (a) AMs games stories (and the optionals that move as leads to them), and (b) game stories designed as new wrapups for PMs:

'AMs' stories should be "BC-Reds-Padres" for the game story and "BC-Reds-Padres, 1st Ld-Writethru," etc., for optionals.

Game "PMs" stories should use the word "Folo" in digest lines and the slug ("BC-Reds-Padres Folo"). When a story carries "Folo" in its slug, it is, by definition, for PMs use. Therefore, it doesn't need "Eds: PMs."

"Folo" is used on PMs versions of game stories only.

On events like major golf and tennis tournaments, when there's a story for PMs papers that will develop with morning action, do it as follows:

**Slug: [ BC-GLF—US Open, Bjt ]**
**Headline: [ Mickelson holds slim lead after first round ]**
**Eds. note: [ Eds: PMs. Changes byline. Will be updated with early action in second round, about 8:30 a.m. EDT. ]**
**Byline: [ By TIM DAHLBERG ]**
**Bytitle: [ AP Sports Writer ]**
PEBBLE BEACH, Calif. (AP) _
or:
**Slug: [ BC-TEN—Wimbledon, Bjt ]**
**Headline: [ Agassi, Sampras advance; Hingis defeated ]**
**Eds. note: [ Eds: PMs. Changes byline. Will be updated with morning matches, about 7 a.m. EDT. ]**
**Byline: [ By STEPHEN WILSON ]**
**Bytitle: [ AP Sports Writer ]**
WIMBLEDON, England (AP) _

Sports Story-type Identifiers:

BBO — Professional baseball (major league baseball: interleague games, All-Star Game, World Series, commissioner's office, Hall of Fame)
BBA — Professional baseball (American League)
BBN — Professional baseball (National League)
BBM — Professional baseball (All minor leagues)
BBI — International baseball
BBC — College baseball
BBH — High school baseball
BBW — Women's baseball
BBY — Youth baseball (Little League, Babe Ruth, American Legion)
BKC — College basketball
BKN — Professional basketball (NBA)
BKO — Other basketball professionals (minors, Europe)
BKH — High school basketball
BKW — Women's college basketball
BKL — Women's pro basketball (WNBA)
BOX — Boxing
CAR — Automotive racing, motorcycle racing
CYC — Cycling
FBC — College football
FBH — High school football
FBN — NFL football
FBO — Other football, including Arena Football, CFL, NFL Europe
FIG — Figure skating
GLF — Golf
GYM — Gymnastics
HKC — College hockey
HKN — NHL hockey
HKO — Other hockey, including minor leagues
OLY — Olympics
RAC — Horse racing
RUN — Track and field
SKI — Skiing
SOC — Soccer
SOF — Softball
SWM — Swimming
TEN — Tennis
VOL — Volleyball

# SPORTS GUIDELINES AND STYLE

# A

**abbreviations** It is not necessary to spell out the most common abbreviations on first reference: AFC, CART, NASCAR, NBA, NFC, NFL, NHL.

**-added** Follow this form in sports stories: *The $500,000-added sweepstakes.*

**All-America, All-American** The Associated Press recognizes only one All-America football and basketball team each year. In football, only Walter Camp's selections through 1924, and the AP selections after that, are recognized. Do not call anyone an *All-America* selection unless he is listed on either the Camp or AP roster.

Similarly do not call anyone an *All-America basketball player* unless an AP selection. The first All-America basketball team was chosen in 1948.

Use *All-American* when referring specifically to an individual: *All-American Pat Ewing,* or *He is an All-American.*

Use *All-America* when referring to the team: *All-America team,* or *All-America selection.*

**Americas Cup** (golf) **America's Cup** (yachting)

**archery** Scoring is usually in points. Use a basic summary. Example:

(After 3 of 4 Distances)
1. Darrell Pace, Cincinnati, 914 points.
2. Richard McKinney, Muncie, Ind. 880.
3. etc.

**AstroTurf** A trademark for a type of artificial grass.

**athlete's foot, athlete's heart**

**athletic club** Abbreviate as *AC* with the name of a club, but only in sports summaries: *Illinois AC.* See the **volleyball** entry for an example of such a summary.

**athletic director** Use the singular *athletic* unless otherwise in a formal title.

**athletic teams** Capitalize teams, associations and recognized nicknames: *Red Sox, the Big Ten, the A's, the Colts.*

**auto racing** Follow the forms below for all major auto races:

Examples:
Qualifying:
ANYTOWN, Fredonia (AP) — Qualifying results Friday for the Fredonia Grand Prix Formula One race on the 3.97-kilometer (2.48-mile) Major Fredonia circuit with driver, country, make of car and qualifying speed:
1. Ayrton Senna, Brazil, McLaren-Honda, 171.103 kph (108.265 mph).
2. Alain Prost, France, Ferrari, 170.297 kph (107.919 mph).
3. etc. for entire starting grid.
Race:
ANYTOWN, Fredonia (AP) — Results Sunday in the Fredonia Grand Prix over the 3.97-kilometer (2.48-mile) Major Fredonia circuit with driver, country (for U.S. drivers, add hometown), make of car,

laps completed, reason out (if any) and winner's average speed:

1. Ayrton Senna, Brazil, McLaren-Honda, 44 laps, 164.297 kph (101.823 mph).

2. Alain Prost, France, Ferrari, 44.

3. Nigel Mansell, Britain, Ferrari, 43.

4. etc. for entire starting grid, adding all non-finishers as follows:

23. Bernhard Bergen, Austria, McLaren-Honda, 12, broken axle.

After the final driver, add:

Time of race: 1:52:53.

Margin of victory: 1.7 seconds.

Caution flags: No full-course yellows.

Lead changes: 2 between 2 drivers.

Lap leaders: Senna, 1-34, Boutsen 35-36, Senna 37-44.

For point leaders:

**World Driver Leaders**

(Points on 9-6-4-3-2-1 basis)

1, Nicki Lauda, Austria, 47 points. 2. Emerson Fitipaldi, Brazil, 53.3. etc.

# B

## backboard, backcourt, backfield, backhand, backspin, backstop, backstretch, backstroke

Some are exceptions to Webster's New World, made for consistency in handling sports stories.

**badminton** Games are won by the first player to score 21 points, unless it is necessary to continue until one player has a two-point spread. Most matches go to the first winner of two games.

Use a match summary.

## ball carrier

## ballclub, ballgame, ballpark, ballplayer

## baseball

The spellings for some frequently used words and phrases, some of which are exceptions to Webster's New World:

| | |
|---|---|
| backstop | outfielder |
| ballclub | passed ball |
| ballpark | pinch hit (v.) |
| ballplayer | pinch-hit (n., adj.) |
| baseline | pinch hitter (n.) |
| bullpen | pitchout |
| center field | play off (v.) |
| center fielder | playoff (n., adj.) |
| designated hitter | put out (v.) putout (n.) |
| doubleheader | RBI (s.), RBIs (pl.) |
| double play | rundown (n.) |
| fair ball | sacrifice |
| fastball | sacrifice fly |
| first baseman | sacrifice hit |
| foul ball line | shoestring catch |
| foul tip | shortstop |
| ground-rule double | shut out (v.) |
| home plate | shutout (n., adj.) |
| home run | slugger |
| left-hander | squeeze play |
| line drive | strike |
| line up (v.) | strike zone |
| lineup (n.) | Texas leaguer |
| major league(s) (n.) | triple play |
| major league (adj.) | twinight doubleheader |
| major leaguer (n.) | wild pitch |

NUMBERS: Some sample uses of numbers: *first inning, seventh-inning stretch, 10th inning; first base, second base, third base; first home run, 10th home run; first place, last place; one RBI, 10 RBIs. The pitcher's record is now 6-5. The final score was 1-0.*

LEAGUES: Use *American League, National League, American League West, National League East,* or *AL West* and *AL East,* etc. On second reference: *the league, the pennant in the West, the league's West Division,* etc.

Note: No hyphen in *major league, minor league, big league* (n. or adj.)

BOX SCORES: A sample follows.

The visiting team always is listed on the left, the home team on the right.

Only one position, the first he played in the game, is listed for any player.

**BC-BBN--BOX-Atl-SD**

**BRAVES 8, PADRES 3**

**ATLANTA**          **SAN DIEGO**

| ATLANTA | ab | r | h | bi | SAN DIEGO | ab | r | h | bi |
|---|---|---|---|---|---|---|---|---|---|
| Ogllen ss | 5 | 1 | 1 | 1 | QVeras 2b | 4 | 1 | 0 | 0 |
| Lckhrt 2b | 5 | 2 | 2 | 0 | SFinley cf | 4 | 0 | 1 | 0 |
| ChJnes 3b | 4 | 2 | 2 | 1 | Gwynn rf | 4 | 1 | 1 | 1 |
| Glrrga 1b | 2 | 1 | 1 | 4 | Cminiti 3b | 3 | 0 | 1 | 0 |
| Klesko lf | 4 | 0 | 1 | 1 | Leyritz 1b | 3 | 1 | 2 | 2 |
| Rocker p | 0 | 0 | 0 | 0 | Joyner 1b | 1 | 0 | 1 | 0 |
| Perez p | 0 | 0 | 0 | 0 | CHrndz c | 4 | 0 | 1 | 0 |
| Seanez p | 0 | 0 | 0 | 0 | RRivra lf | 3 | 0 | 1 | 0 |
| Lgtnbr p | 0 | 0 | 0 | 0 | MaSwy ph | 1 | 0 | 0 | 0 |
| JLopez c | 4 | 1 | 1 | 1 | Gomez ss | 3 | 0 | 0 | 0 |
| AJones cf | 4 | 1 | 2 | 0 | Miceli p | 0 | 0 | 0 | 0 |
| Tucker rf | 2 | 0 | 1 | 0 | Bhrngr p | 0 | 0 | 0 | 0 |
| GerWm rf | 2 | 0 | 1 | 0 | Lngstn p | 0 | 0 | 0 | 0 |
| Neagle p | 2 | 0 | 0 | 0 | GMyrs ph | 0 | 0 | 0 | 0 |
| DeMrtz p | 0 | 0 | 0 | 0 | JHmtn p | 2 | 0 | 0 | 0 |
| Clbrnh ph | 1 | 0 | 0 | 0 | RayMys p | 0 | 0 | 0 | 0 |
| DBtsta lf | 1 | 0 | 0 | 0 | Sheets ss | 1 | 0 | 0 | 0 |
| VnWal ph | 1 | 0 | 0 | 0 | | | | | |
| **Totals** | **36** | **8** | **12** | **8** | | **34** | **3** | **8** | **3** |

Atlanta      000 101 600 - 8
San Diego    000 200 000 - 2

DP_Atlanta 1, San Diego 2. LOB_Atlanta 4, San Diego 7. 2B_ChJnes (1), Gwynn (1), RRivera (2). 3B_Lockhart (1). HR_Galarraga (1), JLopez (1), Leyritz (1).

| | IP | H | R | ER | BB | SO |
|---|---|---|---|---|---|---|
| **Atlanta** | | | | | | |
| Neagle | 5 2-3 | 7 | 3 | 3 | 1 | 7 |
| DeMrtz W, 1-0 | 1-3 | 0 | 0 | 0 | 0 | 0 |
| Rocker | 1 1-3 | 0 | 0 | 0 | 0 | 3 |
| Perez | 0 | 1 | 0 | 0 | 1 | 0 |
| Seanez | 2-3 | 0 | 0 | 0 | 0 | 0 |
| Lightenberg | 1 | 0 | 0 | 0 | 1 | 2 |
| **San Diego** | | | | | | |
| JHamilton L, 0-1 | 6 | 7 | 4 | 4 | 2 | 5 |
| RaMyers | 2-3 | 2 | 3 | 3 | 1 | 0 |
| Miceli | 1-3 | 1 | 1 | 1 | 0 | 1 |
| Boehringer | 1 | 2 | 0 | 0 | 0 | 0 |
| Langston | 1 | 0 | 0 | 0 | 0 | 0 |

Perez pitched to 2 batters in the 8th, JHamilton pitched to 2 batters in the 7th.

Umpires_Home, Bonin; First, Davis; Second, Rippley; Third, Tata; Left, Poncino; Right, Hallion.

T_2:58. A_65,042 (59,772).

## Example of an expanded box score:

**BC-BBA--EXP-BOX-Ana-Tex**

**Rangers 3, Angels 2**

| Anaheim | AB | R | H | BI | BB | SO | Avg. |
|---|---|---|---|---|---|---|---|
| Erstad cf | 4 | 0 | 3 | 2 | 0 | 0 | .750 |
| Gil ss | 3 | 0 | 0 | 0 | 0 | 0 | .000 |
| a-OPalmeiro ph | 1 | 0 | 0 | 0 | 0 | 0 | .000 |
| Nieves ss | 0 | 0 | 0 | 0 | 0 | 0 | .000 |
| Salmon rf | 4 | 0 | 1 | 0 | 0 | 1 | .250 |
| Glaus 3b | 4 | 0 | 1 | 0 | 0 | 1 | .250 |
| GAnderson lf | 3 | 0 | 1 | 0 | 1 | 0 | .333 |
| GHill dh | 4 | 0 | 0 | 0 | 0 | 1 | .000 |
| BMolina c | 4 | 1 | 1 | 0 | 0 | 1 | .250 |
| Spiezio 1b | 3 | 1 | 1 | 0 | 0 | 1 | .333 |
| Eckstein 2b | 3 | 0 | 1 | 0 | 0 | 0 | .333 |
| **Totals** | **33** | **2** | **9** | **2** | **1** | **5** | |

| Texas | AB | R | H | BI | BB | SO | Avg. |
|---|---|---|---|---|---|---|---|
| Greer lf | 3 | 0 | 0 | 1 | 0 | 1 | .143 |
| Velarde 2b | 4 | 0 | 1 | 0 | 0 | 1 | .250 |
| ARodriguez ss | 4 | 0 | 1 | 0 | 0 | 3 | .375 |
| RPalmeiro 1b | 2 | 0 | 0 | 0 | 2 | 0 | .167 |
| IRodriguez c | 4 | 1 | 2 | 0 | 0 | 0 | .250 |
| Galarraga dh | 3 | 1 | 1 | 1 | 0 | 0 | .167 |
| Caminiti 3b | 2 | 0 | 1 | 0 | 1 | 0 | .500 |
| Curtis cf | 2 | 1 | 1 | 0 | 0 | 0 | .500 |
| Mateo rf | 3 | 0 | 1 | 0 | 0 | 1 | .429 |
| **^Totals** | **27** | **3** | **8** | **2** | **3** | **6** | |

Anaheim    001 000 010_2 9 2
Texas      020 000 10x_3 8 0

a-grounded into double play for Gil in the 8th.

LOB_Anaheim 5, Texas 5. 2B_Erstad 2 (2), Glaus (1), BMolina (1), Spiezio (1), Velarde (1), IRodriguez (1), Galarraga (1). RBIs_Erstad 2 (2), Greer (1), Galarraga (1). SB_ARodriguez (1). SF_Greer. GIDP_OPalmeiro, GHill 2, IRodriguez, Curtis, Mateo.

Runners left in scoring position_Anaheim 4 (Salmon, Glaus, BMolina 2); Texas 3 (Greer, RPalmeiro, Caminiti). Runners moved up_Gil 2, Eckstein.

DP_Anaheim 3 (Gil, Eckstein and Spiezio), (Gil, Eckstein and Spiezio), (Eckstein, Gil and Spiezio); Texas 3 (ARodriguez, Velarde and RPalmeiro), (Velarde, ARodriguez and RPalmeiro), (Caminiti, IRodriguez and RPalmeiro).

| | IP | H | R | ER | BB | SO | NP | ERA |
|---|---|---|---|---|---|---|---|---|
| **Anaheim** | | | | | | | | |
| Schoeneweis L, 0-1 | 7 | 8 | 3 | 3 | 3 | 5 | 108 | 3.86 |
| Weber | 1 | 0 | 0 | 0 | 0 | 1 | 13 | 0.00 |
| **Texas** | | | | | | | | |
| Rogers W, 1-0 | 7 1-3 | 7 | 2 | 2 | 0 | 5 | 96 | 2.45 |
| JRZimmermn H, 4 | 2-3 | 0 | 0 | 0 | 0 | 0 | 2 | 0.00 |
| Crabtree S, 1 | 1 | 2 | 0 | 0 | 1 | 0 | 12 | 0.00 |

Inherited runners-scored_JRZimmermn 2-0.

IBB_off Crabtree (GAnderson) 1. HBP_by Schoeneweis (Curtis).

Umpires_Home, Rippley; First, Winters; Second, Barrett, Ted; Third, Marquez.

T_2:31. A_49,512 (49,115).

## LINESCORE: When a bare linescore summary is required, use this form:

**Philadelphia**    010 200 000 - 3 4 1
**San Diego**       000 200 000 - 2 9 1

K. Gross, Tekulve (8) and Virgil; Dravecky, Lefferts (3) and Kennedy. W - KGross, 4-6. L Dravecky, 4-3. Sv - Tekulve (3). HRs - Philadelphia, Virgil 2 (8).

## LEAGUE STANDINGS:
### The form:

**All Times EDT**

**NATIONAL LEAGUE**

|  | EAST | | | |
| --- | --- | --- | --- | --- |
|  | W | L | Pct. | GB |
| Pittsburgh | 92 | 69 | .571 | - |
| Philadelphia | 85 | 75 | .531 | 61/2 |
| etc. | | | | |

|  | WEST | | | |
| --- | --- | --- | --- | --- |
|  | W | L | Pct. | GB |
| Cincinnati | 108 | 54 | .667 | - |
| Los Angeles | 88 | 74 | .543 | 20 |
| etc. | | | | |

### (Night games not included)
### Monday's Results

Chicago 7, St. Louis 5

Atlanta at New York, rain.

### Tuesday's Games

Cincinnati (Gullett 14-2 and Nolan 4-4) at New York
(Seaver 12-3 and Matlack 6-1) 2, 6 p.m.

### Wednesday's Games

Cincinnati at New York

Chicago at St.Louis, night

Only games scheduled.

In subheads for results and future games, spell out day of the week as: *Tuesday's Games,* instead of *Today's Games.*

**basic summary** This format for summarizing sports events lists winners in the order of their finish. The figure showing the place finish is followed by an athlete's full name, his affiliation or hometown, and his time, distance, points, or whatever performance factor is applicable to the sport.

If a contest involves several types of events, the paragraph begins with the name of the event.

A typical example:

60-yard dash — 1, Steve Williams, Florida TC, 6.0. 2, Hasley Crawford, Philadelphia Pioneer, 6.1. 3, Mike McFarland, Chicago TC, 6.2. 4, etc.

100 — 1, Steve Williams, Florida TC, 10.1. 2, etc.

Additional examples are provided in the entries for many of the sports that are reported in this format.

Most basic summaries are a single paragraph per event, as shown. In some competitions with large fields, however, the basic summary is supplied under a dateline with each winner listed in a single paragraph. See the **auto racing** and **bowling** entries for examples.

For international events in which U.S. or Canadian competitors are not among the leaders, add them in a separate paragraph as follows:

Also: 14, Dick Green, New York, 6.8. 17, George Bensen, Canada, 6.9. 19, etc.

In events where points, rather than time or distance, are recorded as performances, mention the word points on the first usage only:

1. Jim Benson, Springfield, N.J., 150 points. 2. Jerry Green, Canada, 149. 3. etc.

**basketball** The spellings of some frequently used words and phrases:

| | |
| --- | --- |
| backboard | half-court pass |
| backcourt | halftime |
| backcourtman | hook shot |
| baseline | jump ball |
| field goal | jump shot |
| foul line | layup |
| foul shot | man-to-man |
| free throw | midcourt |
| free-throw line | pivotman |
| frontcourt | play off (v.) |
| full-court press | playoff (n., adj.) |
| goaltending | zone |

NUMBERS: Some sample uses of numbers: *in the first quarter, a second-quarter lead, nine field goals, a 3-pointer, 10 field goals, the 6-foot-5 forward, the 6-10 center. He is 6 feet 10 inches tall.*

LEAGUE: *National Basketball Association* or *NBA.*

For subdivisions: *the Atlantic Division of the Eastern Conference, the Pacific Division of the Western Conference,* etc. On second reference: *the NBA East, the division, the conference,* etc.

BOX SCORE: A sample follows. The visiting team always is

listed first.

In listing the players, begin with the five starters — two forwards, center, two guards — and follow with all substitutes who played.

Figures after each player's last name denote field goals, free throws, free throws attempted and total points.

Example:

**BC-BKN--Lakers-Hawks, Box, 0165**

**Lakers-Hawks, Box**

**L.A. Lakers (108)**

Jones 0-2 3-3 3, Odom 8-15 12-20 28, Mihm 0-1 0-0 0, Atkins 8-20 6-8 25, C. Butler 3-7 0-0 6, Cook 5-9 0-0 13, Walton 0-1 0-0 0, Brown 8-16 9-11 27, Grant 0-0 0-0 0, Vujacic 1-2 0-0 2, Medvedenko 1-3 2-2 4, Totals 34-76 32-44 108.

**ATLANTA (114)**

Childress 8-10 3-3 19, Walker 10-15 6-10 26, Ekezie 2-5 1-1 5, Anderson 2-7 1-2 5, Diaw 4-9 0-0 8, Drobnjak 1-2 0-0 2, D.Smith 4-6 3-4 11, Delk 7-20 8-9 25, Ivey 3-7 0-1 6, Collier 3-7. Totals 44-88 23-31 114.

**L.A. Lakers 15 30 24 39_108**

**Atlanta 31 31 17 35_114**

3-Point Goals -- L.A. Lakers 8-23 (Cook 3-5, Atkins 3-10, Brown 2-3, Walton 0-1, Odom 0-1, Vujacic 0-1, Jones 0-2), Atlanta 3-8 (Delk 3-8). Fouled Out -- None. Rebounds --L.A. Lakers 48 (Cook 10), Atlanta 58 (Childress 11). Assists_L.A. Lakers 12 (Atkins 5), Atlanta 23 (Delk 8). Total Fouls_L.A. Lakers 29, Atlanta 33. Technical_L.A. Lakers Defensive Three Second. A_15,633. (19,445).

STANDINGS: The format for professional standings:

**Eastern Conference**

**Atlantic Division**

| | W | L | Pct. | GB |
|---|---|---|---|---|
| Boston | 43 | 22 | .662 | — |
| Philadelphia | 40 | 30 | .571 | 5 1/2 |
| etc. | | | | |

In college boxes, the score by periods is omitted because the games are divided only into halves.

**BC-BKC--Connecticut-Syracuse, Box**

**No. 19 CONNECTICUT 74, No. 8 SYRACUSE 66**

**CONNECTICUT** (15-5)

Villanueva 9-13 3-7 21, Boone 2-4 3-5 7, Brown 0-2 5-6 5, Williams 3-11 1-2 9, Gay 6-13 4-4 18, Armstrong 2-2 2-2 6, Kellogg 0-0 0-0 0, Anderson 1-4 2-3 4, Nelson 1-1 2-3 4. Totals 24-50 22-32 74.

**SYRACUSE** (21-3)

Warrick 6-13 4-7 16, Pace 7-9 0-0 14, Forth 0-1 0-0 0, McNarmara 4-18 0-0 9, McCroskey 2-5 0-0 4, Watkins 2-2 0-0 4, Edelin 3-8 1-2 7, Roberts 4-10 4-5 12. Totals 28-66 9-14 66.

Halftime_Connecticut 37-36. 3-Point Goals_Connecticut 4-14 (Gay 2-5, Williams 2-5, Brown 0-2, Anderson 0-2), Syracuse 1-9 (McNamara 1-9). Fouled Out_Roberts. Rebounds_Connecticut 36 (Villanueva 10), Syracuse 34 (Warrick 7). Assists_Connecticut 14 (Williams 6), Syracuse 17 (Edelin, McNamara 6). Total Fouls_Connecticut 15, Syracuse 24. A_27,651.

The format for college conference standings:

| | Conference | | | All Games | | |
|---|---|---|---|---|---|---|
| | W | L | Pct. | W | L | Pct. |
| Missouri | 12 | 2 | .857 | 24 | 4 | .857 |

**betting odds** Use figures and a hyphen: *The odds were 5-4, he won despite 3-2 odds against him.*

The word *to* seldom is necessary, but when it appears it should be hyphenated in all constructions: *3-to-2 odds, odds of 3-to-2, the odds were 3-to-2.*

**bettor** A person who bets.

**bicycle**

**billiards** Scoring is in points. Use a match summary. Example:

Minnesota Fats, St. Paul, Minn., def. Pool Hall Duke, 150-141.

**bobsledding, luge** Scoring is in minutes, seconds and tenths of a second. Extend to hundredths if available.

Identify events as *two-man, four-man, men's luge, women's luge.*

Use a basic summary. Example:

Two-man — 1, Jim Smith and Dick Jones, Alaska Sledders, 4:20.77.2, Tom Winner and Joe Finisher, Mountaineers, 4:31.14.3, etc.

**bowl games** Capitalize them: *Cotton Bowl, Orange Bowl, Rose Bowl,* etc.

**bowling** Scoring systems use both total points and won-lost records.

Use the basic summary format

in paragraph form. Note that a comma is used in giving pinfalls of more than 999.

Examples:

ST. LOUIS (AP) — Second-round leaders and their total pinfalls in the $100,000 Professional Bowlers Association tournament:

1. Bill Spigner, Hamden, Conn., 2,820.

2. Gary Dickinson, Fort Worth, Texas, 2,759.

3. etc.

ALAMEDA, Calif. (AP) — The 24 match play finalists with their won-lost records and total pinfall Thursday night after tour rounds — 26 games — of the $65,000 Alameda Open bowling tournament:

1. Jay Robinson, Los Angeles, 5-3, 5,937.

2. Butch Soper, Huntington Beach, Calif., 3-5, 5,932.

3. etc.

**boxing** The three major sanctioning bodies for professional boxing are the World Boxing Association, the World Boxing Council and the International Boxing Federation.

Weight classes and titles by organization:

105 pounds — Mini Flyweight, WBF, IBF; Strawweight, WBC

108 pounds — Light Flyweight, WBA, WBC; Junior Flyweight, IBF

112 pounds — Flyweight, WBA, WBC, IBF

115 pounds — Super Flyweight, WBA, WBC; Junior Bantamweight, IBF

118 pounds — Bantamweight, WBA, WBC, IBF

122 pounds — Super Bantamweight, WBA, WBC, Junior Featherweight, IBF

126 pounds — Featherweight, WBA, WBC, IBF

130 pounds — Super Featherweight, WBA, WBC; Junior Lightweight, IBF

135 pounds — Lightweight, WBA, WBC, IBF

140 pounds — Super Lightweight, WBA, WBC; Junior Welterweight, IBF

147 pounds — Welterweight, WBA, WBC, IBF

154 pounds — Super Welterweight, WBA, WBC; Junior Middleweight, IBF

160 pounds — Middleweight, WBA, WBC, IBF

168 pounds — Super Middleweight, WBA, WBC, IBF

175 pounds — Light Heavyweight, WBA, WBC, IBF

190 pounds — Cruiserweight, WBA, WBC, IBF

More than 190 pounds — Heavyweight, WBA, WBC, IBF

Some other terms:

**kidney punch** A punch to an opponent's kidney when the puncher has only one hand free. An illegal punch. If the puncher has both hands free, a punch to the opponent's kidney is legal.

**knock out** (v.) **knockout** (n. and adj.) A fighter is knocked out if he takes a 10-count.

If a match ends early because one fighter is unable to continue, say that the winner stopped the loser. In most boxing jurisdictions there is no such thing as a technical knockout.

**outpointed** Not *outdecisioned.*

**rabbit punch** A punch behind an opponent's neck. It is illegal.

SUMMARIES: Use a match summary.

Some examples, with the fighters weights after their names and the number of rounds at the end.

Randy Jackson, 152, New York, outpointed Chuck James, 154, Philadelphia, 10.

Muhammad Ali, 220, Chicago, knocked out Pierre Coopman, 202, Belgium, 5.

George Foreman, 217, Hayward, Calif., stopped Joe Frazier, 214, Philadelphia, 2.

TALE OF THE TAPE:

An example:

# Major College Basketball Conferences
(Football affiliations, where different, are in parentheses.)

**AMERICA EAST** — Albany NY (Northeast); Binghamton (no program); Boston University (no program); Hartford (no program); Maine (Atlantic 10); Maryland-Baltimore County (no program); New Hampshire (Atlantic 10); Stony Brook (Northeast); Vermont (no program).

**ATLANTIC 10 CONFERENCE** — EAST: Charlotte (no program); Fordham (Patriot); Massachusetts; Rhode Island; St. Bonaventure (no program); Saint Joseph's (no program); Temple (I-A Independent); WEST: Dayton (Pioneer); Duquesne (Metro Atlantic); George Washington (no program); La Salle (Metro Atlantic); Richmond; Saint Louis (no program); Xavier (no program).

**ATLANTIC COAST CONFERENCE** — Boston College; Clemson; Duke; Florida State; Georgia Tech; Maryland; Miami; North Carolina State; North Carolina; Virginia; Virginia Tech; Wake Forest.

**ATLANTIC SUN CONFERENCE** — Belmont (no program); Campbell (no program); East Tennessee State (no program); Florida Atlantic (Sun Belt); Gardner-Webb (Big South); Jacksonville (Pioneer); Lipscomb (no program); Mercer (no program); Stetson (no program); Troy State (Sun Belt).

**BIG EAST CONFERENCE** — Cincinnati; Connecticut; DePaul (no program); Georgetown (Patriot); Louisville; Marquette (no program); Notre Dame (I-A Independent); Pittsburgh; Providence (no program); Rutgers; Seton Hall (no program); South Florida; St. John's (no program); Syracuse; Villanova (Atlantic 10); West Virginia.

**BIG SKY CONFERENCE** — Sacramento State; Eastern Washington; Idaho State; Montana; Montana State; Northern Arizona; Portland State; Weber State.

**BIG SOUTH CONFERENCE** — Birmingham-Southern (no program); Charleston Southern; Coastal Carolina; High Point (no program); Liberty; North Carolina-Asheville (no program); Radford (no program); Virginia Military Institute; Winthrop (no program).

**BIG TEN CONFERENCE** — Illinois; Indiana; Iowa; Michigan; Michigan State; Minnesota; Northwestern; Ohio State; Penn State; Purdue; Wisconsin.

**BIG 12 CONFERENCE** — Baylor; Colorado; Iowa State; Kansas; Kansas State; Missouri; Nebraska; Oklahoma; Oklahoma State; Texas; Texas A&M; Texas Tech.

**BIG WEST CONFERENCE** — Cal Poly-San Luis Obispo (Great West); Cal State Fullerton (no program); Cal State Northridge (no program); UC Irvine (no program); UC Riverside (no program); UC Santa Barbara (no program); Long Beach State (no program); Pacific (no program).

**COLONIAL ATHLETIC ASSOCIATION** — Delaware (Atlantic 10); Drexel (no program); George Mason (no program); Georgia State (no program); Hofstra (Atlantic 10); James Madison (Atlantic 10); North Carolina-Wilmington (no program); Northeastern; Old Dominion (no program); Towson (Patriot); Virginia Commonwealth (no program); William and Mary (Atlantic 10).

**CONFERENCE USA** — Alabama-Birmingham; Central Florida (Mid-American); East Carolina; Houston; Marshall; Memphis; Rice; Southern Methodist; Southern Mississippi; Texas-El Paso; Tulane; Tulsa.

**HORIZON LEAGUE** — Butler (Pioneer); Cleveland State (no program); Detroit (no program); Illinois-Chicago (no program); Loyola of Chicago (no program); Wisconsin-Green Bay (no program); Wisconsin-Milwaukee (no program); Wright State (no program); Youngstown State (Gateway).

**IVY LEAGUE** — Brown; Columbia; Cornell; Dartmouth; Harvard; Pennsylvania; Princeton; Yale.

**METRO ATLANTIC ATHLETIC CONFERENCE** — Canisius (no program); Fairfield (no program); Iona; Loyola, Maryland (no program); Manhattan (no program); Marist; Niagara (no program); Rider (no program); St. Peter's; Siena (no program).

**MID-AMERICAN CONFERENCE** — EAST: Akron; Buffalo; Kent State; Miami (Ohio); Ohio; WEST: Ball State; Bowling Green; Central Michigan; Eastern Michigan; Northern Illinois; Toledo; Western Michigan.

**MID-CONTINENT CONFERENCE** — Centenary (no program); Chicago State (no program); Indiana-Purdue-Indianapolis (no program); Missouri-Kansas City (no program); Oakland, Mich. (no program); Oral Roberts (no program); Southern Utah (Great West); Valparaiso (Pioneer); Western Illinois (Gateway).

**MID-EASTERN ATHLETIC CONFERENCE** — Bethune-Cookman; Coppin State (no program); Delaware State; Florida A&M (I-AA Independent); Hampton; Howard; Maryland-Eastern Shore (no program); Morgan State; Norfolk State; North Carolina A&T; South Carolina State.

**MISSOURI VALLEY CONFERENCE** — Bradley (no program); Creighton (no program); Drake (Pioneer); Evansville (no program); Illinois State (Gateway); Indiana State (Gateway); Northern Iowa (Gateway); Southern Illinois (Gateway); Southwest Missouri State (Gateway); Wichita State (no program).

**MOUNTAIN WEST CONFERENCE** — Brigham Young; Colorado State; Nevada-Las Vegas; New Mexico; San Diego State; Texas Christian University; Air Force; Utah; Wyoming.

**NORTHEAST CONFERENCE** — Central Connecticut State; Fairleigh Dickinson (no program); Long Island University-Brooklyn (no program); Monmouth, N.J.; Mount St. Mary's, Md. (no program); Quinnipiac (no program); Robert Morris; Sacred Heart; St. Francis, N.Y. (no program); Saint Francis, Pa.; Wagner.

**OHIO VALLEY CONFERENCE** — Austin Peay (Pioneer); Eastern Illinois; Eastern Kentucky; Jacksonville State; Morehead State (Pioneer); Murray State; Samford; Southeast Missouri State; Tennessee-Martin; Tennessee State; Tennessee Tech.

**PACIFIC-10 CONFERENCE** — Arizona; Arizona State; California; UCLA; Oregon; Oregon State; Southern California; Stanford; Washington; Washington State.

**PATRIOT LEAGUE** — American U. (no program); Army (I-A Independent); Bucknell; Colgate; Holy Cross; Lafayette; Lehigh; Navy (I-A Independent).

**SOUTHEASTERN CONFERENCE** — Alabama; Arkansas; Auburn; Florida; Georgia; Kentucky; Louisiana State; Mississippi; Mississippi State; South Carolina; Tennessee; Vanderbilt.

**SOUTHERN CONFERENCE** — NORTH: Appalachian State; Chattanooga; Elon; North Carolina-Greensboro (no program); Western Carolina; SOUTH: College of Charleston (no program); The Citadel; Davidson (Pioneer); Furman; Georgia Southern; Wofford.

**SOUTHLAND CONFERENCE** — Lamar (no program); McNeese State; Nicholls State; Northwestern State; Sam Houston State; Southeastern Louisiana (I-AA Independent); Stephen F. Austin; Texas A&M-Corpus Christi (no program); Texas-Arlington (no program); Texas-San Antonio (no program); Texas State.

**SOUTHWESTERN ATHLETIC CONFERENCE** — Alabama A&M; Alabama State; Alcorn State; Arkansas-Pine Bluff; Grambling State; Jackson State; Mississippi Valley State; Prairie View A&M; Southern University; Texas Southern.

**SUN BELT CONFERENCE** — Arkansas State; Arkansas-Little Rock (no program); Denver (no program); Florida International; Louisiana-Lafayette; Louisiana-Monroe; Middle Tennessee State; New Orleans (no program); North Texas; South Alabama (no program); Troy; Western Kentucky (Gateway).

**WEST COAST CONFERENCE** — Gonzaga (no program); Loyola Marymount (no program); Pepperdine (no program); Portland (no program); St. Mary's, Cal. (no program); San Diego (Pioneer); San Francisco (no program); Santa Clara (no program).

**WESTERN ATHLETIC CONFERENCE** — Boise State; Fresno State; Hawaii; Idaho (Sun Belt); Louisiana Tech; Nevada; New Mexico State; San Jose State; Utah State.

**INDEPENDENTS** — Indiana-Purdue-Fort Wayne (no program); Savannah State (I-AA Independent); Texas-Pan American (no program).

SAN JUAN, Puerto Rico (AP) — The tale of the tape for the Jean Pierre Coopman-Muhammad Ali world heavyweight championship fight Friday night:

|  | Coopman | Ali |
|---|---|---|
| Age | 29 | 34 |
| Weight | 202 | 220 |
| Height | 6-0 | 6-3 |
| Reach | 75 | 80 |
| Chest Normal | 43 | 44 |
| Chest Expanded | 45 1/2 | 46 |
| Biceps | 15 | 15 |
| Forearm | 13 | 13 1/2 |
| Waist | 34 1/2 | 34 |
| Thigh | 25 1/2 | 26 |
| Calf | 15 | 17 |
| Neck | 17 | 17 1/2 |
| Wrist | 7 1/2 | 8 |
| Fist | 12 1/2 | 13 |
| Ankle | 9 | 9 1/2 |

SCORING BY ROUNDS:
An example:

NEW YORK (AP) — Scorecards for the Muhammad Ali-Joe Frazier heavyweight title fight Friday night:

Scoring by rounds:

Referee Tom Smith

AAA FFF AAA AFA FFF — A8-7

Judge Bill Swift

AAA FFF FFF AFA FFF — F10-5

Judge Ralph Cohen

AAA FFF FFF FFF AFF — F11-4

Scoring by points system:

Referee Tom Smith

A 10 10 10 10 10 10 10 10 10 9 9 9 9 10

F 10 9 9 9 9 9 9 10 10 9 10 10 10 10 10

Total — Ali 146, Frazier 143.

Judge Ralph Cohen

A 10 9 10 10 10 10 10 10 10 10 9 9 9 9

F 9 10 10 9 9 9 9 9 10 10 9 10 10 10 10

Total — Ali 145, Frazier 143.

## box office (n.) **box-office** (adj.)

## bullfight, bullfighter, bullfighting

**bullpen** One word, for the place where baseball pitchers warm up, and for a pen that holds cattle.

# C

**Canada goose** Not Canadian goose.

**canoeing** Scoring is in minutes, seconds and tenths of a second. Extend to hundredths if available.

Use a basic summary. Example:

**Canoeing, Men**

**Kayak Singles, 500 meters**

Heat 1 — Rudiger Helm, Germany, 1:56.06. 2. Zoltan Sztanity, Hungary, 1:57.12. 3. etc.

Also: 6. Henry Krawczyk, New York, 2 04.64.

First Repechage — 1, Ladislav Soucek, Czech Republic, 1:53.20. 2. Hans Eich, Germany, 1:54.23. 3. etc.

**coach** Lowercase as a job description, not a formal title. Capitalize only when substituted for a name as a term of address.

**collective nouns** Nouns that denote a unit take singular verbs and pronouns: *class, committee, crowd, family, group, herd, jury, orchestra, team.*

However, team names such as *the Jazz, the Magic, the Avalanche,* take plural verbs.

**colt** A male horse 4 years and under.

**conferences** A listing of major college basketball conferences is on the previous page. (Football affiliations, where different, are in parentheses.)

**cross country** No hyphen, an exception to Webster's New World based on the practices of U.S. and international governing bodies for the sport.

Scoring for this track event is in minutes, seconds and tenths of a second. Extended to hundredths if available.

**National AAU Championship**

**Cross Country**

Frank Shorter, Miami, 5:25.67; 2. Tom Coster, Los Angeles, 5:30.72; 3. etc.

Adapt the basic summary to paragraph form under a dateline for a field of more than 10 competitors. See the **auto racing** and **bowling** entries for examples.

**cycling** Use the basic summary format.

# D

**decathlon** Summaries include time or distance performance, points earned in that event and the cumulative total of points earned in previous events.

Contestants are listed in the order of their overall point totals. First name and hometown (or nation) are included only on the first and last events on the first day of competition; on the last day, first names are included only in the first event and in the summary denoting final placings.

Use the basic summary format. Include all entrants in summaries of each of the 10 events.

An example for individual events:

Decathlon

(Group A)

100 — 1. Fred Dixon, Los Angeles, 10.8 seconds, 854 points. 2. Bruce Jenner, San Jose State, 11:09, 783. 3. etc.

Long jump — 1. Dixon, 24-7 (7.34m), 889, 1,743. 2. Jenner, 23-6 (7.17m), 855, 1,638. 3. etc.

Decathlon final — 1. Bruce Jenner, San Jose State, 8,524 points. 2. Fred Dixon, Los Angeles, 8,277. 3. etc.

**discus** The disc thrown in track and field events.

**diving** Use a basic summary. See **skating, figure** for the style on compulsory dives.

# E

**ERA** Acceptable in all references to baseball's *earned run average.*

# F

**fencing** Identify epee, foil and saber classes as: *men's individual foil, women's team foil,* etc.

Use match summary for early rounds of major events, for lesser dual meets and for tournaments.

Use basic summary for final results of major championships.

For major events, where competitors meet in a round-robin and are divided into pools, use this form:

Epee, first round (four qualify for semi-finals) Pool 1 — Joe Smith, Springfield, Mass., 4-1. Enrique Lopez, Chile, 3-2. etc.

**figure skating** See **skating, figure** for guidelines on the summary form.

**filly** A female horse under the age of 5.

**football** The spellings of some frequently used words and phrases:

| | |
|---|---|
| ball carrier | lineman |
| ballclub | line of scrimmage |
| blitz (n., v.) | out of bounds (adv.) |
| end line | out-of-bounds (adj.) |
| end zone | pitchout (n.) |
| fair catch | place kick |
| field goal | place-kicker |
| fourth-and-one (adj.) | play off (v.) |
| fullback | playoff (n., adj.) |
| goal line | quarterback |
| goal-line stand | runback (n.) |
| halfback | running back |
| halftime | split end |
| handoff | tailback |
| kick off (v.) | tight end |
| kickoff (adj.) | touchback |
| left guard | touchdown |
| linebacker | wide receiver |

NUMBERS: Use figures for yardage: *The 5-yard line, the 10-yard line, a 5-yard pass play, he plunged in from the 2, he ran 6 yards, a 7-yard gain; a fourth-and-2 play.*

Some other uses of numbers: *The final score was 21-14. The team won its fourth game in 10 starts. The team record is 4-5-1.*

LEAGUE: *National Football League*, or *NFL.*

STATISTICS: All football games, whether using the one- or two-point conversion, use the same summary style.

The visiting team always is listed first.

Field goals are measured from the point where the ball was kicked — not the line of scrimmage. The goal posts are 10 yards behind the goal lines. Include that distance.

Abbreviate team names to four letters or fewer on the scoring and statistical lines as illustrated.

The passing line shows, in order: completions-attempts-had intercepted.

A sample agate package:

**BC-FBN--Super Bowl Summary,0269**
**Super Bowl Summary**
**By The Associated Press**

| New England | 0 | 7 | 7 | 10_24 |
| Philadelphia | 0 | 7 | 7 | 7_21 |

**Second Quarter**
Phi_Smith 6 pass from McNabb (Akers kick), 9:55.
NE_Givens 4 pass from Brady (Vinatieri kick), 1:10.
**Third Quarter**
NE_Vrabel 2 pass from Brady (Vinatieri kick), 11:04.
Phi_Westbrook 10 pass from McNabb (Akers kick), 3:35.
**Fourth Quarter**
NE_Dillon 2 run (Vinatieri kick), 13:44.
NE_FG Vinatieri 22, 8:40.
Phi_G.Lewis 30 pass from McNabb (Akers kick), 1:48.
A_78,125.

| | NE | Phi |
|---|---|---|
| First downs | 21 | 24 |
| Total Net Yards | 331 | 369 |
| Rushes-yards | 28-112 | 17-45 |

| | | |
|---|---|---|
| Passing | 219 | 324 |
| Punt Returns | 4-26 | 3-19 |
| Kickoff Returns | 4-63 | 5-114 |
| Interceptions Ret. | 3-5 | 0-0 |
| Comp-Att-Int | 23-33-0 | 30-51-3 |
| Sacked-Yards Lost | 2-17 | 4-33 |
| Punts | 7-45.1 | 5-42.8 |
| Fumbles-Lost | 1-1 | 2-1 |
| Penalties-Yards | 7-47 | 3-35 |
| Time of Possession | 31:37 | 28:23 |

**INDIVIDUAL STATISTICS**

RUSHING_New England, Dillon 18-75, Faulk 8-38, Pass 1-0, Brady 1-(minus 1). Philadelphia, Westbrook 15-44, Levens 1-1, McNabb 1-0.

PASSING_New England, Branch 11-133, Dillon 3-31, Givens 3-19, Faulk 2-27, T.Brown 2-17, Graham 1-7, Vrabel 1-2. Philadelphia, Owens 9-122, Westbrook 7-60, Pinkston 4-82, G.Lewis 4-53, Smith 4-27, Mitchell 1-11, Parry 1-2.

MISSED FIELD GOALS_None.

The rushing and receiving paragraph for individual leaders shows attempts and yardage gained. The passing paragraph shows completions, attempts, number of attempts intercepted, and total yards gained.

STANDINGS: The form for **professional standings**:

**American Conference**
East

| | W | L | T | Pct. | PF | PA |
|---|---|---|---|---|---|---|
| Baltimore | 10 | 4 | 0 | .714 | 395 | 269 |
| New England | 9 | 5 | 0 | .643 | 387 | 275 |
| Etc. | | | | | | |

The form for college **conference standings**:

**Atlantic Coast Conference**
Atlantic Division

| | Conference | | | | All games | | | |
|---|---|---|---|---|---|---|---|---|
| | W | L | PF | PA | W | L | PF | PA |
| Wake Forest | 6 | 2 | 175 | 145 | 11 | 2 | 289 | 191 |
| Boston College | 5 | 3 | 189 | 133 | 9 | 3 | 313 | 180 |
| Etc. | | | | | | | | |

In college conference standings, limit team names to nine letters or fewer. Abbreviate as necessary.

**fractions** Put a full space between the whole number and the fraction.

# G

## game plan

**gelding** A castrated male horse.

**golf** Some frequently used terms and some definitions:
*birdie, birdies* One stroke under par.
*bogey, bogeys* One stroke over par. The past tense is *bogeyed.*
*caddie*
*eagle* Two strokes under par.
*fairway*
*hole-in-one*
*Masters, Masters Tournament* No possessive. Use *the Masters* on second reference.
*tee, tee off*
*U.S. Open Championship* Use *the U.S. Open* or *the Open* on second reference.

NUMBERS: Some sample uses of numbers:
Use figures for handicaps: *He has a 3 handicap; a 3-handicap golfer, a handicap of 3 strokes; a 3-stroke handicap.*
Use figures for par listings: *He had a par 5 to finish 2-up for the round, a par-4 hole; a 7-under-par 64, the par-3 seventh hole.*
Use figures for club ratings: *a No. 5 iron, a 5-iron, a 7-iron shot, a 4-wood.*
Miscellaneous: *the first hole, the ninth hole, a nine-hole course, the 10th hole, the back nine, the final 18, the third round. He won 3 and 2.*

ASSOCIATIONS: *Professional Golfers' Association of America* (note the apostrophe) or *PGA.* Headquarters is in Palm Beach Gardens, Fla. Members teach golf at golf shops and teaching facilities across the country.

The *PGA Tour* is a separate organization made up of competing professional golfers. Use *tour* (lowercase) on second reference.

The PGA conducts the PGA Championship, the Senior PGA Championship, and the Ryder Cup as well as other golf championships not associated with the PGA Tour.

SUMMARIES — Stroke (Medal) Play: List scores in ascending order. Use a dash before the final figure, hyphens between others.

On the first day, use the player's score for the first nine holes, a hyphen, the player's score for the second nine holes, a dash and the player's total for the day:

First round:

| | | |
|---|---|---|
| Jack Nicklaus | 35-35 | — 70 |
| Johnny Miller | 36-35 | — 71 |

Etc.

On subsequent days, give the player's scores for each day, then the total for all rounds completed:

Second round:

| | | |
|---|---|---|
| Jack Nicklaus | 70-70 | — 140 |
| Johnny Miller | 71-70 | — 141 |

Etc.

Final round, professional tournaments, including prize money:

| | | |
|---|---|---|
| Jack Nicklaus, | $30,000 | 70-70-70-68 — 278 |
| Johnny Miller, | $17,500 | 71-70-70-69 — 280 |

Use hometowns, if ordered, only on national championship amateur tournaments.

| | |
|---|---|
| Jonathan Moore, Oklahoma State | 68-70-69-69 — 276 |
| Chris Kirk, Georgia | 71-71-70-68 — 280 |
| Arnold Palmer | 70-69-68-70—277 |
| Tony Jacklin | 71-70-70-70—281 |

The form for cards:

| | |
|---|---|
| Par out | 444 343 544-35 |
| Watson out | 454 333 435-34 |
| Nicklaus out | 434 243 544-33 |
| Par in | 434 443 454-35 — 70 |
| Watson in | 434 342 443-31 — 65 |
| Nicklaus in | 433 443 453-33 — 66 |

SUMMARIES — Match Play: In

the first example that follows, the *and 1* means that the 18th hole was skipped because Nicklaus had a 2-hole lead after 17. In the second, the match went 18 holes. In the third, a 19th hole was played because the golfers were tied after 18.

Jack Nicklaus def. Lee Trevino, 2 and 1.

Sam Snead def. Ben Hogan, 2-up.

Rachel Teske def. Ikuyo Shiotani, 19 holes.

**Grey Cup** The Canadian Football League's championship game.

**Gulfstream Park** The race-track.

**gymnastics** Scoring is by points. Identify events by name: Men: *floor exercise, vault, pommel horse, still rings, horizontal bar* (or *high bar*), *parallel bars.* Women: *floor exercise, vault, balance beam, uneven bars.*
Use a basic summary. Example:

Parallel Bars _ 1. Joe Smith, Houston, 9.675 points. 2. Ed Jones, Albany, N.Y., 9.54. 3. Andy Brown, Los Angeles, 9.4, etc.

# H

**halfback**

**handball** Games are won by the first player to score 21 points or, in the case of a tie breaker, 11 points. Most matches go to the first winner of two games.
Use a match summary. Example:

Bob Richards, Yale, def. Paul Johnson, Dartmouth, 21-18, 21-19.

Tom Brenna, Massachusetts, def. Bill Stevens, Michigan, 21-19, 17-21, 21-20.

**handicaps** Use figures, hyphenating adjectival forms before

a noun: *He has a 3 handicap, he is a 3-handicap golfer, a handicap of 3 strokes, a 3-stroke handicap.*

**hit and run** (v.) **hit-and-run** (n. and adj.) *The coach told him to hit and run. He scored on a hit-and-run. She was struck by a hit-and-run driver.*

**hockey** The spellings of some frequently used words:

| | |
|---|---|
| blue line | play off (v.) |
| crease | playoff (n., adj.) |
| face off (v.) | power play |
| faceoff (n., adj.) | power-play goal |
| goalie | red line |
| goal line | short-handed |
| goal post | slap shot |
| goaltender | two-on-one break |
| penalty box | |

The term *hat trick* applies when a player has scored three goals in a game. Use it sparingly, however.

LEAGUE: *National Hockey League* or *NHL.*
For NHL subdivisions: *the Central Division of the Western Conference, the division, the conference,* etc.

SUMMARIES: The visiting team always is listed first in the score by periods.
Note that each goal is numbered according to its sequence in the game.
The figure after the name of a scoring player shows his total goals for the season.
Names in parentheses are players credited with an assist on a goal.
The final figure in the listing of each goal is the number of minutes elapsed in the period when the goal was scored.

BC-HKN–Senators-Flyers Sums, 1st Ld-Writethru

Eds: UPDATES with third period penalties.

Senators-Flyers Sums

Ottawa          1 1 1_3

**Philadelphia**      3 1 1_5

First Period_1, Ottawa, Neil 8 (Simpson, Havlat), 4:07. 2, Philadelphia, Lapointe 4 (Somik, Slaney), 10:41. 3, Philadelphia, Recchi 25 (LeClair, Handzus), 11:11. 4, Philadelphia, Markov 6 (Handzus, LeClair), 16:10. Penalty_Amonte, Phi (ob.-holding), 5:17.

Second Period_5, Philadelphia, Johnsson 9 (Zhamnov, Slaney), 5:22 (pp). 6, Ottawa, Chara 15 (Spezza, Schaefer), 14:32 (pp). Penalties_Fisher, Ott (tripping), 3:57; Simpson, Ott (holding), 6:06; Somik, Phi (slashing), 13:08; Fisher, Ott (high-sticking), 17:07.

Third Period_7, Philadelphia, Zhamnov 10 (Gagne, Amonte), 6:54. 8, Ottawa, Bondra 23 (Alfredsson, Schaefer), 19:47 (pp). Penalties_Alfredsson, Ott (rough) 9:03; Zhamnov, Phi (roughing), 9:03; Smolinski, Ott (roughing), 12:18; Sharp, Phi (roughing), 12:18; Simpson, Ott (slashing), 14:21; Philadelphia bench, served by Sharp (too many men), 15:57; Van Allen, Ott, major-double game misconduct (fighting), 18:15; Ray, Ott, major (fighting), 18:15; Lalime, Ott, minor-major-game misconduct (leaving the crease, fighting), 18:15; Simpson, Ott, major-game misconduct (fighting), 18:15 Brashear, Phi, double minor-double major-misconduct-game misconduct; (instigator, roughing, fighting), 18:15; Radivojevic, Phi, major-double game misconduct (fighting), 18:15; Esche, Phi, minor-major-double game misconduct (leaving the crease, fighting), 18:15; Markov, Phi, major-game misconduct (fighting), 18:15; Chara, Ott, minor-major-misconduct-game misconduct (instigator, fighting), 18:18; Neil, Ott, major (fighting), 18:18; Somik, Phi, major (fighting) 18:18; Timander, Phi, major (fighting), 18:18.

Shots on goal_Ottawa 7-9-10_26. Philadelphia 13-11-6_30.

Power-play Opportunities_Ottawa 2 of 6; Philadelphia 1 of 4.

Goalies_Ottawa, Lalime 22-19-7 (30 shots-25 saves), Prusek (18:15 third, 0-0). Philadelphia, Esche 18-7-5 (22-20), Burke (18:15 third, 4-3).

A_19,539 (19,519). T_2:39.

Referees_Marc Joannette, Dan Marouelli. Linesmen_ Jonny Murray, Tim Nowak.

## STANDINGS: The form:

**Eastern Conference**
**Atlantic Division**

|  | W | L | T | Pts. | GF | GA |
|---|---|---|---|---|---|---|
| Philadelphia | 47 | 10 | 14 | 108 | 314 | 184 |
| NY Islanders | 45 | 17 | 9 | 99 | 310 | 192 |
| Etc. | | | | | | |

**horse races** Capitalize their formal names: *Kentucky Derby, Preakness, Belmont Stakes,* etc.

**horse racing** Some frequently used terms and their definitions:

**broodmare** A female horse

used for breeding.

**bug boy** An apprentice jockey, so-called because of the asterisk beside the individual's name in a program. It means that the jockey's mount gets a weight allowance.

**colt** A male horse 4 years old and under.

**entry** Two or more horses owned by same owner running as a single betting interest. In some states two or more horses trained by same person but having different owners also are coupled in betting.

**filly** A female horse under the age of 5.

**furlong** One-eighth of a mile. Race distances are given in furlongs up through seven furlongs, after that in miles, as in *one-mile, 1/1-16 miles.*

**gelding** A castrated male horse.

**half-mile pole** The pole on a racetrack that marks one-half mile from the finish. All distances are measured from the finish line, meaning that when a horse reaches the quarter pole, he is one-quarter mile from the finish.

**horse** A male horse over 4 years old.

**long shot** (two words)

**mare** A female horse 5 years and older.

**mutuel field** Not *mutual field.* Two or more horses, long shots, that have different owners and trainers. They are coupled as a single betting interest to give the field not more than 12 wagering interests. There cannot be more than 12 betting interests in a race. The bettor wins if either horse finishes in the money.

**stallion** A male horse used for breeding.

**horses' names** Capitalize.

See **animals** in main section.

# I

**IC4A** See **Intercollegiate Association of Amateur Athletes of America**.

**indoor** (adj.) **indoors** (adv.) *He plays indoor tennis. He went indoors.*

**Intercollegiate Association of Amateur Athletes of America** In general, spell out on first reference.

A phrase such as *IC4A tournament* may be used on first reference, however, to avoid a cumbersome lead. If this is done, provide the full name later in the story.

# J

**judo** Use the basic summary format by weight divisions for major tournaments; use the match summary for dual and lesser meets.

# K

**Kentucky Derby** *The Derby* on second reference. An exception to normal second-reference practice. Plural is *Derbies*.

See **capitalization** in main section.

# L

**lacrosse** Scoring in goals, worth one point each.

The playing field is 110 yards long. The goals are 80 yards apart, with 15 yards of playing area behind each goal.

A match consists of four 15-minute periods. Overtimes of varying lengths may be played to break a tie.

Adapt the summary format in **hockey**.

**Ladies Professional Golf Association** No apostrophe after *Ladies*. Use *LPGA Tour* in all references.

**left hand** (n.) **left-handed** (adj.) **left-hander** (n.)

# M

**marathon** Use the formats illustrated in the **cross country** and **track and field** entries.

**mare** A female horse 5 years and older.

**match summary** This format for summarizing sports events applies to one vs. one contests such as tennis, match play golf, etc.

Give a competitor's name, followed either by a hometown or by a college or club affiliation. For competitors from outside the United States, a country name alone is sufficient in summaries sent for domestic use.

Jimmy Connors, Belleville, Ill., def. Manuel Orantes, Spain, 2-6, 6-3, 6-2, 6-1.

**metric system** See main section.

**motor sports** (two words unless different in the official name of an event)

**motorboat racing** Scoring may be posted in miles per hour, points or laps, depending on the competition.

In general, use the basic summary format. For some major events, adapt the basic summary to paragraph form under a dateline. See the **auto racing** entry for an example.

**motorcycle racing** Follow the formats shown under **auto racing**.

# N

**National Association for Stock Car Auto Racing** Or *NASCAR*.

**National Collegiate Athletic Association** Or *NCAA*.

**numerals** See the main section on general use and entries on **betting odds**, **handicaps** and **scores**.

# O

**odds** See **betting odds**.

**offseason** (no hyphen)

**Olympics** Capitalize all references to the international athletic contests: *the Olympics, the Winter Olympics, the Olympic Games, an Olympic-size pool.*

Lowercase *the games* in second reference.

# P

**pingpong** A synonym for *table tennis.*

The trademark name is *Ping-Pong.*

**play off** (v.) **playoff, playoffs** (n. and adj.)

**postseason, preseason** No hyphen.

# R

**racket** Not *racquet,* for the light bat used in tennis and badminton.

**racquetball** Amateur games are played to 15 points in a best-of-three match. Professional matches are played to 11 points, unless it is necessary to continue until one player has a two-point spread. Most matches go to the winner of three of five games.

Use a match summary.

**record** Avoid the redundant *new record.*

**right hand** (n.) **right-handed** (adj.) **right-hander** (n.)

**rodeo** Use the basic summary format by classes, listing points.

**rowing** Scoring is in minutes, seconds and tenths of a second. Extend to hundredths if available.

Use a basic summary. An example, for a major event where qualifying heats are required:

Single Sculls Heats (first two in each heat qualify for Monday's quarterfinals, losers go to repechage Friday): Heat 1 — 1, Peter Smith, Australia, 4:24.7. 2. Etc. Heat 2

— 1, John Jones, Canada, 4:26.3. 72, Etc.

## runner-up, runners-up

# S

**scores** Use figures exclusively, placing a hyphen between the totals of the winning and losing teams: *The Reds defeated the Red Sox 4-3, the Giants scored a 12-6 football victory over the Cardinals, the golfer had a 5 on the first hole but finished with a 2-under-par score.*

Use a comma in this format: *Boston 6, Baltimore 5.*

See individual listings for each sport for further details.

**skating, figure** Scoring includes both ordinals and points.

Use a basic summary. Examples:

**Junior Women**
Short Program
1. Mirai Nagasu, Arcadia, Calif., 54.26 points.
2. Caroline Zhang, Irvine, Calif., 53.87.
3. Blake Rosenthal, Newton Square, Pa., 51.67.

**Ice Dance**
Compulsory Dance
1. Tanith Belbin, Bloomfield Hills, Mich., and Ben Agosto, Chicago, 38.23.
2. Morgan Matthews, Fairfax, Va., and Maxim Zovozin, Ashburn, Va., 31.17.
3. Tessa Virtue and Scott Moir, Canada, 30.79.

**skiing** Identify events as: *men's downhill, women's slalom,* cross-country (note hyphen), etc. In ski jumping, note style where two jumps and points are posted. Use a basic summary. Example:

90-meter special jumping — 1, Karl Schnabel, Austria, 320 and 318 feet, 234.8 points. 2, Toni Innauer, Austria, 377-299, 232.9. 3, Etc. Also; 27, Bob Smith, Hanover, N.H., 312-280, 201. 29, Etc.

**ski, skis, skier, skied, skiing** Also: *ski jump, ski jumping.*

**soccer** The spellings of some frequently used words and phrases:

**AFC** (Asian Football Confederation)

**Bundesliga** (German League first division)

**CAF** (Confederation Africaine de Football; refer to as the governing body of African soccer rather than spelling out French acronym)

**Champions League**

**coach** (also known as *manager* on British teams and *technical director* on some Latin American teams)

**CONCACAF** (Confederation of North and Central American and Caribbean Football — use full name somewhere in story)

**CONMEBOL** (Confederacion Sudamerica de Futbol; refer to as South America's governing body rather than spelling out Spanish acronym)

**defender** (rather than defenseman)

**FIFA** (Federation International de Football Association, FIFA acceptable as first reference, refer to as the international soccer football governing body rather than spelling out French acronym)

**forward** or **striker**

**friendly** (use *exhibition game* on U.S. wires)

**goalkeeper** (*goalie* is acceptable but goaltender is not)

**midfielder**

**MLS** (Major League Soccer, MLS acceptable on first reference)

**OFC** (Oceania Football Confederation)

**offside**

**penalty area** (sometimes penalty box — do not refer to solely as box on U.S. wires)

**Premier League** (top league in England; also the name of the top league in Scotland. Note, too, that England, Scotland, Wales and Northern Ireland have separate national teams)

**Serie A** (Italian League first division)

**sideline** (*touchline* for international wires)

**UEFA** (Union of European Football Associations)

In summaries and key lines for international wires, the home team is listed first; on U.S. wires, the visiting team is listed first.

SUMMARY:

At Saint-Denis, France

Italy 0 2 — 2

France 2 0 — 2

(France won 4-3 on penalty kicks)

First half — 1, France, Zidane 4 (Djorkaeff), 12th minute. 2, France, Deschamps (penalty kick), 45th minute.

Second half — 3, Italy, own goal, 88th minute. 4, Italy, R. Baggio 6 (D. Baggio), 90th minute.

First overtime — None.

Second overtime — None.

Penalty kicks — France 4 (Zidane G, Lizarazu NG, Trezeguet G, Henry G, Blanc G); Italy 3 (Baggio G, Albertini NG, Costacurta G, Vieri G, Di Biagio NG).

Yellow Cards — Italy, Del Piero, 26th minute; Bergomi, 28th; Rostacurta, 113th. France, Guivarc'h, 53rd minute; Deschamps, 63rd.

Referee — Dallas (Scotland). Linesmen — Grigorescu (Romania),

Warren (England).

A —77,000

Lineups

Italy — Gianluca Pagliuca; Giuseppe Bergomi, Fabio Cannavaro, Alessandro Costacurta, Paolo Maldini; Francesco Moriero, Dino Baggio (Demetrio Albertini, 52nd), Luigi Di Biagio, Gianluca Pessotto (Angelo Di Livio, 90th); Christian Vieri, Alessandro Del Piero (Roberto Baggio, 67th).

France — Fabien Barthez; Lilian Thuram, Laurent Blanc, Marcel Desailly, Bixente Lizarazu; Didier Deschamps, Emmanuel Petit, Zinedine Zidane, Christian Karembeu (Thierry Henry, 65th); Stephane Guivarc'h (David Trezeguet, 65th), Youri Djorkaeff.

Lineup order is goalkeepers, defenders, midfielders, forwards.

Separate the different positions with semicolons and the players within a position with commas.

STANDINGS: The form:

Scores and standings move in separate files.

Schedule has times GMT instead of EST or EDT.

Schedule lists home teams first.

Sunday, Jan. 31

Bari vs. Lazio of Rome, 0130

Cagliari vs. Juventus of Turin, 0130

Fiorentina vs. Vicenza, 0130

Standings have a different style, starting with *GP* (games played), changing header from *T* (ties) to *D* (draws) and putting draws between wins and losses instead of after.

**Italian League Standings**

By The Associated Press

Division One

| Team | GP | W | D | L | GF | GA | Pts |
|---|---|---|---|---|---|---|---|
| Fiorentina | 18 | 12 | 4 | 2 | 34 | 18 | 38 |
| Lazio of Rome | 18 | 10 | 3 | 5 | 37 | 20 | 35 |

**speedskating** Scoring is in minutes, seconds and tenths of a second. Extend to hundredths if available.

Use a basic summary.

**sports editor** Capitalize as a formal title before a name. See **titles** in main section.

**sports sponsorship** If the sponsor's name is part of the sports event, such as *Pepsi 400* or *Buick Open*, use the name in the title. If there is a previously established name commonly accepted for the event — *Orange Bowl, Sugar Bowl* — use that name even if it currently has a corporate sponsor. *Orange Bowl*, not *FedEx Orange Bowl*. However, mention the sponsor somewhere in the story.

**stadium, stadiums** Capitalize only when part of a proper name: *Yankee Stadium.*

**swimming** Scoring is in minutes, if appropriate, seconds and tenths of a second. Extend to hundredths if available.

Most events are measured in metric units.

Identify events as *men's 4x100 relay, women's 100 backstroke,* etc.

See the **track and field** entry for the style on relay teams and events where a record is broken

Use a basic summary. Examples, where qualifying heats are required:

**Men's 200-meter Backstroke Heats (fastest eight qualify for final Saturday night) heat 1 — 1, John Naber, USC, 2:03.25; 2, Zoltan Verraszio, Hungary, 2:03.50; 3. Etc.**

For diving events, adapt the **skating, figure** entry.

# T

**table tennis** See **pingpong.**

**tennis** The scoring units are points, games, sets and matches.

A player wins a point if his opponent fails to return the ball, hits it into the net or hits it out of bounds. A player also wins a point if his opponent is serving and fails to put the ball into play after two attempts (*double faults,* in tennis terms).

A player must win four points to win a game. In tennis scoring, both players begin at *love,* or zero, and advance to 15, 30, 40 and game. (The numbers *15, 30* and *40* have no point value as such — they are simply tennis terminology for *1 point, 2 points* and *3 points.*) The server's score always is called out first. If a game is tied at 40-all, or *deuce,* play continues until one player has a two-point margin.

A set is won if a player wins six games before his opponent has won five. If a set becomes tied at five games apiece, it goes to the first player to win seven games. If two players who were tied at five games apiece also tie at six games apiece, they normally play a tiebreaker — a game that goes to the first player to win seven points. In some cases, however, the rules call for a player to win by two games.

A match may be either a best-of-three contest that goes to the first player or team to win two sets, or a best-of-five contest that goes to the first player or team to win three sets.

Set scores would be reported this way: *Chris Evert Lloyd defeated Sue Barker 6-0, 3-6, 6-4.* Indicate tiebreakers in parentheses after the set score, using only the lower number: *7-6, (9)*

SUMMARIES: Winners always are listed first in agate summaries. An example:

**Men's Singles**
**First Round**

Jimmy Connors, United States, def. Manuel Orantes, Spain, 2-6, 6-3, 6-2, 6-1.

Bjorn Borg, Sweden, def. Jim Green, United States, walkover.

Arthur Ashe, United States, def. James Peters, United States, 6-3, 4-3, retired.

John McEnroe, United States, def. Guillermo Vilas, Argentina, 7-6 (4), 6-3, 6-7 (3), 6-2.

**track and field** Scoring is in distance or time, depending on the event.

Most events are measured in metric units. For those meets that include feet, make sure the measurement is clearly stated, as in *men's 100-meter dash, women's 880-yard run,* etc.

For time events, spell out *minutes* and *seconds* on first reference, as in *3 minutes, 26.1 seconds.* Subsequent times in stories and all times in agate require a colon and decimal point: *3:34.4.* For a marathon, it would be *2 hours, 11 minutes, 5.01 seconds* on first reference then the form *2:12:4.06* for later listings.

Do not use a colon before times given only in seconds and tenths of a second. Use progressions such as *6.0 seconds, 9.4, 10.1,* etc. Extend times to hundredths, if available: *9.45.*

In running events, the first event should be spelled out, as in *men's 100-meter.* Later references can be condensed to phrases such as *the 200, the 400,* etc.

For hurdle and relay events, the progression can be: *100-meter hurdles, 400 hurdles,* etc.

For field events — those that do not involve running — use these forms: *26 1/2* for *26 feet, one-half inch*; *25-10 1/2* for *25 feet, 10 1/2 inches,* etc.

In general, use a basic summary. For the style when a record is broken, note the mile event in the example below. For the style in listing relay teams, note 4-by-400 meter relay.

60-yard dash — 1, Steve Williams, Florida TC, 6.0 2, Hasley Crawford, Philadelphia Pioneer, 6.2 3, Mike McFarland, Chicago TC. 6.2 3. Etc.

100 — 1, Steve Williams, Florida TC 10.1. 2. Etc.

Mile — 1, Filbert Bayi, Tanzania, 3:55.1, meet record, old record 3:59, Jim Beatty, Los Angeles TC. Feb. 27, 1963; 2. Paul Cummings, Beverly Hills TC. 3:56.1; 3, Etc.

Women's 880 — 1, Johanna Forman, Falmouth TC. 2:07.9. 2. Etc.

4x400 relay — 1, St. John's, (Jon Kennedy, Doug Johnson, Gary Gordon, Ordner Emanuel), 3:21.9. 2. Brown, 3:23.5. 3. Fordham, 3:24.1. 4. Etc.

Team scoring — Chicago TC 32. Philadelphia Pioneer 29, Etc.

Where qualifying heats are required:

Men's 100-meter heats (first two in each heat qualify for Friday's semifinals): Heat 1 — 1, Steve Williams, Florida TC. 10.1. 2. Etc.

# V

**volleyball** International and USA Volleyball sets are won by the first team to score 25 points in the first four sets. If the match is tied in sets after the first four sets, a deciding fifth set will be played to 15 points. In all five sets, teams must win by two points without a cap on points.

U.S. college games are won by the first team to score 30 points in the first four sets. If the match is tied in games after the first four games, a deciding fifth game will be played to 15 points. In all five sets, teams must win by two points without a cap on points.

Use a match summary. Example:

College:

State University def. State Tech 30-22, 31-33, 30-28, 24-30, 15-12.

International:

U.S.-Women def. Korea 21-25, 25-16, 29-27, 16-25, 15-12.

## volley, volleys

# W

**water polo** Scoring is by goals. List team scores. Example:

World Water Polo Championship

First Round

United States 7, Canada 1

Britain 5, France 3

Etc.

**water skiing** Scoring is in points. Use a basic summary. Example:

World Water Skiing Championships

Men

Overall — 1, George Jones, Canada, 1,987 points. 2, Phil Brown, Britain, 1,756. 3, Etc.

Slalom — 1, George Jones, Canada, 73 buoys (two rounds). 2, Etc.

**weightlifting** Identify events by weight classes.

Use a basic summary. Example:

Flyweight (114.5 lbs.) — 1, Zygmont Smalcerz, Poland, 337.5 kg. 2, Lajos Szuecs, Hungary, 330 kg. 3, Etc.

**World Series** Or *the Series* on second reference. A rare exception to the general principles under **capitalization**.

**wrestling** Identify events by weight division.

# Y

**yachting** Use a basic summary, identifying events by classes.

**yard** Equal to 3 feet.

The metric equivalent is approximately 0.91 meter.

To convert to meters, multiply by 0.91 (5 yards x 0.91 = 4.55 meters).

See **foot**; **meter**; and **distances**.

**yard lines** Use figures to indicate the dividing lines on a football field and distance traveled: *4-yard line, 40-yard line, he plunged in from the 2, he ran 6 yards, a 7-yard gain.*

**yearling** An animal 1 year old or in its second year. The birthdays of all horses arbitrarily are set at Jan. 1. On that date, any foal born in the preceding year is reckoned 1 year old.

# BUSINESS GUIDELINES AND STYLE

# BUSINESS GUIDELINES AND STYLE

Our market is the individual reader of business news. We must write in a lively, clear and accessible style that provides explanation and content. We do not talk down to readers and we must avoid insider jargon while laying out complex issues in an understandable, straightforward manner. No story we write is too small or routine to meet this standard: Each has meaning for someone, because they own a stock, are buying some consumer product, have a job or some other connection to the news we are providing.

AP business journalists must not simply be careful with numbers; they have to quickly grasp what those numbers mean, in a cash flow statement, a pension fund report or a worker's paycheck. Only then can they turn those numbers into real stories, not just about companies or profits but about people's lives.

When stories break, or when you set out to break a story yourself, you need experts or insiders who can help you. And you need to know where you can find all the facts you need: in SEC filings, court documents, lists of shareholders and creditors, company histories, etc.

## Covering Corporate Earnings Reports

Federal law requires all corporations whose stock is publicly traded to report revenues and profits or losses each three months in an income statement. This is what business is all about, whether a corporation made money or lost it, and why. These statements are usually released on the major public relations wire services during an earnings "season," a three- or four-week period that begins roughly two weeks after the end of each quarter.

To prepare for an earnings story, first read the AP earnings stories from the previous couple of quarters, then check to see if there have been recent corporate developments at the company. Management changes at the top? Lawsuits or regulatory actions? Major contracts won or lost? Takeovers or divestitures announced? In short, you need to be up to date about issues the company is facing. That will help you better understand how the company makes or doesn't make money and why.

Our goal is to send to members and Web customers a fast file of at least 150 words, or about four paragraphs, within 15 minutes of the earnings release. The standard style for a slug is BC-Earns-Company Name.

The lead should tell the reader what the company does and give the increase or decline of net income, either in percentage or absolute terms, along with the reason. Profits are synonymous with income and earnings. The story should also include the company's revenues, which is sometimes called sales.

Comparisons of profits or losses and revenues/sales should be made with the same period a year earlier, expressed both as a total and as earnings-per-share, which is simply the profit divided by the number of shares of stock outstanding. Company statements often express this figure as *primary* or *basic* and *fully diluted.* AP uses *fully diluted* as a more meaningful figure.

Use active verbs — rose, fell and the like — not passive constructions like were up/down. And to calculate the percentage change in profits, use the year-over-year change in net income, not the earnings-per-share numbers. The number of shares outstanding can, and often does, change year to year, which doesn't make it a clear apples-to-apples comparison.

For subsequent versions, include the year-to-date figures for all of the above. The only quarter when this isn't done is the first quarter. Also include comments on the corporation's performance from the chief executive or outside analysts, and any background that puts the performance in perspective.

Be alert to announcements of job cuts — which, if significant, may share or even take over the lede from the earnings results — as well as warnings of a reduction of future earnings or upward revisions of earnings forecasts. You can usually find these quickly by doing a keyword search for "outlook" or "quarter."

### Why we lead with net income

Net income truly is the bottom line and the benchmark for companies' performance over time. It's what they are required to report to the SEC in accordance with generally accepted accounting principles, and it gives us a standard reporting format that brings a consistency to our news report.

In the rare cases where companies don't provide the net income number in their news release, we need to press their representatives for those numbers. And if they are not immediately available, we need to be as transparent as possible in explaining to readers why we are providing proforma or some other adjusted or non-GAAP representation of the company's results instead of the net income figures, which were not disclosed.

Wall Street analysts have been much more concerned in recent years with operating earnings per share, which are calculated by excluding one-time "extraordinary" gains or charges, and revenue totals. Operating earnings may exclude the costs of a big reorganization, such as severance payments to laid-off workers or penalties for breaking leases on factories that are closed. If a company has no extraordinary events, operating earnings and net earnings can be identical.

In the days and weeks before earnings reports, analysts issue EPS predictions, and these predictions are compiled into a "consensus" figure by research companies such as Thomson Financial.

On the day of the report, investors compare the consensus prediction for operating earnings per share with the actual number and the stock price often moves up or down based on whether the company falls short of, meets or exceeds expectations. When AP says in a story "Company X's performance beat Wall Street analysts' predictions," this is the number we're referring to. In most stories, that means that after we lead with net income, we explain how the adjusted number was calculated and immediately compare the adjusted earnings per share to the consensus Thomson Financial forecast.

It's worth noting that the consensus analyst forecast for earnings and revenues in a quarter often reflect the guidance provided by companies about what they expect their earnings and sales will be. That's why it's important to not only review what the analysts' consensus forecast is, but to determine whether a company has made a public forecast. When earnings or revenue disappoint, it's a much more powerful statement for us to say the company's earnings fell short of its own forecast, as well as analysts' expectations — assuming those facts are obtainable.

"Operating earnings" is sometimes confused with "earnings from continuing operations." Continuing operations is a subset of operations. It refers to business units that existed in the past and will exist in the future. It excludes "discontinued operations" which represent businesses that have been sold or shut down in the past year. Companies often downplay earnings of these operations since they are no longer relevant to future profits.

### Importance of the conference call

Stocks often move within seconds of an unexpected pronouncement by the CEO or CFO on the analyst conference call after the earnings are released. It could come from their response to a question about a big contract, the reason for a revised sales or earnings forecast, or any number of other reasons. That's information you obviously will want in a quick write-thru of your story. But even if there are no dramatic announcements, it's important for you to listen to the call to gain a more complete understanding of how the company is positioning itself going forward. And it may provide you a colorful key quote from a top company executive.

### Make the company come to life

Earnings are the report cards for top corporate executives. The results, more often than not, are a consequence of decisions they made — acquisitions they engineered, factories they convinced their boards of directors to build or shutter, advertising campaigns they signed off on. Using real people to help frame companies' results isn't a call for us to lionize CEOs; it's a reminder that companies are made up of people who win or lose based on decisions they make.

The examples below, contrasting the top of Mike Liedtke AMer from his PM turn for Yahoo's earnings, illustrates this point:

### The AMer:

SAN FRANCISCO (AP) _ Yahoo Inc.'s first-quarter profit doubled as the Internet powerhouse continued to ride a rising tide of online advertising.

The Sunnyvale-based company said Tuesday that it earned $204.6 million, or 14 cents per share, during the three months ended in March. That compared with net income of $101.2 million, or 7 cents per share at the same time last year.

Revenue for the period totaled $1.17 billion, a 55 percent increase from $757.8 million last year. After subtracting the commissions paid to other Web sites in Yahoo's rapidly growing ad network, the company's revenue totaled $821 million, a 49 percent improvement from last year.

Analysts surveyed by Thomson Financial had forecast earnings of 11 cents per share on revenue of $797 million — a figure that stripped out the company's advertising commissions.

### Then the PMer:

SAN FRANCISCO (AP) _ Yahoo Inc. Chairman Terry Semel has embraced an old Frank Sinatra song as his Internet company's unofficial theme song, repeatedly assuring investors during the past few years of steadily rising profits that "the best is yet to come."

The promise is ringing true so far.

Yahoo has emerged as a powerful marketing magnet for advertisers following consumers to the Internet, escalating the company's financial results quarter after quarter.

The Sunnyvale-based company raised the bar again Tuesday when it announced first quarter earnings of $204.6 million, or 14 cents per share. That compared with net income of $101.2 million, or 7 cents per share at the same time last year.

It marked the fifth consecutive quarter in which Yahoo's profit has at least doubled from the previous year.

Revenue for the period totaled $1.17 billion, a 55 percent increase from $757.8 million last year. After subtracting the commissions paid to other Web sites in Yahoo's rapidly growing ad network, the company's revenue totaled $821 million, a 49 percent improvement from last year.

### How to assemble a wrap story

When two or more companies in the same industry report earnings on the same day, we often want an earnings wrap story after the separate earnings stories are out and updated with details from the conference calls. These should read like a seamless narrative with one or more thematic elements holding them together. And in almost every case, a wrap should have a forward-looking element that gives readers a sense of whether the good or bad earnings are likely to get better or worse in future quarters, and why.

The basis for the thematic element may come from one or more of the conference calls that company executives hold after releasing earnings. Or there may be cases where your reporting will take you in a different direction in identifying the unifying theme. Talk to money managers who own the stock, competitors and others who you think can provide insight into what is going on. There also may be cases where the earnings are so divergent that the theme could be that the industry appears to be in disarray. But in all cases, our aim should be to convey to readers who is winning, who is losing and why. That often means that the wrap story may have a more complete explanation of how specific decisions made by executives impacted the earnings.

It also isn't necessary to repeat in the wrap version every number that is in the separate earnings stories. Instead, you should use a common sense approach that asks the question: Is this number necessary to convey the main points we are trying to make? Sales and net income for each company almost always will be needed in the wrap — unless they are a crucial element of the narrative. And they don't have to be lengthy expositions; if you can tell the tale in 400 or 500 words, all the better.

# INTERNATIONAL BUREAUS

### Currency Conversions

International writers should report results in domestic currencies first, then give U.S. dollars for current period results only. There's no need to convert last year's results to dollars. For non-U.S. wires, add a conversion rate for euros as well if the results are in another currency.

If the company doesn't give its own conversion to dollars, you'll have to do it. You should use the current day's foreign exchange rate.

Stock price information in Britain should be expressed in pence per share and not converted to an equivalent figures in pounds.

### Different Accounting Rules

In some countries, companies don't report every quarter. The reports may come out every six months or even annually. Many foreign companies don't report "net earnings" or "earnings per share." Some report "earnings before taxes." If that's all they report, call them to see if they will give you net earnings. If they won't, use whatever number seems closest.

For the companies that report only half-year and full-year results, add a line saying "The company did not break out quarterly results," so it's clear why we're not using them. Similarly, when reporting sales results for French companies, note that they often report sales a week or two before profits.

Foreign companies that sell shares in the United States (called American depository receipts) often issue a separate earnings statement using American accounting standards. Use this when you can.

# BUSINESS GUIDELINES AND STYLE

## A

**accounts payable** Current liabilities or debts of a business which must be paid in the near future (within one year).

**accounts receivable** Amounts due to a company for merchandise or services sold on credit. These are short-term assets.

**acquisitions** The process of buying or acquiring some asset. The term can refer to the purchase of a block of stock or, more often, to the acquisition of an entire company.

**antitrust** Any law or policy designed to encourage competition by curtailing monopolistic power and unfair business practices.

**appreciation** Increase in value of property, as opposed to *depreciation.*

**arbitrage** Buying currency, commercial bills or securities in one market and selling them at the same time in another to make a profit on the price discrepancy.

**asset** Current cash and other items readily converted into cash, usually within one year.

**asset, fixed** Plant, land, equipment, long-term investments that cannot be readily liquefied without disturbing the operation of the business.

## B

**balance sheet** A listing of assets, liabilities and net worth showing the financial position of a company at the specific time. A bank balance sheet is generally referred to as a statement of condition.

**balloon mortgage** A mortgage whose amortization schedule will not extinguish the debt by the end of the mortgage term, leaving a large payment (called balloon payment) of the remaining principal balance to be paid at that time.

**bankruptcy** Federal courts have exclusive jurisdiction over bankruptcy cases and each of the 94 federal judicial districts handles bankruptcy matters. The primary purposes of the federal bankruptcy laws are to give honest debtors a "fresh start" in life by relieving them of most debts, and to repay creditors in an orderly manner to the extent debtors have property available for payment. Bankruptcies can be voluntary or involuntary.

Chapter 7 of the Bankruptcy Code is available to both individual and business debtors. Its purpose is to achieve a fair distribution to creditors of the debtor's available non-exempt property. It provides a fresh financial start for individuals, although not all debt is wiped away; debts for certain taxes, fraudulently incurred credit card debt, family support obligations -- including child support and alimony -- and most student loans must still be repaid. The bankruptcy law that took effect in October 2005 limits Chapter 7 as an option for many Americans: Those deemed by a "means test" to have at least $100 a month left over after paying certain debts and expenses must file a five-year repayment plan under the more restrictive Chapter 13 instead. When a company files for Chapter 7, it usually leads to liquidation. But a company in Chapter 7 proceedings can continue to operate under the direction of a court trustee until the matter is settled, and if it can settle with creditors in the interim, it may not have to be liquidated.

Chapter 11 of the Bankruptcy Code is available for both business and consumer debtors. Its purpose is to rehabilitate a business as a going concern or reorganize an individual's finances through a court-approved reorganization plan. When referring to such a filing, say the company is seeking Chapter 11 protection. This action frees a company from the threat of creditors' lawsuits while it reorganizes its finances. The debtor's reorganization plan must be accepted by a majority of its creditors. Unless the court rules otherwise, the debtor remains in control of the business and its assets.

Chapter 12 of the Bankruptcy Code is designed to give special debt relief to a family farmer with regular income from farming.

Chapter 13 of the Bankruptcy Code is likely to be required for an increasing percentage of individuals seeking to wipe the slate clean. Those deemed by a "means test" to have at least $100 a month left over after paying certain debts and expenses will have to file a five-year repayment plan under Chapter 13 that allows unsecured creditors to recover part of all of what they are owed.

**basis point** The movement of interest rates or yields expressed in hundredths of a point.

**bearer bond** A bond for which the owner's name is not registered on the books of the issuing company. Interest and principal is thus payable to the bond holder.

**bearer stock** Stock certificates that are not registered in any name. They are negotiable without endorsement and transferable by delivery.

**bear market** A period of generally declining stock prices over a prolonged period, generally defined as a 20 percent or larger decline in broad stock indexes such as the Standard & Poor's 500.

**Big Board** Acceptable on second reference for the *New York Stock Exchange*.

**blue chip stock** Stock company known for its long-established record of making money and paying dividends.

**bond ratings** Three private companies, Standard & Poor's Corp., Moody's Investors Service, and Fitch Ratings, sell information -- mainly to institutional investors -- about what they view as the relative risk of various issues of debt. They also charge companies, municipalities and even foreign governments that wish to sell debt and have it rated. The ratings are a fundamental way for investors to form an opinion on whether they are likely to be repaid, and then decide whether the interest rate is high enough to compensate for the risk that they may get back none or only a portion of their investment (in the case of a bankruptcy or some other adverse event). The ratings also effectively set benchmarks for how much interest companies will have to pay to sell bonds, commercial paper, preferred stock and for bank loans they obtain. The higher the grade, the lower the interest rate a borrower must pay.

Standard & Poor's bond ratings, for example, include 10 categories that are referred to as investment grade, from AAA to BBB-, given to borrowers with the strongest ability to repay. Another 6 categories, from BB+ to CCC-, are assigned to more speculative securities that are commonly referred to as *junk* or *high yield debt*. The lowest category, D, is for securities that are in payment default.

A reduction in the rating of a company's debt to noninvestment grade can force some mutual funds and pension funds to sell those bonds because they are prohibited from holding junk debt.

**book value** The difference between a company's assets and liabilities.

The *book value per share*

of common stock is the *book value* divided by the number of common shares outstanding.

**brand names** When they are used, capitalize them.

Brand names normally should be used only if they are essential to a story.

Sometimes, however, the use of a brand name may not be essential but is acceptable because it lends an air of reality to a story: *He fished a Camel from his shirt pocket* may be preferable to the less specific cigarette.

Brand name is a nonlegal term for *service mark* or *trademark*. See entries under those words in the main section.

**bullion** Unminted precious metals of standards suitable for coining.

**bull market** A period of generally rising stock prices over a prolonged period, generally defined as a 20 percent or larger increase in broad stock indexes such as the Standard & Poor's 500.

# C

**capital** When used in a financial sense, *capital* describes money, equipment or property used in a business by a person or corporation.

**capital gain, capital loss** The difference between what a *capital* asset cost and the price it brought when sold.

**central bank** A bank having responsibility for controlling a country's monetary policy.

**cents** Spell out the word *cents* and lowercase, using numerals for amounts less than a dollar: *5 cents, 12 cents.* Use the $ sign and decimal system for larger amounts: *$1.01, $2.50.*

**CEO** Acceptable on first reference as a title before a name or as a stand-alone abbreviation for *chief executive officer.* But spell it out somewhere in the story. (Spell out *chief financial officer* and *chief operating officer,* which are less familiar as abbreviations.)

**charge off** A loan that no longer is expected to be repaid and is written off as a bad debt.

**Chicago Board of Trade** Commodity trading market.

**Chicago Board Options Exchange (CBOE)** Set up by the Chicago Board of Trade, it is the world's largest options exchange.

**closely held corporation** A corporation in which stock shares and voting control are concentrated in the hands of a small number of investors, but for which some shares are available and traded on the market.

**Co.** See **company**.

**collateral** Stock or other property that a borrower is obliged to turn over to a lender if unable to repay a loan.
See **loan terminology**.

**commercial paper** One of the various types of short-term negotiable instruments whereby industrial or finance companies obtain cash after agreeing to pay a specific amount of money on the date due.

**commodities futures contract** A contract to purchase or sell a specific amount of a given commodity at a specified future date.

**commodity** The products of mining or agriculture before they have undergone extensive processing.

**common stock, preferred stock** An ownership interest in a corporation.
If other classes of stock are outstanding, the holders of common stock are the last to receive dividends and the last to receive payments if a corporation is dissolved. The company may raise or lower common stock dividends as its earnings rise or fall.
When preferred stock is outstanding and company earnings are sufficient, a fixed dividend is paid. If a company is liquidated, holders of preferred stock receive payments up to a set amount before any money is distributed to holders of common stock.

**company, companies** Use *Co.* or *Cos.* when a business uses either word at the end of its proper name: *Ford Motor Co., American Broadcasting Cos.*
If *company* or *companies* appears alone in second reference, spell the word out.
The forms for possessives: *Ford Motor Co.'s profits, American Broadcasting Cos.' profits.*
See main section for specific company names.

**company names** Consult the company or Standard & Poor's Register of Corporations if in doubt about a formal name. Do not, however, use a comma before *Inc.* or *Ltd.*

Generally, follow the spelling and capitalization preferred by the company: iMac, eBay. But capitalize the first letter if it begins a sentence.

Do not use all capital letter names unless the letters are individually pronounced: *CRX, BMW.* Others should be uppercase and lowercase.

Do not capitalize "the" unless it is part of the company's official name.

Do not use symbols such as exclamation points, plus signs or asterisks that form contrived spellings that might distract or confuse a reader. Use an ampersand only if it is part of the company's formal name, but not otherwise in place of "and."

**conglomerate** A corporation that has diversified its operations, usually by acquiring enterprises in widely varied industries.

**consumer credit** Loans extended to individuals or small businesses usually on an unsecured basis, and providing for monthly repayment. Also referred to as installment credit or personal loans.

**convertible bond** See **loan terminology**.

**Corp.** See **corporation**.

**corporate names** See **company names**.

**corporation** An entity that is treated as a person in the eyes of the law. It is able to own property, incur debts, sue and be sued.

Abbreviate *corporation* as *Corp.* when a company or government agency uses the word at the end of its name: *the Federal Deposit Insurance Corp.*

Spell out *corporation* when it occurs elsewhere in a name: *the Corporation for Public Broadcasting.*

Spell out and lowercase *corporation* whenever it stands alone.

The form for possessives: *ChevronTexaco Corp.'s profits.*

**cost-plus**

**coupon** See **loan terminology** for its meaning in a financial sense.

**cross rate** The rate of exchange between two currencies calculated by referring to the rates between each and a third currency.

# D

**debt service** The outlay necessary to meet all interest and principal payments during a given period.

**default** The failure to meet a financial obligation, the failure to make payment either of principal or interest when due or a breach or nonperformance of the terms of a note or mortgage.

**deflation** A decrease in the general price level, which results from a decrease in total spending relative to the supply of available goods on the market. Deflation's immediate effect is to increase purchasing power.

**depreciation** The reduction in the value of capital goods due to wear and tear or obsolescence.

*Estimated depreciation* may be deducted from income each year as one of the costs of doing business.

**discount** Interest withheld when a note, draft or bill is purchased.

**discount rate** The rate of interest charged by the Federal Reserve on loans it makes to member banks. This rate has an influence on the rates banks then charge their customers.

**dividend** In a financial sense, the word describes the payment per share that a corporation distributes to its stockholders as their return on the money they have invested in its stock.

See **profit terminology**.

**dollars** Always lowercase. Use figures and the $ sign in all except casual references or amounts without a figure: *The book cost $4. Dad, please give me a dollar. Dollars are flowing overseas.*

For specified amounts, the word takes a singular verb: *He said $500,000 is what they want.*

For amounts of more than $1 million, use up to two decimal places. Do not link the numerals and the word by a hyphen: *He is worth $4.35 million. He is worth exactly $4,351,242. He proposed a $300 billion budget.*

The form for amounts less than $1 million: *$4, $25, $500, $1,000, $650,000.*

See **cents**.

**Dow Jones & Co.** The company publishes The Wall Street Journal and Barron's National Business and Financial Weekly. It also operates the Dow Jones News Service.

For stock market watchers, it provides the Dow Jones industrial average, the Dow Jones transportation average, the Dow Jones utility average, and the Dow Jones composite average.

Headquarters is in New York.

**downside risk** The probability that the price of an investment will fall.

**dumping** The selling of a product in a foreign market at a price lower than the domestic price. It is usually done by a monopoly when it has such a large output that selling entirely in the domestic market would substantially reduce the price.

**durable goods** Long-lasting goods such as appliances that are bought by consumers.

# E

**employee** Not *employe*.

**equity** When used in a financial sense, *equity* means the value of property beyond the amount that is owed on it.

A *stockholder's equity* in a corporation is the value of the shares he holds.

A *homeowner's equity* is the difference between the value of the house and the amount of the unpaid mortgage.

**Eurodollar** A U.S. dollar on deposit in a European bank, including foreign branches of U.S. banks.

**extraordinary loss, extraordinary income** See **profit terminology**.

# F

**factor** A financial organization whose primary business is purchasing the accounts receivable of other firms, at a discount, and taking the risk and responsibilities of making collection.

**Fannie Mae** A government-sponsored and publicly held company traded on the New York Stock Exchange that helps provide money for home mortgages, primarily conventional mortgages, by buying residential mortgages for its investment portfolio and packaging pools of mortgages from lenders.

The nickname *Fannie Mae* is acceptable, but somewhere in the story the company should be identified as the *Federal National Mortgage Association*.

**Federal Farm Credit System** The federally chartered cooperative banking system that provides most of the nation's agricultural loans. The system is cooperatively owned by its farm borrowers and is made up of the regional banks that issue operating and mortgage loans through local land bank associations and production credit associations.

**federal funds, federal funds rate** Money in excess of what the Federal Reserve says a bank must have on hand to back up deposits. The excess can be lent overnight to banks that need more cash on hand to meet their reserve requirements. The interest rate of these loans is the *federal funds rate*.

**Federal Home Loan Mortgage Corp.** See **Freddie Mac** entry.

**Federal National Mortgage Association** See **Fannie Mae** entry.

**firm** A business partnership is correctly referred to as a *firm*: *He joined a law firm.*
Do not use *firm* in references to an incorporated business entity. Use *the company* or *the corporation* instead.

**fiscal, monetary** *Fiscal* applies to budgetary matters.
*Monetary* applies to money supply.

**fiscal year** The 12-month period that a corporation or governmental body uses for bookkeeping purposes.
The federal government's fiscal year starts three months ahead of the calendar year — fiscal 2007, for example, ran from Oct. 1, 2006, to Sept. 30, 2007.

**float** Money that has been committed but not yet credited to an account, like a check that has been written but has not yet cleared.

**f.o.b.** Acceptable on first reference for *free on board*, meaning a seller agrees to put a commodity on a truck or ship, etc., at no charge, but transportation costs must be paid by the buyer.

**force majeure** A condition permitting a company to depart from the strict terms of a contract because of an event or effect that can't be reasonably controlled.

**401(k)** (no space)

**Freddie Mac** A government-chartered organization formed to help provide money for home mortgages by buying mortgages from lenders such as banks and repackaging them as investment securities.

*Freddie Mac*, a publicly held company traded on the New York Stock Exchange, packages conventional mortgages as well as FHA mortgages.

The nickname *Freddie Mac* is acceptable, but somewhere in the story, the company should be identified as the *Federal Home Loan Mortgage Corp.*

**freely floating** Describes an exchange rate that is allowed to fluctuate in response to supply and demand in the foreign markets.

**full faith and credit bond** See **loan terminology**.

**futures** *Futures* contracts are agreements to deliver a quantity of goods, generally commodities, at a specified price at a certain time in the future. *Options*, which also are widely traded on the nation's commodities exchanges, give buyers the right but not the obligation to buy or sell something at a certain price within a specified period.

The purpose of the futures exchanges is to transfer the risk of price fluctuations from people who don't want the risk, such as farmers or metals processors, to speculators who are willing to take a gamble on making big profits.

Major U.S. commodities markets are the Chicago Board Options Exchange, Chicago Board of Trade, Chicago Mercantile Exchange, New York Mercantile Exchange, the New York Cotton Exchange, and the Coffee, Sugar and Cocoa Exchange.

# G

**general obligation bond** See **loan terminology**.

# H

**hedging** A method of selling for future delivery whereby a dealer protects himself from falling prices between the time he buys a product and the time he resells or processes it. A miller, for example, who buys wheat to convert to flour, will sell a similar quantity of wheat he doesn't own at near the price at which he bought his own. He will agree to deliver it at the same time his flour is ready for market. If at that time the price of wheat and therefore flour has fallen, he will lose on the flour but can buy the wheat at a low price and deliver it at a profit. If prices have risen, he will make an extra profit on his flour which he will have to sacrifice to buy the wheat for delivery. But either way he has protected his profit.

**holding company** A company whose principal assets are the securities it owns in companies that actually provide goods or services.

The usual reason for forming

a holding company is to enable one corporation and its directors to control several companies by holding a majority of their stock.

# I

**Inc.** See **incorporated**.

**income** See **profit terminology**.

**incorporated** Abbreviate and capitalize as *Inc.* when used as a part of a corporate name. It usually is not needed, but when it is used, do not set off with commas: *Time Warner Inc. announced* ...

See **company names**.

**Index of Leading Economic Indicators** A composite of 10 economic measurements developed to help forecast shifts in the direction of the U.S. economy.

It is compiled by the Conference Board, a private business-sponsored research group, which took it over from the Commerce Department in 1995.

**inflation** A sustained increase in prices. The result is a decrease in the purchasing power of money.

There are two basic types of inflation:

—*Cost-push inflation* occurs when rising costs are the chief reason for the increased prices.

—*Demand-pull inflation* occurs when the amount of money available exceeds the amount of goods and services available for sale.

**infrastructure** An

economy's capital in the form of roads, railways, water supplies, educational facilities, health services, etc., without which investment in factories can't be fully productive.

**International Monetary Fund** *IMF* is acceptable on second reference. Headquarters is in Washington.

A supply of money supported by subscriptions of member nations, for the purpose of stabilizing international exchange and promoting orderly and balanced trade. Member nations may obtain foreign currency needed, making it possible to correct temporary maladjustments in their balance of payments without currency depreciation.

# L

**leverage** The use of borrowed assets by a business to enhance the return of the owner's equity. The expectation is that the interest rate charged will be lower than the earnings made on the money.

**leveraged buyout** A corporate acquisition in which the bulk of the purchase price is paid with borrowed money. The debt then is repaid with the acquired company's cash flow, with money raised by the sale of its assets or by the later sale of the entire company.

**liabilities** When used in a financial sense, the word means all the claims against a corporation.

They include accounts

payable, wages and salaries due but not paid, dividends declared payable, taxes payable, and fixed or long-term obligations such as bonds, debentures and bank loans.

See **assets**.

**liquidation** When used in a financial sense, the word means the process of converting stock or other assets into cash.

When a company is liquidated, the cash obtained is first used to pay debts and obligations to holders of bonds and preferred stock. Whatever cash remains is distributed on a per-share basis to the holders of common stock.

**liquidity** The ease with which assets can be converted to cash without loss in value.

**loan terminology** Note the meanings of these terms in describing loans by governments and corporations:

**bond** A certificate issued by a corporation or government stating the amount of a loan, the interest to be paid, the time for repayment and the collateral pledged if payment cannot be made. Repayment generally is not due for a long period, usually seven years or more.

**collateral** Stock or other property that a borrower is obligated to turn over to a lender if unable to repay a loan.

**commercial paper** A document describing the details of a short-term loan between corporations.

**convertible bond** A bond carrying the stipulation that it may be exchanged for a specific amount of stock in the company that issued it.

**coupon** A slip of paper attached to a bond that the

bondholder clips at specified times and returns to the issuer for payment of the interest due.

**debenture** A certificate stating the amount of a loan, the interest to be paid and the time for repayment, but not providing collateral. It is backed only by the corporation's reputation and promise to pay.

**default** A person, corporation or government is in default if it fails to meet the terms for repayment.

**full faith and credit bond** An alternate term for general obligation bond, often used to contrast such a bond with a moral obligation bond.

**general obligation bond** A bond that has had the formal approval of either the voters or their legislature. The government's promise to repay the principal and pay the interest is constitutionally guaranteed on the strength of its ability to tax the population.

**maturity** The date on which a bond, debenture or note must be repaid.

**moral obligation bond** A government bond that has not had the formal approval of either the voters or their legislature. It is backed only by the government's "moral obligation" to repay the principal and interest on time.

**municipal bond** A general obligation bond issued by a state, country, city, town, village, possession or territory, or a bond issued by an agency or authority set up by one of these governmental units. In general, interest paid on municipal bonds is exempt from federal income taxes. It also usually is exempt from state and local taxes if held by someone living within the state of issue.

**note** A certificate issued by

a corporation or government stating the amount of a loan, the interest to be paid and the collateral pledged in the event payment cannot be made. The date for repayment is generally more than a year after issue but not more than seven or eight years later. The shorter interval for repayment is the principal difference between a note and a bond.

**revenue bond** A bond backed only by the revenue of the airport, turnpike or other facility that was built with the money it raised.

**Treasury borrowing** A *Treasury bill* is a certificate representing a loan to the federal government that matures in three, six or 12 months. A *Treasury note* may mature in one to 10 years or more. A *Treasury bond* matures in seven years or more.

# M

**margin** The practice of purchasing securities in part with borrowed money, using the purchased securities as collateral in anticipation of an advance in the market price. If the advance occurs, the purchaser may be able to repay the loan and make a profit. If the price declines, the stock may have to be sold to settle the loan. The margin is the difference between the amount of the loan and the value of the securities used as collateral.

**merger** Few business combinations are truly a merger of equals, so be precise and sparing in the use of the word *merger*. It is not a synonym for acquisition or takeover, which should be the preferred descriptive in most stories. Use the following rules for deciding whether it's a merger or acquisition, and as a guide us in concluding who is the acquirer and the company being taken over:

—Is one of the companies' stock being used as the currency? If the answer is yes, that's usually a good sign that company is the acquirer and it is not a merger.

—What is the message from the exchange ratio in stock transactions? Typically when shareholders of Company A are offered new shares in a combined company at a 1-for-1 ratio, and Company B shares are exchanged at something less or more (i.e., each Company B will be exchanged for 0.47 percent of a share of the new company), it's an indication that Company A's stock is being used as the basis for the transaction. But it also could be a sign that the companies' boards have agreed to a merger that uses a formula to compensate for the differing market value (total number of shares multiplied by the closing stock price the day before the announcement) of the two companies to come up with an exchange ratio for stock in the new company.

—What is the message from the stock movements after the announcement? Shares of companies being acquired typically rise and shares of the acquirer often fall after the announcement. Not always, of course, but that's usually the case because most bidders pay a premium, or an above-market price, for the shares of the company being acquired, and investors often are worried about the amount of debt the acquirer is taking on to complete the transaction.

—Whose cash is being used to fund the cash portion of a transaction? If the announcement says Company A's cash will be used or that its existing lines of credit will be tapped to pay for Company B's shares, that's a pretty strong indication that Company A is the acquirer.

—Which company's executives are filling most of the top management rolls? The key distinction usually is who gets the CEO slot. But if one of the two CEOs is named to head the company for a limited period (say two years or less) before his fellow CEO takes over, that's a good sign of a political compromise to paper over the fact that the second CEO's company is going to be in charge long term.

—Which company will end up with the majority of the seats on the new board of directors? This is often a key tie breaker. When Company A and Company B insist it's a merger of equals and other checklist items are inconclusive, if one ends up with 60 percent of the board seats and the other gets 40 percent, that's a good indication of which is going to be in charge. Also, make sure you get not only the short-term makeup of the board of the combined company, but also whether there were any deals cut for some members to retire in short order.

—Where will the company be headquartered? Since CEOs typically do the negotiating and they typically aren't anxious to move, this can be an informative tell.

**monetary** See the **fiscal, monetary** entry.

**moral obligation bond** See **loan terminology**.

**municipal bond** See **loan terminology**.

# N

**Nasdaq** Acceptable on second reference for the Nasdaq Stock Market Inc., the public company whose computerized stock trading network used to be known as the National Association of Securities Dealers Automated Quotations system. Its main stock index is the Nasdaq composite index.

**National Labor Relations Board** *NLRB* is acceptable on second reference.

**net income, net profit** See **profit terminology**.

**New York Stock Exchange** *NYSE* is acceptable on second reference as an adjective for the stock exchange or the exchange for other references. Its parent company is the NYSE Group Inc., whose shares are publicly traded.

**note** For use in a financial sense, see **loan terminology**.

# O

**option** The word means an agreement to buy or sell something, such as shares of stock, within a stipulated time and for a certain price.

A *put option* gives the holder the right to sell blocks of 100 shares of stock within a specified time at an agreed-upon price.

A *call option* gives the holder

the right to buy blocks of 100 shares of stock within a specified time at an agreed-upon price.

**over the counter** A term for the method of trading when securities are not listed on a recognized securities exchange.

# P

**preferred stock** See the **common stock, preferred stock** entry.

**price-earnings ratio** The price of a share of stock divided by earnings per share for a 12-month period. Ratios in AP stock tables reflect earnings for the most recent 12 months.

For example, a stock selling for $60 per share and earning $6 per share would be selling at a price-earnings ratio of 10-to-1.

See **profit terminology**.

## PricewaterhouseCoopers

**prime rate** A benchmark rate used by banks to set interest charges on a variety of corporate and consumer loans, including some adjustable home mortgages, revolving credit cards and business loans extended to their most creditworthy customers. Banks set the rate based on their borrowing costs, as reflected by the interest rate on short-term Treasury bills.

**profit-taking** (n. and adj.) Avoid this term. It means selling a security after a recent rapid rise in price. It is inaccurate if the seller bought the security at a higher price, watched it fall, then sold it after a recent rise

but for less than he bought it. In that case, he would be cutting his losses, not taking his profit.

**profit terminology** Note the meanings of the following terms in reporting a company's financial status. Always be careful to specify whether the figures given apply to quarterly or annual results.

The terms, listed in the order in which they might occur in analyzing a company's financial condition:

**dividend** The amount paid per share per year to holders of common stock. Payments generally are made in quarterly installments.

The dividend usually is a portion of the earnings per share. However, if a company shows no profit during a given period, it may be able to use earnings retained from profitable periods to pay its dividend on schedule.

**earnings per share** (or **loss per share**, for companies posting a net loss) The figure obtained by dividing the number of outstanding shares of common stock into the amount left after dividends have been paid on any preferred stock.

**extraordinary loss, extraordinary income** An expense or source of income that does not occur on a regular basis, such as a loss due to a major fire or the revenue from the sale of a subsidiary. Extraordinary items should be identified in any report on the company's financial status to avoid creating the false impression that its overall profit trend has suddenly plunged or soared.

**gross profit** The difference between the sales price of an item or service and the expenses directly attributed to it, such as the cost of raw materials, labor and overhead linked to the production effort.

**income before taxes** Gross profits minus companywide expenses not directly attributed to specific products or services. These expenses typically include interest costs, advertising and sales costs, and general administrative overhead.

**net income, profit, earnings** The amount left after taxes have been paid.

A portion may be committed to pay preferred dividends. Some of what remains may be paid in dividends to holders of common stocks. The rest may be invested to obtain interest revenue or spent to acquire new buildings or equipment to increase the company's ability to make further profits.

To avoid confusion, do not use the word *income* alone — always specify whether the figure is *income before taxes* or *net income*.

The terms *profit* and *earnings* commonly are interpreted as meaning the amount left after taxes. The terms *net profit* and *net earnings* are acceptable synonyms.

**return on investment** A percentage figure obtained by dividing the company's assets into its net income.

**revenue** The amount of money a company took in, including interest earned and receipts from sales, services provided, rents and royalties.

The figure also may include excise taxes and sales taxes collected for the government. If it does, the fact should be noted in any report on revenue.

**sales** The money a company received for the goods and services it sold.

In some cases the figure includes receipts from rents and royalties. In others, particularly when rentals and royalties make up a large portion of a company's income, figures for these activities are listed separately.

**protective tariff** A duty high enough to assure domestic producers against any effective competition from foreign producers.

# R

**receivership** A legal action in which a court appoints a *receiver* to manage a business while the court tries to resolve problems that could ruin the business, such as insolvency. *Receivership* is often used in federal bankruptcy court proceedings. But it also can be used for nonfinancial troubles such as an ownership dispute.

In bankruptcy proceedings, the court appoints a trustee called a *receiver* who attempts to settle the financial difficulties of the company while under protection from creditors.

**recession** A falling-off of economic activity that may be a temporary phenomenon or could continue into a depression.

**retail sales** The sales of retail stores, including merchandise sold and receipts for repairs and similar services.

A business is considered a *retail store* if it is engaged primarily in selling merchandise for personal, household or farm consumption.

**revenue** See **profit terminology**.

**revenue bond** See **loan**

terminology.

**revolving credit** Describes an account on which the payment is any amount less than the total balance, and the remaining balance carried forward is subject to finance charges.

**rollover** The selling of new securities to pay off old ones coming due or the refinancing of an existing loan.

# S

**savings and loan associations** Once limited to accepting deposits and making home mortgage loans, they are not banks. Since enactment of the Financial Institutions Reform Recovery and Enforcement Act in 1989, they have been regulated by the Office of Thrift Supervision. Use *the association* on second reference.

**service mark** A brand, symbol, word, etc. used by a supplier of services and protected by law to prevent a competitor from using it: *Realtor*, for a member of the National Association of Realtors, for example.
When a service mark is used, capitalize it.
The preferred form, however, is to use a generic term unless the service mark is essential to the story.
See **brand names** and **trademark**.

**short** An investment term used to describe the position held by individuals who sell stock that they do not yet own by borrowing from their broker in order to deliver to the purchaser.

A person selling short is betting that the price of the stock will fall.

**short covering** The purchase of a security to repay shares of a security borrowed from a broker.

**short sale** A sale of securities that are not owned by the sellers at the time of sale but which they intend to purchase or borrow in time to make delivery.

**small-business man**

**spinoff** (n.) A distribution that occurs when the company forms a separate company out of a division, a subsidiary or other holdings. The shares of the new company are distributed proportionately to the parent company holders.

**spot market** A market for buying or selling commodities or foreign exchange for immediate delivery and for cash payment.

**spot price** The price of a commodity available for immediate sale and delivery. The term is also used to refer to foreign exchange transactions.

**Standard & Poor's Register of Corporations** The source for determining the formal name of a business. See **company names**.
The register is published by Standard & Poor's of New York.

**stockbroker**

**stock index futures** Futures contracts valued on the basis of indexes that track the prices of a specific group of stocks. The most widely traded is the future based on the Standard

& Poor's 500-stock index. Speculators also trade options on index futures.

**stock market prices** With the stock markets' conversion to decimalization, prices are quoted in dollars and cents, not fractions. Use active verbs: *Shares rose 15 cents to $48.05 in afternoon trading.*

# T

**trademark** A trademark is a brand, symbol, word, etc., used by a manufacturer or dealer and protected by law to prevent a competitor from using it: *AstroTurf*, for a type of artificial grass, for example.

In general, use a generic equivalent unless the trademark name is essential to the story.

When a trademark is used, capitalize it.

Many trademarks are listed separately in this book, together with generic equivalents.

The International Trademark Association, located in New York, is a helpful source of information about trademarks.

See **brand names** and **service marks**.

**Treasury bills, Treasury bonds, Treasury notes** See **loan terminology**.

# U

**union names** The formal names of unions may be condensed to conventionally accepted short forms that capitalize characteristic words

from the full name followed by *union* in lowercase.

Follow union practice in the use of the word *worker* in shortened forms. Among major unions, all except the *United Steelworkers* use two words: *United Auto Workers, United Mine Workers*, etc.

See entry in main section for more detail and references.

# W

**Wall Street** When the reference is to the entire complex of financial institutions in the area rather than the actual street itself, *the Street* is an acceptable short form.

See **capitalization**.

**wholesale price index** A measurement of the changes in the average price that businesses pay for a selected group of industrial commodities, farm products, processed foods and feed for animals.

Capitalize when referring to the U.S. index, issued monthly by the Bureau of Labor Statistics, an agency of the Labor Department.

# Y

**yield** In a financial sense, the annual rate of return on an investment, as paid in dividends or interest. It is expressed as a percentage obtained by dividing the market price for a stock or bond into the dividend or interest paid in the preceding 12 months.

See **profit terminology**.

# A GUIDE TO PUNCTUATION

# A GUIDE TO PUNCTUATION

There is no alternative to correct punctuation. Incorrect punctuation can change the meaning of a sentence, the results of which could be far-reaching.

Even if the meaning is not changed, bad punctuation, however inconsequential, can cause the reader to lose track of what is being said and give up reading a sentence.

The basic guideline is to use common sense.

—Punctuation is to make clear the thought being expressed.

—If punctuation does not help make clear what is being said, it should not be there.

"The Elements of Style" by E.B. White and William Strunk Jr. is a bible of writers. It states:

"Clarity, clarity, clarity. When you become hopelessly mired in a sentence, it is best to start fresh; do not try to fight your way through against terrible odds of syntax. Usually what is wrong is that the construction has become too involved at some point; the sentence needs to be broken apart and replaced by two or more shorter sentences."

This applies to punctuation. If a sentence becomes cluttered with commas, semicolons and dashes, start over.

These two paragraphs are full of commas and clauses; all of it equals too much for the reader to grasp:

*The Commonwealth Games Federation, in an apparent effort to persuade other nations to ignore the spiraling boycott, ruled Sunday that Budd, a runner who has had a storied past on and off the track, and Cowley, a swimmer who competes for the University of Texas, were ineligible under the Commonwealth Constitution to compete for England in the 10-day event to be held in Edinburgh, Scotland, beginning July 24.*

*The decision on Budd, who has been the object of a number of demonstrations in the past, and Cowley followed an earlier announcement Sunday by Tanzania that it was joining Nigeria, Kenya, Ghana and Uganda in boycotting the games because of Britain's refusal to support economic sanctions against South Africa's government.*

# PUNCTUATION MARKS AND HOW TO USE THEM

**apostrophe (')** Follow these guidelines:

POSSESSIVES: See the **possessives** entry in main section.

PLURAL NOUNS NOT ENDING IN S: Add 's: *the alumni's contributions, women's rights.*

PLURAL NOUNS ENDING IN S: Add only an apostrophe: *the churches' needs, the girls' toys, the horses' food, the ships' wake, states' rights, the VIPs' entrance.*

NOUNS PLURAL IN FORM, SINGULAR IN MEANING: Add only an apostrophe: *mathematics' rules, measles' effects.* (But see INANIMATE OBJECTS below.)

Apply the same principle when a plural word occurs in the formal name of a singular entity: *General Motors' profits, the United States' wealth.*

NOUNS THE SAME IN SINGULAR AND PLURAL: Treat them the same as plurals, even if the meaning is singular: *one corps' location, the two deer's tracks, the lone moose's antlers.*

SINGULAR NOUNS NOT ENDING IN S: Add 's: *the church's needs, the girl's toys, the horse's food, the ship's route, the VIP's seat.*

Some style guides say that singular nouns ending in s sounds such as *ce, x,* and *z* may take either the apostrophe alone or 's. See SPECIAL EXPRESSIONS, but otherwise, for consistency and ease in remembering a rule, always use 's if the word does not end in the letter s: *Butz's policies, the fox's den, the justice's verdict, Marx's theories, the prince's life, Xerox's profits.*

SINGULAR COMMON NOUNS ENDING IN S: Add 's unless the next word begins with s: *the hostess's invitation, the hostess' seat; the witness's answer, the witness' story.*

SINGULAR PROPER NAMES ENDING IN S: Use only an apostrophe: *Achilles' heel, Agnes' book, Ceres' rites, Descartes' theories, Dickens' novels, Euripides' dramas, Hercules' labors, Jesus' life, Jules' seat, Kansas' schools, Moses' law, Socrates' life, Tennessee Williams' plays, Xerxes' armies.* (An exception is *St. James's Palace.*)

SPECIAL EXPRESSIONS: The following exceptions to the general rule for words not ending in s apply to words that end in an s sound and are followed by a word that begins with s: *for appearance' sake, for conscience' sake, for goodness' sake.* Use 's otherwise: *the appearance's cost, my conscience's voice.*

PRONOUNS: Personal interrogative and relative pronouns have separate forms for the possessive. None involves an apostrophe: *mine, ours, your, yours, his, hers, its, theirs, whose.*

Caution: If you are using an apostrophe with a pronoun, always double-check to be sure that the meaning calls for a contraction: *you're, it's, there's, who's.*

Follow the rules listed above in forming the possessives of other pronouns: *another's idea, others' plans, someone's guess.*

COMPOUND WORDS: Applying the rules above, add an apostrophe or 's to the word closest to the object possessed: *the major general's decision, the major generals' decisions, the attorney general's request, the attorneys general's request.* See the **plurals** entry for guidelines on forming the plurals of these words.

Also: *anyone else's attitude, John Adams Jr.'s father, Benjamin Franklin of Pennsylvania's motion.* Whenever practical, however, recast the phrase to avoid ambiguity: *the motion by Benjamin Franklin of Pennsylvania.*

JOINT POSSESSION, INDIVIDUAL POSSESSION: Use a possessive form after only the last word if ownership is joint: *Fred and Sylvia's apartment, Fred and Sylvia's stocks.*

Use a possessive form after both words if the objects are individually owned: *Fred's and Sylvia's books.*

DESCRIPTIVE PHRASES: Do not add an apostrophe to a word ending in *s* when it is used primarily in a descriptive sense: *citizens band radio, a Cincinnati Reds infielder, a teachers college, a Teamsters request, a writers guide.*

Memory Aid: The apostrophe usually is not used if *for* or *by* rather than *of* would be appropriate in the longer form: *a radio band for citizens, a college for teachers, a guide for writers, a request by the Teamsters.*

An *'s* is required however, when a term involves a plural word that does not end in *s*: *a children's hospital, a people's republic, the Young Men's Christian Association.*

DESCRIPTIVE NAMES: Some governmental, corporate and institutional organizations with a descriptive word in their names use an apostrophe; some do not. Follow the user's practice: *Actors' Equity, Diners Club, the Ladies' Home Journal, the National Governors Association.* See separate entries for these and similar names

frequently in the news.

QUASI POSSESSIVES: Follow the rules above in composing the possessive form of words that occur in such phrases as *a day's pay, two weeks' vacation, three days' work, your money's worth.*

Frequently, however, a hyphenated form is clearer: *a two-week vacation, a three-day job.*

DOUBLE POSSESSIVE: Two conditions must apply for a double possessive — a phrase such as *a friend of John's* — to occur: 1. The word after *of* must refer to an animate object, and 2. The word before *of* must involve only a portion of the animate object's possessions.

Otherwise, do not use the possessive form of the word after *of*: *The friends of John Adams mourned his death.* (All the friends were involved.) *He is a friend of the college.* (Not *college's,* because *college* is inanimate).

Memory Aid: This construction occurs most often, and quite naturally, with the possessive forms of personal pronouns: *He is a friend of mine.*

INANIMATE OBJECTS: There is no blanket rule against creating a possessive form for an inanimate object, particularly if the object is treated in a personified sense. See some of the earlier examples, and note these: *death's call, the wind's murmur.*

In general, however, avoid excessive personalization of inanimate objects, and give preference to an *of* construction when it fits the makeup of the sentence. For example, the earlier references to *mathematics' rules* and *measles' effects* would better be phrased: *the rules of mathematics, the effects of measles.*

OMITTED LETTERS: *I've, it's, don't, rock 'n' roll, 'tis the season to be jolly. He is a ne'er-do-well.*

See **contractions** in main section.

OMITTED FIGURES: *The class of '62. The Spirit of '76. The '20s.*

PLURALS OF A SINGLE LETTER: *Mind your p's and q's. He learned the three R's and brought home a report card with four A's and two B's. The Oakland A's won the pennant.*

DO NOT USE: For plurals of numerals or multiple-letter combinations. See **plurals**.

**brackets [ ]** They cannot be transmitted over news wires. Use parentheses or recast the material. See **parentheses**.

**colon (:)** The most frequent use of a colon is at the end of a sentence to introduce lists, tabulations, texts, etc.

Capitalize the first word after a colon only if it is a proper noun or the start of a complete sentence: *He promised this: The company will make good all the losses.* But: *There were three considerations: expense, time and feasibility.*

EMPHASIS: The colon often can be effective in giving emphasis: *He had only one hobby: eating.*

LISTINGS: Use the colon in such listings as time elapsed (*1:31:07.2*), time of day (*8:31 p.m.*), biblical and legal citations (*2 Kings 2:14; Missouri Code 3:245-260*).

DIALOGUE: Use a colon for dialogue. In coverage of a trial, for example:

*Bailey: What were you doing the night of the 19th?*

*Mason: I refuse to answer that.*

Q AND A: The colon is used for question-and-answer interviews:

*Q: Did you strike him?*

*A: Indeed I did.*

INTRODUCING QUOTATIONS: Use a comma to introduce a direct quotation of one sentence that remains within a paragraph. Use a colon to introduce long quotations within a paragraph and to end all paragraphs that introduce a paragraph of quoted material.

PLACEMENT WITH QUOTATION MARKS: Colons go outside quotation marks unless they are part of the quotation itself.

MISCELLANEOUS: Do not combine a dash and a colon.

**comma (,)** The following guidelines treat some of the most frequent questions about the use of commas. Additional guidelines on specialized uses are provided in separate entries such as **dates** and **scores**.

For detailed guidance, consult the punctuation section in the back of Webster's New World College Dictionary.

IN A SERIES: Use commas to separate elements in a series, but do not put a comma before the conjunction in a simple series: *The flag is red, white and blue. He would nominate Tom, Dick or Harry.*

Put a comma before the concluding conjunction in a series, however, if an integral element of the series requires a conjunction: *I had orange juice, toast, and ham and eggs for breakfast.*

Use a comma also before the concluding conjunction in a complex series of phrases: *The main points to consider are whether the athletes are skillful enough to compete, whether they have the stamina to endure the training, and whether they have the proper mental attitude.*

See the **dash** and **semicolon** entries for cases when elements of a series contain internal commas.

WITH EQUAL ADJECTIVES:
Use commas to separate a series
of adjectives equal in rank. If the
commas could be replaced by the
word *and* without changing the
sense, the adjectives are equal:
*a thoughtful, precise manner; a
dark, dangerous street.*

Use no comma when the last
adjective before a noun outranks
its predecessors because it is
an integral element of a noun
phrase, which is the equivalent
of a single noun: *a cheap fur coat*
(the noun phrase is *fur coat*); *the
old oaken bucket; a new, blue
spring bonnet.*

WITH NONESSENTIAL
CLAUSES: A nonessential clause
must be set off by commas. An
essential clause must not be set
off from the rest of a sentence by
commas.

See the **essential clauses,
nonessential clauses** entry in the
main section.

WITH NONESSENTIAL
PHRASES: A nonessential phrase
must be set off by commas. An
essential phrase must not be set
off from the rest of a sentence by
commas.

See the **essential phrases,
nonessential phrases** entry in
the main section.

WITH INTRODUCTORY
CLAUSES AND PHRASES: A
comma is used to separate an introductory clause or phrase from
the main clause: *When he had
tired of the mad pace of New York,
he moved to Dubuque.*

The comma may be omitted
after short introductory phrases if
no ambiguity would result: *During
the night he heard many noises.*

But use the comma if its omission would slow comprehension:
*On the street below, the curious
gathered.*

WITH CONJUNCTIONS: When
a conjunction such as *and, but* or
*for* links two clauses that could

stand alone as separate sentences, use a comma before the conjunction in most cases: *She was
glad she had looked, for a man
was approaching the house.*

As a rule of thumb, use a
comma if the subject of each
clause is expressly stated: *We are
visiting Washington, and we also
plan a side trip to Williamsburg.
We visited Washington, and our
senator greeted us personally.* But
no comma when the subject of
the two clauses is the same and
is not repeated in the second: *We
are visiting Washington and plan
to see the White House.*

The comma may be dropped if
two clauses with expressly stated
subjects are short. In general,
however, favor use of a comma
unless a particular literary effect
is desired or if it would distort the
sense of a sentence.

INTRODUCING DIRECT
QUOTES: Use a comma to introduce a complete one-sentence
quotation within a paragraph:
*Wallace said, "She spent six
months in Argentina and came
back speaking English with a
Spanish accent."* But use a colon
to introduce quotations of more
than one sentence. See **colon**.

Do not use a comma at the
start of an indirect or partial quotation: *He said the victory put him
"firmly on the road to a first-ballot
nomination."*

BEFORE ATTRIBUTION: Use a
comma instead of a period at the
end of a quote that is followed by
attribution: *"Rub my shoulders,"
Miss Cawley suggested.*

Do not use a comma, however,
if the quoted statement ends with
a question mark or exclamation
point: *"Why should I?" he asked.*

WITH HOMETOWNS AND
AGES: Use a comma to set off an
individual's hometown when it is
placed in apposition to a name
(whether *of* is used or not): *Mary*

Richards, Minneapolis, and Maude Findlay, Tuckahoe, N.Y., were there.

If an individual's age is used, set it off by commas: *Maude Findlay, 48, Tuckahoe, N.Y., was present.*

WITH PARTY AFFILIATION, ACADEMIC DEGREES, RELIGIOUS AFFILIATIONS: See separate entries under each of these terms.

NAMES OF STATES AND NATIONS USED WITH CITY NAMES: *His journey will take him from Dublin, Ireland, to Fargo, N.D., and back. The Selma, Ala., group saw the governor.*

Use parentheses, however, if a state name is inserted within a proper name: *The Huntsville (Ala.) Times.*

WITH YES AND NO: *Yes, I will be there.*

IN DIRECT ADDRESS: *Mother, I will be home late. No, sir, I did not take it.*

SEPARATING SIMILAR WORDS: Use a comma to separate duplicated words that otherwise would be confusing: *What the problem is, is not clear.*

IN LARGE FIGURES: Use a comma for most figures greater than 999. The major exceptions are: street addresses (*1234 Main St.*), broadcast frequencies (*1460 kilohertz*), room numbers, serial numbers, telephone numbers, and years (*1876*). See separate entries under these headings.

PLACEMENT WITH QUOTES: Commas always go inside quotation marks.

See **semicolon**.

**compound adjectives** See the **hyphen** entry.

**dash (—)** Follow these guidelines:

ABRUPT CHANGE: Use dashes to denote an abrupt change in thought in a sentence or an emphatic pause: *We will fly to Paris in June — if I get a raise. Smith offered a plan — it was unprecedented — to raise revenues.*

SERIES WITHIN A PHRASE: When a phrase that otherwise would be set off by commas contains a series of words that must be separated by commas, use dashes to set off the full phrase: *He listed the qualities — intelligence, humor, conservatism, independence — that he liked in an executive.*

ATTRIBUTION: Use a dash before an author's or composer's name at the end of a quotation: *"Who steals my purse steals trash." — Shakespeare.*

IN DATELINES:

*NEW YORK (AP) — The city is broke.*

IN LISTS: Dashes should be used to introduce individual sections of a list. Capitalize the first word following the dash. Use periods, not semicolons, at the end of each section, whether it is a full sentence or a phrase. Example:

*Jones gave the following reasons:*

*—He never ordered the package.*

*—If he did, it didn't come.*

*—If it did, he sent it back.*

WITH SPACES: Put a space on both sides of a dash in all uses except the start of a paragraph and sports agate summaries.

**ellipsis ( ... )** In general, treat an ellipsis as a three-letter word, constructed with three periods and two spaces, as shown here.

Use an ellipsis to indicate the deletion of one or more words in condensing quotes, texts and documents. Be especially careful to avoid deletions that would distort the meaning.

Brief examples of how to use ellipses are provided after guidelines are given. More extensive examples, drawn from the speech in which President Nixon announced his resignation, are in the sections below marked CONDENSATION EXAMPLE and QUOTATIONS.

SPACING REQUIREMENTS: In some computer editing systems the thin space must be used between the periods of the ellipsis to prevent them from being placed on two different lines when they are sent through a computer that handles hyphenation and justification.

Leave one regular space — never a thin — on both sides of an ellipsis: *I ... tried to do what was best.*

PUNCTUATION GUIDELINES: If the words that precede an ellipsis constitute a grammatically complete sentence, either in the original or in the condensation, place a period at the end of the last word before the ellipsis. Follow it with a regular space and an ellipsis: *I no longer have a strong enough political base. ...*

When the grammatical sense calls for a question mark, exclamation point, comma or colon, the sequence is word, punctuation mark, regular space, ellipsis: *Will you come? ...*

When material is deleted at the end of one paragraph and at the beginning of the one that follows, place an ellipsis in both locations.

CONDENSATION EXAMPLE: Here is an example of how the spacing and punctuation guidelines would be applied in condensing President Nixon's resignation announcement:

Good evening. ...

In all the decisions I have made in my public life, I have always tried to do what was best for the nation. ...

... However, it has become evident to me that I no longer have a strong enough political base in Congress.

... As long as there was a base, I felt strongly that it was necessary to see the constitutional process through to its conclusion, that to do otherwise would be ... a dangerously destabilizing precedent for the future.

QUOTATIONS: In writing a story, do not use ellipses at the beginning and end of direct quotes:

*"It has become evident to me that I no longer have a strong enough political base," Nixon said.*

Not *"... it has become evident to me that I no longer have a strong enough political base ... ," Nixon said.*

HESITATION: An ellipsis also may be used to indicate a pause or hesitation in speech, or a thought that the speaker or writer does not complete. Substitute a dash for this purpose, however, if the context uses ellipses to indicate that words actually spoken or written have been deleted.

SPECIAL EFFECTS: Ellipses also may be used to separate individual items within a paragraph of show business gossip or similar material. Use periods after items that are complete sentences.

**exclamation point (!)** Follow these guidelines:

EMPHATIC EXPRESSIONS: Use the mark to express a high degree of surprise, incredulity or other strong emotion.

AVOID OVERUSE: Use a comma after mild interjections. End mildly exclamatory sentences with a period.

PLACEMENT WITH QUOTES: Place the mark inside quotation marks when it is part of the quoted material: *"How wonderful!" he exclaimed. "Never!" she shouted.*

Place the mark outside quotation marks when it is not part of the quoted material: *I hated reading Spenser's "Faerie Queene"!*

MISCELLANEOUS: Do not use a comma or a period after the exclamation mark:

Wrong: *"Halt!", the corporal cried.*

Right: *"Halt!" the corporal cried.*

## hyphen (-)

Hyphens are joiners. Use them to avoid ambiguity or to form a single idea from two or more words.

Use of the hyphen is far from standardized. It is optional in most cases, a matter of taste, judgment and style sense. But the fewer hyphens the better; use them only when not using them causes confusion. (*Small-businessman*, but *health care center*.) See individual entries in this book. If not listed here, use the first listed entry in Webster's New World College Dictionary.

Some guidelines:

AVOID AMBIGUITY: Use a hyphen whenever ambiguity would result if it were omitted: *The president will speak to small-business men.* (*Businessmen* normally is one word. But *the president will speak to small businessmen* is unclear.)

Others: *He recovered his health. He re-covered the leaky roof.*

COMPOUND MODIFIERS: When a compound modifier — two or more words that express a single concept — precedes a noun, use hyphens to link all the words in the compound except the adverb *very* and all adverbs that end in *-ly*: *a first-quarter touchdown, a bluish-green dress, a full-time job, a well-known man, a better-qualified woman, a know-it-all attitude, a very good time, an easily remembered rule.*

Many combinations that are hyphenated before a noun are not hyphenated when they occur after a noun: *The team scored in the first quarter. The dress, a bluish green, was attractive on her. She works full time. His attitude suggested that he knew it all.*

But when a modifier that would be hyphenated before a noun occurs instead after a form of the verb *to be*, the hyphen usually must be retained to avoid confusion: *The man is well-known. The woman is quick-witted. The children are soft-spoken. The play is second-rate.*

The principle of using a hyphen to avoid confusion explains why no hyphen is required with *very* and *-ly* words. Readers can expect them to modify the word that follows. But if a combination such as *little-known man* were not hyphenated, the reader could logically be expecting *little* to be followed by a noun, as in *little man.* Instead, the reader encountering *little known* would have to back up mentally and make the compound connection on his own.

TWO-THOUGHT COMPOUNDS: *serio-comic, socio-economic.*

COMPOUND PROPER NOUNS AND ADJECTIVES: Use a hyphen to designate dual heritage: *Italian-American, Mexican-American.*

No hyphen, however, for *French Canadian* or *Latin American.*

PREFIXES AND SUFFIXES: See the **prefixes** and **suffixes** entries, and separate entries for the most frequently used prefixes and suffixes.

AVOID DUPLICATED VOWELS, TRIPLED CONSONANTS: Examples: *anti-intellectual, pre-empt, shell-like.*

WITH NUMERALS: Use a hyphen to separate figures in **odds**, **ratios**, **scores**, some **fractions** and some **vote tabulations**. See examples in entries under these headings.

When large numbers must be spelled out, use a hyphen to connect a word ending in -*y* to another word: *twenty-one, fifty-five,* etc.

SUSPENSIVE HYPHENATION: The form: *He received a 10- to 20-year sentence in prison.*

**parentheses ( )** In general, use parentheses around logos, as shown in the **datelines** entry, but otherwise be sparing with them.

Parentheses are jarring to the reader. Because they do not appear on some news service printers, there is also the danger that material inside them may be misinterpreted.

The temptation to use parentheses is a clue that a sentence is becoming contorted. Try to write it another way. If a sentence must contain incidental material, then commas or two dashes are frequently more effective. Use these alternatives whenever possible.

There are occasions, however, when parentheses are the only effective means of inserting necessary background or reference information. When they are necessary, follow these guidelines:

WITHIN QUOTATIONS: If parenthetical information inserted in a direct quotation is at all sensitive, place an editor's note under a dash at the bottom of a story alerting copy desks to what was inserted.

PUNCTUATION: Place a period outside a closing parenthesis if the material inside is not a sentence (*such as this fragment*).

(*An independent parenthetical sentence such as this one takes a period before the closing parenthesis.*)

When a phrase placed in parentheses (*this one is an example*) might normally qualify as a complete sentence but is dependent on the surrounding material, do not capitalize the first word or end with a period.

MATERIAL FROM OTHER AREAS: If a story contains information from outside the datelined city, put the material in parentheses only if the correspondent in the datelined community was cut off from incoming communications. See **dateline selection**.

INSERTIONS IN A PROPER NAME: Use parentheses if a state name or similar information is inserted within a proper name: *The Huntsville (Ala.) Times.* But use commas if no proper name is involved: *The Selma, Ala., group saw the governor.*

NEVER USED: Do not use parentheses to denote a political figure's party affiliation and jurisdiction. Instead, set them off with commas, as shown under **party affiliation**.

Do not use (*cq*) or similar notation to indicate that an unusual spelling or term is correct. Include the confirmation in an editor's note at the top of a story.

**periods (.)** Follow these guidelines:

END OF DECLARATIVE SENTENCE: *The stylebook is finished.*

END OF A MILDLY IMPERATIVE SENTENCE: *Shut the door.*

Use an exclamation point if greater emphasis is desired: *Be careful!*

END OF SOME RHETORICAL QUESTIONS: A period is preferable if a statement is more a suggestion than a question: *Why don't we go.*

END OF AN INDIRECT QUESTION: *He asked what the score was.*

MANY ABBREVIATIONS: For guidelines, see the **abbreviations and acronyms** entry. For the form of frequently used abbreviations, see the entry under the full name, abbreviation, acronym or term.

INITIALS: *John F. Kennedy, T.S. Eliot* (No space between *T.* and *S.*, to prevent them from being placed on two lines in typesetting.)

Abbreviations using only the initials of a name do not take periods: *JFK, LBJ.*

ELLIPSIS: See **ellipsis**.

ENUMERATIONS: After numbers or letters in enumerating elements of a summary: *1. Wash the car. 2. Clean the basement.* Or: *A. Punctuate properly. B. Write simply.*

PLACEMENT WITH QUOTATION MARKS: Periods always go inside quotation marks. See **quotation marks**.

SPACING: Use a single space after a period at the end of a sentence.

**question mark (?)** Follow these guidelines:

END OF A DIRECT QUESTION: *Who started the riot?*

*Did he ask who started the riot?* (The sentence as a whole is a direct question despite the indirect question at the end.)

*You started the riot?* (A question in the form of a declarative statement.)

INTERPOLATED QUESTION: *You told me — Did I hear you correctly? — that you started the riot.*

MULTIPLE QUESTION: Use a single question mark at the end of the full sentence:

*Did you hear him say, "What right have you to ask about the riot?"*

*Did he plan the riot, employ assistants, and give the signal to begin?*

Or, to cause full stops and throw emphasis on each element, break into separate sentences: *Did he plan the riot? Employ assistants? Give the signal to begin?*

CAUTION: Do not use question marks to indicate the end of indirect questions:

*He asked who started the riot. To ask why the riot started is unnecessary. I want to know what the cause of the riot was. How foolish it is to ask what caused the riot.*

QUESTION AND ANSWER FORMAT: Do not use quotation marks. Paragraph each speaker's words:

*Q: Where did you keep it?*
*A: In a little tin box.*

PLACEMENT WITH QUOTATION MARKS: Inside or outside, depending on the meaning:

*Who wrote "Gone With the Wind"?*

*He asked, "How long will it take?"*

MISCELLANEOUS: The question mark supersedes the comma that normally is used when supplying attribution for a quotation: *"Who is there?" she asked.*

**quotation marks (" ")** The basic guidelines for open-quote marks (") and close-quote marks ("):

FOR DIRECT QUOTATIONS: To surround the exact words of a speaker or writer when reported in a story:

*"I have no intention of staying,"* he replied.

*"I do not object," he said, "to the tenor of the report."*

*Franklin said, "A penny saved is a penny earned."*

*A speculator said the practice is "too conservative for inflationary times."*

RUNNING QUOTATIONS: If a full paragraph of quoted material is followed by a paragraph that continues the quotation, do not put close-quote marks at the end of the first paragraph. Do, however, put open-quote marks at the start of the second paragraph. Continue in this fashion for any succeeding paragraphs, using close-quote marks only at the end of the quoted material.

If a paragraph does not start with quotation marks but ends with a quotation that is continued in the next paragraph, do not use close-quote marks at the end of the introductory paragraph if the quoted material constitutes a full sentence. Use close-quote marks, however, if the quoted material does not constitute a full sentence. For example:

*He said, "I am shocked and horrified by the incident.*

*"I am so horrified, in fact, that I will ask for the death penalty."*

But: *He said he was "shocked and horrified by the incident."*

*"I am so horrified, in fact, that I will ask for the death penalty,"* he said.

DIALOGUE OR CONVERSA-TION: Each person's words, no matter how brief, are placed in a separate paragraph, with quotation marks at the beginning and the end of each person's speech:

*"Will you go?"*

*"Yes."*

*"When?"*

*"Thursday."*

NOT IN Q-and-A: Quotation marks are not required in formats that identify questions and answers by *Q:* and *A:*. See the **question mark** entry for example.

NOT IN TEXTS: Quotation marks are not required in full texts, condensed texts or textual excerpts. See **ellipsis**.

COMPOSITION TITLES: See the **composition titles** entry for guidelines on the use of quotation marks in book titles, movie titles, etc.

NICKNAMES: See the **nicknames** entry.

IRONY: Put quotation marks around a word or words used in an ironical sense: *The "debate" turned into a free-for-all.*

UNFAMILIAR TERMS: A word or words being introduced to readers may be placed in quotation marks on first reference:

*Broadcast frequencies are measured in "kilohertz."*

Do not put subsequent references to *kilohertz* in quotation marks.

See the **foreign words** entry.

AVOID UNNECESSARY FRAGMENTS: Do not use quotation marks to report a few ordinary words that a speaker or writer has used:

Wrong: *The senator said he would "go home to Michigan" if he lost the election.*

Right: *The senator said he would go home to Michigan if he lost the election.*

PARTIAL QUOTES: When a partial quote is used, do not put quotation marks around words that the speaker could not have used.

Suppose the individual said, *"I am horrified at your slovenly manners."*

Wrong: *She said she "was horrified at their slovenly manners."*

Right: *She said she was horrified at their "slovenly manners."*

Better when practical: Use the full quote.

QUOTES WITHIN QUOTES: Alternate between double quotation marks ("or") and single marks ('or'):

*She said, "I quote from his letter, 'I agree with Kipling that "the female of the species is more deadly than the male," but the phenomenon is not an unchangeable law of nature,' a remark he did not explain."*

Use three marks together if two quoted elements end at the same time: *She said, "He told me, 'I love you.'"*

(NOTE: Local style should ensure some differentiation between the single and double quotation marks, either with a "thin" space or by different typography, if not computer-programmed.)

PLACEMENT WITH OTHER PUNCTUATION: Follow these long-established printers' rules:

—The period and the comma always go within the quotation marks.

—The dash, the semicolon, the question mark and the exclamation point go within the quotation marks when they apply to the quoted matter only. They go outside when they apply to the whole sentence.

See **comma**.

**semicolon (;)** In general, use the semicolon to indicate a greater separation of thought and information than a comma can convey but less than the separation that a period implies.

The basic guidelines:

TO CLARIFY A SERIES: Use semicolons to separate elements of a series when the items in the series are long or when individual segments contain material that also must be set off by commas:

*He is survived by a son, John Smith, of Chicago; three daughters, Jane Smith, of Wichita, Kan., Mary Smith, of Denver, and Susan, of Boston; and a sister, Martha, of Omaha, Neb.*

Note that the semicolon is used before the final *and* in such a series.

Another application of this principle may be seen in the cross-references at the end of entries in this book. Because some entries themselves have a comma, a semicolon is used to separate references to multiple entries, as in: *See the* **felony, misdemeanor** *entry;* **pardon, parole, probation;** *and* **prison, jail**.

See the **dash** entry for a different type of connection that uses dashes to avoid multiple commas.

TO LINK INDEPENDENT CLAUSES: Use semicolon when a coordinating conjunction such as *and, but* or *for* is not present: *The package was due last week; it arrived today.*

If a coordinating conjunction is present, use a semicolon before it only if extensive punctuation also is required in one or more of the individual clauses: *They pulled their boats from the water, sandbagged the retaining walls, and boarded up the windows; but even with these precautions, the island was hard-hit by the hurricane.*

Unless a particular literary effect is desired, however, the better approach in these circumstances is to break the independent clauses into separate sentences.

PLACEMENT WITH QUOTES: Place semicolons outside quotation marks.

# BRIEFING ON
# MEDIA LAW

# INTRODUCTION

The legal standards that govern the work of reporters and editors have undergone significant change since the civil rights movement and the Vietnam War, as the courts have given new force and meaning to the First Amendment's protection of speech and press.

In *New York Times v. Sullivan* (1964), the Supreme Court held for the very first time that the First Amendment limits the ability of states to impose damages based upon the content a statement, even when it may be false. Sixteen years later, in *Richmond Newspapers v. Virginia* (1980), the court reached the equally unprecedented conclusion that the First Amendment establishes an affirmative right for the press and public to compel access to information concerning the exercise of government power. The fallout from these two watershed cases has reshaped a great deal of the law that governs the publication of the news and the way it is gathered.

This chapter addresses some of the key legal issues facing journalists. With respect to newsgathering activity, it explores three topics of direct significance:

**Access to government information**, including the rules governing reporter's access to the courts and to government information generally;

**Confidential sources**, including the law relating to promises of confidentiality and the reporter's privilege; and

**Newsgathering conduct,** including common law and statutory rules that may create liability for actions taken while a reporter is seeking out the news.

With respect to news content, this chapter addresses the legal principles in three branches of the law that govern liability for the publication of information:

**Defamation**, including the elements of a claim arising from the publication of a false statement, and the common law and constitutional defenses to liability;

**Privacy**, including claims for the disclosure of private facts, misappropriation and "false light," which can arise when the facts reported are true; and

**Copyright infringement**, including the elements of a copyright claim and the "fair use" defense.

This chapter is intended only as a general primer on some basic principles that are likely to apply across a range of situations. It should not be construed as legal advice and should not substitute for obtaining legal guidance when you are in doubt.

# LEGAL PRINCIPLES OF NEWSGATHERING

Several legal rules have special importance to the way the news is gathered. This chapter takes up three of them: the affirmative rights that can be invoked to compel access to government proceedings and the release of government documents; the legal protections that often allow reporters to obtain information through a promise of confidentiality; and, the "laws of general applicability," such as intrusion, trespass, and misrepresentation, that reporters must usually follow, even when they inhibit the ability to seek out the news.

## Access to government information

Public access to information about the actions of government is essential to the functioning of a democracy. In 1822, James Madison made just this point:

"A Popular Government, without popular information, or the means of acquiring it, is but a Prologue to a Farce or a Tragedy; or perhaps both. Knowledge will forever govern ignorance: And a people who mean to be their own Governors, must arm themselves with the power which knowledge gives."

The press and public have affirmative rights, both constitutional and statutory, to compel access to the type of government information that is essential to the functioning of our democracy. The right of access extends to official proceedings, including court trials, hearings, and the meetings of some legislative bodies and administrative agencies. Access rights also extend to the inspection of documents held by the government, with only specific exceptions. Given the independence of the three branches of government, the scope of access to judicial proceedings and court records is largely governed by constitutional and common law principles articulated by judges, while access to information in the executive and legislative branches are largely governed by statutes and administrative regulations.

These access rights are not absolute; they can be abridged in a number of situations. Nonetheless, clear legal standards define the scope of these rights and the procedures available to reporters to enforce them.

## • *Recognition of a First Amendment right of access*

The articulation by the Supreme Court in 1980 of a constitutional right to certain information about the exercise of government power, and the delineation of the proper scope and application of that right over the ensuing years, would provide a fascinating case study of the meaning of a "living constitution." In *Richmond Newspapers* v. Virginia, the Supreme Court ruled for the first time that the First Amendment encompasses an affirmative, enforceable right of public access to criminal trials. As the court later explained the rationale for this new constitutional right, "a major purpose" of the First Amendment's protection of free speech, a free press and the right to petition the government is the public's need to know what the government is up to, if democracy is to function. Just as other provisions of the Bill of Rights have been read to imply the right to travel, a right to privacy, and the right to be presumed innocent, the court concluded that the First Amendment implies a right of the public to certain information concerning the direct exercise of government power.

In a series of subsequent rulings following *Richmond Newspapers*, the Supreme Court reaffirmed the existence of this constitutional right of access and defined its scope. In 1982, the court said that the right to attend a criminal trial applies even during the testimony of a minor victim of a sex crime. In *Globe Newspaper Co. v. Superior Court* (1982), the court struck down as unconstitutional a Massachusetts statute mandating closed proceedings during all such testimony, saying that the First Amendment right of access requires a judge to determine on a case-by-case basis whether the privacy concerns of a particular victim outweigh the public's right to attend and observe the proceedings. In 1984, the Supreme Court held that the right of access extends to the proceedings to select a jury in a criminal case, *Press-Enterprise Co. v. Superior Ct.*, and two years later said the right extends to preliminary hearings in a criminal prosecution. The First Amendment protects the public's right to attend such judicial proceedings unless specific findings are made, on the record, demonstrating that a closed proceeding is essential in order to "preserve higher values," and any limitation imposed on public access must be narrowly tailored to serve that interest.

While the Supreme Court has not revisited the right of access in detail since 1986, lower federal and state courts have widely considered and applied the right to a large variety of proceedings over the intervening years. Courts have recognized a constitutional right to attend a given type of proceeding if public access will generally play a positive role in the performance of the proceeding (encouraging diligent attention by officials, ensuring that proper procedures are followed, preventing perjury or other misconduct, facilitating public understanding of decisions made), and if it is the type of proceeding that historically has been open to the public.

The constitutional right is generally recognized to apply to all aspects of a criminal prosecution, except to matters involving a grand jury. Grand jury investigations historically have been completely secret, and this secrecy itself advances the important public policy of protecting innocent people in those cases where an investigation does not result in any criminal charge being filed. The right of access has been held to extend to civil trials and proceedings, although in some states there are important exceptions. Family Court proceedings, for example, raise significant privacy concerns, as do juvenile delinquency matters, and these are often closed to the public.

### • *Limits on constitutional access*

As noted, the constitutional right to attend proceedings is not absolute. That a First Amendment right protects public access to a proceeding does not mean that a proceeding can never be closed to the press and public. The Supreme Court has identified four factors that must each be satisfied before the right of access may be restricted:

1. Those who want to close a proceeding must prove that holding a public proceeding would directly threaten some compelling interest, such as a defendant's right to a fair trial or the right of privacy, that outweighs the public interest in openness.

2. There must be no alternative short of closing the proceeding that

could protect the threatened interest.

3. Any limitation on access must be as narrow as possible.

4. The limitation imposed must be effective in protecting the threatened interest or else closure may not be ordered.

Under this standard, courts have required journalists and the public to be excluded from proceedings in a number of situations, such as during the testimony of a sexual assault victim whose identity has not previously been disclosed to the public, or during testimony by an undercover police officer whose effectiveness or safety would be jeopardized by public identification.

Sidebar conferences between the attorneys and the judge generally involve discussions intended to be kept confidential from the jury, but these discussions should usually be available to the press. A transcript is generally kept of such sidebar discussions and should be available for inspection as part of the record of the proceeding. To withhold the transcript of such a sidebar conference held during an open proceeding, the same four-part test would need to be met.

One unsettled issue concerns reporters' access to information identifying jurors, and their right to speak to jurors after a verdict. The Supreme Court has said specifically that the First Amendment right of access extends to jury selection proceedings, where names and other identifying information are normally disclosed. Nonetheless, in some high profile cases such as the Martha Stewart and Michael Jackson prosecutions, courts have sought to keep the identities of jurors private during the trial or to minimize press contact with jurors following a verdict. Sometimes a judge will conduct jury selection by reference only to juror numbers, to prevent public disclosure of juror names or addresses before a trial is over. In other cases, courts have imposed restrictions on reporters barring them from speaking with jurors long after a verdict is returned. While limitations on disclosure of juror identities before a verdict is returned may sometimes be permissible, restrictions after a verdict is returned can rarely be squared with the First Amendment right of access.

Reporters confronted with such court orders should seek legal advice on the validity of the restriction imposed.

### • *What to say if a hearing is about to be closed without prior notice*

Because a constitutional right is at stake when a judicial proceeding is closed, the press has a right to be heard before a proceeding is shut to the public. The following statement should be read in court when confronted with an attempt to close a hearing without advance notice. It allows a reporter, when permitted to address the court, to state the basic concerns and to seek time for counsel to appear to make the legal argument. Any parts of the statement that are not applicable to a specific case can be changed or omitted:

*May it please the Court, I am (name) of The Associated Press (or other news organization). I respectfully request the opportunity to register on the record an objection to closing this proceeding to the public. The Associated Press (or other organization) requests a hearing at which its counsel may present to the court legal authority and arguments showing why any clo-*

*sure in this case would be improper.*

*The press and the public have a constitutional right to attend judicial proceedings, and may not be excluded unless the court makes findings, on the record, that: (1) closure is required to preserve a compelling constitutional interest, (2) no adequate alternatives to closure exist, (3) the closure ordered is narrowly tailored to protect the threatened interest effectively.*

*The Associated Press (or other) submits that these findings cannot be made here, especially given the public interest in this proceeding. The public has a right to be informed of what transpires in this case, the positions being argued by the parties, and the factual basis for rulings made by the court. The court should avoid any impression that justice is being carried on in secret. The Associated Press (or other organization) objects to any closure order and respectfully requests a hearing at which it can present full legal arguments and authority in support of this position. Thank you.*

If the court will not allow a reporter to be heard, a brief written statement — handwritten is fine — should be delivered to the courtroom clerk, making these same points.

### • 'Gag orders'

The tension between the right of a free press and the right of a fair trial is nothing new. Finding an impartial jury for the treason trial of Aaron Burr in 1807 was difficult, the Supreme Court has noted, because few people in Virginia "had not formed some opinions concerning Mr. Burr or his case, from newspaper accounts." Nonetheless, an apparently increasing number of cases involving celebrity defendants or notorious crimes generating intense publicity have led to an increased number of orders preventing lawyers, parties to a case, and sometimes even witnesses, from discussing the case outside of the courtroom.

The Supreme Court has said that speech by attorneys, as officers of the court, may be regulated to protect the integrity of the judicial system. Orders more broadly barring the speech of other trial participants, including the parties and witnesses, are permitted only when absolutely necessary to ensure an accused's right to a fair trial. Such orders have been entered in cases involving extraordinary press coverage that threatens the ability to select an impartial jury, when other measures are not likely to mitigate the effects of unrestrained pretrial publicity.

A typical gag order does not prevent a reporter from asking questions, but it does bar trial participants and court officers from answering them. Because a gag order restricts access to news, a reporter has legal standing to challenge an order, and may be successful if a gag order was entered without adequate factual findings to justify the need for the specific restraint on speech imposed by the court, or if the order is overbroad in the categories of individuals restrained or the range of topics they are prohibited from discussing.

### • Media protocols in high-profile cases

"Decorum orders" regulate the conduct of reporters covering high profile trials. Sometimes requested by the parties and sometimes imposed unilaterally by the court, these orders may restrict the use of cameras and recording devices at specific locations in and around the courthouse, direct that witnesses or jurors not be photographed as they come and go from court, restrict the use of cell phones, or impose other restrictions to protect the decorum of a trial and operations at the courthouse. In the aborted Kobe Bryant prosecution, for example, a Colorado state judge imposed a decorum order specifying such details as where cameras could be positioned outside the courthouse, limiting the times when reporters could enter or leave the courtroom, and specifying where reporters could sit, where they could park their cars and how they could enter the courthouse.

Restrictions on the actions of journalists that directly affect their ability to gather news must be narrowly tailored to protect a compelling governmental interest. Decorum orders that become necessary in high-profile cases to ensure safety, protect physical access to the courts by the public, or prevent interference with the integrity of the proceedings in the courtroom, are likely to be allowed as long as their terms are reasonable, content-neutral and limited to clearly defined restrictions on conduct within the courthouse and its immediate environs. A decorum order likely goes too far, however, if it also controls the content of a news report rather than just the conduct of a reporter. For example, for privacy reasons a court might restrict the taking of photographs of jurors as they enter or leave the courthouse, but could not properly bar the press from ever publishing the image of a juror, even if it were obtained through other sources. One restriction is limited to conduct at the courthouse; the other is aimed at the content of a news report.

### • The right to attend other proceedings

In some instances, the constitutional right of access has been held to extend to proceedings beyond court hearings. For example, in 2004, the U.S. Court of Appeals in Cincinnati held that the public had a constitutional right to attend deportation proceedings conducted by the Immigration and Naturalization Service. (*Detroit Free Press v. Ashcroft,* 2002.) The First Amendment right of access similarly has been found to extend to military courts-martial, proceedings of judicial review boards and hearings of the Federal Mine Safety and Health Administration.

Most states and the federal government also have statutes known as "open meetings laws" or "government in the sunshine" acts that protect the right of the public and the press to attend meetings of public authorities. These laws essentially provide that every meeting where a public board or public authority convenes to conduct business must be open to the public, with only limited exception. The federal law, for example, allows a meeting to be closed only if one of 10 identified categories of information are to be discussed, such as personnel and salary decisions. Even when a portion of a meeting is closed, a transcript or minutes must be prepared, and must be disclosed to the extent that release would not reveal the exempt information.

These access laws apply to executive agencies, but not to the legislative bodies, in most cases. Most state constitutions separately require open legislative sessions, although each house is usually free to make its own rules about access to committee meetings.

## • *The right of access applies to court documents*

The right of access generally includes the right to inspect transcripts of open proceedings, evidence introduced at a trial and most motion papers, orders and other records of open court proceedings. Some courts have concluded that this right to inspect judicial records is implicit in the First Amendment right of access, holding that the right covers any documents relating to a proceeding that is itself subject to the First Amendment right of access.

Other courts analyzed the right of access to documents filed with the court as a common law right that may be more easily restricted, sometimes with unfortunate results. For example, in the famous case of *McConnell v. Federal Election Commission* (2003), a challenge to the constitutionality of the McCain Feingold campaign finance reform act was decided by the courts entirely on the basis of written submissions, without any public evidentiary hearing. A massive record of some 100,000 pages was presented to the court, apparently detailing the types of campaign abuses that justified the restrictions on election speech imposed by Congress. Despite the public interest in knowing the factual basis for the competing arguments being made, the District of Columbia court concluded that the public had only a common law right to inspect the documents presented to the court, and that this right extended only to information "relied upon" by the court in reaching its decision. The court therefore rejected an application by several news organizations to inspect the evidence filed with the court, saying the public was only entitled to inspect specific pages of the record actually cited in the court's opinions.

Whatever the scope of the right to inspect court records, however, it does not generally extend to pretrial discovery documents and other litigation records that are not filed with the courts. While compelled public access to discovery has been afforded on rare occasion involving highly newsworthy disputes, reporters generally have no right to require parties to a lawsuit to allow inspection of litigation material that is never filed with the court.

## • *Access to other government records*

The federal Freedom of Information Act, originally passed by Congress in 1966, creates a presumptive right of access to all documents held in the executive branch, other than documents in the possession of the president and his immediate staff. It does not cover Congress or the courts. All Cabinet agencies, independent agencies, regulatory commissions and government-owned corporations are covered.

Records made available for inspection under the act include virtually anything recorded in a physical medium that can be reproduced. This includes all documents, papers, reports, and letters in the government's possession, as well as films, photographs, sound recordings, databases, computer disks and tapes. A 1996 law expanded FOIA to require federal agencies, whenever possible, to share data in a specific format, such as on computer diskette or CD-ROM. The 1996 amendments also broadened citizen access to government by placing more information directly online.

The act contains nine exemptions that permit — but do not require — agencies to withhold information. Those exemptions are: (1) national security; (2) internal agency personnel rules; (3) information specifically exempt from disclosure by another law; (4) trade secrets; (5) internal agency memorandums and policy deliberations; (6) personal privacy; (7); law enforcement investigations; (8) federally regulated bank information; and (9) oil and gas well data.

Different agencies apply these exemptions in different ways even when issues ostensibly have already been settled in court. If you want something, ask for it. Let the government decide whether it has any grounds or willingness to deny your request. The statutory exemptions allow information to be withheld, but do not require it. Even an exempt document can be released at the government's discretion.

Because of the various exemptions, documents are often produced with large sections blacked out as "exempt." And, because of a lack of manpower assigned to implement the act, there are often long delays in getting documents at all. Under the law, information is supposed to be produced within 20 days, but there is no effective enforcement mechanism when an agency misses this deadline, short of going to court.

### • *Making a request under FOIA*

There is no set format for making an FOIA request for documents. Although most agencies have adopted regulations describing specific steps to follow, any reasonably precise identification of the information sought, submitted to the proper person, will trigger an obligation for an agency to respond. Here are a few elementary steps to consider in making an FOIA request that may help avoid problems:

—Call the public information office of the agency you believe has the records before filing your request, to make sure you have the right agency and the right address for filing it. Ask if the information you are seeking could be released without a written FOIA request.

—Be as specific as possible about what you want. Give dates, titles, and authors for documents if you know them. In your letter, provide your telephone number, e-mail address, and offer to supply any other information that might help narrow the search.

—Even if you are using the letterhead stationery of a news organization, state specifically that you are a reporter for that organization and plan to use the material in news stories. The act does not require you to state your purpose, but disclosures in the public interest are eligible for fee waivers, exemption waivers and in some cases expedited handling.

—Request a waiver of search and copying fees. To avoid delays if the waiver is denied, also state a limit you are prepared to pay, such as $100, without the agency's need to obtain your prior, specific consent.

—If you want field office files checked as well as those at headquarters, be sure to request that specifically. Some agencies, such as the FBI, will not check beyond the office where the request is submitted, unless asked. It is often good practice to send a separate request directly to the FOI officer at the field office of an agency in any event, if you think relevant documents exist there.

—Ask the agency to cite specific exemptions for each item it withholds in the event that any part of the request is denied.

—Request that redacted copies of documents be provided if only a specific portion of a document is subject to an exemption.

—If your initial request is denied, file an administrative appeal. Some agencies take a very different view on appeal. The denial letter will specify to whom the appeal must be sent and the deadline for making an appeal. If you do not first pursue an administrative appeal, you cannot go to court to compel release of the information.

—An appeal can be made through a simple letter that explains why the public will benefit from disclosure and asks for a review of the grounds on which the request was denied. Several exemptions require a balancing effort between private and public interests, and reviewers on an administrative appeal may be more likely to exercise their right to waive an exemption if a good case for disclosure is made.

You may want to consult FOIA experts or manuals before proceeding with a request. An FOI Service Center is maintained by the Reporters Committee for Freedom of the Press. The committee publishes a pamphlet with sample FOIA letters and appeal forms as well as analyses of the act. (Available on the Web at: http://www.rcfp.org/foiact/index.html.) The committee maintains a toll-free hot line (800-336-4243), 24 hours a day, seven days a week, with attorneys available to provide FOIA advice to journalists.

The U.S. Department of Justice publishes an annual "Freedom of Information Case List" which reviews recent cases, contains up-to-date copies of the relevant statutes and, most important, the "Justice Department Guide to the FOIA," which gives the current government understanding of what is covered and not covered by each exemption. This document, published each September, is available for purchase from the Superintendent of Documents, U.S. Government Printing Office, Washington, DC 20402. (On the Web: http://www.usdoj.gov/04foia/index.html.)

It is advisable to check on specific state freedom of information laws. Each individual state also has its own freedom of information laws that apply to state and local government agencies.

## Issues concerning sources

For better or worse, some sources who possess important information of great public significance will speak to a journalist only if they are promised confidentiality. This has been true from the earliest history of an independent press in America. John Peter Zenger, whose New York trial in 1735 is best remembered for establishing the principle that truth must be a defense to a claim for libel, was also the first American newspaperman to establish the tradition that journalists will protect their sources to the point of imprisonment, refusing to divulge to British authorities the anonymous sources of material they claimed to be libelous.

The use of confidential sources remains an important means for reporters to uncover the news. Such sources make available to the public more than the sanitized "spin" of government and corporate press releases. Yale professor Alexander Bickel took note:

"Indispensable information comes in confidence from officeholders fearful of superiors, from businessmen fearful of competitors, from informers operating at the edge of the law who are in danger of reprisal from criminal associates, from people afraid of the law and government

— sometimes rightly afraid, but as often from an excess of caution — and from men in all fields anxious not to incur censure for unorthodox or unpopular views." ("The Morality of Consent," 1975.)

In one study of some 10,000 news reports conducted in 2005, fully 13 percent of the front-page newspaper articles reviewed were based, at least in part, on anonymous sources.

Promising confidentiality to a source always raises a number of issues, legal and journalistic. If a reporter refuses to identify a source, there is always the potential that a publisher may be hauled into court or a reporter thrown into jail. If a publisher is sued for libel, having a story based on sources that were promised confidentiality creates an entirely separate set of concerns: it is hard to prove the "truth" of a statement if the source of the information cannot be revealed. In one recent case, a Massachusetts court entered a default judgment against the Boston Globe for refusing to reveal its confidential source for a story that became the subject of a libel claim. A jury subsequently awarded the plaintiff $2.1 million.

### • *A promise to a source creates an enforceable agreement*

A reporter who reveals the name or identity of someone who was promised confidentiality can be held liable for breach of the agreement.

The Supreme Court decided just this issue in *Cohen v. Cowles Media Co.* (1991), a case involving "dirt" on one political candidate that was provided to a newspaper reporter on the eve of the election by a political consultant for the candidate's opponent. The reporter promised the consultant confidentiality. His editors, however, considered the identification of the source necessary for the public to weigh the significance of the new disclosures, and overruled the reporter. As a result, the no-longer confidential source lost his job, and sued. A jury verdict of $200,000 in favor of the spurned source was upheld by the Supreme Court, which found the First Amendment no defense to a claim for the damages caused by breaking a promise freely made.

The same result was reached by a New York court in a case involving a promise to mask someone's identity in a photograph. A journalist promised a man receiving treatment in an AIDS clinic that he would not be "identifiable" if he allowed his photograph to be taken. The journalist used a rear-angle setup and retouching techniques to obscure his identity, but the man's friends still recognized him when the photograph was published. The New York court held that the burden of carrying out the promise to disguise rested with the journalist who made the promise, and upheld the jury's award of damages to the patient.

Reporters can unwittingly create problems for themselves in making agreements with sources to protect confidentiality, or in failing to clarify with the source the meaning of an agreement. A few common-sense steps can minimize the risk that problems with sources will develop:

—Before making any promise, consider whether it is worth doing: How important is the information that the source is going to provide? Can the information be obtained or confirmed from any "on-the-record" source?

—If a promise of some protection is to be made, express it in terms of the steps that will be taken to protect the source rather than the result to be achieved. For example, promise a source to not use the name, or agree on how the source will be identified in the story (a "high ranking military officer," or a "knowledgeable Defense Department official"), rather than promising "no one will know you gave me this information." If a photograph or videotape is involved, the key is still to promise a specific action ("I will photograph you only from behind") rather than promising a result ("no one will recognize you").

—Make sure the source has the same understanding of the scope of the promise made, as you do. Avoid using ambiguous terms as a shorthand for an agreement, such as "this will be off the record," or this is "confidential." Instead, be specific about the terms of the agreement and how far the promise extends. Must confidentiality be maintained if litigation results? If a court order requires disclosure? Or, will the source allow disclosure in certain situations?

—Follow through with any agreement, making sure to inform editors and others who need to know to carry out the promise. The broader the promise, the more the effort needed to make sure that it is upheld.

The bottom line is this: promises of confidentiality or anonymity should be made cautiously, and only after a determination that the risk of such promises is outweighed by the need for the information. When a promise is made, make sure it is as precise as possible, and then make sure it is carried out.

### • *Reporter's privilege*

Given the importance of confidential sources, reporters have long asserted a right to protect the identity of those to whom confidentiality was promised. All states except Wyoming currently provide some level of protection for reporters who are called to testify about their sources. Thirty-one states and the District of Columbia have enacted "shield laws" that provide legal protection against the disclosure of sources; 18 additional states have recognized some form of a "reporter's privilege" through judicial decisions. About half of the state shield laws provide reporter's with an absolute privilege not to disclose confidential sources, while the remainder establish a high standard that must be met before a reporter's promise of confidentiality can be pierced.

The existence and scope of the reporter's privilege is more confused in federal courts. There is no federal shield law, and the Supreme Court has addressed the "reporter's privilege" only once — in a ruling that is far from clear.

In *Branzburg v. Hayes* (1972), the Supreme Court considered claims of privilege asserted by three journalists who had been subpoenaed to reveal confidential information and sources before grand juries investigating possible criminal activity. The reporters had written stories describing the synthesizing of hashish, conversations with admitted drug users, and eyewitness accounts of events at Black Panther headquarters at a time of civil unrest in the surrounding neighborhood. In each instance, the journalist claimed a privilege under the First Amendment not to answer questions concerning confidential information and sources.

A closely divided Supreme Court held in a 5-4 ruling that it did not violate the First Amendment to require these journalists to testify in the grand jury investigations, conducted in good faith, concerning the identities of persons allegedly engaged in criminal conduct. The court, however, did not reject altogether the notion of a First Amendment privilege. To the contrary, the majority opinion expressed the view that its narrow focus should not apply to "the vast bulk of confidential relationships between reporters and their sources," and emphasized that even grand juries "must operate within the limits of the First Amendment as well as the Fifth."

Justice Lewis Powell cast the decisive fifth vote and wrote separately to underscore further the "limited nature" of the court's holding. He explained that reporters would still have access to the courts, and could move to quash a subpoena if confidential source information were being sought "without a legitimate need of law enforcement."

Court decisions over the ensuing decades have embraced a qualified reporter's privilege that accommodates the interests of the press and those who seek to obtain information through judicial process. The United States Courts of Appeals in 10 of the 12 federal circuits have specifically applied the First Amendment reporter's privilege in civil lawsuits, and the remaining two circuits have not rejected the privilege in civil litigation.

Courts, however, have read *Branzburg* more restrictively in the criminal context, sometimes declining to recognize a privilege at all, or allowing only a very limited balancing of interests. Recently, three different federal appellate courts affirmed contempt citations requiring reporters to be jailed for refusing to reveal confidential sources sought in criminal investigations. In 2001, freelance writer Vanessa Leggett served nearly six months in a Texas prison for declining to reveal sources of information related to a notorious murder, almost four times longer than any prison term previously imposed on any reporter by any federal court. In 2004, James Taricani, a reporter for WJAR-TV in Rhode Island, completed a four-month sentence of home confinement for declining to reveal who leaked a videotape capturing alleged corruption by public officials in Providence. And, in 2005 The New York Times reporter Judith Miller was jailed in Virginia for several months for refusing to disclose her confidential source for a story she never wrote about CIA operative Valerie Plame.

These aggressive court actions in criminal investigations have encouraged private litigants and federal courts adjudicating their civil cases also to demand confidential information from reporters. In one civil suit, five reporters (including two Pulitzer Prize winners) were held in contempt and subjected to fines of $500 per day each for declining to reveal their confidential sources of information about Dr. Wen Ho Lee, who contended information about him was provided to reporters by government agents in violation of the Privacy Act.

While the state of the reporter's privilege in the federal courts is somewhat unsettled, reporters have one additional protection in federal criminal investigations in the form of Department of Justice guidelines that severely limit the circumstances under which U.S. attorneys may attempt to subpoena reporters. Adopted by Attorney General Elliot Richardson in the wake of the Watergate scandal, these guidelines remain in effect and are published in the Code of Federal Regulations at 28 C.F.R. 50.10. In general, the guidelines require:

—All reasonable attempts must be made to obtain the information sought from other sources before a subpoena to a reporter is even considered,

—Negotiations for the information should be pursued with the reporter before a subpoena is sought.

—No subpoena may be issued to a reporter without the personal approval of the attorney general.

—The attorney general's approval may not be sought unless the information held by the reporter is essential to the investigation and not available from other sources.

—Except in exigent circumstances, subpoenas should be used only to verify published information and to confirm the accuracy of the circumstances surrounding published information.

These regulations provide the same types of protection contained in some state shield laws, and the Department of Justice has demonstrated in the past a serious desire to enforce these regulations strictly. Any time a subpoena is received by a reporter from a U.S. attorney, the first question to ask the attorney is: Did you comply with the media guidelines at 28 C.F.R. 50.10 before issuing this subpoena? Not infrequently, just asking the question results in the subpoena being withdrawn.

## • *Policies and practices for handling subpoenas*

AP declines to provide any of its news stories and photos to non-subscribers without a valid subpoena. Although AP does not invite subpoenas, it advises litigants and government officials that it will accept service of validly issued subpoena narrowly requiring production of news stories and photos as they were transmitted, and will otherwise enforce its rights to resist disclosure to the full extent of the law.

Procedures for responding to a narrow subpoena for published material should be consistently applied, without taking sides, in order to preserve neutrality and objectivity, both in fact and in appearance. In appropriate cases, AP may provide a letter or affidavit authenticating a published story or photo, confirming that a fair and true copy has been provided of an item transmitted by AP on a particular date and time. Whenever possible, AP seeks reimbursement of its copying costs and other costs of compliance.

Subpoenas that go beyond published reports should be resisted routinely by AP reporters in order to avoid becoming perceived as an investigative arm of the government or private litigants. AP does not produce reporters' notes or photos or negatives which have not been moved, nor does it produce drafts or any editorial material, including internal memorandums concerning the newsgathering process. AP never reveals the identity of sources to which it has promised confidentiality.

AP does not invite sanctions by ignoring subpoenas. It will affirmatively oppose subpoenas that seek privileged work-product and unpublished information of every kind.

A couple of practical pointers that can avoid subpoena problems:

—Always avoid giving out information about stories to lawyers over the phone. Providing information may only whet a lawyer's appetite to serve a subpoena, and it can create an argument that grounds for objecting to a subpoena have somehow been waived. It is always better to refer any questions from lawyers to AP's lawyers in New York.

—Subpoenas from criminal defense attorneys seeking published, local news copy to demonstrate the extent of pretrial publicity can often be deflected by reminding the litigants that AP has no means of determining whether or which AP members used AP copy. The reliable sources for information about what was disseminated to the public are articles stored in news databases and video clips available from television stations and electronic "clipping" services.

### • *Liability for newsgathering conduct*

A reporter for Mother Jones won a national award in 1984 for posing as a job applicant at a chemical factory and covertly taking photographs documenting illegal pesticides being manufactured for the export market. That conduct today would more likely win a lawsuit.

In holding that a reporter's promise of confidentiality is legally binding, the Supreme Court in *Cohen v. Cowles Media, Co.* (1991) announced that "generally applicable" laws having only "incidental effects" on the ability of the press to gather the news do not offend the First Amendment. Ever since, a flow of lawsuits have been filed against reporters asserting claims for such "generally applicable" torts as intrusion, trespass, and fraud. From the muzzling effect of the tobacco industry's threat of "tortuous interference" liability against CBS for an expose based on a confidential source who was party to a standard confidentiality agreement as an employee of a tobacco company, through *Food Lion's* claim of trespass, fraud and breach of duty leveled against ABC and a spate of other hidden camera lawsuits, reporters since *Cohen v. Cowles Media*, have faced an increased number of claims alleging misconduct in the gathering of the news.

Some of the legal theories that can create problems for the unwary reporter.

### • *Intrusion upon seclusion*

A claim for intrusion exists in most states if someone intentionally commits a "highly offensive" intrusion upon another's solitude or seclusion, invading either a physical space or the private affairs of the plaintiff, such as reviewing private financial statements or personal e-mail without permission. Intrusion claims against the press most commonly arise in three contexts: (1) surreptitious surveillance; (2) trespass of private property, and (3) instances where consent to enter a private setting for one purpose has been exceeded (as where a reporter gains access to information under false pretenses).

Intrusion is a branch of the law of privacy. Where the potentially offending conduct occurs is therefore important. For example, a person generally has no legitimate basis to complain if a picture is taken in a public place, but if the picture is taken in or around the person's home, a claim for intrusion may exist if the person had a "reasonable expectation" of privacy where the photograph was taken.

In one noted lawsuit a few years back, the family of an officer of a large health care corporation successfully obtained an injunction against the elaborate efforts of a news organization that was seeking information about the family. The organization's camera crew followed the children to school, and sat in a boat outside the family's Florida home with a camera having a high-power telescopic lens. In issuing an injunction, the court concluded that "a persistent course of hounding, harassment and unreasonable surveillance, even if conducted in a public or semi-public place," could support a claim for intrusion upon seclusion.

A claim for intrusion generally requires (1) an intentional intrusion, (2) that impinges upon the solitude or seclusion of another, or his private affairs, and (3) that would be highly offensive to a reasonable person. The term "highly offensive" is ill-defined, but can include harassing behavior, surreptitious surveillance, or the use of high-power lenses and listening devices to invade typically private places.

The tort of intrusion is based on wrongful conduct rather than on the publication of any information, so a claim may exist even when the news story being pursued is never published. For this reason, in many states it is no defense to an intrusion claim to assert the newsworthiness of the information that was being sought. The issue is whether a reasonable person would view the conduct as highly offensive under all the circumstances.

Some examples where courts have upheld claims for intrusion illustrate the nature of the tort:

—Two journalists in California, without discussing who they were, gained access to the home of a disabled veteran who purported to provide healing aids in the form of clay, minerals and herbs. While there, they surreptitiously photographed and tape-recorded the veteran, for use in a magazine report. The court allowed a claim for intrusion even though the reporters were invited into the home by the veteran. While a person takes the risk that someone allowed into their home is not what he seems, and even though a visitor is free to repeat anything he sees or hears, the court held that the homeowner's risk does not extend to the risk that secret photographs and recordings will be transmitted to the world at large.

—The unauthorized recording of an unplanned interview conducted when the plaintiff answered his own front door has similarly been held to constitute an actionable "intrusion," while secretly recording an interview of a person who stepped from their home onto a public sidewalk was held not to be an intrusion.

—Televising an image of a person's home is not an intrusion if the broadcast shows no more than can be seen from the street, and secretly recording a conversation in a place of business was held not to be an intrusion if the reporter was invited into the office and the state wiretap law permitted the secret recording.

### • Trespass

A person commits a trespass by entering property that is in the possession of another, without authorization or consent. To avoid a claim, permission must be obtained by an owner, a tenant or someone acting on their behalf. Like intrusion, a trespass claim arises from conduct in gathering news, not from the content of any report that may subsequently be published.

Permission to be on private property can be implied by custom or by the nature of the premises. For example, someone has implied permission to enter a store or restaurant during business hours, even though it may be located on private property. There is similarly an implied right to approach someone's house on a driveway or sidewalk to see if they are home. Permission, whether express or implied, can also be revoked. If a posted sign says "Do Not Enter," or if the owner came to the door and said to leave, remaining on the property would be a trespass.

Trespass is also a strict liability tort. Entering on someone's property without permission, even by accident or mistake, will constitute a trespass. On the other hand, trespass protects only against a physical invasion of property; it does not limit the collection or use of information. The law of trespass does not restrict a reporter on a public sidewalk from using what can be seen or heard on the adjacent private property.

The impact of trespass on newsgathering is also tempered by the nature of the damages that may be recovered through a claim for trespass. The trespass tort is intended to protect property, not privacy or reputation. A trespasser therefore can be held responsible only for physical harm done while on the land and other injury that is a "natural consequence" of the trespass. Courts generally will not recognize injury to reputation or emotional distress caused by the later publication of a photograph obtained during a trespass to be a "natural consequence" of the trespass itself.

A vivid example of a trespass claim involved a television camera crew that was preparing a report on credit card fraud. The United States Secret Service obtained a warrant to search an apartment for evidence of credit card fraud, and a news magazine camera crew followed the Secret Service into the apartment. Part of the search was taped, including a sequence of a mother and child cowering on the couch asking not be photographed. In refusing to dismiss a lawsuit asserting claims for trespass and a constitutional tort (for improperly accompanying federal agents in executing a search warrant), an outraged court said the reporters "had no greater right than that of a common thief to be in the apartment." Like intrusion, the trespass was complete once the invasion of private property occurred. The trespass claim could be asserted even though the news report being pursued was never broadcast.

In situations rife with the potential for trespass, common sense can once again minimize the risk of litigation:

—Whenever possible, ask the property owner or those who appear to be in charge for permission to enter, or seek their approval to remain. In situations where police or fire officials have taken control of a crime or disaster scene, they may stand in for the owner and grant or deny access. Their presence does not defeat the owner's rights, however, and the owner can still require a reporter to leave private property.

—Always identify yourself — verbally, by displaying a press credential, and through insignias on clothing and cameras — so that those present know you are a reporter and will not assume you are part of any police or emergency response team. If not asked to leave, the very fact that your status as a reporter was disclosed may be sufficient to establish an implied consent to remain.

—If asked to leave, retire to the sidewalk, street, or other position on public property.

—Consent obtained through fraud or misrepresentation will not be considered valid consent and will not defeat a claim for trespass.

—Consent obtained from minors or others who are not legally capable of giving consent (mentally incapacitated people, for example) will not defeat a claim for trespass.

### • *Electronic eavesdropping*

Both state and federal law regulate the electronic recording of conversations, including telephone conversations.

Under the federal law, a conversation may not be recorded without the consent of at least one of the participants. That means reporters are not prohibited by federal law from recording any conversation that they participate in, whether or not they disclose that the conversation is being recorded. But, leaving a hidden tape recorder in a room to record a conversation between others, secretly listening in on an extension phone and recording the conversation, or recording a telephone call picked up on a scanner or listening device, is a violation of federal law if done without permission of one of the parties.

The law in most states is similar to the federal law, allowing a conversation to be recorded so long as one party to the conversation consents. The laws in a minority of states are more strict, and prohibit recording any conversation unless permission is given by all the parties to the conversation. States where the consent of all parties is required in order to record a conversation are: California, Connecticut, Florida, Illinois, Maryland, Massachusetts, Michigan, Montana, Nevada, New Hampshire, Pennsylvania, and Washington. This requirement extends only to conversations where there is some expectation of privacy, and does not prohibit tape-recording at speeches, press conferences and similar public events.

### • *Misrepresentation and similar forms of wrongdoing*

Laws of general applicability govern the actions of reporters, yet conduct that might sometimes be deemed "deceit," "misrepresentation" or "fraud" can be useful in ferreting out the news. Reporters are often less than candid in dealing with those from whom they want information. Recognizing this reality, some courts have held that claims such as fraud and misrepresentation cannot be pursued against journalists unless the wrong is "particularly egregious," or part of a broader pattern of wrongdoing. For example, courts have rejected claims for fraud based on a false message left on a telephone answering machine to induce the disclosure of information, and for fraudulently promising that no "ambush" techniques would be used if an interview were granted.

Other courts have been less willing to weigh the public interest in a news report against the allegedly wrongful conduct. In one instance, a judge allowed claims for fraud and breach of contract to proceed against Business Week after a reporter gained access to records of a credit reporting agency by misrepresenting that a subscription to the credit service was being sought in order to conduct background checks on potential Business Week employees. In reality, information was sought for an exposé on the credit-reporting industry, and the reporter promptly obtained the credit history of then-Vice President Dan Quayle without his consent. The court held that such "wanton misconduct" can result in liability, and allowed a recovery of the costs incurred by the credit agency as a result of the misrepresentation.

Remember, the basic rule says that reporters must obey rules and regulations when they are gathering the news. While there are some exceptions, the First Amendment will not generally provide a defense to a reporter whose conduct while gathering the news violates the law.

# LEGAL PRINCIPLES OF PUBLICATION

When a news report is published, the nature of its content poses three principal legal risks to a journalist: that the report contains incorrect information that harms someone's reputation, contains correct information that invades someone's privacy, or contains material that is subject to someone else's copyright. This section provides an overview of the law of libel, privacy and copyright infringement, by examining what a plaintiff is required to prove against news organizations to succeed on such claims and the defenses that are available.

## Defamation

In 1967, shortly after *New York Times v. Sullivan* was handed down, Associate Justice John Harlan remarked that "the law of libel has changed substantially since the early days of the Republic." Unfortunately, the news stories that still generate the most claims of injury to reputation – the basis of libel – are still the run-of-the-mill.

Perhaps 95 of 100 libel suits result from the routine publication of charges of crime, immorality, incompetence or inefficiency. A Harvard Nieman report makes the point: "The gee-whiz, slam-bang stories usually aren't the ones that generate libel, but the innocent-appearing, potentially treacherous minor yarns from police courts and traffic cases, from routine meetings and from business reports."

Most lawsuits based on relatively minor stories result from factual error or inexact language – for example, getting the plea wrong or inaccurately making it appear that all defendants in a case face identical charges. Libel even lurks in such innocent-appearing stories as birth notices and wedding announcements. Turner Catledge, former managing editor of The New York Times, noted in his autobiography, "My Life and the Times," that people sometimes would "call in the engagement of two people who hate each other, as a practical joke." The fact that some New York newspapers have had to defend suits for such announcements illustrates the care and concern required in every editorial department.

In publishing, no matter what level of constitutional protection, there is just no substitute for accuracy.

### • *What is libel?*

Libel is one side of the coin called "defamation," slander being the flip side. At its most basic, defamation means injury to reputation. Libel is generally distinguished from slander, in that a libel is written, or otherwise printed, whereas a slander is spoken. While defamation published in a newspaper universally is regarded as libel, it is perhaps not so self-evident that, in many states, defamation broadcast by television or radio also is considered libel, rather than slander: Because broadcast defamation is often recorded on tape and carried to a wide audience, it is viewed as more dangerous to reputation than a fleeting, unrecorded conversation, and so is classed with printed defamation. In any case, the term defamation generally includes both libel and slander. Words, pictures, cartoons, photo captions and headlines can all give rise to a claim for defamation.

The various states define libel somewhat differently, but largely to the same effect. In Illinois, for example, libel is defined by the courts as "the publication of anything injurious to the good name or reputation of another, or which tends to bring him into disrepute." In New York, a libelous statement is one that tends to expose a person to hatred, contempt or aversion or to induce an evil or unsavory opinion of the person in the minds of a substantial number of people in the community.

In Texas, libel is defined by statute as anything that "tends to injure a living person's reputation and thereby expose the person to public hatred, contempt or ridicule, or financial injury or to impeach any person's honesty, integrity, virtue, or reputation or to publish the natural defects of anyone and thereby expose the person to public hatred, ridicule, or financial injury."

### • *Liability for republication: the 'conduit' fallacy*

A common misconception is that one who directly quotes a statement containing libelous allegations is immune from suit so long as the quoted statement was actually made, accurately transcribed and clearly attributed to the original speaker. This is not so. In fact, the common law principle is just the opposite — a republisher of a libel is generally considered just as responsible for the libel as the original speaker. That you were simply an accurate conduit for the statement of another is no defense to a libel claim.

In many circumstances, therefore, a newspaper can be called to task for republishing a libelous statement made by someone quoted in a story. This rule can lead to harsh results and therefore exceptions exist. For example, reporting the fact that a plaintiff has filed a libel suit against a defendant could, in certain circumstances, lead to a claim against a newspaper for repeating the libel alleged in the complaint. In most states, a "fair report privilege" shields the publisher of an accurate and impartial report of the contents of legal papers filed in court to avoid this result.

Many states also recognize that newspapers under the pressure of daily deadlines often rely on the research of other reputable news organizations in republishing news items originally appearing elsewhere. In such cases, reliance on a reputable newspaper or news agency often is recognized as a defense to a libel claim. Of course, this so-called "wire service defense" may not be available if the republisher had or should have had substantial reason to question the accuracy or good faith of the original story.

The fair report privilege and the wire service defense are exceptions to the basic rule. When the press reports that X has leveled accusations against Y, the press may be held to account not only for the truth of the fact that the accusations were made, but also for the steps taken to verify the truth of the accusations. Therefore, when accusations are made against a person, it generally is prudent to investigate their truth as well as to obtain balancing comment with some relation to the original charges. Irrelevant countercharges can lead to problems with the person who made the first accusation.

In short, always bear in mind that a newspaper can be held responsible in defamation for republishing the libelous statement made by another, even when the quote is correct.

## • *The five things a successful libel plaintiff must prove*

Although the terminology may differ from state to state, a libel plaintiff suing a reporter or a news organization will have to prove five things in order to prevail on a claim for defamation:

1. A defamatory statement was made.
2. The defamatory statement is a matter of fact, not opinion.
3. The defamatory statement is false.
4. The defamatory statement is about ("of and concerning") the plaintiff.
5. The defamatory statement was published with the requisite degree of "fault."

By developing an understanding of the legal elements of a claim for libel, reporters and editors can fashion guideposts that will assist them in practicing their craft in a way that avoids wrongfully injuring the reputation of the subjects of their stories – and thereby to reducing the legal risk to the publications for which they write.

### 1. A defamatory statement was made

It may seem self-evident that a libel claim cannot exist unless a defamatory statement was made, but subjects of news stories (and their lawyers) often bring claims for libel without being able to demonstrate that what was written about them is capable of conveying a defamatory meaning. Put differently, not every negative news report is defamatory.

Generally, statements accusing someone of being a criminal, an adulterer, insane or infected with a loathsome disease are considered automatically "capable of defamatory meaning," as are statements that injure someone's professional reputation (such as that they are corrupt or incompetent). However, to determine whether any particular statement is susceptible of defamatory meaning, reference must be made, first, to the definition of libel adopted in the relevant state, and second, to the full context in which the challenged statement appeared when it was published.

For example, a New York court found that a statement identifying an attorney as a "flashy entertainment lawyer" was not, without more, defamatory, although a statement that a lawyer was an "ambulance chaser" with an interest only in "slam dunk" cases would be. The reasoning is that the first statement would not necessarily damage a lawyer's reputation, while the latter would. Likewise, in New York, allegations of drunkenness, use of "political clout" to gain governmental benefit, membership in the "Mafia," communist affiliation or that someone has cancer may or may not be defamatory, depending on the circumstances of the case.

In Illinois, courts make determinations about defamatory meaning on a case-by-case basis, though in Illinois, most statements will not be considered defamatory unless they charge a person with commission of a crime, adultery/fornication, or incompetence or lack of integrity in their business or profession. Under this approach, the statement that plaintiff left his children home at night and lost his job because of drinking was held to be defamatory as an accusation of child neglect and inability to discharge the duties of his job due to alcoholism. Similarly, reporting that an alderman had disclosed confidential information was held to be defamatory as indicating that the official lacked the integrity to properly discharge the duties of his office.

In Texas, a statement may be false, abusive and unpleasant without being defamatory. For example, a Texas court held that describing someone as resembling a "hard boiled egg," referring to baldness and pudginess, was not defamatory. Likewise, describing a political candidate as a "radical," "backed and financed by big-shot labor bosses" was not considered defamatory in Texas. On the other hand, an insinuation that a person is connected with gambling and prostitution was found to be defamatory. The assertion that a person who had made an allegation against another of child molestation had fabricated and since recanted the allegation was defamatory when no recantation had, in fact, been made.

While each potentially defamatory statement must be assessed in its own context, particular caution is in order where the statement involves allegations of crime or similar wrongdoing, incompetence or unprofessionalism, or infidelity.

## 2. The defamatory statement is a matter of fact, not opinion

To be actionable as libel, a defamatory statement must be provably false (or carry a provably false implication). Stated differently, only factual statements that are capable of being proven true or false can form the basis of a libel claim. "Opinions" that don't include or imply provably false facts cannot be the basis of a libel claim. Similarly, epithets, satire, parody and hyperbole that are incapable of being proven true or false are protected forms of expression.

The Supreme Court, in *Gertz v. Robert Welch Inc.* (1974), recognized a constitutional dimension to the prohibition of libel claims based on opinion, stating that "there is no such thing as a false idea." In a later case, *Milkovich v. Lorain Journal Co.* (1990), the Supreme Court denied that there is a distinct constitutional "opinion privilege," but held that any claim for libel must be based on a statement of fact that is provably false, thus shielding purely subjective opinions from liability. Under this approach, a statement is not protected "opinion" merely because it contains qualifying language such as "I think" or "I believe," if what follows contains an assertion of fact that can be proven true or false (e.g., "I believe he murdered his wife.").

Some examples of actual cases can provide a better sense of the distinction between an actionable false fact and a protected opinion:

In Virginia, "pure expressions of opinion" cannot be the basis of a claim for defamation. Under this standard, the statement "I wouldn't trust him as far as I could throw him" and the caption "Director of Butt-Licking" were held to be nonactionable opinion. The Virginia Supreme Court has found words charging that an architect lacked experience and charged excessive fees, or accusing a charitable foundation with failing to spend a "reasonable portion" of its income on program services, also to be protected opinions rather than to be verifiable facts.

In New York, the test for distinguishing a fact from an opinion asks whether: (1) the statement has a precise core of meaning on which a consensus of understanding exists; (2) the statement is verifiable; (3) the textual context of the statement would cause an average reader to infer a factual meaning; and (4) the broader social context signals usage as either fact or opinion. The first two factors focus on the meaning of the words used, the latter two factors consider whether the content, tone and apparent purpose of the statement should signal to the reader that the statement reflects the author's opinion.

Under these principles, calling a doctor a "rotten apple," for example, is incapable of being proved true or false and is therefore protected as an expression of opinion. Similarly, a statement that someone lacked "talent, ambition, initiative" is a nonactionable expression of opinion, since there is no provable, common understanding of what quantum of talent or ambition constitutes a "lack." In one New York case, a letter to the editor published in a scientific journal submitted by the International Primate Protection League and which warned that a multinational corporation's plans for establishing facilities to conduct hepatitis research using chimpanzees could spread hepatitis to the rest of the chimpanzee population was, given its overall context, protected as opinion.

Even when a fact is implicit in an opinion, the common law often protects the statement from liability. In many states, a statement of opinion based on true facts that are themselves accurately set forth is not actionable. Where the facts underlying the opinion are reported inaccurately, however, and would adversely affect the conclusion drawn by the average reader concerning the opinion expressed, the publication may give rise to a claim for libel. For example, the statement, "I believe he murdered his wife because he was found with a bottle of the same kind of poison that killed her," likely would not be actionable even if the plaintiff could prove he did not murder is wife *if* it is true that he was found with a bottle of the same kind of poison that killed her. The true facts on which the (erroneous) opinion was based were disclosed to the readers. If there was no bottle of poison, however, the suggestion that he was a murderer would certainly be actionable. If an opinion suggests or appears to rely on an undisclosed fact, however, a libel claim may still be brought upon the unstated, implied facts if they are both false and defamatory.

The statement that a sports commentator was a "liar" without reference to specific facts, under this approach, was considered to be protected opinion. Taken in the total context of an article, the statement that the plaintiff was "neo-Nazi" was protected as opinion. Likewise, a statement calling a plaintiff a "commie," suggesting that he does not understand the subject he teaches and that he is "not traveling with a full set of luggage," was also protected as opinion. Statements accusing doctors of being "cancer con-artists," of practicing "medical quackery," and of promoting "snake oil remedies," were also protected. A newspaper column and editorial characterizing a nudist pageant as "pornography" and as "immoral" were also protected.

A court in California held that three questions should be considered to distinguish opinion from fact: (1) does the statement use figurative or hyperbolic language that would negate the impression that the statement is serious? (2) does the general tenor of the statement negate the impression that the statement is serious? (3) can the statement be proved true or false?

Under this test, a commentator's statement that a product "didn't work" was not an opinion because, despite the humorous tenor of the comment, it did not use figurative or hyperbolic language, it could reasonably be understood as asserting an objective fact and the fact could be proven true or false. Likewise, a statement made in a newspaper interview that plaintiff was an "extortionist" was not protected as opinion.

The common thread to these variations is that opinions offered in a context presenting the facts on which they are based will generally not be actionable. On the other hand, opinions that imply the existence of undisclosed, defamatory facts (i.e., if you knew what I know) are more likely to be actionable. In addition, a statement that is capable of being proven true or false, regardless of whether it is expressed as an opinion, an exaggeration or hyperbole, may be actionable.

### 3. The defamatory statement is false

In almost all libel cases involving news organizations, the plaintiff has the burden of proving that the defamatory statement is false. (The states are divided on whether a purely private individual has to prove falsity when the defamatory statement does not involve a matter of public concern.) Nonetheless, as a practical matter, a libel defendant's best defense is often to prove that the statement is true. While this may sound like six-of-one-half-dozen-of-the-other, there is considerable significance to placing on the plaintiff the legal burden of proving falsity: Where a jury feels it cannot decide whether a statement is true or false because the evidence is mixed, it is required to rule against the plaintiff — ties go to the defendant.

In almost all states, the question is not whether the challenged statement is literally and absolutely true, in every jot and title, but whether the statement as published is "substantially true." That is, a court will consider whether the gist or sting of the defamatory statement is accurate, or whether the published statement would produce a different effect in the mind of a reader than would the absolutely true version.

For example, most courts will dismiss a libel claim brought by a person charged with second degree burglary, if a newspaper mistakenly reported that he had been charged with first degree burglary: The gist of the story (that the man is an accused burglar) is true, and most readers would not form a better opinion of the man had they been correctly informed that it was only second degree burglary with which he had been charged. But, where a newspaper mistakenly reports that the accused burglar has been charged with murder (or that a person thus far only accused of murder has been convicted of it), a court might well conclude that the "sting" of the statement is not substantially accurate, and that readers would think less of the person based on the false statement than they would have had the published report been accurate.

### 4. The defamatory statement is about the plaintiff

Since the law of libel protects the reputation of an individual or a business entity, only the individual or entity whose reputation has been injured is entitled to complain. Thus, a libel plaintiff must prove that the defamatory statement was "of and concerning" the plaintiff. It often is obvious whether a statement is about a particular person (for example, because it gives his or her full name, place of residence and age). But even where no name is used, a libel claim may be brought if some readers would reasonably understand the statement to be about the plaintiff. For example, the statement referring to "the woman who cooks lunch at the diner," when there is only one woman who cooks at that diner, will be considered "of and concerning" the female cook.

In a recent Illinois case, a news report on the commencement of a murder trial referred to the defendant as "suburban car dealer John Doe." While "John Doe" was indeed on trial for murder, he was not a suburban car dealer. His brother, "Joe Doe," was a suburban car dealer, but was not on trial for murder. The court concluded that reasonable readers could have understood the report to be about Joe (despite the fact that Joe's name was never mentioned, while John's was correctly used), and that Joe therefore would have the opportunity to show the statement was understood to be "of and concerning" him.

A few words about "group libel." Where a statement impugns a group of persons, but no individual is specifically identified, no member of the group may sue for libel if the group is large. For example, the statement, in a large city, that "all cab drivers cheat their customers out of money," does not allow any cab driver to sue for libel as a result, no matter how many fares the plaintiff cab driver may have lost because of the published statement. But, beware of publishing the same statement in a newspaper in a town with only a handful of cab drivers, where a court might well conclude the readers would reasonably think the statement was specifically referring to each of the town's four cab drivers, despite the absence of their names in the statement. Some courts have questioned whether the First Amendment permits claims for group libel under any circumstances, because the Supreme Court has said that the requirement that the statement be "of and concerning" the plaintiff is constitutionally required.

Finally, a word about the dead: It is mostly correct that you cannot defame the dead. Again, because libel protects personal reputation, and one has no practical need for a good personal reputation in this world after one has departed it, most states do not permit a person's survivors to bring a claim for statements made after the person's death.

### 5. The defamatory statement was published with the requisite degree of fault

For almost 200 years, libel in this country was a tort of strict liability. It did not matter whether the defendant was at fault or had acted in some improper way. The mere fact that a libel was printed was sufficient to establish liability

*New York Times v. Sullivan* changed everything. In that case the Supreme Court first recognized the constitutional requirement that a public official must demonstrate not only that an error was made, but also a high degree of fault by the publisher in order to prevail on a libel claim. This additional burden was required under the First Amendment, the court said, in order to provide the "breathing room" for the exercise of free speech that is essential to public discussion by citizens on matters concerning their self-government.

The court considered the *Sullivan* case "against the background of a profound national commitment to the principle that debate on public issues should be uninhibited, robust and wide-open, and that it may well include vehement, caustic and sometimes unpleasantly sharp attacks on government and public officials."

The ruling in *Sullivan* with respect to libel claims by public officials was extended three years later to libel claims by public figures, in *The Associated Press v. Walker*. The court reversed a $500,000 libel judgment won by former Maj. Gen. Edwin A. Walker in a Texas state court against the AP, after it had reported that Walker "assumed command" of rioters at the University of Mississippi and "led a charge of students against federal marshals" when James H. Meredith was admitted to the university in September 1962. Walker alleged those statements to be false.

In ruling for the AP, the Supreme Court found: "Under any reasoning, Gen. Walker was a public man in whose public conduct society and the press had a legitimate and substantial interest." It therefore held that Walker, too, was required to prove fault by the publisher even though he was not a public official.

The rulings in *Sullivan* and *Walker* cases were landmark decisions for freedom of the press and speech. They established safeguards not previously defined, but they did not provide news organizations with absolute immunity against libel suits by officials who are criticized. Rather, they stand for the principle that, to encourage public debate on matters of public concern, when a newspaper publishes information about a public official and publishes it without actual malice, it should be spared a damage suit even if some of the information turns out to be wrong.

The *Walker* decision made an additional important distinction concerning the context in which an article is prepared. In a companion case consolidated before the Supreme Court, Wallace Butts, former athletic director of the University of Georgia, had obtained a libel verdict against Curtis Publishing Co. His suit was based on an article in the Saturday Evening Post accusing Butts of giving his football team's strategy secrets to an opposing coach prior to a game between the two schools.

The Supreme Court found that Butts was a public figure, but said there was a substantial difference between the two cases. Unlike the AP report on the actions of Walker, "the Butts story was in no sense "hot news" and the editors of the magazine recognized the need for a thorough investigation of the serious charges. Elementary precautions were, nevertheless, ignored."

Chief Justice Earl Warren, in a concurring opinion, referred to "slipshod and sketchy investigatory techniques employed to check the veracity of the source" in the Butts case. He said the evidence disclosed "reckless disregard for the truth."

The differing outcomes against The Associated Press and the Saturday Evening Post should be noted carefully. Although both involved public figures who were required to establish "actual malice," the evidence required to make this showing differed in the context of a "hot news" report from investigative reporting.

By 1974, in *Gertz v. Robert Welch, Inc.*, the Supreme Court had extended the requirement that a libel plaintiff show some fault on the part of the defendant to include all defamation claims against news organizations, although not all types of plaintiffs must show the highest degree of fault. The level of "fault" that a plaintiff must prove will vary depending on who the plaintiff is.

### • Fault required for public officials and public figures

If the plaintiff is a public official or public figure, the plaintiff must establish by clear and convincing evidence that the publication was made with "actual malice," an unfortunate choice of phrase by the Supreme Court for a concept that might better have been called "constitutional fault," since the standard has little to do with whether a reporter harbored spite or ill will against the plaintiff.

The court has explained that "actual malice" means publication with knowledge that a statement is false, or in reckless disregard for whether it is true or false. The concept of "knowing falsity" is easy to understand. "Reckless disregard" has required further elaboration by the courts, which have described it as publication of a statement "with a high degree of awareness of its probable falsity." Put differently, a reporter may act with reckless disregard for truth if he or she publishes despite holding serious doubts about the truth of the published statement.

The test for actual malice thus looks to the subjective state of mind of the reporter/publisher at the time of publication. It inquires into whether the reporter or publisher believed the statement was false or whether they proceeded to publish despite recognizing that there was a good chance that the statement was false. Because most reporters and publishers are not in the business of publishing news reports unless they have good grounds to believe them to be true, generally speaking, it is difficult for a plaintiff to show that a newspaper published a story with actual malice.

As one Illinois court phrased it, actual malice is shown only when a reporter's investigation "has revealed either insufficient information to support the allegations in good faith or information which creates substantial doubt as to the truth of published allegations."

Thus, as interpreted by most states, "actual malice" cannot be proven simply by showing that a reporter made mistakes (either by getting facts wrong or by failing to talk to one or more key sources), or that the reporter disliked the plaintiff, or that the newspaper frequently published items critical of the plaintiff. Rather, the test focuses on whether the reporter in fact disbelieved, or strongly doubted the truth of, the published statement. In some cases, plaintiffs may establish actual malice if they can show that a reporter willfully turned a blind eye to the truth and, if acting in good faith, would have known that the statement was false.

### • Fault required for private individuals

Under the First Amendment, even private individuals must show some degree of fault before they can recover for a libel by a news organization in a report on a matter of public concern. States are free to set the standard of care that must be met in reporting on private individuals, so long as they require at least a showing of negligence.

Most states have decided to adopt the minimum standard and require a private libel plaintiff to show only that a reporter was negligent. That means the plaintiff must show that the reporter's conduct was less careful than one would expect of a reasonable journalist in similar circumstances. In Texas and California, for example, the question in a private figure libel case is whether the defendant should have known, through the exercise of reasonable care, that a statement was false.

The courts have looked at a number of factors to evaluate whether "negligence" exists. The considerations include:

—Did the reporter follow the standards of investigation and reporting ordinarily adhered to by responsible publishers. In many libel cases plaintiffs will use "expert" witnesses to testify about what are the "acceptable journalistic practices."

—Did the reporter follow his or her own normal procedures? Any time that you do something differently from what you usually do in reporting a story — particularly if the change involves exercising less care, rather than more care — you'd better have a good explanation for why that was done.

—Did the reporter have any reason to doubt the accuracy of a source, or any advance warning that the story might not be right? Was it possible to find out the truth? This — like many of the factors the courts consider — is a matter of common sense. If you have received information that just doesn't ring true to you, and it is something that is easily checked, check it out before you run with the story!

—How *much* did the reporter do to check out the facts? Did the reporter take steps to confirm the information received, or simply run with the story without checking it out?

—Who are your sources of information? Are they reliable, and objective — or known "flakes" or people with a clear ax to grind? Are they anonymous sources? How many independent sources do you have (and how do they know the information they are giving you)?

Some courts set different fault levels for private figures depending on whether the publication at issue involved a matter of "public concern" or of "private concern." New York, for example, has held that if the plaintiff is a private individual involved in a matter of legitimate public concern, the plaintiff must establish by a preponderance of the evidence that the publication was made in a "grossly irresponsible" manner without due regard for the standards of information gathering and dissemination ordinarily followed by responsible parties involving similar matters. In cases involving matters of private concern, New York, too, applies a negligence standard, although New York courts typically defer to the press in determining what constitutes a matter of "public concern" (and thus the vast majority of New York private figure cases apply the "gross irresponsibility" standard).

Finally, a handful of states apply the actual malice standard to all libel cases, regardless of the plaintiff's status. These states include Alaska, Colorado, Indiana, and New Jersey.

### • *Who is who?*

Being able to determine whether the subject of a news story is a public official or figure or a private figure bears directly on the amount of legal risk posed by the story.

While it is clear that not every government employee will be considered a public official for purposes of what they must prove in a libel case, the Supreme Court has yet to lay down definitive standards. Thus, the definition varies somewhat from state to state.

In New York, public officials are those who are elected or appointed to office and who appear to have substantial responsibility for control over public and governmental affairs. Judges, police officers, state troopers and corrections officers have all been held to be public officials under this standard. Similarly, in California, a public official is one who has, or appears to the public to have, substantial responsibility for or control over the conduct of governmental affairs. In California, people found to be public officers have included a police officer, an assistant public defender, and an assistant district attorney.

Texas, in contrast, looks to the following criteria are relevant to determine whether a libel plaintiff is a public official: (1) the public interest in the public position held by the plaintiff; (2) the authority possessed by the plaintiff to act on behalf of a government entity; (3) the amount of governmental funds controlled by the plaintiff; (4) the number of employees the official supervises; (5) the amount of contact between the plaintiff and the public, and (6) the extent to which the plaintiff acts in a representative capacity for the governmental entity or has any direct dealings with the government.

Under this standard, (1) a county sheriff, (2) a Child Protective Services specialist with authority to investigate charges of child abuse, remove children from their homes and place them in foster care, (3) an undercover narcotics agent employed by the state's law enforcement agency, (4) a ranking officer in charge of a narcotics squad of four men, (5) an individual who was a high school athletic director, head football coach and teacher, (6) an assistant regional administrator of a branch office of the Securities and Exchange Commission and (7) a part-time city attorney have all been found to be public officials.

But under the same Texas test, the following people were found not to be public officials: (1) a high school teacher; (2) a prominent member of two private organizations affiliated with a state university; (3) a former special counsel for a court of inquiry into county fund management; (4) a court reporter; and (5) an appointed justice of the peace (where the article appeared in a city where plaintiff was not justice of the peace and did not refer to plaintiff's official capacity).

While, at least at higher ranks, it is relatively easy to identify public officials, both reporters and the courts have confronted substantial difficulty in the area of public figures, particularly in separating those who are merely socially or professionally prominent from those who, because of their influence over public matters, are properly considered public figures for libel purposes.

For example, the 1976 case of *Time v. Firestone* stemmed from Time magazine's account of the divorce of Russell and Mary Alice Firestone. The magazine said she had been divorced on grounds of "extreme cruelty and adultery." The court made no finding of adultery. She sued. The former Mrs. Firestone was a prominent social figure in Palm Beach, Fla., and held press conferences in the course of the divorce proceedings. Yet, the Supreme Court said she was not a public figure because "she did not assume any role of special prominence in the affairs of society, other than perhaps Palm Beach society, and she did not thrust herself to the forefront of any particular public controversy in order to influence resolution of the issues involved in it."

Similarly, Sen. William Proxmire of Wisconsin was sued for $8 million by Ronald Hutchinson, a research scientist who had received several public grants, including one for $50,000. Proxmire gave Hutchinson a "Golden Fleece" award, saying Hutchinson "has made a fortune from his monkeys and in the process made a monkey of the American taxpayer." Hutchinson sued. The Supreme Court held in 1979 that, despite the receipt of substantial public funds, Hutchinson was not a public figure because he held no particular sway over the resolution of matters of public concern.

Note also the case of Ilya Wolston, who pleaded guilty in 1957 to criminal contempt for failing to appear before a grand jury investigating espionage. A book published in 1974 referred to these events. Wolston alleged that he had been libeled. In ruling on *Wolston v. Reader's Digest*, the Supreme Court said that he was not a public figure. The court said people convicted of crimes do not automatically become public figures. Wolston, the court said, was thrust into the public spotlight unwillingly, long after the events of public concern had ended. (But, the Supreme Court also has said, in a different context, that allegations of criminal activity by public officials, no matter how far in the past the conduct may have occurred, is always relevant to their fitness for public office.)

At bottom, although the Supreme Court has yet to definitively resolve the issue, the point appears to be that public figures are those who seek the limelight, who inject themselves into public debate, and who seek to influence public opinion. A person who has widespread influence over public opinion on many matters may be deemed a "general purpose public figure" and required to prove actual malice no matter the subject of a particular allegedly defamatory statement. Oprah Winfrey is an example of someone who likely would be deemed a general purpose public figure.

A person who seeks to influence public opinion in only one area (such as, for example, by leading a campaign to enact animal rights legislation), however, may be deemed a "limited purpose public figure" and required to prove actual malice only with respect to allegedly defamatory statements about his or her animal rights activities. Limited purpose public figures have included: a prominent attorney; religious groups; a belly dancer; and a "stripper for God," among others.

Texas courts generally ask three questions in order to determine whether someone is a limited purpose public figure: (1) is the controversy truly a public controversy? (i.e., (a) are people talking about the controversy and (b) are people other than those immediately involved in the controversy likely to feel the impact of its resolution?); (2) does the plaintiff have more than a trivial or tangential role in the controversy?; (3) is the alleged defamation relevant to the plaintiff's participation in the controversy? Under this standard, an abortion protester on a public street in the vicinity of an abortion clinic was considered a limited purpose public figure, as was a zoologist who appeared on television shows and gave interviews on his controversial work.

On the other hand, a public school teacher whose participation in public controversy did not exceed that which she was required to do by school district regulations (except that she responded to media inquiries), was not a public figure in California. Similarly, a corporation which conducted a closeout sale for a landmark department store was not a public figure simply because it was doing business with a party to a controversy.

A note on corporations: In many states, the same standards that determine whether an individual is a public figure apply to corporations. Some states, however, conclude that corporations are always public figures, while others apply a narrower standard. For example, a British corporation that did not deal in consumer goods and had not received significant past publicity was a private figure for the purposes of a Texas libel claim.

In addition, a few lower courts have embraced the concept of an "involuntary public figure," in which an otherwise private person becomes a public figure by virtue of his or her having become drawn into a significant public controversy.

While this area of the law is freighted with subtleties to which lawyers and judges devote considerable energy, the practical bottom line is that, while public officials and public figures always bear a high burden of proof in making out a libel claim, where a news story concerns a private individual, whether involved in a matter of public concern or not, his or her burden is likely to be lower, perhaps much lower, if the story is wrong. Accordingly, there are more legal risks to publishing reports about private individuals (especially where the matter is not of legitimate public concern).

## • Defenses commonly available to news organizations

Where a news story is written in such a way that a plaintiff might be able to prove all five of the elements of a libel, the law nevertheless affords defenses to news organizations in certain circumstances. Among the most prominent are the "fair comment privilege," the "fair and accurate report privilege," and the "neutral report privilege." They are referred to as privileges because, where properly invoked, a news organization is "privileged" to print what otherwise would be an actionable libel.

### 1. Fair comment

The fair comment (sometimes, "fair criticism") privilege long predates the opinion doctrine and continues, in most states, to exist as an independent matter of state law. The right of fair comment has been summarized as follows: "Everyone has a right to comment on matters of public interest and concern, provided they do so fairly and with an honest purpose. Such comments or criticism are not libelous, however severe in their terms, unless they are written maliciously. Thus it has been held that books, prints, pictures and statuary publicly exhibited, and the architecture of public buildings, and actors and exhibitors are all the legitimate subjects of newspapers' criticism, and such criticism fairly and honestly made is not libelous, however strong the terms of censure may be." (*Hoeppner v. Dunkirk Pr. Co.*, 1930.)

Some states, such as Texas, have recognized the fair comment privilege as a matter of statutory law. The Texas statute protects reasonable and fair comment or criticism of the official acts of public officials and of other matters of public concern when published for general information.

Not all states recognize this privilege, and the specifics of its application vary among the states that do recognize it. But where an otherwise potentially libelous story is important to the public interest, careful consideration of whether this privilege might protect publication of the report may be appropriate.

### 2. Fair and accurate report

Under this privilege, a fair and accurate report of a public proceeding (such as a city council hearing) or document (such as a pleading filed in court) generally cannot be the basis of a libel suit.

Pursuant to the Texas fair report statute, for example, the privilege applies to "a fair, true and impartial account" of: (a) judicial proceedings; (b) an official proceeding to administer the law; (c) all executive and legislative proceedings; and (d) the proceedings of public meetings dealing with public purposes. New York and several other states likewise have created the privilege by statute along similar lines; in some states, the privilege is a product of judge-made law.

In order to qualify for the privilege in the states that recognize it, the account must be both substantially accurate and fair. This does not mean the newspaper is required to publish a verbatim account of an official proceeding or the full text of a government document, but any abridgement or synopsis must be substantially accurate and fairly portrayed. Where it applies, the privilege relieves a news organization of responsibility for determining the underlying truth of the statements made by the participants in these contexts, precisely because the very fact that the comments were made in an official proceeding is newsworthy regardless of whether the statements are actually true.

It bears emphasis, however, this privilege is limited to statements made in the contexts defined under state law, and it behooves practitioners to learn the particulars of the privilege in the states in which they practice journalism.

Statements made by government officials outside of official proceedings (e.g., statements by police or a prosecutor or an attorney on the courthouse steps), or in documents that have not been officially made part of the government record (e.g., a draft pleading provided by a lawyer that has not yet been filed with the court) may or may not qualify as privileged, depending on what state you are in and on the circumstances in which the statements are made. Some states only extend the privilege to such out of court statements if made by specified top officials. At least one New York trial court, however, has applied this fair report privilege to a news report based on information provided "off the record" by police sources.

In New York and some other states, court rules provide that the papers filed in matrimonial actions are sealed and thus not open to inspection by the general public. It is not clear whether the fair report privilege will attach to publication of the contents of such papers, which by court rule, or order of the judge, are to be kept confidential.

In one case where this very situation arose, the vice president of a company filed a libel suit in New York alleging that he was fired because a newspaper published his wife's charges of infidelity set forth in divorce proceedings. The newspaper responded that its report was a true and fair account of court proceedings. The New York Court of Appeals rejected that argument on grounds that the law makes details of marital cases secret because spatting spouses frequently make unfounded charges.

The lesson of this case is that information gleaned from "confidential" court documents might not be covered under the fair report privilege. In such a case, the paper will be put to the test of proving that it made a reasonable effort to determine the truth of the allegations before publishing them.

There are other "traps" to be aware of when relying on this privilege. For example, statements made on the floor of convention sessions or from speakers' platforms organized by private organizations may not be privileged under the fair report privilege. Strictly speaking, conventions of private organizations are not "public and official proceedings" even though they may be forums for discussions of public questions.

Similarly, while statements made by a governor in the course of executive proceedings have absolute privilege for the speaker (even if false or defamatory), the press' privilege to report all such statements is not always absolute. For example, after a civil rights march, George Wallace, then governor of Alabama, appeared on a television show and said some of the marchers were members of communist and communist-front organizations. He gave some names, which newspapers carried. Some libel suits resulted.

### 3. Neutral reportage

Once viewed as a promising development in the law likely to spread across most states, the advancement of the neutral report privilege has not proceeded as once anticipated. Many states have declined to consider whether the privilege should exist, while others have rejected it outright (most recently, in Pennsylvania in 2005). Where recognized, the neutral report privilege protects a fair, true and impartial account of newsworthy statements, regardless of whether the reporter knows or believes those statements to be true, if the statements have been made by prominent and typically responsible persons or organizations. The rationale is that some statements are newsworthy, and should receive public attention just because of who has made them.

Thus, for example, a news report concerning a statement by Michael Jordan concerning corruption in basketball, or by the NAACP regarding discrimination committed by a business, likely would be privileged as a neutral report, even if it should later turn out that Jordan or the NAACP was mistaken, since the mere leveling of charges by such prominent sources typically is of public concern.

Significantly, the privilege, where it exists, does not apply when the author of an article goes beyond reporting the fact the statements made and espouses or adopts the charges as the author's own.

California is one of the few states to recognize the neutral report privilege. There, the privilege is available when the plaintiff is a public figure, the defamatory statement is made by one who is a party to a public controversy and the publication is accurate and neutral. One California court applying the privilege found that a newspaper's account of an accusation that a police officer had improperly obtained a false confession to a crime from a person later released as innocent was not actionable where the newspaper also printed the officer's denial of the charge.

In some states, courts appear to have applied the principle without naming the privilege as such. In one 1997 case in Texas, the court held that a story that accurately reported that parents of school children had accused a school teacher of physically threatening and verbally abusing their children was substantially true regardless of whether the parents' allegations themselves were accurate. Similarly, in Illinois, a federal appeals court in 2004 held that several stories that accurately reported that a charitable organization was the target of a federal investigation into terrorism funding were not actionable because the fact that the organization was under investigation was true, regardless of whether it was actually guilty of funding terrorism.

New York state courts do not recognize a privilege for neutral reportage, though a federal court in New York has actually found a neutral reportage privilege grounded in the U.S. Constitution. As the federal court described the neutral report privilege in that case, "when a responsible, prominent organization ... makes serious charges against a public figure, the First Amendment protects the accurate and disinterested reporting of those charges, regardless of the reporter's private views regarding their validity." (*Edwards v. National Audubon Society*, 1977.)

## • *Summary of practical points*

Although every AP story is expected to be accurate and fair, stories that involve negative reports about individuals or companies warrant particular attention. When evaluating such a story, it usually is prudent to ask these questions:

1. Are any statements in the story capable of defamatory meaning? In this regard pay close attention to the use of certain "red flag" words that may sound more negative (and thereby more defamatory) than if a different, but similar, word had been chosen. Words such as "fraud," "crony," "linked," "suspicious," and "contaminated" may suggest or imply bad conduct or have criminal connotations (like: "connected" to the Mafia or organized crime). Careful editing can ensure that the facts get reported without the use of "buzz words" that may trigger a libel claim.

—Remember that the fact that police are questioning someone about a crime does not necessarily justify the label suspect. Witnesses are obviously also questioned about a crime.

2. Are those statements ones of fact (capable of being proven true or false), or protected as opinion, or simply rhetorical hyperbole that no reasonable reader would understand as a statement of fact?

3. Could someone reading the report reasonably understand it to be about a specific person, whether or not the person is actually named? Could readers understand it to be about more than one person – the person we intend, but also someone else?

—Remember to be careful of descriptive phrases that may give rise to cases of mistaken identity. A report that "an elderly janitor for a local school" was arrested could lead to suits from every elderly janitor in the school district.

4. Could you prove that the statements in question are true (and do so without violating promises to any confidential sources)?

5. If it turns out that you have the facts wrong, would a jury think you did not do something that any reasonable journalist would have done to get it right?

6. Assuming there is some possibility that the first five questions could be answered in the plaintiff's favor, is there a privilege that nevertheless justifies proceeding to publish? For example, is the report a fair and accurate report of an official government proceeding or document?

—If a privilege applies, remember that the privilege does not remove the need for careful reporting and the use of editorial judgment. In many cases, courts have held that it is up to the jury to decide whether a particular publication was a fair and accurate report or whether there was "actual malice."

Headlines, photos and captions must be as accurate and objective as news stories. Remember that each of these elements of a story can also give rise to claims of libel.

### • Corrections and retraction demands

A correction acknowledges an error in a story and sets the record straight. Published studies have shown that lawsuits against the press can sometimes be avoided if requests for corrections or clarifications are dealt with seriously, promptly and fairly. Anyone making a retraction demand should be dealt with courteously, and the request should be communicated promptly to the appropriate editor.

Do not be too hasty in drafting a correction, however. It is important to ensure that the correction is actually warranted, that it corrects all aspects of the story that may need correction, and that the correction itself is accurate. Some states have "retraction statutes" that limit the damages a plaintiff can recover or provide other benefits if an error is corrected when brought to the attention of the publisher. You should be aware of any legal requirement in your state setting a time within which a correction must appear.

Transmitting a corrective does not necessarily safeguard the AP against legal action. In fact, transmission of a corrective may itself have legal consequences because it formally acknowledges an error. Because of potential legal implications, a news manager or supervisor in New York needs to approve all correctives and clarifications, before they are transmitted.

Any time that a kill or corrective is filed, it is crucial to ensure that it is transmitted on all wires that transmitted that original report. In addition, the bureau chief or news editor must prepare and maintain a file containing:

1. Wire copy of the original story and of the kill or corrective that was sent.

2. Wire copy of the substitute story, corrective or clarification filed.

3. A copy of any source material used by the writer or editor in preparation of the story, including member clip, reporter's notes and the like.

In addition, a factual e-mail stating why the story was killed or corrected should be sent to the New York manager designated to handle correctives. This statement should be prepared either by the bureau chief or the news editor, in consultation with the staff members involved. If legal action is a possibility, this explanation should not be prepared without prior consultation with a deputy managing editor.

The statement should include relevant details, such as any contact with outsiders on the matter. The letter should be a factual report of what happened. It is not the place for extraneous comments about staff members or bureau procedures. Nor is it the place for apologies, nor any legal or factual speculation or conclusions.

Do not make any response to any letter or other communication in connection with any case where legal action seems possible, especially if a lawyer is involved, without first seeking advice from AP's lawyers in New York.

### • Document preservation and discovery

A 1979 Supreme Court ruling, *Herbert v. Lando*, has had a significant impact on what materials a libel plaintiff can compel a news organization to disclose. The case ruled that retired Army Lt. Col. Anthony Herbert, a Vietnam veteran, had the right to inquire into the editing process of a CBS "60 Minutes" segment, produced by Barry Lando, which provoked his suit. Herbert had claimed the right to do this so that he could establish actual malice.

The decision formalized and called attention to something that was at least implicit in *New York Times v. Sullivan*: that a plaintiff had the right to try to prove the press was reckless or even knew that what it was printing was a lie. How else could this be done except through inquiry about a reporter's or editor's state of mind?

Despite an admonition in *Herbert v. Lando* that lower courts should carefully monitor (and, if necessary, reign in) discovery in libel cases, reporters and publications involved in libel suits are often forced to expend significant time and resources on discovery concerning their newsgathering, writing and editing activities.

Different reporters follow different practices about retaining their notes. There are potential litigation advantages and disadvantages from following a policy of either keeping notes for a number of years or disposing of notes as soon as they are no longer needed for reporting. The best practice is the one that best advances a reporter's journalistic goals. Whatever practice you follow, however, should be followed uniformly. A difficult issue is presented in litigation if a reporter generally keeps notes, but just doesn't happen to have the notes for a disputed story. Similarly, a reporter who never keeps notes, but happens to save them for a story that ends in litigation, can send a message that the story posed some unique concerns. Adopt a policy and follow it consistently.

Of course, once a lawsuit arrives, no documents should be destroyed, regardless of your usual practice. At that point any notes and drafts are potential evidence and their destruction, with knowledge of the lawsuit, may be illegal.

## • *Motions practice*

If litigation arises, lawyers for a reporter will often seek to dispose of the claims without the necessity of a trial. A number of issues, such as whether a story is "of and concerning" the plaintiff or conveys the defamatory meaning alleged, can often be decided by a judge as a matter of law before any litigation discovery begins.

Courts also can impose "summary judgment" dismissing a case at any point when the evidence developed by the parties demonstrates that the plaintiff's claims are legally defective. A judge may not enter summary judgment if it rests on any facts in dispute. Only the jury may decide disputed issues of fact.

In a 1986 decision, *Anderson v. Liberty Lobby*, the Supreme Court held that summary judgment should be granted in libel actions against public officials and public figures unless the plaintiff can prove actual malice with "convincing clarity" or by "clear and convincing evidence." This rule further facilitates the dismissal of unmeritorious claims without the expense and burden of proceeding to trial.

## • *Trials and damages*

The huge jury verdicts that often result in libel cases have caused much concern among legal commentators and the press. A number of remedies have been proposed, including statutory caps on both compensatory and punitive damages. A 1996 non-press Supreme Court case, holding that some excessive damage verdicts might violate the Constitution, holds out some possible promise of relief.

The Supreme Court addressed libel damages in *Gertz v. Robert Welch, Inc.* (1974), and held that in private figure cases, where "actual malice" has not been proven, any award of damages must be supported by competent evidence, represent compensation only for actual damages, must not be "presumed," and must not be punitive. "Actual damages," however, may include compensation for injury to reputation and standing in the community, personal humiliation, and mental anguish and suffering -- all items to which a jury assigns a dollar value. In cases where a plaintiff has proved "actual malice," he or she may also recover "presumed" and "punitive" damages.

While the First Amendment imposes severe restrictions on libel claims, and court rules encourage the dismissal of meritless cases at the earliest point, litigation can be a long, expensive, and disruptive process. The key to avoiding the distraction of litigation is always to remember AP's credo: Get it fast, but get it right.

## • *Invasion of privacy*

The roots of the right of privacy are often traced to an article titled "The Right to Privacy" that appeared in the Harvard Law Review in 1890, and was co-authored by Louis D. Brandeis, who later became a Supreme Court justice. The article asserted that the press of the day was "overstepping in every direction the obvious bounds of propriety and decency," and urged courts to recognize a distinct cause of action that would protect the individual's "right of privacy." As a Supreme Court justice, Brandeis later wrote:

"The makers of our Constitution recognized the significance of man's spiritual nature, of his feelings and of his intellect. They knew that only a part of the pain, pleasure and satisfactions of life are to be found in material things. They sought to protect Americans in their beliefs, their thoughts, their emotions and their sensations. They conferred, as against the government, the right to be let alone — the most comprehensive of rights and the right most valued by civilized men." (*Olmstead v. United States*, Brandeis, J. dissenting.)

Over the following decades, legal commentators have vigorously debated the scope and nature of a cause of action for privacy, and identified four distinct forms of the "right of privacy:" (1) misappropriation of someone's name or likeness for a commercial purpose; (2) public disclosure of private facts; (3) unreasonable intrusion upon seclusion; and (4) false light in the public eye. In recent times, these causes of action have taken on significance to the press as plaintiffs have attempted to avoid the heavy burdens of proof placed on the libel plaintiff by alleging an invasion of a form of the right of privacy, instead.

The four distinct "branches" of the privacy tort each seek to protect a different aspect on individual's privacy. The "intrusion" tort primarily seeks to protect against physical intrusions into a person's solitude or private affairs. The tort does not require publications of information for recovery, and it is discussed previously as a newsgathering tort. The other three branches of privacy all require publication of some information in order for the plaintiff to have a claim.

States vary widely both in terms of their acceptance of any of these right to privacy claims and in terms of the rules governing any such claims. Of the four forms of the "privacy" cause of action, New York only recognizes the claim for misappropriation of name or likeness for commercial purposes. Texas recognizes claims for intrusion upon seclusion, public disclosure of private facts and misappropriation of name or likeness for commercial purposes. The California state constitution expressly incorporates a right of privacy and California courts recognize all four forms of the right of privacy cause of action. Illinois courts also recognize all four privacy torts, except there is some disagreement among them regarding whether to recognize the tort of intrusion upon seclusion, with some districts recognizing the cause of action, and others rejecting it.

The right of privacy creates liability for the publication of facts that are true, and thus raises particular concerns under the First Amendment. In a number of contexts the Supreme Court has struck down rulings imposing liability for reporting information that was both true and newsworthy, but it has consistently declined to hold that the First Amendment always bars such liability altogether.

It can generally be said that when people become involved in a news event, voluntarily or involuntarily, they forfeit aspects of the right to privacy. A person somehow involved in a matter of legitimate public interest, even if not a bona fide spot news event, normally can be written about with safety. However, the same cannot be said about a story or picture that dredges up the sordid details of a person's past and has no current newsworthiness.

Paul P. Ashley, then president of the Washington State Bar Association, summarized the privacy concern for reporters at a meeting of the Associated Press Managing Editors Association:

"The essence of the wrong will be found in crudity, in ruthless exploitation of the woes or other personal affairs of private individuals who have done nothing noteworthy and have not by design or misadventure been involved in an event which tosses them into an arena subject to public gaze."

### • *Publication of private facts*

When most people speak of an "invasion of privacy," they have in mind the public disclosure of highly embarrassing private facts. In those states where such a claim is recognized, the elements of a cause of action generally include: (1) "publicity" given to private information, (2) that a reasonable person would find highly offensive, and (3) which is not of any legitimate public interest.

In some states the lack of "legitimate public interest" or lack of "newsworthiness" is an element of the tort, meaning it is a plaintiff's burden to prove. In others, this element is an affirmative defense and the defendant must show how the information was indeed a matter of legitimate public concern. In all cases, newsworthiness is a complete defense to the tort. The First Amendment bars a claim for the true and accurate disclosure of a private fact so long as the information is newsworthy.

The first element of the tort requires "publicity" given to private information. This requires some element of widespread disclosure to the general public, not simply a communication to a single person or small group of people. Conversely, facts that are already known to the general public can not be the basis of a public disclosure claim, while facts known only to a small group can be.

For example, a California court allowed a privacy claim to be based upon the publication of a photograph of a Little League team in a national magazine to illustrate a story about the team's coach who had sexually abused some of the athletes. Although the photograph had been given to all the members of the team, the identities of the minors shown in the photograph were not known to a broader national audience. The court said their identities could therefore be considered "private" in the context of the story about sex abuse. Some courts have similarly ruled that a person who is recognizable in a picture of a crowd in a public place is not entitled to the right of privacy, but if the camera singled him out for no news-connected reason, then his privacy might be invaded.

The second element of the tort requires that the disclosure be "highly offensive" to a reasonable person. This factor goes to the embarrassing nature of the information itself. Reporting someone's age, for example, would not be highly offensive to a reasonable person, even if that information were not widely known. Reporting, over their objection, that someone was a victim of sexual abuse or suffered from an incurable disease might be.

Finally, no claim will lie if the information is newsworthy, or of legitimate public concern. Courts generally will defer to reporters and editors to determine what is "newsworthy," but the line is not always clear. Even in the context of a report on a plainly newsworthy topic, the disclosure of a highly embarrassing private fact may give rise to a claim for invasion of privacy if the facts are not logically related to the matter of public concern. For example, disclosure of the intimate sexual practices of a celebrity might support a claim for invasion of privacy if it were unrelated to any newsworthy report and amounted to prying into someone's life for its own sake.

Some examples can help to demonstrate the nature of this branch of the privacy tort:

—In a case against a Chicago newspaper, an Illinois trial court held that a mother had stated a cause of action for invasion of privacy where she alleged that she told the newspaper reporter that she did not want to make any public statement about her son's death and where the reporter nevertheless remained in the private hospital room with the mother, recorded her grief-stricken last words to her son and subsequently published a picture of the son's dead body and the mother's "last words" to her son.

—The unsavory incidents of the past of a former prostitute, who had been tried for murder, acquitted, married and lived a respectable life, were featured in a motion picture. She sued for invasion of privacy by public disclosure of private facts. The court ruled that the use of her name in the picture and the statement in advertisements that the story was taken from true incidents in her life violated her right to pursue and obtain happiness.

—Another example of spot news interest: A child was injured in an auto accident in Alabama. A newspaper took a picture of the scene before the child was removed and ran it. That was spot news. Twenty months later a magazine used the picture to illustrate an article. The magazine was sued for public disclosure of private facts and lost the case, the court ruling that 20 months after the accident the child was no longer "in the news."

—In another case, a newspaper photographer in search of a picture to illustrate a hot weather story took a picture of a woman sitting on her front porch. She wore a house dress, her hair in curlers, her feet in thong sandals. The picture was taken from a car parked across the street from the woman's home. She sued, charging invasion of privacy by intrusion upon seclusion and public disclosure of private facts. A court, denying the newspaper's motion for dismissal of the suit, said the scene photographed "was not a particularly newsworthy incident," and the limits of decency were exceeded by "surreptitious" taking and publishing of pictures "in an embarrassing pose."

## • *False light invasion of privacy*

A claim for false light basically complains about publicity that places the plaintiff in a false light in the public eye. In those states that recognize this tort, the publicity must be of a kind that would be highly offensive to a reasonable person, and the defendant generally must have acted with the same level of fault that would be required if the plaintiff had filed a libel claim.

One form in which a claim for false light occasionally arises occurs where an opinion or utterance is falsely attributed to the plaintiff. In another version of the claim, the plaintiff's picture is used to illustrate an article to which he has no reasonable connection, as where the picture of an honest taxi driver is used to illustrate an article about the cheating propensities of cab drivers.

The Supreme Court of the United States ruled in 1967 that the constitutional guarantees of freedom of the press are applicable to claims for invasion-of-privacy by false light involving reports of newsworthy matters. *Time, Inc. v. Hill* (1967). The ruling arose out of a reversal by the Supreme Court of a decision of a New York court that an article with photos in Life magazine reviewing a play, "The Desperate Hours," violated the privacy of a couple who had been held hostage in a real-life incident. In illustrating the article, Life posed the actors in the house where the real family had been held captive.

The family alleged violation of privacy by false light in the public eye, saying the article gave readers the false impression that the play was a true account of their experiences. Life said the article was "basically truthful."

The court said:

"We create grave risk of serious impairment of the indispensable service of a free press in a free society if we saddle the press with the impossible burden of verifying to a certainty the facts associated in a news article with a person's name, picture or portrait, particularly as related to non-defamatory matter."

The court added, however, that these constitutional guarantees do not extend to "knowing or reckless falsehood." A newspaper still may be liable for invasion of privacy if the facts of a story are changed deliberately or recklessly, or "fictionalized." As with The New York Times and The Associated Press decisions in the field of libel, "The Desperate Hours" case does not confer a license for defamatory statements or for reckless disregard of the truth.

An Illinois court allowed a "false light" claim to proceed where a news report allegedly broadcast the plaintiff's comments (which were covertly recorded) out of context. More recently, federal appeals court concluded that Gennifer Flowers could maintain a false light claim against James Carville for publishing facts suggesting she had lied about the nature of her relationship with President Clinton. The court said the false light claim could compensate for emotional injury that would not be covered by a claim for defamation.

### • Misappropriation

The final form of invasion of privacy recognized by the courts is misappropriation of the name or likeness of a living person for purposes of trade or advertising without that person's consent. In recent years, some states have included voice as well as name or likeness. This tort is intended to allow people to control the commercial use and exploitation of their own identities. The First Amendment provides for at least some exceptions to such a right — as where a candidate for public office includes his opponent's name and likeness in campaign advertisements.

The misappropriation tort is not generally a concern to reporters because it applies to the *commercial* exploitation of a person's name and likeness. It does not bar editorial uses and provides no remedy when a person's name or image (questions of copyright aside) is used in a news report. This branch of privacy is of little concern outside of the advertising department of a news organization.

## Copyright infringement

Copyright is the right of an author to control the reproduction and use of any creative expression that has been fixed in tangible form, such as on paper or computer desk. The right of Congress to pass laws protecting copyright is itself protected in the Constitution, and the First Amendment is therefore no defense to a valid claim for copyright infringement under the Copyright Act.

The types of creative expression eligible for copyright protection include literary, graphic, photographic, audiovisual, electronic and musical works. In this context, "tangible forms" range from film to videotape to material posted on the Internet. Personal letters or diaries may be protected by copyright even though they may not have been published and may not contain a copyright notice. Probably of greatest concern to reporters and editors are the copyrights in photographs used to illustrate a news report.

A copyright comes into existence the moment an original work of expression is captured in a tangible form. No government approval or filing is required for a work to be protected by copyright. Upon creation of the work, ownership of the copyright in that work is vested in the "author" of a work — the person to whom the work owes its origin.

The owner will generally be the author of the work, or the photographer in the case of an image. Under certain circumstances, however, someone other than the person who actually created the work may be deemed to be the work's "author" and thereby own the copyright. Under the work made for hire doctrine, copyright ownership of a particular work vests with the employer of the author when the work is created by an employee who is acting within the scope of his or her employment.

The owner of a copyright is given the exclusive right to reproduce, distribute, display and prepare "derivative works" of the copyrighted material. These rights exist for the life of the author plus 70 years. In the case of a "work for hire" owned by a corporation, the right exists for 95 years from the first publication or 120 years from creation, whichever is shorter.

### • *Limitations on copyright*

Not all uses of copyright material constitute infringement. The most important limitation on the reach of copyright law for journalists is that ideas and facts are never protected by a copyright. What is protected by the copyright law is the manner of expression. The copyright pertains only to the literary, musical, graphic or artistic form in which an author expresses intellectual concepts.

For example, an author's analysis or interpretation of events, the way the material is structured and the specific facts marshaled, the choice of particular words and the emphasis given to specific developments, may all be protected by copyright. The essence of a claim for copyright infringement lies not in taking a general theme or in covering specific events, but in appropriating particular expression through similarities of treatment, details, scenes, events and characterizations.

This printed page illustrates the distinction between protected expression and nonprotected ideas and facts. Despite the copyright protecting this page, a subsequent author is free to report any of the facts it contains. The subsequent author may not, however, employ the same or essentially the same combination of words, structure, and tone, which constitute the expression of those facts.

A second limitation of the reach of copyright is the doctrine of "fair use." This doctrine permits, in certain circumstances, the use of copyright material without its author's permission. Courts will invoke "fair use" when a rigid application of the copyright law would stifle the very creativity the law is designed to foster.

To determine whether a particular use is "fair" and hence permitted, courts are required to evaluate and balance such factors as: (1) the purpose of the use; (2) the nature of the copyrighted work that is being used; (3) the amount and substantiality of the portion used in relation to the copyright work as a whole; and (4) the effect of the use upon the potential value of the copyright work. In addition, courts generally consider how "transformative" the use is. Uses that can be said to have transformed the original work into something new by building upon it in some fashion are more likely to be considered fair uses. Uses that merely supplant the work by presenting it essentially as was in the original version tend not to be fair.

News reporting, criticism, and comment are favored purposes under the fair-use doctrine, but "scooping" a copyright holder's first use of previously unpublished material is not. Note, though, that "purpose" is only one of the fair-use factors. Thus, a use for a proper purpose may nevertheless constitute an infringement if other factors weigh against that use's being fair.

Here are some general guidelines to keep in mind when dealing with material written by others:

—Fair use is more likely to be found if the copyrighted work is informational rather than fictional.

—Documents written by the federal government are not protected by copyright, but documents written by state and local governments may be.

—The greater the amount of the copyrighted work used, the less likely that a court will characterize the use as fair. The use of an entire copyrighted work is almost never fair. Size alone, however, is not decisive; courts have found uses not to be fair when the portion used was small but so important that it went to the heart of the copyrighted work.

—Uses that decrease any potential market for the copyrighted work tend not to be fair. For instance, if a literary critic reproduces all five lines of a five-line poem, the potential market for the poem will be diminished because any reader of the critic's piece can also obtain a copy of the poem for free.

It is always possible to obtain permission from the copyright holder. Reporters and editors having questions about whether their use in a news story or column of copyright material is a fair use should review these factors. No mathematical formula can yield the answer.

It bears emphasis that the First Amendment provides no greater right to use copyrighted materials than those provided by the copyright law. If a use is not "fair" within the meaning of copyright law, it will be no defense to claim the use of the copyrighted material was newsworthy and therefore protected by the First Amendment. Moreover, proper attribution alone cannot transform an infringing use into a fair one.

In using copyright material in a news story or column, writers should make sure that no more of a copyrighted work than is necessary for a proper purpose is used, and that the work is not used in a way that impairs its value. Photographers in particular pose copyright issues. Any use of a photograph without permission of the owner of the copyright is likely to raise legal issues.

# PHOTO CAPTIONS

# PHOTO CAPTIONS

Nearly all AP captions follow a simple formula:

* The first sentence of the caption describes what the photo shows, in the present tense, and states where and when the photo was made. It must ALWAYS include the day and date the photo was made (e.g., Friday, Jan. 29, 2003).

* The second sentence of the caption gives background on the news event or describes why the photo is significant.

* Whenever possible, try to keep captions to no more than two concise sentences, while including the relevant information. Try to anticipate what information a newspaper editor or reader will need. Nonpublishable information in the body of the caption should be set off by dual asterisks (**) as in the examples below.

### THIS IS AN EXAMPLE OF THE STANDARD AP CAPTION:

The Mississippi River flows through a hole in the Snay Island, Ill., levee, flooding farmland and homes 10 miles south of Quincy, Ill., Sunday, July 25, 1993. About 2,000 people were evacuated from the 44,000 acres that flooded. (AP Photo/Bill Waugh)

### FOR HANDOUT PHOTOS (provided or released by governments, armies, companies or other official sources):

In this photo released by the White House, President Bush receives a phone call in the Oval Office of the White House, Wednesday, Nov. 3, 2004 from Democratic presidential candidate Sen. John Kerry, D-Mass., as he concedes the elections. (AP Photo/White House, Eric Draper)

The caption should begin with *In this photo released by*, followed by the name of the providing body.

The name of the releasing body is then repeated in the photo credit: (AP Photo/White House, Draper)

The name of the releasing body should be translated according to AP style, where applicable.

The special instructions header should have: Photo provided by the White House (or the relevant body)

### DO NOT use DESCRIPTIVE OVERLINES such as:

1. SAFE AT SECOND—For a baseball play at second base, or PRESIDENT ADDRESSES WOMEN—For a presidential speech to a women's group. Regular captions have NO overlines.

### INSTRUCTIVE OVERLINES will be used in the following cases:

1. For FILE PHOTOS the word FILE will be the OVERLINE, set off by twin asterisks.

Example: **In this May 12, 1993, file photo, New York Knick's Patrick Ewing is bowled over by Charlotte Hornets' Larry Johnson during the NBA Playoffs in New York. (AP Photo/Ron Frehm. File)

2. For ADVANCES the OVERLINE is the word ADVANCE and the RELEASE DATE. Do not use story slugs or writer's name in the OVERLINE.

Example: **ADVANCE FOR MAY 15-16** Sean Smith, a fish culturist at Vermont's new fish hatchery in Grand Isle, Vt., one of the Lake Champlain islands, moves young rainbow trout on May 4, 1993, to a new tank. (AP Photo/Toby Talbot)

3. For SPECIALS the OVERLINE should be the word SPECIAL and the name of the publication. Do not use the authorizing editor in the OVERLINE. Also, if the city is not part of the formal title of the publication's name, add it. Put SPCL in the subcategory field of the NAA/IPTC header.

Example: **SPECIAL FOR THE CLEVELAND PLAIN DEALER** Diana Holmes participates in the second day of the 66th annual National Spelling Bee in Washington Thursday, June 3, 1993. (AP Photo/Ron Edmonds)

4. For EMBARGOED photos the OVERLINE should be the word EMBARGOED with the RELEASE TIME and DATE. Also, add HFR (Hold for Release) in the SUPPLEMENTAL CATEGORY field of the NAA/IPTC header for embargoed photos for same day release.

Example: **EMBARGOED UNTIL 9 P.M. EDT, June 1, 1993** Jan Smith, right, leaves the courtroom at the Travis County courthouse with friends Tuesday, June 1, 1993, in Austin, Texas, after her assailant William Johnson was found guilty of assault. (AP Photo/Austin American Statesman, Chuck Johnson)

If the date is unknown, state "date of photo unknown" in the body of the caption and in the INSTRUCTIONS field of the NAA/IPTC header.

The SIGNOFF for an AP staffer or stringer is, in parentheses, AP Photo followed by a slash and the name of the photographer. Don't use str or stf. Example: (AP Photo/Rick Bowmer). If the name of the photographer is not known or needs to be withheld, the signoff is: (AP Photo).

MEMBER PHOTO SIGNOFF: (AP Photo/USA Today, Anne Ryan). Put MBR in the BYLINE TITLE field of the NAA/IPTC header.

HANDOUT PHOTO SIGNOFF: (AP Photo/General Motors, HO). If photographer is known: (AP Photo/General Motors, John Smith, HO).

POOL PHOTO SIGNOFF: (AP Photo/Bill Waugh, Pool). For pool photos, do not name the newspaper or agency that shot for the pool in the caption signoff. However, put the name of the organization that shot the pool in the BYLINE TITLE field of the NAA/IPTC header.

SPECIALS PHOTO SIGNOFF for photo shot by AP: (AP Photo/Al Smith). If made by member's own photographer: (Chicago Tribune Photo/Bill James).

FILE PHOTO SIGNOFF: (AP Photo/Lenny Ignelzi, File). If the name of the photographer who shot the file photo is not known the signoff should be: (AP Photo/File)

AP GRAPHIC SIGNOFF: (AP Graphic/Karl Tate).

HANDOUT GRAPHIC SIGNOFF: (AP Graphic/AccuWeather, HO).

TV FRAMEGRAB PHOTO SIGNOFF: (AP Photo/CNN)

MANDATORY CREDITS, OUTS, CORRECTION INFORMATION and ED-ITOR'S NOTES should only appear in the caption box in unusual cases, such as when a source demands, and should be set off by twin asterisks. They also appear in the INSTRUCTIONS field of the NAA/IPTC header. When necessary in the caption box, they appear AFTER the signoff.

HANDOUT PHOTOS should be marked NO SALES in the INSTRUC-TIONS field of the NAA/IPTC header with two exceptions: Do NOT put NO SALES on federal government (such as NASA, FBI, NOAA, military, etc.) handouts or POOL images.

# CAPTION CORRECTIONS, ADDITIONS, ELIMINATIONS

An AP captions **CORRECTION** is moved when a simple and nonlibelous error occurs in a caption. Examples would be a misspelled name, wrong hometown, sports score or slug. The procedure AP uses to file a caption correction form on PhotoStream is to point out the information that is being corrected in the **INSTRUCTIONS** field of the NAA/PTC header and write a corrected caption in publishable form. The word **CORRECTION** and the original photo's **TRANS REFERENCE** number are added to the **OBJECT NAME** field in the NAA/IPTC header. The form is followed by the photo again with a corrected publishable caption noting so in the **INSTRUC-TIONS** field of the NAA/IPTC header. The same procedure is followed for an AP caption **ADDITION**.

An AP caption **ADDITION** is moved when the original caption is incomplete but otherwise accurate. An AP caption **ADDITION** may add the name of someone in the photo or other important background information.

An AP caption **ELIMINATION** is moved for an acceptable photo that has a caption field that misrepresents the photo or is in bad taste. When this occurs, an AP caption **ELIMINATION** form is moved alerting members. Then the photo is rerun with the corrected caption using procedures for an AP caption **CORRECTION** transmission.

# PHOTO KILLS AND ELIMINATIONS

An AP photo KILL is moved on PhotoStream and DataStream for a photo that is objectionable and calls into question the threat of legal action, libel or copyright infringement. Photo KILLS move in consultation with the New York Photos desk supervisor and senior photo management.

An AP photo ELIMINATION is moved on PhotoStream and DataStream for a photo that carries no threat of legal action but is objectionable for other reasons, such as error, poor taste or inaccuracy. When these occur, either an AP photo KILL or ELIMINATION is moved in consultation with the New York Photos desk supervisor and senior photo management, alerting members.

# TEXT WIRE FORMATS

PHOTO ADVISORIES — For routine notifications to members on major stories.

**Slug: [ BC-PHOTO ADVISORY-School Siege ]**
**EDITORS:**
**Photos on the Arizona school siege will move within 30 minutes.**
**The AP**


CAPTION CORRECTIONS — For significant corrections that should be pointed out on text wires, e.g., misidentification or other serious error.

**Slug: [ BC-CAPTION CORRECTION-Blind Cyclist ]**
**EDITORS:**
**A correction, NY107, has moved on photo services to AP Photo BUF108 of Oct. 24, 2000, Blind Cyclist, from Buffalo, N.Y. The cyclist had been riding for 5 miles, not 50 miles.**
**The AP**

PHOTO ELIMINATIONS — For major factual errors, poor taste or other circumstance that would require removing a photo from the report and archives.

**Slug: [ BC-PHOTO ELIMINATION-Blind Cyclist ]**
**EDITORS:**
**AP Photo BUF108 of Oct. 24, 2000, Blind Cyclist, from Buffalo, N.Y., has been eliminated. The bicycle rider is not blind. Ensure that the photo is eliminated from your archives and is not published. The photo will not be retransmitted.**
**The AP**

CAPTION ELIMINATIONS — For captions on otherwise acceptable photos that misrepresent the photo or present problems with bad taste or sensitivity.

**Slug: [ BC-CAPTION ELIMINATION-CEO Resigns ]**
**EDITORS:**
**The caption on AP Photo BUF112, CEO Resigns, from Buffalo, N.Y., has been eliminated. Smith did not resign during his speech. The photo will be retransmitted with a corrected caption.**
**The AP**

PHOTO KILLS — For photos that present potential legal problems.

**Slug: [ BC-PHOTO KILL-School Standoff ]**
**EDITORS:**
AP Photo GLE122 of Oct. 24, 2000, School Standoff, from Glendale, Ariz., has been killed. The person in the photo is not under arrest. A kill is mandatory. Make certain the photo is not published. The photo will not be retransmitted. (Or: The photo will be retransmitted with a corrected caption).
**The AP**

PHOTO CORRECTIVES — These are publishable stories designed to aid members that might have published a photo that was killed. In addition to the Corrective itself, we need to move an advisory. Use both formats below, as separate items.

**Slug: [ BC-School Standoff, PHOTO CORRECTIVE ]**
**EDITORS:**
**Members who used AP Photo GLE122 of Oct. 24, 2000, School Standoff, from Glendale, Ariz., showing police and a handcuffed man outside a school, are asked to use the following story. ]**
GLENDALE, Ariz. (AP) _ The Associated Press reported erroneously in a photo caption Oct. 24 that John Doe, shown in the accompanying photograph, had been arrested. Doe had not been arrested.

**Slug: [ BC-PHOTO CORRECTIVE-School Standoff, Advisory ]**
**EDITORS:**
**Please note a0444, BC-School Standoff, PHOTO CORRECTIVE, which corrects an error in the caption on AP Photo GLE122 of Oct. 24, 2000, School Standoff, from Glendale, Ariz.**
**The AP**

PHOTO WITHHOLDS — Used to temporarily remove a photo that may or may not be incorrect, but which we are in the process of checking.

**Slug: [ BC-PHOTO WITHHOLD-Iraq ]**
EDITORS: Withhold AP Photo BAG123, transmitted Tuesday. The photo shows a U.S. Army soldier comforting a dying child wounded Monday in a car bomb blast in Mosul, Iraq. The U.S. Army, which initially said the photo was taken by the Army, has since said it was taken by an embedded photographer. The military asks that the picture not be used further in print or online until the photographer can be contacted to determine the availability of the photo.
**The AP**

# NAA/IPTC HEADER FIELDS

Byline: The Byline field lists the name of the person who made the photo.

Byline Title: The Byline Title field lists the title of the person who made the photo.

Caption: The Caption field is the text that accompanies the photo, containing the who, what, when, where and why information.

Caption Writer: The Caption Writer field lists the initials of all the people who wrote or edited the caption, header fields or image file. This includes toning and pixel editing.

Category: The Category field lists codes that aid in a more detailed search. (See category definitions in this section.)

City: The City field lists where the photo was originally made. For file photos, do not use the transmission point's city.

Country: The Country field lists the three-letter country code where the photo was originally made. For file photos, do not put the transmission point's country.

Create Date Time: The Create Date Time field is the date the photo was originally made. For file photos, use the date the photo was originally made, if known. If the complete date is not known, Leafdesk 8.3 software will allow the field to be left blank. The field will not accept a partial date. The time is not needed.

Credit: The Credit field is the name of the service transmitting the photo.

Headline: The Headline field lists keywords to aid in a more detailed search for a photo.

Instructions: The Instructions field lists special notations that apply uniquely to a photo, such as file photo, correction, advance or outs.

Object Name: The Object Name field lists the story slug associated with a photo. For photos without a story, Associated Press photographers or photo editors will make up a logical slug to aid in a search and note it as a "stand-alone photo" in the INSTRUCTIONS field of the NAA/PTC header. If a related story moves on DataStream, the photo will be retransmitted with the appropriate OBJECT NAME to match the story.

Routing: The Routing field is used by The Associated Press to route photos on to PhotoStream.

Source: The Source field lists who is the original provider of a photo, such as: AP, an AP member, pool photo provider or handout photo provider.

State: The State field lists the state where the photo was originally made. Use U.S. postal code abbreviations. For file photos, do not use the transmission point's state.

Supp Categories: The Supplemental Categories field lists codes that aid in a more detailed search for a photo. (See supplemental categories definitions in this section.)

Trans Reference: The Trans Reference field lists a call letter/number combination associated with a photo. It includes an originating transmit point's call letters and picture number from that point's sequence of offerings for a given day. Example: NY105.

# SUPPLEMENTAL CATEGORIES

## GENERAL:
ADV  Advance
APN  APNewsfeatures
ENT  Entertainment, celebrities (don't use the word people)
FEA  Feature pictures of a non-news nature
FILE  File photo
HFR  Hold for Release (embargoed photos for same day release)
OBIT Obituary
SPF  Special Features package
SPCLSpecial
WEA Weather

## NEWS EVENTS:
CVN  National political conventions
ELN  For election cycles only
XGR  State legislatures

## SPORTS:
BBA  Professional baseball (American League)
BBN  Professional baseball (National League)
BBO  Professional baseball (minor league or related to neither league)
BBC  College baseball
BKN  NBA basketball
BKC  Men's college basketball
BKW  Women's college basketball
BKO  Other basketball including high school and semipro
BOX  Boxing
CAR  Racing (car, speedboat or motorcycle)
FBN  NFL Football
FBC  College football
FBO  Other football including high school and semipro
GLF  Golf
GYM  Gymnastics
HKN  NHL hockey
HKC  College hockey
HKO  Other hockey including high school and minor league
OLY  Olympics
RAC  Racing (animals)
RUN  Track and Field
SKI  Skiing
SOC  Soccer
TEN  Tennis

# AP Caption and NAA/IPTC Header Quick Reference Guide

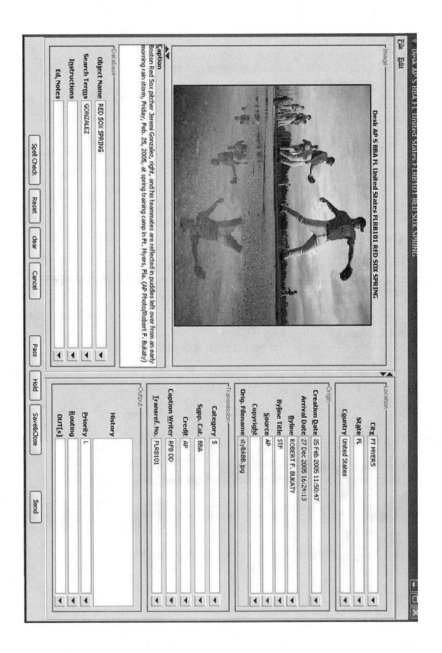

# GRAPHICS

# GRAPHICS
## WIRE FORMATS

**GRAPHICS ADVISORIES**
Slug: [ BC-Graphics Advisory ]
EDITORS:
The APWebGraphics server is down. We expect to restore operation by 11 a.m. EST.
The APWebGraphics ...
The AP

**GRAPHICS WITHHOLDS**
Slug: [ BC-GRAPHICS WITHHOLD-BLINDCYCLIST ]
EDITORS:
AP Graphic BLINDCYCLIST of Oct. 24, 2000, has been withheld. Questions have been raised about whether the person referred to has been arrested.
The AP

**GRAPHICS CORRECTIONS**
Slug: [ BC-GRAPHICS CORRECTION-BLINDCYCLIST ]
EDITORS:
A correction, BLINDCYCLIST_FIX, has moved to graphics subscribers, correcting AP Graphic BLINDCYCLIST of Oct. 24, 2000. The cyclist had been riding for 5 miles, not 50 miles.
The AP

**GRAPHICS KILLS**
Slug: [ BC-GRAPHICS KILL-BLINDCYCLIST ]
EDITORS:
AP Graphic SCHOOLSTANDOFF of Oct. 24, 2000, has been killed. The person referred to in the graphic is not under arrest.
A kill is mandatory. Make certain the graphic is not published.
The graphic will not be retransmitted. (Or: The graphic will be retransmitted in corrected form.)
The AP

**GRAPHICS CORRECTIVES**
Slug: [ BC-School Standoff, GRAPHICS CORRECTIVE ]
Headline: [ AP Correction: School Standoff graphic ]
Eds. note: [ Eds: Members who used AP Graphic SCHOOLSTANDOFF of Oct. 24, 2000, are asked to use the following story. ]
GLENDALE, Ariz. (AP) _ The Associated Press said erroneously in a graphic Oct. 24 that John Doe had been arrested in the Glendale school standoff. Doe had not been arrested.

# FILING THE WIRE

# FILING THE WIRE

These guidelines are intended to help editors handle newspaper copy easily and efficiently.

Codes in the heading of a story tell AP computers where to send it, how quickly it should be moved out, and in what format.

See:
**Coding Requirements**
   **File Name**
**Priority Codes**
   **Category Codes**
**Format Identifiers**
   **Keyword (Slug)**
      **Version Section**
**Reference Number Section**

## Filing the Wire: Coding Requirements

The **file name** received by newspaper members consists of a letter of the alphabet and four numbers. The letter is called the **Service Level Designator** and shows the type of service the file belongs to. Usually stories are numbered in sequence. But some stories or fixtures — digests, for example — are given predetermined numbers. The first AP News Digest of the new cycle is always a9000 on a-level DataStream.

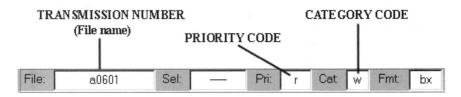

These are the letters and types of service most common in nationwide transmissions:

**a** — Spot DataStream news.
**B** — AP Basic service.
**b** — Most advances.
**c** — Weekly Features service.
**f** — Business and financial DataStream news.
**p** — Limited DataStream news.
**s** — Sports DataStream news.
Other letters used by the AP include:
**h** — Sports news for Limited DataStream members.
**r** — Race report.

**t** — Sports news for Limited DataStream members who want an expanded sports report.

**u** — Special stock and markets package.

**Priority codes** are used by the AP to assure that stories are sent in the order of their urgency. At newspapers, the codes can be used by computer systems to determine the order in which stories come to an editor's attention.

The principal priority codes, in order of urgency, and their use:

**f** — Flash, highest priority, used for flashes only.

**b** — APNewsAlerts, bulletins, kill notes.

**u** — Urgent, high-priority copy, including all writethrus containing corrections. It must be used on all items that carry an *URGENT* tag. It also may be used on items that lack this tag but must move on an urgent basis.

**r** — Stories of a routine nature.

**d** — Deferred priority: Used on spot copy that can be delayed.

**a** — For weekday advances designed for use more than 12 hours after transmission. (Hold-for-release material sent for use less than 12 hours after transmission carries a spot news priority.)

**s** — For Sunday advances designed for use more than 12 hours after transmission.

**Category codes** help newspapers sort copy into various categories. For example, domestic stories may go in one place in the queue, Washington stories in another, and foreign stories somewhere else.

The principal category codes and their uses:

**a** — Domestic, non-Washington, general news items.

**b** — Special events.

**d** — Food, diet. For use primarily on standing advance features on food, recipes and the like. Frequently used with stories on c-level DataStream.

**e** — Entertainment news and features.

**f** — News copy, regardless of dateline, designed primarily for use on financial pages.

**i** — International items, including stories from the United Nations, U.S. possessions, and undated roundups keyed to foreign events.

**j** — Lottery results only. (Stories about lotteries or lottery winners carry standard news category codes.)

**k** — Commentary. Material designed primarily for editorial and op-ed pages. (The code is not used on national DataStream services.)

**l** — Weekly Features package.

**n** — Stories of state or regional interest under domestic datelines. If a regional item has a Washington dateline, use the w category. If a regional item has an international dateline, use the i category. If a regional item is designed primarily for financial pages use the f category and if it is designed primarily for the sports pages, use the s category.

**o** — Weather tables and forecast fixtures. Do not use on weather stories.

**p** — National political copy. Generally used in months before an election.

**q** — Use only for result or period score of a single sports event. The code is designed to help newspaper computer systems build a list of scores or ignore individual scores and wait for transmissions that group them.

**s** — Sports stories, standings, results of more than one event.

**t** — Travel copy.

**v** —Advisories about stories that may carry any of the category letters. This code is also used for news digests and news advisories.

**w** — Washington-datelined stories. Change to the *a* or *i* category code if a subsequent lead shifts to a different city.

The **format identifier** is comprised of two letters, which appear after the category code.

Use **bx** if the item is intended to be set in body type or standard text.

Use **bt** if the item is intended to be set in body type and contains even one tabular line.

Use **at** if the item is intended to be set in agate type and contains even one tabular line.

Use **ax** if the item is intended to be set in agate type but contains no tabular lines.

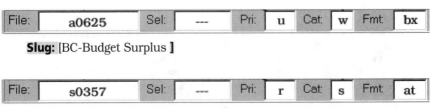

| File: | a0625 | Sel: | --- | Pri: | u | Cat: | w | Fmt: | bx |

**Slug:** [BC-Budget Surplus ]

| File: | s0357 | Sel: | --- | Pri: | r | Cat: | s | Fmt: | at |

**Slug:** [BC-BKN--Celtics-Knicks, Box ]

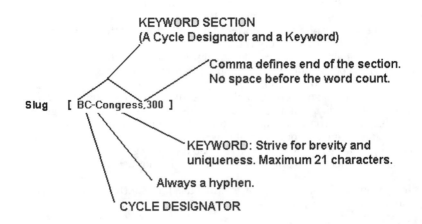

KEYWORD SECTION
(A Cycle Designator and a Keyword)

Comma defines end of the section. No space before the word count.

Slug    [ BC-Congress,300 ]

KEYWORD: Strive for brevity and uniqueness. Maximum 21 characters.

Always a hyphen.

CYCLE DESIGNATOR

### Special note: Format Identifiers on DataStream

The letters **bx**, **at**, etc., shown in the examples convey information about whether the item is meant to be set in agate or body type and whether it contains tabular material.

# Filing the Wire: Keyword Slugline

Every news item in the AP report has a keyword section that consists of a cycle designator, a hyphen and a keyword or keywords. A comma marks the end of the section.

Because the keyword section provides the basic identification of a story for automatic linkup routines, it must be repeated in exactly the same form on all subsequent leads, adds, inserts, subs, etc. filed for a story.

The cycle designator is always BC-, to indicate that the story may be used by morning or afternoon newspapers.

The **keyword** or slug (sometimes more than one word) clearly indicates the content of the story.

The keyword or keywords should not total more than 21 characters.

Use of easily recognized abbreviations and acronyms, such as *Scotus* for the Supreme Court of the United States and *XGR* for legislature, is encouraged. (Also, the keyword of an item sent on a state service contains the postal code for the state of origin.)

Some computer systems automatically add a word count at the end of a line.

For budgeted stories, note that Bjt is
not repeated in filing a lead.

Slug:  [ BC-Smith, 1st Ld,300 ]

Slug:  [ BC-Smith, 2nd Ld-3Takes-Writethru,450 ]

Slug:  [ BC-Smith, 2nd Ld-1st Add-Writethru,400 ]

Note the form when three terms from
the versions list are needed.

The keyword section of the line is followed by the version section, which provides additional information.

The version vocabulary is broken into two lists. If more than one term is necessary in a keyword line, use them in the order listed here. If a term from the second list is needed, it must follow any term from this list:

**1st Ld, 2nd Ld, 10th Ld,** etc.
**Adv01, Adv31,** etc.
**Advisory**
**HFR** (Hold for Release)

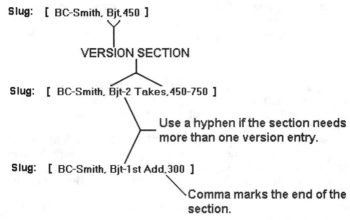

**Slug:** [ BC-Smith, Bjt 450 ]

VERSION SECTION

**Slug:** [ BC-Smith, Bjt-2 Takes,450-750 ]

Use a hyphen if the section needs more than one version entry.

**Slug:** [ BC-Smith, Bjt-1st Add,300 ]

Comma marks the end of the section.

**KILL**
**WITHHOLD**
**CORRECTIVE**
**CLARIFICATION**

A term from the second list may stand alone in the version section if no term from the first list is needed. If there is an item from the first list, the item from the second list should start with a hyphen. Examples:
1st Ld-Writethru
Smith text, 1st Ld-1st Add
Adv15-2 Takes

**2 Takes, 3 Takes,** etc.
**1st Add, 2nd Add,** etc.
**Writethru**

Story-type Identifiers used in the United States:
BC-APN (Special Newsfeatures package)
BC-BRF (Briefs)
BC-ELN (Election)
BC-ENT (Entertainment)
BC-LOT (Lottery)
BC-Scotus (Supreme Court of the United States)
BC-SPE (Special Edition)
BC-TRV (Travel)
BC-WEA (Weather)
BC-WKD (Weekend)
BC-XGR (Legislature)

# FILING PRACTICES

AP news moves in a 24-hour cycle. For U.S. papers, the cycle begins at midnight Eastern time on national wires, and usually at midnight local time on state wires. On World Service wires, the cycle starts at midnight GMT.

Each story is filed on a 24-hour basis, with a single lead sequence from midnight to midnight. The first story after midnight on a major fire, for example, might be slugged BC-Fire. As the story develops, it might be slugged BC-Fire, 1st Ld-Writethru by 8 a.m., BC-Fire, 4th Ld-Writethru by 1 p.m., BC-Fire, 6th Ld-Writethru by 6 p.m. and BC-Fire, 10th Ld-Writethru by 11 p.m. After midnight, the new-cycle story will once again be simply BC-Fire.

On a developing story, it's important to retain the same basic slug (BC-Fire in this case) whenever possible from cycle to cycle. Don't switch, for example, from BC-Fire to BC-Inferno. If a slug must change because of the nature of the story, start a new numbering sequence with the new slug and make reference to the earlier series:

### Slug: [ BC-Town Burns ]

### Eds. note: [ Eds: Incorporates BC-Block Burns ]

For U.S. members, if a story is developing strongly beyond midnight and still needs to be updated for late AMs papers, the lead sequence can be continued past the start of the new cycle. In the example above, the story might be BC-Fire, 12th Ld-Writethru by 1 a.m. and BC-Fire, 13th Ld-Writethru by 2 a.m. Each post-midnight lead intended for morning newspapers should say Eds: AMs. When it's late enough that AMs papers are no longer publishing (about 4 a.m. Eastern time), begin the new-cycle sequence, sending the new story for use by PMs papers as BC-Fire. In such a case, the first story for PMs will carry an Eds: PMs label (see below: Filing Practices: Eds: AMs and Eds: PMs).

## Keeping copy fresh

Just because there is a single numbering sequence from midnight to midnight doesn't mean an important story should remain the same in approach. The new story moving after midnight should take a different approach to the copy that moved in time for AMs. The version of the story moving in late afternoon - the story aimed at AMs -- should take a different approach to what PMs papers have published.

Many PMs papers aren't publishing after 4 p.m. Eastern time, but the leads moved before that time with PMs in mind should continue to be updated even after that hour for Web and broadcast needs, until the version of the story aimed at AMs papers is ready.

## Day of the week

Style is to use the day of the week in spot copy, rather than "today" or "tomorrow." However, if a spot story is something of a feature, it makes sense to lower the time element to the second graf to make the story more useable for both AMs and PMs papers and Web purposes.

## Corrections and clarifications

Stories can be written through for the purpose of correcting them only in the same 24-hour cycle in which they originally moved. (Exception: If a developing story is continuing to be written through with a running lead sequence past the midnight hour, it can still be written through.)

If, say, at 5 a.m., a significant error is discovered in a story that moved at 8 p.m., do a new story, noting in an Eds: note that it corrects an error in the version of the story moved in the previous cycle. There may also be a need, in AMs time, for a corrective to the original story. The same approach applies to clarifications.

See also the **Procedures** section at the end of this chapter.

## ADDS

Use adds only to break up copy that is too long for a single take (more than 10,000 words).

In filing an add, place below the keyword line a pickup line that lists the name of the datelined community followed by a colon. (Use UNDATED if the item does not have a dateline. The name of the community usually is adequate; include the state or country name only if needed to avoid confusion.)

—The last two words of the previous take.

**Slug: [ BC-Smith Text, 1st Add ]**
**Pickup line: [ WASHINGTON: this year. ]**

## ADVANCE SLUGS

Stories transmitted in advance on nationwide services require a minimum of two additional slugs.

The first allows computer systems to key on the item. Use the notation Adv followed by the two-digit release date shown in the keyword line.

The second slug line specifies the release date in more detail.

*To send an advance, do not simply type the format shown here. Use the template in Reporters Workbench to format it precisely. This is essential for archive and other purposes. To use the template, click Templates, then click Insert Field, then click Advance.*

**Slug: [ BC-New Team, Adv15-2 Takes ]**
**Adv date: [ Adv15 ]**
**Adv/HFR note: [ For release in AMs newspapers of Monday, May 15 ]**

When filing a series use a consistent keyword but differentiate the parts by use of a Roman numeral.

**BC-Regulators I, Adv10-3 Takes**
**BC-Regulators II, Adv11-3 Takes**

For weekend or two-day advances:

**Slug: [ BC-CA--Balance of Power, Adv09-10,930 ]**
**Adv date: [ Adv09-10 ]**
**Adv/HFR note: [ For release weekend editions of May 9-10 ]**

Do not add such designations as *End Adv* or *End Advance* at the bottom of the story.

## ADVISORIES AND DIGESTS

All advisories and digests carry the *v* category code. Most advisories have the word Advisory in the version field, separated from the keyword by a comma. Some fixture advisories also have a three-letter identifier in the keyword line to make them easier to find.

Spot news advisories with information on a particular story should have the same keyword as the story. Use Reporter's Workbench template to set up advisories.

**Slug: [ BC-Airfares, Advisory ]**
**Headline: [ ]**

**EDITORS:**
**The embargo on BC-Airfares has been broken. The story is available for immediate use.**
**The AP**

# BULLETINS

A decision on whether to designate a story *bulletin* or *urgent* rests with the supervisor. The *bulletin* tag always must be used judiciously.

A *bulletin* should be kept short — usually, one publishable sentence.

A *bulletin* should not carry a byline, photo, or graphics slug or an editor's note. Include a very brief headline.

Use *b* priority and do not put *More* at the bottom of a *bulletin*.

**Slug: [ BC-Fire, 4th Ld ]**
**Urgent [ BULLETIN ]**
**Headline: [Dormitory fire kills 29]**

An undated *bulletin* should carry a byline or *By The Associated Press in the Reporters Workbench 'Byline' field*.

A *bulletin* is always preceded by an *APNewsAlert*. (See **NewsAlerts** entry.)

When more information is available, call up the *bulletin* that has moved, add the new material and refile the new story as a writethru, with the next lead number. Do the same with further information, until the story is complete.

# BYLINES

Except for prefixes such as *Mac, Mc, Le,* or *De* (writer's preference) and *Sr.* or *Jr.*, a writer's name is entirely in capital letters.

The standard underline for full-time AP employees is *Associated Press Writer*. Abbreviate *Associated Press* to *AP* for specialty underlines such as *AP Sports Writer* and *AP Special Correspondent*.

**Byline: [ By H. JOSEF HEBERT ]**
**Bytitle: [ Associated Press Writer ]**

**Byline: [ By RACHEL ZOLL ]**
**Bytitle: [ AP Religion Writer ]**

**Byline: [ By CHARLES J. HANLEY ]**
**Bytitle: [ AP Special Correspondent ]**

For undated stories when a writer's name is not used:
**Byline: [ By The Associated Press ]**
For dual bylines, put the word *and* on a separate line between the names. To do this, type ctrl-enter after the first author's name and again after 'and.'
**Byline: [ By SAMPLE AUTHOR**
**and**
**EXAMPLE WRITER ]**
**Bytitle: [ Associated Press Writers ]**

When a story has been written by someone who is not an AP employee, a byline without an underline is sometimes used.

When a writer works for a newspaper, use the byline with the name of the newspaper:

**Byline:** [ By NEWSPAPER WRITER ]
**Bytitle:** [ Hometown Citizen-Times ]

## CHANGING DATELINES

The designation of *2nd, 3rd, 4th Ld*, etc. continues in sequence even if the dateline changes on a story.

If a new lead does shift the dateline, note the change in the editor's note:

**Slug:** [ BC-Airfares, 6th Ld-Writethru ]
**Eds note:** [ Eds: Changes dateline from WASHINGTON ]

## CLARIFICATIONS

For a full explanation, see **Procedures** section at the end of this chapter. The format:

**Slug:** [ BC-Airfares, CLARIFICATION ]
**Headline:** [ Clarification: Airfares story ]
**Eds. note:** [ Eds: Members who used BC-Airfares of May 8 may wish to use the following, which explains that not all fares on domestic flights are subject to change. ]
**WASHINGTON (AP)** _ In a story May 8, The Associated Press reported that fares on domestic flights will increase beginning in April. Fares will increase for flights in the continental United States, but not for flights to Hawaii or Alaska.

For clarifications on undated stories, use **By The Associated Press**

*To send a clarification, do not simply type the format shown here. Use the template in Reporter's Workbench to format it precisely. This is essential for archive and other purposes. To use the template, open the story for which you are doing a clarification, click Templates, click Kill or Correct This Story and select what you want to do.*

Use *v* priority and the same category code as the original story.

## CORRECTIONS

When a story is still live, use a writethru with an editor's note explaining specifically the location of the correction and what it is.

For a full explanation, see the Procedures section at the end of this chapter. The format:

**Slug:** [ BC-Airfares, 2nd Ld-Writethru ]
**Headline:** [ Airlines raise fares before Christmas ]
**Eds Note:** [ Eds: SUBS 20th graf, 'The company ...', to CORRECT airline from American to Delta. Pickup 21st graf, 'Joe Smith ...' ]
**WASHINGTON (AP)** _

In corrections on undated stories, use **By The Associated Press** and no dateline.

Always give the reason for a correction. Be specific. Do not use vague phrases such as *to correct a figure* — give the correct figure and the one it replaces. If correcting a typo, say, for instance, 'to correct spelling of adequate.' The objective is to let editors who may be on deadline know the severity of the error without having to go back to the original copy.

Use this format to correct an APNewsAlert (if a kill is not necessary):

**Slug: [ BC-APNewsAlert, CORRECTION ]**
**NEW YORK _ A prosecutor says state legislator John Smith has been charged with eight counts of perjury. (Corrects APNewsAlert that said he had been charged with five counts.)**

Use *v* priority and the same category code as the original story.

## CORRECTIVES

For a full explanation, see the **Procedures** section at the end of this chapter. The format:

**Slug: [ BC-Fed-Indictments, CORRECTIVE ]**
**Headline: [ Correction: Federal Indictment story ]**
**Eds. note: [ Eds: Members who used BC-Fed-Indictments, sent Oct. 22 under a New York dateline (or with no dateline), are asked to use the following story. ]**
**NEW YORK (AP) _ In an Oct. 22 story about federal indictments of city officials, The Associated Press reported erroneously the first name of one of those indicted. The correct name is Joseph Arnold, not John Arnold.**

For correctives on undated stories, use **By The Associated Press** in the Reporters Workbench 'Byline' field, and no dateline.

*To send a corrective, do not simply type the format shown here. Use the template in Reporter's Workbench to format it precisely. This is essential for archive and other purposes. To use the template, open the story for which you are doing a corrective, click Templates, click Kill or Correct This Story and select what you want to do.*

## CREDIT LINES

Use credit lines at the end of a story to note staffers who contributed significantly to the story other than the byliner. Place them under an indented three-underscore line.

___
**Associated Press writers John Jones and Susan Smith in Omaha, AP business writer Jane Brown in Paris and researcher Jim Doe contributed to this report.**

## DISREGARDS

For a full explanation, see the **Procedures** section at the end of this chapter.

Use disregards to advise of routine material sent on the wire inadvertently, including old stories, duplicate stories and copy not meant for the wires. The disregard should say why the material should be disregarded.

The form:
**Slug: [ BC-Turkey-Quake Survivors, DISREGARD ]**
**Headline: [ ]**
**EDITORS:**
**Disregard BC-Turkey-Quake Survivors. The story moved in a previous cycle.**
**The AP**

Use this format for disregarding an APNewsAlert:

**Slug: [ BC-APNewsAlert, DISREGARD ]**
**WASHINGTON _ Disregard the APNewsAlert on the House spending vote. The House is still voting. The measure has not been approved.**
**The AP**

*Do not simply type the format shown here. Use the template in Reporter's Workbench to format it precisely. This is essential for archive and other purposes. To use the template, open the story to be disregarded, click Templates, click Kill or Correct This Story and select what you want to do.*

Use v priority and the same category code as the original story.

## "Eds: AMs" and "Eds: PMs" Slugs

The movement of the new version of a developing story aimed at AMs or PMs can be pointed out to editors with an 'Eds: AMs' note or 'Eds: PMs' note on the story itself.

The 'Eds: PMs' note is used only in early PMs time (usually around 1-6 a.m.). It's used to designate the version of a story aimed at PMs papers when the AMs story has been led beyond the midnight cycle divide, or when a story broke very soon after midnight and the earlier copy was likely to have been used by AMs papers.

Example of a story developing over the midnight barrier:
The wire carries BC-Fire, 9th Ld-Writethru at 11 p.m., BC-Fire, 10th Ld-Writethru at 2 a.m. and the desk is ready at 3 a.m. to send the new story for PMs. Include 'Eds: PMs' on the 3 a.m. story with the PMs approach:
**Slug: [ BC-Fire, Bjt ]**
**Headline: [ Fire destroys three city blocks ]**
**Eds. note: [ Eds: PMs ]**
(There's no writethru number because this is the start of a new lead sequence. The previous sequence was carried over, past the midnight barrier, from the previous cycle.)

Example of a story developing shortly after midnight:
BC-Fire, a new and important story, moves at 12:30 a.m. It is led with BC-Fire, 1st Ld-Writethru at 1 a.m., BC-Fire, 2nd Ld-Writethru at 2 a.m. and the desk is ready at 3 a.m. to send the new story for PMs. Include 'Eds: PMs' on the 3 a.m. story with the PMs approach:

**Slug:** [ BC-Fire, Bjt, 3rd Ld-Writethru ]
**Headline:** [ Fire destroys three city blocks ]
**Eds. note:** [ Eds: PMs ]

(The 3 a.m. story will be BC-Fire, 3rd Ld-Writethru. The story started entirely in the current cycle so a single lead sequence is used throughout the cycle.)

The 'Eds: AMs' note is used only in AMs time, usually late afternoon. It's used to designate the version of a story aimed at AMs papers when the story has been developing during PMs time. Suppose, for example, that BC-Fire, 3rd Ld-Writethru moves at 6 a.m., BC-Fire, 7th Ld-Writethru moves at 4 p.m. and the desk is ready at 5 p.m. to send the new story for AMs. Include 'Eds: AMs' on the 5 p.m. story with the AMs approach:

**Slug:** [ BC-Fire, 8th Ld-Writethru ]
**Headline:** [ Fire destroys three city blocks ]
**Eds. note:** [ Eds: AMs ]

'Eds: AMs' should be used only when making a substantial change in the approach or content of a story. If a story runs at 9 a.m. and is written through at 5 p.m. to add minor information, the writethru should not carry 'Eds: AMs.'

Use precisely the formats 'Eds: AMs.' and 'Eds: PMs.' The notes should be letter-perfect for archive systems to identify them. The notes should go ahead of other matter in Eds. notes:

**Eds. note:** [ Eds: PMs. Updates with court testimony. ]

On a very fast-moving story, in order to make clear that newspapers on deadline can go to bed, use a separate advisory to highlight the change in approaches.

Example:
**Slug:** [ BC-Governor's Illness, Advisory ]
**Editors: BC-Governor's Illness, 7th Ld-Writethru will stand for AMs. Upcoming is a new story for PMs papers, BC-Governor's Illness.**

## FLASHES

Use as an underline immediately below the APNewsAlert slug on the rare occasion when an APNewsAlert represents a transcendent development — one likely to be one of the top stories of the year.

A flash carries an *f* priority code, a dateline and attribution if appropriate. Use the template in Reporters Workbench. The format:

**Slug:** [ BC-APNewsAlert ]
**Urgent:** [ FLASH ]
**Headline:** [ ]
**SPACE CENTER, HOUSTON (AP ) _ A man has landed on the moon.**
(See **NewsAlerts**)

## GLANCES

Glances are brief listings of information that accompany a story, although some may occasionally stand alone.

Glances and other layering devices, such as biographical boxes, chro-

nologies, lists and highlights, are always undated and carry a line referring to the main story. Avoid beginning glances with words like "Here is"
or "The following are."

**Slug:** [ BC-Budget-Dollar-Glance ]
**Headline:** [ Where the money comes from, and where it goes ]
**Sidebars:** [ With BC-Budget ]
**Byline:** [ By The Associated Press ]
Where the federal government gets a typical dollar and where it goes:

Layering devices provide expanded detail, give editors a way to dress
up a page and serve as points of entry for readers.
They should be listed with related stories on digests and advisories.

## HEADLINES

All stories should have headlines giving the essence of what the story
is about.
Headlines should be written to stand alone in Web page directories.
The location of the event, for instance, must be clear.
Only the first word and proper nouns are capitalized.
Follow story style in spelling but use numerals for all numbers and
single quotes for quotation marks.

**Slug:** [ BC-Airfares ]
**Headline:** [ Airfares going up 'dramatically' at 3 airports ]

For online headlines:
—Label opinion pieces. Short and long headlines for news analyses
must begin with *Analysis*, followed by a colon. Likewise, *reviews must
begin with Review*.
—Attribute carefully. Attribute the source in the headline when appropriate, particularly if it is an anonymous source, a government official or
a report from another news organization.
—Identify location. Locators should be used in headlines when neces-
sary to tell the story. They should be spelled out if there is room or abbre-
viated according to AP style. (Wisconsin is *Wis.* — not *WI.*)
—Acronyms Acceptable in headlines for well-known entities such as
NAACP, FDA, IRS, SEC.
—Co. Try not to use this or *cos.* to abbreviate for company or compa-
nies.
—Federal Reserve *Fed* is acceptable in headlines.
—EU, U.S., U.N. Note AP style: Use periods in *U.S.* and *U.N.*, but not in
*EU.*
—Government Can be abbreviated to *govt* in headlines as a last resort,
but it is preferable to list the specific agency, such as *SEC* or *IRS.*
—Millions, billions These figures can be abbreviated in headlines. For
example, $45 million would be *$45M*, and $5 billion would be *$5B*.
—Numerals. Use numerals; do not spell out numbers.
—Percent Try not to abbreviate. If necessary, use *pct.*, not *%.*
—Quarters Use *4Q*, not *Q4.*
—Quotes Always use single quotes.

## HOLD-FOR-RELEASE SLUGS

All embargoed copy contains *HFR* (Hold for Release) in the version field of the keyword line.

Place the necessary cautions about release on a second slug line immediately under the keyword slug line. For example:

**Slug: [ BC-State of the Union, HFR-4 takes ]**
**Adv/HFR note: [ HOLD FOR RELEASE UNTIL 12:01 a.m. THIS STORY MAY NOT BE POSTED ONLINE, BROADCAST OR PUBLISHED BEFORE 12:01 a.m. ]**

If parts of a story are embargoed, make that clear:

**Slug: [ BC-Polls-2004, HFR, 1st Ld-Writethru ]**
**Eds: [ Final three grafs EMBARGOED for release 1 a.m. Sunday. ]**

*Do not simply type the format shown here. Use the template in Reporters Workbench to format it precisely. This is essential for archive and other purposes. To use the template, click Templates, then click Insert Field, then click Hold for Release.*

## INSERTS

Make inserts with writethru leads, with an editor's note saying what is being updated.

## INTERNET CITATIONS

Place them at the ends of stories, on a separate line or lines under an indented three-underscore line, with the title or a brief description of the Web site to tell readers what to expect.. Example:

___
**On the Net:**
White House: http://www.whitehouse.gov/report
National Diabetes Education Program: http://ndep.nih.gov/

If there is other material to put at the end of a story, such as the names of other staffers contributing, put the Internet citation last.
(See **Nontransmitting Symbols**.)

## KILLS

Bulletin kills should move with a *b* priority and the category code of the original story.

For a full explanation, see the **Procedures** section at the end of this chapter. The format:

**Slug: [ BC-Smith Charged, KILL ]**
**Headline: [ BULLETIN KILL ]**
**NEW YORK _ Kill BC-Smith Charged. Smith was charged with robbery, not murder.**
**The AP**

On print wires, but NOT on online wires, follow the KILL immediately with an advisory. State whether a substitute story is planned:

**Slug:** [ BC-Smith Charged, KILL Advisory ]
**EDITORS:**
The New York story BC-Smith Charged has been killed. Smith was charged with robbery, not murder.
A kill is mandatory.
Make certain the story is not published.
A substitute story will be filed shortly. (Or: **No substitute story will be filed.**)
The AP

*Do not simply type the format shown here. Use the template in Reporter's Workbench to format it precisely. This is essential for archive and other purposes. To use the template, open the story to be killed, click Templates, click Kill or Correct This Story and select what you want to do.*

If a substitute story is filed, mark it as the next lead-writethru to the previous story. Include a nonpublishable editor's note advising that it replaces an earlier story that was KILLED.

The form is:
**Slug:** [ BC-Smith Charged, 4th Ld-Writethru ]
**Eds: SUBS 7th graf "Smith ... year," which was killed, to CORRECT that Smith was charged last year with armed robbery but was not convicted. No pickup.**

Use this format for killing an APNewsAlert:
**Slug:** [ BC-APNewsAlert, KILL ]
NEW YORK _ Kill the APNewsAlert saying John Smith was charged in the murder. Smith was charged with robbery, not murder.
The AP

## LEADS

All leads should be writethrus with editor's notes saying what is being updated.

File a new lead to a story whenever developments warrant. Provide a nonpublishable editor's note explaining the reason for the lead:
**Eds. note:** [ Eds: ADDS statistics on death rate. ]

The designation of *2nd, 3rd, 4th Ld,* etc., continues in sequence even if the dateline changes. See the Changing Datelines entry.

An **optional** lead is a separate, complete version of a story, used to offer a different approach for those desiring it. An *Eds: note* should be used to explain this. Like the main story, it needs to be updated with new developments.
**Slug:** [ BC-Presidential Helicopters-Optional ]
**Headline:** [ Lockheed Martin wins presidential helicopter contract ]
**Eds. Note:** [ Eds: For those desiring an alternative approach ]
**Byline:** [ By LOLITA C. BALDOR ]
**Bytitle:** [ Associated Press Writer ]

An **optional** is updated using its own numerical series of writethrus:
**Slug:** [ BC-Presidential Helicopters-Optional, 1st Ld-Writethru ]
**Eds. Note:** [ Eds: For those desiring an alternative approach. ADDS 1 graf after 3rd graf pvs with White House comment ]

# LOGOS

Follow the dateline by the AP logo enclosed in parentheses without spaces. Put spaces on both sides of the underscore that follows:

**LOS ANGELES (AP) _ An earthquake struck the city Monday.**

Logos are not used in digest and advisory lines.

# MORE LINES

A MORE indication, if needed at the conclusion of a take of copy, such as a long text, is indented:

**MORE**

# NEWSALERTS

A short headline, just one line whenever possible, that briefly reports a development about to move as a bulletin or urgent. A NewsAlert just reports a fact; it is not the place for background or detail. An APNewsAlert must be followed quickly by a bulletin or urgent.

APNewsAlerts should move with a *b* priority. They always carry a dateline, and the simple slug **BC-APNewsAlert**. They should conform to AP practices on attribution.

APNewsAlerts should be written in a style that broadcasters can use immediately on the air. Place the attribution, for example, at the beginning. Use appropriate verbs, often the perfect tense (*has signed, have announced.*) Use articles (*a, the,* instead of telegraphese). For instance, *The Senate has passed the Smith Amendment* rather than *Senate passes Smith Amendment.*

A sample:

**Slug: [ BC-APNewsAlert ]**
**WASHINGTON (AP) _ President Bush has signed the Iraqi war resolution.**

In cases in which the APNewsAlert is undated, use this format:

**Slug: [ BC-APNewsAlert ]**
**(AP) _ Text.**

Use this format for killing an APNewsAlert:

**Slug: [ BC-APNewsAlert, KILL ]**
**NEW YORK _ Kill the APNewsAlert saying John Smith was charged in the murder. Smith was not charged with murder.**
**The AP**

Use this format to correct an APNewsAlert (if a kill is not necessary):

**Slug: [ BC-APNewsAlert, CORRECTION ]**
**NEW YORK _ State legislator John Smith has been charged with eight counts of perjury. (Corrects APNewsAlert that said he had been charged with five counts.)**

Use this format for disregarding an APNewsAlert:

**Slug: [ BC-APNewsAlert, DISREGARD ]**
**WASHINGTON _ Disregard the APNewsAlert on the House spending vote. The House is still voting. The measure has not been approved.**
**The AP**

## NONPUBLISHABLE EDITOR'S NOTES

Use the "Eds. note" field of Workbench:
The form:
**Eds. note: [Eds: Adds statistics on death rate. ]**
See also **Publishable Editor's Notes**.

## NONTRANSMITTING SYMBOLS

The following are symbols that should not be used in standard AP wire transmissions.

The symbols can be sent and received by some computers but are not generally used because they are not available throughout the newspaper industry or may act as control characters to make a computer perform a function rather than print a character.

**accent marks** Do not use them; they cause garbled copy in some newspaper computers.

**asterisk** * Rarely translates and in many cases cannot be sent by AP computers or received by newspaper computers.

**at sign** @ Do not use in text. In computer addresses, use (at). Example: *president(at)whitehouse.gov*.

**brackets [ ]** Rarely translates and in many cases cannot be sent by AP computers or received by newspaper computers. Use parentheses.

**bullets** • Do not use because they cannot be transmitted without causing problems with some newspaper computers. Use dashes instead.

**cent** ¢ Does not exist. Spell out.

**equals** = Spell out, including in Internet addresses.

**percent** % Rarely translates and in many cases cannot be sent by AP computers or received by newspaper computers.

**pound sign** £ or # Frequently a control character. Rarely translates and in many cases cannot be sent by AP computers or received by newspaper computers.

**tilde** ~ Do not use the symbol. If necessary for Internet addresses, write out the word and put it in parentheses.

**underscore** _ Do not use the symbol for Internet addresses. If needed, write out "underscore" and put it in parentheses.

**Others:**
Symbols and combinations of characters and symbols used by languages other than English generally can be transmitted or received only by AP and newspaper computers programmed for those languages. Leave the symbols off or use generally accepted equivalents. For example, German umlauts are represented using two regular letters when they are needed: In "Goethe," the "oe" is the "o" with an umlaut.

Typesetting symbols such as tab-line-indicators, tab-field-indicators, en, em, thin should only be used to set tabular copy.

Typefaces such as bold and *italic* cannot be sent on AP news wires.

## PACKAGE ADVISORIES

If a story is strongly developing with many elements, use a Package Advisory to keep members and subscribers up to date. Package Avisories also provide a place to tell members about how AP is covering a story; to

advise on coverage plans; and to draw attention to exceptional AP work.
Example:
**Slug: [ BC-Saddam, Package Advisory ]**
EDITORS:
Our package on the execution of Saddam Hussein:

MAIN STORY:

SADDAM
BAGHDAD _ Iraqis awoke to television images of a noose being slipped over Saddam Hussein's neck and his white-shrouded body _ the pre-dawn work of black-hooded hangmen. But some Iraqis wondered if their tormentor's execution would change anything. "He's gone, but our problems continue," mused a Shiite candy store owner in east Baghdad. By Steven R. Hurst.

IRAQ
BAGHDAD _ At least 68 Iraqis die in bombings as they prepare to celebrate Islam's biggest holiday _ their first without Saddam Hussein. Six more American troops die, making December the deadliest month of 2006 for U.S. forces. At least 2,998 members of the U.S. military have been killed since the Iraq war began in March 2003. By Lauren Frayer.

SIDEBARS:

_ SADDAM-AMERICA'S VILLAIN _ When U.S. leaders decided it was time to despise Saddam Hussein, he made the perfect villain. America's quarter-century fascination with the Iraqi leader ended Friday at the gallows.
_ US-IRAQ _ President Bush called Saddam's execution a milestone in Iraq, but was monitoring reaction. He warned it will not halt the bloodshed and political discord splitting the country.
_ SADDAM-PALESTINIANS _ Palestinians mourn and struggle to accept the demise of Saddam, one of their most steadfast allies. His last words were reportedly "Palestine is Arab."

BOXES:

_ SADDAM-QUOTE BOX.
_ SADDAM-CHRONOLOGY.

MULTIMEDIA:

Photos:
IRAQ SADDAM HUSSEIN: NY114, Guards place a noose around Saddam Hussein's neck moments before the former Iraqi leader was executed.

Interactives:
_ SADDAM SPECIAL SECTION: For Hosted Custom News subscribers, a section front slugged IRAQ contains the latest text, photo, video and multimedia coverage.

_ SADDAM PHOTO GALLERY: Photo gallery of archive images, _international/saddam_pix folder.
_ SADDAM TIMELINE: Interactive with photos and timeline on Saddam's life and recent trial, _international/saddam_timeline folder.
_ SADDAM STAY OF EXECUTION REQUEST: Copy of request filed by Saddam's lawyers, _documents folder, slugged 1229saddam.pdf.

AP Online Video Network:

In addition to spot coverage, a large package of file video will be posted online.

Graphics:

IRAQ US DEATHS: Chart shows the monthly number of U.S. soldiers' deaths for 2006.
THE WEEK IN IRAQ: Graphic provides a look at some of the events in Iraq during the previous Sunday through Saturday.
SADDAM TIMELINE: profiles life and trial of former Iraq president Saddam Hussein.

**The AP**

## PHOTOS LINE

Use this format for listing photos to accompany AP stories, unless you are dragging a photo link directly into the story:
Photo: [ AP Photo NY101 ]
Photo: [ AP Photos NY101-NY104 ]
When a date is needed, list it before the photo number, even if there is just one photo:
Photo: [ AP Photo of Dec. 25: NY101 ]
Photo: [ AP Photos of Dec. 25: NY101-NY104 ]

## PUBLISHABLE EDITOR'S NOTES

Publishable editor's notes should be placed in the Pub Eds Note field. They should begin with EDITOR'S NOTE in all caps, followed by a space, an underscore and a space, followed by the text of the note.
Pub eds. note: [ EDITOR'S NOTE — This is the second installment of a three-part series on governmental agencies. ]

## SUMMARY BOX

It can contain three or four items, but the text (excluding the header material) must be under 100 words.
The format:
Slug: [ BC-Arthritis Recall-Summary Box ]
Headline: [Summary Box: What's wrong with Vioxx? ]
Sidebars: [ With BC-Arthritis Drug Recall ]
Byline: [ By The Associated Press ]

WHY VIOXX IS BEING PULLED: The popular arthritis drug doubled the risk of heart attack and stroke compared to people taking a dummy pill, according to a study.

WHAT IT MEANS: People should stop taking it and ask their doctors for alternatives.

THE FALLOUT: Could boost sales of other similar prescription drugs and over-the-counter pain relievers.

BIG PICTURE: A blow to high hopes that Vioxx, in addition to fighting arthritis pain, might help prevent certain cancers.

## TABLES

The following rules are designed to help build simple tables:

I. Every story or file that has even one line of tabular material in it must have a tabular format identifier in the priority-category code line.

The identifier may be *bt* for body-tabular or *at* for agate-tabular, but it MUST be there.

Examples: *rnbt, rnat.*

II. Every tabular line must begin with a tab line indicator symbol called a *tli.*

III. Immediately before the first character of the first tabulated column there must be a tab field indicator symbol represented by a *tfi.* There must be at least one space between the last character of the first column following the *tli* and the *tfi* preceding the first tabbed column.

Example:

tliReagantfi000 000 00

tliVerylongnametfi000 000 00

IV. The number of the columns and the width of the entire format are restricted by how they will fit in a newspaper and not by the margin of the services on which they are being sent. A good rule of thumb is to use as many abbreviations as possible while keeping the table understandable.

The basic rule for AP tables is that a line in an agate table may not exceed 392 units and lines in a body type table cannot exceed 293.

Each letter and number has a unit count. By totaling the units of all of the characters you will find whether the table will fit.

The unit count is fixed and does not change for the various newspaper type fonts. Theoretically it will fit all.

Here are the counts:

| | | | |
|---|---|---|---|
| A -14 | a -11 | T -13 | t -7 |
| B -14 | b -11 | U -15 | u -11 |
| C -13 | c -13 | V -14 | v -11 |
| D -15 | d -11 | W -18 | w -15 |
| E -15 | e -10 | X -15 | x -11 |
| F -14 | f -7 | Y -15 | y -11 |
| G -15 | g -11 | Z -12 | z -9 |
| H -15 | h -11 | | |
| I -8 | i -6 | 0 -9 | 1 -9 |
| J -11 | j -7 | 2 -9 | 3 -9 |
| K -15 | k -11 | 4 -9 | 5 -9 |
| L -13 | l -6 | 6 -9 | 7 -9 |
| M -18 | m -18 | 8 -9 | 9 -9 |

| N -15 | n -11 | , -6 | . -6 |
|-------|-------|------|------|
| O -14 | o -10 | | |
| P -14 | p -11 | EM18 | |
| Q -14 | q -11 | EN9 | |
| R -15 | r -9 | Thin6 | |
| S -11 | s -9 | Fractions18 | |

As you can see from the above table, all characters are not 18, nine or six units, but vary. However, you can use *em, en* and *thin* symbols to get within one unit of a character's width.

By figuring out how to set the line with the most characters, you can get the basic table width and all other lines should fall properly into place.

You can put in the *em, en* or *thin* symbols manually but frequently the standard AP computer will do it adequately once the file is stored in the system.

## URGENTS

A decision on whether to slug a story *URGENT* rests with the supervisor.

A story with an urgent tag should always have an urgent priority code. The urgent priority code also may be used if an item is not urgent but needs to be moved on an urgent basis.

The slugging of a typical urgent:

**Slug: [ BC-Quake ]**
**Urgent: [ URGENT ]**

For the first break on an *urgent* story, the initial *urgent* should be no more than two paragraphs.

When more information is available, call up the *urgent* that has moved, add a paragraph or two of new material and refile the new story as a writethru with the next lead number. Do the same with further information, until the story is complete.

## WITHHOLDS

Use *u* priority and the same category code as the original story.

For a full explanation, see the Procedures section at the end of this chapter.

The form for a WITHHOLD is:

**Slug: [ BC-Gold Find, WITHHOLD ]**
**Headline: [ WITHHOLD ]**
**DENVER _ Withhold BC-Gold. Authorities say the miner's story has been questioned.**
**The AP**

*Do not simply type the format shown here. Use the template in Reporter's Workbench to format it precisely. This is essential for archive and other purposes. To use the template, open the story to be withheld, click Templates, click Kill or Correct This Story and select what you want to do.*

## WORD COUNTS

Most computers automatically put in the word count.

If the word count is not automatic, put it in at the end of the keyword line immediately following the final comma, without a space.

## WRITETHRUS

Writethrus are used to update or correct a story, to add photo numbers and similar material, and to add details in a bulletin or urgent series. Do not retransmit stories with the same writethru number.

**Slug: [ BC-Governor's Illness, 2nd Ld-Writethru, a0584 ]**
**Eds. note: [ Eds: ADDS new Smith comment. ]**

# PROCEDURES FOR HANDLING KILLS, DISREGARDS, WITHHOLDS, CLARIFICATIONS AND CORRECTIVES

This chapter summarizes how to make critical corrections to stories that have already moved, and how to remove them completely or temporarily from the news report if needed. We use KILLS, WITHHOLDS, CORRECTIVES and CLARIFICATIONS in these cases.

The rules for the use of these items are more complex than for ordinary in-cycle corrections, which are described in the Filing Practices section of this Stylebook.

The Supervisor's Desk in New York or the New York manager designated to handle correctives must approve a KILL, CORRECTIVE or CLARIFICATION before it is filed. The New York Photo Desk must be consulted for photo problems.

In many cases, the story involved may have been transmitted over more than one service. Any corrective action must be taken on all services where the story moved.

### 1. KILLS, DISREGARDS AND WITHHOLDS

**KILLS AND DISREGARDS** are used to permanently remove from the wire material that is still "alive" — usually, copy that has been transmitted in the current 24-hour cycle. For material transmitted in a previous cycle, use a CORRECTIVE or CLARIFICATION.

KILLS advise an AP member not to use a story at all in its publication and to remove it from its Web site. They may be used when the entire basis of the story is found to be wrong, and on stories with particularly damaging errors or that are potentially libelous. A KILL informs a member that the story, or part of a story, must not be used.

DISREGARDS have a similar effect, but are used in less serious cases — for instance, when an old story is retransmitted inadvertently or material moves on a service where it is not supposed to move.

**WITHHOLDS** are used to temporarily remove from the report a story that may or may not be incorrect, and which we're in the process of checking.

If the check finds that the story was correct as originally filed, an advisory canceling the WITHHOLD and releasing the story can be filed.

If the check finds some material to be in error, send an advisory noting the upcoming changes. The advisory should be followed quickly with a writethru incorporating the changes.

If the story is found to be substantially in error or potentially libelous, the WITHHOLD should be followed by a KILL.

## 2. FORMATS FOR KILLS, DISREGARDS AND WITHHOLDS

Workbench templates and the formats below should be used. For broadcast services, follow broadcast style.

Datelines on withholds and kills should be the same as on the original stories. Withholds, disregards and kills should carry the same category code as the original story (*a* for national news stories, *n* for state news stories, *s* for sports, etc.). Kill advisories should carry a *v* category code.

### KILLS

A KILL should say succinctly what was wrong with the original story — for example, 'Smith was charged with robbery, not murder.' Do not make any legal conclusions in the KILL — e.g., 'the story is potentially libelous' — when transmitting the KILL.

The form for a KILL:

**Slug: [ BC-Smith Charged, KILL ]**
**Headline: [ BULLETIN KILL ]**
**NEW YORK _ Kill BC-Smith Charged. Smith was charged with robbery, not murder.**
**The AP**

If only part of a story is killed, it should be followed by a writethru, eliminating the offending paragraph. The form for a partial kill is:

**Slug: [ BC-Smith Charged, KILL ]**
**Headline: [ BULLETIN KILL ]**
**NEW YORK _ Kill BC-Smith Charged. Smith was charged with robbery, not murder.**
**The AP**

Follow the KILL immediately with an advisory. State whether a substitute story is planned:
**Slug: [ BC-Smith Charged, KILL Advisory ]**
**Editors:**
**The New York story BC-Smith Charged, filed Monday, has been killed. Smith was charged with robbery, not murder.**
**A kill is mandatory.**
**Make certain the story is not published.**

**A substitute story will be filed shortly. (Or: No substitute story will be filed.)**
**The AP**

If a substitute story is filed, mark it as the next lead-writethru to the previous story. Include a nonpublishable editor's note advising that it replaces an earlier story that was KILLED.
The form is:
**Slug: [ BC-Smith Charged, 4th Ld-Writethru ]**
**Eds: SUBS 7th graf "Smith was ...," which was killed, to CORRECT that Smith was charged last year with armed robbery but was not convicted.**

Use this format for killing an APNewsAlert:
**Slug: [ BC-APNewsAlert, KILL ]**
**NEW YORK _ Kill the APNewsAlert saying John Smith was charged in the murder. Smith was not charged with murder.**
**The AP**

### WITHHOLDS
The form for a WITHHOLD is:
**Slug: [ BC-Gold Find, WITHHOLD ]**
**Headline: [ WITHHOLD ]**
**DENVER _ Withhold BC-Gold Find. Authorities say the miner's story has been questioned.**
**The AP**

The form to release a story that has previously been WITHHELD is:
**Slug: [ BC-Gold Find, WITHHOLD ADVISORY ]**
**Headline: [ WITHHOLD ADVISORY ]**
**DENVER _ The story BC-Gold Find is available for use. The miner's story has been confirmed. (Or: The story BC-Gold has been confirmed. A new version with additional information will be sent shortly.)**
**The AP**

### DISREGARDS
The form for a DISREGARD is:
**Slug: [ BC-Practical Joke, DISREGARD ]**
**Editors:**
**Disregard BC-Practical Joke. The story moved Tuesday and was inadvertently repeated today.**
**The AP**

## 3. CORRECTIVES and CLARIFICATIONS
A CORRECTIVE is a publishable story that acknowledges an error in a story and sets the record straight. The news manager or supervisor in New York needs to approve all correctives and clarifications.
Do not be hasty in transmitting a CORRECTIVE. When you take the

step of transmitting a CORRECTIVE, it is important to ensure that the correction is actually warranted, that it corrects all aspects of the story that may need correction and that the correction itself is accurate.

Transmission of a CORRECTIVE does not necessarily safeguard the AP against legal action. In fact, transmission of a CORRECTIVE may itself have legal consequences because it formally acknowledges an error.

You should be aware of any legal requirement in your state setting a time within which a correction must appear.

CORRECTIVES and CLARIFICATIONS should identify the previous incorrect story by slug and date. They should carry the dateline and category code of the original story. Use Workbench templates and the formats below. For broadcast services, follow broadcast style.

CORRECTIVES and CLARIFICATIONS should carry headlines. The headlines should begin with the word CORRECTION or CLARIFICATION, followed by a colon. In most cases, the slug and the word *story* will follow:

**Slug: [ BC-Church Expenses, CORRECTIVE ]**
**Headline: [ Correction: Church Expenses story ]**
or
**Slug: [ BC-Church Expenses, CLARIFICATION ]**
**Headline: [ Clarification: Church Expenses story ]**

Note the slug of the story, *Church Expenses*, is uppercase, while *story* is down.

Occasionally, you will want to use something other than the slug after the word Correction or Clarification, to help online readers know what the content is. For example, the slug on a Benton Harbor riots story was *Crash Death-Disturbance*. An appropriate corrective headline in that case might be:

**Slug: [ BC-Crash Death-Disturbance, CORRECTIVE ]**
**Headline: [ Correction: Benton Harbor Riot story ]**

The format for a corrective:

**Slug: [ BC-Fed-Indictments, CORRECTIVE ]**
**Headline: [ Correction: Fed-Indictments story ]**
**Eds. note: [ Eds: Members who used BC-Fed-Indictments, sent Oct. 22 under a New York dateline, are asked to use the following story. ]**

**NEW YORK (AP) _ In an Oct. 22 story about federal indictments of city officials, The Associated Press reported erroneously the first name of one of those indicted. The correct name is Joseph Arnold, not John Arnold.**

For correctives on undated stories, use **By The Associated Press** and no dateline.

The proper form for a CORRECTIVE story often will be the straightforward statement that a previous AP report contained an error. However, where the AP did not originate the error, the CORRECTIVE should make that clear. For instance, "The Associated Press, quoting state police, on Tuesday erroneously identified a man charged with embezzlement. The man charged was Robert Smith, not Reginald Smith." When the original story cited a member as a source, consult with the member. We will usually cite the member in the corrective. If the original story used member material as a source but did not attribute it to the member, we sometimes handle the corrective as if the AP itself made the error. Consult local or New York news managers if necessary.

### CLARIFICATIONS

A clarification is a publishable story used to clarify or expand upon a previous story which, while factually correct, may be unfair or subject to misinterpretation.

A clarification must NOT be used as a substitute for a kill or a corrective. The clarification is used to provide background or detail in the interest of clarity or fairness. It is not used to correct factual errors in copy.

The format:

**Slug: [ BC-Airfares, CLARIFICATION ]**
**Headline: [ Clarification: Airfares story ]**
**Eds. note: [ Eds: Members who used BC-Airfares of May 8 may wish to use the following, which explains that not all fares on domestic flights are subject to change. ]**
**WASHINGTON (AP) _ In a story May 8, The Associated Press reported that fares on domestic flights will increase beginning in April. Fares will increase for flights in the continental United States, but not for flights to Hawaii and Alaska.**

For clarifications on undated stories, use **By The Associated Press** and no dateline.

## 4. Sending KILLS, WITHHOLDS, CORRECTIVES AND CLARIFICATIONS

Every KILL, WITHHOLD, CORRECTIVE and CLARIFICATION must be sent to the same services as the original story. To ensure that distribution is complete, the news editor in charge of the bureau or desk where the problem arose should fully advise the New York news manager or supervisor of all services to which the original item was sent.

The Text news desks, Broadcast News Center, AP Digital, Graphics and Photos are responsible for ensuring that these items are filed wherever necessary in their services.

## 5. Report Requirements

Any time that a kill or corrective is filed, the bureau chief or news editor must maintain a file for the period of the statute of limitations for defamation claims in your state or country. The file must contain:

1. Wire copy of the original story and the KILL and substitute story that were sent. Include material transmitted on broadcast.

2. Wire copy of the original story and CORRECTIVE or CLARIFICATION filed.

3. A copy of any source material used by the writer or editor in preparation of the story, including member clip, handout and the like.

In the case of a KILL, or a CORRECTIVE or CLARIFICATION with potential ramifications, include a factual statement by the bureau chief or the news editor, in consultation with staff members involved, on the circumstances. If legal action is a possibility, the explanation should be prepared in consultation with a deputy managing editor or the general counsel.

The statement should cite relevant details, such as any contact with outsiders on the matter. Do not include extraneous comments about staff members or bureau procedures. It is not the place for apologies, or any legal or factual speculation or conclusions. Do not respond to any letter or other communication in connection with any case where legal action seems possible, especially if a lawyer is involved, without prior consultation with the New York manager handling correctives and kills.

4. Procedures for filing CORRECTIVES, CLARIFICATIONS, AND KILLS.

New York must approve all such items. Message the relevant information to "sup," addressed "NY-supervisor." You may attention the New York manager handling correctives. Say what was wrong and who contacted AP about it. Explain the source of the error. (If the matter is sensitive, phone an explanation.)

Include a proposed, fully formatted CORRECTIVE, CLARIFICATION OR KILL for each service the story moved on, using the format in "Templates" in Reporters Workbench. Attach the original story to your message.

Immediately after transmitting the approved item, record it in the AP Correctives Database, along with the required explanations. You can access the database via staff-only links in Inside AP.

# EDITING MARKS

¶ ATLANTA (AP)—The organization
said Thursday. It was the first
the last attempts.
With this the president tried

indent for paragraph

paragraph

no paragraph

the Jones Smith company is not

transpose

over a period of sixty or more years

use figures

there were 9 in the group.

spell it out

Ada, Oklahoma is the hometown

abbreviate

The Ga. man was the guest of

don't abbreviate

prince edward said it was his

uppercase

as a result This will be

lowercase

the accuser pointed to them

remove space

In these times it is necessary

insert space

the order for the later devices

retain

The ruling a fine example

insert word

according to the this source

delete

BF By DONALD AMES

boldface, center

J.R. Thomas

flush right

J.R. Thomas

flush left

insert comma

insert apostrophe

insert quotation marks

⊗ or ⊙

insert period

hyphen

dash

# ABOUT THE AP

Without The Associated Press (www.ap.org), the planet would be a very different place. AP is the world's largest news network, a not-for-profit cooperative whose content — across subjects, formats and continents — reaches half of Earth's population every day.

AP provides coverage of news, sports, business, weather, entertainment, politics, lifestyles and technology in text, audio, video, graphics, photos and online interactives. AP's services are distributed by satellite and the Internet to more than 120 nations, and AP is also a leader in developing and marketing newsroom technology.

More than 240 bureaus worldwide contribute to the AP report, which is administered out of the cooperative's New York headquarters. Two-thirds of AP's worldwide staff of more than 4,000 employees are journalists.

The extensive network that is the AP grew from a single notion more than a century and a half ago: that cooperation can help accurate news reach readers faster.

In late April 1846, hostilities began in what would become the Mexican War. American newspapers, most based in the Northeast at the time, faced huge obstacles in reporting the conflict.

War reports for the New York Sun were sent from Mexico to Mobile, Ala., by boat, rushed by special pony express to Montgomery and then 700 miles by U.S. Mail stagecoach to the southern terminus of the newly invented — and costly — telegraph near Richmond, Va. That express gave the Sun an edge of 24 hours or more on papers using the regular mail.

But Moses Yale Beach, the Sun's publisher, relinquished that advantage by inviting other New York publishers to join a cooperative venture. Five newspapers signed on: the Sun, the Journal of Commerce, the Courier and Enquirer, the Herald, and the Express. It was the beginning of the AP.

AP assumed its modern legal form in 1900 when it incorporated as a not-for-profit cooperative under the Membership Corporation Law of New York state. Today, the AP membership elects the board of directors, the cooperative's governing body.

AP staffers are governed by a comprehensive ethics statement, available for viewing at http://www.ap.org/pages/about/whatsnew/wn_112905.html

The Associated Press is the essential global news network, delivering fast, unbiased news from every corner of the world to all media platforms and formats. AP today is the largest and most trusted source of independent news and information.

**HEADQUARTERS**
**The Associated Press**
**450 West 33rd St.**
**New York, NY 10001**
**(212) 621-1500**